Upon My Words

Volume One
Essays, Lectures, and Addresses

Alexander S. Kohanski
1902–1987

Upon My Words

Essays, Lectures, and Addresses

Alexander S. Kohanski

Bloch Publishing Company
New York
1987

Also by Alexander S. Kohanski:

Lossky's Theory of Knowledge
From Kishinev to Babi Yar
Philosophy and Technology
An Analytical Interpretation of Martin Buber's 'I and Thou'
Martin Buber's Philosophy of Interhuman Relation
The Ethical Will of Rabbi Joseph Moses Abraham Levinski
The Greek Mode of Thought in Western Philosophy

Library of Congress Catalogue Card Number:

Kohanski, Alexander Sissel, 1902–1987
Upon My Words

Bibliography: p.
1. Judaism—20th Century. 2. Philosophy, Jewish. 3. Jews—Politics and government. 4. Zionism. 5. Israel. 6. Jewish religious education—United States. I. Title.
BM45.K58 1987   296   87-30942
ISBN 0-8197-0553-5
ISBN 0-8197-0550-0 (pbk.)

Printed in the United States of America

Bloch Publishing Company
37 W. 26th Street, 9th floor
New York, N.Y. 10010

To my grandchildren

Michael Aaron
Anna Leah
Samson Elazar

When you grow up to the age
of independent reading, you
will find much in this book that
will give meaning to your
independence.

Contents

Part V
Philatelic Briefs

Bibliography

Pictures

Acknowledgments

I gratefully acknowledge the permissions granted to me to reprint my articles which appeared in the following publications. Each article is identified by the number assigned to it in my Bibliography at the end of this volume.

Bnai Brith Bulletin. San Francisco, December 1951. No. 91.
Cleveland Jewish Center Bulletin. March 6, 1942. No. 65.
Contemporary Jewish Record. New York, September-October 1940. No. 51.
Israel Philatelist. New York, March and June 1961, December 1961-March 1962-March 1963, February 1962, November-December 1963, September-October and November-December, 1966. Nos. 99, 102, 103, 106, 112.
Jewish Education. New York, Fall 1953, Spring-Summer 1966. Nos. 97, 113.
Jewish Frontier. New York, February 1938, June 1941, February 1952. Nos. 45, 62, 93.
Jewish News. East Orange, N.J., September 13, 1963, July 2, 1965, September 9, 1966, September 12, 1969, September 29, 1970, September 17, 1971, September 7, 1972, September 20, 1973 September 4, 1975, September 23, 1976, September 18, 1977, September 28, 1978, September 20, 1979, September 4, 1980, September 24, 1981. Nos. 108, 110, 114, 124, 126, 127, 129, 132, 145, 150, 155, 156, 159, 167, 169.
Jewish Social Service Quarterly. New York, June 1938, March 1939, Nos. 46, 47.
Jewish Social Studies. New York, vol. XXIX, No. 3 (July 1967). Pp. 155-170. No. 116.
Linn's Weekly Stamp News. Sidney, Ohio, September 30 and October 7, 1963, September 28, 1964. Nos. 105, 107.
New Palestine. Washington, D.C., January 10, 1941. No. 59.
Phil W. Lown: A Jubilee Volume. New York, 1967. No. 115.
Reconstructionist. New York, January 29, 1954, February 2, 1962, June 11 and 25, 1965, February 23, 1968, September 28, 1969. Nos. 98, 104, 109, 119, 125.
WINS Radio Station. New York June 2, 1945. No. 74.

A.S.K.

Preface
Literary Autobiography

The essays, lectures, and addresses which I have collected in this volume and the poems which will be included in Volume II were written in the course of seven decades. Most of them were published in various periodicals, and the rest, especially the poems, have remained private until now. They may be regarded as gleanings between my published main works, which include fifteen books that I have written or edited. The present volume is arranged in five parts. I have placed the philosophical writings first because ever since I started on the literary road I have always leaned toward the philosophical mode of expression, and subsequently developed it into my major interest. When I was still a student in the Hebrew Realgymnasium in my native town, Vilkavishk, Lithuania, I was inclined more toward the natural sciences and mathematics. But even then they interested me for their speculative implications rather than their experimental values. As I look back on those student days, I can still feel the sense of freedom I had experienced in the surroundings of my fellow students and our faculty. Hebrew was not yet the sole language of instruction in the Gymnasium, primarily because not all our professors had as yet mastered the language. The other two languages of instruction were German and Russian. The students were brought up in Hebrew Schools, and they had also studied German and Russian privately or in schools and at home.

I was born on a Friday, July 4, 1902, in the village Shelmi, a substation of Vilkavishk. My childhood education started at home about the age of three. I recall one evening when I was sitting at the table practicing my reading lesson from the *Reshis Da'as* (the proverbial Hebrew Primer of many generations of Jewish children), and my maternal grandfather Abraham Kollekandt (I never knew my paternal grandparents) was standing behind me listening in. From time to time, when he liked my reading especially, he would drop a coin from behind me on my book, saying, this is a present from an angel. Thus from my early childhood I was brought up with the idea that learning is a sacred duty, watched over by angels from above. Before I started school at the age of four-and-a-half, I was already able to read the Siddur fluently and I would often join my father in the morning prayers. At that time we lived in the village of

Novodoliye on a farm-estate which my father had rented from the Government. On Sabbath days the Jewish farmers in the neighborhood would gather in one of their homes for services. When it was held at a neighbor's farm I always looked forward to our walk through the forest where I would watch the sun coming in and out through the branches, spreading light on the lush green grass, and the trees casting their shade and cooling our path.

My first school, which I attended in the nearby town of Kibarti (on the German border), was a *Heder Metukan*, a modern Hebrew school in which the language of instruction was Hebrew. When I would come home on weekends, I would immediately resort to the orchard, climb the trees and pick some pears, plums, and cherries off the branches, find myself a corner on a heavy branch and sit there in quiet solitude musing over my limited expanse of nature around me. I had no contact with the children of the Lithuanian peasants who worked on my father's farm. My life was centered at home with my parents, my brother, and sisters (I was then the eighth and youngest child in the family). Evenings we would gather around mother who would tell us stories and sing songs, while her hands were occupied with knitting, sewing, or mending clothes for the family. Father would retire early to bed, because his work day started at three in the morning. When I was at home for some length of time, I was left alone most of the days. Yet I was not lonesome. I would walk in the fields, ride a horse, or hide on top of a hay wagon on the way to the barn. The natural surroundings engaged my attention; the trees and the wide expanses of the fields fascinated me most. When I learned to write, my first composition was a letter which I wrote in Yiddish (my home language) to my grandfather in Vilkavishk. I addressed the envelope also in Yiddish and sent it off without a postage stamp. The kind Russian postman must have consulted a Jewish neighbor in town for the translation of the address, for the letter reached its destination without delay.

When we later moved back to town, I attended a Heder of a somewhat modernized nature, for the teacher, probably influenced by the *Haskala* (Hebrew Enlightenment) also taught us German, which we wrote in Hebrew characters. This was my first introduction to a foreign language. The Russian language I first learned at the age of ten, when I attended a modernized Talmud Torah (a Hebrew Day School) in Pinsk-Karlin (White Russia), where I was also introduced to Hebrew grammer and literature, the

Bible, Talmud, history, and geography. I was invited to come to Pinsk by my uncle and aunt (my mother's sister) Leyser and Rivka Grayevsky, who had two daughters, Haya and Tauba, and a son, Beryl, of my age, who became my classmate and close companion. Pinsk was a metropolitan center of Russian culture, and many Jewish families sent their sons to the Russian Gymnasium and introduced the Russian vernacular into their homes. My uncle's home, however, remained traditionally Jewish and its language was Yiddish. The same traditional atmosphere prevailed in the Talmud Torah, where the language of instruction was Yiddish, although it extended its curriculum to include some secular studies in Russian. The Talmud Torah was a well organized and educationally highly motivated school, with a well-planned eight-year curriculum and a staff of competent instructors, each a specialist in his field. It was there that I received a thorough grounding in the Hebrew language, its grammar and literature, and a broad spectrum in biblical and talmudic lore, which we covered in the original texts. Student-teacher relationships were warm with much personal attention given to each pupil and his needs. At one time the students decided that they would like to have pictures of their faculty as a memento, and that request was granted by all our teachers, including the School Superintendent (called in Hebrew the *Mashgiah*) who was also my teacher in Talmud. I cherish these photos, which I still have in my personal album. School discipline was hardly ever broken. I don't know how it operated, but I have no recollection of anyone having been subjected to corporal punishment. We carried our inner discipline with us from home where supervision of our studies was regular and homework was an accepted practice. We studied hard and we played hard. Every school day during recess we played outdoors a kind of one-base baseball game. After school we rode bicycles, skated on the sidewalk snow or on the frozen river, the Pina, and in the summer we played croquet, went swimming and boating or on an outing in the woods. Evenings, after homework, we played chess and other games.

I returned to my home town, in Vilkavishk, during the first World War, in 1915. I continued my Hebrew studies together with a group of friends and I also had private instruction in German and Russian. Later I attended a *Stadtschule* conducted under the auspices of the German occupying forces. At the end of the war I enrolled in the newly founded Hebrew Realgymnasium (in 1918).

As I have described it above, the student body was well versed in Hebrew, German, and Russian and felt comfortable with the trilingual method of instruction in the classrooms. But the atmosphere of the school was on the whole Hebraic; and in that atmosphere reigned the spirit of the Jewish national revival. The Hebrew Gymnasium represented to us the inner sanctum of our national independence, almost hermetically sealed off from its surroundings. The Gymnasium building was our territory and its Student Council, of which I was the first President, was our sovereign governing body: we felt as if we were running a Jewish State. My cultural horizon was then extended to the arts, music, and the sciences and mathematics, and I also took a course in English, perhaps in anticipation of my future prospects. It was in that period, before and during my Gymnasium days, that I started to write Hebrew poetry and to keep a diary. Only one of my poems of that time (*Hamilhama*) has remained in my possession.

Many of my friends and fellow students, after graduation, went to Palestine to participate in the upbuilding of the Jewish homeland. Others entered the Lithuanian University, which was established by the newly liberated Republic of Lithuania in Kovno, and they became involved in the political-cultural life of the country as a whole. My path led me in a different direction. I was never a part of the Lithuanian national reconstruction, for I left the country (in December 1920) while it was still in its formative stages, and proceeded with my parents, Samson and Hanna Feigl, and my two sisters, Sylvia and Rose on our way to Montreal, Canada, where my brother, Morris, and two other sisters, Ethel and Sarah, had preceded us about a decade earlier. Another sister of mine, Beatrice, lived in New York. Passing through Berlin I was delayed for a couple of months and there I became acquainted with the German theater and I started my collection of German classics: Goethe, Schiller, Heine, and above all the works of Kant. Jewish immigration from Eastern Europe to Canada and the United States was then at its peak and there were many obstacles in our way. I was thus delayed for another three months in Antwerp, where my parents and sisters caught up with me shortly before we embarked on a ship sailing for Montreal. In Antwerp I had frequented the Museums and came into contact for the first time with some of the treasures of Flemish painting, and I roamed the quaint streets and marketplaces of the town and observed its architecture and business enterprises.

We arrived in Montreal in June 1921. Having still been under the influence of my mathematical and scientific schooling, I matriculated that same year at McGill University, in the Department of Engineering. My dream was to become a civil engineer. Home circumstances changed and I had to leave the university and was engaged as a teacher in one of the Jewish Communal Talmud Torahs, and later in the Yiddish Peretz Folkshule. My free time was spent mainly in the City Library, where I became absorbed in the humanities, chiefly in the field of philosophy. After two years (in October 1923) I left Montreal for New York.

The cultural centers of immigrant Jewish life were then still on the East Side. I attended courses at the Jewish People's University, one in Biblical History with Hayyim Schauss (author of *Di Groisse Yiddishe Geshichte*) and another in Jewish philosophy with Yehudah Kaufman (Yehudah Ibn Shmuel, author of a *Perush* on Maimonides' *Moreh Hanevukhim*). I also frequented the Jewish Division of the New York Public Library where I intensified my interests in Judaica. At that time I started writing Yiddish poetry, but I never aspired to become a professional poet. My poems, then and later, have a personal lyrical character and have remained unpublished until now, and they will be issued in a separate volume.

I moved from New York to Memphis, Tenn. to occupy a position of Principal-Teacher in the Yiddishe Folkshule of the Jewish National Workers Alliance (in 1925), and there I enrolled in the college Southwestern, that was originally Southwestern Presbyterian University (in Kentucky). This was my first contact with the internal life of a Christian institution of higher learning. While it had dropped the appellation of "Presbyterian University" and operated under the new name and in a new location, its faculty was still composed mainly of Ministers of the Church, and its prescribed curriculum included the Old and New Testaments, attendance at daily Chapel, and on Sundays at a church service. My personal relationship with my fellow students and with the faculty was free and open. I was given special credit for my Gymnasium courses, some of which were on a college level, and was placed in the Sophomore year. As one of the Jewish students (there were only eight of us in the college) I was given the privilege of attending Chapel on a voluntary basis, but was expected to attend a synagogue for Sabbath services. That year I made the

"Dean's List," was promoted to the Senior year, and graduated in June 1927.

In those two years new horizons were opened to me in world literature, including ancient Greek drama, Shakespeare, religious poetry, the Greek language, philosophy, and American history, and also the New Testament. In the class on religious poetry, when the subject was the biblical poetic writings, I was often called upon to explain the Hebrew text. I was expected to know my Hebrew Bible. There was no Christian proselytizing at school. As I look back on it, I would say that my Jewish beliefs were reinforced by my experiences in a Christian environment, for the faculty showed great appreciation of the Jewish origins of their own beliefs. I recall a sermon in Chapel given by one of the professors on the veracity of ancient historical records. He noted that one could not find greater objectivity in ancient documents than in the historical narratives of the Old Testament. My personal approach to the New Testament was one of deep respect and the search for an understanding of the Christian religion that has molded the lives and destinies of hundreds of millions of human beings in the course of almost two millenia. And this search has continued after I graduated from Southwestern, even to this day. When I took up graduate work in the Department of Philosophy at Vanderbilt University, one of my courses was in New Testament Greek (we read the Book of Mark). In later years I started to delve into church history and philosophy, trying to clarify for myself not only how far Christianty was indebted to Jewish precepts but wherein it differed from the basic forms of Jewish thought and belief.

In my first year at Vanderbilt I directed my attention to the field of esthetics and wrote my Master's thesis "Einfühlung and Painting," a discussion of Theodor Lipps's theory of esthetics as applied to modern painting. This topic was suggested to me by my professor, Herbert C. Sanborn, who was a student of Lipps's in Germany as well as of Kuno Fischer and other leading philosophers of the time. On the basis of my grades that year, the University offered me a scholarship of merit toward my doctoral work. This was renewed for a second year and at the end of that academic year (June 1930) I completed my residence requirements for my doctoral degree, which I was granted six years later, after I finished my dissertation (on the Russian philosopher, Nicolai Onufreyevich "Lossky's Theory of Knowledge"). As my interest deepened in classical philosophy particularly in Plato, it dawned on me that in order to grasp the essence of Christian thought I must look to its Greek sources for its metaphysical-theological origins. I then discovered that one learns to know a religion other than his own not so much by comparing their similarities as by gauging their differences, provided one shows a healthy respect for the other religion that differs from his own. And thus I turned my attention to the basic variations between the Greek mode of thought and the Jewish. I was versed in the Greek mode, which has dominated Western thinking; but I was convinced that there was a Jewish mode which has a different origin from that of the Greek and also follows a different path. I then came to the realization that Western thought, insofar as it is expressed in the Greek mode, is essentially Christian; or rather, Western thought is fundamentally Greco-Christian.

Philosophy to me has always been a way of expressing living interhuman relations, and not a mere speculative enterprise of abstract notions. Each philosophical mode is thus grounded in the living experiences of a people that has cultivated it through its social, political, cultural, and religious institutions and has articulated it in forms of thought peculiar to its own language. These are the parameters of the discipline of philosophical thinking. My own philosophical horizon was not limited to academic institutions but extended into Jewish educational, communal, and religious organizations on a local and national level. After two years of training in the Graduate School for Jewish Social Work (in New York), where I also had a course in Jewish history with Salo W. Baron, and in "Judaism as a Civilization" with Mordecai M. Kaplan, I served as Executive Director in the Jewish Center field, as National Director of the League for Labor Palestine, Executive Educational Director of the Cleveland Jewish Center (a Conservative Congregation), Director of Research for the American Jewish Conference (and was attached to its Delegation of Observers at the United Nations Conference in San Francisco, in 1945), Executive Director of the Maine Jewish Council, Dean of the College of Jewish Studies and Executive Director of the Jewish Education Society of San Francisco, and Director of other institutions. Last I joined the faculty of Kean College of New Jersey (at Union) as Adjunct Professor of Philosophy.

In all these capacities I deepened my insights into the American way of life and its history as well as into the life of the Jewish community and its aspirations. I gave literary expression to my thoughts in writing and lecturing, as documented in my Bibliography at the end of this volume. Besides my regular lectures at the College of Jewish Studies and at Kean College I also read papers at philosophical conferences and gave talks at the Townsend Lecture Series of Kean College, at the Adult Education Institute of Congregation Adas Israel, in Passaic, N.J., at educational conferences and many other places, and lately at the Lecture Series of Temple Judea, Laguna Hills, California. Many topics in this book formed the subject of literary-philosophical discussions at home with my wife Dorothy and our sons Daniel and Ronald, which have been a source of inspiration in my writings. My theses are varied in interest, reflecting my involvements in various areas of interhuman relations. But my main interest has always been the different world outlooks of the Greek and Jewish modes of thinking. I have presented the former in my book *The Greek Mode of Thought in Western Philosophy*, and now I am engaged in writing the companion volume, The Jewish Mode of Thought.

Laguna Hills, California
November 24, 1986.   *Alexander S. Kohanski*

My Home

in Vilkavishk, Lithuania. Pencil drawing. I sketched the house in 1919 at home and completed the sky in 1981 in Passaic, N. J.

Introduction

The Legacy of Rabbi Yehudah Hakohen of Budvich

We have come together here from several corners of the earth. — South Africa, Israel, England, Canada, and the United States — to celebrate the first reunion of the Kahanski family, the descendants of Rabbi Yehudah Hakohen of Budvich.* Now what is Budvich and where is it? Budvich is a village, about a good jogging distance from the town of Vilkavishk in Lithuania. In the western world of Enlightenment, every town in Eastern Europe is conceived as a *shtetl*, which may be translated as a small township with very low standards of modern living conditions, whose inhabitants are mostly poor, unsophisticated people, with a very limited grasp of the wide universe of human civilization. There is some element of truth in this appraisal, if we measure civilization by the standards of science and technology that had their inception in the western Age of Enlightenment in the seventeenth and eighteenth centuries. As a rule this sort of scientific-technological awakening did not reach Eastern Europe until two centuries later. But if we gauge the people in the shtetl by standards of human values, they were not so unenlightened as the West conceives them. The following story will illustrate the difference.

After the first World War, when the gates of the United States were still open to the large influx of East European Jewish immigrants, a young man from Bialystok arrived in New York and was met by his uncle, who had been living there since he came to the United States two decades earlier and who considered himself already Americanized. To impress his nephew with the wonders of New York City, the uncle took him on a tour of the town. But no matter what he showed him — the Forty Second Street Library, the

*Address at the First Kahanski Family Reunion, at the Sheraton Heights, Hasbrouck Heights, N. J., July 4, 1982.

Metropolitan Opera House, the Woolworth skyscraper, and the like — the young man remained unimpressed, remarking: "In Bialystok hob ich gezen gressers un sheners." (In Bialystok I have seen bigger and more beautiful things.) The uncle was at his wit's end. Then he thought to himself: I am going to show him Chinatown, which I am sure he has not seen in Bialystok. When they reached the downtown area and walked through the streets full of Chinese shops and stores with a conglomerate of signs in Chinese characters, the young man did not say a word. Then they walked into one of the stores and when he saw the dazzling display of Oriental merchandise and the storekeeper with a Chinese looking white beard, he could no longer contain his dismay and murmured, "Dos hob ich in Bialystok nit gezen" (This I did not see in Bialystok.) The storekeeper heard him very clearly and greeted him with delight: "Ir zait a Bialystoker? sholem-aleikhem a landsman!" (You are from Bialystok? Welcome, my countryman!)

Now what was the young man trying to tell his uncle by insisting that he had seen bigger and more beautiful buildings in his home town than those he saw in New York? Surely there was nothing in Bialystok equal to the Woolworth skyscraper or the Metropolitan Opera House. He did not mean to deny that, but the Yiddish word "gresser" means both "bigger" and "greater" and he used it to convey to his uncle that in his home town he had experienced "greater" and more beautiful things than those he was shown in New York. The popular American notion that "bigger" is "better" and more beautiful did not impress him. What he and others like him brought with them from the shtetl was quite a sophisticated world outlook on the essence of human values that overshadowed technological expansion.

Their lives in the small towns were not so backward as some of us are prone to view them. Western culture, insofar as it had reached Eastern Europe, also penetrated Jewish homes and schools. Many young men and women attended Russian Gymnasia (High Schools) and universities and specialized in various professions. There was, besides, a revival of the Hebrew language and literature, and Yiddish too assumed literary form in prose, poetry, history, sociology, and philosophy. After the first World War Hebrew and Yiddish Gymnasia began to flourish in large and small towns in Poland, Lithuania and Latvia, with modern curricula, including foreign languages. Thus large numbers of those who emigrated to various countries indeed came from small towns, but they were not what one might call "klein-shteteldike mentshen" (countryside folk). However, in order to grasp the full import of their world outlook, we must see them in the light of their struggle against the oppressive rulers of the Russian Empire, from which they hailed.

The Jewish historian Simon Dubnow characterized the Russian policy toward the Jews in the period 1881-1911 as the "Czar's thirty years war against the Jewish people" (an allusion to the cruel and devastating Thirty Years War of 1618-48 of the Spanish rulers in the Netherlands). Starting with pogroms and expulsions from the countryside in various parts of Russia the government continued, with all manner of economic and educational repression, its policy of eliminating the Jewish population from the empire. But the Jews could not be vanquished. They responded with a drive for self-emancipation, with the strengthening of their cultural and religious forces, the launching of the Zionist movement, and, wherever possible, the organization of self-defense squads against the pogromists. The Kahanski families were in the forefront of these inner fortifications, and some of their members also joined the pioneers who went to Eretz Israel to rebuild their homeland.

In the booklet "Memories" issued for our present Family Reunion, we read Bernard Cohen's recount of how the Budvicher young men dealt effectively with the Lithuanian hooligans (calling themselves "The Sons of John") who broke into Jewish homes and plundered their goods. We also read in these "Memories" Shmuel Kahana's description of his experiences as a pioneer in the Moshavim and Kevutsot, and in the defense of the Yishuv against Arab attacks. Those Jews who remained in Russia continued to brave the storms of periodic repressions by strengthening their inner institutions and by developing new avenues of economic enterprise. Others who emigrated to various lands brought with them the necessary working skills, business acumen, and intellectual capacities that stood them in good stead in making a rapid adjustment in their new habitations.

The contribution that Jews have made to the general progress of their countries of immigration are of a twofold nature. There has been a trend in American Jewish historiography to overemphasize the role of the individual Jew in the development of various aspects of American life — in medicine, jurisprudence, literature and the performing arts, in academic and scientific pursuits as well as in commerce, labor and industry, and in political leadership. These contributions have indeed been substantial, and members of our family have had their full share in them. To mention but a few: Senator Lazarus Phillips of Canada, Sir Horace R. Cohen, O.B.E. (Order of the British Empire), Lawrence Lande, bibliogragapher, who established the Lawrence Lande Foundation for Historical Research at McGill University, Judge Bernard Gillis of the Central Criminal Court in London, Jules Stein of Beverly Hills, California, founder of the Music Corporation of America (MCA), Professor Joseph Cohen of the State University of Washington, Martin Cohen of West Hartford, Conn., Lt. Colonel in the U.S. Air Force, Richard Cohen of Montreal, Lt. Colonel in the British Army. But no less a contribution has been made by members of our family who organized and built social, religious and educational institutions on a local, national, and international level, that have enhanced not only the lives of their own communities but have strengthened the cultural and religious life of their respective countries in general. In Montreal, Canada, where the largest segment of the Budvicher descendants dwell, the families of Lazarus Cohen [Kahanski] and of his brother, Rabbi Zvi Hirsch Cohen, the late Chief Rabbi of Montreal, of Hirsch Lande, and of Moshe Coviensky, have been among the initiators and builders of the communal United Talmud Torahs, the Jewish People's Library, the founders of the Zionist Movement in Canada and the Canadian Jewish Congress, and of synagogues and other religious and cultural institutions. In the United States, Rabbi Cohen's daughter, Miriam Fierst, carried on her Zionist work as a member of the National Board of Hadassah, and her son, Herbert Fierst, continues in the same tradition in Washington, D.C. In England, Rabbi Judah Julius Kyanski spread Torah study among parents and children in his congregations and Hebrew Schools in London. In Israel, Adina Kahanski of Rishon Lezion, the Kovensky families of Karkur and the families of Shmuel Kahana of Buston Hagalil, Batya Lapidus of Tel Aviv, Shifra Mitkovsky of Holon, Rabbi Dov Cohen of Jerusalem, and of Abraham and Dora Kahn in Savyon, have pioneered in the development of Moshavim and Kevutzot, of the Labor movement, and of scientific advancement as well as in the spreading of Torah study, from the days of the Second Aliyah (in 1904) to the present.

My purpose here is not to write a full biography of the many members of our family who have made important contributions toward the development of Jewish communal life in all the countries of their habitation. I have cited only a few names to illustrate the source from which this kind of activity emanated. It came to them as the legacy of our common ancestor, Rabbi Yehuda Hakohen of Budvich and his seven sons and four daughters, our great-grandparents, grandparents and parents. We did not just inherit, but we grew up in it, as it was cultivated through the generations in our own homes and became embedded in our character. We may call it the *ethos* (which is the Greek term for character, meaning habit acquired through performance), which Rabbi Yehuda left us as his legacy.

The distinction between an inheritance and a legacy was noted by Goethe (in his *Faust*: 682-83): "Was du ererbt von deinen Vätern hast, erwirb es, um es zu besitzen" (What you have inherited from your fathers, you must acquire it in order to possess it). An inherited characteristic may become a legacy if it is worked on and cultivated thus turning it into an *ethos* — one's character. We find this distinction drawn more clearly in the Torah. In Hebrew, the word for inheritance is *nahala*, and for legacy (or heritage), *morasha.* When the daughters of Zelophehad claimed their right to their father's portion of land, the Divine instruction reads: כן בנות צלפחד דוברות... והעברת את נחלת אביהן להן (What Zelophehad's daughters say is right . . . and you shall ו shall transfer their father's inheritance (*nahalat avihen*) to them. - Numbers 27:7). That is, an inheritance is transmitted to a person as a matter of legal right and the inheritor receives it passively, without having to cultivate it in order to make it his possession. On the other hand, when Moses passed on the Torah to the Sons of Israel, the Hebrew text says, תורה צוה לנו משה, מורשה קהלת יעקב (Moses bequeathed the Torah to us, a legacy (*Morasha*) to the community of Jacob. Deut. 33:4). Rashi comments on this verse: תורה אשר צוה לנו משה, מורשה היא לקהלת יעקב; אחזנוה ולא נעזבנה (The Torah that Moses bequeathed to us is a legacy to the community of Jacob; we have acquired it and we shall not forsake it). A legacy (or heritage) may be considered one's possession after one has worked on it, thus making it his own product. The application of this to a person's character (his *ethos*) may be illustrated by the following Hasidic story, which Martin Buber relates in his *Tales of the Hasidim* (Early Masters, 1964, "The Driver," p. 298). Once Rabbi Yitzhok of Vorki took his young son Mendel with him on a visit to Rabbi Yisroel of Rizhyn. The host invited his friend to go driving

29

with him. The child wanted to join them, but Rabbi Yisroel would not allow it. Making a play on the Hebrew word *merkava*, which means a carriage, but also refers to the mystic connotation of Ezekiel's chariot, Rabbi Yisroel told the boy that one who cannot expound the mysteries of the "merkava" is not ready to ride in it. The boy promptly retorted, "But I know how to drive!" The Rabbi was somewhat taken aback and said, "You do? Then drive!" And the boy climbed into the carriage, took hold of the reins and drove on like a master coachman. On the way, the host asked his friend, "Rov of Vorki, how did you deserve such a son?" Rabbi Yitzhok replied, "It is an undeserved gift."

The unusual capacities of a child are an hereditary gift; but the development of those capacities and their proper use require guidance and direction from parents and teachers. In the home of Rabbi Yehudah of Budvich and his sons and daughters, the young generations were given a proper upbringing in the traditional precepts of Torah and good deeds. While they lived in a village and were engaged in farming and innkeeping, they sent their sons to yeshivot and some of them received Rabbinic ordination. This is the legacy that has come to us, their descendants, and our families in the far reaches of the globe. We have cultivated it and made it our own way of life and have carried on its tradition.

Remembering the Abiding Faith of Our Forebears

An Account of an Ethical Will

In the past few years my wife has been engaged in tracing the distant backgrounds of our respective families in Hungary and Lithuania. In her search for the roots on my mother's side she discovered the existance of an "Ethical Will," a tsava'ah, written about 1823 by my great-great-great-grandfather, known as the Tsaddik of Lazday. Copies of this will are extant in two editions (1845 and some 65 years later) in the New York Public Library, in the library of the Jewish Theological Seminary of America, and among members of my family in this country. This tsava'ah belongs to the literature of ethical wills which goes back to Biblical days, to the testament that our patriarch Jacob left to his children (Genesis 49) and to the Blessing that Moses bestowed on the twelve tribes of Israel (Deuteronomy 33). Through the generations that followed, fathers left similar wills to their children which have become a souce of inspiration to all those who have had an opportunity to read them.

The Hebrew word "tsava'ah" is related to the word mitzvah or mitzvot — that is, moral and ethical precepts which every Jew is enjoined to observe in his everyday life. It is called a "will" when one writes it at an advanced age as a last testament to his offspring. However, it does not deal with one's worldly possessions, but rather with instructions how to cultivate the highest possible standard of moral conduct. Such is the nature of the Ethical Will of the Lazdayer Tsaddik, Rabbi Joseph Moses Abraham. Lazday (spelled Lazdijai on recent maps) is a small town in the Province of Suvalk in Lithuania, which since 1795 was part of the Russian Empire. Between the two world wars, in accordance with the Versailles Peace Treaty of 1919, Lithuania was an independent state. But in 1940 it was incorporated as one of the republics of the Union of Soviet Socialist Republics, and Lazday is now again part of Russia, while Suvalk and its environs belong to Poland.

Rabbi Joseph Moses Abraham was born in 1753 and died the 14th of Iyyar 1823. He lived in Lazday, where he was rabbi of the Jewish community and conducted a yeshiva for Talmudic students who came to him from many parts of the country. This was before the rise of central yeshivot in Lithuania, which started in Volozhin (1802) and later spread to Radin, Telsha, Lida, Mir, and other places. Prior to that time, Jewish youths who wanted to pursue the study of the Talmud would join a group under the guidance of a well known Talmudic scholar in a given town, where they would spend many years until they were ordained as rabbis and felt ready to continue their studies on their own. Some of them would take rabbinic positions in various towns, but many would continue their studies independently while engaging in some business or other gainful occupation as a source of their livelihood. Thus the Lazdayer Rabbi's own seven sons received rabbinic ordination but most of them never occupied an official position. One of those seven sons was named Alexander Siskind and he was my maternal grandmother's grandfather. When I was a small boy, my grandmother, Mindl Hodes Kollekandt, who lived at the time in Vilkavishk (my native town), used to call me "Zeide" because I was named after her zeide, the Tsaddik's son. The appellation "Tsaddik" or "saintly person" (not the same as a Hasidic Tsaddik, who was hardly known in Lithuania) was given to the Lazdayer Rabbi by his townsfolk and all who knew of him, because of his exemplary piety and high ethical conduct in all walks of life with his own family, with the members of his community as well as with people of other faiths. After he died, some of my relatives, other Jews, and also non-Jews in the vicinity of Lazday would go to pray at his grave for health and parnoso (a livelihood). I recall that my uncle, Layzer Grayevsky (the husband of my mother's sister Rivka), who was a staunch believer in the Tsaddik's influence, would frequent his grave whenever he was in the neighborhood.

The tsava'ah which the Lazdayer wrote is addressed to his sons, sons-in-law, his wife and other members of his family as well as to friends and relatives. It consists of two parts. The first is a short section in which he prescribes 22 specific instructions how to prepare his body after death for burial and how to conduct the funeral service, enjoining the Hevra Kadisha (the burial society) not to deviate from his instructions in the slightest. The second part, which is much larger and is the main burden of his will, bequeaths detailed guidelines for the moral life of his children and their descendants in keeping with the precepts of the Torah and the Talmud. We can only grasp the full import of this will if we gauge it in the light of the moral climate of the time and of the role which ethical wills played in the life of Lithuanian Jewry in general. There were quite a few of these tsava'ot in circulation in many Jewish households, and they constituted a moral code in their own right, which served as the foundation of what later became known as the Mussar Movement (of ethical practice) in Lithuania. The following description of this movement will give us a proper insight into the character of the tsava'ah before us.

Origin of the Movement

The founder and spiritual mentor of the Mussar Movement was Rabbi Israel Lipkin (born in Zager, Lithuania, 1810, and died in Koenigsberg, Prussia, 1883), known as Israel Salanter after the small town of Salant, near Bialystok, where he spent several years as a married youth (at the age of 12) at the home of his father-in-law, and came under the influence of Rabbi Zundl Salanter (1786-1866), the prototype of this movement, whose saintly conduct was the embodiment of its ethical precepts. The study of Talmud and rabbinic lore was always considered in Lithuania as the highest and noblest endeavor of every Jew, and this received greater impetus through the newly founded yeshivot led by the most prestigious of all, the Yeshiva of Volozhin, founded in 1802 by Rabbi Hayyim Volozhiner, the most outstanding disciple of the Gaon of Vilna. What Rabbi Zundl, who attended Volozhin, learned from his master, Rabbi Hayyim, and transmitted to his own followers was a new direction in Talmudic study, which was first introduced by the Vilna Gaon, and which aimed at a deep penetration into the substantive of Halacha (Talmudic law) to be applied in all practical everyday affairs, not just for the sake of abstract discussion and argumentation. To this Zundl added his own innovation of extending the same discipline to all matters affecting moral behavior besides ritual observance. For him the chief goal of Talmudic learning — and that meant a mastery of its vast and ramified literature — was the improvement and refinement of the human person, and this also became the goal of the Mussar Movement which had its inception in Zundl's personal life work, and which was later spread throughout the land by his most loyal disciple, Rabbi Israel Salanter. A brief glance at the mood of the time in retrospect will bring to light what was at stake in this enterprise.

Economic, Social, and Cultural Factors

In the 17th Century the Jewish population in the Ukraine and Poland suffered great losses during the Chmielnizki uprising (1848-49). Many communities were wiped out and organized life everywhere was disrupted. In the aftermath of these tragic events, the Sabbatai Zvi messianic movement sprang up, promising immediate redemption to the suffering people. But this upsurge of hope soon dissipated as the Sabbatean claims proved to be an illusion. At the same time, the social economic decline brought a certain degree of moral decay, and when the Polish Government abolished the Jewish Community Council, rabbinic leadership all but lost its influence over the masses who were struggling against insurmountable odds just to eke out a living. Another factor that shook the foundations of rabbinic Judaism was the rise of enlightenment in the general intellectual spheres, which began to make inroads also in Jewish intellectual circles. This trend fostered an individualistic self-assertion and a concomitant weakening of communal authority. In response to all those forces which undermined the traditional Jewish structure there arose the Hasidic movement, founded in the first half of the 18th Century by Rabbi Israel Ba'al Shem Tov (1700-1760), which met the moral and spiritual needs of the masses as individuals and also organized them under the aegis of a new type of leadership, the Hasidic Rebbe, whose authority was derived from the staunch loyalty of his followers and their unquestioned belief in his spiritual powers.

It is not my function here to dwell on the historical development of Hasidism, which is still a potent factor in Jewish life throughout the world. The point to be noted, however, is that for various reasons it did not strike root in Lithuania but, on the contrary, met its strongest opposition there from the established rabbinic leadership, notably from the Gaon of Vilna. One main reason was that the havoc which Polish and Ukrainian Jewry had suffered from the Chmielnizki uprising did not spill over into the Lithuanian regions, and the Jewish communal foundations there remained intact. Nevertheless, the other factors, such as, the spread of secular enlightenment and the lowering of moral climate took their toll in Lithuania as well. And although the influence of the rabbinate was still strong, its rigid emphasis on Talmudic erudition created a caste of scholars who failed to meet the moral and spiritual needs of the people. It was mainly to fill this gap that Rabbi Israel Salanter set in motion what became known as the Mussar Movement.

Organizing the Community

We mentioned earlier that this movement grew out of the ethical literature, books on mussar and ethical wills of past generations, which had circulated in Jewish homes, especially among the descendants of the will makers, and had a great impact on certain individuals. Their personal involvement consisted chiefly in isolating themselves periodically from their mundane affairs and devoting an hour or two each day to the study of mussar books. In his early stages, Israel Salanter followed the same path, which had been paved for him by his master, Rabbi Zundl. But after a while he realized that individual edification and purification of character, though lofty as such, would not by itself reshape the social ethical character of the community as a whole. He then stepped out of his self-imposed isolation into the public arena and actively sought to gain adherents to his cause and to forge it into a vibrant force of communal regeneration. Yet his goal was not to rise in opposition to rabbinic teaching or authority but, on the contrary, to bring the masses closer to that teaching on their own level of comprehension and through their own ways of self-expression. At the same time, he sought to bring the Talmudic scholars into a more intimate relationship with the people.

In his public lectures, which were attended by the learned as well as the unlearned in large numbers, Rabbi Israel employed the pilpul-argumentation of the former in order to meet them on their own ground, and then converted those arguments into the simple language of persuasive reasoning to suit his general audience. In both instances he aimed to demonstrate from Talmudic sources that mussar (morality) is the foundation of all Torah learning. In essence he tried to emulate the dictum of the Talmudic sages which are replete in rabbinic literature, such as Rav's statement, "The mitzvot were given only to purify human character" (Bereshit Rabba 44a), or as Joseph Albo spelled it out explicitly in his Book of Principles, III:27), "All the commandments, whether positive or negative, are a means to the attainment of human perfection, or a certain degree thereof, if they are done with the [heart's] intention." And it is the "heart's intention" which Israel Salanter especially tried to open up to all the precepts of the Torah, for it is the inner intention that may lead man to moral improvement. Rabbi Israel thus took mussar out of the customary realm of Aggada (story, aphorism and preachment) and placed it in the field of Halacha (law) on an equal footing with all other aspects of law and deserving the same attention and learned exposition. Once Israel Salanter came out with his teachings into the open, he used not only his vast Talmudic scholarship but also his outstanding organizing abilities to form groups of laymen who would meet regularly in synagogues to study mussar books and, most important, he introduced regular courses of mussar study in the yeshivot of his time. His main influence was felt in the two metropolitan centers of Lithuanian Jewry, in Vilna and Kovno; but he also traveled, taught and organized in other towns as well as abroad, such as Paris and Koenigsberg.

Character Training

Moral conduct is fundemantally grounded in human character which is molded by habit. Torah study had been inculcated in the

Jewish character as a matter of habit through the ages, and in the life of the Lithuanian Jew this habit became his second nature. Even those who could not devote time to study considered it a personal privilege to support Torah students. Hence the Mussar Movement found its way to the soul of the Lithuanian Jew through study. It was only a matter of convincing the learners that the study of ethical works was as important as the study of Halacha and that, indeed, those works carried the same weight as Halacha. And thus through the new habit of learning mussar came the process of character development which, in turn, led to the habit of moral conduct. All the mussar books emphasize love of God and fellow man, modesty and honesty in relationship with others and in one's own self-esteem. But in order to cultivate these traits a person must gain a deep understanding of their values in his own life and, what is most significant, he must be moved by them through personal experience. Mussar training demands not just an outer show of love, modesty and honesty, but a deep conviction and an inner transformation to be realized through the very manner of study. We, therefore, find in the mussar books the admonition that the learner should become absorbed in his studies to the point of being moved to shed tears over his shortcomings and to confess and repent his transgressions — not confessing to someone else, but in his innermost self before the Divine Presence. In Jewish tradition Torah study was always regarded as a form of Divine worship. Now mussar study sought to elevate it still higher through the purification of the heart as well as of the mind.

The Individual as the Center of Attention

We noted above that the rise of secular enlightenment was accompanied by a trend toward individualism. Basically, the Mussar Movement was intended as a counteraction to the disrupting forces of enlightenment, yet it utilized its principles for the strengthening of the character of the Jew as an individual. In this respect, mussar study followed the general individualistic trend of the time. This placement of the individual at the center of attention brought a reaction on the part of some communal leaders, including heads of yeshivot, who resisted the spread of mussar study as an isolationist anti-social phenomenon and a threat to communal stability. This struggle curtailed the movement from becoming the accepted norm of the organized Jewish community.

Within its restricted scope, mussar study was a process of self-education in which the individual assumed full responsibility for his character training. Besides an understanding of the ethical precepts and the experience of an inner transformation, there was also the need for a tangible application of those precepts to everyday affairs in each individual's personal behavior. The model for this kind of practice was created by Rabbi Zundl, but it was Rabbi Israel who systematized it as a sort of "science of mussar" based on tradition and "worldly wisdom," or as he phrased it, "being wise to the ways of the world."

As a student of secular sciences and especially of human psychology, Rabbi Israel considered such knowledge essential to the training and practice of ethical conduct. He conceived the life of man as a struggle against evil temptation, which may be overcome only by deliberate planning, by a kind of strategy against the enemy, to "foresee consequences, anticipate the evil day before it arrives, take counsel and plan how to conduct oneself in relation to others, and to diminish or lighten the threat of temptation, to the extent that one's fear of God becomes greater than his desires" — in a word, to use the cunning of modern psychology and wordly wisdom as far as possible toward the realization of the ethical way of life.

While the Mussar Movement was limited to small circles of laymen and yeshiva students, it had a remarkable influence on the lives of its adherents and also permeated the consciousness of the Jewish population in Lithuania in general. This is not the place to detail its impact on the various social-political movements which spread in the Jewish community in the latter part of the 19th and the early part of the 20th centuries. Suffice it to say that it fostered social and ethical ideals which are valid for all time, and it gave the individual Jew an anchor in human reality grounded in his own tradition.

The Moral Instruction of the Lazdayer's Will

As a forerunner of the Mussar Movement, as described above, the Lazdayer Tsaddik's "will" was written in the rabbinic language and style of its time, grounded in the moral precepts of Torah and Talmud, and addressed to a generation that was steeped in that lore and to whom Torah study was the highest good in life. It is noteworthy that its guidelines are reflected very clearly in the concepts and practical instructions of the Mussar Movement which followed closely upon it. Yet its teachings and methods of realization are applicable also to other modes of thinking and to different lifestyles in every generation. The Lazdayer Tsaddik, too, considers character development as the prime goal of Torah study, and he too bases it on Halacha, but as it is exemplified in ethical writings, which he recommends for regular daily study together with the Talmud and Midrash. Following Hillel's interpretation of the Biblical dictum, "Love thy neighbor as thyself," he emphasizes the authentic moment of this trait, saying: "Love every human being truly as yourself . . . for all the mitzvot put together depend on it, as has been elaborated in many books." And the best way to attain it is by being humble in relation to all people and not to humble them, even members of one's own family. And if one finds it necessary to correct his children and lead them on the right path, he should "not do it with anger in his heart, but always with a heart full of joy and attachment to the Creator."

The Tsaddik sees anger, in particular, as a source of many evils, and he dwells on it at length, prescribing certain ways of avoiding it, such as not to respond immediately to a situation which arouses one's anger, but to allow time for it to subside; to think before uttering a word; to train oneself not to get angry at all; and, even when anger is justifiable, not to let oneself be caught in its trap, but weigh its consequences and act with restraint. The best antidote to this evil is the cultivation of modesty, which one should "pursue to perfection." This may be done through a regimen of daily study of an ethical work with innermost intent. Quoting a Midrash, he writes: "One should always be modest with respect to Torah and fear of Heaven, to one's father and mother, wife and children, and all members of one's family as well as to neighbors, relatives or nonrelatives, so that he may be beloved by people and spend his days and years with a good name." The Tsaddik practiced what he taught, as he says to his children: "Follow my example and do the same and thereby you will be privileged to rejoice in this [world] and in the world to come." He instructed them by persuasion and with solicitude for their welfare. "My sons, sons-in-law, and relatives," he writes, "beloved of my soul, the pleasure of my eyes, accept my instruction and do not turn away from the words of my mouth, and you will understand and gain wisdom, and will know and observe all that is written before you. Then it will be for your good and mine."

He shows his utmost tenderness when he asks his wife's forgiveness for anything he might have done to offend her, even unwittingly. "My beloved wife," he says to her in his will, "my precious dove, I beg you, forgive me with complete forgiveness . . . whether I caused you grief or sinned against your body or dignity." The same personal concern for others runs through the entire text of his will.

Like all moral teachers, the Tsaddik regards excessive passion as the chief cause of sin. "All of man's lusts and passions," he writes, "come from the Serpent," the relentless tempter. Yet, while he urges man to learn how to control his passions, he does not deprecate them as evil forces in themselves, but rather advises that they could be turned to good through the performance of mitzvot: "They should be directed toward holiness and the worship of God." And if in moments of weakness one succumbs to temptation, he should cleanse himself through an examination of his deeds, confession and repentance, the same method that was later prescribed by Rabbi Israel Salanter and in the same manner, that is, not just on formal occasions of public worship, but in solitude with "bowed head and a broken heart," until one is touched to his innermost core. This, the Tsaddik felt, was of great import to the purification and refinement of one's character. Despite the solemn tone of his dissertation, the Tsaddik repeatedly stresses full enjoyment of life, but in moderation, whether in food, drink or sexual relation. "During a meal," he advises, "one should be very careful not to have worries or a sorrowful heart . . . but should eat with joy, in good spirit and with attachment to the Creator." "One should greet all persons in a cheerful manner, and even when one is worried he should show himself to them with a smile on his face." And we have already noted his admonition to treat one's family "always with a heart of joy." Above all, it is the joy of family life that shines forth in the Tsaddik's instruction to his children. There is no gap there between generations. The father speaks with a deep faith in Jewish tradition and with complete trust in his children that they will continue it in their personal lives and pass it on to their own children in succession. This continuity may assume different forms of self-expression and, indeed, in the course of the generations that have followed it has undergone many changes. What is abiding is the faith of our forebears in the intrinsic values of Jewish life and their trust that these values will never cease from among their offspring.

1981

My Religious Belief

A Letter to a Friend

July 30, 1984.

Dear Ida Pearl,

I received your lovely letter in April, before Dorothy and I left on a prolonged trip to Israel and Italy. On the way back we spent a few weeks in New York, New Jersey, and Baltimore with our children, waiting for the birth of a second grandchild, who arrived *in a mazeldike shoh* July 10th. Her name is Anna Leah Kohanski (first name after my late mother), a pretty little girl. We then returned home and have now settled down to our various activities as heretofore.

I am glad to hear that you have enjoyed reading my items which I sent you. Somehow you have become intrigued with the quotation on the title page of the Lazdayer Tsaddik's "Ethical Will" and felt that there must be some straight line of religious belief between my ancestor and myself. That is so, but not in the same orientation or expression. The difference between us is basically a matter of direction: his toward the other world, mine toward this world.

The Tsaddik saw the other world as a continuation of this world, only in greater purity of moral conduct, free from the vicissitudes of earthly travail (which is what he meant by "proper rest"), but full of zest and activity in a "life eternal," that is, a life of eternal values, according to the precepts of the Torah, as they may be applied in the heavenly domain. As talmudic lore has it, God, too, busies Himself with the Torah every day.

My own way in religion is in man's relation with God (which is the fundamental meaning of the term *religion*) directed to this world of nature and fellowman. One who does not believe in God does not have that relation and is therefore outside the religious field of discourse. Belief cannot be taught. One grows up with it at home or in school. Otherwise, one may come to it through personal experience, after having realized that life without religious belief remains unfulfilled, incomplete. By the way, this is implied in the original meaning of the word *tsaddik*, as we find it in Genesis, 6.9: נח איש צדיק, תמים היה בדורותיו, את האלהים התהלך נח , "Noah was a tsaddik, a complete (self-fulfilled) man in his generation: [for] Noah directed himself toward God."

While I see fulfillment in life possible only in moral conduct (within human possibilities in life on earth), this is not the main thrust of my religious belief. Rather it has to do (philosophically speaking) with a complete world outlook which cannot, in my view, be contemplated without the reality of God as creator and provider of the world of nature and man. I have found no answer for it in science or in the secular philosophies.

In Jewish tradition the Torah is the central source for this kind of outlook. Other religions have their respective sacred literatures that help them come nearer to God. In the Jewish way, the choice of belief and worship was made in ancient times by the people as a whole. Today each individual decides for himself or herself. Nevertheless the decision must be based on a given tradition, on the way a given people relates itself with God. (See, e.g., Exodus, ch. 24, and Joshua, ch. 24.)

I trust that this brief excursion has somewhat lightened your burden of self-fulfillment. The rest is as Hillel, whom you have quoted, said as a corollary to his advice to the God-seeking, go on and study.

As ever, yours,

Alexander

PART I

Philosophy

Through philosophy I find freedom
in my relationship with fellowman,
nature, and the Supreme Being. I
have cultivated it as a discipline
of thought to gain insight into the
reality of the human condition in
the world.

Solomon Ibn Gabirol

Bronze by the British sculptor H. Reed Armstrong
in the Jardin de Alcazabilla, Malaga, Spain

From the Jewish Heritage in Spain
The Statue of Solomon Ibn Gabirol

Several years ago I visited Spain in search of some tangible remains of what is known as the Golden Age (11th to 13th centuries) of Jewish life and letters in that country. In Madrid, where I made my headquarters, I became acquainted with David Gonzalo Maeso, professor of Hebrew and Arabic studies at the University of Granada (emeritus), a leading Christian scholar in his field, author of many books on the subject and a true lover of the Jewish heritage, and particularly a most ardent admirer of Solomon Ibn Gabirol, "poet, philosopher and theologian," as he called him, a native of Malaga. Gonzalo Maeso presented me with a copy of his monograph on Gabirol with a reprint of his statue on the front cover. I did not know until then that there was such a monument in existence and I immediately prepared myself for a pilgrimage to Malaga, where it is located.

Remains of a Glorious Past

Going through the southern parts of Spain, I came across the towns where Jewish life had flourished during the Middle Ages. I roamed through the streets and alleys of Sevilla, Cordoba, Toledo and Granada, before I reached my destination in Malaga. In Sevilla I lodged in a small hotel in the Plaza de los Curtidores (the Square of the Tanners), which was in the old Jewish ghetto in the 14th Century. In a nearby street named Levies there is the church of San Bartolome, converted from an old synagogue still bearing Hebrew inscriptions on its portals. In the same area there is another church, Madre de Dios, converted from a synagogue in 1396. The Jewish district had covered some 18 to 20 square blocks, from Calle San Esteban to Santa Teresa, south of the main avenue Mendez Pelayo, named after the famous literary critic and historian who translated Judah Halevi into Spanish.

In Cordoba I wound my way through Plaza de Juda Halevi into Calle Judios where I stopped at the monument of Maimonides, a native of that city, and at the Sinagoga, built in 1315, and I continued to the end of the street at Puerta de Almodovar, called in Arabic Bab al Yahud (The Jewish Gate), which had enclosed the Jewish quarter in former days. Around the Mezquita-Cathedral (the famous cathedral converted from a Mosque) I came upon the Hotel Maimonides, the Meson de la Juderia on Calle Juderia, and Edificio Leiva Aguilar on the corner of a street by the same name. Further than that I found no traces of Jewish habitations. In Toledo, the jewel of medieval Spain, rich in Jewish legend since the end of the First Temple, the birthplace of Judah Halevi, I saw the two most impressive remains of the Jewish past, the Sinagoga de Santa Maria Blanca, or the Main Synagogue, built in the 12th Century, and the Sinagoga del Transilo, also known as the Synagogue of Samuel Levi, the ill-fated Minister of Finance to Pedro I, who built it in 1336. The former synagogue is now but an empty shell, and the latter is partly a Jewish museum containing old tombstones, Megilla and Torah scrolls, some sacred books of modern times, and tablets with inscriptions of Jewish families of many past generations. Near the Sinagoga del Transito is the Palace of Samuel Levi, later taken over by El Greco and now housing his paintings, furniture and artifacts. The only sign of an active Jewish presence in Toledo is the "Sinai" Restaurant, opposite the Sinagoga del Transito, owned by Alberto (Abraham) Zuckerman, a French-born Jew, who had spent 15 years in Brooklyn, N.Y., then left the United States for Israel, stopped over in Madrid, where he opened a kosher restaurant, and has lived there to this day. Recently he transferred his restaurant to Toledo (to serve Jewish tourists), but continued his residence in Madrid. There were no Jewish residents then in Toledo, as there were none in Cordoba, Sevilla or Granada — a phenomenon which was, and most likely still is, indicative of the Jewish position in Spain now and of its prospects for the future.

The Jews in Modern Spain

When I was there in 1975, there were some 9,000 Jews in the country, most of them originating from Eastern and Western

Europe, North Africa, and South America, who came there during and after World War II and established themselves largely in Madrid, Barcelona and Malaga, and some smaller communities. In 1965 Generalisimo Franco formally recognized the Jewish community of Madrid, and in 1968 he permitted it to build its Center-Synagogue. It also operates an elementary Hebrew School and conducts a summer camp. In Malaga the Jews maintain a synagogue on the sixth floor of a commercial building, which is open only on weekends. Although the inscription on the plaque dedicating the synagogue in Madrid notes that this "will be the harbinger of the revival of Judaism in Spain," there does not seem to be a real tie between the present Jewish community and the glorious past of the Middle Ages, nor is there a real indication that a bridge might be thrown from that era into the future. Spain is a Catholic country which is only moderately tolerant of other religions. Whatever it inherited from the Jews and the Arabs it has integrated into its own cultural image. The Spanish scholars and intelligentsia are very proud of this heritage, but only insofar as it has become native to their ethnic way of life. Maimonides, Halevi, Gabirol and the rest are to them like Moses, Isaiah or Jesus, part and parcel of their Christian mode of thought.

A typical expression of this approach to Judaism we find in a book *Elegio y Nostalgia de Toledo*, by the late poet laureate of that city, Gregorio Maranon. While he speaks of "the miracle of holy tolerance in the existence of the synagogue and the mosque side by side with the Catholic church as the three are united by the same ardor for knowledge," he does not hesitate to justify "the expulsion of the Jews, who [as he claims] threatened to smother the Spanish populace. In Granada I met Pascual Pascual Recuero, professor Hebrew and Arabic at the University of Granada. In the course of our conversation I asked him what prospects there were for a revival of the Jewish community in Spain as a cultural factor in the life of the country. He answered plainly and openly, "None" that he could foresee. Yet he felt very possessive of the Jewish legacy of the past and was very proud of his role in getting the municipality to name a street Tibonidas, in honor of the famous Jewish translator Judah Ibn Tibon, who was born in Granada in 1120, and "who rescued scientific and philosophical works for universal culture," as a brief notice in the local newspaper read.

A more benevolent opinion, though no less proprietary, is voiced by Gonzalo Maeso in his book *El Legado del Judaismo Espanol*, in which he concludes: "These important parts of universal culture which constitute the legacy of Israel and the legacy of Islam, and in which the legacy of Spanish Jewry stands out with unique significance, encompassing many mysterious Spanish fermentations, are the glories on our escutcheon. This phase must always be taken into account for our evaluation [of this legacy]." The Spanish Jews, of whom a larger number remained in the country than was expelled at the end of the 15th Century, were subsequently absorbed into the general populace, physically and spiritually. It may be to the credit of present-day Spanish scholars and cultural leaders that they are so vitally interested in the Jewish heritage that they have established special institutes and courses of study for its understanding and perpetuation. But all these grand efforts are only for the sake of uncovering the "mysterious Spanish fermentations." which they seek in that heritage and wish to engrave them as the "glories on [the Spanish] escutcheon." The basic character of this escutcheon has been well described by Gonzalo Maeso in one of his articles, "Espana es Catolica" (1967).

I have interrupted the account of my itinerary in order to reflect on what is actually left of the Jewish legacy in a land where great Jewish minds had produced a Golden Era of the highest of their creative powers. Among them was Solomon Ibn Gabirol who perhaps made the greatest contribution of all to Spanish religious thought. It seems, to use a phrase of Goethe's as if "two souls had dwelt in his breast." As a philosopher he left no trace of his Jewishness in his Arabic work, *The Source of Life*, but as a poet he poured out his heart to the God of his fathers and wrote Hebrew liturgies which adorn our High Holiday services. We may say of his philosophical output, in the words of the Paytan in the Sukkot prayers, "I have paid on this festival for all the 70 nations." For Gabirol not only contributed to Spain but to all of Christendom. Before I describe these two strands in our philosopher-poet, let us first go to Malaga and see how a modern sculptor portrayed this remarkable man.

Before the Statue of Ibn Gabirol

Malaga is a summer resort on the Mediterranean Sea which attracts visitors from every part of the country and from all over the world. It is also a very active business and cultural center, enlivened by a sizable contingent of American summer residents. The statue of Ibn Gabirol is situated in the Jardin de Alcazabilla in the eastern section of the town. I had some difficulty in reaching it. I was directed from one cultural institution to another until I finally came to the Archeological Museum. Then I discovered that my problem was due to my English pronunciation of Ibn Gabirol (accent on the second syllable), of whom no one had heard by that name. At last, an official in the Museum detected my error and said, "You mean Aben Gabirol" (accent on the last syllable), took me outside and pointed to a small garden across the street. And there it was, the only monument in that garden, standing all alone in the midst of trees, shrubs and flowers, bathing in bright sunlight under a deep blue sky.

There is a legend that Gabirol was murdered and buried under a dead trea by an Arab who had been jealous of his fame. Soon that tree came to life and began bearing fruit, which alarmed the authorities. After thorough investigation the culprit was apprehended and brought to justice. It is thus fitting that Gabirol's indomitable spirit has now (in 1970) been immortalized in a bronze statue, conceived and formed by a British sculptor, H. Reed Armstrong, and placed among live trees and flowers in his native city. An inscription on the pedestal reads, "ExCmo Ayuntamiento de la Ciudad Erigio esta Bronce en el IX Centenario de ABEN GABIROL, Poeta y Filosofo de Malaga" (The very distinguished municipal government erected this bronze on the 9th Centennial [of the death] of Ibn Garirol, Poet and Philosopher of Malaga.) The statue is in full length, robed in a loosely flowing garment, the head covered with a turban, the right hand stretched by his side and the left holding a scroll pressed against his chest. His facial features are elongated, with hollow cheeks and a slightly humped nose, and his eyes are turned downward in deep contemplation — altogether the portrayal of a man who had experienced great suffering throughout his life, and who had been consumed physically by constant pain and spiritually by an insatiable drive for knowledge.

Gabirol's Life and Character

Solomon Ibn Gabirol was born in 1021 and was orphaned in early childhood. Left alone without parents, brother or friends, he was then taken to Saragosa, where he was brought up by a prominent man, named Yekutiel, who was later immortalized by his protege's poems. When Yekutiel died (at the hands of his political enemies), Gabirol, still only a youth of 18 years, left the city for Granada, where he was taken under the wing of Rabbi Samuel Ha-Nagid, the famous scholar, poet and statesman, and Secretary to the Calif's Grand Vizier in Granada. Gabirol suffered from a debilitating disease, apparently tuberculosis, which tormented him all his life and cut off his years at the age of 49 (some say 30), in 1070. His burning desire for knowledge, coupled with his remarkable poetic talents, stood in perpetual conflict with his bodily affliction, to which he gave poetic expression from his early youth. His first poems that have come down to us were written when he was 16 years of age. The following selection (cited in my translation from the Hebrew) will give us an insight into his life and character. In his very first poem we read of the burden of his lot, which never abated.

My joy breaks forth in a sigh,
My song is filled with sorrow,
Any laughter resounds like a cry,
My life is short, my days I borrow.

My heart is rent with searing pain
Through endless seasons — no help in store.
How long for a healing can I hope in vain?
What if balm came, and I was no more?

Because of his absorption in his studies and the frailty of his body he had difficulty in making friends, which weighed heavily on his mind.

I do not bemoan my lot;
But when I do, it is for knowledge that I cry.
And I do not rejoice, but if I do,
To gain a friend is my greatest joy.

Gabriol was fully aware of his poetic powers even from his youth, and he did not hesitate to declare them openly. In several

poems he described the struggle going on in him, as he was trying to
subdue his physical pain which often prevented him from creative
writing. In his young days he declared almost defiantly,

I am the master and song is my slave;
I am the harp unto singers and bards.
My song is a crown unto kings
And a miter on heads of the lords.

In later years, when this incessant strife had sapped his strength,
he sadly realized his limitations, even though his goal remained
lofty. He gave it expression in a lengthy poem called "I Am the
Man."

I am the man who has girded his loins
And will not desist until he reaches his goal;
Whose heart abhors the rule of his heart,
Who disdains the flesh that embeddeth his soul.

I am one who has chosen knowledge from his youth.
And even though he suffer a thousand blows,
His edifice shattered, his fences broken,
And his shoots uprooted — he will fulfill his vows.

Were he not fettered by affliction
And imprisoned by daily pains,
He would have reached the heights of understanding,
He would have scaled the pinnacles of wisdom's domains.

If only my heart would not grow faint untimely
Then I could verily fulfill my vow.
But one is caught, my friends, by what he fears;
And what I have feared has come to me now.

After describing a stormy nocturne in which he sees his spirit, like
the moon, entrapped in dark clouds, he ends his poem in a tone of
submission to his fate.

Thus has God restrained my will
And my heart's desire did He arrest.
He put my mind in fetters dark
And from His Tower foiled my quest.

No, my friends, I shall not hope
For lunar light to guide my path;
The clouds moved swiftly over it
As if to pour on me their wrath.

Yet I yearn for its unveiling;
To see its face again I long.
Like a slave remembered by his master
I would rejoice, burst forth in song.

But like a man in combat, weary of his armor,
Falters as he throws his dart;
So is one weighed down by sorrows,
Though on stars he set his heart.

I stood before Gabirol's statue in the little garden a long time, peered into every twist and furrow of his pensive face, and I felt those lines which he had written in his youth and in later years surging in their rhythmic cadences through his mind.

Philosopher-Theologian

The knowledge to which Gabirol had dedicated his life was philosophy as a means of attaining a knowledge of God, and he expounded it in his work *The Fountain of Life*. Originally written in Arabic, it was later translated into Hebrew, entitled "M'kor Hayyim," only in excerpts, by Shem Tov Falakera (13th Century), but received scant notice in Jewish learned circles and none among general readers. However, this work had been previously (in the 12th Century) translated into Latin under the title "Fons Vitae" with the author's name transformed into Avicebron, and became a source of doctrinal dispute among the medieval Christian philosophers, the Franciscans siding with its teachings, and the Dominicans opposing it. Neither side was aware of the fact that the author was a Jew, some thinking he was a Mohammedan and others, a Christian. The Arabic original was lost and the Hebrew short version was all but forgotten. The main reason that this work of Gabirol's had no influence on Jewish religious thinking is that it could not be identified basically as a Jewish view of the world or of God. It tended to explain reality in terms of a triune of principles, which appealed especially to the

Christians, although Gabirol had no intention of leading in that direction. It was not until 1846 that Solomon Munk, a French Jewish scholar, discovered the only extant copy of the Hebrew short version in the national library in Paris, and after comparing it with the Latin "Fons Vitae" was able to identify the two versions as one and the same work of Ibn Gabirol. Thus for centuries Gabirol's philosophy fructified the thinking of Chrisitan theologians, but left no imprint on the Jewish mind. Recently, the full text has been translated from the Latin into Hebrew, *Sefer M'kor Hayyim*, by Jacob Blaustein, and rehabilitated in the Jewish fold "with the aid of Mosad Harav Cook" (Tel Aviv 1950).

Poet of Hebrew Liturgy

Ibn Gabirol wrote numerous liturgical poems that have entered into the Sephardic and Ashkenazic prayerbooks for the Sabbath, the Three Festivals, and Rosh Hashanah and Yom Kippur. They are all filled with religious fervor and strong national sentiment, steeped in Biblical and Talmudic lore. In many of them a refrain would run through every stanza ending in a Biblical quotation appropriate to the theme of the poem. Thus in the "Introduction to Shofarot," each stanza ends with a reference to the shofar.

God dwells high above human dwellings.
Praise Him, ye multitudes, honor Him,
Shout for joy before God the King
"With trumpets and the voice of the shofar."

Thy people, summoned to ascend the Mount of Olives,
Flock there at Thy command;
"The entire nation perceives the thunders,
The lightning and the voice of the Shofar."

In a "Song of Redemption for the Fourth Sabbath after Passover," the poet presents a dialogue between The Holy One Blessed be He and the Community of Israel.

The Holy One:
You, who are consumed by bereavement,
Why do you cry?
Has your heart despaired of waiting so long?

Israel:
Thine end is extended, and I continue in darkness.

The Holy One:
Do not lose hope, for soon
I will send my angel to clear your way.
I will anoint my king on Mount Zion;
A messenger will come to clear your path.
"Say unto Zion, the Lord rules."
"Behold your king will come again."

Israel:
In days of yore my mulitiudes
Were drowned by one king only,
And rescue from Egypt and Babylon came very soon.
Now I am surrounded by all "the four kings"
Who like vultures devour my flesh and do not desist.

The Holy One:
Trust the Rock who has given His oath
That your lover who has gone will return.

Ibn Gabirol's greatest religious poem is "Keter Malkhut" (The
Royal Crown), comprising 40 long stanzas. Following is the 34th
stanza which has been incorporated into the penitent prayers of the
Yom Kippur services, called "Ashamnu." In the prayerbook it is
recited in the plural, in keeping with communal worship, but in
Gabirol's version it is an individual confession and thus written in
the singular.

My God, I know that my sins are too many to recount
And my faults too numerous to remember.
But I will recall only a few, like a drop in the sea,
And I will confess.
Perhaps I can still the roar of their dashing waves,
"And Thou wilt hear in Heaven and forgive."

I have been guilty of breaking Thy Torah,
I have disdained Thy commandments;
In my heart I have abhorred
And with my mouth I have spoken rashly.

I have been iniquitous, wicked and insolent,
I have done violence, have imputed falsehood;
I have counselled evil without ground,
I have defected, revolted, blasphemed;
I have harassed and have been stubborn.

I have ignored Thy rebukes and have done evil,
I have corrupted my ways
  and have gone astray from my paths;
I have transgressed Thy commandments
  and have turned away.
"But Thou art just in all that has come upon me,
For Thou hast dealt in truth
  and I have done wrong."

Gabirol also composed "Introductions" (Reshuyot) to certain prayers, which are in a joyous, even playful, mood, as shown in the following Reshut to "Yishtabach" in the Sabbath morning service.

My beloved, rise at dawn
And come with me, for
My heart yearns to see
The sons of my people.

I will spread before you
Golden couches in my court;
I will set for you a table
And prepare for you a meal.

I will fill you a goblet
Of the finest grapes in my vineyard
To please your taste, and you will drink
To your heart's desire.

I will greet you with a joy
That fits my people's prince,
The son of Jesse,
God's servant, the Bethlehemite.

On my return from this pilgrimage, I still was searching for the glories of the Golden Age, though no longer in the land where it had once flourished, but close at home. For indeed, that heritage is stored up among the treasures of the Jewish creative spirit and is preserved in the hearts and minds of its people.

1980

Martin Buber — An Appreciation

Volumes have already been written about Buber and, now that he has passed away, many more studies of his life and works will follow. On first learning of the passing of this sage of Jerusalem, and being deeply moved by the suddenness of the fateful news, one is not apt to engage in a lengthy dissertation on the place of this singular man in the world of ideas, his role in reviving the ancient Hebraic spirit, his unique influence on Christian theologians, or his particular, often divergent, path toward Jewish national redemption. Rather, one would search for a brief statement on the quintessence of his message to modern man.

At an early age, Buber began to delve into universal problems of our time. Born in 1878 in Vienna, he was raised in the Jewish traditional home of his grandfather, in the Hasidic town of Lemberg, Galitia. Yet, he also imbibed the critical thinking that prevailed in that home, and he tried to blend the old with the new, the sacred with the profane. His Bar Mitzvah speech was on the German poet of the era of emancipation, Friedrich Schiller. One need not discuss here to what extent this apostle of human worth and freedom had influenced Buber's later thoughts. But in one of his philosophical poems, Schiller says "to the Metaphysician," who is perched on the pinnacle of Plato's ideas, "Of what use is it all to you now, except to look into the valley?"

Apparently, Buber, as a lad, did not heed the poet's admonition, for he kept soaring higher and higher into metaphysical speculation, until he came on the verge of suicide. As quoted by Meyer Levin, who interviewed the octogenerian less than four years ago (New York Times Magazine, Dec. 3, 1961), the 14-year-old youth was overcome, to the point of self-destruction, by a "mysterious and overwhelming compulsion [to visualize the] limiting brink of time — or its limitlessness."

The Classical Tragedy

Reason, enlightenment, science brought no surcease from his torments. Is this not the Faustian tragedy of our generation? After studying, "with utmost diligence, philosophy, law and medicine, and alas also theology," as Goethe's Faust ruefully soliloquizes, man is still ignorant of his fellow-man and nature around him and of the Divine Presence above him, even more so than heretofore. At the time of his great agony, Buber was saved by the master of "pure reason," Immanuel Kant. On reading Kant's *Prolego-mena* he learned that time is only man's way (*Handlungsweise*) of approaching and gauging reality, but is not reality itself.

Buber thus accepted the limitations of pure reason — limitations, as Kant taught, bound by sense perception and the categories of human understanding. He knew there is a beyond, "an eternal, far removed from the finite and the infinite"; but it could not be reached by reason. Knowledge derived from reason is limited by reason's own faculties, which can yield only a scientific account of things as we see them around us, but not as they really are in themselves. That was the essence of Kant's teaching, and it may have abated Buber's "overwhelming compulsion" to visualize the limits of time, but it did not quench his thirst for a full knowledge of reality.

A Different Approach

If science does not lead to certainty, what will? Buber struck out on his own path to find the answer. Some 30 years later, in 1923, he formulated it in his book *I and Thou.* Of all his writings on philosophy, psychology, education, sociology, mysticism, Hasidism, and including his monumental German rendition of the Holy Scriptures, Buber's little volume, *I and Thou*, — really the size of an essay — has made the greatest impact on his contemporaries, scholars as well as laymen. There are two contributing factors, one personal-subjective, the other philosophical-objective.

Kant said of himself that he was awakened from dogmatic rationalism by David Hume's skepticism. Buber was awakened from enlightened rationalism by a deep-moving personal experience. After he became well known through his Hasidic tales, there came to him one day a young man, as one would come to a "Tsaddik," to relieve his soul of a very pressing burden. The master did not open himself to the young man and the latter left without being able to divest himself of his troubles, and shortly thereafter committed suicide. This event shook Buber to his innermost depths. He felt he had not "turned to the other"; he had only been philosophizing about reality, but had not lived it. That set him on a new path, which led to *I and Thou.*

If we read carefully this concise volume, attuning ourselves to its cadences and tensions, we may re-live with the author his ascent from the shattering experience to the purification of his soul. However, while this may be its underlying tone, expressed in many lyric, religious passages, *I and Thou* is not a "confession." It is first and foremost an objective-philosophical essay on fundamental problems of knowledge — knowledge of nature around us, of fellow-man with us, and of God beyond us.

Man has been concerned with these problems ever since the ancient Greeks posed them before him. The predicament of our age is that too many leaders of thought have all but given up hope of ever attaining a knowledge of God or even of man. Instead, they have put their faith in a knowledge of nature, and of man as a part of it, through scientific investigation and discovery. But the more the scientists have probed into the recesses of physical nature and into the depths of the psychological, anthropological and sociological behavior of man, the more they have come to realize their inability to achieve true knowledge of either man or nature. Some scientists-philosophers have ventured the proposition that there is a "great unknown" in the physical universe which cannot be fathomed by the human mind. This has led man to despair and is at the root of modern skepticism, insecurity, and mistrust that pervades the relationships of men and nations in the world today.

Shows an Exit

In *I and Thou* Buber tries to point the way out of this predicament. His message to modern man is that he need not despair of his quest for certainty, because man has in himself also the capacity of knowing reality as is. Does one have to give up science? No. But there is another way of seeing reality besides the scientific one. In his very opening statement, Buber lays down this basic principle: "To man the world is twofold, in accordance with his twofold attitude," which is at the core of his being. In the one attitude man deals with objects, parts of things, insofar as he may use them or contemplate their theoretical meaning. This is the "I-

It" relation. In the other attitude, man meets realities as they are, without being aware of their use or even understanding their functional interconnections. This is the "I-Thou" relation.

Buber's example of considering a tree illustrates the dual attitude with remarkable simplicity. In one way, I may see the tree as a partial thing for making furniture or some other wooden object. I may also look at it with regard to its structure and growth or other aspects belonging to the realm of plants. In either case, the tree is an "It" for an "I" who investigates, classifies or uses it, cuts it down or lets it grow. It is an object of the theoretical or practical consideration of the "I" — that is, of scientific interest, pure or applied. In the other way, I see the tree as a whole, immediately, without classifying or analyzing it and without contemplating its use for art or artifact. The tree is then a "Thou" in relation to an "I", or "I" meet the tree as a "Thou."

This twofold viewing of reality pertains to all spheres — to our life with nature, our life with fellow-man, and our life with God. One view does not negate the other, but both cannot function simultaneously. Buber further cautions that we cannot possibly tarry too long in the "I-Thou" relation, for it is too overwhelming, too consuming. Only at moments can we enter into such relation with reality. Yet, those moments, when truly lived, give us sufficient awareness of reality as is. This is non-scientific knowledge, and that is exactly what Buber investigates in his work, *I and Thou*. It is of great importance in our quest for certainty and, for that matter, in our struggle for individual and national security.

1965

Buber Speaks to Jewish Youth on the Meaning of Return (Teshuvah)

Martin Buber addressed himself to the Jewish youth directly on many occasions, from his earliest "Speeches on Judaism" to some of his utterings in his last essays. He himself began as a youth speaking with other youths of his people on the needs of the time — the needs of renewal, rebirth, identification, response, and responsibility — on the essence of "return." These are as real today as they were some seven decades ago when he first started to shape his ideas on Jewish life and to convey them to his own generation. As he later reminisced of those early days, he wrote (in 1941): "When 40 years ago, a circle of young people, to which I belonged, began to direct the attention of Jewry in the German speaking countries to the idea of a rebirth of the Jewish people and of the Jewish person, we designated the goal of our endeavors as a Jewish renaissance."

Jewish spiritual life in the English-speaking countries today resembles very much the spiritual condition of the youth to whom and with whom Buber spoke in the German lands of his day, and that is, that large numbers of our gifted, thinking, striving, idealizing youths are breaking away from the Jewish fold to seek their self-realization in a whirl of abstract humanity.

Found the Way

Buber, too, went through that stage, but he found his way back, for he knew the meaning of return (teshuvah) yet from his childhood. Thus, he tells how in his student years toward the end of last century, in the centers of German culture, he had lived in "the whirl of the age . . . in a world of confusion a mythical habitation of roving souls with the fullness of spiritual agility but without Judaism, and thus without humanity." How descriptive this is of our age as well! When he came out of that state he discovered that his humanity could be realized only through his own people. His return or teshuvah was not in the nature of "repentance" or "regret," but rather a return to something that his people represented but he had failed to recognize it; nor was it a matter of going back to a historical past, to days gone by, but rather a return to something fundamental which he could resume and go on to realize in his personal life. He shared his findings with his own generation, and also endeavored later to transmit it to the new generation through speech and the written word. What are these findings?

Bible as Source

One is the spirit of the Bible as actually lived and expressed in the language of the Bible. Buber considered its language as such, as lived life. In a lecture he once gave on this subject to students at the *Freies jüdisches Lehrhaus* in Frankfurt am Main, he said: "If I attend as faithfully as I can to what it contains of word and texture, of sound and rhythmic structure, of open and hidden connections, . . . I find something, I have found something. And if I show what I have found, I guide him who lets himself be guided to the reality of the text." That, too, is his meaning of "return." The baalteshuvah, the one who decides to return to the source of Jewish life, must "attend faithfully," with his whole being to the very rhythm of the pulsating life that speaks out of the ancient text in order to make it real in his own life today. Buber laid great stress on the prophetic teachings of our Scriptures, but he did not deny the intrinsic values of law and ritual; he only wanted to see them constantly renewed and revitalized by the spirit of revelation at all times in the actual events of everyday life. He wanted to bring the spirit of the Bible, its humanizing powers, into the life of the modern Jew.

Another area of vital concern that Buber brought to the attention of Jewish youth is the role of the Jewish people in building "the genuine community" of mankind in truth and righteousness. Not a universal type of community of all in one, but a community of communities, each people fulfilling the task in its own way of life within and in relation to others. This task, he pointed out, devolves particularly on the Jewish people, because not only was it revealed to this people directly at Sinai, but this people's existence has always depended on it throughout its history. This is the meaning of "return" to the Divine commandments — a return to the essence of the revelation at Sinai, which is the demand that Israel establish itself as the true community in and for itself, and thereby also serve as an example to other peoples on earth. Those young Jews who may go out into the world to seek the realization of humanity, in general, will find upon their "return" that genuine humanity, inasmuch as it can be realized only in true communal life, starts with their own people, for it is the people Israel that heard the demand of this realization and accepted it from its very inception as a people.

Attuned to Youth

Buber was not unaware of the difficulty in speaking to modern youth in a religious vein. He was well attuned to the voice of youth — to their drive for experience, their passion for a cause, their all-out defense of the position they have assumed, but also their refusal very often to hear the other side for fear of putting in question their own views. He was also aware of what is nowadays designated as the "generation gap," of youth's rebellion against the "establishment," their disregard of history, and their passion to do things differently by themselves and, hopefully, better. He saw in all these tendencies something "fine and fruitful," but at the same time he cautioned against the pitfalls generated by youthful prejudice and lack of faith that prevent "the living stream of tradition from entering their souls." Hence, when he spoke to them about their "return" to the ways of God, he pointed to the power of faith, truth, and responsibility, which are human expressions of the Divine. How can we find truth in a world of relative, changing, ephemeral values, without standard or norm? There is no ready made answer to it, but, said Buber, "one can have an honest and uncompromising attitude toward truth," and that means to strive to realize it through one's own life by assuming personal responsibility for one's word and deed in relation to fellow men. Therein lie truth and faith.

Buber was also mindful of youth's complaint about religious institutions that do not live up to their professed faith and truth. However, he did not think this could be changed by devising new formulas of behavior, because human daily action cannot be regulated entirely by formulas. Rather, the man of faith meets life by holding himself open to become engaged in it, or as we say, involved, at every moment of its unpredictable encounters. Ultimately, this is faith in God, Who calls on man in many ways and through many channels to realize his humanity, to build the true community together with his fellow men of his own people, and with his neighboring peoples throughout the world. In Jewish tradition such faith is expressed through trust in God, Who is ever present to the man who responds to His call — trust in the Divine Presence. This is man's way to God in all generations. Teshuvah, in its ultimate meaning is therefore a "return" to God. Let youth, then, listen to the voice of God which is never silenced; "it speaks to the men of all generations, makes demands upon them, and summons them to accept their responsibility. . . . It does not matter what you name it. All that matters is that you hear it."

1972

Martin Buber and the Quest of Scientific Knowledge

Science deals with experience, regardless of its ultimate ground, be it in sensibility, intellection, supersensibility, or in any of their combinations. Therefore, a scientific knowledge of any field of investigation must account for our experience in that field. In modern times, since the days of Galileo and Newton, all the sciences have been directed toward a knowledge of nature and what it contains, including man, with the aim of establishing its objective reality, that is, to know the natural world as it may exist independently of the knowing subject. But this quest of scientific knowledge has produced a most disturbing paradox: If science deals with experience, how can it reach the world of nature apart from the knowing subject who experiences it? Is the subject merely a passive recipient of this knowledge which he uncovers in nature, or does he have an active role in determining its real character? The question becomes even more troublesome when we consider another aspect of science, namely, that it is based on observation. Does the knowing subject observe events as an outsider, without influencing them, or does he become part of the events through the very process of his observation, whether directly or through instruments which he has contrived especially for it?

These fundamental questions about human experience of the world and man's subjective role in determining its nature have been raised by philosophers who have shown a vital interest in science as a valid method of gauging reality. They have not tried to supplant it, but rather to set its claims within proper bounds, and at the same time to probe into other modes of knowledge which have forced themselves upon their attention. In order to understand Buber's contribution in this regard, I will state briefly the reaction to Newton's physical theory on the part of two leading thinkers of the early stages of our modern era, David Hume and Immanuel Kant.

Newton's brilliant career as a natural scientist was of such tremendous force that his method became the touchstone of scientific knowledge during his life-time and has remained so, in very large measure, to this day. Chiefly, he confirmed the domain of the science of nature to be the relationship between objects of observation and its translation into mathematical language. He espoused Galileo's dictum that nature speaks in the language of mathematics. A scientist then who observes physical occurrences is not so much concerned with the inner nature of things, as with what takes place between them, even though the occurrences may be due in part to their nature as such. Let us take, for example, the growth of a tree. To explain it, the botanist investigates the relationship between the tree and its environment, and in this relationship he discovers the causes of the tree's growth. Without a knowledge of the manner in which the elements of the soil, the sun, and the climate pass through to the seed, the roots, the trunk and the leaves of the tree, the scientist would not be able to tell how a tree grows and contains itself. All sciences therefore study the "between" of things, or, as Aristotle called it, the "middle." "In all our inquiries," Aristotle said, "we are asking either whether there is a 'middle' or what the 'middle' is: for the 'middle' here is precisely the cause, and it is the cause that we seek in all our inquiries" (Post. An. 90 a5).

Now when Newton sought a universal cause of physical motion, terrestrial as well as celestial, he found it to be the force of gravity, or that which occurs between bodies and causes their mutual attraction. The tremendous impact of this hypothesis on science was due not to the concept of gravity as such, for Newton did not invent or discover it, but to his mathematical formulation of it into a universal law that proved to be applicable to all observable phenomena (or almost all) in the universe. Yet with all that, Newton could not account for the source of gravity, as he did not conceive it to be a property inherent in bodies, only an occurrence between them. When restless minds pressed him for a cause of this mysterious force, he could only shrug them off with his famous statement "hypotheses non fingo" (I feign no hypotheses), that is to say, he would not invent an imaginary physical explanation of its origin or even its locus. "Whether this agent is material or immaterial," he said, "I have left it to the consideration of my readers."[1]

One of his admiring readers was David Hume, who was not only dissatisfied with his enigmatic answer, but also saw in it the main weakness of his scientific method itself. What troubled Hume was that Newton accepted gravity as the cause of all physical occurrences dogmatically, without investigating where such a

1. *Newton's Philosophy of Nature.* Selections. Edited by H. S. Thayer (New York 1953), pp. 5-6

cause and, for that matter, causality in general, might come from. Our physicist assumed the existence of a world order which he set out to explain in terms of physical reality but could not account for the reality of its basic force. All he could say was that "gravity does really exist," even though not in the "true physical sense," and left it at that. This is where Hume became skeptical of "scientific demonstration": Can it give us a knowledge of the world in reality? To "mitigate" his skepticism (he later called himself a "mitigated skeptic" in distinction from the "excessive skeptics"),[2] he proposed to investigate human nature as a possible source of the concept of causality, which may also provide a knowledge of objective causal relations.

> 'Tis evident [he said] that all the sciences have a relation, greater or less, to human nature . . . . Even *Mathematics, Natural Philosophy* and *Natural Religion* are in some measure dependent on the science of Man; since they lie under the cognizance of men, and are judged by their powers and faculties; . . . and consequentlly we ourselves are not only the beings, that reason, but also one of the objects, concerning which we reason.[3]

What differentiates Hume's quest for scientific knowledge from Newton's is that whereas the latter investigates the relationships between *things* in nature, the former does it between *human nature* and *general nature*, thus seeking to discover a human faculty that mediates between them. This is Hume's chief philosophical contribution to scientific knowledge. He brought man as an active agent into the field of a knowledge of the world. Science as such may be dealing with objective experience and with relationships between things, but a philosophy of science deals with man who experiences and relates.

Kant's Question "What Is Man?"

Windelband's apt description of Newton's science of nature will give us a clue to Kant's reaction to it. Newton, says Windelband, tried to free his system from metaphysics. "Through this single

2. David Hume, *An Enquiry Concerning Human Understanding*, Sec. XII, Part III, "Mitigated Scepticism."
3. David Hume, *A Treaties of Human Nature*, Introduction, p. XIX.

hypotheis [of gravitation] the general axiom of modern science that nature forms an independent causal interconnectedness, assumed a real image. The world of gravitation lives in itself."[4] But Newton failed to explain the life-giving implulse of his system, namely, the source of gravity. In the final analysis, he had to resort to some metaphysical speculation on this subject, which other scientists of his own and succeeding generations challenged repeatedly. Kant met this challenge head on by proposing to show "How a science of metaphysics is possible." Without it, he maintained, the natural sciences can never attain completion, because they cannot see their own limits. Metaphysics shows what we *can* know, and it thus establishes the bounds of our knowledges of the universe.

In Kant's view, Hume's skepticism was a worthy transition between dogmatism and critical philosophy. The skeptic only breaks down dogmatic metaphysics; what is required is to rebuild it on new foundations, which is the task of the critic. Thus Kant went further than Hume in bringing man's knowing capacities into full play in relation to reality. Since science deals with experience, Kant's question is not just what capacity does man have for a concept of causality, but what makes his experience altogether possible?[5] Science can answer this question only if it can construct a complete system of a knowledge of our experience. Such a system is made possible through the fullest participation of all our knowing capacities as the powers that set the laws of objective knowledge through the categories of the understanding, the principle of purposiveness through judgment, and the ideas of completeness through reason.

We cannot enter here into a discussion how far Kant succeeded in bringing his system to completion. The more important question is: In what manner and to what extent did he, as philosopher-scientist, allow man to play an active part in it? To be sure, he assigned a specific function to each of man's higher knowing faculties, but he did not see in the knowing process his role as a human being as a whole. Kant must have felt this imcompleteness in his system when he mused, in later years, in his *Lectures on Metaphysics*, about the philosopher's true function in gauging reality.

4. Wilhelm Windelband, *Die Geschichte der neueren Philosophie.* Leipzig 1899, p. 300.
5. Immanuel Kant. *Prolegomena,* 365.

A philosopher [he said] is one who has certain purposes setting maxims for the use of our reason. . . .

The field of philosophy. . . reduces itself to the following questions:

1) What can I know? This is answered by metaphysics.

2) What ought I to do? This is shown by morals.

3) What may I hope? This is taught by religion.

4) What is Man? This is taught by anthropology.

One could name it all anthropology [he concluded], because the first three questions are related to the last one.[6]

Kant never answered his last all-embracing question. But this was the pivotal problem in his own Era of Enlightenment and has since become more and more the concern of modern thought in general. When Buber started out on a path of his own, he conceived it as the central issue of our time and sought its resolution in what became known as "philosophical anthropology." If, following Kant's dictum, man can grasp the world only through a *complete science* of a knowledge of his experience, such knowledge, Buber maintains, is possible only through man himself becoming a *complete human being.* He must become involved in it not merely with his higher knowing faculties, but with his being as a whole, even with his so-called irrationality. Like all scientific knowledge this kind is also of our experience and of the between, but in a twofold way, one in "lived experience" (*Erlebnis*) expressed in the I-Thou relation, and the other in "experiencing" (*Erfahrung*) in the I-It connection. The difference will become clear in the course of our discussion. For the moment I want to pursue its scientific import.

Buber's Answer to the Question "What Is Man?"

Buber characterizes the human predicament of our time in regard to science, technology, and religion as the "crisis of the between," that is, the crisis of relations. In essence, it is a problem of scientific knowledge in all these areas, for what we *can* know is only our relation to others, be it to things in nature, to fellow-man, or to the divine Being. The fundamental scientific question then is, Who establishes the relation and under what conditions? We shall grasp the full meaning of this question if we bear in mind that in

6. Kant, *Vorlesungen über die Metaphysik.* Erfurt 1921, pp. 3-4.

modern science we hardly observe phenomena in their undisturbed natural condition. The scientist subjects everything to laboratory tests; even in astronomy, not to speak of biology and physics, his instruments of observation influence his findings. The natural scientists are becoming more and more aware of the fact that man not just measures things but is also, to a certain extent, a constitutive factor of his measuring rods, as Kant has taught us in his *Critique of Pure Reason* (note his emphasis on the categories of the understanding as ''constitutive'' principles or our experience). Henry Margenau, one of today's leading philosopher-scientists, has brought this situation forcefully to our attention in his treatment of what is known in physical theory as "the operator," that is, a factor which converts one mathematical function into another in the general form of $w(x) = Qy(x)$, Q being the operator. The typical condition is to establish an "operator" and then find the objects that go with it. It is like setting up a "seeing" apparatus and then bring in all objects that may be seen. Anything that may be "heard" will not fit this situation. What is happening in modern scientific research, as Margenau describes it, is this: It "defines its systems, selects observables for these systems, and combines a significant set of these observables into states."[7]

Religion and the Science of the Between

Continuing now with our theme, we can see how man creates the betweens of his experience. In Newton's way of thinking, the relation is between things; in Hume's and Kant's views, it is between a knowing subject and his objects of knowledge. Buber has introduced another dimension, namely, a relation between subject and subject, in addition to that between subject and object. These are the twofold relations we spoke of above, and they are designated by him as I-Thou for the first, and I-It for the second. The former, man may establish only by entering into it with his being-as-a-whole. Man, says Buber, is the only kind of being who has the potencies of entering into relation with other beings in this manner. It is an ontic act of his "category humanum." (I call it ontic rather than ontological, because in Buber's philosophical anthropology this act establishes the possibility of a science or ontology of being.) This kind of relation renders knowledge of the

7. Henry Margenau, *The Nature of Physical Reality.* New York 1950, pp. 331-34.

other complete inasmuch as the one who takes his stand in it is a complete being and sees the other also as a complete being. In the I-It relation, on the other hand, one sees the other as an object, taken apart into elements and seen only partially from a given point of view as the other may fit into a specific scheme of things in nature, society, or other aspects suitable to the viewer's interests, that is, making use of the other for whatever purpose one may see fit. Each relation passes froml I-Thou to I-It and back again to I-Thou. Buber describes it like a pendulum swinging between Thou and It. The I-Thou encounter is too consuming to be sustained for any length of time and, therefore, every Thou must be turned into an It. But in order to realize oneself as a human being, one may turn the It as often as possible into a Thou. This holds true in relation to fellow-man as well as to all things in nature. But when it comes to one's relation to God, the possibility of I-It does not occur, because God, as the Absolute Thou, cannot be turned into an It, or an object. This specific mode of knowledge of the Divine renders Buber's science what I would.designate as a science of religious relation. The term stems from his own concept of religion; I only call attention to its central position in his world outlook.

In a short essay entitled "Über Religionswisseschaft," Buber raises the question whether the field of religion may be investigated by the scientific method. The reality of religion, he notes, consists of a reciprocity between the the Divine and the human, which involves the human act of entering into relation with God. It is this relation, when detached from the reality of the reciprocity and is reflected upon, that may become the subject of scientfic study, provided, Buber cautions, that we do not trespass the boundary which the detachment has created for us. That is, we can investigate the conditions of entering into relation and how it affects our life, but not the reciprocity as such, that is, not God's nature or His part in it. This is what Buber calls a *Religion-swissenschaft*, which I render into English as a "science of religious relation," to emphasize his concept of religion as a relationship with the Divine, and "not human thinking about the Divine."

Many difficulties may arise from such a scientific view of reality, which, however, we cannot consider in this discussion. Our concern here is rather how it affects our knowledge of the world and all that is therein. We live in an "open world", Buber says, and we have to find our own way in it. The authentic way to a knowledge of things, as said, is through entering into relation with them fully, without holding oneself back. But this relation is at best relative. The Thou we encounter in everyday life is always turned into an It. How then can we "see the world steady and whole," as Matthew Arnold put it? There is one relation which is constant and unchangeable and that is with the Absolute Thou or God, who cannot be turned into an It. It is complete and man may therefore achieve his own completeness through it, as long and as often as he may tarry in it at certain moments in his life. When he steps out of it, as he must each time, and the Divine calls to him again, he may respond by renewing it. Each such encounter puts its stamp on all finite relations between man and nature and his fellow-men. As Buber states, "The extended lines of relation intersect in the eternal Thou."[8] By this he means to say that man cannot reach out to God except as he goes through a genuine relation with all of God's creatures. And in reverse, in all finite relations with other creatures there is a spark of the Divine. This, in essence, is what renders all human interrelations religious in character.

If we now contemplate the philosophical meaning of the scientific quest of knowledge as it has come down to us from the dawn of our modern era, we find tht its emphasis has been on the centrality of man who has the capacity to know the world objectively, that is, as an object of his knowledge. Buber's added dimension of a knowledge of others also as subjects reveals man in the fulness of his category humanum, that is, as one who can know not merely through the categories of his understanding, which is mediated knowledge and belongs to the province of the natural sciences, but also through his very category of being human, which brings him into immediate relation with the world-order as a whole. In each genuine encounter with others there is an intimation of this world-order, for all such encounters stem from the primal sources of reality. Buber's science of religious relation is thus a science of man, in answer to the question "What is man?" which he conceived to be the paramount question of our time.

1978

---

8. Martin Buber, *I and Thou.* Opening statement, Part Three.

Is Martin Buber a Personalist?

Reflections on Harold Schulweis's Article "Buber's Broken Dialogue"[1]

Some twenty years ago Harold S. Schulweis tried to associate Martin Buber with "Personalistic" philosophy[2] and he still views him in this light in his article, now under review. Regrettably, nowhere in his two writings does Schulweis tell us what he means by personalism, but speaks of "Buber's personal God," "personalistic faith," "personalistic theodicies," "personalistic theologies," and the like, without accounting for the intrinsic connection between Buber's concepts and the attributes which he (Schulweis) ascribes to them. This is not the place to go into a discussion of the diversified branches of the personalistic world-view. I will adduce only its main features as presented by one of its outstanding protagonists, Ralph T. Flewelling, who was also the founder of the magazine *The Personalist* (in 1920).

Basically, Personalism is a metaphysic centered in the concept of person as an independent, self-conscious, self-directing, and self-organizing unity, "both in finite individuals and in a supreme creative intelligence which is the world-ground and source of reality." "To personalism, personality is of supreme value; . . . all reality is in some sense personal" and what persons create. Moral character, in this view, is "the supreme creative achievement"; and "the cosmic order, being personal, is also ethical." The cosmic creative process, which manifests itself in the person, implies "permanence and duration" and therefore calls for a "Supreme Creative Intelligence" which has the same qualities as the human creative intelligence, only in a higher, or in a highest, degree. In sum, Personalism is "the trend toward naming the qualities of personality as the ultimate reality."[3] One of the most succinct statements on the personalistic trend was expressed by another illustrious thinker of this movement, William Stern, author of *Person und Sache*. The fundamental presuppositions of philosophical personalism, he wrote, "are that Weltanschauung, science, and the conduct of life can be established only through a metaphysic, and

1. See *Reconstructionist*, December 1972.
2. Cf. "The Personalism of Martin Buber," by Harold S. Schulweis, *The Personalist*, Spring 1952, pp. 131-34.
3. Cf. Ralph T. Flewelling, "Personalism," in *Twentieth Century Philosophy*, edited by Dagobert D. Runes. New York: The Philosophical Library, 1947, pp. 324-27.

that for our epoch and the succeeding one the basic metaphysical category must be that of 'person.'"[4]

Now the use which Buber makes of the term "person" as applied to the human being or to the divine Absolute does not stem from this world-view, as described above. To begin with, Buber does not deal with metaphysical speculations about the essence or existence of man, nature, or God. He does not propose to construct a metaphysical system out of categories of the human person to be posited in nature or in God. He only investigates the category *humanun* as such, insofar as man enters into relation with nature, fellow-men, and the Absolute, whatever these beings may be in their essences, and whether or not man can fathom them. Since Shulweis interprets Buber from the standpoint of personalistic metaphysics, he ascribes to him concepts and ideas which are alien to his philosophy.[5] In what follows I will indicate some of the discrepancies in his argument.

Schulweis's main contention is that Buber deprives God of the quality of the moral ideal which contradicts his own concept of a "personal God," since in essence "personal," from the personalistic viewpoint, means moral character.[6] Further, Buber raises the Person God to the status of the "Supergood" and thus, Schulweis maintains, puts the divine Absolute beyond the reach of goodness, making Him totally indifferent to the fate of His creatures, who can do nothing but submit to the hidden powers of their Creator. "The absolute personality" of Buber's Person God, Schulweis writes, "transcends the moral ideal. God is, as it were, the good beyond the good. . . . A supra-good absolute personality will produce no Jobian discontent." And, Schulweis asks, "wherein [does] such a faith in a supra-personal, supra-moral God differ from a religious masochism which finds love in the signs of indifference or hostility?" (p. 8). I don't know of any place in Buber's writings

<hr>

4. Cf. William Stern, "Selbstdarstellung," in *Die Philosophie der Gegenwart in Selbstdarstellungen.* Herausgegeben von Dr. Raymund Schmidt, Leipzig: Felix Meiner Verlag, 1927, p. 162.

5. In a similar vein, Charles Hartshorne tried to find metaphysical self-contradictions in Buber, to which the latter replied: "You begin, dear Hartshorne, with the sentence, I am no metaphysician and I am one of the greatest metaphysicians . . . . I am . . . convinced . . . that we can make only the first half of your sentence the basis for an understanding." *Cf. The Philosophy of Martin Buber.* Edited by Paul Arthur Schilpp and Maurice Friedman (LaSalle, Ill. 1967), p. 717.

6. Schulweis, "Buber's Broken Dialogue," *op. cit.,* p. 8. "For personality is too bound by moral associations to prevent Jobian disillusionment with God." See p. 11. Other page references to this article will be indicated in parentheses in my text.

where he comes even remotely to the notion that God is indifferent or hostile. But this is not the real issue. What concerns us is the meaning of his term "absolute Person God," and of his statement "The oneness of God is not the good but more than the good."[7] More important, what does he mean by "love of God" apart from the idea of moral goodness? We shall start with the last concept, which will lead us to the other two.

We must bear in mind that for Buber, as he often stated, "the question is not about god but only about our relationship to him."[8] This relation is one of faith, embracing also love, cognition, even imaging, that is, of man as a whole with all his potencies. On the other hand, the primary relation between human beings is love, connoting a mutuality of accepting the other as he is, as an independent being, without attempting to dominate or use him for one's own purposes.[9] This is what Buber means by the term "person" as applied to a human being. man becomes a person insofar as he realizes his *humanum* through the mutuality of love between himself and other human beings. When the relationship of love is manifested between man and God, as part of faith, we can speak of it in terms of mutuality that occurs between persons, because "a mutual relation with us can be only as between persons (*eine personhafte*)."[10] And when we apply the word Person to the Absolute, we can only mean that man loves God as Person and, in turn, God as Person loves man. Buber's objection to Hermann Cohen's concept of God as the moral ideal does not concern so much the "moral" as the "ideal," because the latter does not account for God's love of man. For even admitting, as Cohen maintains, that man can love God only as an ideal, he (man) cannot be loved by an ideal. Love takes place between actual

7. Martin Buber, *Werke* I (Munich, 1962). "Die Liebe zu Gott und die Gottesidee," p. 547 ff. The German original reads: "Die Einheit Gottes ist nicht das Gute, sondern das Übergute." The English translation by I.M. Lask in *Eclipse of God* is based on an earlier Hebrew text (published in *Knesset*, Tel Aviv, 1943-44). Several terms in Lask's translation do not convey the full intent of the German text, which must be taken as the more authentic one. For example, Buber never uses the word *Persönlichkeit* (personality), which has a psychological connotation, but rather *Person* in its ontic sense. (The Hebrew *ishiyut* can mean both.) Also, *das Übergute* is best rendered as "more than the good," that is not only the idea of good but more than any idea. Cf. *Eclipse*, p. 58. "He who loves God loves Him precisely insofar as He is not 'only an idea.'" Similarly, by *Einheit Gottes* Buber means "the oneness of God," not "the unity" as a unification of all qualities, which is the personalistic view.

8. Buber, *I and Thou* (Walter Kaufmann's translation, 1970), p. 180.

9. Cf. Martin Buber, *Knowledge of Man*, p. 182.

10. Buber, *Werke* I, p. 576 (my translation. See *Eclipse*, p. 97).

73

persons, even when one may idealize the other in certain respects.[11]

At the same time, Buber cautions not to take the term Person as applied to God to mean that God *is* a person, because the very concept "person" is a relative one (man becomes a person only relative to others), which contradicts the Absolute.[12] He therefore speaks of God as absolute Person only to distinguish between the infinite and the finite. For the term "absolute Person" is paradoxical if taken metaphysically, that is, if Person signifies God's essence. Nevertheless we may use this term if, speaking humanly, we mean the mutual relation of love between man and God. This can only mean that man who seeks a relationship with God can achieve it best if he approaches him *as if he were* a Person, but this does designate God's essence.,[13]

Schulweis raises many objections to this manner of speaking, all of which stem from his misinterpretation of two main concepts in Buber's philosophy of religion, namely, experience and the Absolute. According to Buber, he says, "we are allowed by God, 'so to speak,' to experience Him as person," and he asks, "Is the personalistic language allowed as an accommodation to man's conceptual limitations in describing his relationship to the Absolute? Or does it affirm an independent ontologic status of personality to God?" (p. 9). Neither is the case. Accepting not just the conceptual but all other limitations of man, Buber does not philosophize about God and does not ascribe to Him any ontological status, but takes Him as an existing reality, whatever His status may be in a philosophical system (which is what "status" signifies). On the contrary, he holds that the philosopher who might want to relate to God in genuine mutuality "would be compelled to renounce the attempt to include God in his system in any conceptual form. . . . [He would] only point toward God, without actually dealing with him."[14] He certainly would not speak of God as allowing us "to experience Him as person," because

11. *Eclipse of God*, p. 59.
12. *I and Thou* (2nd ed.), p. 134. Buber speaks there of "the paradoxical combination of a substantive concept with an adjective which contradicts its normal content." Schulweis paraphrases it in a totally contrary sense, as follows (p. 8): "The substantive concept 'personality' combines with an adjective 'absolute' *in order* 'to contradict its normal *concept*'" (italics mine). Buber's intent is not "in order to contradict" but rather to clarify that "which contradicts its normal content."
13. *I and Thou* (Kaufmann's transl.), pp. 181-82.
14. *Eclipse of God,* p. 50.

God is not an object of experience. What we experience is the *relation* to God, that which occurs *between* man and the Absolute in the immediate encounter, and when we reflect on it (after stepping out of the experience), we speak of this relation as one of love between mutually independent beings, of man as person and of God "*also* as Person." This "*also* as Person," as Buber says, "is both permitted and necessary to say . . .," not "allowed by God" but permissible in our way of relating.[15] In the philosopher's language, Buber points out (taking a cue from Spinoza), it could also be said, God reveals the attribute of *Personhaftigkeit*, like a Person. However, speaking not as metaphysicians but as men experiencing an encounter with the Absolute, what we are talking about is the relation, not God.

The meaning Schulweis ascribes to the Absolute leads him further to a misinterpretation of Buber's statement "God is not the good but more than the good" or, as Schulweis quotes, the "Supergood." Schulweis conceives of the Absolute in terms of the quality of justice as inherent in the quality of perfection. Moreover, he holds that we must have knowledge of this specific divine quality ("a common understanding of goodness," p. 12), if our religious experience is to help us direct our life in justice and righteousness. " To exclude the moral ideal of divine perfection from religious belief," he says, "is a costly strategy for religion" (p. 12).

Now Buber does not exclude the moral ideal from religious experience; he only sees it in a different connection. Religion, as the fundamental relation between man and God, sanctifies the ethical, which is expressed in human life on earth. But God is not the Lord of religion, but the Lord of existence[16] This is the real answer given by God to Job), and he could not be qualified by a moral ideal without ascribing the same ideal to all of existence, which is a personalistic view, not Buber's. However, the main question is whether the Absolute can be qualified at all. Buber views "the absolute . . . [as] a power which cannot be identified with any attribute accessible to human understanding." It can be expressed only as the absolute Person addressing man and commanding him ("there is no revelation without commandment") to distinguish between good and evil, righteousness and unright-

---

15. *I and Thou*, p. 181. See Kaufmann's note on the word *Personhaftigkeit.*
16. Cf. Martin Buber, *Pointing the Way* (New York 1957), p. 210.

eousness. "Our own life is, therefore, the only sphere in which we can point him out, and then only through this life of ours."[17] What is good and righteous is thus not conceived as a quality of the Absolute *per se*, nor that of the cosmic order, but only distinguishable in human life. This is what Buber means by "God is more than the good," that is, He is not identifiable with the good as such. If we place him in this category, we become baffled, disillusioned nonbelievers when calamities strike our lives and we cannot square them with the category of the "good God." This too would be the case if we placed him under any other ideal category which we could not reconcile with the exigencies of our existence on earth, because God is neither an idea nor an ideal, although he may demand of us to strive toward certain ideals.

In his *Eclipse of God,* from which Schulweis draws most of his references, Buber points out that what is *incomprehensible* in our viewing the Absolute is not God Himself, but his hiding and revealing. For we *do* know him when we relate to him, but not in categories. We therefore pray, "Do not hide Thy countenance from us," so that we may enter into relation with the divine Presence and thus find our way to the good, for the good lies in direction to God.[18]

1973

17. Martin Buber, *Israel and the World* (New York 1948), p. 209. Cf. *Eclipse,* p. 104.

18. Cf. Martin Buber, *Between Man and Man* (New York 1965), pp. 78-9. Cf. *Ten Rungs: Hasidic Sayings,* collected and edited by Martin Buber (New York 1962), p. 93, The "Way."

Martin Buber's Way in Judaism

A Tribute on the Centennial of His Birth

In the preface to his last four speeches on Judaism, entitled "At the Turning" (1951), Buber wrote: "In these hours of destiny, the four speeches are to be read as directed by a Jew to Jews. Yet what he says concerns present-day man and his humanity."

Buber's entire process of thinking, no matter what he thought and wrote, centered on the human predicament in modern times. But as an "arch-Jew," as he called himself, he was bound to seek a way out of this predicament in the sources of Judaism, "from the Decalogue to Hasidism." He found in the Jewish Bible a prospect of human existence that expresses itself in "a dialogue between above and below"; and as for Hasidism, "it is the fulfillment of Judaism." His problematic, then, was mankind, and his guidelines for resolving it came from the teachings of the Prophets, the Talmudic Sages and Hasidic lore.

The Human Problematic

Man, according to Buber, is by nature a duality, torn between good and evil impulses, harboring finitude and infinity, concerned with the conditioned and unconditioned, full of contradiction which splinters his life and leads him astray in his personal, social and cosmic existence. This duality or polarity lies at the root of all critical stages in the history of mankind and is particularly manifest in the present-day crisis of man's life with fellowman, with nature and with the Divine Being or God. But man is also constituted of potencies which help him overcome his inner duality and realize his destiny as a human being-as-a-whole. This occurs whenever he enters in relation with another, be it a creature on the animal or lower level, fellowman, or a higher being, and responds to that other with his whole self, without reservation, in complete mutuality. The most effective and all-embracing potency is that of faith, which operates in interhuman relations and which is also the gateway to life with nature and in the Divine Presence. This, in essence, is Buber's principle of dialogue or the I-Thou relationship. Man may strive toward his destiny, and attain it in various degrees, not as an individual by himself, but through his life with fellowman, "completing one another in mutual contribution, together showing forth man.... Only man with man provides the full image" of the human being-as-a-whole. The fullest expression of this way of life is realized in the community, the people, and in the nation, if it is constituted out of fundamental communal entities.

This general human problematic Buber testifies to have experienced in his life as a Jew. Moreover, he feels that in the Jews, as individuals and as a people, the duality is more pronounced than in any other group. At the same time, the drive toward overcoming it is also stronger in the Jewish people than in others. The Jewish people and Judaism have thus become for Buber an example or "a paradigm of humanity" in whom the process of unification "is purer, stronger and clearer than in any other human group." "No man knows the abyss of inner duality as does the Jew." he said in one of his early speeches on Judaism, "but none like him knows the wonder of unifying, which cannot be believed but only experienced." And this is the key to an understanding of Buber's way in Judaism. He does not philosophize about it in the accepted sense of metaphysical or theological speculation. Rather, he regards himself a philosophizing man who translates his "decisive experiences into human thought-values," experiences he had lived through in his Jewishness, and thought-values, notably the dialogical principle, he had learned from the fountainhead of Judaism: "The Biblical word," he discovered, "preserves the dialogical character of living reality without disguise or restraint."

Formative Years: Estrangement, Return

Mordecai (Martin) Buber was born on Feb. 8, 1878, into an affluent Jewish family in Vienna. When he was about three years old, his parents separated and he was placed with his paternal grandparents in Lemberg, Galicia, then part of the Austria Hungarian Empire. His education was from the start Jewish traditional as well as secular, under the tutelage of his grandfather, Shlomo Buber, a rich landowner and a prominent scholar in Midrash-Aggada, and under his grandmother, Adele, a highly cultured woman, self-educated in German and world literature. His mother, Elise, never came to see him; but his father, Carl, a successful mine operator and a follower of the Sadagorer Hasidic Rebbe, used to take him along on visits to the Rebbe and on summer vacations at his own nearby estate. The Hasidic way of life made a deep impression on young Buber. At the age of 14 Martin went back to live with his father, who had remarried and settled in Lemberg. He attended a Polish gymnasium, gave up his traditional Jewish observances and started to devote himself more to the study of German literature, philosophy and linguistic. As he delved into the philosophical issues of the time he became estranged not only from Hasidism but also from Judaism, in general. In his student days, which followed in Vienna, Berlin and Leipzig, he was swept away by the esthetic-cultural current which then prevailed in the intellectual centers of Germany and Austria. As he later described those years, he lived in a "world of confusion, a mythical habitation of roving souls with the fullness of spiritual agility, but without Judaism, and thus without humanity and without the presence of the divine." At the age of 21 Buber married a Christian girl, Paula Winkler of Munich, a gifted writer, whom he had met at the University of Zurich. She converted to Judaism and became his life-long faithful and inspiring co-worker for Zionism and other Jewish ideals.

The zionist movement, which then came to world prominence under Herzl's leadership, brought Buber back into the Jewish fold. But this was only a first step. He saw in Zionism not just the prospect of a Jewish State but rather the revival of the creative forces of the Jewish people, the road to a regeneration of Judaism and the redemption of the individual Jew through his own people. Another important step on his way back to the fold was his becoming absorbed in a study of the Hasidic way of life in which he sought to gain "the immediate knowing . . . of the people in its creative primal hour." However, he never turned into a practicing Hasid, but was only an inside observer and interpreter. Yet his closeness to this movement brought a transformation in his personal life; through it he learned to experience a primary relation between man and God. This brief sketch of Buber's formative years gives us an insight into the problems of the intellectual Jews of his generation in Western Europe, their struggle with the "spirit of the time" (Zeitgeist) and with biologial and cultural assimilation, and their inner conflicts on the road which some of their finest spirits, among them Buber himself, were able to hew for themselves toward a renewal of their Jewishness.

When Buber first started to speak to that generation on the subject of Judaism (in 1909-1911), he wanted to share with them his personal experiences of estrangement and return. Some of his listeners had come by the same road, but many more who had been alienated from their roots did not know how to return and came to him to find the way. It will be instructive to our appreciation of Buber's further development of his Jewishness if we dwell for a moment on the manner of his response to the needs of the hour; for his entire mode of thinking and acting was in the nature of a response to others, which was to him the essence of moral and intellectual responsibility. One was his response to his people, and the other his response to the voice of the prophets. To these two he devoted the best of his creative years over half a century. It is noteworthy that his writings on Jewish themes and on the Bible comprise more than three-quarters of his entire intellectual output, and that his general philosophy on the human condition in cosmic terms sprang from the sources of his philosophy of Judaism (a subject which cannot properly be treated in this short essay).

The Teacher Pointing the Way

Due to the deep stirrings of the Jewish national movement in its early stages and, perhaps, also under the influence of Herzl's magnetic personality, the people who sought their way back to Judaism generally looked for a leader to bring them to their goal. Buber was not unaware of this folk yearning, but for himself he chose the role of teacher. When he later contemplates this matter from the vantage point of his social philosophy, he finds that he is more in keeping with the basic needs of the people than the leaders. The leader of a group or people, he points out, decides for members of the group and shows them how to carry out his decision in order to reach their prescribed goal. When necessary, the leader may use force and disregard the individual strivings of his constituents. Not so the teacher. He uses persuasion and gives direction toward the goal, but "not the manner in which one must strive for this direction: that each one must discover and acquire for himself." Nevertheless, Buber recognizes the value of true leadership. "Certainly," he says, "the people that has no leader is unfortunate; but thrice unfortunate is the people whose leader has no teacher."

Response is Responsibility

Buber anticipates a personal commitment from his listeners. The response of each individual to the problems of his time must be that of personal responsibility; for how else, he says, "except through such expectation could we learn how much the individual is capable of?" Buber risks misunderstanding, which is not slow in coming, when he disregards the demand of the masses for a leader who will design a definite program and a plan of action. He has neither, for he does not consider it to be his specific task. His main concern is the individual Jew who has lost his way as a human being and who can be brought back on the way only through a realization that his humanity stems from his identification with his own people as a whole. This is not a matter of planned programatic activity, but of living one's Jewishness in his innermost self. That each Jew must experience personally through his mutual

80

relationship with fellow Jews. The teacher can only point the way.

Experiencing the Words of the Prophets

The second area of response, namely, to the voice of the prophets, had even more far-reaching effects on Buber's own life and on his Jewish thinking than his response to the people. Here we deal with past events, teachings, revelations and recorded experiences which have come down through the ages in various interpretations, codifications and institutionalized forms of conduct. Buber's approach to the Biblical text is that in reading it he must himself experience the primal force that prompted the prophets and seers to speak the way they spoke, That is, he sought in his own way to gain from the words of the Bible a direct living relationship with the Divine Presence as those who had spoken those words had experienced through the revelations in their time. He does not claim the powers of prophecy but maintains that the human being, as such, has the potency of faith which brings him in communication with God, at all times, whenever he directs himself to Him wholly, completely. This is the teaching that he brings to his fellow Jews and, for that matter, to men of all faiths. Moreover, he claims that this was the real function of the true Pharisees (not the "painted ones," in allusion to the Talmud, Sota 22b), and that he himself is only following in their footsteps — to "put the Torah in the living tradition, which modifies it as it interprets it." "The pharisee," he writes, "is the man who is concerned with nothing but that the Word (of God) assume an image in all things: the man who affirms the world as God's world actively, not just with some of his life-expressions but with all of them."

In the Manner of Pirke Avot

And here, too, Buber assumes the role of teacher rather than that of leader. We may consider his teachings on Judaism in the light of the tractate "Pirke Avot" (Sayings of the Fathers), which deals not with laws, statutes and commandments, but with the character of man and his destiny in the world; that is, with man-as-a-whole in relation to fellow man, to the world and to God. The centrality of the six chapters of this tractate is the Torah, but the emphasis is on how the study of Torah molds man's character and leads him to the realization of his human destiny. What is most significant in those "Sayings" is that they are addressed to individual man, calling him to personal responsibility in all walks of life. There are only two references to the communal and national aspects, namely, "Do not separate yourself from the community" and the love of God for his people Israel, both of which are tenets in Buber's view of Judaism as well. Like Hillel and Rabbi Zadok of old (Avot II.5 and IV.7), Buber stresses the essence of communality in Jewish living, and like Rabbi Akiba (III.18) he emphasizes Israel's experience of divine revelation as a people. "Israel," he writes, "was and is a people and a religious community in one, and it is this unity which enabled it to survive in an exile no other nation had to suffer. . . Snatch from Akiba his phrase about 'special love' which God has for Israel, and you snatch the heart out of his body."

I have referred to the tractate "Pirke Avot" as a model of Buber's approach to Judaism not only because of their parallel intrinsic "thought-values" about man and the Torah, but also because the time in which the Sages of the Talmud composed that tractate bore the same signs of crisis and turmoil in Jewish national survival as Buber witnessed in his youth and as all of us still see in our own day. His response was similar to that of the teachers of former times: to bring Judaism back into the heart of each individual Jew, which, according to Buber, was the primary intent of these Sages of the Talmud. Like those teachers of old he learned this prescription from his favorite prophet, Jeremiah (31:32): "I will put my Torah in their inwardness, and I shall inscribe it in their heart." This is what he proposed to bring to the attention of the Western Jew of his generation, and it may well be applied to the American Jew of our generation. In the following pages I will present his message to his contemporaries as he delivered it in his early speeches on Judaism, and as he later deepened it in his teachings on Zionism and the messianic idea.

The Jewish Question

The "Jewish Question" was then uppermost in everybody's mind. The Western Jews and their gentile neighbors saw it as a problem of how the individual Jew could adjust himself to his non-Jewish environment. His Jewish life, especially among the upper social strata and the intellectual elite, was being emptied of content as a culture, a national entity or even a religion. It almost ceased to have an autonomous reality. In Buber's view this was a manifestation of the duality in the Jewish soul in its lowest state: the Western Jew was aware only of his surroundings but not of his own being. His condition in exile had split him apart most grievously. It penetrated his innermost self and corroded his very humanity which he was trying desperately to realize through his surroundings. The "Jewish Question," as Buber sees it, is thus a problem not from without but from within, not how the Jew may cope with the outside world but with his Jewishness in relation to his own people. As posed by Buber, the question is, "What is it that makes a man's people an autonomous reality in his soul and in his life? What makes him feel the people not just about him but in him?" Buber then addresses himself to that question as a problem of inner duality and how it may be overcome through self-identification with a people one may call truly his own. His listeners, reared in universalistic and cosmopolitan ideas, could well follow him on the subject of duality as a general human condition; but how could they be made to appreciate the reality of a people of whom they had had no personal experience, except perhaps as a vague recollection of a distant past? Buber develops his theme on three levels: the biological, the ideational and the religious.

a. *The Substance of Jewishness*

Buber recognizes that in the Diaspora the Jew lives in two cultural worlds, but he deplores the fact that under the conditions of the time the Jew is master of neither the surrounding world nor his own. Granting that "we are a mixture of cultures," he writes, "we don't want to be slaves of this mixture but its masters." We must decide "what ought to be dominating and what dominated in us," and for that we must know ourselves as a people. The usual earmarks of a people are a common language, a land and customs, which obviously the Jews in the Diaspora do not possess in fact. And even with the modicum of sameness they may have in these areas in a given country, the three criteria are external, acquired and changing and do not constitute the substantial elements that every member of the group could feel as his personal possession. Buber, therefore, suggests that the true and absolute common bond of Jews everywhere is their blood relationship which has been transplanted through the generations from their remotest ancestors.

Through this bond each individual or "I" feels himself as the bearer of the substance of his people. Through this awareness the Jewish people becomes a reality for every Jew in his life at present and in his striving for the future. The humanity he yearns for is now within his power to attain, because it dwells in his innermost self. Once again Buber brings to his listeners "thought values" which he gained from his own living experience. This self-identification with one's ancestral roots played an important role in the revaluation of his Jewishness when he returned to the fold. He rediscovered them close to home in his grandfather, who labored in the vineyard of Torah and Midrash. In a congratulatory letter on the latter's birthday (Jan. 31, 1900), he wrote: "I cannot show you my gratitude and love better than when I — in my domain — emulate your manner, and like you place my life at the service of the Jewish people. . . . In this sense I can well say that I am continuing your life's work. . . . I am in truth your, *your* faithful grandson."

b. *Three Basic Jewish Ideas*

The main burden of Buber's message to the young generation is to renew the three tendencies or ideas which he considers to be primary in the Jewish folk character. He designates them as unity, deed and the future, and views them as essential not only to Jewish self-realization but also to the attainment of humanity's ultimate goal, as such. Unity is the wholeness of community through which each of its members strives to overcome his inner dualilty. Deed is observed in the Jewish tendency to action, which is stronger than in any other group. The idea of the future expresses itself in the people's search for unconditional justice and love or, generally, in its yearning for the days of the Messiah. These tendencies, Buber maintains, have been weakened and are lying dormant in the folk character in Exile. Those who have found their way back to their people through their awareness of blood relationship are called upon to awaken these primal tendencies in themselves, for they are but the expression of their real Jewishness, the expression of their wholeness as human beings.

c. *Jewish Religiosity*

The three basic ideas described above are permeated with a religious fervor, which is also peculiar to the Jewish people and which Buber calls religiosity. This is the third level of his central theme of overcoming the duality in the soul of the individual Jew. In both the biological and ideational aspects of Buber's concept of Judaism there are two dominant factors: the *act* and the *realization.* In order for the individual to realize himself he must decide to act. This "act of decision," as Buber calls it, is not so much a matter of ethics as of religiosity. That is, the self-realization is an activity of bringing the unconditioned divine presence into the conditioned and limited life of man on earth, whether it be of justice or love or any other of the religious precepts of Judaism. "The specific religious worth of Judaism," according to Buber, is the deed which has eternal value, designated as the unconditioned, and is grounded in "the basic feeling that it needs to be done"(et la'asot). The deed must be directed toward the ultimate goal of establishing the true community, for it is only through mutuality of communal life that the individual may realize himself as a being-as-a-whole. Those who direct themselves toward this end may often fail on their road in specific undertakings, but the influence of their activity bears fruit through the ages, leading to the goal. Buber's meaning of religiosity may be better understood in contrast to what he designates as "religion." The first, as described, is expressed in acts of the unconditioned as decided upon freely by each individual; the second consists of formal laws, rituals and ceremonies which are prescribed and codified in rules and regulations and administered by a ruling hierarchy or, as Buber calls it, "official Judaism." "Thus religiosity is the creative principle, religion the organizing one," The two have contended for supremacy in Jewish life throughout history and, while the organizing forces always have the upper hand, the dynamic principle of religiosity, acting in the depth of the folk spirit, breaks out from time to time and propels itself toward its ultimate goal. On its way it does not propose to abrogate the rites and ceremonies but to renew them through the deed of true intention. This deed of renewal, to which Buber exhorts his listeners, he finds exemplified in two historical movements, in Zionism and Messianism.

Zionism

Buber sees in Zionism a force that will enable the Jewish people to renew its primal religious deeds for the establishment of a true community, and he considers the Halutz movement as the vanguard of this enterprise. He says this is possible only in the Land of Israel, because there the Jews are in a position to reawaken their creative forces which have been lying dormant during their sojourn among the Western nations. He regards the Jewish people essentially as a people of the Orient. Although the Jews have been greatly influenced by Western culture, their yearnings and aspirations have remained true to the Oriental mode of thought, from Asia Minor to the Far East, of which they are the most representative type. "On this overt or latent Orientalism, this foundation of the soil of the Jew," he writes, "I build my faith in a new spiritual-religious creation of Judaism." Therefore, he advises that Western nationalism must not be the goal of Zionism, "because Zion is more than a nation"; it is a place where something unique, something above all nations, is to occur. To be sure, the Jews will rebuild themselves in their ancient land as a nation, but they must not strive to become "like all other nations," as some branches of the Zionist movement have advocated. This also explains Buber's approach to Jewish-Arab relations. He regards the Arabs too as an Oriental people and sees an historical opportunity for the two peoples to join forces for the renewal of human society and for their own regeneration. But he miscalculates the Arab intentions. While he demands of the Zionists to become impervious to "European state politics" and to cultivate, instead, the social principle of their national rebirth, he overlooks, though he sees clearly, the political-national forces among the Arabs that militate against the entire Jewish enterprise. He envisions Zionism in its messianic dimension, as the fulfillment of Israel's goal as a people on its own soil and as an example of the true community to be emulated by all other nations. "The true way leads through Zion for the renewal of human society." When the Jewish State was founded in 1948, he declared: "I have accepted the form of the new Jewish community, which emerged from the war, as my own." At the same time, he hoped for a real rapport with the Arabs through the instrumentality of the new State. "The commandment to serve the spirit," he then worte, "is now to be fulfilled by us through the State."

Messianism

The central place of Buber's religiosity or "act of decision" is the true community, and this is also his idea of the messianic faith.

"We expect a theopahany [a divine revelation]," he writes, "of which we know nothing but the place, and the place is called community"; and "a community of faith truly exists only when it is a community of work." This central messianic idea he considers to be an extension of the prophetic faith. Interpreting Jeremiah 7, he explains: God "desires a human people. . . . Out of a human community He wills to make His kingdom; community there must be in order that His kingdom shall come."

Fulfillment Here and Now

While Buber views Messianism in its historical development since the time of the prophets, he speaks of its realization "here and now" on earth and not in the beyond or in some distant future. Nor does he consider its fulfillment to be the exclusive task of a single person, as seen by traditional Judaism. Rather, he emphasizes the Talmudic concept of the Days of the Messiah (yemot hamashiah), for which all Israel is responsible and toward which it must work as a people every day of its existence. "A drop of messianic fulfillment must be mixed into every hour," he says, "or else it is godless despite all piety," (See Sanhedrin 97b and 98a. The coming of the Messiah "depends only upon repentance and good deeds"; and "If you [Israel] are worthy, I will hasten it.") However, since to this day the Jewish people as a whole has not fulfilled this task, there may now come forth selected individuals who will do its work. Every one of them may become what Isaiah calls God's servant. His prophecy, "My servant art thou, Israel, in whom I will shine forth," Buber interprets to mean that God addresses himself not only to the People Israel but also to individuals who will carry out the messianic deed, thus embodying the truth of Israel's existence, which is the establishment of the true community on earth. The striving of the Jews toward this end epitomizes Buber's entire philosophy of Judaism. The identification of each Jew with his own people on the biological level and his renewal of the three basic Jewish principles on the ideational level converge in his religious deed of self-realization as a human being-as-a-whole through an act of decision to build the true Jewish community in Zion.

1978

A Note on Buber's Approach to Jesus[1]

In his essay "Two Types of Faith", Buber makes the well-known distinction between what Jesus said about himself and what others (notably Paul) said about him, as recorded in the New Testament.[2] It has been suggested that Buber's real issue in this respect is the problem that has existed between the Judaizers and anti-Judaizers which has produced different views of Jesus. I maintain that the Judaizing controversy is an internal matter of Church doctrine, which Buber does not propose to arbitrate, and it would be incorrect for anyone to place him in the midst of it.

Originally, the Judaizing issue was whether or to what extent the Church was to adopt Jewish traditions and practices, an issue that was first raised in Acts 15. This was later developed into the question about "separation of Law from Gospel." and "to Judaize" came to mean "to teach false doctrine" in this regard.[3] Another form of Judaizing, or rather anti-Judaizing, involved the Old Testament as to whether it was Jewish or Christian Holy Scripture and who had a legitimate right to interpret it. Any one who upheld the Jewish claim was regarded a Judaizer. A third aspect took the turn of labeling as "Judaizing" any manner of heresy that the Church authorities might detect among followers of Christ.[4] Eventually it was debased to a game of name calling. Even to tolerate a Jewish community in the midst of a Christian population was branded Judaizing. This was one of the grounds for the establishment of the Ghettos and for the forced conversion of Jews. The term took on a totally degenerate form in Nazi Germany, where a group of Christian theologians, led by Dr. Walter Grundmann who held an official position in the Reich, undertook to de-Judaize the New Testament by expurgating all references to Jews and Jewry and converting its characters into pure Aryans. (Jesus, Grundmann "proved," could not have been born a Jew.) Ironically, the Reich Propaganda Ministry repudiated their efforts, telling them in no uncertain terms that all of

---

1. In reference to my treatment of Buber's essay "Two Types of Faith" in my book *Martin Buber's Philosophy of Interhuman Relation*, pp. 198-212.

2. See ibid., pp. 202 and 241, n. 422.

3. Cf. Jaroslav Pelikan. *The Christian Tradition.* Chicago: The University of Chicago Press, vol. 1, 1971. pp. 71f.

4. Cf. ibid., pp. 55f., 200f.

Christianity, no matter how reshaped is nothing but a Jewish scheme in disguise.[5]

Now Buber's position cannot be made to fit into any of those categories: nor does he discuss them in his approach to Jesus. His question is of an entirely different character, not how *Jesus the Jew* is related to the Church, but rather how *Buber the Jew* may relate himself to Jesus as far as he knows him from the New Testament. In other words, Buber seeks to establish what he considers to be a "Jewish view" of Jesus not for Christians but for Jews. The person, then, he deals with, though taken from Christian sources, is not the person Jesus Christ that the Church or any Christian finds in those sources. We may trace Buber's question to Mat. 16, where Jesus "asked his disciples. 'Who do men say that the Son of man is?'" Jesus himself did not clarify their answers directly and left them open. But on the bedrock of what one of them (Peter) said, he built his Church. Buber does not take issue with this, but he wants to know, as he put it, for "Jesus' sake" and his own, how Jesus himself saw his place in the Basilea and in his mission to mankind. After probing Jesus' own words in the New Testament, Buber comes to the conclusion that he did not consider himself a divine being and never intended to declare himself the Christ. My discussion centers on this issue and, as the reader of my book may observe, my analysis of the evidence leads me to conclude that Buber does not prove his case from the sources which he has adduced.

1980

5. See *Hitler's Professors*, by Max Weinreich. New York: Yivo, 1946, pp. 62-67.

רוח המזרח ורוח המערב לפי שיטתו של מרטין בובר

איש המזרח

1. איש התנועה והמניע.
2. כל מה שעושה רושם בנפשו יוצא לפעולה.
3. לחשׁב משמעו לעשות לפעל.
4. חוש השמיעה שלטת בו ביותר.
5. מרגיש את הייחסים בין דברים־הדדיות.
6. חושב ביחס לזמן יותר מביחס למקום.
7. הנביא חוזה חזון כדי לשמע דבר ה׳.
8. העולם צריך להתממש על ידי האדם.
9. העיקר הוא הדרך שילך בה האדם אל מטרתו לאחד את עולמו הפנימי.
10. נקודת מבטו היא מתוך הפנימיות־סוביקטיבית: מה שמתרחש מסביב לאדם נוגע בו בעומק נפשו.
11. מודה על האמת. האמת גלוייה והאדם רק מודה עליה.

איש המערב

1. איש המחוש.
2. כל מה שעושה רושם בנפשו נהפך לדמות פלסטית.
3. לחשב מובנו ליצר תבנית.
4. חוש הראיה שלטת בו יותר מכל החושים.
5. מרגיש דברים כשהם לעצמם.
6. חושב ביחס למקום יותר מביחס לזמן.
7. החזון הוא רק מראה, חזון לדמיון. האידאות שלו שקועות במנוחה נצחית מבלי להשתנות ולכן אין להם תנועה (למשל, האידאות של אפלטון).
8. העולם עומד להוודע על ידי שכל האדם.
9. העיקר הוא שהאדם יודע את האופן (מֶתודה), שיטה נכונה לאחד את עולם הטבע.
10. נקודת מבטו היא מתוך דברים חיצוניים — אוביקטיביות: דברים מתהווים מחוץ לנפשו בטבע.
11. מגלה את האמת. האמת נסתרה והאדם מגלה אותה. הדבר נחבא והאדם מוציא אותו ממחבואו.

*הרצאה ב"שבוע העברי" של ההסתדרות העברית באמריקה, 1973.

הלאומיים. הוא כתב באותו זמן: "אני קבלתי עלי את הדמות של הצבור היהודי החדש שעלתה מן המלחמה. המצווה של עבודת הרוח תתקיים עכשו על-ידי המדינה".

משיחיות

מבטו של בובר על המשיחיות גם כן מתרכז על הצבור האמתי בתפקידו לתקן את חיי החברה. "אנחנו מצפים להגלות השכינה", הוא כותב, "ואיננו יודעים שום אדותיה אלא מקומה; והמקום שלה נקרא צבור." הוא מפרש פרק ז' בספר ירמיהו במובן שהאלקים "רוצה בעם אנושי... ברצונו להקים ממלכתו מצבור אנושי. יש צורך בצבור כדי שתוקם ממלכתו." בובר דן הרבה בהתפתחות ההיסטורית של רעיון המשיחי. אבל ההטעמה תמיד על ממושו "עכשו ופה" עלי אדמות, ולא בעולם הדמיון או בעתיד הרחוק. "נָחוּץ לַמֵזֶג טפה של משיחיות בכל שעה ושעה", אומר, "כי בלי זאת הרעיון איננו אלהי, למרות כל דְבֵקות." הוא גם אינו רואה את ממוש הרעיון המשיחי כשליחותו של איש יָחיד הנקוב בשם מן השמים. לאמתו של דבר, התפקיד הוא של כל עם ישראל, כעם מיוחד. אך מפני שעד הנה העם לא התמכר לזה כלל או רובו, צריך שיופיעו אנשים יחידים שמסוגלים למלא את הפקודה שנטלה על עמם. כל אחד יכול לקבל על עצמו את העול של "עבד ה'", שדבר עליו ישעיהו הנביא, ולהגשים את המציאות של עם ישראל צעד על צעד בכל מה שיֵעשה לשם הָקמת הצבור האמתי.

תמצית דבר

שאיפת היהודים למטרה זו מתארת את תמצית משנתו של בובר על היהדות בכל ענפיה. התיַחדות של כל איש-יהודי עם עַמו דרך הכרת קרֵבות-הדם השוטֵף בעורקָיו, או הדרך הביאולוגית; הַחיָאַת שלשת הכוונים היסודיים בכל מעשיו, או הדרך האִידאולוגית; שתי אלה משתלבות עם דרך הדתיות וכֻלן מוליכות אותו להשתלמותו האנושית בהקימו את הצבור היהודי האמתי בארץ ציון.

(ג) המבט הדתי : דתיות ודת

בובר מציין את הדרך השלישית במושג דתיות שלפי דעתו שונה הוא מהמושג דת. המושג הראשון משתתף במעשה לשם שמים או, כשהוא גוזר, מעשה לפי המחלט, שכל אחד מחליט מתוך הכרה פנימית שבאה לו על ידי יחסו של דו־שיח לעֲמיתו ולמקום גם יחד. "ערך הדתיות המיוחד של היהדות", הוא אומר, נגלה במעשים שיש בהם ערך נצחי, וזה נובע מן הרגש העקרי "שיש צורך לעשות" או, כמו שאמרו חז"ל, "עת לעשות". זאת היא דתיות.

המושג השני, דת, משמעו חוקים, מצוות ופולחן, שנערכו ונמסרו רשמית בספרי ההלכה ונגזרים על ידי שומרי הדת בכל דור ודור. בקצור, "דתיות היא הכח היוצר, ודת, הכח המארגן." בתולדות עם ישראל שני הכחות התרוצצו בקרבו, ואף־על־פי שכח המארגן תמיד ידו על העליונה, הכח היוצר פורץ לתקופות מתחתית נפש העם וממריץ אותו אל המטרה. בובר איננו גורס שמגמת כח היוצר היא לבטל את הכח המארגן, מפני שהוא מכיר בתועלתו לצבור, אלא להפיח בו רוח חיים חדשה, שלא יתאבן לקפדנות צחיחה. איך מתגשמים שלשת הכוונים האלה, לפי שיטת בובר, בחיי העם למעשה ? אעבר בקצרה על שתי תנועות הפועלות בחיינו מיום היותנו לעם עד הנה ובחזוננו לעתיד : **ציונות ומשיחיות.**

ציונות

כמו שראינו, הצבור האמתי הוא נקודת הכובד במשנתו של בובר על היהדות וגם על האנושות בכללה. הוא סָכָה בציונות תכשרה היסטורית לעם היהודי להקים צבור כזה על אדמת אבותיו שרק שם אפשר לו לממש אותו. בעבור־זה תלה את תקוותו בקבוצות החלוצים שתהיינה לא רק למרפא נפש היהודי הנפקעת, אלא גם מופת לכל העמים.

לפי דעתו של בובר, העם היהודי הוא עם המזרח, ולמרות זה שהיה מֻשפע הרבה מתרבות המערב, נשאר לאמתו עם המזרח הטפוסי ביותר, מִיַם התיכון ועד מזרח הרחוק. "על יסוד זה של המזרחיות, בגלוי או בנסתר", הוא אומר, "אני תולה את אמונתי בכח היצירה הרוחנית־הדתית של היהדות". ולכן הוא מציע שהציונות לא תלך בדרך הלאומיות־הפוליטית המערבית, "כי הלא ציון עולה מֵעל לאום." ציון היא המקום שבו יתרחש דבר־מה מיוחד, דבר־מה מעל לעמים. בלי ספק עם ישראל יקים שָם את לאומיותו, אבל לא יהיה "ככל העמים", כפי שדרשו מנהיגים שונים בתנועה.

מזה אנו למדים גם את יחסו של בובר אל שאלת הערבים בארץ. הוא ראה את העם הערבי גם־כן כעם המזרח וקווה ששני העמים יתקרבו זה לזה ויֵעשו לכח יוצר שיחדש את חיי החברה האנושית וגם יתקדמו אל מַטרת תחיָתם בארץ המשותפת להם. אך הוא טעה טעות טראגית בזה שלא הביא בחשבון, אף־על־פי שראה זה בפועל, את הכוון הערבי שהתנגד ליישוב היהודי מיסודו בלי תנאים ובלי וִתורים. גם אחרי שקמה מדינת ישראל לתחיה בשנת 1948, ובייחוד אחרי נצחונה במלחמת השחרור, קווה בובר שהמדינה תתאמץ לשתף את הערבים להגשמת מגמותיה

92

אבות): "איזו היא דרך ישרה שיבור לו אדם" יהודי כדי להגשים את שאיפותיו?
בובר מראה לו את הדרך מתוך שלשה מבטים: מבט חיוני (או ביולוגי), מבט שיטתי
(או אידאולוגי), ומבט דתי.

(א) המבט החיוני

אמרנו שדו-שיח משמעו שהוויה עצמאית אחת מתייחסת להווייה עצמאית
אחרת מבלי להשתלט בה; שכל אחת מהן נמצאת בפני עצמה וחותכת את גורלה לפי
כחותיה הפנימיים יחד עם הזולת. אבל יחס כזה אין בין עם ישראל והעמים האחרים
בגולה. האחרים שולטים בו ושוללים את חפש רוחו. בובר מכיר שבגולה היהודי חי
בשני עולמות תרבותיים, אבל חס על זה שהוא איננו שולט לא בעולם הסביבה ולא
בעולם שלו. "אנחנו בני תרבות של תערובת," הוא כותב, "אבל אין אנחנו רוצים
להיות משעבדים לתערובת הזאת, אלא להתגבר עליה." אנחנו בעצמנו נחליט מה
צריך להיות שליט ומה משעבד. ולזה אנו צריכים להכיר את עצמנו כעם.

בדרך כלל, הציונים של עם הם שפה משותפת, ארץ מולדת, ומנהגים משותפים,
אבל למעשה אין לנו הציונים האלה בגולה. ועד כמה שיש לנו דברים משותפים
באיזו ארץ שהיא, הדברים האלה אינם יסודיים, שכל אחד ממנו יכיר בהם את נחלתו
האישית. ולכן בובר סובר שהנחלה המשותפת היחידה שיש לכל אחד מאתנו בכל
ארצות מגורינו היא ירושת-הדם של אבותינו השוטף בעורקינו. בזה כל יהודי מכיר
את מוצאו היסודי מעם אחד מדורות שעברו עד עתה: ומי שבא לידי הכרה זו מרגיש
את עמו בקרב לבו ובתוך נפשו בכל מקום שיגור. כדאי להעיר, שבובר בא לידי הכרה
זו לא רק מהתבוננות בחיי היהודים אלא אף מחייו הפרטיים. הוא הרגיש את עברו
היהודי וקשרו אל עמו כירושה שבאה לו מקרבות-הדם של בני משפחתו. במכתב־
ברכה ששלח לסבו ביום הולדתו (באחד בינואר 1900) כתב: "אינני יכול להביע לך
תודָתי ואהבתי היטב מזה שאני, בתחום שלי, הולך בדרכך, וכמוך אני מקדיש את חיי
לשרות העם היהודי.... במובן זה, מותר לי לומר שאני ממשיך את מלאכת חייך....
אני מברך ונושק אותך ואת הסבתא היקרה באהבה לבבית; ואני באמת הנכד שלכם,
הנאמן לכם."

(ב) המבט השיטתי: שלשה כוונים יהודיים מן היסוד

הדרך השניה שבובר מראה לדור הצעיר היא להחיות בקרבם את שלשלת הכוונים
או האידאות שיסודם בנפש העם היהודי, והם: ייחוד, פעולה, ועתיד. הוא גורס
שהכוונים האלה הם יסודיים לא רק להגשמת הייעוד היהודי אלא גם להשגת מטרת
האנושית העולמית. האידיאה של ייחוד משתקפת בשלמות הצבור שממנו כל אחד
שואב את כחו כדי להתגבר על השניות שבו. פעולה אנו רואים כנטיה כבירה בכל
דרכי היהודי בחיים. והאידיאה של עתיד מתבטאת בשאיפתו של העם לחיי נצח של
צדק ואהבה, או לחיי ימות המשיח. במדה שכל יהודי יחדש את הכוונים האלה בנפשו
ויעשה אותם קבע, ימצא את דרכו הנכונה אל עמו ואל ייעדו האנושי.

93

ונהיתה לעוזרת נאמנה לבעלה בתנועה הציונית וביהדות בכלל.

התנועה הציונית הביאה את בובר שוב למקורו היהודי. אז גם החל להתעמק בתורת החסידות ובחיי החסידים שמהם בקש לשאב "את הידע הבלתי־אמצעי... של העם בשחר יצירתו". הוא לא קבל עליו את עול החסידות, אלא נשאר כמתבונן ומפרש מבחוץ. אך התקרבותו אל התנועה גרמה הפכה עמוקה בנפשו: הוא עמד בנסיון של יחס עיקרי בין אדם למקום. וזה גם היה המניע הראשי של תורת הדו־שיח שלו שגלה אחרי שנים אחדות בספרו "אני ואתה".

רשימה קלה זו של ימי התפתחותו של בובר משקפת את בעית היהודים של דורו במערב אירופה, את התנגשותם עם "רוח הזמן", התלבטותם בהתבוללות ביולוגית ותרבותית, וסערת רוחם של יחידי סגולה, וביניהם בובר עצמו, שמצאו את דרכם לשוב ולהחיות את זיקי היהדות שרתחו בקרבם. כשהחל בובר לדבר אל הדור ההוא על היהדות חפש את האופן הנכון לגלות לפניו את לבטי ההתנכרות והתשובה שהוא עצמו נתנסה בהם. מעט מספר של שומעיו שבו בעצמם באותו הדרך, אך רובם לא ידעו איך לשוב ובאו אליו לבקש את דרכם.

נבדק נא את השאלה ששאלנו לעיל מתוך מבטו של הדור ההוא במערב אירופה; ונכון לומר שהיא הולמת גם היום אל הרוב של הדור הצעיר שלנו פה בארצות הברית. שאלנו, מה הקשר בין עקרון הדו־שיח ותחית העם היהודי? בני הדור שבובר דבר אליהם, אלה שחונכו באידאות של אוניברסליות וקוסמופוליטיות, יכלו בנקל להמשך אחרי משאת נפש של גאולה אישית, כפי מוסג הדו־שיח בין אדם ואדם; וזהו ענין הנוגע באנושות האוניברסלית. אבל איך היו יכולים להתיחד עם משאת נפש של העם היהודי השואף לגאולה מיוחדת, כשלא היה להם שום מגע עם העם הזה, אולי מלבד זכרונות של עבר מערפל?

כבר הערתי לעיל שבובר מצא את עקרונו במקורות היהדות, מדברי הנביאים ועד תורת החסידים. אבל המקורות האלה היו דברים חיצוניים וזרים בעיני דורו. הכח המניע היה צריך לבוא מבפנים כל אחד מהם, כי הלא הם היו "הנפשות הנודדות" שבובר ראה בעודנו באבו. הוא ציין את השאלה הזאת בשם "השאלה היהודית" לאמתה, לאמר: מהו הגורם שחולל אדם יהודי למצא עצמאות בנפשו ובחייו היהודיים? מה גורם לו שירגיש את הלאם לא רק מסביבו אלא בקרב לבו? את תשובתו מצא בעקרון שני אשר יסודו בנפש היהודי כיחיד וכעם. הוא גרס, שהשניות הטבעית שבאדם נמצאת בנפש היהודי ובעם היהודי במדה היותר גדולה מבכל בני אדם. אך נוסף על זה, גם האמץ להתגבר עליה פועם בלב היהודי ובעמו ביתר עוז. באחד מנאומיו על היהדות כתב: "שום איש לא ידע את תהום השניות כמו שיודע אותו איש יהודי; ברם אין אחר כמוהו שידע גם את הפלא של שלמות, אשר אין רק להאמין בו, אלא לבוא אליו דרך הנסיון." בשתי התכונות האלה מצטיין עם ישראל כגוי אחד למינו. איש יהודי ששואף לגאולת הווייתו בשלמות לא ישיג את מטרתו אלא על ידי התיחדותו הנפשית עם עַמו, כי הלא שניהם היחיד והעם, מטיב אחד הם. והנה נצבת לפנינו שאלה שנייה, יותר חמורה (בדגמת השאלה ששאל רבי בפרקי

עצמה. במפגש כזה שתי ההוויות מאשרות זו את זו, ומתוך האישור בא אמון הדדי ביניהן. יחס של דו־שיח זה בין אדם לאדם גובר על השניות שבכל אחד מהם, וכל אחד מוצא את שלמותו יחד עם עמיתו. כלל־דבר: אין השתלמות של אדם בעצמו, אך ורק של אדם עם הזולת. זהו היסוד שעליו נבנים — עדה, צבור, לאום, ועם. היחידה שממנה מתהווה הצבור האנושי היא התא שנוצר על ידי היחס הזה בין יחידים או עדות. הלאום או העם, שתאים יסודיים כאלה פועמים בקרבו, חי חיים שלמים וקיימים. אך במדה שהלאום או העם מתרחק ממקורו האנושי, עצמתו מתפוררת, ואם אין בו רוח להחיות את הכחות היסודיים שלו, ירד לאבדון.

היוצא לנו מעקרון הדו־שיח של בובר הוא, שלאומיות תלויה בצבור אנושי אמיתי, וצבור כזה מתהווה מיחס הדדי של אנשים הנפגשים על ידי תעצומות האהבה והאמונה שבלבם. והנה תשאלו בתמהון, מהי הנקודה הסגלית של עקרון זה שממנה ילמד אדם־יהודי את קשרו ליהדותו ולעמו?

טרם, שנוכל להשיב דבר אנו צריכים לדעת על איזה מין אדם־יהודי השאלה מדברת, ומהי נכונות השאלה. פרטים אחדים מחיי בובר, בייחוד בגילו הרך בבית הורי אביו ובראשית דרכו בתרבות המערב, יועילו לנו להבין את הענין יותר לנכון.

רשימות ביאוגרפיות

מרדכי (מרטין) בובר נולד בשמונה לפברואר, שנת שמונה עשרה מאות שבעים ושמונה בן למשפחה יהודית אמידית בווינה. בעודו פחות משלש שנים הוריו הפרדו והוא יצא לגור בבית הוריו של אביו בלמברג, במזרח־גליציה, שהיתה אז מחוז בממלכת אוסטריה־אונגריה. ראשית חנוכו בשפה העברית ובלימודי קדש היתה תחת השגחת סבו, שלמה באבער, תלמיד חכם מופלג וחוקר במדרש אגדה, הנודע בכל רחבי היהדות המסורתית. את לימודיו בשפות לועזיות ובמקצועות אחרים קבל בעזרת הסבתא שלו, אדעל, בעלת תרבות גבוהה שרכשה בעצמה בספרות הגרמנית והעולמית. אמו, עליזה, לא באה לראות את בנה מיום שעזבה אותו. אך אביו, קרל, שהיה חסיד לבית הרבי מסאדיגורא, היה לוקח אותו עמו כשבקר את הרבי וגם היה מבלה אתו ימות החפש בעונת הקיץ שלו. בבקוריו אצל הרבי בובר הצעיר למד את דרכי החסידים שעשו רושם גדול עליו.

בהיותו בן ארבע־עשרה בובר שב לגור בבית אביו, שנשא אז אשה שניה והשתקע בלמברג. הוא בקר בגמנסיון פולני, פרק עול מצוות מעשיות, ועסק לרוב בספרות העולמית, פילוסופיה, ובלשנות. כשתקע את עצמו בבעיות הפלוסופיות של הזמן, התרחק לא רק מהחסידות אלא מהיהדות בכלל. בימי לימודיו באוניברסיטאות של וינה, ברלין וליפסיה נגרר אחר הזרם האסטטי־תרבותי שסחף את מרכזי ההשכלה האירופית באוסטריה וגרמניה. כשנזכר בובר אחרי שנים שעברו אודות אותם הימים הוא כתב שהיה חי אז "בעולם נבוך, במגור מֵתִי של נפשות נודדות, המלאות זריזות רוחנית, אבל בלי יהדות ולכן בלי אנושות ובלי קדושת השכינה." כשהגיע לשנתו העשרים־ואחת נשא אשה נוצרית, פאולא ווינקעל מינכן, שהיתה סופרת בעלת כשרון רב וכתבה ספורים ונובלות שיצאו לאור בשם עט גיאורג מונק. היא התגיירה

95

משנתו של מרטין בובר על היהדות *

בעית האדם

במבוא לנאומיו האחרונים על היהדות (1951) בובר כותב : "בימים הגורליים האלה, ארבעת הנאומים צריכים להקרא כמו שנכתבו מאת יהודי אל יהודים. אך מה שנאמר שם נוגע לאדם ואנושותו בכלל. כל מחשבותיו של בובר תמיד היו סובבים על בעית האדם בזמננו. אלא כ"יהודי חרוץ" (כשקרא את עצמו) הוא נאלץ לחפש תשובה על בעיה זו במקורות היהדות, כמו שאמר, "מעשרת הדברות עד החסידות". הוא מצא בפסרי המקרא את הדגמה של הווית האדם שמתבטאת על ידי "דו־שיח בין מעלה ומטה." ואת החסידות ראה "כהתקימות של היהדות". ולכן השאלה הנמרצת שלו היתה על גורל האנושות, ואת הדרך לפתרון שאלה זו מצא בדברי הנביאים, בהוראות חז"ל, ובאמרות רבני החסידים.

לפי דעתו של בובר, האדם הוא בעל דו־צירים או בעל שניות טבעית : הוא מתלבט בין יצר הרע ויצר הטוב, נאבק עם סופיות ואין־סופיות, ומפרכס בין המוגבל והבלתי־מוגבל. הנגודים האלה ויתר הסתירות שבקרבו פוקעים את רוחו ודוחפים אותו מדרכו הרצויה בחייו. שניות זו רובצת בכל משבר סוציאלי שבא עליו בימי חלדו ביחס לעמיתו, בינו לטבע, ובינו למקום. משבר כזה בא על האנושיות המודרנית בכל נבכי חייה. אבל, גורס בובר, ישנן בנפש האדם גם תעצומות שמתאימין לו כדי להתגבר על שברונו זה ולאחד את עצמו כהווייה שלמה.

בובר מונה ארבע תעצומות כאלה, שכולן דיאלוגיות, כולן של דו־שיח, ואלו הן : הכרה, אומנות, אהבה, ואמונה. לא אבוא כאן בעבי ההתפלספות שלו בעניין זה מפני שהוא נוגע למחשבתו הכללית. רק אציין שהאמונה היא התעצומה היותר כבירה, והיא משתתפת עם יתר התעצומות ומוליכה את האדם ליחס בלתי־אמצעי אל כל ההוויה. מזה אנו למדים שתורתו של בובר על דו־שיח היא דתית במהותה. וכמו שציינתי לעיל, הוא למד את העקרון הזה מספרי הקודש. ומזה אנו למדים עוד דבר עקרי, שתפקיד האדם הוא למצא את דרך האמונה שתוביל אותו לשלמותו האנושית.

עקרון הדו־שיח

אבאר בקיצור נמרץ את מהותו של עקרון הדו־שיח, כי בלי הבנה של עקרון זה אי־אפשר לנו לתפש את משנתו של בובר על היהדות. כל הגותו מסתובבת על ציר זה.

דו־שיח אפשר להתרחש בין אדם וכל יצור, מהמדרגה הכי נמוכה עד היותר עליונה שבטבע, וגם בין אדם למקום. אך מפני שהאדם הוא היצור היחידי שיש בו כשרון זה, יחס הדו־שיח בין אדם לאדם משתרר על כל היקום. יתר על כן, אין אדם יכול לבוא ביחס לבוראו אלא דרך התייחסותו אל אדם אחר. ובכן יחס זה הוא גורלו של האדם כהווייה היוצאת מן הכלל, ועליו לעשות אותו הרגל בכל דרכיו ומעשיו, כי רק על ידו הוא מגשים את אנושותו. היחס של דו־שיח בין אנשים משמעו שאיש נענה אל הזולת בתם לב, מבלי לחפש להשתלט בו ומבלי להתרחק ממנו, אלא מקדם את פניו כהווייה מצד עצמה הבאה בקשר עם הווייה אחרת שגם היא חפשית מצד

96

Some Observations
on a Discussion between Norbert Samuelson and Shubert Spero Concerning Maimonides' Concept of Relations as Divine Attributes

Samuelson states: "In consequence of Friedlander's mis-translation of the original text, Rabbi Spero erroneously reasoned that Maimonides distinguished between 'a strong and a weak sense of relational attributes' and that 'Maimonides was convinced that in a strict and literal sense' relations can be affirmed of God. In fact, Maimonides made no such claim. Rather, he said that of the four kinds of false divine predications, relations are less objectionable than the others" (p 361).[1]

1. In the first place, Friedlander's translation of the passage under discussion (*Guide* I, 72) does not differ materially from Pines' translation quoted by Samuelson. To say "They are forgivable with reference to what is predicated of God" (Pines) is the same as "These are to be employed, in a less strict sense, in reference to God" (Friedlander). Ibn Tibbun supports the latter rendition, as he translates אלא שהוא הראוי שבתארים אשר צריך שיקלו בתאר ה' בו. The word שיקלו conveys the meaning of a lighter or "a less strict sense." Second, Spero does not say that "Maimonides was convinced that in *a strict and literal sense* relations can be affirmed of God," as Samuelson quotes him, but on the contrary, that Maimonides concluded that they could "be employed, *in a less strict sense*, in reference to God," which is what Maimonides did claim.[2]

2. However, the real issue is not a matter of exact English wording ("forgivable," "in a less strict sense," or "less objectionable"), but rather, why Maimonides felt that attributes of relation could be used *in some way* with reference to God, when in the same breath he ruled them out as accidents inapplicable to the Divine Name, even though they did not affect its essence. The answer is that he permits the use of relations as divine attributes, but cautions that they should not be understood, "as some people understood them" (כפי מחשבת בני אדם), as qualities, definitions, or certain kinds of relation which contain elements of accident.

---

1. See *Judaism,* Winter and Summer 1973, pp. 66-78 and 359-63.
2. Ibid, p. 71.

Indeed, Maimonides not just tolerates their use but himself indulges in them when he speaks of God's relation to the world. Thus he says, the Hebrew word ישב (sit), when applied to God, "is to be taken in the sense: 'Thou, O Lord, abideth (תשב) forever, . . . in His relation to other things; for there is no relation between Him and any other being that He might change in that relation." And further, the verse "'The Lord sitteth upon the flood,' means: though earthly things change and become corrupt, God's relation does not change."[3]

3. In order to clear up these discrepancies, we must understand in what sense Maimonides uses the category "relation." This has nothing to do with equivocation, but with logical and existential aspects of the term as such. Existentially Maimonides realizes, as every philosopher ought to, that if there is no relation between God and man whatsoever, man cannot speak of God at all, for speaking of someone is relating. Maimonides now asks himself the philosophical question, What can I say about God that is logically consistent (or not inconsistent) with His Divine Name, that is His Oneness?

4. The Greek word *Kategorein* means to express or to say. The above question may thus be rephrased: What categories does Maimondies use as attributes of the Divine Name? He divides Aristotle's ten categories into two main parts: (1) Substance and (2) the other nine which are accidents.[4] Since he does not permit the use of any category signifying accidence to be applied to God, how can one express (categorein) God's relation to the world and man, unless one can find a form among the other nine categories which does not imply accidence? Upon examining the category of relation, Maimonides finds that all its forms, as enumerated by Aristotle (Cat. 6a-8b), are inapplicable, because they indicate changeability and plurality in the divine essence. But Maimondies labors under the difficulty created by Aristotle's restricted definition of relation, namely, "Those things only are properly called relative in the case of which relation to an external object is a necessary condition of existence" (which Aristotle himself regards as "not complete." See Cat. 8a30). Moreover, he follows Aristotle's dictum that "all relations are correlatives," that is, are

3. *Guide* I, 11, my translation from the Hebrew according to Ibn Tibbun in Yehudah Ibn Shmuel Kaufman's edition, Tel Aviv, 1935.
4. See his *Logic* I, ed. X. Efros, p. 53: "The first of these categories is substance and the rest are accidents."

reciprocal, whether actually expressed or implied (cf. Cat. 6b25-7b10). Hence, if we introduce a reciprocal relative between God and external things, we make His existence conditioned by those things, which is inconceivable.

5. Nevertheless, Maimonides recognizes, as Aristotle himself states: "The fact that a thing is explained with reference to something else does not make it [that thing] essentially relative" (Cat. 8a30), and he emphasizes this fact several times in his analysis of relation in the *Guide* I, 52. His main concern there is to ascertain "whether some real relation exists between God and any of the substances created by Him, by which He could be described," for he still feels that relations "are the most appropriate of all attributes to be employed. . . in reference to God." He therefore tries to "ease up" (להקל) the restriction imposed by Aristotle's definition, and he finds a leeway in the relation of *action*, which also refers to something else (to an other), namely a product, but does not point to any faculty of quality of the one who acts, and does not imply reciprocity.

6. That the category of action, as developed by Maimonides in the *Guide* I (chaps. 52 and 53), falls under the category of relation can be illustrated from Kant's three categories of Relation, which, we might say, were anticipated by Maimonides. Those categories come in pairs, expressing the relations of a thing to something else as (1) Substance and Accident, (2) Ground and Consequence, and (3) Community of Disjunctives related to each other in reciprocity or under subsumption of a common sphere.[5] Now Maimonides rules out the first and third kinds (accidental quality and correlation or subsumption) but admits the second, namely, that God may be described as the Ground (Creator) of all His creatures, who are consequences of His action, without in any way diminishing His Unity and Perfection. God is thus related to the world existentially and without contradiction in His Divine Name, for in this kind of relation He is not affected by His creatures.

7. The closing sentences of chapter 53 of the *Guide* summarize Maimonides' view on the relational attribute of action as applied to God. When we speak of the four attributes of God — life, potency, wisdom, and will — (he says there) we do not speak of Him as if He consisted of a plurality of essential qualities but, on the contrary,

5. Cf. Kant, *Kritik der reinen Venrunft,* Bill-12, Third Observation.

99

that He is One Substance who lives, is potent, is wise, and wills. "As for the changing attributes, there is no difference whether they refer to His actions or to the changing relations between Him and His creatures; for as we have explained [in ch. 52], they also express the truth of relation but in the way people understand them generally."[6] But when relation is applied to God, it can be only His action. "And this is what we must believe concerning the attributes mentioned in the books of the Prophets."[7]

1973

6. It should be pointed out with regard to this phrase that Friedlander's translation, "exists only in the thoughts of man" (p.74), or Pines' translation, "its being merely something that is in thought and not in reality" (as Spero adds) is out of context. The discussion in this passage, and in the entire preceding chapter of the *Guide*, is not whether what we have in our thought regarding the divine attribute *corresponds* to what is in God in reality, but rather whether our *thinking* about the attribute of God's relation as action is consistent without *thinking* of His Oneness and Perfection.
7. My rendition from the Hebrew of Kaufman's edition of the *Guide*, pp. 259-60.

A Critique of Religious Humanism

Humanism may be broadly said to be turning man's attention to man, not only to his needs but also to his power to meet those needs. In this respect, Eugene Kohn follows in the footsteps of Jewish tradition, which has always recognized human worth and has credited man with the ability to realize his aspirations on earth. For, as we read in the biblical account of man's coming into being, he was endowed by his Maker with the power to "subdue the earth and have dominion over the fish of the sea and over the fowl of the air and over every living thing that creepeth upon the earth." Even in spiritual matters early man received Divine admonition not to allow evil, crouching at his door, to engulf him, for he can rule over it. What prompts Kohn to go beyond tradition is the claim of natural science to bestow on man greater powers than tradition, which views man as a creature, is willing to grant him. For what displeases modern man most is his creaturely status. Humanism, with the aid of natural science (or naturalism), holds forth the promise of freeing him from his fetters.

An Attempt at Reconciliation

Humanism and science, however, hold divergent and often conflicting views on the subject. From their earliest inception in

100

the fifteenth century, the natural scientists have advocated, for the most part, a dissociation of religion from science (such as, the theory of double truth or double revelation held by Campanella and Paracelsus). The humanists, on the other hand, have felt that the two can be reconciled and their contradictions eliminated (as was tried by Pico della Mirandola, Erasmus and Thomas More). Such an attempt at reconciliation has been made by the author of *Religious Humanism,** with particular reference to Jewish tradition.

Kohn writes in a very readable style and his analysis is a clear presentation of the Reconstructionist approach to the problems of faith in our day. He furthermore imbues his discourse with a deep sense of personal religious commitment, which is ultimately the true touchstone of reaching out toward the Divine. Kohn's essay will thus inspire its readers to seek God, even though many of them may not follow the path he has charted for them. The book discusses many aspects of religion, all centering on the question, "What is the role of religion in human life?" I shall limit myself to an investigation of Kohn's conception of the idea of God, and whether his humanistic interpretation of that idea resolves the difficulties he poses.

Scientific Methodology

Of particular interest and merit is Kohn's determination not to break with tradition, but only to reinterpret it so as to make the age-old idea of God fit into the world outlook of modern man. For this purpose he embarks upon a methodological excursion, bringing into play scientific as well as ideational modes of reasoning, which he considers as "criteria for validating religious beliefs." On the scientific side, he proposes to proceed on the principles of empirical observation and experimentation. For in religion as in science, he says, propositions must be verified by facts. However, he realizes that facts in themselves, without underlying rules of explanation, will not yield certainty. Observed data are changeable and elusive, and may point in different directions on different occasions. He therefore introduces (on the ideational side) what he regards as intuitions and definitions, which are

---

Religious Humanism, A Jewish Interpretation, by Eugene Kohn, The Reconstructionist Press, New York, Second Edition, 1963.

constant, and which are to cement the observable data into a system where the main idea, namely, of God, must of necessity play a part. Basically, then, Kohn's methodology is to yield a system of facts and ideas functioning in mutual interaction. The question is to what extent these ideas are related to the facts. Are they also performing the functions which he has ascribed to them in his system? One difficulty Kohn encounters at the very outset of his analysis is that in religion, unlike science, "it is impossible to employ the experimental method, since we would be both the subject and the object of our experiment." Moreover, Kohn points out, "religious belief, of necessity, involves an *a priori* commitment, a moral hazard consciously assumed." Hence, he substitutes for the "test of experiment" the "test of experience," maintaining that "experiment is nothing but controlled experience." Under these circumstances, Kohn can hardly claim scientific validity for his method of investigation. The difference between "experience" and "controlled experience" is precisely the difference between non-scientific and scientific observation.

The Elements of Experiment

In experimentation, the scientist introduces elements which are not derived from experience, but which are designed to solve a problem on the basis of an accepted hypothesis or principle. The scientist selects the data and sets up the physical conditions of their observation in line with his hypothesis. The control is exercised by the instruments of observation, which have been designed specifically for the experiment. In the scientific experiments with light, for example, no one ever experienced ether as an element transmitting waves. Yet ether was a factor in interpreting the data observed in the experiments. Following the same wave-theory, Michelson-Morley designed instruments of observation to calculate the movement of light, and those instruments, in turn, enabled science to modify the wave theory. When Einstein introduced the principle of a light-constant, he did not derive it entirely from experience but posited it in the experiment as a standard of measurement. Then, new instruments of observation were designed in line with this principle to test its validity. (Cf. Einstein on what he terms "the fictitious character of fundamental principles" in "The Method of Theoretical Physics," *Essays in Science*, Philosophical Library, 1934, p. 17).

"Test of Experience" Not Enough

From experiment, then, we can calculate and interpret data obtained by instruments of observation. We may also verify the hypothesis on which an experiment is based. From experience, on the other hand, we can only describe and enumerate what we perceive. We may even classify and compare on the basis of an observable element (as shape of leaves in plants or color of skin in human races). The moment we try to calculate and intrepret the data, we must introduce hypotheses or principles which lie outside the realm of pure experiences. In that case, the hypotheses or principles must be submitted to the test of experimentation or controlled experience. The "test of experience" by itself, which Kohn proposes to apply, is not sufficient if he is to abide by the principles of empirical science.

An even greater methodological difficulty is created by the author's introduction of "an *a priori* commitment" in the experience of religious belief, which is entirely foreign to empirical science. An *a priori* commitment is not subject to scientific test or verification, for the commitment itself (if and when made) is a fact and need not be verified by other facts. Nor does it confirm or deny other facts. It is an act of self-readiness to accept ideas that may be attained through means other than its own. The test of experience may show what happens when a commitment is made; but it does not verify the truth or falsehood of the object to which it was made. One could make a commitment to erroneous religious beliefs, which might result in idol worship. The sources of truth of the belief must be derived by other means. That is not subject to investigation by the methods of empirical science and certainly not by those of pure experience. The hypothetical approach to faith does not bear real fruit. (Pascal tried it with respect to the doctrine of original sin, trying to adjust himself to the scientific mood of his day, without effect.) As will be shown later, the hypothesis Kohn introduces not only cannot be verified by experiment, but does not even explain the experience.

Speculative Reason

It appears that Kohn's methodology is rather one of speculative reason. The test for that is not experience in itself, but experience interpreted within a consistent system of thought. To what extent Kohn is consistent with his speculations may be seen from his treatment of the criteria he designates as intuitions, and how he applies them in his derivation of religious ideas, especially the God-idea. Intuition is purported to do what concepts cannot do (as maintained, for example, by Bergson, who distrusted conceptual knowledge), that is, to know real things immediately without resorting to the categories of the understanding. It is a kind of higher perception. In the realm of ideas, intuition is also non-perceptual as well as non-conceptual, that is, completely non-mediated knowledge. It is sometimes called intellectual intuition or speculative reason. Since Kohn investigates religious-ethical ideas and not perceptual data, his intuitions must fall within the area of speculative reason. In either case, intuitive knowledge may be applied to things and ideas as they are, even though we may never be able to see them (perceptually) or infer them from other things (conceptually). But intuition can hardly be used for things as they *ought to be*, unless the *ought* is transcendent, that is, not posited by the intuiting self. In other words, intuition is an immediate, non-causal relationship of knowledge between one subject and another. I may, for example, have an intuition of a Divine commandemnt, "Love thy neighbor as thyself." But if I am the one who posits that dictum, I am aware of it not by intuition but by my act (cause) of positing. There is no speculation about it.

Criteria of Intuition

The four intuitions adduced by Kohn, and quoted below, do not fall entirely within the meaning of this term, as they contain also elements not given by intuition.

"1. The human being is not merely a body or an organism, but is also a person, or, in traditional terminology, a soul." Although this is stated in the form of a definition, we may accept its implication that the knowledge of one human being by another is ultimately possible only through intuition.

"2. Other human beings are, equally with ourselves, persons or souls and should possess an equal right to the maximum fulfillment of their personal wants." The first part of this statement is contained in the first intuition, above, which is formulated as a universal proposition. The second part contains an "ought," which may be regarded as an intuition only if not posited by the self. (This is questionable in Kohn's system of immanence.)

"3. All men are organically akin, belonging to the same

biological order of species." This is a conclusion drawn from the science of organic life, and is not an intuition.

"4. All men are dependent on their natural environment, and human life is part of the life of the universe, akin to all other forms of life." This, too, is inferred from the physical and biological sciences, and, while it contains elements of direct observation, is not an intuition. Besides, the phrases "human life is part of the life of the universe" and "akin to all other forms of life" are ambiguous. Taken together, they may mean that human life functions in all respects as a part of the general functioning of life. Or, they may mean that human life is only in part functioning like general life, but has other factors not found in non-human life. In any event, they are analytical judgments obtained by inference and not by intuition, and are subject to scientific (empirico-logical) proof. The balance of the fourth proposition is an intuition, namely: "Human personality and society express an emergent purpose that transcends them and upon which they depend. That purpose is not capricious; it is manifest in natural and moral law, and is commonly identified as Divine" (p. 6). The last element, "Divine," however, is not intuited but just "commonly identified," that is, named as such.

It is from the first intuition (the person) and the fourth (the purpose) that Kohn finally derives his concept of the God-idea. What we are concerned with here is to find out, following the author's analysis, whence the "purpose" emerges, what is the locus of its transcendence, and how this purpose, together with the intuition of the human being as a person, leads to the God-idea.

The Soul

In the second chapter, "The Soul's Testimony to God," Kohn offers a succinct analysis of the nature of human personality or, as he also designates it, the human soul. Contrary to the general position of the naturalists, the author recognizes "the mystery of human personality," that is, that not all is known about it and "we cannot frame an adequate idea of the self," not to speak of the "other." It is therefore correct to maintain with Kohn that our knowledge of "personality" is intuitive—it is more than can be derived form our sense-data and the categories of the understanding in analyzing the physio-biological findings about the human being.

The same holds true of psychological analysis which the self, as a whole, eludes. "Psychology may analyze a man's state of consciousness," he writes, "his instinctual drives or his conditioned reflexes, his libido and his super-ego, etc., but the self, of which all of these are so many aspects or activities, transcends them all." Granting, then, our intuitive knowldege of the human personality as a whole, how do we identify it in our system of reality? Here Kohn deviates sharply from the traditional view, which regards the soul as a substance. He calls the biblical account of the origin of the soul a myth, referring to *Genesis*, 2:7, where it reads: "Then the Lord God formed man of the ground, and breathed into his nostrils the breath of life; and man became a soul." If one may digress for a moment into biblical exegesis, the account in *Genesis* is more in keeping with Kohn's intuition of the nature of the soul than is his own final definition of it.

A Disturbing Ambiguity

Kohn regards the soul at one time as a whole, and at another time as a factor or aspect of the whole. This is due to his inconsistent use of the terms "person" and "soul." In his analysis of human personality he applies the terms person-soul-ego-self-I interchangeably. When it comes to identifying the soul, he defines it as an "aspect of the human personality." He thus posits "personality" as a whole and the "soul" as the unifying, integrating factor of all its "conflicting impulses." He is still left with the problem of how to identify personality. On the other hand, in the Bible there is no such division between person and soul or, for that matter, between body and soul. While the origin of the body is dust (and can be analyzed in biology and psychology), "man [as a whole] became a living soul." In this respect, Kohn would be justified in saying that the soul (or person) transcends the human body—its physiological as well as psychological aspects. He starts in that direction but, yielding to the naturalists, he lapses into their errors. His difficulty can be traced to conflicts in his methodology. He views the soul (or person, which he treats synonymously, as seen from his first intuition, quoted above) under the concept of causality and not of substance. The elimination of the concept of substance from an account of reality has been a dogma of the natural scientists since the 18th century—the Age of Enlightenment. Kohn tries to follow this mode of thinking in his definition of the soul, which he calls "the reality behind the myth." But he cannot escape the myth when he searches for the "soul" and finds it in "personality"—definitely a substantial concept. The soul, he says, "enables" the impulses of personality "to fulfill *its* vital functions." In this connotation, the soul can no longer be regarded as an intuition. It appears rather as a hypothesis or an abstract principle of unity (perhaps in the Kantian sense).

The God-Idea

From his definition of the soul, Kohn ventures out to reach God. And here he comes up against the greatest stumbling block in his system, namely, the meaning of transcendence and immanence with reference to the soul and the God-idea. To prepare the ground, he makes a further distinction between the "soul" and the "ego," the latter being the individualistic "selfish self," whereas the former has the task of relating the individual to society. Thus the soul receives an additional function. While it unifies "the conflicting interests of the individual, [it] must also endeavor to bring them into harmony with the similar interests of the other human beings, without whose cooperation it would be impossible to live a human life. The soul, therefore . . . compels man to recognize *a Source of authority outside his individual ego. . . .* The soul [is thus] *the self-transcendent of the human personality"* (p. 20, author's italics). In the underscored lines of the last sentence, the author introduces two factors—a Source of authority, and self-transcendence—which are not derived from his analysis of the nature of the soul. The societal aspect of the soul may well come from its own recognition that in order to fulfill its aspirations it has to get along with other souls. Outside authority does not come into question here. If, by authority, is meant (and it could mean nothing else in this context) that a limitation is to be set on the "conflicting interests" of the individual, that is to be done by the soul itself. According to the author's definition, it is the function of the soul "to bring them [the conflicting interests] into harmony with the similar interests of other human beings." The soul might well enter voluntarily into a mutual relationship with other souls to fulfill its own interests and also to allow others to fulfill theirs. Rousseau's "social contract," for example, and not a selftranscendent authority, would be sufficient to satisfy that purpose.

Dual Use of Transcendence

The difficulty here is in Dr. Kohn's dual use of the term transcendence, as he applies it to the single soul and to all souls in the aggregate. A soul may transcend itself with reference to other souls by recognizing their existence and interests. When they all get together, voluntarily, for the furtherance of their respective or mutual interests, there is no further transcendence necessary, unless the "society" thus formed is regarded as transcending them all, which would serve no purpose. All the souls, according to Kohn's definition, could fulfill themselves by their cooperation in the society which they may found, without the aid of any factor transcending themselves. What prompts Kohn to look for an extra power transcending the aggregate of souls, and why does he not bestow this power on society itself, as some humanists do? (p. 20). Apparently, he feels that society cannot really fulfill itself without the aid of a transcending power, which is quite in keeping with the traditional religious view. "We must assume, therefore," he says, "that the Source of authority which our souls recognize must transcend not only the individual, but also society. That source must be found in the very Source of life, in the *Hai Ha-olamin*, the Life of the Ages, in God" (21). We may go along with the author on the proposition that the *Hai Ha-olamin* is the source of authority for human life, but this proposition does not follow from his analysis of the nature of the soul, nor from "our self-identification with the interests of society." But the second, larger type of transcendence, namely, of the Source of society's authority, has no necessary relation to the single soul or the aggregate of souls.

Recognition of God

One must bear in mind that the recognition of God or the "Source of authority" in Kohn's system is not in itself intuited, but is here inferred from his intuition number two, discussed above, namely, that "other human beings, equally with ourselves, are persons and should possess an equal right to the maximum fulfillment of their personal wants." As pointed out, this statement contains an *ought* which cannot be the subject of intuition unless it is issued by a power transcending the self. But Kohn does not grant such power, or any transcendent power, to the Source of authority or God. The weakness of his argument is manifest in his next step, when he reverts the God-idea back to its original place, namely, the soul, which he further defines as "the immanent or in-dwelling aspect of Divine nature . . . in us" (21). The transcending (not really transcendent) "source of authority" derived by the author from the human self (self-identification or self-transcendence is an act of the self) has found no locus outside the self, and has therefore been returned to where it came from.

Concept of God—An Hypothesis

What, then, is the relationship of soul (or souls) to God, and how does the God-idea function in Kohn's system of religious humanism? This he develops in his chapter on "The God Idea Reinterpreted." The motivation for a new interpretation of the God-idea—man's attainment of the highest good—is a pivotal factor in the author's formulation of his concept of God. He maintains that the traditional interpretation is beset with insurmountable contradictions, inasmuch as it fails to reconcile the problem of good and evil with God's attributes of goodness, omnipotence, etc. This, he says, is due to the old "conception of God as a person" (36). Instead, he recommends a concept of God as an "hypothesis of the power that makes for human salvation," and all inner contradictions will be eliminated (35). All the hypothesis has to do is satisfy the conditions of "man's ethical behavior and . . . affect his orientation in life" (34), which must be all to the good, there being no evil in it.

The difficulties Kohn finds with the old theories of divine attributes do not really lie in his inability to reconcile them with the problem of good and evil. He does not solve this problem any more than they did. He just cuts the Gordian knot, first by removing evil from the "Source of authority" and then by naming it "unrealized good" (38). (Anyone who has suffered real evil at the hands of man will hardly be inclined to accept such a euphemism.) The real difference between Kohn and the traditional view has deeper roots. In Jewish tradition, God is not only ineffable but also undefinable. To define God as a concept is completely alien to Jewish awareness of the Divine Presence. Jewish tradition aims to *find* God, not *define* Him, because any definition would negate His very Being. (That is why Kohn excludes being or entity from his God-idea.) The medieval philosophers kept that tradition inviolate. The Rambam explicitly stated: "Anything predicated of God is totally different from our attributes; no definition can comprehend both." And, "it is a well known principle, received by all philosophers, who are precise in their statements, that no definition can be given of God" (*Guide,* Friedlander's translation, 1942, pp. 49, 70). Spinoza broke with tradition when he chose to comprehend the Divine Being by definition.

Argument by Definition

The inadequacy of definition in certain realms of thought is a matter not only of theology but also of pure reason. Kant, for example, denies the possibility of defining *a priori* concepts, such as substance or causality, etc., and all empirical concepts, because a definition could not exhaust the nature of such concepts, or might even be a misstatement of their intrinsic character. What he means is that one may state in explicit terms what one understands by using a given concept, but one does not thereby define a real thing. ("*. . . aber ich kann nicht sagen dass ich dadurch einen waren Gegenstand definiert habe." Kritik d.r.V.,* Kirchmann, 1870, p. 569-70.) Kohn, on the other hand, thinks (though he may not know for certain, p.42) that he has obtained adequate knowledge of the real God by defining Him. We may be mindful of his admonition that his "definition of a concept like the idea of God does not exhaust God's attributes," or that he does not pretend to know the unknowable. Yet, he does say that the terms of his definition "identify those aspects of our experience in which we see the manifestation of the deity." (28). On the other hand, if we accept his statement that all he proposes in defining the concept of God is to make "clear what we mean when we name it," and no adequate knowledge is attained, he is just attaching a mere name to something which is not really God. One could well agree, then, with Sidney Hook, for example, that the religion of the humanists is not justified in using the term "God." (*The Quest for Being,* 1961, p. 135.)

What is problematic about Kohn's account of "divine manifestation" is that he presents God as a concept. The argument of the non-believer (whom he is trying to refute) that such a concept is superfluous in his scheme of things, remains unanswered. It is superfluous because Kohn cannot demonstrate its transcendence. His concept, by its very function, is immanent in the human soul, and no amount of self-transcending will bring it out of there. Indeed, the author is constrained to whittle down the idea of transcendence to an abstract notion devoid of the fullness of reality. He thinks "of God, not as an entity or spiritual person with transcendent powers, but *more abstractly*, as a cosmic process on which we depend for life worth living and holy . . ." (33). Adopting Dr. Kaplan's formulation, he quotes: ". . . in using the term 'God,' men of the past and of the present have been trying to express the same fundamental affirmation concerning the *basic rightness* and *the ultimate achievability* of men's aim to leave the world better for their having lived in it" (30, italics mine). Kohn's concept of the God-idea resolves itself into an hypothesis that is to serve a double function: 1) as a foundation for man's striving to realize his highest good, and 2) as a guarantee that his striving is possible of attainment. The attributes of God he interprets as divine "aspects" not of God but of human ethical behavior. Accordingly, he sees the first purpose fulfilled when he attributes "divine manifestation" to man's ethical striving. Does his hypothesis actually fulfill that function? The author himself holds that "it is a sound principle in . . . a scientific hypothesis not to assume anything which is unnecessary for an explanation of the phenomena to which it refers" (34). To assure that, the hypothesis must be subject to verification by the phenomena whose operation it seeks to explain. Dr. Kohn observes or intuits the phenomenon of human striving for the highest good and he names it "diving manifestation." His hypothesis of the God-idea is thus identical with the phenomenon. His God-idea has no other Being except "being manifest" in the phenomenon itself. Nor does it perform the function of directing man's striving, and since it is not transcendent, it cannot be the cause or origin of the striving. It *is* unnecessary.

Pure Phenomenalism

To extend the hypothesis to cosmic dimensions is of no avail. The God-idea, as a cosmic process, he says elsewhere, "is viewed rather as the 'sum of everything in the world that renders life significant and worthwhile' . . ." (30). Apart from the question whether "worthwhileness" is observable (or intuited) and not read into life below the human level, it does not demonstrate the need for the hypothesis; it only shifts it to different phenomena. The result is pure phenomenalism. We have here another example of the position reached by Edmund Husserl, who developed a phenomenological system to a high degree of inner consistency, but for the sake of consistency removed being from reality. His disciple, Martin Heidegger (*Sein und Seit),* tried to save his master by restoring being to reality, but was able to go only far enough to reach man, not God. (*"Das Sein dieses Seienden ist je meines."*— *"The being of this Being is forever mine."*)

The second function of Kohn's hypothesis is to guarantee man that his striving shall not be in vain. One might ask if, according to Kohn's view, man is able to achieve the highest good through his own efforts, why does he need divine intervention? Again, to say that man's very striving is a divine manifestation and that the divine manifestation guarantees his striving is talking in circles. There must be a distinction made between man's efforts and the divine function for the latter to be considered as a guarantee of any kind. Kohn finds such a distinction between man's inability to conceive the endless possibilities of human betterment, on the one hand, and the infinity of the God-idea, on the other. "Our mind," he writes, "cannot conceive of any end to the process by which life yields value, nor any spatial limit to the operation of the Power on which man must depend for his self-fulfillment... [yet] we need not despair, for God is everlasting" (p. 39).

Infinity and Eternity

By infinity, the author means "endlessness of space; eternity is endlessness of time," in the sense of "infinite series or processes," and he wants to assure man that as he wanders through the "infinite series or processes" of endless space and time, his goal will be reached "at some time in the eternal life of God" (p. 39). Man may have a little difficulty in orienting himself in accord with this outlook. Contrast this with the prophetic view of "the end of days." Man's road to redemption, though it may take a long time, has a terminus. According to Rabbinic interpretation, it will come by an act of God when man deserves it. Man could even hasten it by repentance and good deeds (*Sanhedrin,* 97b). A secularist will say, it will come at such time and as speedily as man resolves to realize it himself. But, in either case, man may look forward to a definite goal in limited time and space. Kohn, on the other hand, holds out a promise for man's achievement of his strivings at an end in an endless series, which man cannot even conceive. And how, short of a miracle, can God guarantee an end in an endless series that is manifest in man's own striving? Contrast again this outlook with another theory, evolved by Hermann Cohen, which also posits the idea that God assures man the possibility of fulfilling his ethical aspirations. Hermann Cohen makes a distinction between the ethical and the religious, the one, in which God guarantees human society that it will attain its ethical ideal on this earth in good time; and the other, assuring the individual that he will receive his rightful share in it. For man, having no absolute control over nature, cannot be sure that the world will persist long enough for him to reach his goal and that it will continue thereafter. God, the Creator and Ruler of the universe, can assure him both, for He can guarantee the existence of the world in space and time. But He Himself is not conceived as an endless series of a spatio-temporal character.

When Eugene Kohn speaks of God's infinity as endlessness in space and His eternity as endlessness in time, both of which are manifest in man's striving, man is destined never to attain his goal in actual reality.

The hypothesis of God as a guarantor is untenable. His only assets, according to the author's interpretation of divine attributes, are those that may be manifest in man; He has none of His own to validate His guarantee.

"Where in All This is the Ribono-shel-Olam?"

Upon reading Kohn's *Religious Humanism* one is convinced of the author's deep-seated religious sentiment. Far less convincing is his reinterpretation of tradition or his approach to the religious issues of our time. It is related of Hermann Cohen (before he wrote *Die Religion der Vernunft*) that he tried to expound his ethical concept of God to an old Jew in Marburg. The old man listened with great respect and, when Cohen finished, asked: "But where in all this is the *Ribono-shel-Olam*" (God)? Tears came to the eyes of the Sage of Marburg; he had no answer.

Similarly, when Eugene Kohn faces the religionist's crucial question, "Do you or do you not believe in a personal God?" he replies, "It is a tricky question that cannot be answered categorically" (p. 42). And the reason is that at the end of his religious discourse, Kohn has not found God. Spinoza starts with a definition of Substance and, being unable to reach the phenomena, he winds up with absolute Pan-entheism—everything is in God. Kohn starts with phenomena, intuitions and the definition of an hypothesis and, not being able to reach the Substance, he ends with relative (ethical-vitalistic) Pantheism—God is "the sum of everything" worthwhile in life. As Hermann Cohen, in later years, restated the issue very pointedly: *"Die Unterscheidung des Monotheismus vom Pantheismus haengt vom genauem Begriffe der Schoepfung ab."* ("The differentiation between Monotheism and Pantheism depends on the precise meaning of creation." *Religion der Vernunft,* Leipzig, 1919, p.74).

1965

Hermann Cohen and Mordecai M. Kaplan

The recent publication of Mordecai M. Kaplan's *Purpose and Meaning of Jewish Existence* adds another dimension to the author's place in the realm of Jewish thought. In his previous writings Kaplan developed his concepts of Jewish religion, peoplehood, ethics, and modern man in a thought-complex which he designated as "Reconstructionism" or "Judaism as a Civilization." In his latest book he posits his conceptions of Judaism in direct comparison with those of other thinkers in Jewish history, Philo, Maimonides, Buber and, notably, Hermann Cohen's *Die Religion der Vernunft aus den Quellen des Judentums* (Religion of Reason from the Sources of Judaism).[1]

As the author states in his Preface: "The main portion of this book deals with Hermann Cohen's exposition of Judaism as a rational religion." In Part I, after a brief analysis of the Mosaic Torah, Philo, and Maimonides, there follows an essay on Cohen. Part II, which is more than half of the book, is devoted to an Epitome of the *Religion der Vernunft,* chapter by chapter, with a

---

1. The main references in this article are: Kaplan's book under discussion, published by The Jewish Publication Society of America (Philadelphia 1964), referred to by page number in parentheses; Hermann Cohen's *Die Relgion der Vernunft aus den Quellen des Judentums* (Leipzig 1919), referred to as RV; Kant's *Kritik der reinen Vernunft,* Kirchmann, zweite Auflage (Berlin 1870), referred to as *Kritik.* Other references will be noted in the next text. All translations from the sources are by the writer of this article.

114

running commentary in the form of extensive footnotes.

The added dimension in this latest of Kaplan's writings is a philosophical one. The author juxtaposes his own philosophy of "functional rationalism" and "Judaism as a Civilization" against what he considers to be Cohen's "ideationist rationalism" and "Judaism as a religion, and a religion only." It is due to this difference in philosophical outlook that he finds Cohen's view a "misunderstanding of Judaism." In the biographical account of Cohen (1842-1918), Kaplan points to his early Jewish and general education, his unconsummated preparation for the rabbinate, his later estrangement from the Jewish people, even to advocacy of total assimilation. Cohen became professor of philosophy at Marburg University in Germany and was a leading spirit in the neo-Kantian movement. He wrote several important works on ethics and religion, but they were basically unrelated to Judaism, as such, which he had thought would in time merge with a newly created "German Religion." Toward the end of his life, however, he returned as a penitent to the Jewish fold. He then worte his *Religion der Vernunft*, which was published after his death, in 1918.

Kaplan glosses over Cohen's personal break with the past as of no great consequence to his later views. He still considers the *Religion der Vernunft* as Cohen's "final formulation of what he regarded as the rational and viable element in Judaism, . . . [which] he believed would ultimately become the religion of the entire German nation" (48). The author, thus, does not distinguish between the several stages in Cohen's development which led him to the writing of his last work, and which are relevant to an understanding of his position in the last years of his life. This is not the place to go into a full analysis of this aspect of Cohen's personal life. Suffice it to compare his earlier assimilationist tendency with a statement in his last book, where among other things he pleads passionately for the preservation of Hebrew in Jewish prayer and in the instruction of Judaism. Concerning the relationship of Jews to the general culture in Germany, he writes: "The principle [of that relationship] is the specific content of Jewish monotheism and its inevitable isolation" (RV, 461).

Kaplan's Epitome

On the whole, Cohen comes out very pale from under Kaplan's scalpel. It does not "shock the reader," as the author forewarns, that he should "go to the trouble of publicizing" Cohen's treaties if he thinks it "is a misunderstanding of Judaism" (v). The sages of the Talmud went to the trouble of publishing a whole Tractate of unaccepted views in order "to teach the future generations" not to fall into the same errors (*Eduyot,* 1:4). Rather, what may be puzzling the reader is that in presenting Hermann Cohen, Kaplan does not allow him to appear his full-blooded self. To reduce a volume of 544 pages of German philosophical writing to about a tenth of its size in an English summary is in itself a grand undertaking on the part of the author. However, the brevity of many passages in the Epitome very often obscure their meaning and sometimes convey a misconception of the original. There are some difficulties in translation which have not been totally overcome, including the rendition of the very title of the book as *Rational Religion,* instead of *Religion of Reason.* Another obstacle, and not the least one, is the reflection of Kaplan's own mode of thinking in the summary. Large portions of the Epitome read like Cohen "reconstructed" in Kaplan's terminology. For the author feels that those "insights" that are valid in Cohen's book are his (Kaplan's) own philosophical province. He, therefore, allows himself to say that "Cohen arrives at his second seminal idea, that God is the correlate of man. In other words, Divinity is to be conceived as that aspect of nature which impels and helps man to transcend his animal nature" (58). Both the phrasing of the meaning of correlation and its expansion into "other words" are, to be sure, Kaplan's views, but not Cohen's. In his own words, the latter states: ". . . man as a rational being is the correlate to the God of revelation."[2] As will be shown later, this is an entirely different conception of God, man, and animal nature and their interrelations than the one rendered by Kaplan.

Basic in Kaplan's summary of the *Religion der Vernunft* is his argument "that Judaism was to Cohen a philosophical religion . . . compatible with absolute reason" (v, 54). Cohen, however, spends his entire Introduction and many lengthy passages in the body of his book to establish his thesis on the opposite ground, that "philosophy is not religion" and that absolute reason is not a religious criterion. This leads to many serious discrepancies between Cohen's original text and Kaplan's Epitome.

---

2. RV, 92: ". . . der Mensch, als Vernunftwesen, ist das Korrelat zum Gotte der Offenbarung."

In order to obviate a battle of words, it is necessary to place Cohen in the proper perspective of Kant's philosophy, of which, with modifications, he was one of the chief exponents. Nineteenth-century German philosophy is often characterized as having been in a state of confusion. Perhaps it would be more correct to say, it was in a state of fermentation. The field of science was teeming with new discoveries through research and practical application. That field was dominated by natural laws formulated in the seventeenth century by Newton, who reigned supreme in the scientific domain till well in the twentieth century. Even Einstein's theories of relativity, though deviating from some of Newton's principles, still remain under his dominance. Equally strong was Kant's impact on the century. In his *Critique of Pure Reason* Kant laid down the philosophical foundations as well as the limitations for Newton's laws of nature. Newton had based his laws on three main principles: the existence of absolute space, the concept of mechanical causation, and the method of scientific hypothesis. Kant investigated these principles, expanded them into a system of percepts and concepts which, he claimed, could be found a priori in pure sensibility and pure understanding, respectively. He thus set the boundaries of scientific knowledge within the limits of *human* understanding (Kant's emphasis).

But the burst of scientific speculation in the century following Kant's death, in 1804, kept pushing out against his boundaries. The German scientific and philosophical world, stimulated further by Hegel and Fichte, was split asunder in fragmentary cells. Into this fragmentation stepped Hermann Cohen trying to help bring the fermentation to its fruition and to promote the cause of science. It may be recalled here that Cohen earned his full professorship at Marburg University shortly after he had published a major work on Kant. The problem he then faced was that of certainty in the natural sciences. Even Newton had noted the uncertainty of hypotheses and cautioned against their multiplicity and abuse. On the other hand, Kant's transcendental deduction of the categories of understanding aimed at giving scientific knowledge universality and necessity, that is, certainty. But the scientists could not be restrained either by Newton's admonition or by Kant's refusal to allow more than his table of twelve categories. Cohen's interpretation of Kant (which is known as one kind of Neo-Kantianism) followed the master's path of "Critical Idealism"

(Kant's own phrase) to its logical conclusion. In his *Logik der reinen Erkenntnis* he introduced a number of new categories, such as, origin, motion, continuity and function. He also tried to remove the veil from Kant's "thing-in-itself" by reducing it to a mathematical calculus, on the concept of the infinitesimal, and thus to enable the scientist to come to grips with the thing-itself as well. In this manner, many scientific hypotheses were given the status of categories, that is, certainty. On the other hand, the Kantian categories a priori as well as Cohen's new categories assumed an hypothetical character, that is, uncertainty.

In Germany, philosophy has always been taken more seriously, that is, more personally, than in any other Western country. Not only were there fierce intellectual battles among the different post-Kantian and Hegelian schools, but sundry philosophers staked their careers on the right or the wrong side of the battlefield. Kaplan therefore correctly points out the stake Hermann Cohen had in expressing his philosophical and religious *Weltanschauung* when he appeared before Professor Lange for his appointment on the faculty at Marburg. We shall appreciate more fully the problem of certainty in nineteenth-century German philosophy if we realize that it is the same problem we face today, except that in our "age of psychology" we call it the problem of security. It became even more apparent as a life problem when Nietzsche raised the issue, why seek truth? "Why not prefer untruth? And uncertainty, even not-knowledge (*Unwissenheit*)?" One step further and he came to the thesis, "To acknowledge untruth as a condition of life: . . . And a philosophy that dares this, places itself thereby alone beyond good and evil."[3] Nietzsche's classic interpreter, Hans Vaihinger, the philosopher of "As-If," took the next step and declared all categories as "fictions," falsifications of reality, including the self. These trends spread confusion and hopelessness among the ranks of philosophers. The search for truth became overwhelming even for many a stout heart. In this fluid state between certainty and uncertainty (which again in our day has become the battleground of quantum mechanics) Cohen evolved his theories of ethics and religion, based at first on a scientific philosophy of mathematical rationalsim. The best he could offer was a science of ethics in which he posited a God-idea that was actually little more than an

3. Cf. Nietzsche, *Jenseits von Gut und Böse* (Leipzig 1924), Nos. 1, 4, "Von den Vorurteilen der Philosophen," pp. 7, 10.

hypothesis of a guarantor for the ultimate attainment of man's ethical striving. In this, he anticipated very much Kaplan's hypothesis of a God-guarantor, although Cohen's concept was logically the more tenable one. That is perhaps why Kaplan feels that Cohen trespassed on his territory (and apparently got away with it).

Cohen's Break with His Past

Toward the end of his Marburg period (he left the University in 1912), when he was moved by the spirit of faith, as has often been said of his old age, Cohen realized that by means of mathematical rationalism he had not reached the living God. For Cohen was not so much in search of a rationale for Jewish existence as he was in search of God. How deeply he was moved by his problem and how he suffered sometimes from his particular mathematical bent of mind is revealed in a letter he wrote to a friend in 1909, where he said:

> Mine is a peculiar kind of fate. If there are people who sacrifice reason, I sacrifice feeling. You know how much I am attached to the Jewish religion, with the most deep-lying fibres of my heart and with the innermost feelings of my soul. But there, too, my fate is—abstraction. And only men of truth are capable of understanding my spirit and will bear with me patiently.[4]

God as Being

In his "Transcendental Dialectic," in the Second Division of the *Kritik*, Kant bears down his full weight against the rationalist arguments for the proof of the immortality of the soul and the existence of God. But, continues Kant, even though we cannot prove the existence of God, as the rationalists claim, we need not despair of finding in Reason such concepts that would enable us to speak of God in relation to the totality of human experience. He termed such concepts *ideas* or principles of speculative reason. Such an idea is God as Being, which cannot be further identified or defined as to its content, substance or purpose.[5] And this is Cohen's starting point. Since he is looking for an idea to express God, he must be able to find it first and foremost in the place where

4. Cf. Bergmann, Hugo, *Hoge ha-Dor* (Tel-Aviv 1935), p. 225.
5. Cf. *Kritik*, pp. 503, 529, 540 ff.

all ideas come from, namely, Reason. He then goes to the historical sources of the Jewish religion (which he regarded as the primary source of all religion) to find whether that idea is manifested in those sources. To be sure, the idea or concept (the words are here interchangeable) is taken from speculative reason but that does not make it less valid, even though it does not possess the categorical status of a concept of the understanding, namely, the certainty of scientific knowledge. For if we are to grasp religion in thought at all, we can only do so by means of reason.[6]

This background of concepts is overlooked in Kaplan's summary of the passages under consideration. "Reason in Religion," we read in the Epitome, "stresses the unreliability of sensate experience and emotion and affirms the dominion of Law. Reason is the foundation of Law." And he further notes in his commentary: "He [Cohen] refers to ideationist rationalism, insofar as it leads to the good life. . . . Whether ideationist or functional, reason demands of religion that it be spelled out in laws of human behavior and the regulation of human relations. Hence Cohen's affirmation: Reason is the foundation of law" (64-65). This summary statement does not convey Cohen's meaning, and the commentary is thus out of context. In his original text (RV, 11-12) Cohen goes to some length in trying to show that the idea he has found in speculative reason is not just a figment of the imagination, which would have no binding validity for the world of experience. For Cohen does not altogether accept the role that Kant assigns to the God-idea, namely, of a unifying principle of the totality of human experience. Kant emphasizes that in this respect the Idea has no binding scientific necessity and hence no certainty, as it cannot be deduced from the "synthetic unity of apperception" of the understanding (which is the only source of necessity). In this limited role, the Idea for Kant may refer only to a Deity but not to a living God of history. "Thus," he says, ". . . the concept which merely speculative reason gives us of God is, most strictly understood, *deistic*."[7] But Cohen wants to extend the Idea to the

6. Cf. *Kritik*: "Kritik aller spekulativen Theologie," p. 529: "Die Ideen der reinen Vernunft verstatten zwar keine Deduktion von der Art, als die Kategorien; sollen sie aber im mindesten einige, wenn auch nur unbestimmte, objektive Gültigkeit haben und nicht bloss leere Gedankendinge vorstellen . . ." (Although the ideas of pure reason do not permit a deduction of the same kind as the categories, if they are to have at least some objective though indeterminate validity, and not present just empty notions . . . [then there must be some other kind of deduction for them] . . .)

7. Cf. *Kritik*, p. 533: "So ist der . . . Begriff, den uns die bloss spekulative Vernunft von Gott gibt, im genauesten Verstande *deistisch* . . ."

120

God of Israel and he cannot rest satisfied with Kant's limitation on it.

What Cohen says, then, in the passage referred to, has nothing to do with "spelling out . . . laws of human behavior." Rather, it has to do with finding certainty in the idea of God offered by reason, which is Cohen's main concern as it is also the burden of our own age. Reason in religion, he therefore goes on to say, expresses rules (*Gesetze*) of religious thought with as much binding force as do other aspects of reason, scientific or philosophical. For reason, in general, stands for orderliness according to rule (*Gesetzlichkeit*); it is the organ, the instrument, of rules. "Where orderliness has its sway, reason's domain is assured" (RV, 12). And this orderliness according to rule, this certainty of reason, is the foundation of the prime source (*Ursprünglichkeit*), which we have only validated in history, but which "has its ground beyond the boundaries of all history."[8]

Specific Mode of Thought in Jewish Sources

The Jewish sources that Cohen is now going to examine are, therefore, not just a conglomeration of historical "contingence, caprice or illusion," as some may claim; for in them runs through an " origin" that is grounded in *Gesetzlichkeit* of reason. But how can one reconcile the Jewish historical sources, which seemingly "have no part in philosophy," with reason which is basically a philosophical problem? That depends on the meaning of philosophy. "Reason does not exshaust itself in science and philosophy," says Cohen.[9] It also has other modes of thought. And here Cohen directs our attention to a most illuminating distinction that touches the essence of discursive thought and that has manifested itself in two divergent trends in the history of Judaism. The one is rooted in the consciousness of the Jewish people, generally identified as traditional, while the other has been grafted on Jewish awareness as a recurrent modernism but has never really taken root in it.

The section in his book where Cohen deals with this matter is summarized by Kaplan as follows: "Rational reason is as much a

---

8. Cohen, RV, 12: "wo Gesetzlichkeit waltet, da ist das Gebiet der Vernunft gesichert." . . . "Die Ursprünglichkeit, die wir bisher nur als eine geschichtliche geltend machen, erscheint nunmehr über die Grenzen aller Geschichte hinaus begründet. . . ."

9. RV, p. 8: ". . . die Vernunft erschöpft sich nicht in Wissenschaft und Philosophie."

creation of the human mind as are science and philosophy. . . . The Greeks were as original in science and philosophy as were the Jews in religion. The Jews accepted certain concepts of Greek philosophy, but not the Greek science, because Judaism is inherently philosophic." And he comments: "Both philosophy and rational religion—which, for Cohen, had to be based on a rational conception of God—had a bearing on ethics, on what we *ought to do*, whereas science had a bearing only on knowledge as such, on what we *ought to know*. That is why Jews, in Bible times, were not interested in Greek science" (64). In the first place, it is not correct to say that Jews in Bible times were not interested in Greek science because they did not stress what we "ought to know." On the contrary, they were very much interested in the problem of knowledge but not in its Greek formulation. Their quest for knowledge and their admonition to right deed were so interwoven that in the biblical Hebrew idiom both functions were placed in the heart. Similarly, they were interested in the sciences of their time, as such, but not in the Greek mode of scientific methodology. And this is the meaning of Cohen's basic differentiation. He does not say that "the Jews accepted certain concepts of Greek philosophy." Quite the contrary, he stresses the fact that they neither borrowed nor imitated it. The Greeks, he says, have given to their philosophy a specific character and to their science, which they borrowed from the Orient, a particular philosophic bent. They created a "scientific philosophy" and a "philosophical science," whereas the Jews, having "created the religion of reason," cultivated a "speculative philosophy." And he concludes: "The religion of reason preserves in the sources of Judaism their original, natural, human association with philosophical speculation which can, therefore, be as little an imitation of the Greeks as it is borrowed from them. The philosophical in the biblical sources must therefore have a specific character of its own. . . ."[10] This represents most clearly Cohen's break with mathematical rationalism and his return to the traditional mode of thinking when he set out on his quest for the living God.

10. RV, p. 11: "Die Religion der Vernunft wahrt den Quellen des Judentums ihren ursprünglichen, natürlichen, menschlichen Zusammenhang mit der philosophischen Spekulation, die ebenso wenig griechische Nachahmung daher sein kann, als sie griechische Entlehnung ist. Das Philosophische in den biblischen Quellen nuss ebenso Eigenart haben..."

A Special Characteristic of the Hebrew Language

To make the distinction between the Greek and Hebrew modes of thought, as drawn by Hermann Cohen, more relevant to our discussion, I shall point briefly to a special characteristic of the Hebrew language in contrast with Greek and other European languages. Ernst Cassirer, in his comprehensive study of speech, indicates that the sentence, not the word, is the basic formation (*Grundgebilde*) of language.[11] This, however, may be said of the modes of expression in Western culture which have been inherited from the Greek legacy of "scientific philosophy," but it may not be said of the Hebrew mode of thought. In the Greek mode, a judgment is expressed in the form of a *triad*, such as we find in the logical laws of identity and contradiction, "A is A" and "A is not not-A." That is, two related entities always have a third one that mediates between them. Translated into metaphysical concepts, the copula "is" as a mediator became the *Logos* for Philo or *The Holy Ghost* in Christianity.

By contrast, the most remarkable characteristic of the Hebrew language is that it does not possess a term for the copula "is." Its mode of thought is the *dyad* or that of immediate relation. The primary element of Hebrew expression is therefore not the sentence but the word, which is pregnant with content. The relational connection between words is direct, without a mediator. The sentence *ha-yeled gadol* (the boy is big) is often innocently translated by the Hebrew beginner as "the boy big," because he cannot find the word "is" in it. It would never have occurred to the ancient Hebrews to make a statement "A is A," and they refused to borrow this mode from the Greeks, because it implies definition of Being and thus its limitation.

This contrast between the two modes of thought is fundamental to an understanding of Cohen's meaning of "origin," "correlation," and other concepts he has drawn from the sources of Judaism. Correlation, for him, represents the mode of the *dyad*, that is, immediate relation. (Buber later developed his own mode of the *dyad* in the *I-Thou* relation.) It is therefore incorrect, as pointed out above, to use this term in the form of a logical judgment, "God *is* the correlation of man," as Kaplan rephrases it (58). In this

11. Cf. Cassirer, Ernst, *Philosophie der symbolischen Formen.* Dritter Teil (Darmstadt 1958), p. 526.

latter mode, God is conceived as a function of man, which may be in keeping with Kaplan's functional rationalism, but not with Cohen's speculative reason. In the more than fifty passges in the original text that deal with the primary word, there is nowhere a direct statement or indirect implication that God *is* the correlate of man. Cohen always uses the form "correlation of God and man," "the correlation of man and God," or "correlation between God and man," and the like.[12]

Negative Attributes and Creation

The specific mode of Jewish thought is also reflected in Cohen's insight of "divine negative attributes," which he develops along the lines taught by Maimonides. Kaplan leaves this section entirely out of his Epitome. But without this insight, Cohen's idea of creation as causality in reference to oneness of Being is, philosophically speaking, unintelligible. That is why Kaplan can come to the conclusion that "the traditional conception of creation out of nothing, as an event in time, is meaningless (99). Parenthetically, tradition does not teach creation "as an event in time." Maimonides, as an Aristotelian, certainly could not have taught it, for Aristotle does not take time as an absolute. In the *Guide*, Part II, Chapter XIII, Maimonides specifically warns against the doctrine of creation in time. Neither did Cohen, as a Kantian, teach this doctrine.[13] Briefly stated, Cohen maintains that negative attributes do not negate positive attributes (which, he says, would be senseless) but they deny the private ones. For instance, the statement, "God is not inert," means the negation of the privative idea of inertness, even though or especially because the word "inert" is not stated in the negative form of "not-active." This denial of the privative, furthermore, "affirms a new positivity, so that the negation has been completely rooted out," and the positive idea of action, creation, has been conveyed (RV, 73). What is important for the understanding of Cohen is that this whole conception of creation is *not* a logical one, even though it has a logical counterpart in the category of " origin."

---

12. Cf. RV, pp. 133, 151, 251, etc.
13. Cf. Kant, *Kritik der praktischen Vernunft,* Erster Teil, I, 3, Kritische Beleuchtung der Analytik: ". . . weil die Schöpfung ihre intelligibele, aber nicht sensibele Existenz betrifft." (. . . creation pertains to its intelligible, but not sensible, existence [that is, not to space and time]).

Kaplan notwithstanding Cohen's direct argument to the contrary, summarizes the section under discussion as follows: "The doctrine of God as creator means that God is the *logical* ground of existence. . . . Nature and becoming derive *logically* from being. Thus the creation of the world is to be inferred logically from the Being of God" (98-99). But in the *Religion der Vernunft* Cohen emphatically denies that creation is a *logical* inference from Being. "Insofar as creation is regarded from the point of view of causality," he writes, "it demands a parting of the way with logic. In the light of this [logic] it appears as a miracle. But reason maintains it can resolve the anomaly of the miracle into normalcy of thought."[14] And at this normalcy of thought Cohen arrives through his lucid presentation of the doctrine of negative attributes. This doctrine, again, is borne out by the specific character of the Hebrew language which, as indicated above, does not have the mediating copula "is." The Hebraic mode of thought does not use the mediating logical form for positive attributes because it does not think of them in logical terms. The verses in Exodus 34:6-7, which are known as the thirteen Divine Attributes, do not contain a single word that might suggest the copula "is." "The Lord, the Lord, God merciful and gracious. . . ." It does not say, "God *is* merciful," etc., which is a logical form of definition. The only possible attributive use of an implied copula is contained in the negatives *en, lo* (not), as for example, in 2 Samuel 15:29, *Ki lo adam hu le-hinnahem* "For *He is* not man that He should repent." But even there the word *hu* (He is) does not take the place of the copula but rather of the personification of Being as contrasted with anthropomorphism.

How far Kaplan deviates from the Hebrew mode of thinking and what it leads him to, is illustrated by the issue he takes with Cohen on the meaning of the word *hayetah* in the biblical account of creation. Cohen says that the mythological view of creation assumes a pre-existing chaos, whereas in the Hebrew account chaos was the state of the earth *after* creation (RV, 74). "And the earth was unformed and void." On this Kaplan notes: "Here Cohen misunderstands the meaning of the Hebrew *hayethah* in

---

14. RV, p. 81: ". . . die Schöpfung, sofern sie unter dem Gesichtspunkte der Kausalität steht, nur die Auseinandersetzung mit der Logik fordert. Dieser gegenüber erscheint sie als ein Wunder, und die Vernunft erhebt den Anspruch, die Anomalie des Wunders aufzuheben in die Normalität des Denkens."

Genesis 1:2. It is used there in the *pluperfect* sense, implying that the earth had been null and void before creation set in" (98). This interpretation is very well in accord with Kaplan's own concept of *creativity* (rather than creation) which can mean only composition out of preexisting elements. In the cosmic act he thus presupposes an eternal chaos before the world came into being. But the traditional view and the very character of the Hebrew biblical text are on Cohen's side. The past tense in Hebrew does not differentiate between imperfect, perfect and pluperfect. It has no separate words or word-forms for these. For that matter, the Hebrew temporal sense is expressed only two-fold, in terms of past (*hayah* or *hayetah*) and continuity (*howeh* and *yiheyeh*—historic present and future). With the absence of "is" for the present, the Hebrew substantive cannot be predicated, because it already expresses being. The predicate in the Hebrew sentence appears as the object of action. That is why the *verbum* is the dominant form of biblical style, and Cohen's treatment of action (*Handlung*) in relation to Being (*Sein*) is in the spirit of Hebraic thought.[15]

Kaplan's Functional Rationalism

Besides his commentaries on Cohen's *Religion der Vernunft*, Kaplan supplies at the end of his book a brief chapter on his own approach to Judaism entitled, "A Modern Functional Rationale." It is an excellent "epitome" in its own right of his views developed in his previous voluminous writings, and since it is a statement of his own position, it must be accepted as authentic. As indicated above, Kaplan follows a line of reasoning which is patterned after the Greek mode of thinking rather than the traditional Jewish mode. This becomes more directly evident on reading the Introduction and the last chapter of the book. Kaplan finds justification for his "reconstructionist" approach to Judaism in the fact that in former generations there were similar attempts to reinterpret Jewish religion and to find new meaning in it, in order to meet the challenges of time. That will, no doubt, be acceptable to every Jew who is at all concerned (or "worried," according to Kaplan's favorite expression) about Judaism as a living reality. One may thus agree with Kaplan about the need for reinterpretation but hold serious reservations as to what it is in Judaism that he

15. Cf. RV, Ch. VI, p. 109 ff.

reinterprets. This depends largely on one's conception of change, which is a constituent factor of reinterpretation.

Kaplan follows Heraclitus's dictum, "Everything flows, nothing abides." But while the Greek philosopher has the Logos put some order and reason into the flux, Kaplan tries to derive reason from the flux itself, that is, reason, for him, flows along with the changing stream. Therefore, in the ancient philosopher's metaphor, when he "steps in the river" to take a look at the stream, he never finds the river to be the same. If one were to ask, as Cohen did, what it is that changes, Kaplan would answer, the "what" has no meaning outside the concept of "change." His reconstruction is thus a rational as well as a practical attempt to rebuild Jewish life in accordance with the constant changes that are taking place in our day. Reconstruction, as such, may mean the rebuilding of something out of its old materials into a new design; or rebuilding it in the old design out of new materials. Kaplan tries to do both, with emphasis on the new design. First he selects "from the mass of traditional lore and custom the psychological aspect which testifies to the presence of ethical and spiritual strivings."[16] But then he also reinterprets that "psychological aspect" to make it "relevant for our day." Such of the old materials as do not fit into his new design he either reinterprets to make them fit or else declares them out of existence because, according to him, they have ceased to "function" for "modern man." This is basically what he means by "functional interpretation," "functional reinterpretation," or "functional rationalism."[17]

Functional Existence of the Jew

Many difficulties arise out of Kaplan's use of the concept of function. In the first place he identifies it universally with existence. "Whatever performs a function of any kind exists" (3). And since he also puts it in the logical converse—"for anything to exist, it has to function"—the two, function and existence, are synonymous or identical. By function in this sense he apparently understands "operation," performance, in and for itself and not necessarily in relation of dependence on another existent. His other uses of the concept are important in his arrival at the

16. Cf. Kaplan, *Judasim as a Civilization* (New York 1935), p. 390.
17. Ibid., p. 389.

particular function, and thus existence, of the Jewish people. In the next step he speaks of function of a *given kind* which identifies existence: "For anything to exist, it has to function in some specific manner" (3). That is, an existent is identified by the nature or essence of its function. " 'Jewish existence,' accordingly, means 'functioning as a Jew,' " The third step is to ascertain what *it* is that enables a Jew to *function* as a Jew. This leads him to the concept of function as relational *dependence*, where "A is a function of B." or A depends on an independent variable B (a mathematical function). This independent variable is the Jewish people whose existence can be identified only by its function in the first sense, that is, by its manner of *operation*, since, "For the Jewish people to exist, it has to function as a people." In sum: the Jew functions as a Jew, that is, exists as a dependent of the Jewish people, which in turn functions or exists in its operation as a people. This poses a dual question: What are the general earmarks of a people and what are the specifics of a Jewish people? One might answer this question by simply observing how a people, in general, and our people, in particular, operate (function) and thus ascertain their manner of existence. But Kaplan avers that the Jews of today do not function as a people, hence they do not exist as a people. At best, he sees their existence as that of a *veteran* people, on the analogy of soldiers who ceased to be soldiers because they left the army and became veternas. There being no real people in existence to show us its manner of function (operation), Kaplan resorts to a *definition*: An existent Jewish people is one that functions as "a civilizational people." but what will prompt a veteran people to reconstruct itself into a "civilizational people?" This is the real burden of Kaplan's "rationale" for Jewish existence.

If the "veteran" people has no abiding elements of a real people left in it, its efforts toward reconstruction are hopeless. Kaplan, like Hermann Cohen before him, therefore delves into the Jewish past to find such elements that might spell "Jewish function as a people" and hence "Jewish existence as a people." But unlike Cohen, Kaplan not just reinterprets the elements of the past, but completely transforms them by his "functional rationalism." For "nowadays," he says, "the Jewish situation is such that reinterpretation is far from enough" (10). First the Jews "have to find a way of functioning as a civilizational people," that will "assure the existence of the Jewish people" and then "proceed to reinterpret the traditional values which spell out the purpose and meaning of that existence" (10). Reconstruction thus precedes the finding of a rationale and yet it rests on such a rationale. For if the "veteran" Jewish people can "find a way of functioning as a civilizational people" without a rationale, why does it need one *after* it has assured its own existence? A living being does not need a rationale for its existence. A "rationale," on the other hand, is inevitable if it is to be *rationally* reconstructed. One must then give a good and valid reason for wanting to reconstruct it in the first place. Actually Kaplan does not see the possibility of establishing the Jewish "civilizational people" without his rationale, for that is what he intends his "Judaism as a Civilization" to be—a rationale. This explains also the title of his latest book *The Purpose and Meaning of Jewish Existence.* For him, the Jews at present do not exist as a people and hence the Jew does not exist as a Jew. This is the pivotal problem of his entire conceptual approach to Judaism. He does not start with *the existence* of the Jewish people as a people. That status, he says, they lost in 1807, with the acceptance of the Napoleonic Sanhedrin and have not recovered it since, at least not as a world people.

A Bridge between Existentialism and Rationalism

It is of more than passing interest to note that Kaplan separates himself from all exponents of Jewish life who betray even a semblance of existentialism. For the latter starts with existence, whereas he starts with concepts. He finds Cohen's *Religion der Vernunft* "extremely illuminating" for his own thesis because he considers Cohen a rationalist like himself, except that Cohen's rationalism is of the wrong brand. But a careful study of Cohen's *magnum opus* of his old age will reveal that his work has built a bridge between existentialism and rationalism, as Hugo Bergmann for example, has pointed out.[18] Some of those who have followed him have continued building various approaches to the bridge which may now be in the planning or developing stage. Kaplan, on the other hand, has remained in the rational sphere of thought. He has made a concerted effort at a different method of concept-forming, namely, functional rationalism. By this method (and that

18. Bergmann, *op. cit.,* p. 219. Cf. Martin Buber, *Pointing the Way* (New York 1963), p. 91, where he speaks of "Hermann Cohen's masterly legacy . . . *The Religion of Reason. . . .* where he advanced from the idealism of his system to the existentialism of 'correlation,' . . ."

is what he calls his "Reconstructionism") he has undertaken a gigantic task of shaping new concepts of God, Torah and peoplehood, out of which, he hopes, a new Jewish "civilizational people" will emerge. Whether or not such a new structure can be founded and whether, if erected, it can be firmly established, depends on its cornerstone, namely, Kaplan's concept of God, which will receive our attention in the following paragraphs.

Kaplan's God-Idea

Kaplan defines God as "that aspect of nature as a whole which makes for the maximum fulfillment of man's highest ethical and creative potentialities. That is the God of whom we have immediate experience whenever we deliberately act out of a sense of responsibility, honesty, loyalty or love, and creativity. Such ethical conduct reflects cosmic traits which are manifest throughout the universe" (295). This, he maintains, is a "naturalist's" concept of God and, as such, is best suited "for the modern intellectual Jew."

One must bear in mind that Kaplan derives his naturalistic view from concepts of ethical value and not from a scientific account of nature which, he claims, does not yield values. From his "functional-rationalist" point of view, then, in order for God to exist he "must function in some specific manner." What manner of function does this God-idea perform? As an "aspect" it cannot have any operational function, though this is the basic category of functional rationalism. All the God-idea can stand for is a relational function of dependence—on man's "sense of responsibility, honesty, loyalty or love, and creativity." And if that sense of responsibility were to diminish or reduce to zero, the God-idea as a dependent function would diminish accordingly or become non-existent. Even if nature revealed the ethical cosmic traits Kaplan ascribes to it and all of it were permeated by the sense of responsibility, that sense would still be only a "natural" responsibility and the God-idea would be only one of the variable functions of nature (for nature has other manifestations besides the ethical).[19] In and for itself it does not, nay cannot, do anything, for

19. Cf. Kaplan, *Ha-Emunah weha-Musar* (Jerusalem 1954). The author develops there his ideas of the relation of ethics to religion from a naturalistic viewpoint. *See* especially ch. 5, p. 121 ff., where the concept of "responsibility" is derived form principles of natural evolution.

Kaplan does not ascribe to it any being, only existence in the functional sense. But in that sense, its existsence is in jeopardy because it is conceived as a numerical function (besides being a dependent function), a "summation" of all that is or might be regarded as ethical values. In and for itself Kaplan's God-idea has no empirical evidence, no scientific necessity, and no metaphysical validity.

Kaplan seems to have felt this implicit difficulty in his definition of the God idea, for in another passage in his book he tries to find an active, operational function for it. And since "creativity" is one of the manifestations of his God-idea, he assigns to this creativity a special power: "It is that in the cosmos which prevents its entropy from having the last word" (99). Here his "naturalism" comes into direct collision with "natural science." Entropy is a physical principle of "The Second Law of Thermodynamics." According to this principle, the irreversible process of the loss of heat may eventually lead to the extinction of the world. Unless Kaplan has a scientific refutation of this natural law, how will his God-idea, as the aspect of "creativity," prevent entropy? His God-idea thus remains a mystery of nature. Throughout the ages some mystics have sought to *experience* God in nature through sense perception. He remained a mystery to them because they could not *perceive* Him there. So does Kaplan posit a God-idea in nature which he expects to reach through "immediate experience" of human ethical conduct. But his God-idea cannot be found in nature through such experience except as a "meaning" attached to man's behavior. Kaplan has constructed a logical triad: "Ethical conduct *means* the God-idea," and he is trying to elevate the mediating copula "means" to an active, cosmic function.

The Problem of Man

Man in Kaplan's naturalism and, in particular, the individual Jew in the Jewish "civilizational people" also undergo some hardships within the confines of his "functional rationalism." Kaplan starts with a functional concept of the Jew as he started with a concept of God. As analyzed above, according to him, Jews exist as Jews if they function as Jews; and they "can function as Jews only by virtue of their belonging to the Jewish people," which means a "civilizational people." Since that people has not yet been constituted, the individual Jew is bound to lead a life of quasi-existence. Into this anatomy Kaplan hopes to infuse a new spirit that will bring salvation to the modern, emancipated Jew.

It would take us too far afield to dwell here at length on the impact that emancipation and enlightenment have had on the modern Jew and on modern man in general. Those two forces, like meteors, tore man not only out of the bosom of church or synagogue but also from family, community and state authority. It meant the individualization of man. Suddenly man found himself burdened with superhuman tasks which he was now called upon to face as an indivudial and he began to wonder with the Psalmist: "What is this human . . . whom thou hast made a little less than the mighty ones," and hast transferred unto him all their responsibilities? This is where the winds blow from so fiercely in our day and forcibly remind us of "forlornness," "anxiety," "despair." To reconstruct individual man back into a societal or communal entity, as Kaplan proposes, without resolving his status as an emancipated individual, intellectually and morally, is well-nigh impossible. August Comte, a century earlier, tried by means of his "Western Committee" to found a new society with a positivist "Religion of Humanity" in which the evils of emancipation, as he saw them, would be overcome. But the forces of emancipation could not be arrested or set back. Kaplan, in our day, acknowledges that emancipation is a factor to reckon with. As a matter of fact, it is the background for his portrait of the modern Jew. But he does not see the Jew as a Jewish individual existent in and for himself. He has not met with him in real confrontation, for he has not resolved his problems as an emancipated, individual Jew, as he went forth to search for the living God, through the sources of the Jew's tradition. He sought the individual as an "I" not only in relation to organized society or to mankind as a whole, but also in and for himself. It is paradoxical that in this age of individualism, individual man has become the most neglected of entities. True, individualism has fostered the ideas of individual enterprise, equal rights and opportunity before the law, and similar freedoms that benefit man as an individual. But individual man as a moral being has been very much left out of account. In this age of freedoms, the individual has found many things in his favor; but has he found himself as man?

Ethics and Religion

Hermann Cohen presents in his book an extensive analysis of this very intricate problem of man in his categories of a socio-ethical being and of an individual "I." Cohen draws a clear distinction between the ethical and religious aspects of morality, the first being related more directly to the social problem, while the second aims to resolve the problem of the individual. How far apart Kaplan and Cohen are on this issue can be illustrated by the former's interpretation of the chapter dealing with the "discovery of man" in the *Religion der Vernunft*. Kaplan writes: "It is difficult to grasp the thought of this chapter if we read it in the light of ideational rationalism [*i.e.,* by Cohen's method]. What Cohen tries to say is more understandable in the light of functional rationalism [*i.e.,* by Kaplan's method]. According to the latter, moral responsibility is a function of reason. Moral responsibility is an *ethical* principle, because it derives from cosmic polarity which, when it operates in man, enables him to achieve his role as man. That polarity is the synthesis of individuation and interaction with the environment. Cohen discusses in this chapter how a human being discerns in another human being a person like himself" (122).

Here Kaplan visualizes the moral human being as an abstraction of an interaction between the ethical principle, which is a function of reason, and the religious principle, which is a function of cosmic polarity. Hermann Cohen leads in the opposite direction, away from abstract man to the real individual. He wants to see man as an "I" who is not abstracted from humanity, society, polarity, or a derivative of any kind. How then, according to Cohen, does man discover himself as an individual "I"? Not as Kaplan interprets, that the "human being discerns in another human being a person like himself." Quite the contrary, when a man becomes aware of fellow-man, says Cohen, he does not see himself at all. (That, he says, is Schopenhauer's view, which he rejects.) In fellow-man or in the "Thou" one discovers the ethical principle of pure will, the ought, but not yet himself as a moral "I." Even fellow-man is not yet an individual which might be designated as an 'I.' "[20] Thus far, he continues, through the correlation of God and man as a rational being, even as an ethical being, man still remains an abstraction and the task is now "to resolve this abstraction and to transform it into an individual, living human being."[21] And to emphasize the

20. RV, p. 193: "Auch der Mitmensch ist noch kein Individuum, welches als Ich Zur Bestimmung Käme."
21. Ibid., ". . . die Abstraktion wieder aufzuheben und diese in ein lebendiges menshcliches Einzelwesen umzuwandeln."

religious aspect, he states: "The question is whether this absolute individual is a justified concept. However, one must not believe that this question has already been disposed of through the [idea of] fellow-man. Yet, in the solution of this question the specific character of religion is brought out more definitely and more clearly than in the [idea of] fellow-man." The problem now before Cohen is to show how "the correlation of God and man assumes for man the more restricted meaning of an individual and of an 'I.'[22] This he develops through man's feeling of guilt and awareness of sin which, he says, was first brought to light by the Prophet Ezekiel.

In brief, Cohen states that ethics of pure will can enjoin man what he ought to do or ought not to do, and, insofar as it is carried into practice by organized society, he can be held to account for his unethical actions, declared guilty and punished. But ethics of pure will, either as teaching or in practice, cannot make man accept his guilt and sinfulness of his own accord. Society can even hold him responsible as a moral being, but it cannot make him into a moral being by mere enforcement of ethical action. And unless and until man discovers in himself the awareness of guilt and sinfulness, he is not really a moral being. This is the particular, concrete status of individual man in correlation with God. And this, says Cohen, is the specific character (*Eigenart*) of monotheism which he found in the sources of Jewish tradition. The Jew who sees this tradition as his own, finds himself as a Jew.

What is most important in this path that Cohen took on his way to finding God, man, and the Jew in himself, is not whether he reached his ultimate destination, but the distance he traveled, the light in which he posed the question, and the deep insights of his proposed solution. If one were to pursue Dr. Kaplan's analogy of the soldier and the army, one would find that a soldier does not cease to be a soldier when he steps out of the army but when he stops fighting. Sergeant York fought a battle without an army. And Kaplan himself is the most illustrious example of a Jewish fighter (or "happy worrier," as he calls himself, one who worrries over the

---

22. RV, pp. 193-194: "Es ist die Frage ob dieses absolute Individuum ein berechtigter Begriff ist, aber man darf nicht glauben, dass durch den Mitmenschen diese Frage schon erledigt wäre. In der Lösung dieser Frage aber erst vollzieht sich die Eignart der Religion bestimmter und deutlicher als beim Mitmenschen." And "... dass die Korrelation von Gott und Mensch die engere Bedeutung zum Menschen, als Individuum und als Ich annimmt."

Jewish people) without a body politic. The Jews have to find themselves through their tradition first and foremost, and the kind of people they will then constitute will be operating as a Jewish body to the core.

1967

Mordecai M. Kaplan's Vision of a Modern Judaism

On June 11 of this year Mordecai M. Kaplan, one of the foremost Jewish thinkers of our time, reached his 95th birthday. When my wife and I visited Dr. and Mrs. Kaplan this past January in Jerusalem, we were delighted to find them both in good health and actively engaged in their respective literary and artistic pursuits, Dr. Kaplan wrestling with some Biblical aspects of his God-idea as the cosmic moral power of human salvation, and Mrs. Kaplan-Riger, an artist of great talent, painting her reconstructions of the Israeli landscape. As a one-time student and a long-time friend of Dr. Kaplan's, I have always admired his intellectual vigor and followed with keen interest his searching analysis of the Jewish condition in our time and his contributions toward resolving its problems. Whether or not I agree with all his conclusions, I have always been inspired by the strength of his argument, his deep sense of commitment, and the clarity of his thinking, which has not diminished to this day — a "supernatural" feat (if Dr. Kaplan will forgive the use of this term) for a man of his venerable age. In this essay I will review the main features of Dr. Kaplan's vision of a viable modern Judaism which he has promulgated under the name of "Reconstructionism." As we reflect on his writings from the time he first gave full expression to his concepts of Judaism as a civilization, some 40 years ago, to the present, and as we contemplate his personal involvement and the high caliber of his leadership in Jewish affairs, we find one particular quality permeating all his intellectual and practical endeavors: trust in God. It is his highest personal act of commitment, and it is also the abiding element in his ceaseless striving for new forms and concepts to enhance Jewish living.

In order to understand the basic changes which Kaplan has introduced in traditional Judaism, we must know what he means by "Reconstructionism." This term performs a specific function in his entire mode of thinking, it expresses the essence of his world-view and also relates him to the spirit of modern times. He did not coin it but rather grew into it, as it became the dominant method of revaluating the social and spiritual trends in the early part of this century, when he began to strike out on a path of his own. Its first comprehensive formulation we find in John Dewey's "Reconstruction in Philosophy" (1920), which focuses on the conflict between the new scientific trend and the moral, social, and logical conceptions of the time. The reconstruction Dewey called for meant not just changing old concepts into new forms, but a fundamental, radical turn in our way of thinking. It called, as one prominent scientist put it, for "a ministry of Disturbance, a regulated source of annoyance; a destroyer of routine; an underminer of complacency." Similar forces of "reconstruction" were then active also in western Europe with the avowed purpose of liberating modern man from the otherworldly orientation of traditional thinking. Kaplan embraced these ideas and, assuming what he called "the function of the gadfly," set out to apply them toward a reconstruction of Judaism in a new mold. The radical changes that Kaplan wants to bring about in the Jewish orientation are motivated by his sense of urgency for an adjustment to changing times. As individuals, he says, modern Jews have caught up with the new trends, but as a community they keep losing ground. If they do not find new ways of setting their house in order, they will also cease to exist as individual Jews, for they cannot prevail as such without a reconstructed Jewish community. In past generations, he points out, there were methods of adjustment which were suited to whatever variations took place within the Jewish fold; it was strong enough to withstand outside pressures. Now the challenge of science and the impact of modernity demand a fundamental change. The methods of adjustment from within that were used in the past were effective as long as the House of Israel remained intact. Now that its walls are bending and its quarters are too narrow to accommodate the ever growing number of its emancipated children, the house as a whole has to be rebuilt from its foundations up. This, he says, requires a more deliberate and more effective method than the Jews had heretofore. The new method is "Reconstructionism" which, says Kaplan, is adaptable to the thinking of the modern Jew, because it grew out of his modern way of thinking.

In Answer to the Epikoros

Kaplan's writings reflect the spoken rather than the written word. He addresses himself to a listening people, whom he is trying to arouse to an awareness of the new Jewish realities. He is, as he calls himself, a "Jewish worrier." He does not theorize for others, but seeks to communicate with them on what worries him in regard to Jewish existence today, its communal structure, its contacts with the world, and particularly its relation to "the God of our fathers." That is why he speaks in a new terminology and searches for new ideas. "I myself," he said in answer to a question about his God-idea, "find the conception of God, as the Power that makes for salvation, compelling and comforting and . . . I find it conducive to worship, prayer and ritual." While this statement reveals the true motive of his striving for new concepts, it has been a source of much misunderstanding about his "definition" of God. It is often contended that Kaplan has converted God into a conceptual process so he could grasp Him in thought. This is not entirely the case. As a deeply religious man, Kaplan, to use his own words, has "never been satisfied with an awareness of God merely as an intellectual concept." "For God," he emphasizes in the same context, "must not merely be held as an idea; He must be felt as a presence, if we want not only to know about God but to know God." Why then, we may ask, look for a concept of God if it does not actually help "to know God" but only to form "an idea" about Him? Kaplan's answer is directed to those who doubt whether there is a God to be known at all; and for that matter, to those who question the realities of the Jewish people and the validity of the Torah, in a word, those who are dubious about their identity as Jews, religiously or otherwise. "Reconstructionism," says Kaplan, "addresses itself primarily to Jews who are hesitant about the values of Judaism and are teetering on the brink of assimilation, but who have not yet determined to take the plunge. Such Jews probably constitute today the majority of Diaspora Jewry." Kaplan sees this type of Jew as the modern Epikoros, who professes a scientific outlook on the world and who doubts everything that is not empirical fact, verifiable through observation and experimentation. In order to speak to such a person about Jewish values, Kaplan maintains, one must use a vocabulary that makes sense to him, that is, the language and method of modern science; and this is what Reconstructionism proposes to do. To save the Jews who "are teetering on the brink of assimilation," they must be given a convincing rationale of Jewish existence. This, Kaplan says, requires more than a reinterpretation of "traditional ideas about God, the world, and man;" it calls for a radical rebuilding of the whole structure.

Kaplan places the three realities of Judaism in a certain order of relationship, first the People Israel, then God, and then the Torah. It means that his outlook is anthropocentric, his primary reality being the members of the Jewish people, or in general, man as an individual and social existent. Nevertheless, his main issue is a religious one, inasmuch as his God-idea plays a dominant role in the life of the people whose civilization is in constant change. That is, as the people evolves its religious ideas change. Religion assumes different meanings at different times in Jewish history. There is a "modern Jewish religion" as there was a pre-modern, ancient, or medieval one. The meaning of God in each era differs accordingly. What characterizes the present age, Kaplan would say, is that it has not yet found an adequate concept of God in consonance with the modern scientific-empirical outlook on reality. This constitutes today's religious crisis in general, not just in Judaism. This is not a crisis in the existence of God, as some non-Jewish theologians see it, but in the existence of man, more specifically, as Kaplan sees it, in his existence as a moral being. God as a transcendent Being, says Kaplan, may not become known to man, but his manifestations are ever present in the human art of living, in man's moral behavior. It is therefore up to man to transcend his own condition and approach the divine through his moral conduct. This expresses itself fully through one's life with his people which is the only way that may lead one to personal salvation.

The Idea of Peoplehood

Kaplan looks at the problem of modern Jewry as it affects the emancipated Jew, particularly the man of enlightenment who seeks individual freedom or self-fulfilment in everyday life on earth. If this emancipated Jew, he says, is to develop a bond with his people, as a people or nation, he must be in a position to view it as playing a decisive role in his quest for personal liberation. Kaplan recognizes three main properties of Jewish peoplehood: salvation, chosenness, and organic community which have sufficient force to attract the individual Jew; but these properties, he maintains, have been constricted within a religious frame of reference that is no longer acceptable to the modern mind, They need not just reinterpretation but complete reconstruction.

Individual Salvation

Nothing expresses Kaplan's spirit of reconstructionism more empathically than his concept of salvation. He considers the supreme value of individual freedom and its "progressive self-assertion . . . almost . . . a law of human history." Salvation of the individual Jew thus becomes the central idea of the reconstructed Jewish community, whose "chief aim . . . is to help him attain those objectives which constitute for him his complete self-realization." All three realities of Judaism, the very essence of peoplehood, the God-idea, and the Torah serve the same end. According to Kaplan, salvation is an observable process in human nature as part of the cosmic natural order, in contrast to the traditional view of Jewish redemption which Kaplan regards as supernatural or otherworldly. By supernaturalism he means basically miracles, which operate on a suspension or abrogation of the empirical laws of nature, performed by an omnipotent, transcendent God who is not subject to these laws. This concept, he says, cannot be reconciled with the modern scientific outlook, which rejects God's miracles as well as His transcendence. As a naturalist, modern man looks for divinity in whatever may be observed in human life or in the universe as a whole, and not in miraculous acts of a power beyond this universe. Insofar as salvation is related to the idea of divinity, the divine power is manifest in man's own actions of creativity, responsibility, and integrity, Kaplan's three natural moral virtues which man ought to cultivate in cooperation with fellow-man. The real drive for salvation is thus grounded in man's own moral capacities. If we disregard for a moment Kaplan's objection to the traditional promise of eternal life in the hereafter, his naturalistic moral goal for man on earth does not differ basically from the earthly goal set for man by Jewish tradition in the past or in our own time. The progressive improvement in Jewish existence is paramount in both views. There is, however, a fundamental difference between them in two respects, namely, in the role Kaplan assigns to the Jewish people for the salvation of the individual, and in the kind and manner of help he expects "from above."

Although Kaplan speaks of Judaism as a civilization being an end in itself and not "an indispensable means to some universal good," he nevertheless considers the Jewish people or peoplehood as a means toward the attainment of personal ends. "Its fundamental purpose," he says, "is to humanize and civilize:" it is "an instrument for human development." The instrumental character of the people serving the individual is the basic element of his very concept of peoplehood, which is little more than an operational or functional factor of salvation. Even when he reinterprets the significance of the Pesah Festival, he omits the hero of the drama, the People Israel, and speaks only of the "redemptive energies which exist in nature and in man." Now, if the redemptive energies, according to the naturalistic view, exist in individual man, what exactly is the part played by the people in the salvational process? What energies flow from the people or, as Kaplan himself phrases the question, "How can the Jewish people, then, become a means to the Jew's this-worldly salvation?" On the other hand, since man is not only the center of this process but also its starting point, what is there in his nature that prompts him to seek salvation through a group identification and how does the latter function in meeting his quest? Kaplan tries to resolve this problem on the Faustian pattern of "two souls dwell in my breast" in conflict with one another. One is an aggressive force manifested through self-indulgence, envy, hatred, and arrogance which are characteristic of the human drive to satisfy one's physiological needs. The other is a moral force which manifests itself after those needs have been satisfied and which then strives to counteract the aggressive traits. This striving or counterstriving is designated by Kaplan as "man's salvational behavior," his "true destiny" of self-realization. However, since individual man is not physiologically and psychologically self-sufficient to be able to reach his destiny all alone, he must submerge his "selfish salvation" within a social structure that aims at the attainment of the common destiny of all its members. That is why the individual, though starting from his own needs, will identify himself with a given group or people in order to promote his welfare jointly with others. In the case of the Jew, this is his rationale for seeking to identify himself with the Jewish people.

From this naturalistic viewpoint of individual salvation we can understand why Kaplan rejects categorically the idea of the chosen people, without granting it even the possibility of reinterpretation in his own mode of thinking. Before we discuss his objections to it, let us examine its essential role in Jewish life; I believe, we shall have no difficulty in assigning it an honorable function in modern times, without violating our sense of moral and spiritual propriety. The idea of chosenness, whether of a person or a group, does not necessarily imply superiority above everyone else. It does imply certain unique outstanding characteristics, "choice" qualities, which single out a person or group from its surroundings. This is an observable fact by whatever criteria it may be gauged and regardless of who does the choosing, God or Mother Nature; for nature too does her work selectively. The same outstanding qualities may be observed in different persons or groups, though each one is unique in its particular chosenness. We can safely say, then, that Jewish tradition has for the most part not considered the idea of a chosen people as synonymous with absolute superiority above other nations. We only have to recall how often the Prophets and Sages, from Moses down, have chided the Jewish folk for its shortcomings, indeed how God Himself often showed His displeasure at its extreme stubbornness. Whether or not we know the purpose of Jewish chosenness by God or by Nature, the Jews certainly were not chosen for their superiority or perfection, and they have never claimed that. At the same time, it should be noted that Jewish tradition does claim that its Torah is complete in all its ways, and that God has chosen the Jewish people from among the nations, despite its shortcomings and imperfections, to accept His Torah and to fulfill it in everyday life on earth. This does not impute a divine rejection of other nations. On the contrary, tradition relates that God had first offered the Torah to others, but for various reasons they did not accept it. Essentially, the chosen people idea signifies now as in the past that the poeple Israel as a whole has been chosen by a power higher than it to become an end in itself and not an instrumentality for some other ends. The individual members of this people, therefore, are not the ones to choose it, or just to choose it, as a means for their personal salvation. Those who belong to it unconditionally will become active participants in its redemption and be redeemed with it.

Kaplan discards the chosen people idea on the contention that it not only connotes superiority but also that, if this idea be taken literally, it "is part of the original supernaturalism of the traditional religion." Yet he does not deny that the Jews in fact possess unique qualities which others do not possess. Indeed, he extolls them on every occasion. The Jews, he says, "experienced the moral and spiritual importance of nationhood as a factor in the development of human personality to a more intense degree than any other people." "The Jewish civilization stands out unique in having festivals to commemorate past events." "Judasim came to be the first civilization to have a national history" (Judaism as a Civilization," pp. 257, 261, 262). However, he sees all these qualities mainly as instruments for "the individual Jew [who] can experience the privilege of divine election only as he identifies himself with the whole of Israel." It is Kaplan's emphasis of the "divine election" of the individual, rather than his objection to supernaturalism, that explains his rejection of the idea of a chosen people. In his scheme of salvation, the people Israel is not the one to be redeemed as an end in itself, but rather the individual who sees in it a means to his own ends. Thus Kaplan shifts the idea of divine election from the people to the individual, but fails to show why an individual Jew who yearns for the "experience of divine election" should want to identify himself with a people that is not divinely chosen. More important, Kaplan has never been able to demonstrate how a Jew "teetering on the brink of assimilation" and denying all Jewish values, may be convinced that his personal salvation can come through his identification with the Jewish people rather than with the people with whom he seeks to assimilate. For as long as salvation is a matter of a purely personal striving for the good life, assimilation will have the upper hand.

The Organic Community

In order for the Jewish people to perform its function as a vehicle of salvation, Kaplan says, it must be reconstituted as an organic community. It may seem difficult to grasp how such a task can at all be undertaken. Leaving aside recent claims by some biologists that they have succeeded in synthesizing an organic cell, scientific advancement is still at a stage where we have to accept organic structures as natural existents. If the Jewish people are not an organic body now, there is nothing we can do to reconstitute it as such. What Kaplan then means is that we must reconstruct our approach to Jewish existence from an organic viewpoint and we shall recognize that the Jewish people is and always has been an organic entity except that it is not at present functioning in that capacity. It is now a sick organism, inasmuch as its established institutions and overall structure are deficient in the life-giving energies that would naturally activate the salvational drive of its members. If the people is to be regenerated, it must first reorganize itself in a network of organic communities on a local level and on a national scale with an appropriate apparatus for global inter-relations. The foundation of this entire new structure is the reconstructionist view of Judaism as a civilization functioning in a given space or land and evolving through historical time. Each civilization can function successfully only in its own land where it is the dominant mode of life. The Jewish community in the Land of Israel, therefore, is the ony one in world Jewry which may realize its particular civilizational existence. In other lands, such as in the United States, for example, Judaism must be satisfied to live as a secondary civilization within the framework of the American civilization which is primary for this land. We may accept Kaplan's civilizational concept of Judaism insofar as it may attract Jews who seek salvation through this medium. But if we regard the Jewish civilization in the Diaspora, as Kaplan does, in a secondary light, it loses its redemptive character. It certainly does not possess the magic force of the chosen people idea which it purports to supplant. Kaplan cannot resolve "the predicament of the modern Jew" by placing him in two civilizations, unless he can recompense him for the loss of primacy in his non-Jewish environment. The reconstructionist concept of religion does not fulfill this function, because it itself is relegated to an adjectival, that is secondary, position as is indicated by the adjective "religious" in a reconstructed "Judaism as a religious civilization." This leads us to Kaplan's concept of God in relation to man.

Cosmic Power of Salvation

In designating Judaism as a civilization, Kaplan emphasizes that it is "far more comprehensive than Jewish religion. It includes that nexus of a history, literature, language, social organization, esthetic values, which in their totality form a civilization." At the same time, he regards religion as a "quality inherent in the very substance of a civilization." That is, while a civilization possesses other qualities as well, religion is its most pervasive one. What then is the nature and function of this religious property and how does it permeate Judaism as a whole? Furthermore, if it does inhere in every facet of Jewish life, why can it not be said that Judaism is "inherently" a religion? What Kaplan means is that Judaism as a religion in the old sense cannot be accepted today, but that it may be regarded as religious in a new reconstructed socio-psychological sense. That is, religion permeates Judaism insofar as the latter serves a religious purpose and insofar as this purpose grows out of human nature. But what is the reconstructionist meaning of the term "religious?" Once Kaplan has established the socio-psychological need of man's striving for the good and full life (salvation), he simply asserts that this striving is religious in the sense that it is sacred and of the highest good. If it is to pass the functional test of reconstructionism, it must operate in some manifest human behavior, and the only kind of behavior that fits a religious designation is "salvational behavior." Religion thus becomes synonymous with salvation as an act of striving toward human self-fulfiment. The same reasoning leads Kaplan to his God-idea. Salvation, he says, is "the promise from which we can arrive at a meaningful conception of God." The moral traits of human nature, which are part of the cosmic order, point to a Power in the Cosmos that fosters those traits. Moreover, this power guarantees the possible achievement of the moral goal, for the nature of striving presupposes the possibility of attainment. The God-idea is thus none other than the "Cosmic Power that makes for salvation." Now religion must foster belief. However, in the "salvational behavior" belief is directed not toward God but toward man's capacity to achieve his goal. The religious man here believes in his own ability to reach a matured sense of integrity, responsibility, and creativity (the three main moral virtues), in a word, salvation. Thus, religious behavior means salvational behavior, and religious belief means belief in one's own capacities to attain the salvational goal. This kind of "religion without supernaturalism," as Kaplan calls it, puts all trust in man's moral powers and transposes God to the realm of a moral cosmic order. In this order God may be viewed as transcending man insofar as the order is greater than man, and at the same time as being immanent in man insofar as man is part of the order. Man becomes aware of the God-idea in himself as he becomes fully conscious of his own moral power of striving for salvation. The "self-conscious will to salvation," Kaplan writes, "is the immanent aspect of that cosmic reality for which no term can be more appropriate than 'God.' "

Kaplan's God-idea raises more questions in the mind of the believer than we can possibly entertain here. I will only touch on one of its aspects which must satisfy all believers, and especially those to be turned into believers, and that is the problem of God's immanence and transcendence in relation to man, which Kaplan has tried to resolve but which has strained his naturalism almost to the breaking point. Kaplan tries to reconcile God's dual relationship to man (being in man and at the same time beyond him) by means of a two-way pointer. Issuing from man's salvational moral behavior, he says this behavior points necessarily to a cosmic moral power in man because he is part of the cosmic process. But the cosmic process generates man's nature, including his moral nature; therefore it points to the fact that it is beyond man and infinitely greater than he. By naming this moral "Power in the Cosmos" God, Kaplan finds Him both immanent in man (as man's salvational behavior) and transcendent to man (as the cosmic power that generates this behavior, to begin with). Kaplan must have felt the difficulty of this circular reasoning, which grew out of his attempt to establish a self-operating naturalism of "only one universe within which man and God exist." To overcome it, he introduced in his later writings a new concept, called "trans-naturalism."

It would take me too far afield to enter here into a discussion of its multiple implications. I will only indicate what Kaplan has tried to overcome by his new term. His original problem stems from the fact tht he posits the God-idea as a Power functioning within the natural laws of the cosmos and at the same time not being affected by those laws. The second position clearly places God as acting beyond the confines of the laws of nature, that is, as a supernatural power, a concept which Kaplan tries to avoid at all costs. He therefore draws a distinction between "natural" laws as understood by science and technology, on one hand, and, on the other, "transnatural" laws which come into play in man's moral activities of integrity, creativity, and responsibility. The latter are not supernatural because they operate within man's moral nature; yet they are transnatural because they are outside the narrow range of the mechanical, positivistic natural sciences. They constitute the spiritual realm of human life in "the language of symbol, myth and drama," as expressed primarily in the Torah, which is the third reality of Judaism.

Torah an Instrument of Salvation

In keeping with his reconstructionist method, Kaplan reinterprets the Torah as "the ethico-religious, or spiritual, civilization of the Jewish people." Its full import is "meant to be an instrument for the improvement of human nature, both individual and social. . . ." It teaches man that the purpose of religion is his salvation and it directs him toward this end. There may be nothing contradictory between this view and tradition, except when it comes to the meaning of the Masoretic text of the Torah. Here Kaplan introduces a new Midrash in terms of myth and symbol not of what the text actually presents, "but what it impels us to affirm as a means of salvation." "What we affirm," he says, "may be the very antithesis of what the Torah teaches."

What Kaplan is seeking in the text of the Torah is general principles, ideas, and concepts that will serve his primary purpose of individual salvation. By reinterpreting the Torah in terms of these principles, and by ascribing to them symbols and myths, he hopes to avoid what he considers to be its supernatural aspects, on the one hand, and, on the other, to discover in it a cosmic transcendence and a human immanence in consonance with the strivings of the modern Jew for personal freedom. Speaking in terms of Jungian psychology, which Reconstructionism has adopted, the Torah, according to Kaplan's Midrash, represents the "collective unconscious" that manifests itself throughout Jewish history in symbols and myths and, as it reaches the fully self-conscious level, prompts and guides the individual Jew toward his destiny, toward salvation. Many trends of modern thought converge in Kaplan's vision of a reconstructed Judaism. My brief exposition of its main tenets does not claim to cover adequately all the phases and nuances of his rich intellectual output, but may well serve as a stimulus to further exploration of his contribution to Jewish thinking in our time.

1976

Correspondence with Dr. Kaplan on His "Vision of a Modern Judaism"

October 3, 1976

Dear Dr. Alexander S. Kohanski:

Please accept my heartfelt thanks for the publication, in the September 23 issue of the Jewish News, of your elaborate article entitled *Kaplan's Vision of a Modern Judaism.*

Permit me to mention the two points wherein it falls short of what might have been an authentic exposition of Reconstructionism:

(1) In the first place, what you say about individual salvation being the essence of Reconstructionism is far from adequate. To be "modern," Judaism has to stress the fact that to be "modern" the conception of salvation has to be this-worldly and to reckon fully with the two statements, one by Hillel and the other by Rabban Shimon ben Gamliel quoted toward the end of the first chapter of פרקי אבות , as compared with the traditional statement at the beginning of that chapter by Shimon Hatsaddik.

(2) Moreover, you wrongly assume that I regard "Jewish civilization in the Diaspora in a *secondary light.* You seem to ignore the Reconstructionist contribution to America's *civil religion*, known as The Faith of America published by Henry Schuman, N.Y. 1951. It consists of Readings, Songs and Prayers for the celebration of American Holidays, chosen from the standpoint of Judaism as a civilization. We invited Prof. J. Paul Williams of Connecticut University (?) to be one of the three editors. The book is used in numerous public schools throughout the United States. Does that mean loss of primacy, as you put it for Jewish civilization.

I hope you will try to undo the harm to our movement by reading the chapter in The Future of the American Jew entitled "The 'Chosen People' an Anachronism," and by reckoning with the following comment by the well-known popular American philosopher Harry A. Overstreet:

"Dr. Kaplan's variation from Aristotle's declaration that man is a political animal, and the substitution of the view that man is characteristically an animal that cares about maximum life, goes to

147

the roots. It should be the starting point for new patterns in philosophy and religion, and it should invest science with the dignity of being coexplorer with them in man's quest for salvation."

I leave it entirely to you to counteract the effect of the two serious mistakes in what is otherwise a brilliantly written article about the Reconstruct [ionist] version of Judaism.

With all good wishes for the Jewish New Year,

Sincerely,

Mordecai M. Kaplan

October 13, 1976

Dr. Mordecai M. Kaplan
3 Ibn Ezra Street
Jerusalem, Israel

Dear Dr. Kaplan:

Thank you for your response to my article "Kaplan's Vision of a modern Judaism." מכל מלמדי השכלתי , I learn from all my teachers and especially from my revered teacher Dr. Mordecai M. Kaplan. Far be it from me to want to harm the Reconstructionist Movement by word of mouth or in print. The views I have expressed in my article are the result of a careful study of your works over many years. Allow me therefore to comment on the several points which you consider erroneous in my presentation. I should say at the outset that I appreciate the fact that you find the general burden of my essay as a fair exposition of your teachings. As I said at the end, I did not claim to have covered them all but only dwelt on some highlights as a starting point for further exploration, which should involve also many of your students and followers. For, if I may be so bold as to say, Reconstructionism has not as yet been subjected to the kind of critical study that has been accorded to other currents of thought in our age.

Let me start with your reference to Professor Harry A. Overstreet's statement, as it has a bearing on the issue of individualism. If we look at Overstreet's quotation from Aristotle ["man is a political animal"] in its full context, we shall find that the contrast between Aristotle's view of man and your view is not between "a political animal" and "an animal that cares about maximum life," as Overstreet sees it (for these two aspects of man may be perfectly compatible), but rather between "community" and "individual." In his *Politics*, Book I (from which the quotation is excerpted), Aristotle (in his very opening sentence) declares: "Every state is a community of some kind and every community is established with a view to some good. . . . But. . . the state or political community. . . aims at the highest good." The state, he says further, is the natural form of society. "Hence, it is evident that the state is a creation of nature, and that *man is by nature a political animal*" (ibid., 1252a1, 1252b7, 1253a2, my *ital.*). Aristotle does not use the term "political" in its modern connotation of political power but in its social-communal sense, viewing, as he does, the comunity as the source that gives purpose or a goal (*to telos*) to individual man's life on earth. (In Book III he emphasizes the concept "that man is a political animal. And therefore, men, even when they do not require one another's help [for personal salvation, as you would say], desire to live together" 1278b20). In this respect there is a marked difference between his view of man and yours, namely: he puts the primacy of man in his *community*, [whereas] you place it in *individuality*. Your reference to *Pirke Avot* and to your *Future of the American Jew* corroborate this point.

Judging Hillel's view from his statement in *Pirke Avot*, אם אין אני לי מי לי, and Raban Shimon ben Gamliel's view from his statement על שלשה דברים העולם עומד, על הדין ועל האמת ועל השלום , I would say their teachings are individualistic, Hillel starting with the "I" and Shimon concluding with the "world," but both leaving out the "people" as the central figure in the drama of interhuman relation. (Interestingly enough, the Rambam does well by adding in his Perush: הדין הוא הנהגת המדינה ביושר . It is the *Polis* or community that gives intrinsic worth to man's justice.) To be sure, these two statements also express your own view. However, this moral stance will not induce the individual Jew to seek personal "salvation" particularly through the Jewish people; for any other group of individuals who comply with these dicta may band together for their fulfillment. And since you don't grant the Jewish people any *chosenness*, there is no reason why a Jew should choose this people for his self-realization in this world. I will return to the Chosen People idea later, but let me continue now with your other reference.

In the same chapter 13 of your *Future of the American Jew* in which you contend against the "Chosen People Idea [as] an Anachronism," you make the followign statement: "*Judaism can certainly not afford to harbor any doctrine which is in conflict with the ethical basis of democracy* [ital. in original]. That basis is the intrinsic worth of the individual soul, a worth which is independent of the people, race or church to which one belongs. This implies that no people, race or church can confer upon its members a higher human status than does any other" (p. 224). Your statement is crystal clear but your implication does not follow. For the statement implies only what it says: the people does not bestow on the individual his intrinsic worth, because his worth is independent of the people. This has nothing to do with one people being considered greater than another, but is has to do with the worth of the individual not being derived from his people at all. Aristotle says of such an individual that he "is either a bad man or above humanity" (ibid., 1253a4). And I side with Aristotle.

Returning now to the Chosen People idea, you maintain that "the very assumption of a predetermined and permanent superiority, no matter in what respect, does not lend itself to reinterpretation" (*The Future of the American Jew*, p. 217). I respectfully submit that this is begging the question. The reinterpretation to be sought is not of the "superiority" but of the "chosenness" which need not entail the notion of greater than others. For, while the chosen people idea in traditional sources contain this notion it is not its main thrust, as I have pointed out in my article. Moreover, your substitution of "vocation" for election only postpones the issue. A vocation which is "compatible with our highest ethical standards," as you demand, is in the nature of human destiny, that is, predetermined and permanent. Otherwise, man's ethical basis [being contingent] may be converted into an evil ground. Who then, or what, determines this destiny? Who chooses this particular vocation for individual man? You say it is cosmic determination, or a divine determination of the cosmos called God. Whichever way it is phrased, the idea of election is inescapable. For one, like myself, who uses the communal approach, the election is of the people as a whole. But you speak only of the individual being elected, not the people. Then why, speaking in functional terms, should the individual who has been chosen through a divine cosmic power want to associate with a people who has not been chosen by the same power? How can the people "function" in the individual's election for salvation if "the intrinsic worth of the individual soul . . . is independent of the people"? If nothing else, this calls for a pragmatic answer.

A final note on the Reconstructionist view of Jewish civilization in the diaspora. My observation that it puts the Jewish civilization in a secondary role in relation to the dominant one is derived from a study of all its aspects. In my brief article, of course, I could only touch on one or two points. But your evidence to the contrary adduced from "the Reconstructionist contribution to America's *civil religion*" leaves me as much in doubt as heretofore. If this "contribution" should take hold and spread widely through its Public School usage, as you indicate, it would lead to a new "common religion" of the American nation (similar, I might say, to Hermann Cohen's religion for the entire German nation, which you criticized in your *Purpose and Meaning of Jewish Existence*, p. 48), supplanting the Jewish religion not only in the eyes of the Gentiles (it will not supplant their Christian religion), but also and especially in the eyes of those Jews to whom Reconstructionism addresses itself. I doubt whether this can be regarded as Judasim's " primacy" in the diaspora.

Reconstructionism has made important contributions to Jewish life in modern times. It has many seminal ideas which ought to be brought to fruition. I feel that those of your followers who have dealt with its underlying principles have not given it the necessary critical analysis that it deserves. It is through such an analysis that its strengths as well as its weaknesses will be brought to light and, most important, will stimulate young minds to a greater participation in its evolving thought formation and reformulation. This was my real intention and hope, as I had expressed it at the conclusion of my article in *The Jewish News*.

I remain as ever with cordial greetings from Dorothy and myself to you and Mrs. Kaplan.

Sincerely

Alexander S. Kohanski

June 15, 1966

Dear Dr. Kaplan:

I join with Dorothy in sending you our greetings and felicitations on the blessed occasion of your reaching the eighty-fifth birthday כן ירבו ימיך ושנותיך .

My own reminiscences lead me back to my days at the Graduate School for Jewish Social Work, when I first came in contact with your vigorous mind. I had just come from the wilds of Tennessee and was promptly introduced to your "Civilization." As I recall, you opened the text to us by reading from manuscript, and an avalanche of ideas came rolling down upon us. To gain a firm foothold, I wrote a term paper on "Kaplan and Ahad Haam" and that started me off on a long road of reading your works, contemplating their import, and forming ideas on Jewish life and thought in our generation. The clarity of your style, your straightforward statement, and your unmistakable position have served me as guideposts and highlights in the development of my own ideas.

I am grateful that I have found Mordecai M. Kaplan, who has enriched my life, even though I have not yet found his God. The roads may be different, but the goal is the same.

With warm regards, I am as ever,

Alexander S. Kohanski

Will Herberg's Existentialist Judaism

What is the meaning of human life? is an age-old question. In generations past the answer was sought in "a system of values anchored in ultimate reality." What disturbs Will Herberg and many others in our generation is that man today has not committed himself to any system of values.* Modern man's life has been devaluated and is therefore meaningless, purposeless, without significance—insecure. His perplexing problem is that he tries to place himself as an object of existence among other objects of nature in a universal scheme of things, and he just cannot find himself there, not as a free living being. According to Herberg, "man finds the meaning of his existence in his capacity for decision, in his freedom of choice." But, does modern man, in his own estimate of himself, stand on firm enough ground to be able to decide and to choose freely? Herberg approaches this question from an "existentialist" viewpoint.

The seventeenth and eighteenth century philosophers, who grappled with the problem of freedom, thought they had proved man's (or his soul's) free and indestructible existence by rational argument. Then came Kant's shattering demonstration of the limitations of pure reason and its inability to prove the existence or non-existence of the free soul. Later, Schopenhauer made an attempt to find man through "will," a very real thing indeed, but he lost him again when he allowed the human will to disappear without a trace in the Universal Will. In the late nineteenth century, Nietzsche, as Franz Rosenzweig pointed out, was the first of modern thinkers who rebelled against the philosophies that reduced man to an object of logical demonstration. He placed the problem of man as an existing living being against the problem of the universe, and against God Himself, even though he negated God's reality. Thus, philosophy may postulate, but cannot deduct, human freedom. Modern man, however, considers himself primarily as a scientist. He acknowleges only facts that can be observed, tested, proved or disproved. As to the question of security, the modern man-scientist may well argue that science has

*Judaism and Modern Man, by Will Herberg. New York: Farrar, Straus and Young.

helped in no small measure to make the objective world a more secure place for human beings to live in. And yet, when man toys with the instruments of power which scientific invention or discovery has placed in his hands, he trembles at the possible use he could make of those instruments for good or for evil. Security thus becomes an uncertainty, an illusion, unless man is able to decide at all times that the instruments of science shall be used for good. But, decision, choice, can be made only by a free moral being on the basis of an accepted set of values. In this, science has failed man, for it could neither demonstrate his freedom nor establish for him a set of values.

This is where the *existentialist* approach to the human problem comes in. The existence of man as a subject—as a person—is the starting point of a world outlook that can give man his freedom. Man's existence is a reality which cannot, and need not, be demonstrated by logical proof or objective analysis. The moment one makes man the object of demonstration, one destroys him as an *existing* subject, and no amount of reasoning or scientific induction will restore his real existence. Only as an existing person can man choose a set of values, for outside his existence values are meaningless. To be able to decide, to choose, makes man free; but it also places upon him a tremendous responsibility. Can he bear that responsibility in terms of human existence alone? Man feels he cannot; for he knows his limitations, his relativism, changeability, and finally death. Herberg calls it "man's existential predicament" out of which he can extricate himself by reaching out to the absolute. Man cannot prove the existence of the Absolute, or God any more than he he can demonstrate the existence of his own free being. But while he can start with himself as a person in real existence, he cannot do so with reference to God, who is "beyond" the human person. How, then, does man reach God? Through "a leap of faith" says Will Herberg. Man may use intellectual speculation and sense experience as an anchor for the springboard from which he may leap into the "beyond," but not as a bridge to span the abyss that lies between himself and the Absolute. The "leap of faith," Herberg warns, is the most critical existential decision of man's life. Man may even have to risk his very life for it. And yet, it is not something one may expect to attain as "a permanent acquisition. Faith is a never-ending battle against self-absolutization." It is "never final" though "always possible" (p. 40).

Thus, Herberg places man "at the brink of the abyss" and advises him to jump into the beyond where he will find, or "has *already* found," *the outstretched hand of God to* receive him. What leaves one in doubt about the author's advice is not whether one is to make the "decision for God" but whether the springboard is securely anchored for the leap. For Will Herberg leads man to the brink, telling him all along the road that reason and science are incapable of finding God. That may be so. But reason and science are realms best known to man. If he is to venture beyond them, he must feel that they are not illusions but a strong pavement upon which he may walk securely and which holds firmly at least one end of the springboard on this side of the brink. Herberg, however, does not allow man to stand securely enough in reason which would help him make the existential decision, even though the decision itself may be an act of faith. Reason may not provide for man a safe landing in the beyond but it can give him a safe jumping point, so that he does not just fall off the brink.

In the next two discourses of his book, the author analyzes the relationships of "God and Man" and of "Religion and Society." He draws a fine distinction between the Graeco-Oriental concept of God, which is basically pantheistic, immanent and impersonal, and the God of Hebraic religion Who is a transcendent "living, active, 'feeling' God." Herberg does not try to *define* God, but to *find* Him, which is the true quest of religion. He also correctly expresses the point of view of Hebraic (really Jewish) religion, when he speaks of idols as illusions and of idolatry as the cardinal sin of man. Furthermore, he does not view man as being basically sinful. Man's attempt to attain absolute self-sufficiency, his self-centeredness, Herberg indicates, is the source of his great perplexity and of sin. Man will find salvation, the author advises, if he will ony "transfer the center of his existence from within himself to the Living God" (p. 119). So far, Herberg has stood solidly on the ground of Jewish religious tradition. But when he tries to lead man out of his sinful state to salvation, he wanders off into some by-paths of Christological interpretation. It should be pointed out that Herberg discusses the spiritual problems of modern man from the point of view of what he terms "Hebraic religion" as distinguished from "Judaism," the former being the foundation of both Judaism and Christianity. However, in order to make room for both on common ground, he narrows the Jewish foundation too much. This is evident in his treatment of the relation between justice and love.

According to Herberg, man may attain salvation "by the power of his faith and love" (p 119). Justice or righteousness, the author relegates to a secondary position, at best to a function of love. "Law may not be the final word of the will of God, but so long as men remain sinful, that is, so long as they remain human—it is the will of God in a form that is indispensable and authoritative for the everyday conduct of life" (p 107). "It is because love fails that justice is instituted among men" (p. 148-149). In essence, Herberg does not differ from Paul, who, speaking to the Graeco-Oriental world, said: "Wherefore then serveth the law? It was added because of transgressions. . . . Before faith came, we were kept under the law. . . . The law was our schoolmaster . . . that we might be justified by faith." (*Galatians*, 3:19, 23, 24). Herberg considers law and justice as relative in terms of human limitations, whereas love he regards in terms of the Absolute. Therefore, he cannot find an "ultimate criterion of justice" except in "the divine imperative, the law of love" (p. 148). But on the level of human limitations, love, too is relative. On the other hand, justice as a divine command is as absolute as love. Furthermore, he finds only one source of sin, namely self-absolutization. Jewish tradition, however, recognizes several sources, including simple human error (*hataah*), iniquity (*avon*), and transgression (*pesha*). (Cf. *Yoma*, 36b.) Through faith man may overcome his willful iniquity of self-absolutization. But as a creaturely human being he will always be subject to error. Love will not eliminate it, because man may err even in love. Herberg also erroneously limits the idea of justice to "impartiality" and "rightfulness." But in Jewish tradition, justice stresses *equality*, to make room for everyone. Love, on the other hand, seeks to establish harmony. Yet harmony may exist even where there are flagrant inequalities. Love without justice is insufficient for the salvation of man and society. If man is to take an active part in bringing of the Kingdom of God, he needs both love and justice: love, to overlook the shortcomings of his fellow-men; justice, to help correct and overcome those shortcomings.

In his last discourse entitled "The Mystery of Israel," the author deals with the Jewish people in relation to the Absolute and to world history. One who accepts the reality of God as a power beyond that can be reached through faith, must accept the possibility of revelation; otherwise, man in his limitation would never know the ways of God. What is the meaning of revelation? Herberg's position, following Buber, Rosenzweig, and others, and differing from the fundamentalists and modernists, is understandable in a religious frame of reference that takes into account human experience. "Revelation" he defines, "is the *self-disclosure of God in his dealings with the world.* Scripture is thus not itself revelation but a humanly mediated record of revelation" (p. 246). What Mr. Herberg finds hard to explain is why revelation is through Scripture only. Furthermore, granted that revelation, as a personal relation of the Living God to man, must be concrete and particular, the question still remains why God chose to reveal himself especially "to, and in the history of, Israel" and not to another people. It is the mystery of Israel, Herberg says, "the divine covenant into which God entered with Israel at Sinai." This covenant brought Israel into existence as a people, to fulfill God's redemptive purpose in the world. This is a traditional view, ancient as well as modern.

Herberg advances many authentic references in his attempt to vindicate this tradition, but the modern Jew will find little comfort in his exposition of Israel's role among the nations. The author elevates the Jewish collective to the heights of a supernatural community, "the covenant-folk," which is the bond that unites all natural particular Jewish communities, the former being eternal, while the latter are changeable, appearing and disappearing in time and space. Israel's task in relation to the outside wold, he explains, is that of an "outgoing service," to be a "light to the gentiles," and "by an active effort to bring the peoples of the world to acknowledge the Holy One of Israel" (p. 272). Its history is the redemptive history of the world. Apart from this, Herberg concludes, "the very being of Israel is a blank mystery and its history an anomaly without sense or meaning" (p. 269). The assignment of a specific function or vocation to the Jewish people has been a subject of speculation since the days of the prophets. What is most distrubing to the modern Jew, however, is that of all peoples Israel alone has been used as the instrument for the salvation of mankind. What is even more disconcerting is the contention that without this vocation Israel has no reason for existence. Whether the role of instrument is by divine appointment or by the human strategem of some mundane potentate, it is equally unacceptable to the Jew of today.

In the earthly realities of Jewish history, the instrument idea has assumed the ugly form of "usefulness" to dominant groups and states. Herberg will no doubt protest against such an application of his mission idea. The difficulty in his interpretation of the Jewish role in the world is that he applies the "I-Thou" relationship to individuals but not to peoples. The human individual, he says, following Buber, must be regarded as a "Thou," that is, as a person or an end in himself, and not as an object (an "It") to be used by others. The same, then, should hold true of the relationship between peoples. If a mission must be assigned to Israel, it would be more in keeping with the thinking and with the spiritual needs of modern man to have a special vocation given to each of the other peoples as well. All nations should share alike in the bringing of the Kingdom of God and none should be used as a vehicle for others. Another difficulty is that Herberg makes the mission of Israel the condition of the people's existance. He then asks of the individual Jew "an existential self-intregation into the sacred history of Israel" (p. 287). This would be utterly unattainable if one were to try to integrate himself with a supernatural community, unless one could first identify himself with a particular community which is real and natural as the individual himself is real. Existential identification is possible if the particular community, even in its transient state, exists as an end in itself—has existential validity— and does not require any special "reason for existence."

In the closing pages of his book Herberg tries to chart for the modern Jew a way of life in accordance with Torah, written and oral. The Jew today, he says, is perplexed not by "the ethical laws included in the halakha," but by "the so-called 'ritual observances.'" He distinguishes observances "that are of a *general-religious* type, more or less common to all religions (prayer, communal worship...), [from] those of the *special-Jewish* type that are held to apply to Jews and to Jews only (circumcision, kashrut, Sabbath, etc.)" (p. 298). He seems to feel that only the latter are disturbing to the Jew, because they tend to separate him from his gentile neighbors. But this is really not the problem that perplexes the modern Jew. It is not the type that makes an observance specifically Jewish but its *mode*. Those Jews who feel strongly against any degree of "separation" have modelled their religious observances after the manner of the Protestant church. Those who accept "separation" look for modes of Jewish observation, old or new, within the Jewish fold. What perplexes the modern Jew is the lack of authority for a specific manner of Jewish observance. Granting

Herberg's interpretation of religious observation as "the *acting out* of one's religious convictions" as an affirmative decision "to take the way of the Torah," the modern Jew is still left in the dark as to "how" to *act out* or *live out* his decision. For the traditionalist (or fundamentalist) the specific way is prescribed in *halakha* as handed down in Talmudic-Rabbinic law. Some moderns, notably the Reconstructionists, have tried to turn *halakha* into *aggada*, that is, into folk-lore or folkways, which do not possess the binding character of prescribed law. Herberg wants to retain the binding force of *halakha* but he reduces it to an abstract principle on a supernatural plane. "Jewish ritual observance is *halakha*," he says. But "the special discipline to which the *halakha* subjects [the Jew] is the commandment of God involved in the election of Israel" (p. 298).

One may agree with Herberg that *halakha* is divine commandment though not in its particular detailed observances. However, Herberg, like other moderns, leaves the particular observances without binding force, except as they may be appropriated personally by each individual Jew as "*halakha*-for-me." "No man," he says, "can decide for another what he can or cannot make his own; each must decide for himself, in responsible recognition of the claim that the tradition of the Law has upon him, but for himself nevertheless" (p. 300). But such individual appropriation destroys the very nature of the law. "*Halakha*-for-me" actually becomes "*halakha*-by-me," which is not *halakha* at all. What makes a particular observance binding, according to Jewish tradition, is its legislative character. One may accept this as the human aspect of the divine commandment. Its force, however, is derived from the collective responsibility for the covenant, if you will, in which, as Herberg himself points out, the divine and human are in a "unique and inseparable combination" (p. 299). Once this responsibility is shifted from the collective to the individual, as Herberg proposes, the observance is no longer *halakha*. Particular observances are changeable; but in Jewish tradition they did not just change by themselves, as Herberg and other moderns maintain. They *were changed* by legislation or by interpretation of given laws. Change is needed now too. The responsibility for it rests with an authoritative collective body. Then the modern Jew will welcome it.

Judaism and Modern Man is a profound study of the religious problems that perplex mankind, particularly the Jew, of today.

Herberg's style is clear and precise. He maintains throughout the book an inspired, reverent tone. He does not present so much a rational argument, as he affirms the faith of his people as he sees it reflected in traditional writings, ancient as well as modern. His illustrations are always apt and very illuminating. His copious references to Talmudic-Rabbinic sources are a good reminder to Jews and non-Jews alike, that the living fountain of Judaism was not sealed off with the close of the Bilblical Canon, but that it has continued to well up as a creative force throughout the ages, to our day.

1952

Max Scheler's Metaphysical Anthropology

The Kantian Problem of Man's Limits

A critical investigation of reason led Kant to the discovery of two main human faculties, one of pure understanding and the other of pure reason. The categories of the first are concepts that the understanding uses to construct objects of experience; those of the second are principles which reason uses to form ideas. As for the latter, insofar as we can at all have concepts of them, they come under the three conceptual categories of relation. But while the ideas find a necessary anchor in human reason for the construction of a moral order, there is nothing in reason that will lead man to the idea of God, such as is taught by revealed religion. Man's place in the realm of Kant's ideas is doubly inadequate to satisfy the human desire for completion in the world of experience or beyond it. First, the ideas do not correspond to any real thing; they are only unifying *schema* of relation. This is particularly discomforting to man who wants to see himself as a unity or soul in reality. Second, as relation, the ideas do not establish a connection between man and the living God, either through the idea of a soul, a cosmos, or even of the God-idea itself, which is at best only deistic.[1]

---

1. Cf. Kant, *Kritik der reinen Vernunft*. Kritik aller spekulativen Theologie, B708. "So ist der transzendentale . . . Begriff, den uns die bloss spekulative Vernunft von Gott gibt, im

160

Among those who have continued to probe into the recesses of the human being, Max Scheler is one who proposes to find another faculty in man, besides the capacity of relation, which will account for the idea of the absolute in reality. His method is that of philosophical anthropology, which he extends into a "critical metaphysic," beyond the confines set by Kant. He accepts the latter's dictum on the limitations of the natural sciences, namely, that they cannot reach beyond the bounds of their empirical domain, but argues, contrary to Kant, that this limitation does not prevent man from knowing the beyond; we only need to know *what* we are looking for, *where* it may be found, and *how* we can know it.[2] Furthermore, Scheler, like Kant, investigates the human knowing capacities and finds that the understanding is the faculty of constructing concepts of things, and that reason is the faculty of forming ideas. But unlike Kant he maintains that, when properly used, the understanding too can know ideas as they are in themselves. He contends that Kant and his predecessors, Hume and the others, did not go far enough in their investigation of the human faculties.

Scheler proposes a philosophical anthropology that seeks in man not only his specific humanum, as distinguished from the beast, but also the reflection of what lies beyond that specific, namely, the absolute. This, he says, calls for "a free philosophical investigation of the absolute, [which] is possible not only because metaphysics is always actual, [but also because] man very well possesses the appropriate cognitive means . . . of knowing the ground of all things."[3] And although he deviates from the "critical school," he wants to build a "critical metaphysic" of his own that will answer the question "How is the knowledge of the absolute a priori possible?"[4] His task in philosophical anthropology is to find in man the a priori conditions of a knowledge of the absolute, which lie beyond man himself as a living being; and he significantly designates his world-view as a "metanthropolgy."[5] He views man

genauesten Verstande *deistisch.*" (Thus the transcendental . . . concept which mere speculative reason gives us of God is, strictly understood, *deistic.*)

2. Max Scheler, *Philosophische Weltanschauung* (Bonn 1929), p. 9. "Weder kann ein echtes Wesen selbst, noch kann das Dasein von etwas echten Wesens jemals durch die positive Wissenschaft erklärt und verständlich gemacht werden." (Neither a genuine being itself nor the existence of any genuine being can ever be explained or made understandable through positive science.)

3. Ibid., p. 3.

4. See ibid., p. 8.

5. Ibid., p. 12.

as a *microcosmos* and a *microtheos* and hopes to derive from him
the essences of both the world and God. But man is steeped in
everyday experiences of controlling his environment of spatio-
temporal sense-perception. How can he divest himself of this and
rise to a knowledge of the absolute, which lies outside that
experience? For that Scheler establishes what he calls "action-
metaphysics."[6] Metanthropology and action-metaphysics thus
constitute a closed system so that the one is unthinkable without
the other, the first corresponding to Kant's theoretical reason and
the second to his practical reason.

A Metaphysical Anthropos

Like Kant, then, Scheler also sees a boundary between the world
of perceptual experience and the world of things-in-themselves,
but the character of this boundary is not the same as for Kant.
Scheler's boundary consists of conceptual essences, which have a
real (not illusory) double application: on the inner side of the
boundary (that is, for the positive sciences) they set limits to the
highest presuppositions of the sundry fields of scientific research,
and on the outer side (that is, for metaphysics) they are the
openings into the absolute.[7] In order that the concepts may account
for all types of being on both sides of the boundary, Scheler
proposes to discover a *what* or essence of being (*Wassein*) that
would serve as ground for all of them. That, he says, is the "highest
goal of the philosophical formation of all metaphysical world-
views: to think and perceive the absolute self-being so that . . . it
corresponds and conforms to the essential structure of the world
(*Wesensstruktur*) as discovered in 'first philosophy' [of concepts];
to the evolving real existence of the world (*Dasein*), which is
accessible to us in its resistance to our striving; and to the
contingent, particular things as such (*Sosein*)."[8] That is, he
proposes to find the kind of self-being that will show itself in the
essential structure of the world, in the real existents as well as in
the particular things of experience. What is the essence of this self-
being and *where* can we find it? Scheler says we can find that
essence in man and draw conclusions from it to its existence
outside man. This is the undertaking of his philosophical

6. Ibid.
7. Ibid., p. 8.
8. Ibid., p. 9.

anthropology whereby he seeks to establish a metanthropology. The essence of absolute being, which is meta-anthropological (beyond man), can be inferred from the essence which is anthropological (in man). The means that Scheler uses in drawing such a conclusion is "philosophical," and it appears that it is derived from his ontology rather than his anthropology. That is, his starting point is not man as a certain kind of being, which may be characterized as man specifically, but a philosophy or what he calls "first philosophy" of being as such.[9] His metaphysics thus becomes a metanthropology (beyond man) because he starts not *with* man but *beyond* him, and he only tries to locate the beyond in man as the only place where it may manifest itself. But this man is a metaphysical Anthropos to start with.

Passing through the Bounds of Nature

Scheler faces the same problem as Kant did, to relate the world of nature to the world of the things-in-themselves by setting a boundary between them and constructing two sets of metaphysical realities. He sets up a realm of the positive sciences of life, matter, etc., which he calls "the metaphysics of the first order," and a realm of the absolute which he calls the "metaphysics of the second order."[10] He also follows the Kantian method of passing from one realm to the other by means of drawing conclusions from the first (given) to the second (which must be). But Kant showed that drawing conclusions from natural science, which is based on man's experience, to the objective existence of things-in-themselves, which we cannot experience, involves us in insurmountable contradictions, and that a metaphysics built on such conclusions is just an illusion. The Scheler agrees; but that is not exactly his method. His conclusions stem from a different source, not directly from the given of scientific nature. Between the realms of positive science and the absolute he introduces a third sphere, his philosophical anthropology; and he now proposes to draw conclusions to the essence of the absolute not from cosmology (natural science) but from anthropology (man).[11] We shall see later whether this intermediary sphere enables our philosopher to

9. Cf. ibid., p. 10. He calls 'first philosophy' "the ontology of the essence," "Wesensontologie" of the world and the self.
10. Ibid., p. 10.
11. Ibid., p. 11.

pass through the bounds of nature to the absolute. What we are concerned about now is, where did he get the idea of an absolute being to begin with? Since he does not accept it on faith, as the theists, for example, do, how does he arrive at the existence of such a being, regardless of its essence? This is the critical question of his "critical metaphysics." Acutally he does not derive the idea of an absolute from anthropology but from his own philosophy. Before he ever reaches man as an actual living entity, he goes to the fountain of reason from which he draws some fundamental verities that lead him to the notion of absolute being. Unlike Kant, who arrives at the idea of an unconditioned realm as a necessary bound to the conditioned things of experience because the latter cannot set their own bounds, Scheler seeks the idea of an absolute in reason itself, in first principles, without regard to the conditioned world. He thus reverts to the old ontological metaphysics, despite Kant's interdict against it.

Logical Foundation of Scheler's Metaphysics

Scheler starts with three "insights" of reason, which, he asserts, are evident and need no proof. Their order, he says, is basic, and it is with this problem of the *"order of the most fundamental evidences"* that all philosophy begins.[12] (1) The first and most immediate evidence is the insight that there can not be nothing (*dass nicht Nichts sei*). (2) The second evidence is the insight that there is an absolute being (*dass ein absolut Seiendes ist*), on which every relative being depends for its being. (3) The third evidence is the insight that every possible being necessarily possesses an essence or a what (*Wassein*) and an existence (*Dasein*), regardless of what it may be, or of the sphere of being to which it may belong.[13] These three insights constitute the foundation of Scheler's metaphysics; in their logical evidence they resemble very closely Kant's threefold category of relation: substance, dependence, and reciprocity.

Scheler's first insight, which is his most fundamental and immediate one and not derived from any other insight, is nothing but the logical law of contradiction. That "there can not be nothing" is the same as "there can not be not-being." Stated in its

---

12. Max Scheler, *Vom Ewigen im Menschen*. 4. durchgesehene Auflage (Bern, 1954). Vom Wesen der Philosophie, p. 93.
13. Ibid., pp. 93-96.

positive content, it means, there cannot be not-a-thing in general, that is, not a substance of some kind, whatever its nature may *be*, whether of being-so or being-as-such, being-an-object or being-an-act, and the like, all of which are subordinate categories of being.[14] It is the same logical cornerstone which Aristotle laid at the foundation of his metaphyscial structure, namely, the "principle which every one must have who understands anything. . . that it is impossible for anything at the same time to be and not to be. . . . [No principle] is more self-evident than the present one."[15]

The other evident insight that there must be an absolute being, which Scheler places second in order, as it is founded on the first insight, is of the same character as the concept of dependence in Kant's second category of relation. By the law of the impossibility of infinite regress, we must accept the proposition that dependence of one being on another, whether one-sided or reciprocal, must find its ultimate in an absolute, independent being.[16] It is virtually through this second insight that Scheler posits the absolute in man. In the first insight there are two elements "being" and "nothing" (*Sein* and *Nichtsein*). While the first element may be either relative or absolute, the second can be only relative. Now in the things of our everyday experience, which are relative beings, we apprehend not only being but also relative not-being, for they may be and not-be. As long as we look at things this way, we do not fall into the snare of absolutization, and thus do not regard all of reality as relativistic. For the Relativist is one who overlooks the not-being which is alongside "relative being" and identifies the latter with the absolute, without his realizing the delusion. (While he calls all things in experience relative beings he actually views them as interrelated absolutes without end.) But, Scheler argues, if we can take the attitude to this philosophical insight that there can be only being and not nothing as such (*überhaupt*), we will find that we ourselves are not not" (*dass wir selber nicht nicht sind*), that is, we possess real absoluteness.[17]

In the third insight, which follows the other two evidences, Scheler ascribes certain properties to essence or the what-content,

---

14. Ibid., p. 93. "Die eminente Positivität des Inhalts der Einsicht [ist] dass überhaupt Etwas ist und nicht lieber Nichts." (The eminent positive content of insight [is] that in general there is something and not just nothing.)
15. Cf. Aristotle, *Met.* 1005b-1006a.
16. Cf. Scheler, *op. cit.,* p. 94.
17. Ibid., p. 96.

which differentiate it basically from all knowledge of contingent existence. First, the insight of essence is closed (*abgeschlossen*), that is it cannot be extended or diminished, and as such is strictly *evident*, whereas contingent existence has only hypothetical evidence, which may be changed by further experience. Second, it is an *insight* and is valid (in the form of a judgment) a priori for all possible existence of the same essence, whether known or unknown to us at the moment. "To this extent, all true a priori is a priori of essence." Third, as pure insight of essence, it is contained in all of its forms from the most fictitious to actually existing objects.[18] It is especially this last property which enables our philosopher to find the *what* of a ground such that will meet his "highest goal . . . of all metaphysical world-views: to think and perceive absolute self-being so that . . . it corresponds and conforms to the essential structure of the world."[19] By setting an ontological distinction between essence and existence, Scheler finds the source of his absolute in a being which *is* in itself, without any limiting determination. This, he says, is not a matter of *conclusion (eines Schlusses)* but of "immediate intuitive insight."[20] Indeed, the absolute itself demands such a source for its existence; or, its existence is derived from its very esence, by the three properties of essence noted above.

Despite Scheler's contention that this is an insight and not a matter of conclusion, his argument for an absolute existent betrays faulty reasoning. The absolute being, which, he says, "by its concept cannot be determined by any other possible being, can also *not* be contingent in its existence; its existence, moreover, must be so determined that it follows exclusively out of its own essence (whatever it may be)."[21] If essence and existence are separable elements of being (which Scheler postulates for all being in general), then the above line of reasoning is what Kant would call a paralogism or a conclusion of a *quaternio terminorum*.[22]

18. Ibid., pp. 97-98.
19. Ibid., p. 38.
20. Ibid., p. 95.
21. Ibid., p. 98. Das absolute Sein, "da es seinem Begriffe nach in seinem Sein überhaupt von keinem anderen möglichen Sein abhängig, auch dem Dasin nach *nicht* zufällig sein kann, sein Dasein vielmehr so beschlossen sein muss dass es aus einem Wesen (welch immer dies sei) selbst und ausschliesslich notwending folge."
22. Ibid., p. 97. "Fur jedes mogliche Sein überhaupt gultige Scheinbarkeit von *Wesen* und *Dasein*." (The separability of essence and existence is valid for all possible being as such.) In sylogistic form the reasoning is: 1. An absolute being is a being (in essence) that is not determined by any other possible being. 2. A being (in existence) that is not determined by

The middle term — a being "which cannot be determined by any other possible being" — is used here in two senses. In the major premise it means "not determined" in essence (logically, by definition); in the minor premise it stands for "not determined" in existence (really). We cannot therefore conclude that absolute being can *not* have contingent existence, not so long as its determination hinges on essence as distinguished from existence. If, on the other hand, essence and existence are not separable (as Scheler postulates for the absolute),[23] then the above reasoning is a tautology. The non-contingent existence of the absolute is already implied in the particular concept of its essence.

This is the conceptual foundation with its logical scaffold that serves Scheler for the construction of his metaphysical universe. It is the philosophical phase of his "philosophical anthropology" which, he maintains, it structured out of "immediate intuitive insights" into absolute being. Actually, however, all his three evidences are axioms ot logical thought founded on the law of contradiction (the first insight) and its duality of being and not-being. In the realm of experience contradiction is inevitable, because all things are relative, being as well as not-being, and the two must go together to maintain the relative validity of our scientific knowledge. But in the realm of the absolute only being as such, not not-being, may be thought; for there cannot be absolute nothing. Those who claim there is no absolute only transform the notion of relative being into an absolute concept by omitting the relative not-being from the empirical objects. They absolutize the relative. The last insight of "essence" and "existence" follows the first two, if we look at being and at the absolute *essentially*.[24] In the world of experience, these two elements are separated and require different cognitive processes in establishing their evidence, validity, and attainability.[25] But in the case of absolute being,

any other possible being cannot have contingent existence. 3. Absolute being (in essence) cannot have contingent existence. The *quaternum terminorum* of this reasoning is obvious.

23. Ibid., p. 98.

24. Ibid., p. 96. "Die *dritte* Einsicht, die in der 'Ordnung der Evidenz' folgt, d.h. so folgt,' dass wir unter den Gliedern dieser Ordnung das je vorhergehende, je schon wesensmässig einsahen." (The third insight, which follows in the 'order of evidence,' that is 'follows' so that we have already had essential insight into that which precedes under the members of this order.)

25. Ibid., p. 97.

"essence" and "existence" coalesce into one,[26] so that when they are separated in relative cognition the existence *follows* from the essence. The knowledge of the absolute being is thus a cognition of essence, which also establishes its existence. How does one attain the essence of that being?

Two Primary Attributes of Being

Having established the philosophical base for his "philosophical anthropology." Scheler proceeds to its anthropology, from which he seeks to derive the *essence* of being as such, and then to apply it also to the absolute ground of *all* being or the world-ground. His method of application he designates as the "transcendental manner of conclusion" (*die 'transzendentale Schlussweise'*).[27] But Scheler can find in anthropology only what he has already posited in the philosophical phase, which is the background of his search for man's essence. In his philosophical world-view he has already separated the realm of sensible experience from that of super-sensible reality of values and ideas by a boundary which the positive sciences of nature cannot bridge. It is best for those sciences, he says, to exclude questions of essence from their province. "The essential structure as well as the existence of the world must be reduced, in the final instance, to the absolute being, that is to the common primary ground of the world and the human self."[28] In that ground or absolute being he distinguishes two fundamental attributes (*Grundattribute*) one, an endless *spirit*, which releases from itself a Reason capable of forming ideas and values that are common to the essential structure of both the world and man; and the other, an irrational *drive*, a dynmic force of organic nature, which establishes irrational existence (*Dasein*) and contingent being (*Sosein*, die 'Bilder') of individuals and of all kinds of life appearance.[29] When Scheler now returns to man to look for his specific *humanum* that singles him out of all other creatures, he finds it to be none other than the spiritual attribute of the absolute ground, which manifests itself in him as Person. The specific character of spirit is the "act of ideation," and its spatial nature, as it reveals itself in man, is the human capacity to

---

26. Ibid., p. 98. "Da-Sein und Wesen fallen im absoluten Sein in eins zusammen." (Existence and essence fall together in absolute being into one.)
27. See *Philosophische Weltanschauung*, p. 11.
28. Ibid., p. 9.
29. Ibid.

differentiate essence from existence and constantly to form out of the essence ideas, values, thoughts, perceptions, love.[30] This is the capacity of pure spirit, also called Reason, which makes man specifically human. Scheler thus merges the two Kantian faculties of "pure understanding" and "pure reason" into a single idea-forming faculty of "pure spirit." By means of his "transcendental conclusion" he then passes back from the spirit in man to spirit as an attribute of absolute being. Contrary to Kant's admonition that reason cannot have the things-in-themselves or the ideas as objects of thought, Scheler maintains that that is exactly what the spirit *can* have. Man alone, in so far as he is Person, that is the manifest spirit, can transcend himself as a concentrated being, a "center," and thus have everything beyond the spatio-temporal world, including himself, as an object of cognition.[31] Yet this "center" from which man fulfills the acts of objectification cannot be part of the sensible world at any definite place or time; it can have its locus only in the highest ground of being. "Thus man is the essence which transcends himself and the world."[32]

Relation between the Two Primary Attributes

Scheler now has to establish the relationship between the *spirit* and the other primary attribute of the ground, the *drive*. He conceives of the first as a static principle and the second as dynamic. This distinction, it must be noted, falls back on Kant's third category of relation, which is that of reciprocity between the active and the passive.[33] The spirit has no power, force, or activity whatsoever. All these are functions of the drive. Spirit is the passive attribute of the ground and drive is the active one, and they stand in correlation to each other within the ground. The specific

30. Cf. Scheler, "Die Sonderstellung des Menschen," *Mensch und Erde* (Darmstadt 1927), pp. 206-207. This will be referred to below as "sonderstellung."
31. Ibid., p. 202.
32. Ibid., p. 203.
33. Cf. *Kritik d.r. V.* Transzendentale Analytik, 1.3, paragraphs 10-11, Tafel der Kategorien. The third category of relation according to concept is "Wechselwirkung zwischen dem Handelnden und Leidenden" (B106). It should be pointed out that Kant designates "relation" and "modality" as *dynamic* categories, which are directed toward the *existence* of objects of the first two sets of categories, "quantity" and "quality," which he calls mathematical. Another important observation made by Kant entails a disjunctive judgment, that is one in which the parts of a whole are *coordinated* and not subordinated to one another (B112). We shall see shortly that Scheler follows the same order, as he places the 'spirit' and the 'drive,' or man and the world, in coordination to each other within the same ground.

function of the spirit is the act of ideation and the positing of its
ideas and values before the life-producing drive, so that they may
influence the latter toward spiritualization, that is the unification
(or fusion) of the spirit with the drive. Absolute being is in itself not
an actuality but in the process of becoming, effectuated by the
drive as it fuses with the ideas and values of the spirit. The spirit, as
the passive correlate, can do nothing but constantly form and
present ideas and values and guide the drive toward their
realization. This process of eternal becoming, Scheler holds,
exemplifies itself most clearly in human history.[34] Man, insofar as
he is the only creature in whom the spirit is manifest as Person, is
the only living being in whom the self-realization of the ground
takes place. What is the place of God in this process?

Scheler's position in the last stages of his philosophical
development is anti-theistic. His idea of God is that of deity, a
godhood or *deitas*, which is just another name for the primary
spirit, as the passive attribute of the world-ground.[35] The ground
itself must engage the world-creative drive in order to realize the
deity, for the latter has no power of its own to set itself in motion.
That is, the ground realizes its spiritual essence through the active
world process in time and it thus becomes the being-thought-itself
and may then be called a divine existence. This is effected through
the history of man. "The 'being' through itself, in Scheler writes,
"will be a being that may be worthy to be called a being of divine
existence, only to the extent that it realizes the eternal *Deitas* in the
striving of world history in man and through man."[36] Contrary to
the theists, Scheler maintains that God is not the starting-point of
the self-realization of finite being (man and the world) but its
fulfillment. Man can strive for it through self-abnegation (an
asceticism of worldly experiences though not a negation of life but
rather its sublimation), and that is his hope for salvation.

34. *Philosopsche Weltanschauung*, p. 10.
35. "Sonderstellung," p. 225. "Nennen wir das geistige Attribut im obersten Grunde alles
endlichen Seins 'deitas,' so kommt ihr, kommt dem, was wir den Geist und die Gott-heit in
diesem Grunde nennen, keinerlei positive schöpferische Macht zu." (If we name the
spiritual attribute in the supreme ground of all finite being 'deitas,' then what we call spirit
and God-hood in this ground does not imply any positive creative power.) Cf. ibid., p. 251.
"Weil wir die theistische Voraussetzung leugnen — 'eines geistigen, in seiner Geistigkeit
allmächtigen persönlichen Gott.' " (For we deny the theistic presupposition of a spiritual
personal God who is all-powerful in his spirituality.')
36. Ibid., p. 226. See also ibid., p. 251. "Dass dieser Grund . . . sich im Menschen selbst
unmittelbar erfasst und verwirklicht." (That this ground . . . comprehends and realizes itself
immediately in man himself.)

In brief, Scheler's metaphysical anthropology teaches a doctrine of salvation through a modified incarnation of God (or rather Godhood) in man. The absolute ground is not itself God, but one of its attributes is godhood (*deitas*), which is spirit transcending all life. This spirit manifests itself in man as Person, whose specific faculty is to form ideas and values. It stands in essential contrast to life (*Gegensatz von Leben und Geist*), but the two are interralated as principles of passion and action (*Leiden und Wirken*). The function of the spirit is to influence the life-giving drive to overcome this contrast by guiding it toward fusion with the ideas and values and thus spiritualizing it. But the active principle here is the elemental drive not the spirit, which is altogether powerless. The latter can only watch over the daemonic drive, place the values and ideas before it so that it may fuse with them as it rushes on turbulently and aimlessly. To the extent that this spiritualization of life takes place, the godhood is realized and becomes God, or man realizes God in himself, and that is his salvation.[37] In the ultimate course of time, the godhood will thus (through human history) be realized in the world-ground, which is striving to make itself the being that may truly be called "divine existence."[38]

Scheler's conceptual metaphysics, like every closed conceptual structure, has a built-in dynamic circularity. In trying to combine being and becoming in one closed system, it posits a passive and active principle in one ground. This ground, however, is conceived as prior (*vorher*) to its separation into essence and existence. It is then man's special human faculty that is able to cognize such a separation, and since this faculty is of an ontic character, it stems

37. Cf. "Sonderstellung," pp. 252-53. "Von vornherein also ist nach unserer Anschauung die Mensch- und die Gottwerdung gegenseitig aufeinander angewiesen . . . .Geist und Drang . . .sind . . .in sich nicht fertig: sie wachsen an sich selbst eben in diesen ihren Manifestationen in der Geschichte des menschlichen Geistes und in der Evolution des Lebens der Welt." (From the start, according to our view man-becoming and God-becoming depend on each other reciprocally . . . . Spirit and drive . . . are . . . not finished by themselves: they grow of themselves in their very manifestations of the history of the human spirit and in the evolution of the life of the world.)

38. Scheler's principle of 'spirit' is a sort of Aristotle's *hypokeinenon* in reverse. It is like a substratum which never becomes an object but objectifies ("der selber nie gegenständlich werdende, aber vergegenständlichende Geist') It is itself indeterminate but determines ('die höhere Seinsform determiniert'). In Aristotle's metaphysics this is the role of the material cause, which is passive, while the formal or 'spiritual' cause is the active one. Scheler reverses the order. Cf. Aristotle, *Met.* 983a, and VII,3. Cf. Scheler, "Sonderstellung," p. 211f., on the contrast between his concept of spirit and the Greek classical theory'; also. pp. 221, 237.

from the absolute ground itself. This, in the final analysis, is man's
a priori knowledge of the ground and of its dual attributes. The
process of realization moves from the bifurcation of the absolute
being into an active and passive principle, back into a fusion of
these principles through man, and ultimately, again through man,
into the original oneness of the absolute. If we now ask, with Kant,
"What may man hope for" in this process of realization? Scheler
can only suggest that man's hope is not in the absolute being but in
the becoming of godhood into a God.[39]

1974

39. Cf. "Sonderstellung," pp. 253-54. "Sur Stützung des Menschen . . . ist das Absolute
Sein nicht da. Wohl gibt es auch für uns eine 'Stützung'; . . . auf das gesamte Werk der
Wertverwirklichung der bisherigen Weltgeschichte, so weit es das Werden der 'Gottheit' zu
einem 'Gott' bereits gefördert hat." (The Absolute Being is not there for the support of man.
However, there is a 'support' for us . . . in the entire work of realization of value in world
history to date, insofar as it has already advanced the becoming of 'godhood' into a 'God.')
For the sources of these ideas in Heraclitus's *Logos* and in Hegel's *Spirit*, see my *Greek
Mode of Thought in Western Philosophy*,. chs. 7 and 42.

Kant's Moral Problem of Freedom

Kant introduced a new type of philosophizing man in the
modern world and that is the philosopher-scientist, as distinguished
from the philosopher-king in the world of Plato and the
philosopher-saint in medieval times. As philosopher-scientist,
then, Kant bequeathed to us two counterproductive legacies: one
the primacy of the moral law over theoretical reason, and the other,
the absolutization of individual man.

When we speak of Kant as having wrought a Copernican
Revoltion in modern thought or, as he conceived it, in the thinking
of the Age of Enlightenment, we mean to say that he inaugurated
the philosophical-scientific view of man as the center of universal
reason around which the world turns. This view then became
pregnant with a multitude of problems that man still faces in our
own time. To be sure, the scientific factor was already dominant in
the minds of Kant's predecessors, notably, Descartes, Locke, and
Leibniz, but it was the Critical Philosopher who first established its
principles on a philosophical basis and, what is more important,
gave it moral justification. As is well known, in his *Critique of Pure*

172

Reason he uncovered the philosophical ground of Newton's science of physics, and in his *Critique of Practical Reason* and his other writings on morals he laid the foundations for a science of ethics or, as Karl Vorlander observed, he "became the Newton of ethics."[1]

The paramount issue of the Age of Enlightenment, of which Kant was both a product and a guiding light, was the problem of individual freedom against the encroachments of organized society. To resolve this issue, the social philosophers of the time adopted the method of logical analysis (Galilei's method of "resolutivo" and "compositivo") whereby they searched for man's nature for certain drives for freedom that could also serve as ground for a new society in which the individual would be reconciled with his social order. They looked for elements of freedom in individual man that would at the same time become the basic entities of his social structure. This method gave rise to the logic of individualism which has governed our social thinking to this day.[2]

The method of logical analysis dissolves a thing into separate parts and tries to compose them into a new totality. But it often happens that the sundered parts assume an independent existence and refuse to subordinate themselves to the whole, that is, they make an existential claim against it when they are pressed into it. This is the paradox of the logic of individualism: when individuals are conceived as independent entities, they cannot be unified into a social whole without being subordinated to it, that is without losing their independence. The new method then tried to find in the make-up of individuals such patterns or laws that would of their own accord unite themselves into a social structure. But this did not obviate the logical paradox of individual freedom which stands in conflict with the social principle. Logically, the two are irreconcilable, and to this day we still stand in the shadow of this paradox. Galilei's method may have worked here in its "resolutivo" or analysis, but fell far short in its "compositivo" or synthesis.

When Kant looked into this scientific problem in general, he noticed that the promoters of the new method posited the synthetic

---

1. *Kritik der praktischen Vernunft.* Einleitung von Karl Vorländer, p. xli. References to Kant's works are in the edition of the Philosophische Bibliothek, Verlag von Felix Meiner in Hamburg. Pages are given according to the original edition as listed in the margins. All translations from the German are my own.
2. Cf. *Ernst Cassirer, Die Philosophie der Aufklärung.* Tübingen 1932, pp. 339ff.

force in the elements which they derived from their analysis of the individual instead of seeing the latter as the synthetic factor to begin with, that is *a priori*. He then reformulated Galileo's principle of "compositivo" into his own famous question: "How are synthetic judgments a priori possible? in man's experience as such, and he spent his entire *Critique of Pure Reason* in establishing their possibility, function and limitations in theoretical and speculative reason. But at the end of his "Critique," in the discussion of "The Canon of Pure Reason," he came to a remarkably disquieting conclusion. Theoretical reason, he said, may establish a science of nature according to universal and necessary laws of causality, but if it tries to build a self-contained system of a world-order, such an order can be only of a speculative character. That is, as Kant emphasizes repeatedly, science of nature or theoretical reason has only negative value as "a discipline for the limitations of its domain" in the experience of phenomena. But in the world of reality as a whole it gives no certainty, as it can only tell man where not to go but cannot help him find his way to regions where he wants and strives to go. Yet man continues to explore those regions — the ideas of a Supreme Being, a soul, and freedom — and demands that philosophy provide him as much scientific certainty about those ideas as it claims for the natural sciences.

A Science of Ethics

It is in response to this demand that Kant developed his science of ethics as formulated in his three main works on this subject, in the *Groundwork of the Metaphysic of Morals,* the *Critique of Practical Reason,* and the *Metaphysic of Morals.* It should be noted that in each of these works he had set himself a different task. In the first he sought to ascertain whether there are principles or laws on which a science of ethics might be founded; in the second he investigated the human capacity to conceive such principles as operative in human experience; and in the third he proposed to construct these principles into a system or doctrine that would serve as a guideline or canon for their universal application. These are the areas of any scientific theory which a philosopher must investigate.

According to Kant, science is a doctrine of causal relations, and therefore, a science of morality, although identical with free will, must also have its necessary laws of causation. The difference between a science of nature and a science of morals lies in their respective sources of causality. In nature it comes from outside the thing, whereas in morality it emanates from within. A stone or animal always has some outside force determining its movement, but a free will moves of its own accord without any outside determination. Nevertheless, both must have laws which govern their direction. In the case of natural science, the law only says what takes place, but in moral science, which deals with willed action, the law tells the will what to do. The question now is: if the will is considered free, who sets the law commanding it to act one way rather than another? This depends on Kant's concept of free will.

We know from experience that we have a faculty of willing, but this faculty, says Kant, cannot be free under conditions of spatio-temporal determinations, that is, in the phenomenal world. Its freedom is possible only in the noumenal or intelligible world where it need not relate to the intuitions of space and time or generally to spatio-temporal experiences. Consequently, the categories of pure understanding which have jurisdiction only over spatio-temporal intuitions do not prevail in the intelligible world. There the sole legislator of the moral law is free will itself, which may form its own commandments autonomously and unconditionally. This act of the free will is designated by Kant as the "categorical imperative," indicating its universality and necessity as well as its non-hypothetical character. Now this issuing of an imperative by the will to itself may sound like a strange business. Why does it not just act as it ought to without going through the motion of telling itself how to act? Moreover, what certainty is there that by following an unconditional imperative from the noumenal world man will be able to act freely in a conditioned world of phenomenal everyday life? In truth, Kant does not hold out much promise for real freedom in the world of phenomena. But even in the world of noumena he can guarantee it only if there is a Supreme Being who rules both worlds and if the human soul is immortal so that its freedom may be attained in the fulness of infinite time. God's existence and the soul's immortality are postulated by Kant alongside his categorical imperative. "For," as he says, "when morality commands that we *ought* now to become better men, it follows that we must be *able* to be better men."[3]

3. *Religion Within the Limits of Reason Alone.* Harper Torchbooks 1960, p. 46.

However, the goal is so far away and the demand on man's limited power is so great that without the aid of God and his promise of eternal life man cannot hope to attain his freedom.

Here Kant's system of morality reaches its culmination in a law issuing from supersensible reality and grounded in speculative ideas of God and immortality. Man is supposed to receive the message from the intelligible domain through the categorical imperative. However, the messenger fails to reach him in everyday life. The obstacle is created by Kant's transcendental logical individualism, which counteracts the moral principle.. The main weakness of the categorical imperative is not so much that it comes from another world as that it has been implanted in man as an individual, autonomous lawmaker. This imperative is each man's self-directed will. There is no social imperative to direct him with equal categorical determination. Kant's imperative tells man individually to will to act in such a manner that the same may be willed by everyone else, and that if everyone willed in the same manner all of them would attain their freedom. This "if" turns the categorical into a hypothetical imperative. For if all others, or a good many others, do not will to act according to this law, the universal condition is not met and therefore no one can attain freedom. This situation is due to the fact that the categorical imperative is tied to a maxim whose origin and final determination are outside the intelligible world where the moral law has its sway. In his everyday life, man may set himself any code of behavior according to his desires and goals he is striving to realize, as for example, to pursue a career, to amass wealth, or to attain social status. Such a code becomes his maxim which guides him in his daily activities. What the categorical imperative then tells him is that before applying his maxim to a given situation he must ask himself whether it can become a universal law applicable to and by everyone under all conditions. As Kant formulates it, "I ought never *to act* except in such a way that I can *also will* that my maxim should become a universal law."[4] Evidently, the command "to act" and "also will" implies two wills. One tends to act according to the rules of its own maxim, while the other warns it not to act unless the maxim may be converted into a universal rule. Since both wills are in man, they actually represent two aspects of one

4. *Grundlegung zur Metaaphysik der Sitten.* 402.

human will, one acting as the commanding subject and the other as the obeying object. Kant accomplishes this bifurcation of the will by placing it simultaneously in two different worlds, one noumenal and the other phenomenal. In the first world the will acts freely by its very nature as a free existent, but in the second it is encumbered by spatio-temporal limitations. To free itself of these encumbrances, the will in the phenomneal world must obey the inner law of the will in the noumenal world and act in conformity with it.

Now while the moral law comes from the noumenal world, the maxim which man follow, as said, does not come from that world. Nor is it set in the phenomenal world as a necessary rule; for if this were so, man would have to follow this rule necessarily and could not submit to the categorical imperative. Furthermore, there are many maxims to choose from and one must have a criterion for choosing the right one. From the noumenal world man gets only the command to convert the maxim into a universal law but not guidance for choosing the right maxim so that it may lend itself to becoming universal. (Evidently, not all maxims are suitable for such conversion and are therefore to be discarded.) The criterion supplied by Kant does not come from his moral law as such, but rather from his formulation of the ethical principle of human worth, which reads: "In all creation, everything that one may want or have in one's power can also be used *as a means only*; man alone and with him every rational creature is an end in himself."[5] The same principle, stated by Kant as "practical imperative," says: "*Act in such a way that you treat the humanity in your own person as well as in the person of any other, never just as a means, but always at the same time as an end.*"[6] The two wills implied in the categorical imperative thus assume two distinct forms, one as a *moral law* and the other as an *ethical ground*, and by placing each in a separate world Kant has created an "unbridgeable gap" between morality and ethics.

5. *Kritik der praktischen Vernunft* 155-56.
6. *Grundlegung zur Metaphysik der Sitten*, 429. The four illustrations of this imperative have the same examples as in the illustrations of the universal law, earlier, 421f. Cf. Hermann Cohen, *Ethik des reinen Willens* (Berlin 1921), p. 321, on three meanings of the Categorical Imperative. The idea of humanity is the content of the categorical imperative. Cf. Karl Vorländer, *Kant und Marx* (Tübingen 1926), p. 119. "It has been forgotten that in the second formulation of his categorical imperative Kant declared its content to be the idea of humanity."

Morality and Ethics

Kant himself does not draw this distinction directly, but we are justified in inferring it from the distinction he makes between *purposive* and *non-purposive* action. The first may be designated ethical and the second moral. Kant's fundamental principle of freedom, which he identifies with morality as such, has to do with action that is willed without purpose or end in view. When the action is directed toward an end or purpose it becomes an ethical principle. Ethical action is in the phenomenal world of becoming; "the moral law itself" issues from "an intelligible world through the realization of the concept of freedom."[7] That is, the principle of morality in found in man's state as he *is* — a rational will in a rational world where there is no discrepancy or contradiction between the two. The principle of ethics, on the other hand, is in man's action in relation to himself and to others in a phenomenal world where his will comes into conflict with his inner drives and outer spatio-temporal contingencies. Accordingly, morality has to do with man's being a free will, ethics with his becoming free under diversified conditions. Morality sees man as autonomous in

7. *Kritik der praktischen Vernunft* 168. Cf. *Metaphysik d. Sitten* 381 f. Cf. Jeffrie G. Murphy, "Kant's Concept of a Right Action," *The Monist*, 51:4 (1967), pp. 574-98. Murphy tries to find "a very useful distinction between *Ethik*, on the one hand, and *Sitten* or *Moralität*, on the other — between 'ethics' and 'morality' — in Kant's own statement in *Metaphysik der Sitten*, 379. But all Kant says there is that the name *Ethik* is now applied to those duties which are not subject to outside laws, called in German *Tugendlehre* (doctrine of virtue). Then he draws a distinction between this "Tugendlehre (*ethica*)" and "Rechtslehre (*jurisprudentia*)," the latter being subject to outside laws. Furthermore, Murphy's entire argument that Kant could not mean that "an action has no real worth unless performed from the proper purpose," and that for Kant "legaltiy and ethics — both . . . fall under morality" is, in my opinion, a misinterpretation of Kant's very idea of morality. Kant says that, if the motive of action is not free, the action itself is not free, meaning not moral. The only motive that can be designated as free is one which is self-set. Such a motive is the law of duty, and that makes the action moral. (Cf. *Grundlegung* 399. "The worth of character is moral, and without comparison the highest. . . . in that it does good, not from inclination but out of duty.") See also *Metaphysik der Sitten*, 214, where the distinction is drawn between *Legalität* and *Moralität* of action. In his differentiation between *maxim 1* and *maxim 2*, one without a motive and the other with a motive, Murphy fails to clear up the meaning of motive with reference to inner and outer action, on the one hand, and to inner and outer law, on the other. These terms are clarified in the German original. Kant distinguishes between *innere* and *aussere Handlung*, and also between *Handlung* and *Tat* (*Hanglung*) according to law). Cf. *Met. d. Sitten*, 220, 230, 386 (*Tat* as act). 399, (relation of *Handlung* to law of duty in becoming a *Tat*), 227, and 438 (judging whether a *Handlung* is a *Tat* according to law). Kant's emphasis is not on "legality" but on "law." The difference is brought out in his *Grundlegung* in which he seeks to establish that will is governed by its own Laws (causes) in the science of ethics, on the analogy of *nature* which is governed by its own laws in the science of physics. He did not intend in that book to write a theory of ethics, a task which he fulfilled in his *Met. d. Sitten*,

himself; ethics leads him toward an end which is determined by a judgment of values as to what constitutes right and wrong in relation to others not only with reference to a given end but also concerning the manner of attaining it. In this repect, ethics acts on the basis of an ought. The moral will does not presuppose an end and sets no ought for itself, but for the other, the actualizing will. Morality expresses the nature of man in his pure rational state, as *is*, and commands ethical man to become a "better person," as Kant puts it, or to rise to the state of higher existence that he ought to be. In Kant's terminology, "this better person... insofar as it is a member of the intelligible world, . . . is conscious of posessing a good will which, on his own admission, constitutes the law for the bad will belonging to him as a member of the sensible world."[8] Yet, what is right and wrong is determined by the ethical principle inherent in the "practical imperative," not in the categorical one. This distinction between the moral *is* and the ethical *ought*, although not designated this way by Kant directly, is spelled out unmistakably in his summary of the two principles in his *Grundlegung der Metaphysik der Sitten.* "The moral ought," it says there, "is thus man's own necessary willing as a member of the intelligible world, and it is conceived by him as an ought only insofar as he considers himself at the same time a member of the sensible world."[9] Clearly, in the first world there is the higher "will as is" or as Kant calls it, "pure will" (*reiner Wille*), and in the second world there is the lower will (Willkür) directed by an ought coming from that same world. For, as pointed out above, the norm for choosing the right maxim as a possible candidate for the moral law, that is the actual decision as to what one ought to do, is not supplied by the intelligible world from which the pure will emanates, but rather by the ethical principle in phenomenal reality.

The significance of this gap between morality and ethics cannot be over estimated if we consider Kant's metaphysic of morals and the social structure he has founded on it. Like Rousseau, whom he admired greatly, Kant proposes to show how the individual may be free while being subjected to the laws governing society and

8. *Grundlegung zur Metaphysik der Sitten* 455.

9. Ibid., In general, Kant separated the "ought" from the "is" in nature and published a new "is" in the moral world, where the ought may exist without hinderance, or where actually there is no ought, for the "is" acts as it "ought to" by itself without an imperative.

mankind as a whole. Both stress the idea of *moral duty* as the basic principle of freedom, meaning duty without outside coercion. But what they are really trying to do is to resolve the paradox of free man's duty to obey others when his duty in freedom is to obey only himself. This is the paradox of the absolutization of the individual as final authority for setting his own laws and, by the same token, the laws of his social order. Rousseau tries to find a solution in a "social contract" whereby all individual wills are fused into a general will, which becomes the sovereign or supreme legislator. It is then the moral duty of every individual to obey the general will, because the latter contains all individual wills, and each individual is thus obeying only himself. This is a blatant fallacy of a paralogism or a double meaning of will.

Kant, as philosopher-scientist and as the more astute logician of the two, establishes the same principle of freedom through a general will not on Rousseau's ground of the empirical fusion of particular wills, but on the basis of an a priori universal law legislated by each will, the same being true of all rational wills; that is, all individual wills are legislators and obey their own individual legislation. In Kant's words, it is "the idea *of the will of every intelligible being as a will which is a universal lawgiver.*"[10] Freedom is thus derived neither from the phenomenal-sensible world nor from the noumenal one, but out of the intelligible being as lawgiver. It appears that, in order to avoid the gap between the two worlds, Kant took freedom out of both worlds and posited it entirely in the individual as an autonomous being who is independent of either one of them.[11] This is Kant's moral vindication of his logic of individualism. Its practical implication may be illustrated by contrasting his attitude toward the Prussian Kingdom, in which he lived, with the Greek Polis of Plato's *Republic.* Plato conjoined the king with the philosopher and thereby endowed the combined personage with a social imperative. But Kant did not put his trust in such a combination, for he claimed that the king would corrupt the philosopher. He therefore perferred

10. Ibid., 431.

11. Cf. Ernst Cassirer, "Die Freiheitslehre im System des kritischen Idealismus," in his *Freiheit und Form* (Berlin 1916), pp. 237-38, on the autonomly of will as legislator, not given in objective experience but presupposed as a condition of that experience. See further p. 239. Kant cannot deduce freedom and the moral law from the constitution of an "intelligible world," because freedom would then lose its autonomy. For Kant, therefore, "freedom does not follow from the intelligible being but it posits and establishes this being out of itself as a primary datum."

to let the latter obey the ruler so long as the ruler allowed him to "dare think" freely (*sapere aude*). To think but not to act freely; and the scientist-philosopher was compelled to abandon his practical (moral) superiority by relegating his active will to theoretical speculation. In this scheme of things, the only individual who may be regarded as free is the monarch.

1976

Observations On Hans Reichenbach's Ethical Imperative

As developed in his book *The Rise of Scientific Philosophy*, Hans Reichenbach's approach to ethics is quite positive, though in contrast to the ethics of the philosophers, notably that of Kant, who is also his target on general philosophical grounds. (Page references to the above mentioned book are in the Paper-bound edition of the University of California Press, 1963.)

1. Reichenbach rejects Kant's synthetic judgment a priori and establishes the science of physics on an empirical basis, following Hume's principle of "habit" of perception and causality as repetition (158-59), but forgetting Hume's other principle of "belief" which is not a perceptual experience, any more than are Kant's concepts of the understanding.

2. He views the science of physics, and all sciences, as an expression of cognitive statements of what *is* true in fact. Ethics, he holds, is expressed in terms of imperatives or directives ("he should"), which are neither true nor false, and hence does not constitute scientific knowledge. Therefore, he contends that to put ethics on a cognitive basis, parallel to the physical sciences, as Kant does in his ethico-cognitive parallelism, is untenable.

3. Imperatives ("should") are expressions of one person's will directed to an other that he would do as directed by the speaker. Imperatives are thus volitional "linguistic utterances" to influence the action of others. Reichenbach demonstrates this by a "grammatical analysis of the phrase 'he should,' which can be regarded as the grammatical form of a moral directive" (287-88).

181

But he also asserts that there is no "objective moral law from which the imperative is derivable" (188), and there is no obligation for anyone to accept the imperative if it is contrary to one's own will. Yet every one has a right not only to express but also to try to project his own will on others. The question then is, how can an imperative issuing from a subjective will become a course of action to be followed by others, which would make it morally valid?

4. Reichenbach distinguishes between what he calls "personal imperatives" (subjective), and "moral imperatives" (objective), the latter involving a "feeling of obligation" to accept the will of the speaker and to subordinate one's own will to it. (284-85) in that case one's own will becomes "secondary" to the obligation. But the feeling of obligation, Reichenbach argues, has its source in the social group to which one belongs and which has imposed it on its members in the form of oral precepts of the past. Generally, "the ethics of our social and political life is a conglomeration of group ethics of various strata" which have accumulated through the generations and have created a "muddle of moral rules of present-day society" (286-87). This muddle cannot be cleared up by a philosophical system of ethical principles, because "the feeling of moral obligation cannot be transformed into a source of the validity of ethics" (291). Our obligation to observe ethical rules is derived from a false notion that they are true laws of reason, which gives them a cognitive meaning, contrary to their volitional character; that destroys our sense of ethics altogether. To save the situation Reichenbach restores the moral imperative to its rightful place in the will of every individual. "Let us forget about the appeal to obligation," he admonishes us. "Let us stand on our own feet and trust our volitions . . . because they are our own volitions," not "secondary ones" subordinated to the will of an other or imposed by standard group morals from the past.

5. If this sounds like anarchy, Reichenbach says, he is not perplexed. On the contrary, he finds his ethical experiences in the political institutions grounded in a "democratic principle," which he formulates as follows: "Everybody is entitled to set up his own moral imperatives and to demand that everyone follow these imperatives" (295). The place to decide which of these imperatives is acceptable to the group is in the political entities of a democratic society. "Whoever wants to study ethics," he continues, "should not go to the philosopher; he should go to where moral issues are fought out," in the actual communal groupings and there learn to

"adjust oneself to group will" (297). "Open your ears to your own will, and try to unite your will with that of others" (302). "The friction between volitions is the propelling force of all ethical development" (301).

6. Now all the above admonitions are procedural steps toward a group decision as to which of the individual imperatives should be accepted for all its members to follow. But the mere acceptance of an imperative by a group does not make it moral. Here Reichenbach introduces two new elements, one that may pass as a criterion of moral validity, and the other to serve as a guide for the formation of a group will that would supersede all individual wills. The first is that the proponent of an imperative, though issuing from his own individual will, be ready to share in the directive which he demands of others to follow. That is, a personal commitment to abide by one's own imperative is a moral commitment, and if the others follow, their action is moral. Reichenbach calls this reference to the speaker "token-reflexive" (the imperative reflects on the speaker), and concludes: "The recognition that the phrase 'he should,' in its moral meaning, is a token-reflexive term is the indispensable basis of a scientific analysis of ethics" (290).

7. The second element is the transformation of moral issues into logical issues. That is done by discussing the "fundamental aims" that are entailed in the imperatives. This is obviously a cognitive process that, according to Reichenbach, may result in "a readjustment of our volitional attitudes." The logical discussion of our fundamental aims, which most of us have in common simply as members of the human species (299), together with the "group influence" in carrying on the discussion has the power to modify individual wills and bring them to an acceptance of the "group will." These two elements, the personal commitment of the proponent of an imperative and the cognitive discussion (not just a clash of wills) of its fundamental aim, mould a group will that renders the imperative moral.

8. Reichenbach adduces an example from jurisprudence on the question whether "a sentenced criminal should be put into a penitentiary." This, he says, is not "a moral issue" but a psychological question of a more fundamentals aim, namely, to adjust as many citizens as possible to society. If examined by psychological facts, this aim will convince us "that a criminal should not be punished, but should be put into an environment that

offers him possibilities of a readjustment." The logic of the argument and the influence of the group in the course of the discussion may modify the volitional attitude of those members who demand punishment of the criminal, and the "group will" may prevail. This, we may say, is the crucible in which ethical principles are formed and become acceptable by a given society.

Summary

(a) Ethics cannot be regarded as a science in the modern sense of scientific knowledge, because science is by nature *cognitive*, expressing the *truth* of a thing as it *is* in *fact*, whereas ethics expresses an *imperative* or directive issued by one person to another what *he should* or should not do.

(b) An analysis of the phrase "he should" shows that an imperative is a volitional "linguistic utterance" to influence others and is thus a "grammatical form" of a "moral directive," which is not derivable from any objective *moral law*.

(c) Imperatives may be *personal* (subjective) or *moral* (objective), the latter involving a feeling of *obligation*. But such a feeling comes from various traditionally ordained group morals imposed upon individuals through home, school, and church and resulting in a "muddle of moral rules of present-day society." The mere feeling of obligation cannot be transformed into valid ethics, because obligation stems from the false impression as if a "a law of reason" is behind it, of which there is none in moral imperatives. Morality has its source in the *will* of each individual.

(d) Moral issues are developed and decided through a *conflict of wills* in the political institutions of our democratic society, in which a "group will" is formed, overriding all individual wills.

(e) An individual imperative is considered moral if the speaker directing his will for all others to follow also includes himself in the action he demands of others. This is the token-reflective criterion of moral imperatives.

(f) As an aid in the process of deciding which moral imperative is to be accepted by the group, a moral issue may be transformed into a logical issue of fundamental aims (a cognitive process) that are entailed in the imperative. The cognitive discussion of such aims, which are generally common to all individuals of a given society (or to mankind as a whole), combined with the group will resulting from such discussion, may influence the members to readjust their individual wills and make common cause with the group will.

Critical Notes on Reichenbach's View of the Science of Truth and the Nature of Ethics

(a) A science of truth is not a priori

Reichenbah's empirical view that truth lies in verified facts is a contradiction in terms. Facts in themselves are neither true nor false unless they are part of a theory of relations between them. Human relations, too, must have a rational basis in certain aims for the well being of society and mankind as a whole, which cannot be derived from mere observation but must spring from the human natural strivings and recognized by each individual as well as by the community. The moral good stems from a moral truth.

On the whole, Reichenbach misinterprets Kant's meaning of a priori, which is without any admixture of experience at all. Reichenbach illustrates what he himself understands by causality a priori, and attributes it to Kant as follows, "When we see the tides of the ocean in their periodic rhythm, we know from pure reason that this occurence has a cause (110). but, contrary to Reichenbach, this is an argument from empirical observation and not from pure reason. Kant is quite clear about it, when he writes, "We understand by cognitive a priori not that which is independent of this or that experience, but that which is independent of all experience. . . . Of the a priori cognitions only those are pure which have no empirical admixture at all. For example, the statement, Every change has its cause, is an a priori statement, but not pure, because change is a concept which can be inferred only from experience" (*Critique of Pure Reason* B3).

Furthermore, Reichenbach tries to show that Kant deduces "the notion of cause by finding particular causes." (112). But Kant repudiates it, when he writes: "To attempt an empirical deduction [such as Reichenbach suggests] would be entirely a fruitless task, because their [the categories, including causality] natural differentiation lies in that they relate to their objects without deriving their representation from experience. Therefore, if we have to deduce them [the categories] it will always have to be transcendental, i.e. apart from experience" (*Critique of Pure Reason* B118-119).

185

It should be noted that Reichenbach disregards Kant's Transcendental Analytic and Transcendental Logic, which are the mainstay of the *Critique*; and even the Transcendental Dialectic he puts out of gear by confusing "transcendental" (which makes experience possible) with "transcendent" (beyond experience altogether). See R's book, pp. 65-66, 252-53. Cf. my discussion of these matters in my *Greek Mode*, chapter on Kant, p. 297 n. 426.

Of Reichenbach's misrepresentation of Hume's empiricism I will cite only one (but major) example, again on the subject of causality. Reichenbach writes: "The interpretation of causality in terms of generality, clearly formulated in the writings of David Hume, is now generally accepted by the scientist. Laws of nature [referring especially to the law of causaiilty] are for him statements of an exceptionless repetition" (159). I have dealt with this aspect of Hume's theory in my *Greek Mode*, pp. 180-82, 291-92 n. 377. Suffice it here to point out that Hume places the "necessary connection" of causality not in mere repetition but in "repetition of their union . . . in imagination," which is a synthetic act of the mind. Indeed, Hume, like Kant, looks for a mental faculty, an "act of mind," to establish causality as a "necessary connection," and he does not, as Reichenbach claims, regard "the addition to knowledge supplied by the mind . . . [as] of an empty nature" (86). It is this drive by Hume to discover mental faculties that brought Kant out of his "dogmatic slumber." See my discussion of Kant's relation of the unity in imagination to the categories of the understanding in my *Greek Mode*, 207, 300 n. 439).

(b) Ethics is not a science

Of course, if one issues from Reichenbach's notion of science as grounded in empirical evidence of facts alone, it is contrary to Kant's view of science and even to that of many notable modern scientists, not the least of whom is Albert Einstein. (See my chapter on Einstein in my *Philosophy and Technology*, especially "Between Illusion and Reality," pp. 33-34.) Insofar as ethics deals with the good, even the "good will" (as Kant emphasizes in his *Lectures on Ethics*, "Bonitas moralis" (p. 15), and "morality . . . requires a good will" (p. 18), it must be tested and guided by the understanding, and in this respect it has a scientific basis. However, Reichenbach does not regard ethics as a problem of the good, but rather as a conflict of interests and their adjudication by political groups.

(c) An imperative is a grammatical form of a moral directive

Reichenbach's linguistic analysis of the imperative term "he should" only tells the various meanings it may contain, but not how one is to differentiate the moral form from other forms if there is no moral law, or any other rule, from which it is derivable.

(d) A moral imperative is the will of the individual

Reichenbach removes the "feeling of obligation" as a determining factor in the constitution of the moral imperative or directive. But by placing the moral directive in the will of each individual, without any obligation (emotional or rational) on the part of the given individual to follow it, or of the others to whom it is directed, to accept it, what is the earmark of its morality? We shall see later that instead of obligation Reichenbach uses the term "to share," that is, the person issuing the imperative commits himself to share with the others in its action, and that renders it moral. Yet we still are not told what would prompt the given individual (or as Kant would say, what motive would he have) to do it?

Here the distinction between Reichenbach's and Kant's ethics comes to the fore. Reichenbach, like Kant, places the moral directive in the individual will, who issues it of his own accord, without external compulsion. But whereas Kant tells the individual to check his directive against the *categorical imperative*, issuing from the higher intelligible will in conformity with a universal rule of moral action (which implies "human worth" and a universal action that would not go contrary to this worth), Reichenbach tells the individual will just to assert itself ("trust our volition") without any guideline at all. The guidelines he adds later do not issue from his ethics but from his notion of politics and its democratic form of operation, which is a cognitive operation and, as we shall see shortly, is fraught with some serious difficulties.

(e) Democratic principle of ethical development

Ethical action, according to Reichenbach, takes place in the political institutions of a democratic society, where the conflict between wills irons itself out in free play, without preconceived moral rules, but simply through a clash of wills. The political group where this clash occurs is like a conglomeration of atoms, each flying off in different directions and gaining eventually some form of organization by chance collisions with each other which deflect them from their individual tracts into a unified operation. When the individual wills are thus brought together, their action is said to be functioning according to the "group will." However the group will does not make a moral judgment, only a numerical decision (if the group consists of 9 members it takes 5 to pass an imperative, whether or not it is good for the group). Reichenbach seems to be aware of this incongruency in his democratic process of ethical development and he introduces a moral criterion and a cognitive guideline that may render the group decision morally valid.

(f) Moral criterion of an individual imperative

As indicated above (4), in order to give one's imperative moral validity, the speaker has to commit himself "to share" in the action that he proposes for all the others to follow. It is a form of a show of "good will" though not of the same kind that Kant speaks of, because in the latter the speaker has to show to himself, to his own conscience, and match it with the categorical imperative, whereas in Reichenbach's case it is only a public statement that has to be accepted at its face value (as it usually happens in political commitments).

(g) Cognitive guidance for moral group decision

Although Reichenbach originally excluded rational argument from moral imperatives, which are only of a volitional character, he realized that when it comes to group decisions a mere clash of wills cannot bring the desired moral results. He therefore advises now to convert the "moral issue" into a "logical issue" by uncovering the "fundamental aims" that may be entailed in the proposed imperatives and have the group discuss their merits on the basis of empirical evidence (such as psychological, sociological, or economic, and the like, as the case may call for. See his example from criminal jurisprudence in #8). If the fundamental aim is recognized by all members, the group discussion may succeed in influencing the individual wills to change their attitudes and follow the logical consequence of the evidence by adopting such action that may bring the aim to fruition. This is tantamount to saying that each individual should forego "to share" in his own imperative, which makes it moral, and adopt the group decision on cognitive grounds, which are outside the moral sphere. For the group will is not an act of volition, despite its nomenclature, but the result of rational deliberation of observable facts. Reichenbach has thus transformed Kant's categorical imperative into a group imperative but in the process lost the moral force of the former. The psychological, sociological, or economic facts brought into the argument may not be verifiable and may turn out to be contrary to the fundamental aim of the social entity. Moreover, by throwing the moral issue into the political hopper, the decision reached is of a legal-coginitive nature absolving the members from their moral committments.

One has only to observe (in Reichenbach's own empirical manner) how political officials who have gained their positions through "group will" engage in all kinds of morally questionable activities (judged by the people who have a healthy tradition of moral values), but are exonerated from prosecution by government appointed investigators on legal-cognitive grounds. These officials cannot be indicted on legalities and remain untouchable even though they have not answered for their morally questionable behavior.

Thus Reichenbach has been constrained to bring back into the moral imperative cognitive judgments which he had eliminated at the start, only to forfeit the moral ground of his ethical principle. Without a moral law morality cannot be created out of sheer individual wills.

Note: In placing Reichenbach's ethical principle against Kant's categorical imperative, I did not mean to defend Kant's position as the only possible solution of ethical problems. I only wanted to point out that Reichenbach's arguments against Kant rest on a misrepresentation of the latter's "science of ethics." I have examined Kant's ethical theory more critically in my book *Philosophy and Technology*, chapter 4.

1984

Is Nietzsche a Metaphysician?

Anyone who says anything about Nietzsche's metaphysic is bound to run into the controversy going on among Nietzsche scholars about source and system: where in his writings does one find a metaphysical system, are the sources authentic, and if so, are they organized and sufficiently developed to be rightfully regarded as a metaphysic? One of the main issues centers on the reliability of the collection of notes published under the title *The Will to Power*, from which one may cull most of the philosopher's metaphysical concepts. It appears that no one questions their authenticity, only their value as a system. Walter Kaufmann, for example, points out that those notes were jotted down by Nietzsche at different times in the course of his later philosophical development (1883-1888), and that they cannot be taken as systematic thinking but rather as raw material, "full of sketches, drafts, abandoned attempts, and unfinished dreams."[1] He does not doubt their authenticity, but questions their validity and cautions on their use. Karl-Heinz Volkmann-Schluck, on the other hand, holds that "... the collected pieces under the title 'Will to Power' show Nietzsche at work on conceptual analysis which does not fall behind the work of system-formation by his predecessors."[2] Karl Jaspers regards *The Will to Power* and the entire *Nachlass* of which it is a part as representative of the philosopher's thinking as is any of his other writings. "Nietzsche's work," he says, "is really not centralized anywhere; there is no main work."[3] And Jaspers himself quotes from the *Nachlass* and *Der Wille zur Macht* as freely as he does from the other writings.

The real question, however, is whether Nietzsche has a metaphysic at all. We see him fighting it throughout his writings and now we want to saddle him with one of his own, tied to his

---

1. Cf. Friedrich Nietzsche, *The Will to Power.* Translated by Walter Kaufmann and R. J. Hollingdale. Edited by Walter Kaufmann (New York 1968), Appendix, p. 557, and Editor's Introduction, pp. xv-xvi. See comments on Karl Schlechta's attempt to discredit the volume "Will to Power" altogether. Taking a clue from Schlechta, Geoffrey Clive, editor of *The Philosophy of Nietzsche* (New York 1965), which is based on the former's German edition, omits "The Will to Power" from his anthology, because, he says, it adds "little of significance to the Nietzsche canon" (p. xxii).

2. Karl-Heinz Volkmann-Schluck, *Leben und Denken, Interpretationen zur Philosophie Nietzsches* (Frankfurt am/Main 1968), p. 64.

3. Karl Jaspers, *Nietzsche. Einführung in das Verständnis seines Philosophierens.* Dritte unveränderte Auflage (Berlin 1950), p. 12.

concept "will to power." In his defense Kaufmann observes that "Nietzsche's central concern is with man, and power is to him above all a state of the human being. The projection of the will to power from the human sphere to the cosmos is an afterthought."[4] But I maintain that this projection to the cosmos, even as an afterthought, is what constitutes Nietzsche's metaphysic. All metaphysics came as an afterthought. Kant, for example, never intended to write his *Prolegomena* except as an afterthought to his *Critique of Pure Reason*.[5] Similarly, Aristotle's *Metaphysics* came only after (*meta*) he had established his system of physics.[6] And so does every metaphysical speculation follow a given science of physics, whether the *physis* is of things, man, life, or the universe as a whole.

Now Nietzsche set out to revaluate all values about the nature of man through a science of physico-psychology, and not just man but with him the entire universe and all the sciences that aim to interpret it.[7] For all that, he was not a natural scientist but rather a philosopher, and since he raised philosophy above the sciences (that in itself is a metaphysical assertion — witness Aristotle),[8] he was constrained to pose and answer philosophical questions as to what he was actually revaluating and how he came about it. He did not expect the total answer from empirical science and therefore had to venture beyond it. The metaphyscial issue is thus not being imposed on him but arises from his particular approach to the

4. Walter Kaufmann, *Nietzsche. Philosopher, Psychologist, Antichrist.* Third Edition. Revised and Enlarged (Vintage Books, New York 1968). p. 420.

5. Cf. Immanuel Kant, *Prolegomena zu einer jeden künftigen metaphysik.* Ed. by Karl Vorländer (Hamburg 1965). Vorrede 261 and Anhang 372. For that Kritik (of Pure Reason), he says, must stand on its own before one can even think of letting metaphysics come up.

6. The books on "Metaphysics" were not just placed by the compilers after the Books on "Physics" accidentally, as is commonly understood, but were actually written as a projection of the theories of the *Physics* into the realm of the *First Principles.* Cf. Werner Jaeger, *Aristotle* (Oxford Paperback 1960), pp. 378-79.

7. Nietzsche, *Beyond Good and Evil* 23, on "psychology . . . as the morphology and theory of development of the will to power . . . as I conceive it." It "will be required that psychology be recognized again as the master of all sciences and that the rest of the sciences are at its service and predisposition." Note: All quotations from Nietzsche's works are in my own translation from the German edition of *Kröners Taschenausgabe.* References are by numbers of the aphorisms or sections, as the case may be.

8. Cf. ibid. 204 on the overbearing attitude of the scientists in relation to philosophy; also 211 on the superiority of the true philosopher who is not to be confused with the scientists "his servants."

problem of man or, as he puts it, the problematic of human morality.[9] How does he face this problem.

Nietzsche places man at the center of a given world-view and urges him to "become what he is." What kind of world-view is it and how does man orient himself in it, both as he *is* and as he *becomes* what he is? Moreover, how can he become what he already is unless the "is" changes from what it "is-not?" And what becomes then of his world-orientation? Is it the same world with a different orientation or the same orientation in a different world? These questions are metaphyscial precisely because Nietzsche seeks to revaluate human morality in terms of physico-psychological concepts grounded in the will to power which is neither derived from those concepts nor observable in actual behavior. The will to power is posited by our philosopher not as a hypothesis but, I would say, as a first principle.[10]

One might still raise the question, if Nietzsche has no system, by what right do we ascribe to him a metaphysic, which by its very nature is systematic? Are we not imputing something alien to his thoughts by our very attempt to systematize him? That depends not on what we read into his writings by implication but rather on what we read out of them by selection, for systematization is just that, selecting all prime elements which constitute a unified whole. If we mean by system a totality held together through causal connectives, then Nietzsche has no system, for he does not operate with those connectives, not as criteria of truth anyway. By the same token, his metaphysic does not fall back on the logical principle of "no infinite regress" which requires a prime, unmoved mover (Aristotle) or an unconditioned *Grenzbegriff* (Kant). But he does deal with a totality which is held together by certain inner relationships, constituting some kind of system of relations, though not of relata (there are no "things").

Now, if Nietzsche had left it at that, he would have constructed just a natural science in terms of physical or physico-psychological correlatives, such as we find today in the theory of relativity, and the like. But he went beyond that and brought all his correlatives

9. Cf. Nietzsche, *Genealogy of Morals* iii, 23. "Science today has absolutely no faith in itself, not to speak of an ideal above itself."

10. As principle it is neither deductive nor inductive but *thetic*. This is particularly evident from Nietzsche's account of time as eternal recurrence, which is also posited by him to accommodate "the will to power."

into perspective with one overriding immanent principle, namely "the will to power." This points to his systematic thinking, even though it is not carried out in schematic form in his writings. If now we mean by system a coherent, directional world-view, Nietzsche has such a system or, to use his own words, a free "incomplete system." "It requires a totally different strength nd mobility," he observes, "to hold fast with free, unbound perspectives in an incomplete system, rather than in a dogmatic world."[11] His is not one of the "great systems" built by "schematic heads," as he calls them, but a dynamic world-view of *becoming*, and its metaphysical problem is to ascertain the ultimate *dynamis* which gives it a state of *being*. As he tells us in the opening sentence of his "Recapitulation" of the section on Science, "To impress the character of being on becoming — that is the highest will to power."[12] Having prepared the ground for a new immanent and dynamic metaphysic, he went forth in search of "new philosophers . . . to revaluate 'eternal values'. . . . "[13] But on his way he had to devise the tools that these philosophers could use for their orientation in a world of sheer becoming, sheer doing. For in that world, he said, "there is no 'being' behind the doing, acting, becoming; 'the doer' is only an innovation added to the doing — the doing is everything."[14].

Revaluating the Metaphysics of Morals

Nietzsche does not revaluate morals but the metaphysic of morals. He directs his metaphyscial arrows against Kant more than against any other of his predecessors. Kant, he says, came to the odd conclusion that the intelligible world is unintelligible, that is, the true world which Kant postulates beyond the sensible world is inaccessible to the concepts of the understanding. To resolve this paradox, Nietzsche takes two bold steps: he denies the existence of a world of noumena and he downgrades the value of the understanding as an instrument of real knowledge of the world of phenomena; he shakes the foundations of Kant's practical world and unhinges the categories of the understanding which are fastened to his theoretical world. What kind of reality and what

---

11.Nietzsche, *Nachlass* ii, 220. Cf. ibid. 223 on the pedantry of "schematic heads."
12. Nietzsche, *Will to Power* 617.
13. *Beyond Good and Evil* 203.
14. *Genealogy of Morals* i. 13.

means of knowing it does Nietzsche substitute for Kant's dual kingdom? "The true world," he says, "we have abolished; which world remains? perhaps the phenomenal? — Not so! With the true world we have also abolished the phenomenal one!"[15] But with it he did not abolish metaphysics, any more than Kant did. He only revaluated the old into a new world-orientation.

Nietzsche traces the history of the error of positing a "true world" beyond the phenomenal one from Plato through Christianity to Kant. After Kant came "dawn" of positivism, which threw a dim light on the unattainability of that world, followed by "bright day" when its uselessness became visible and one could abolish it altogether. Thus "noon" arrived, when the "shadow of error" was at its shortest and a new metaphysic became incipient in the bright light of day.[16] To understand Nietzsche's revaluation of Kant's dual kingdom, we must note the philosophical problem which both philosophers have had to cope with.

Fundamentally, Nietzsche as well as Kant tries to set limits to a scientific account of reality by placing the physical sciences within a philosophic frame of reference. Both recognize that science is useful as a tool of cognition and action but that, in a sense, it falsifies reality. The metaphyscial issue between them centers on the meaning each ascribes to reality from a different outlook of the physcial sciences. Kant built his scientific theory on the foundations of Newtonian physics, while Nietzsche, by a stroke of genius, projected his on the principles of modern nuclear physics. I shall resist the temptation to draw a parallel between Nietzsche's "interpretation" of the world and modern theories of mathematical physics, as this would lead me far outside the limits of my present study. I will only indicate how some of his concepts project themselves into those theories. On the general concept of "points of force" which prevails in today's physics, he writes: "The mathematical physicists cannot use the atomlumps for their science; hence they construct for themselves a world of points of force which may be reckoned with."[17] On giving up the principle of causality, as is now being advocated by the Copenhagen school of quantum mechanics, and generally on the use of sign language to

---

15. Nietzsche, *Twilight of the Idols.* "How the 'True World' Finally Became a Legend," item 6.
16. Ibid., items 1-6.
17. *Nachlass* ii, 271.

describe rather than explain physical states, he says: "The development of the mechanistic-atomistic mode of thinking is today not yet aware of its necessary goal. . . . It will end up with the creation of a system of signs: it will forgo explanation and will give up the concept of 'cause and effect.' "[18]

Many of his other observations anticipated modern connotations of such concepts as movement, atomic structure, disregard of the singular, contingency of combination, law of probability, relative character of simultaneity, and the like, which are today the building blocks, cement, and scaffolding of the mathematico-physical structure of the world. He even dared to think of the physicist's concept of force and motion not as action at a distance but as "symptoms of inner occurrences," and of the concept of "time as a property of space."[19]

Will to Power, a Metaphysical Principle

With these and similar concepts, notably space, time and recurrence, Nietzsche constructs an immanent world of nature to which he underpins a metaphyscial first principle — the will to power. This principle is metaphysical inasmuch as it is not accounted for by the same concepts as are the natural elements, but is posited beyond nature, though immanent in the phenomena. It is the ultimate *dynamis* from which everything flows. Stated briefly, this world structure is of a voidless, finite space and endless time, constituting a complete whole of cyclic recurrence, within which actions take place endlessly, never attaining equilibrium, never diminished in their potencies, ever in the same distribution, always now as they have ever been and ever will be. This world is never in the past nor in the future but always in the *now*, for every "now" even "this instant . . . has always been once and many times and will return the same, all forces distributed exactly as now. . . ."[20] "That everything recurs," Nietzsche says, "is the extremest approximation of a world of becoming to that of being,"[21] and this eternal recurrence of the "now" is in essence his metaphysic of time — not as cause but as the *fatum* of being, imagined in the

18. Ibid. 273. See also 230.
19. *Will to Power* 619, 862.
20. *Nachlass* ii. 1332.
21. *Will to Power* 617.

becoming. "If one is a philosopher," he says, ". . . one sees only being (*das Seiende*). But since there is no such thing as being, what is left for the philosopher is only the imaginary, saved up as his 'world.' "[22]

Perspectivistic Interpretation

Is everything in this world, then, an illusion, a lie? Yes, says Nietzsche, and of necessity, because life itself demands that it be so. If we ask, what moves within the totality? the answer is, not a thing, for there is no thing as there is no movement in itself. There is only "interpretation" relative to a given "perspective." There are many perspectives, each issuing from a certain drive, and there are many interpretations.[23] Nietzsche's "perspective interpretations" are analogous to the coordinate systems of modern physics. Both are innumerable, and anyone who wants to make use of them must choose from among their endless number. However, since there is no purpose or goal in Nietzsche's world of nature or morals, as there is none in modern physical reality, there is no way of deciding on a given perspective interpretation in preference to any other. Modern physical theory has circumvented this problem by adopting a certain geometry as a basis for its coordinates. How does our philosopher get around it when he advises man to choose "to become what he is?" What kind of perspective interpretation will enable man to move in that direction? And that, as we recall, is Nietzsche's primary task, namely, to give man direction in a world of sheer becoming. Without some constant guideline man will be totally disoriented in the becoming, will be unable to hit upon the right perspective, and will remain in the condition of nihilism from which Nietzsche has tried to extricate him through a revaluation of all values. What are man's new horizons?

In the past, Nietzsche maintains, man interpreted the world from a narrow perspective of a belief in God as the creator and preserver of the universe, which, while having served certain life needs, has now become untenable. But what are the new

22. Ibid. 570.

23. *Genealogy of Morals* iii, 12. "There is only a perspectivistic (*perspektivistisches*) seeing, only a perspectivistic 'cognition'; and the more drives we allow to come to expression over a thing . . . the more complete will be our 'concept,' our 'objectivity' of that thing." Cf. *The Gay Science* v. 374, on the possibility of endless perspectives and interpretations.

alternatives? Actually, Nietzsche does not deny God, only the Christian doctrine of a supernatural, transcendent Being who also demands a given moralilty. Such an interpretation, he holds, is inconsistent with the new, emerging view of reality.[24] That is, Nietzsche denies the life-giving values of Christian theology and its metaphysic of morals, which are grounded in a dual world of being and appearance, such as theologians and philosophers, notably Kant, had built up in the past. And if now he wants to revaluate those values and not, as he says, abolish them, he must establish new religious concepts, a new metaphysic or theology, which will be in keeping with his own viewing of the world of nature. This should not be too difficult if he could only find a guideline for choosing the right perspective for his new interpretation. This is like having to choose the proper geometry for a new set of coordinates.

Nietzsche considers the old theologies and metaphysics of morals as interpretations that have lost their anchor in reality, because their God, that is the anchor, had died, or they themselves have killed him. But what is reality? According to our philosopher, all there is is becoming. Any being that we might ascribe to it could come only through interpretation. Reality, then, *is* interpretation of becoming.[25] This is "The interpretative character of all occurrence. There is no event in itself. What occurs is a group of appearances, selected and comprehended through an interpreting being."[26] And here we come to the fundamental question of his metaphysic: Who is that "interpreting being?" If there were such a being apart from the interpretation, it would be unreal, because a being in reality arises only through interpretation. Having dethroned the principle of causality, Nietzsche may deny the need of an Aristotelian prime mover, but he cannot forgo the principle of a prime interpreter. And that is exactly what he arrives at in good metaphysical tradition — a prime interpreter interpreting itself, which is none other than "will to power." Its role as a first principle is stated in the following aphorism: "The will to power not a being, not a becoming, but a *pathos* — is the most elemental fact, out of which a becoming, an action first arises."[27]

24. *Nachlass* ii, 994. "The refutation of God: — actually only the *moral* God is refuted."
25. Jaspers, *Nietzsche,* ch. v. "Weltauslegung," pp. 290-330. He gives a detailed analysis of Nietzsche's view of the world as interpretation.
26. *Nachlass* ii, 245. "Der interpretative Charakter alles Geschehens."
27. *Will to Power* 635.

As pointed out earlier, Nietzsche objects to Kant's dual kingdom chiefly because it posits an intelligible world which is inaccessible to the intellect; he therefore tries to substitute for this duality a unified world which is intelligible from within. But what he actually does is revaluate intelligibility to mean not only reason but also sensibility and affections so that they all stem from one source, namely, will to power as the supreme drive. That is, of all the drives that effectuate different perspectives he chooses one overall drive which he regards as the right perspective of an intelligible world. This is his "geometry" for the coordinates he proposes to use in his new structuring of reality — bringing into existence, sensing, feeling, understanding, guaging, and measuring, in a word, will to Power interpreting itself in its various manifestations in nature, in life, and in man. Nietzsche forwarns, "One should not ask: 'who then interprets?' for the interpreting itself is a form of will to power, has existence (not, however, as a 'being,' but as a process, a becoming) as an affect."[28] Even if we were to heed his admonition we would still want to know, who or what is this will to power that can do all those things, and how does our philosopher come by it?

The will to power is a oneness posited by Nietzsche in place of the Kantian-Christian dualism of two worlds. This new oneness also contains a dualism, but its two terms, "will" and "power," are conceived as inseparable from each other. Will in itself, according to Nietzsche, even in its most determinate form, is only a vague abstraction or illusion. "To reduce everything to will," he says, is "a very naive distortion!" and he calls for "Abolishing the will, free and unfree, the 'ought' and 'necessity,' 'knowledge in itself' and the 'thing in itself,' "[29] all of which are expressions of an illusory concept of will. In its place he recommends a new kind of will, not as a concept of a human capacity or a quality of reason, but of a more primal nature.[30]

---

28. Ibid. 556.

29. *Nachlass* ii, 83 and 842. Cf. *Nachlass* i, 61. "The expiring will (the dying God) crumbles in the individualities. Its striving is always the lost oneness, its *telos* always further disintegration."

30. *Will to Power* 692f. Cf. *Twilight.* "Reason" in Philosophy, 5. "To start with, there is the great fatality of error that will is something that acts,—that will is a capacity — Today we know that it is only a word —" Nietzsche's complaint is that the rationalists, notably Kant, could not establish the kind of will that has something real for its object according to which it must act or direct itself, and they therefore went beyond the phenomenal world to find such an object. It should be noted that Kant repudiates the notion that such an object can be found beyond the phenomena. See my *Greek Mode of Thought,* pp. 200-203.

Actually, Nietzsche is looking for a something that will wills, or its object, the same as Kant did, only he seeks to overcome the logical duality in the subject-object relationship through an amazingly simple device of converting the static copula "is" into a dynamic connective "to" in a happening (*Geschehen*) in which neither subject nor object prevails. His first principle is not a definition (as for example, Aristotle's substance) but an assertion which is undefinable and unconditioned by logical laws (again, Aristotle would expect it to conform to those laws).[31] He does not assert that "will is power," "will has power," or "will wills power," but simply posits "the will *to* power." In the first three assertions there is a logical duality governed by the laws of identity and contradiction, which can never lead to a real unity. In the last one there is a oneness with a built-in manifold in internal conflict — an original *dynamis*, a drive or, as he calls it, a *pathos*.[32] Everything in it is in an inchoate state of becoming, assuming various forms of organic and inorganic nature, of life and man, unto its highest form of the supreme man. If "the ultimate question is whether we really acknowledge will as active, whether we believe in the causality of will,"[33] Nietzsche says, then let us get to the one and only kind of will which is the actual ground of it all. This cannot be the will of a logical, abstract subject which is unable even to get off its starting point. It can only be "the will to power" as an endless drive of something toward something, speaking out of all its forms as they become reality through the self-interpretation of that drive. Even

The philosopher is only a kind of opportunity, making it possible that the drive may come to utterance. . . . In them [in the philosophers] the drive brings itself to light with the greatest impudence and innocence of a basic drive: — it wants to be lord and possibly the purpose of all things, of all happening. . . . It is clear that here spesaks the sovereign drive, which is stronger than man.[34]

31. Cf. Aristotle, *Metaphysics* 1005b, 1006a, 1061b.
32. *Will to Power* 556. "The 'essence,' the 'beingness' is something perspectivistic and already presupposes a manifold."
33. *Beyond Good and Evil* 36.
34. *Nachlass* ii, 717.

The second term, power, of the duality "will to power" is also inseparable from the oneness, for in itself power may be conceived as force and, like will in itself, be only an illusion or abstraction. As such, it is subject to rules, to laws of necessity and calculation, as it would be in any scientific account of the world. However, says Nietzsche, if we do assume that the world has a necessary calculable course, we may also assume that this is "not because there are laws ruling it, but because laws are absolutely lacking, and each power at every instant draws its own consequence. Granted that this too is only interpretation. . .—then, the better.—"[35] Basically, Nietzsche conceives of power as its own lawmaker, in distinction from mechanistic force as a concept of causality. Power is thus expressed spontaneously in its effect and resistance to hindrance; there is no mover or cause pushing or pulling it. Mechanical force is gauged by a moving cause. " 'Attraction' and 'repulsion' in the purely mechanistic sense is a total fiction: a word."[36] This duality of meaning of the term "power" is not worked out by our philosopher systematically; but neither has he systematized any of his other concepts and terms. Nevertheless, his pattern is clear. Once he introduced the immanent duality "will to power," he had to live with it all the way through, as it split, like Plato's dichotomy, into sub-dualities:[37] two kinds of will, two kinds of power, two kinds of philosophers, and so on, in endless interpretation. There is no contradiction in this kind of duality if one looks at it from Nietzsche's perspective of will to power as such. Any immanent duality has this characteristic of subdivision; the moment one of its elements is singled out for specific interpretation, it splits into a duality of its own; otherwise it could not be interpreted. Every interpretation, like every coordinated mesh, requires a minimum of two elements at cross purposes or directions to each other. Thus, by interpreting the world as an

35. *Beyond Good and Evil* 22. Cf. *Will to Power* 634. Critique of mechanistic interpretation. "There is no law: each power at every instant draws its last consequence. It is exactly because there is no ability to be otherwise that there is calculability."

36. Ibid. 627.

37. Cf. Plato, *The Sophist* 219d-221c. Plato uses dialectics (in his own sense) to arrive at the reality of being. Neitzsche proceeds in the same manner, although his dialectic has a dynamic character. Plato applies to appearance both "separation" and "participation," whereas Nietzsche never spearates the oneness "will to power" whatever appearance it may assume — will to know, will to rule, will to govern, will to lust, and the like. Plato operates with the copula "is"; Nietzsche substitutes for it the particle "to." Cf. Ernst Hoffmann, *Platonismus und christliche Philosophie* (Zurich, 1960), p. 49, on Plato's use of the copula.

immanent duality in oneness, Nietzsche has tried to make it an intelligible world accessible not only to the intellect but also at the same time to sensibility and the affections: " 'Purpose and means,' 'cause and effect,' 'subject and object,' 'action and passion,' 'thing in itself and appearance,' as interpretations (not as facts) . . . all in the sense of a 'will to power.' "[38]

Nietzsche thus arrives at this first principle not by induction or deduction, but by positing it as the world-interpreter. He proceeds very much in accord with the modern mathematical-scientific methodology of establishing a unified science, namely, by positing one and only one, all-embracing and simplest functioning factor as the interpreter of a world of becoming. This, he says,

> is dictated by the conscience of method, Not to assume many kinds of causality, so long as no attempt has been made to reach out with a single one to its outermost limit. . . . Suppose that one succeeded in explaining the entire life of drives as a formation and ramification of a basic form of will — namely of the will to power, as is my proposition; — . . . then one would thereby be given the right to determine univocally all active force as: will to power. The world seen from within, the world determined and designated as to its 'intelligible character'—it would just be 'will to power' and nothing besides that."[39]

The New Gods: Philosophers-Lawgivers

After he established his first principle as the "one great fact of evaluations (logically and morally)" in the manner of the philosopher-scientist, Nietzsche found this type of philosopher insufficient unto himself, and he pursued his search of the "true philosopher," the one who is the "lawgiver of such evaluations,"[40] the kind he envisioned as the highest man on earth. When he therefore speaks of man "becoming what he is," he means that man should strive for the highest interpretation, even toward the outermost state of will to power, to become the Supreme Man. Will to power, speaking through its manifestations, has not yet become

---

38. *Will to Power* 589.
39. *Beyond Good and Evil* 36.
40. *Will to Power* 972. A distinction is made between these two kinds of philosophers. Cf. ibid. 979. "For us the philosopher must be a lawgiver."

fully what it is; man is to reach out for its fulfillment, that is "become what he is" in will to power as such. "There can be endless kinds of the ability-to-be-different, even of the ability-to-be-God."[41] Man is to sublimate himself unto his manifest destiny of the artist-philosopher becoming a god.[42] Thus Nietzsche hoped to overcome the nihilism of his age and of succeeding epochs for thousands of years by setting a new goal and purpose in human life — the creation of supreme man, "the future caste of rulers. . . . These lords of the earth, now, shall replace God and acquire for themselves the deep unconditional trust of those who are ruled."[43]

When Nietzsche proclaimed "All the gods are dead: now we want that the Supreme Man shall live," he postulated with *Zarathustra*, as he also did with the Madman in *The Gay Science*, that it is possible for God to die or, more correctly, for man to kill him. At any rate this is the way he posed the problem: "either we die of this . . . artificially inoculated religion . . . or religion dies of us. I believe in the old-German word: all the gods must die.[44] However, Nietzsche intended by this act to save humanity from nihilism, and he would not have presumed to have killed God unless he had assumed that man created the old God and could therefore also kill him and create other gods in his stead. "And how many new gods are still possible!" he exclaims. "Type of god according to the type of the creative spirits, of the 'great men.' "[45] The old God, he said, was fashioned by man out of weakness. . . "[46] which brought about the crisis of nihilism. The new gods, the philosophers who are to be sublimated toward becoming Supreme Men, are all to be created out of the will to power.

Nietzsche's theory of sublimation does not set a goal for man as such or for mankind as a whole, but for select individuals, the great, superior men, for whom the entire human species is to sacrifice

41. Ibid. 1005.

42. Originally Nietzsche had three types of supreme men in mind, the artist, the philosopher, and the saint. But after he elimianted the Kantian-Christian "real world," he had no place where to put the saint, and he therefore left him out of account in the final reckoning. Cf. Daufmann, *Nietzsche,* p. 285: "The saint has dropped out of the picture," and p. 322. "Nietzsche was not primarily a moral philosopher at all."

43. *Nachlass* ii, 1414.

44. *Nachlass* i, 1. Cf. *The Gay Science* 125. "The Madman." Cf. *Nachlass* ii, 141. "The time of his [Zarathustra's] coming. . . . The greatest event; God is dead."

45. *Will to Power* 1038. Cf. *Nachlass* ii, 927. "Men have created God, there is no doubt."

46. Ibid. 54.

everything needed in order to bring them forth; ". . . humanity on the whole has no goals. . . . "[47] Its task is to produce individual great men; its goal lies not in an end of its own, but in its highest specimens. For "man is a bridge and not an end: to count himself blessed that his noon and evening are a road to new dawns."[48] The superior men are to be "The Lords of the Earth," to whom the governing forces are to be subordinated. "Beyond the governors, relieved of all ties, live the highest men: and in the governors they have their tools.[49] Not 'humanity' but *Supreme Man* is the goal!"[50] For "the destiny of mankind lies in the attainment of its highest type."[51] "All virtue and self-overcoming has meaning only as preparation of the ruler!"[52]

One could cite many more passages in the same vein, all of which intersect in the following entry: "About the ruling types. — The 'Shepherd' in contrast to the 'Lord' (— the former a means to sustain the herd; the latter, end for which there is a herd)."[53] These Lords form a breed of philosopher-gods who are detached from the rest of mankind, assuming a sort of transcendence within a universal immanence, removed on a new Olympus, and from its clouds they flash the words *nolle me tangere*. No wonder our philosopher himself was awed by his own creation. "When I created the supreme man," he said, "I arranged the great veil of becoming around him and let the sun stand over him at noon." "When he [Zarathustra] leaves the people he turns back unto himself. It retreats from him like a cloud. Type of how the supreme man must live: like an Epicurean god."[54]

As the reality of will to power, as the highest "perspective interpretation," this philodopher-god "is a man who constantly experiences extraordinary things, . . . who is himself perhaps a thunderstorm pregnant with new lightnings: a fateful man around whom there is always pealing, growling and yelping, and things go weird. . . ."[55] Nietzsche often speaks of man as *die Pflanze Mensch*

---

47. *Human All Too Human* i, 33.
48. *Thus Spoke Zarathustra* iii. "On Old and New Tablets" 3.
49. *Will to Power* 998. Cf. *Antichrist* 57. "The highest caste . . . the fewest — being perfect . . . the most spiritual human beings." "The second are the executive arm of the most spiritual."
50. Ibid. 1001.
51. Ibid. 987.
52. *Nachlass* ii, 1279.
53. *Will to Power* 902.
54. *Nachlass* ii, 1273, 1359.
55. *Beyond Good and Evil* 292.

— the plant humanum which exists only to produce the topmost, finest fruits. However, in whatever metaphyscial soil he may plant this man of nature he cannot elevate him to an ethical being. That is why he sees "Morals and Anti-Nature," and "the single [human being as] a piece of *fatum* from the front and from the rear. . . ."[56] Such is Nietzsche's Supreme Man, like a storm without an ethic. He may be a sublimated manifestation of nature, but he is not the man who will bring salvation to his fellow-men, no matter how sublime the heights to which he himself may rise.

1973

56.*Twilight of the Idols.* "Morals as Anti-Nature" 6.

Postscript on Nietzsche's Metaphysics

April 30, 1973

Professor Walter Kaufmann
Princeton University
Princeton, N. J. 08540

Dear Professor Kaufmann:

I was pleased to make your personal acquaintance at the session of the New Jersey Philosophical Association, even though only for a few moments. Having read your works and admired the clarity of your thinking, I found your comments on my paper quite stimulating, although our views run in somewhat different directions. Since you had to leave the session early, I wish to clarify a few points in my paper on Nietzsche's metaphysics which, because of the brevity of my exposition (due to time limitations), were not altogether evident to the listener. I should mention, first of all, that my paper is a short resume of a larger essay on Nietzsche included in my book *The End of Enlightenment* [later published as *Philosophy and Technology*]. My scope was not a full length study of this philosopher, only his role in the scientific and moral crisis of our time. Included in my work are also Einstein, Skinner, Sartre,

Wittgenstein, and others. Now as far as your comments are concerned I will note four areas that you touched upon: (1) The title of my topic, (2) System in relation to metaphysics, (3) Psychological hypothesis versus first principle, and (4) Metaphysics as an afterthought.

1. You said that you were distrubed by the fact that I chose to discuss Nietzsche as a metaphysician at all. He was many things, etc. Now, your book *Nietzsche* has the subtitle *Philosopher, Psychologist, Antichrist.* I could as much be disturbed by your calling him a psychologist as you are by my calling him a metaphysician. But I am not, because one view does not preclude the other. Einstein, eg, has been evaluated as "scientist," "philosopher," and even a propounder of "a theory of knowledge." But the question is not what I call Nietzsche, but rather whether I can justify the appellation. I think I can.

2. *System.* You did not think it was necessary for me to connect system with metaphysics, as you felt that the two have nothing to do with each other. There are many systems which are not metaphysical at all. Quite so. But it is a logical truism that, while not all systems are metaphysical, one may still assert that all metaphysics are systematic. On the other hand, if all we can find in Nietzsche's works are a few scattered statements that may be considered "metaphysical," [as you indicated], then we cannot speak of any kind of metaphysical thinking in his writings, because sundry remarks and sketchy phrases, as you call them, cannot be regarded metaphysical under any philosophical aspect, unless they are tied together into a coherent world-view, incomplete as that may be. This is what I meant by N's "incomplete system" (his term). To bring together such a coherent world-view out of the writings of a philosopher who "mistrusts all systematizers" and wants "to stay out of their way," may be a daring undertaking. But that is the risk I have taken, and I have not been amiss of N's own position in this matter. We both agree that he is a philosopher. What he says of this type of thinker is very much in line with my approach to his metaphysical speculations. The "true philosopher," he says, has no right to speak in sundry thoughts; his ideas grow out of him like the fruits of a tree "related and all in all interconnected, and are witness of one will, one whole someness, one earthly domain, one sun" (*Genealgy*, Preface 2). While he abhors the "schematic heads," he admits that "Rational thought is interpretation according to a *schema*, which we cannot reject" (*Will to*

Power 522). I have encountered the same difficulty in trying to "systematize" Buber (not as a metaphysician, to be sure) who shuns all system-writing, in my book *Martin Buber's Philosophy of Communication* (later published as *Martin Buber's Philosophy of Interhuman Relation*). I found the solution in his own appraisal of his works, as I did for Nietzsche in his self-appraisal. In both cases there is a selfcontained, unified thought complex which, for lack of a better term we call "system," but mean a coordinated world-view, in Buber's words, "ein in sich schlussiger trans-mittierbarer Denkzusammenhang." And I have found enough in N's writings to present a metaphysical *Denkzusammenhang.*

3. You maintain that N's "will to power" is a psychological hypothesis and not a universal first principle. If this were so, it could explain only psychic phenomena, if indeed it explained anything. But N. extends "will to power" as "the highest perspectivistic interpretation" in nature, life, and man, in a word, as the world drive interpreting itself. Moreover, he does not consider it as a capacity of the mind at all. For its aspect that mght conceivably be psychological is "will" not "power"; and of will as such our philosopher says it is a vague abstraction or illusion: "there is the great fatality of error that will is something that acts — that will is a capacity" (*Twilight,* "Person" in Philosophy 5). "To reduce everything to will is a very naive distortion. . . . Abolish will, free or unfree." (*Nachlass* II, 83, 842. cf. *Nachlass* I, 61). In its place he recommends a new kind of will, not as a human capacity or a quality of the mind, but more fundamentally as a world drive, as a first principle —"The interpretation interpreting itself as a form of will to power" (*Will to Power* 556). "It is clear that here speaks the sovereign drive, which is stronger than man" (*Nachlass* II, 717).

Your suggestion that N's idea of "Eternal Recurrence" would be the more appropriate metaphysical subject of investigation is well taken, but that is not my purpose, as I presuppose this subject in my analysis, without going into its ramifications. For N's "Eternal Recurrence" could be conceived equally well as a theory of physics, and it would therefore still need a first principle to lead it beyond into the realm of metaphysics. By analogy, Einstein's physical world is one of "eternal return" (spherical or elliptical). But Einstein could not close its cycle and he needed a metamathematics. This, by the way, is the theme of my essay "Einteins's Metamathematics" [in my *Philosophy and Technology].*

Apropos your comment that Newton contends he "invented no hypotheses," I would say that he is begging the question. He means to tell us that he deals only with observable facts, but he never observed gravitation as a fact; nor did anyone else. Newton too resorts to metaphysics. This leads me to the next item.

4. *The Afterthought.* Since this was questioned rather emphatically by you and Professor Darnoi, I will say a few more words about it. I am sure that when you wrote in your *Nietzsche* (p. 430) that his "projection of the will to power from the human sphere to the cosmos is an afterthought," you did not mean that it is just a casual notion which is not to be taken seriously, or is an "atavism" of Schopenhauer's influence. The application of the will to power to the universe as a whole plays a fundamental role in N's world-view and only a derivative one in the human sphere when regarded psychologically (as will"), as I have indicated above in item 3. I use the word "afterthought" meaning the metaphysical thought which follows with logical, not psychological, necessity out of physical thought. Kant is no exception to this procedure. For his *K.d.r.V.* is primarily not a dissertation on metaphyscial principles but rather a treatise on the certainty of the science of physics without a metaphysic of any kind. This *Kritik* (d.r.V.), he says, "must stand as a science, systematic and complete in its minutest detail, before we can even think of allowing metaphysics to arise" (*Prolegomena*, Vorrede, 261). After the publication of the *Kritik* and under the impact of critical reviews, Kant put forth his thought on the possibility of the science of metaphysics as such. In this sense his *Prolegomena* is his "afterthought." Of course, he had thought it out previously, but as a logical outgrowth of his views on physics. It is noteworthy that he wrote considerably on problems in physics before he developed into a critical philosopher and started his attack on traditional metaphysics. He proceeded similarly with his theory of ethics. First he wrote the *Kritik der praktischen Vernunft* (1788) which investigates the moral capacity, that is the *physis* of morals, and then the *Metaphysik der Sitten* (1797), which develops the system of a doctrine of morals, that is a *metaphysik*. But regardless of the chronology of his writings and publications, the anterior-posterior relationship is a logical one.

In sum, I consider Nietzsche's metaphysics as one of "perspectivistic interpretation," as an open-end world-view, which differs from some other metaphyscial speculations in that it is a dynamic approach to reality. N's "perspectivism" has always fascinated me, but I have not had the occasion to delve into it. I visualise it in the form of a traveler on a train with the entire net of railroad tracks extending in full view toward the horizon. When the train stops the traveler sees the tracks converging into a unified point, but when the train is in motion he can visualise this point only as a possibility which he hopes to attain beyond the horizon or, if he is of a nilhilistic or pessimistic disposition, perhaps never. His saving grace would then be if he could hope for its return in repeated cycles. He could then grasp it in its universality even while the train is in motion, and he would gain a clear view only of the particulars at every stop. This is the meaning of N's "Eternal Return," which is essentially a doctrine of salvation. But Western man is obsessed with the Faustian tragedy that, if he stopped to enjoy even a fleeting moment of reality he would fall into perdition: "Werd' ich gern zum Augenblicke sagen: Verweile doch! du bist so schön! . . . Dann will ich gern zugrunde gehn. . . . Nur rastlos betätigt sich der Mann." Nietzsche wants to assure him eternal salvation even if he should tarry for a while.

In a metaphysic of "interpretation" such as N's, the tracks and their convergence are meaningless without the traveler. In recent years Fritz Heinemann, taking a clue from our philosopher, no doubt, propounded a metaphysic of *Perspektivismus* in terms of *Interpretations-kategorien* rather than *Seinskategorien* (cf. his *Die Philosophie* d. 20. *Jahrhunderts*, pp. 375-78). Is Nietzsche then a metaphysician or a psychologist? I would say he is both, for in essence he is a Christian philosopher. In your book on *Nietzche* you have treated the Christian aspect of his philosophy with keen insight from a psychological viewpoint. I say there is also a metaphysical side to it. All Christian philosophy (and that is all medieval and modern Western thought) harbors a conflict between psychology (the Socratic *eidos*) and metaphysics (the Aristotelian *logos*), which it tries to reconcile in the person Jesus. Nietzsche too was troubled by this conflict and by the problem of its reconciliation. For he must have felt strongly that anyone who declares God dead [as he did] must answer for it both to man and to God, or in the Christian mode of thinking, both psychologically and metaphysically. You are looking for the Socratic side of Nietzsche, I see in him also a good deal of Aristotle.

I remain cordially yours,
Alexander S. Kohanski

The American Revolution and the Age of Englightenment

In a recent TV production, "Meeting of Minds," on Channel 13 (January 22, 1977, 8 P.M.), Thomas Paine, echoing John Adams, described the American Revolution not as it was fought on the battlefield, which, he thought, was too often a sorry affair, but as it took place in the hearts and minds of the people. In a similar vein, Max Lerner, in his book *America as a Civilization,* seeks to determine what he calls "the American Spirit" " at the point where cultural norms . . . shape personality and character, and where in turn the human material and the energies of Americans leave their impact on the fabric of the culture" (p. 69). I would look for the two most salient features of this character in the American norm of the human individual and in its concept of space, both of which had their inception in the eighteenth century Age of Englightenment, which in turn gave rise to the spirit of the American Revolution.

The Quality of Freedom

Historically, the Age of Enlightenment may be said to have started with John Locke's first "Letter Concerning Toleration," in 1689, and, if we add a few extra years from now until 1989, we shall have rounded out three centuries of one continuous era of the greatest advancement in scientific, technical, and cultural endeavors that Western Civilization has yet been capable of. In our own American civilization it has progressed in the direction of technology, and it is this particular endeavor that has shaped the American character to the point where it may become its destiny for good or ill, depending on a new turn in its outlook toward the future. This is the way of life our forebears chose when they raised the banner of freedom, and this is the burden we must bear on the road to our liberation from whatever shackles it has placed on us.

What quality of freedom did the Americans hope for in their quest for independence? We must look for its roots in the revolution that occurred at the dawn of that era in man's self-evaluation as a human being. I have already mentioned that one of its characteristics was individualism. The general goal of freedom in eighteenth century western Europe was liberation from the tutelage of church and state. It was like the revolt of an adolescent striving for maturity. In Kant's words, "Enlightenment is man's emergence out of his self-encumbered immaturity," that is, an overcoming of one's "incapacity to make use of his own understanding without direction from another." In its broader sense, it means that every one must be free to exercise his personal capacities without outside restriction or interference in thought or action. It then became necessary for man to find out what kind of being he is, what are his strengths and weaknesses, and how he could order his life by himself collectively, but above all individually. The study of man's nature thus became the chief concern of the social philosophers of the time. Alexander Pope expressed this mood in his well-known epigram: "Know then thyself, presume not God to scan./ The proper study of mankind is man." Jean Jacques Rousseau stated it more boldly in his *Confessions.* He said: "I dared to unravel human nature and to look upon it in its nakedness."

The search was on for a faculty in man that is most effective and most reliable in establishing him as an autonomous creature on earth, capable of coping with the forces of his environment in order to procure for himself the conditions of "life, liberty, and the pursuit of happiness," as our Declaration of Independence phrased it. The faculty best suited for that purpose was found to be reason in its various connotations. This was discovered by Locke and Hume, by the French *philosophes* and Encyclopaedists, by Kant, Herder, Lessing, and Mendelssohn. Locke, whose *Essay Concerning Civil Government* was the source of our Declaration of Independence (many passages were taken out verbatim), spoke in that Essay of "the right rule of reason . . . the common rule and measure God has given to mankind." Kant urged his readers: "Have courage to use your own understanding!" and all the rest had the same end in view: to demonstrate man's rational capacity for self-liberation. Rightly or wrongly, that age called itself the Age of Reason, and it is in that light that Thomas Paine wrote his book by that title, and Thomas Jefferson acquired "the habit of testing everything by reason." Summing up the spirit of Englightenment, Wilhelm Windelband states in his *History of Philosophy (Die Geschichte der neueren Philosophie*, I, p. 245): "Having been awakened to the consciousness of its own maturity, modern thought wished in every respect to set its own laws, to find the principles of action and inaction through rational deliberation, and to recognize no other judge over itself."

The second main concern of that age was a knowledge of nature. I shall limit myself to two of its aspects: atomism and the concept of space, as both have a bearing on the temper of the American people before and after the Revolution. The study of natural reality, like the study of human reality, had as its goal the attainment of freedom. It seems as if nature and reason had conspired to reshape the world into the image of rational man. An astute observer like Hegel wrote of that age in his *Philosophy of History* (p. 447): "Never since the sun had stood in the firmament and the planets revolved around him had it been perceived that man's existence centers in his head, i.e in Thought, inspired by which he builds up the world of reality.'

Atomistic World View

The revival of atomic theory, beginning with the 17th century, was concerned with the discovery of the smallest physcial particle or, as it was called, the doctrine of *minima naturalia*. The problems were how to differentiate elements from compounds, whether the elements differed only quantitatively or also qualitatively, and whether they changed their qualities when combined in a compound. Various views prevailed among scientists, such as those of Daniel Sennert, Peirre Gassendi, René Descartes, and Robert Boyle, until they were resolved in the 18th centruy by Antoine Lavoisier who established a method of distinguishing elements from compounds, and later in the beginning of the 19th century by John Dalton, who conceived of the atom as possessing qualities that do not change in the compound. At the same time, the divergent views of the science of nature had their impact on the science of man. Individualism, which came into vogue at that time, is fundamentally a social atomism. Like the atom, each individual is regarded as an entity in and for itself, possessing certain qualities, but indivisible and capable of combining with similar entities into a social compound. We can readily see how the questions about the physical atom and its combinations may be raised also with regard to the human individual and his relationship to society, especially the question whether he changes or loses some of his qualities or natural rights upon entering into a social structure. As we shall note shortly, this was the cardinal issue in the great debate between the Federalists and the anti-Federalists in the framing of the American Constitution. Before we get to this point, we have to examine the role of space in the natural and social sciences of that age.

Limitless Space

Until the time fo Galileo Galilei in the 17th century, the science of physics as well as of man in general, was moving according to Aristotle's metaphysic of space or, speaking more correctly, his notion of place. In Aristotle's world-order a thing moves into a given place by nature and is contained therein as in a vessel filled to the brim, without a separation between the thing and its place, which forms it bounds. There being no void between things and their places or between places, when one thing changes its place it can do so only if another thing makes room for it. Some things move upward and some downward, but under no circumstances can a thing of the lower, that is sublunar regions, occupy the place of a thing in the upper, celestial regions. This was the natural order of the universe, the divine order of the gods in heaven, and the social order of men on earth. Vestiges of this scheme of things on the social level could still be found in the beginning of the twentieth century, as we have witnessed in the Masterpiece Theater production of "Upstairs-Downstairs."

Under these restrictions, atoms could not move about freely from one compound to another. They needed a wide expanse of empty space extended in all directions without hindrance. Therefore, when Galileo introduced his method of quantitative measurement of physical phenomena as they group and regroup themselves in numerous spatial arrangements, he had to give up the Aristotelian view of place and adopt the Platonic concept of an endless space that envelops everything and goes through the entire universe. This then became the new foundation of the natural sciences and also made its inroads into the social-political sciences which started developing during that century. The most effective spokesman of this new social policital outlook was Jean-Jacques Rousseau who, as I quoted him earlier, "dared to unravel human nature and to look at it in its nakedness."

In his *Second Discourse* (on the Origin and Foundations of Inequality Among Men), Rousseau, speaking in terms of physical and moral forces, conceives of natural man as a being who is absolutely free to roam by himself, unencumbered by social or even family ties, and not limited by spatial encroachments through fellow man or beast. Natural man, Rousseau argues, lost his freedom when civilized society imposed itself on him against his will. Therefore, in order to set himself free he must now form a new kind of society through a contract mutually agreed upon by all individuals of equally free disposition. Such a contract must be so constructed that the individual shall not forfeit his free will to the physical forces of society and, moreover, that each phase of the new social order shall derive its powers from the free will of its members.

This credo of individualism, although paradoxically it was turned by Rousseau into an absolute authoritarianism, was hailed by the enlightened world as the basic principle of the rights of man. The American colonials embraced this principle (whether they received it from Rousseau's writings or from other sources), and in their new land they found the opportunity of applying it in their everyday affairs. How did this opportunity present itself? What did the colonials discover in the new world which they had lacked in their old habitations? It was space. Here they found almost endless stretches of fertile territory which every one could virtually roam as he willed, or settle down if he wished, and build his world to his heart's desire. It is these open spaces that molded the American character. These wide expanses also shaped the specific mode of American thinking that was later formulated in the philosophy of Pragmatism, as they also determined the particular American bias toward the mechanical arts which established our technological supremacy.

Much has been written about the fact that in early America, before and long after independence, there were no great theoreticians in the natural as well as in the social sciences When we read a volume such as Brooke Hindle's *The Pursuit of Science in Revolutionary America*, we are struck by the constant emphasis on the practical aspects of all scientific endeavors. Even "Astronomy was a study which fused the utilitarian with the utterly useless in a way that could be twisted to conform to the prevailing assumption that all science is useful" (p. 166). This was not because there were no great minds in the colonies, but rather that these minds directed their attention to the business of carrying theories into practical effects, for which the open spaces provided such tremendous possibilities. The pragmatic bent of inquiry which deals with "functional possibilities," with the way ideas and things work, equating the true with the useful and the good, became

213

manifest yet in the early stages of American society. This was especially evident in its ethical and political writings which assumed the form of maxims and pronouncements rather than theoretical treatises.

Ethical Norms

The ethical norms of the time were markedly individualistic, which, as said, was then the dominant social creed. Some modern social scientists may feel dubious about the real worth of these norms; some, indeed, regard them as shallow or hypocritical. However, in order to evaluate them correctly, we must bear in mind the temper of the generation to whom they were addressed. The people then were not concerned with a speculative ethical system, and none was offered to them. They were interested in virtues that would lead to personal success. Accordingly, they were advised that the most suitable virtues for that purpose were industry, frugality, temperance, justuce, moderation, and the rest of Benjamin Franklin's well-known list of thirteen moral precepts. These were not put forth as moralizing preachment, but as practical instruction. It was generally believed that man is by nature an ethical being, or, as Thomas Jefferson put it, the "moral sense is as much a part of our constitution as that of feeling, seeing, or hearing." Hence, one who cultivates his natural virtues will be able to apply them in everyday life. Undoubtedly Jefferson was speaking to the entire youth of his time when he advised his young nephew Peter Carr:

> Exercise all your virtuous dispositions, and exercise them whenever an opportunity arises: being assured that they will gain strength by exercise, as the limb of the body does, and that exercise will make them habitual. (*The Dem. Enlight.*, pp. 117, 120).

Seemingly, this as well as Franklin's advice has no social import, for it does not relate directly to the good of society as a whole. Nevertheless, it contains an admonition, as implied in the virtue of justice, that one's personal success cannot be bought without due regard for the public weal. Thus Franklin himself was not abashed to advertize his *Almanack* as a publication issued "For the benefit of the Public, and for my own Profit." Society was conceived as the sum-total of its individual members, and the success and wellbeing of all individuals as constituting the good of the totality. Now what is noteworthy about this ethic, regardless of its other implications, is that the individual was judged by his qualities or virtues, and that one of these virtues was his self-interest, which was considered to be proper to his nature like all the other qualities.

I would say that moderation was probably the most valued virtue, at least as we find it in Franklin's code of morals. It was akin to the ancient Greek dictum *oudén ágan,* nothing in excess. Self-interest, when pursued to the extreme, turns into selfishness, and frugality into niggardliness, and so on. But we may rightfully ask, what is to prevent one who lives in an individualistic atmosphere from doing just that: follow his personal ambitions without restraint, even to the detriment of his fellow citizens? Strange as it may seem, this was not viewed as a specifically ethical issue.

Political Planning

The founding fathers were fully aware of this social dilemma, for they knew well also the other side of man's nature, his passions and drives which put self-love above the love of others. However, they had an uncanny insight into the different aspects of the human condition and were able to single them out in their most elemental states. They saw ethics as the problem of individual man and his freedom, but politics as the concern of society as a whole. Not that they regarded the two unrelated to each other, but found from experience that each required specific treatment or, we might say, a different kind of technology. The ethical moment demands unrestricted individual liberty, whereas the political calls for a social authority to control that liberty. Moreover, while the ethical sense, as pointed out above, is a natural individual quality, the political structure is a product of social planning. It was then a problem of finding the best plan that the framers of the American Constitution set out to resolve, and to do it in such a manner that the ethics of personal interest would harmonize with the polity of society. Indeed, their proposed solution was grounded in the ethical principle; for they recognized that unless man was endowed with an ethical capacity he would be totally uncontrollable. At the same time they realized that this capacity is not in a position to generate a sufficient amount of self-control requisite for the good of the body politic. The restraint has to come from a source superseding the individual, namely, from the political power of the organized state.

James Madison presented the issue most pointedly in his famous paper Number 10 of the *Federalist Papers*, in which he argued for the adoption of the proposed American Constitution. "To secure the public good and private rights," he wrote, ". . . is the great object to which our inquiries are directed." But, he warned, if the passion or interest of one group contrives to oppress all the others, "we well know that neither moral nor religious motives can be relied on as an adequate control." And here we come to the core of the social significance of the American Revolution.

Having lived now for two centuries under the aegis of the American Constitution and having experienced some serious disappointments in many phases of its application, we are apt to overlook the fundamental principle which has been the source of its strength; and instead of trying to renew the living forces contained in this principle, we look for a *radical* solution to our social ills, meaning, for the *eradiction* of their underlying causes — types of solution which have been propounded by political theoreticians through the ages, in one form or another, from utopias to scientific socialism. What is revolutionary about the American Constitution is that it was founded on a principle diametrically opposed to a radical solution. Again I shall refer to Madison who unravelled this basic principle through his practical insight into the human condition. In substance he says that, since man is morally so constituted that his interhuman relations are always beset with conflicting factional interests, his political strategy should be not to try to eradicate the causes of this conflict, namely the private interests, which would be contrary to his nature and would destroy his freedom, but rather to set up a governmental structure that would control its effects. It is this kind of structure that our founding fathers envisaged when they established a republican form of government consisting of three branches, namely, the legislative, the executive, and the judicial, and made them all subject to the will of the people, but kept them separate and independent from one another, having each act as a guard against the other two so that none may make its own rule absolute. The art of governing thus becomes a matter of maintaining a balance between factional interests and of adjusting their respective jurisdictions through compromise.*

If now we ask ourselves whether this dream of our founding fathers has been realized, we must answer that, in truth, they were not dreaming but were wide awake to the stark realities of the time as they tried to resolve its inner tensions. The same tensions, we may observe, have existed in American society all along to this day, and the methods which the framers of our Constitution devised for resolving them then have proved to be workable in the course of time with considerable success. The founding fathers did not undertake to create a fool-proof system and they made no claim to perfection: their aim was to devise an adjustable apparatus for their own generation, leaving it to future generations to make further adjustments. I would hesitate calling this a dream. For a dream can never be actualized, because it already is complete or actual in idea. It may serve as a model, but then it may also be a grand illusion because of its perfect form. What can be actualized is the potential, and that is all the American Constitution proposes to provide: a functional potency of government which is constantly being actualized. Without going into the details of all its potentials, I shall indicate only one of its main features, perhaps the main one.

I used several times the phrase "factional interests and conflicts," because this was the central issue of the great Constitutional debate. Speaking on behalf of all concerned in this debate, Madison wrote in the *Federalist Papers* (No. 10): "Among the numerous advantages promised by a well-constructed Union, none deserves to be more accurately developed than its tendency to break and control the violence of faction." The function of government is to "break and control violence," but not to abolish the factions or, as they were also called, the classes. A classless society is a dream without a potential basis in reality. On the other hand, factions or classes are real and potentially adjustable though constant reconciliation. An open recognition of this reality and a firm resolve to cope with it in all its social

*It should be noted that our founding fathers neglected to define more strictly the prerogatives of our judicial branch, especially of its highest body, the Supreme Court. Unlike the other two branches, the Supreme Court is not an elected body; yet very often it exercises what is tantamount to legislative and administrative functions with great, almost absolute authority, which the elected branches do not enjoy. I cannot enter into this matter in my present essay, but it will require basic readjustments through a constitutional amendment.

217

ramifications, is the most important feature of the American Constitution.

Corroding Elements

Now taking a leap from the distant past to the immediate present, and looking at our condition of social turmoil and political disorientation, we may ask ourselves, what went wrong? Who threw a monkey-wrench into the apparatus and made it rasp? And why does our generation feel so helpless when it comes to making the necessary repairs? I will indicate but briefly three elements that have had a corroding influence on the fabric of our social structure. These are a drive for the conquest of nature, the proliferation of technology, and the spirit of mercantilism. They are all interrelated and were inherent in the atomistic outlook of the Age of Enlightenment.

(a) Conquest of Nature

The conquest of nature is the most prenicious goal that the men of the Age of Enlightenment set for themselves. It has all the earmarks of the carefree warrior: plunder, rape, reckless destruction, willful neglect. To use a hyperbole associated with king Pyrrus of Epirus (3rd c. BCE), who was reputed to be a military genius, we may view man's conquest of nature as nothing but a Pyrrhic Victory. As history relates, when this king was congratulated on defeating the Romans at Askulum, though he himself had sustained heavy losses, he remarked: "One more such victory over the Romans and we are utterly undone." We in this century are not very far removed from this kind of victory over nature.

(b) Technological Proliferation

As for our technological advancement, all the material benefit we have gained from it is far outweighed by the loss of human worth we have sustained through its unchecked proliferation. It too is a self-destructive race, not just in the field of nuclear weaponry but also in every phase of our social, governmental, educational, even spiritual activities. When we say that technology has dehumanized man, we mean it has emptied him of content and brought him down to the level of a non-descript entity, like the atom, without qualitative differentiation. The individual is no longer regarded as possessing qualities or virtues by nature, and he is therefore not expected to cultivate them, as he was expected to do in our early past. Individuals are now viewed as mere elements of space and time, as "bits of information" fed into, and coming out of, automated machines. This is true of our industrial and commercial establishments as well as of our social, governmental, and other agencies that deal with the human condition. (Witness the avalanche of questionaires and forms under which every bit of information is buried in these agencies.) By means of the automated media of communication we can now be simultaneously everywhere in space but nowhere at home. As Marshall McLuhan put it in his *The Medium is the Massage* (p. 63), "Ours is a brand-new world of allatonceness. 'Time' has ceased, 'space' has vanished. . . . We live in a . . . simultaneous happening." At the same time, the communications media have magnified the individual beyond measure. The qualitative individualism of the Age of Enlightenment has been transformed into a quantitative individualism without bounds.

(c) Spirit of Mercantilism

The third corroding element in our society, the spirit of mercantilism, is a rather strange vestige of pre-revolutionary days, which we managed to glorify and perpetuate, forgetting all along that our very Declaration of Independence was a reaction against the mercantilistic legislation which the English Parliament had imposed on the American colonies. The United States was born and reared as a capitalist country. It is of interest to note that Adam Smith's *The Wealth of Nations,* the bible of capitalist enterprise, was issued in 1776, in the first year of our independence. Prior to that the prevailing economic view was that of mercantilism which held that wealth consists of gold and silver, or money, and that a country that can accumulate the greatest possible amount of money is wealthy. Thus the American colonies were taxed and used as a conduit for filling the coffers of the English merchants with gold and silver.

Adam Smith changed this outlook by declaring, or by demonstrating from the manufacturing and commercial conditions of his time, that the wealth of a nation consists not of money, as such, but of consumable goods. Therefore, one who possesses capital will invest it in the production of goods for home consumption. Money then serves only as a means of exchange. While the Americans entered into this new mode of economic relations with alacrity, they always, for some reason, retained a mercantilistic attachment to money as the manifestation of real wealth. Even in our time, John Dewey spoke ruefully of "the excessive mercantilism of American life" ("The Development of American Pragmatism," in *Pragmatism*, ed. by H. S. Thayer, p. 38). Be this as it may, the pursuit of money has been a chief goal of the American way of life. This in itself would not be such an evil if money, more specifically paper money, did not become an end in itself on a national scale.

It was sheer prophetic foresight on the part of our founding fathers that they warned us against "a rage of paper money," which they looked upon as "an improper or wicked project" (*Federalist Papers*, No. 10). Whatever they meant by it, this rage has now come upon us like the biblical flood, not that everyone wants to earn as much money as possible, which has its useful purpose, but that our industrial and financial enterprises are converting our natural resources into a gigantic project of producing paper money. Forests are denuded, millions of acres of soil are stripped of verdure, precious wild-life extinguished, rivers and oceans polluted, and mineral wealth wasted — all to no real purpose in human life, but to amass paper money.

In all three of these corroding elements — the conquest of nature, technological proliferation, and mercantilism — man's self-interest has overreached itself. The ethic of individualism has turned into license. This sort of liberty can lead only to enslavement. Violence against nature breeds violence against fellow man and ultimately against oneself. Can our governmental apparatus, which was designed "to break and control violence," still perform its rightful task? Does our Constitution still provide the safeguards built into it under conditions so far removed from ours? No doubt, this Constitution can be made to serve our generation if we face its realities with the same openness of mind and determination of will as our founding fathers faced the realities of their generation. They gave us an instrument which, though it has sustained some cracks, has stood the test of time. It is now up to us to repair its breach and to renew its strength so that we can redirect ourselves on the proper path.

1971

The Problem of Modernity
To Establish the Bounds
of Human Freedom

a. A Crisis in Orientation

In the Spirit of Enlightenment

Our concept of freedom in modern times had its inception in the outlook on reality in the eighteenth century Age of Enlightenment, and to this day it is still dominated by that outlook. Whether or not man may consider himself free depends on his orientation in the world of nature and fellow-men, and when such an orientation becomes obsolete or inadequate in the light of contemporary experience, freedom loses its meaning or at best turns into a problem.

By orientation I mean here a frame of reference in which the category *humanum* and the category *natura* are the two coordinates. In the Age of Enlightenment these categories were given certain dimensions of a scientific world outlook which brought them into conflict with one another. The central question of that age, "What Is Man?" set up the human category as a problematic existent, in that it was conceived as a part of nature and at the same time as a being *sui generis* which is essentially different from all the other parts. To compound its problematic existence, it was further singled out as a self-contained individuality whose tendencies are contrary to its social environment. Thus there arose the negative notion of human freedom, on the one hand as freedom from the exigencies of nature, and on the other hand as freedom from social impediments, which, in turn, made man a problem unto himself. He sought to escape his natural self in order to realize what he conceived to be his superior or true self, and he tried to subdue his social character in order to safeguard his individuality. A brief sketch of the mode of thinking of the Age of Enlightenment will bring to light the rationale of this kind of orientation.

No other philosopher of the eighteenth century expressed the spirit of Englightenment better than Immanuel Kant, when he admonished man, "have courage to use your own understanding. This, then, is the motto of Enlightenment" (opening statement in his essay "what is Enlightenment," *Beantwortung der Frage: Was ist Aufklärung?* October 1784). Indeed, the appeal to reason was the earmark of that age. Kant's plea was for freedom of the individual in matters of thought and belief, for the use of one's own mind without having to depend on "guidance from an other," and, more important, not to be dictated dogmatically by an official body on what is right and wrong to think or to believe, because, as Kant held, "it is every man's calling to think for himself."

In a similar vein, Friedrich Schiller, adopting, as he said, some "Kantian basic ideas," expressed the spirit of the time in his writings on esthetics. Commenting on a motto from Lessing's *Nathan the Wise,* "No man must be coerced" (*Kein Mensch muss müssen*), he wrote: "All things are coerced (müssen): only man is a being that wills." And pondering this essential distinction between man and nature, he further observed:

> But this claim to absolute freedom from everything that is coercion seems to presuppose a being who possesses enough power to ward off any other power against itself. If this claim is found in a being who does not rank highest in the domain of powers, there arises an unfortunate contradiction between drive and capacity; and this is the predicament in which man finds himself (see his essay *Ueber das Erhabene*).

Another distrubing contradiction in the human drive for freedom was pointed out by Moses Mendelssohn in his essay "What does it Mean to Enlighten?" (*Ueber die Frage: Was heisst aufklären?* September 1784). Mendelssohn, who together with Lessing carried on the Leibnizian tradition of metaphysical speculation (a tradition going back to Aristotle), saw the human predicament as a conflict between the contemplative life or philosophy and the practical aspects of social intercourse or art and technology, thus anticipating the specter of technological proliferation in our own time. He designated the first as "Enlightenment" which affects man as an individual, and the second as "Culture" which pertains to a nation or state as a whole. Both, he said, are essential determinations of human destiny, but if they do not proceed in harmony with each other, exercizing mutual controls, each by itself can be detrimental to man's individuality as much as to his role as a member of society. "Misuse of Enlightenment weakens the moral feeling, leads to a rigid view, egotism, irreligion, and anarchy. Misuse of Culture generates profligacy, superficial glitter, softness, superstition, and enslavement." Without elaboration, Mendelssohn called attention to the problem of Culture in the technical and artificial sense and its effects on the social structure when it comes into conflict with the individual urge to rise above the animal level unto higher spheres of thought. In that philosopher's view, the ultimate goal of "Enlightenment . . . is toward (objective) rational knowledge and (subjective) readiness for rational contemplation about things of human life according to their importance and influence in human destiny, . . . which is the measure and goal of all our strivings and efforts."

In general, as the drive for freedom swept the Age of Enlightenment, the leading thinkers of the time saw it from the start in its inner problematic, namely, man's limitations as compared with the forces of nature, and the conflicts between the individual and his social order, both of which dimmed their confidence in man's ability to attain true freedom. Nevertheless, some viewed it as an ideal to strive for, even though it may never be reached.

This is how Kant saw it, as he thought that his generation was really "not living in an enlightened era . . . but rather in an era of enlightenment." That is, while "everyone," he said, "was given an opportunity to avail himself of his own reason," the individual had not yet emerged "from his self-encumbered immaturity," which rendered him "incapable of making use of his understanding without direction from others." Kant's emphasis then was on maturity, which meant individual independence, and thus Enlightenment, or to become enlightened, came to signify man's becoming of age as a totally independent being. Describing the dawn of modernity, Wilhelm Windelband writes (*Die Geschichte der neueren Philosophie* I, Leipzig 1899, p. 245):

Having been awakened to consciousness of his own maturity, modern thought wished in every respect to set its own laws, to find the principles of action and inaction through rational deliberation, and to recognize no other judge over itself.

The means of attaining this goal was through the methods of natural science. To this day, maturity of thought is identified with the sciences; immaturity with theology and metaphysics, which modern man is advised to shun. Thus we hear a logical empiricist warn us, in a volume on *Twentieth Century Philosophy* (New York 1947, p. 376), that

Immature attitudes are associated with attempts to explain experience in ways which lack the distinguishing marks of science. Certain of these pre-scientific modes of explanation, ... like the theological and metaphysical, still prevail.

Scientific method was the dominant orientation of that age, even in the field of philosophy. Writing in the middle of the 1800's, the French mathematician Jean Le Rond d'Alembert characterized that century as the "Age of Philosophy." By that he meant (in Newton's sense of "natural philosophy") that the method of natural science was extended to all fields of knowledge, to problems of metaphysics, taste, politics, morals, as well as to the presuppositions of revealed religion.

The same trend prevailed in England, the cradle of Newtonian mathematical physics, although there reason was subordinated to sense-perceptual experience. David Hume, whom we may regard as the spokesman for English Enlightenment, tempered his scientific view of reality with what he called a "mitigated scepticism" about man's claim to rational certainty. Nonetheless, his method was scientific in the Newtonian sense, only his attention was shifted from physical nature to human nature. His aim was to establish a science of man as the ground for all other sciences.

> 'Tis evident [he wrote in *A Treatise of Human Nature*. Oxford 1964, Introduction, p. xix] that all the sciences have a relation, greater or less, to human nature. . . . Even *Mathematics, Natural Philosophy, and Natural Religion*, are in some measure dependent on the science of Man: since they lie under the cognizance of men and are judged by their powers and faculties.

The true knowledge of man's powers and faculties became the passion of that age, because in order to free himself from all possible coercion man had to be assured of possessing the powers which surpass all things that may coerce. At the same time, as Schiller pointed out, he was faced with the predicament of his own limitations. Science and its concomitant technological advancements held forth to modern man the high promise of enabling him to overcome his limits, surpass the overwhelming forces of nature, and also assert the supremacy of his individual will against social impediments. This gave rise to two phases of the modern orientation in reality: (1) the absolutization of the individual as the supreme rational being, and (2) his relentless drive for the conquest of nature. These two aspects of modernity have turned out to be the Scylla and Charybdis which endanger man's journey toward freedom.

The Irrationality of Individualism

It is not science or technology as such that poses a threat to man's aspiration to freedom, but rather his unwarranted expectation from them. As handed down from Galileo and Newton, the scientific method is that of *resolutivo* and *compositivo*, as the former named it, or that of resolving things into their irreducible elements and restructuring them into an organized knowledge of the world. The most important aspect of this method is that it has to be carried on within a system of principles and laws that may be expressed in mathematical formulae and constituted into a unified whole. It is this particular feature that gave the natural sciences their rightful claim to a rational view of reality. Science then became synonymous with system-building, which could be applied to any field of investigation, not just to mathematical physics. Thus Kant, the great architect of a philosophical structure, considered science (*Wissenschaft*) not an "aggregate" of cognitions but a "system" which is an articulated, organic whole based on an Idea that holds it together. More specifically, "A whole of knowledge which is systematic," he said, "may be called science, and when the connection of knowledge in this system is an interrelationship of grounds and consequences it is a *rational* science" (*Met. Anfangsgründe d. Naturwissenschaft.* Vorrede, 3rd paragraph).

The pursuit of philosophy as science reached a high point in Hegel's system of *Logic.* However, our concern here is what makes a scientific system rational or the meaning of "rational" and *pari passu* "irrational," in this kind of world outlook. In Aristotle's world structure rational means a proper relationship between things within a larger entity. The world is conceived as a cosmos and all its parts are well ordered in certain relationships among themselves as well as with the whole. Its underlying principle is that all things are complete in themselves, have definite magnitudes, and are arranged in harmonious forms. This is called rational. Its opposite is confusion, which is inconceivable or irrational. This pertains to all beings in nature, including man. Thus when Aristotle says, "the state is a creation of nature, and . . . man is by nature a political animal" (*Pol.* 1253a2), he sets the essence of man as that of his proper relationship within a state-community (*polis*), and through the community with the cosmos as a whole. In this kind of world order the Greek person could feel free and secure, because he saw himself as an integral part of a small order (*microcosmos*) which was in turn an integral part of a large order (*macrocosmos*). What is noteworthy here is that the microcosmos is the polis, not the individual, for an individual by himself is not a "cosmos," not an order, to begin with. This also is Aristotle's meaning of man as a rational animal. "Animals," Aristotle says, "lead for the most part a life of nature. . . . Man has a rational principle, in addition, and man only . . . . .And it is characteristic of man that he alone has any sense of good and evil, of just and unjust, and the like, and the association of living beings who have this sense makes a family and a state" (*Pol.* 1334b4, 1253a15). In other words, it is man's communal relationship as one whole being with other whole beings that characterizes his rationality concerning "what is just . . . as well as those [matters] concerned with nature and other aspects of truth" (*Protrepticus*, fr. 30). This may be designated a philosophical view of reality, as contrasted with the physico-mathematical, which goes back to Pythagoras and Plato.

The Pythagoreans saw all things in the world in their numerical proportions, that is, as commensurable with each other like whole numbers, such as 1:2, 3:4, etc. This was regarded as rational because it expressed a *ratio* of things complete in themselves, "not only in the world of the gods, but likewise in all of men's deeds and intercommunications, in the realm of technical skills, and in music. The nature of number as well as of right proportion admits no deception" (Philolaos, fr. 11). But when one of the Pythagoreans, Hypassus of Megapont, discovered that, according to the Master's theorem, the diagonal of a square is incommensurable with its side $(d = a\sqrt{2})$, there was great consternation among the disciples and they were forbidden even to talk about it. They called it an *alogon*, an "unutterable" or irrational.

What happened as a result of that discovery is that for the first time two contrasting world-views came into prominence, the philosophical and the physico-mathematical. In the first the datum of deliberation is man as a human being as a whole; in the second it is any object exclusive of man. Moreover, in the physico-mathematical fields of knowledge in which man is the subject of investigation he is abstracted as just another concept or filtered through as "bits" of information, but not treated as the full living being that he is. The Pythagoreans' world view was basically philosophical, for their prime concern was man as a moral being and not sheer numbers. They applied mathematical principles of relation, or ratios, in order to establish his existence in a rational world. When, therefore, they stumbled on an irrational element in their world structure they were troubled not so much by the mystery of a mathematical deviant as by the fact that it disrupted their view of the world in which man was to exercise his moral functions. The incommensurable entity made the natural order irrational, and man as a whole could have no place in it. This gap between man and nature was unacceptable to them, and they preferred to remain silent until, perhaps, they could come up with a plausible solution. Such a solution was later given by Plato as far as the mathematical sciences are concerned, and only indirectly, or rather in a negative sense, concerning the human condition.

In Plato's dialogue *Theaetetus* (151e), a brilliant young mathematician by the same name investigates the truth of sense-perceptual knowledge in the case of two squares whose sides are not commensurable with each other in length, as for example, $a^2 =$ 3 square feet, and $b^2 = 5$ square feet. The lengths of their sides stand in a ratio of $a:b = \sqrt{3}:\sqrt{5}$. Theaetetus comes up with the following very interesting solution. A number composed of a number multiplying itself he calls "square" or "rectilinear," and all other intermediate numbers in the number series he calls "oblong." The lines forming a rectilinear area he designates as "lengths," and those forming an oblong area "roots" or "surds." If we now consider the above two areas in these terms, they are both oblong, $a^2 = 3 \times 1$, and $b^2 = 5 \times 1$. The areas are communsurable with each other ($a^2:b^2 = 3:5$), but their sides are incommensurable, because they are not lengths, only surds, meaning that they have no independent existence as wholes. Thus Plato accepts the surds for what they are, namely, irrational, but gives them meaning in the context of a structure on a higher level.

Now while Plato does not apply his solution directly to the human condition, it has a philosophical import in its negative aspect. That is, when we take an individual thing out of its appropriate area it appears as an irrational entity, without real independent existence. This holds true of all things in nature when they are decomposed into irreducible elements by the method of physico-mathematical science. Their recomposition may form a system, in which each element is validated in its relationship with all the others. However, in this process not all the decomposed elements are included, only those that fit into the system, and the result is that the things as such cannot be interrelated rationally. The scientists have devised mathematical schemata for "rationalizing" such elements by raising them to a degree above their own level, thus forming a new entity of which they become an inseparable part (according to Bernhard Riemann's formula, whereby a group of n dimensions is explicable in a system of $n+1$ dimensions). Thus a three-dimensionl world is rationalized in a four-dimensional continuum. However, in the new higher entity the constituent elements cease to exist independently. This is dramatically brought to light in the theory of relativity, which adopted Minkowski's four-dimensional space-time continuum. In Minkowski's own words, in this new structure, "space by itself and time by itself are doomed to fade away into mere shadows, and only a kind of union of the two will preserve an independent reality" (*The Principle of Relativity*, by A. Einstein, et alia. New York, 1923, p. 75).

This schema of the Galilean method of *resolutivo* and *compositivo* has its legitimate role in the advancement of the natural sciences, because the fragmentized things, upon entering into a mathematical system, need not be reconstituted as wholes. As a matter of fact, they cease to be things as such altogether and are turned into functions of relation, expressed in mathematical parameters. This is what Bertrand Russell meant when he "defined ... mathematics ... as the subject in which we never know what we are talking about." That is, the *what* can be "about *anything*, and not about one or more particular things" (*Mysticism and Logic*. Anchor Books, p. 71). With the giant strides made in the mathematization of all our sciences in modern times, we are close to the state of a "mathesis universalis" anticipated by Plato and dreamed of by Descartes.

Now man is the sort of "thing" that refuses to lose his identity in this kind of system-building, because he is the only being who strives for freedom; and to be free means to be complete, to be whole. If we look at any of the scientific structures dealing with the human condition in our time, whether physical, psychological, or sociological, we don't find man there as a being as a whole. Whatever semblance of individuality he may be assigned in these structures, it can have no real existence in itself, because it is only a "surd," an irrational element in a contrived complexity (see below on Camus's "freedom of the absurd"). The irony of it is that whenever someone dares to assert his individuality he soon learns to his dismay that the structure is so complicated that he could never extricate. himself from it. Thus modern man is placed in a universe in which he does not find himself as a whole, and he is contrived as an individual in whom he does not recognize his living human experiences. In the modern parlance, he is alienated from the world as well as from himself.

b. The Bounds of Freedom

Absolutization of the Individual

Against this manner of orientation in reality man of today is struggling to produce a rationale for the complexities in which he has become enmeshed, trying to live with them and at the same time hoping to find a meaning in his striving for freedom. As he is groping for a real frame of reference, he tries to absolutize his own individuality as its focal point. A few observations taken from literature, art, and philosophy will exemplify the human predicament of this world outlook.

Albert Camus, in his *The Myth of Sisyphus* (New York, 1955), finds man on the verge of suicide (not "philosophical suicide," he says, but "plain suicide," p. 37), and he tries to save him by showing him the logic of "freedom of the absurd." On the face of it, such reasoning may seem jestful if not ludicrous. But what Camus is telling us in all seriousness is that individual man is an absolute being who can justify his existence only with reference to himself alone. Not only does Camus refuse to accept a scientific schema of placing man within a natural structure of a higher dimension, but he also rejects all philosophical consideration of relating him to a higher human entity.

This is why | he writes| I cannot get lost in the glorification or the mere definition of a notion which eludes me and loses its meaning as soon as it goes beyond the frame of reference of my individual experience. I cannot understand what kind of freedom would be given me by a higher being (p. 42). And thus Camus (in that

229

particular essay, though he later modified his position) is satisfied to set man in the dimension of a "surd," so that his freedom becomes a freedom ad *ab-surdum*; and this, he says, is "true liberty."

When man is "decomposed" and "recomposed" in the paintings of Pablo Picasso, he appears as an irrational being, detached from any organic relationship with nature or fellow-men. Insofar as Picasso pursued this manner of art (which covered his entire career), he could never recompose man as a whole or a group of men as a higher unity, except through geometric design. If we look, for example, at his numerous sketches and paintings of *The Women of Algiers* from A to M, all we see is three or four individualized figures manipulated into various relations of surfaces. In picture C, as one admiring critic observed, "the humanity of the left-hand figure is kept in abeyance; she looks engineered, rigid, solidified, her efficient parts mounted like traffic signals" (Leo Steinberg, *Other Criteria,* p. 131). It is remarkable that this prodigious artist who was pre-occupied throughout his life with the human physiognomy, brought forth, for the most part, individuals torn out of their human and natural existence. He himself characterized his view of man and things very succinctly in the following self-appraisal.

> It is my misfortune — and probably my delight — to use things as my passions tell me. . . . In my case a picture is a sum of destructions [decompositions]. . . . I put all the things I like into my pictures. The things — so much the worse for them; they just have to put up with it ("Conversation, 1935," in *Theories of Modern Art,* by Herschel B. Chipp, 1968, p. 267).

The same goes for his treatment of humans in his paintings.

This is not the place to discuss the influence of science on modern art, but a couple of citations from two leading artists-theoreticians, Albert Gleizes and Jean Metzinger who were colleagues of Picasso, will illustrate their general penchant for the irrational and the individual. They tried to reach their goal by "banishing things" and painting relations. However, as Gleizes and Metzinger saw it,

> The diversity of *relations* of line to line must be indefinite; on this condition it incorporates quality, the *incommensurable* sum

of the affinities perceived between what we discern and that which pre-exists within us: on this condition a work of art is able to move us. . . . There is nothing real except the coincidence of a sensation and an *individual* mental tendency (ibid., pp. 213, 214, italics added).

In the field of philosophy, Jean-Paul Sartre is perhaps the strongest protagonist of this view of reality. What is a logical "absurdity" for Camus becomes an ontololological "nullity" for Sartre. According to the latter, for man to be truly free, he must be "an absolutely independent being," an "absolute event," to the point of self-creation. His drive for freedom is a conflict between himself and the ontic reality of Being, which swallows his existence. He then pecks a nullity or "a hole in the heart of being" and emerges from it as an independent existent. Thus Sartre transforms the theological doctrine of *creatio ex nihilo* into a metaphysical "upsurge" of man creating himself out of his own nothingness. (For a fuller treatment of this subject see my book *Philosophy and Technology.* New York, 1977, ch. 12.) In this schema man emerges as a lonely self who must assume responsibility for all situations he may encounter, because he alone is the founding foundation of them all. The irrationality of this absolutization of the individual is well expressed in Sartre's pithy statement (*Being and Nothingness.* New York, 1956, p. 39), "I have to realize the meaning of the world and of my essence; I make my decision concerning them — without justification and without excuse."

The Conquest of Nature and the Paradox of Freedom

An individual presumably absolutized as a rational being is in fact an irrational entity in reference to a scientific system of nature, because in such a system he appears as a fragment. The two coordinates, *humanum* and *natura*, are broken up into divergent segments, each militating against the other. Not being able to see himself as an integral part of natura, man tends to subordinate it to his humanum and eventually to conquer it entirely. He wants to create an environment which is altogether of his own making and always under his control. This is essentially the meaning of his striving for freedom as far as nature is concerned; but it also represents his aim to free himself from social hindrances. As an absolute individual he must feel free from all outside restrictions. Nature and society are only to serve his individual desires and interests. What has contributed most to this view of the world is modern man's tremendous success in devising scientific and technological instruments for the manipulation of the natural as well as the social order. It fostered in him the notion that those instruments actually reveal the truth of his human condition and that they will augment his capicities beyond all bounds. Indeed, he has already proclaimed this truth to be not far from its realization. But in actuality, it is a paradox of his concept of freedom.

A paradox is an idea which is unbelievable (*paradoxos*, contrary to belief), yet accepted as truth; in contradistinction to a paralogism which is unreasonable (*paralogismos*, false reasoning), yet accepted as belief. In modern times, paradoxical thinking is very much in vogue. We find it unbelievable that man, being a part of nature and a member of society, should be able to master all the forces of nature and establish a social order that will give him absolute individual freedom. Yet this is today the accepted truth of human liberty. This paradox cannot be resolved unless man changes his present orientation in reality.

A Frame of Reference

Of the two main world views which I have traced back to Pythagorean days, the philosophical view prevailed alongside a slow scientific development until the late Renaissance. At the dawn of the Modern Era Galileo set the two worlds apart and inaugurated the physico-mathematical view which has dominated our thinking to this day. Each of these orientations has a different frame of reference and, consequently, a different meaning of freedom. Needless to say that in contemporary thought there is no unitary concept of freedom in either orientation; but I venture to say that we now stand at the end of the Age of Enlightenment and its scientific outlook, as depicted above, and that we are ready to embrace a philosophical outlook, without necessarily abandoning our scientific-technological advancements. For it is not a question whether science and technology are true or good or useful, but how we relate them in a given orientation in which man as a whole and nature in its entirety constitute its two coexistent coordinates. Nor is it a matter of plotting a monolithic goal of freedom, but rather of finding direction toward balancing man and nature within variable limits and bounds. Such a frame of reference may be designated a philosophical orientation in reality, and within it we may reach a general understanding of human freedom and also establish some principles for setting its bounds.

Meaning of Freedom

When we speak of freedom within any frame of reference, and not in the abstract, we must always ask, freedom in reference to what? In the philosophical view it means in reference to both man and nature which are two inseparable entities in our orientation. I am leaving out the religious issue, because it would take me beyond the confines of this paper. Besides, even on the religious level, the problem of man's relation to fellow-men and to nature must be resolved through a human justification, regardless of our theodicy.

The philosophical question that was raised in the past was whether man had a faculty of freedom and how he could exercise it against the surpassing forces of nature. It was couched under the general inquiry "What is Man?" Today we are still pursuing the same quest, broken down into a multiple of compartments, such as, capacities, drives, intuitions, powers, and the like, all of which taken together or separately do not answer the general question nor resolve the particular one of freedom. We know that man is striving for something we call freedom, but we have not given it a real determination, because a determinate freedom seems like a contradicition in terms, as for example, Rousseau's dictum, man is "*forced* to be free," or in Sartre's more ominous words, "man is *condemned* to be free." Perhaps, then, we ought to reexamine our question and, instead of asking what man is and what faculties he has, ask what goes on between him and fellowman and between him and nature, and what it contributes to either side.

As an individual, detached from his community and from his natural environment, man is neither free nor not-free. When therefore, society or nature compels him, so to speak, to do certain things or behave in a certain way, he is not being deprived of freedom, because as an individual he never possessed it or had any notion of it. For freedom is neither a human faculty nor a possession which might have existed prior to his life with fellowman and nature. Rather it comes into existence as a result of this life, that is, as one enters into relations with others; or, freedom is, in fact, *a relation.* It is not on either side of the relation but both sides are *in* it as and when they relate to each other as wholes, as complete entities. To be free, as I pointed out earlier, is for each side to be whole or complete in their interaction. In this respect it is a rational state of affairs, because the ratio is of one whole being to another. Outside of it it has no meaning, whether rational or irrational, because it has no determination, and we must side with Aristotle that, what is not determinate in some form cannot be known and is thus meaningless. Furthermore, this kind of determination of freedom cannot be absolute because neither side is complete in itself. Each may realize its completeness through the relation insofar as it acts in reciprocity.

Here we must draw a distinction between man's relationship with fellowman or the community, on the one hand, and with nature, on the other. I hold with Aristotle that the human community is an outgrowth of man's natural existence and not an artificial contrivance, as Hobbes and Rousseau maintain. Man's relationship with fellowman, therefore, is of the same process as his relationship with nature as a whole. However, in regard to nature, only man is the conscious active partner and as he completes himself through this relationship he also completes nature. On the other hand, in regard to the community, both sides are consciously active partners and their completion grows in direct proportion to their reciprocal interaction.

Evidently, there is a tension in this process, as in all living processes in which both sides try to promote their respective goals. One side may try to utilize or suppress the other for one's own advancement, not recognizing that this would be contrary to the interests of either side. This danger lurks not only in relations between man and community, where it is more pronounced, but also between man and nature. This leads us to the problem of establishing bounds within which the reciprocal relationship, or the process of freedom, may find its proper realization.

Limits and Bounds

The distinction between limits and bounds, as drawn by Kant (*Schranken und Grenzen*, KdrV, B789ff. and *Prolegomena*, ## 57f.), may be adapted here to good advantage. Conceptually, an extended entity may be diminished by subtraction or increased by addition endlessly. We may put a provisional stop in this process by setting a limit to the contraction or extention at any point, as we may find desirable for a given purpose. There are three main features of this concept which make it particularly adaptable to the physico-mathematical sciences. First, the limit is homogeneous with the entity which it limits and is therefore measurable and calculable by the same parameters as the latter, as for example, a point sets a limit on a line, a line on a plane, etc. Second, what lies on one side of the limit is of the same nature as that on the other side, and the limit may thus be shifted from point to point in endless possibilities. Third, the limit does not establish a complete unity, because it always leaves an indeterminate extension of the same entity unaccounted for. In general, then, a limit sets off partial, fragmented objects of extension for specific measurements and calculation, expanding or contracting them, but never reaching a unity of their sum total, because the possibilities of fragmentation (setting limits) are endless. Such is the characteristic of the physico-mathematical sciences: they never complete themselves. Without going into further analysis of this concept, we may observe it also in all fields of technology. Whatever limits we may set in these various fields, they always lend themselves to further extension and thus remain open to endless proliferation.

A bound, on the other hand, is a concept which embraces a totality or schema in all their aspects, forming a complete universe of thought and discourse. It is like a fence around a field which circumscribes it entirely and does not permit it to extend beyond the bounded lines. It is heterogeneous from the object which it bounds, and the two are not measurable by the same parameters; it cannot be shifted at will, because what lies outside of it is of a different nature from that within it; and it gives completion to the objects in all their manifestations, because they cannot get beyond the confines of the established totality. These features of the bound make it adaptable to the philosophical world view.

Role of Philosophy

Kant's comparison of the limit with an indefinitely extended plane and of the bound with a well rounded sphere is very instructive to an understanding of the role which philosophy may play in bringing the two world outlooks together. The limits of the plane are indeterminate and can be known only in segments on contingent grounds, whereas the bounds of the sphere are determined by its contour whose entire curvature as well as its inner dimensions may be gauged with greater assurance from its surface. The sphere represents our world view expressed through speculative concepts and ideas in a philosophical outlook on reality. Within this sphere we may set an indefinite number of planes, expand or contract them, let them shift or rest for any length of time, according to the advancement of our scientific knowledge of each of the parts. But the setting and shifting of such limits must be in harmony with the two coordinates of the sphere as a whole, that is, with man and nature which constitute our universe. The function of philosophy, or rather of the philosopher, then, is to establish the bounds of a world orientation as a guildeline for setting the limits of what is reasonable within it. While the limits of the physico-mathematical sciences may be extended in geometric progression, the bounds of our philosophical orientation may be reshaped only as a complete world view in accordance with our living human experiences (not our empirical sciences). A generation without such bounds loses its bearings in reality. In our Western mode of thinking, which has its roots in the ancient Greek rational view of the world, only the renewal of a philosophical orientation may show us the way to freedom.

Postscripts

It has not been my function in this paper to chart a blueprint of a new orientation for the present generation. My purpose has been to establish its rational ground and to point to its necessary consequences. I have dealt with two contrasting world views, the mathematical-scientific and the philosophical, which call for a reconciliation. But our modernity is beset also with the problem of technology, which more than any other factor threatens to block our road to freedom. However, technology as such is not a world outlook and is therefore outside the confines of my present discussion. Yet it dominates our life and must be accounted for in any new orientation. I will comment only on one of its features, which may tip the scale in favor of philosophy.

Technology, like philosophy, is by its very character teleological. Philosophy gives meaning to human existence only if its outlook is purposive, striving toward a goal in which man is an end in himself, but not the only end. Technology, insofar as it is directed toward the improvement of the human condition, it also purposive, that is, having man's wellbeing as its ultimate goal. However, the trend of modernity is to subordinate nature entirely to human needs, without giving heed to the concept that both, man and nature, are ends in themselves. A true philosophical orientation may bring technology within a universal teleological outlook that will harmonize man and nature toward the same end.

1979

PART II

The Jewish People among the Nations

To my sister Rose Mitchell with whom I have shared our love of Jewish history

Jewish Representations at the United Nations Conference in San Francisco*

The world events that have taken place since the United Nations met in San Francisco — the Berlin Meeting of the Big Three and end of the war with Japan — have almost overshadowed the Charter for peace and security that was created at the San Francisco Conference. What is uppermost in everybody's mind now is a reconversion to a peace economy, the setting of boundaries, reparations from the enemy, and reconstruction of the devastated areas in Europe and Asia. While victory over the enemy and preparations for peace were planned at other meetings of the great powers, the United Nations Conference at San Francisco welded an instrument for the future maintenance of peace. How well or how long this instrument will function will depend on how it will be used by the powers bearing the greatest responsibility under its terms. Nevertheless, the ultimate responsibility must be shared by all the participating states and their respective peoples. Peace and security may be enforced through economic sanctions or military intervention; but it cannot be maintained unless the people have learned to live together in harmony as individuals and as nations. At San Francisco the nations learned to negotiate together; but the settlements and agreements they have reached serve only as a basis for the possibility of living together. To realize this possibility there will have to be a spirit of give and take in the social, economic, and cultural intercourse among the peoples of the world.

For the Jewish people the rehabilitation of its surviving remnants in Europe, insofar as this may be feasible, and the

*Radio address on WINS, New York, June 2, 1945.

establishment of Palestine as a Jewish Commonwealth are the two most pressing tasks in this postwar period. The Charter of the United Nations has a direct bearing on these problems, especially with regard to human rights and the principle of trusteeship over dependent areas. The three major Jewish bodies that sent representatives to the San Francisco Conference were the American Jewish Conference, The World Jewish Congress, and The Board of Deputies of British Jews.

The American Jewish Conference was formed in September 1943, as the representative body of American Jews, comprising 379 delegates democratically elected by all the communities in the country, and 108 delegates designated by sixty-three national Jewish organizations. It may rightfully speak for the overwhelming majority of American Jews on postwar Jewish reconstruction in Europe and on the questions regarding Jewish settlement in Palestine, the two major areas that the American Jewish Conference has adopted as its main concern. The American Jewish Conference was one of forty-two national organizations that were accredited with one consultant each to the American Delegation at San Francisco.

The World Jewish Congress was established by delegates of Jewish organizations and communities from twenty-nine countries who met in Geneva in 1936. Without prejudice to, but in direct support of, the loyalty of the Jewish communities to their various homelands, the World Jewish Congress serves as the organizational expression of Jewish solidarity, that is particularly urgent in the present difficult world situation.

The Board of Deputies of British Jews consists of representatives of congregations and Jewish organizations in Great Britain. Founded in 1760, the Board has throughout its existence watched over the interests of the Jewish communities in the British Isles. It also uses its best offices to mitigate oppression and misfortune of Jews in other countries.

Those three bodies, it may well be said, speak on behalf of 80% to 90% of the Jews in the world, excluding the Soviet Union. Having sent their respective representations to the San Francisco Conference, those three bodies formed a Joint Committee to make presentations to the United Nations on matters of importance to the Jewish people. Another Jewish representative body at San Francisco was the Jewish Agency for Palestine, which is the official representative body of the Jewish people in regard to

Palestine, recognized under the Palestine Mandate by the League of Nations and by the United States of America. The Joint Committee worked in close cooperation with the Jewish Agency on all matters pertaining to Palestine. Among other Jewish organizations that sent representatives to San Francisco mention should made of the American Jewish Committee who had its own accredited consultant to the American Delegation.

Now what was the particular concern of the Jewish representation in San Francisco that could not be taken up as part of the national interests that Jews share with their fellow citizens in their respective countries? They all have the same stake in universal peace and security and in the safeguarding of the rights of each country and its inhabitants. What were the Jewish demands at the United Nations Conference that were not covered by the general resolutions on peace and security for each of the member countries including their Jewish citizens? To be sure many of those resolutions had no specific bearing on Jewish conditions, and generally the Jewish Joint Committee worked together with the non-Jewish American representations for their common interests. But there were two areas which affected Jews in the occupied countries in Europe and in Palestine which bore a specifically Jewish character, and those were some aspects of the principle of human rights and the whole question of trusteeship over dependent territories, notably Palestine.

Human Rights

The promotion of human rights and fundamental freedoms is obviously intended for those who do not enjoy such rights and freedoms. For the Jewish people, which has suffered age-long disabilities and prosecutions in various lands in the old world, and particularly now that a third of its total population has been decimated by the Nazis, the question of human rights assumes very great importance. The Dumbarton Oaks Proposals that were adopted by the United Nations prior to their Conference in San Francisco, recommended a clause on the "promotion of respect" for human rights, but left it to each state to carry it into effect within its own territorial boundaries. From past experiences the Jewish people has learned not to trust such vague promises without effective international control. Hence the Jewish Joint Committee in San Francisco urged the United Nations Conference to add one word in its resolution on this subject, namely, "protection" under its Charter with all the enforcing instruments at its disposal. It should be noted that many of the other representations at the Conference supported this proposal and together they succeeded in strengthening the human rights resolution. Nevertheless, the final phrasing in the section of the Charter dealing with this matter did not fully satisfy the Jewish demands; nor did it meet the expectations of the other representative bodies, but some progress was made. The promotion of human rights was made part of the Charter's purposes, and the General Assembly of the United Nations and its Economic and Social Council have been charged with its implementation though their general organs and also through a special Commission on Human Rights.

Trusteeship Territories

The second sphere of special interest to the Jewish people, namely, the trusteeship plan for dependent areas, had many more hurdles to overcome. One should remember that the chapter on trusteeships does not, and is not supposed to, mention any given territory. A general draft covering all colonial, mandated and other dependent territories may thus be formulated in such a way that the rights of the Jewish people to Palestine under the present mandate may be overlooked, if not jeopardized. Such rights are immigration, colonization, and the upbuilding of the Jewish National Home which are of the essence of the Jewish undertaking in Palestine. And in fact, several governments submitted to the Conference a preliminary trusteeship draft which not only failed to include special safeguards of those rights, but actually prejudiced the rights already recognized. For example, one of the objectives of the proposed trusteeship plan was to promote the welfare of the inhabitants in the trust territories. In this formulation, such a provision might well preclude hundreds of thousands of destitute Jews from entering Palestine, now their only hope for survival. Furthermore, there was no provision made by the draft proponents that if and when the present mandate areas came under the new trusteeship system, the terms of the existing mandate, especially with regard to immigration and colonization, should not be impaired or curtailed.

The Jewish Joint Committee together with the Jewish Agency for Palestine made their objections clear on these proposals, and they received a favorable response by the leading delegations of the Conference. The issue was now on giving the resolution a specific character that would meet the particular needs of each dependent territory; and here the contention was about changing the word "people" to "peoples," to include all those peoples who have a stake in a given territory besides its present inhabitants. In its final form, the resolution now speaks not just of the promotion of the welfare of the inhabitants of a territory, but rather of insuring "the economic and social advancement of the *peoples concerned*." And when it comes to the progressive development of the territories toward self-government or independence, this aim is specified by the phrases "as may be appropriate to the particular circumstances of each territory and its peoples, and as may be provided in each trusteeship arrangement." It further safeguards that "nothing in this chapter should be construed in and of itself to alter in any manner the rights whatsoever of any states or any peoples, or the terms of existing international instruments to which member states may respectively by parties." These amendments and safeguards, referring as they do not just to the inhabitants of the territories, but to the peoples concerned, and specifying further that the terms of existing international obligations may not be altered, give us reason to believe that the rights of the Jewish people to Palestine under the present mandate or its successors will not be abrogated in a new trusteeship system.

It does not follow from the United Nations Charter that the Jewish rights to Palestine will be automatically implemented by the mandate government. The whole struggle around the trusteeship plan at the Conference was to prevent the undermining, if not annulment, of these rights that have previously been acknowledged by recognized international bodies. The Jewish claim to Palestine has the same validity now as before the Charter was written. There were at the Conference certain hostile forces that tried to invalidate that claim; but the obligations of the mandate government, and now also of the United Nations, toward the upbuilding of the Jewish National Home in Palestine remain inviolate.

Recent Jewish Colonization Projects

In the past decade, at least nineteen projects were offered for Jewish immigrant colonization in one part of the world or another, outside Palestine. They all emanated from authoritative government sources, and were given serious consideration by Jewish and general public opinion. In some cases, expeditions were sent to investigate the territories and extensive reports were issued on the possibilities of settlement. Thus far, only one of these projects — succeeded in establishing a very small non-sectarian colony at Sosna in the Dominican Republic; all the others have not reached beyond the stage of preliminary discussion. The following territories came under consideration: in *Africa* — Abyssinia, Angola, Kenya, Madagascar, Rhodesia, Tanganyika; in *Australia* — the Kimberleys; in the *Western Hemisphere* — Alaska, British Guiana, Costa Rica, Cuba, Dominican Republic, Ecuador, French Guiana, Peru, Uruguay; in the *Pacific Ocean* — New Caledonia, New Hebrides, Philippines.

Before we proceed to analyze the nature of these projects and their promise for success or failure, it will be well to discuss the general principles underlying present-day immigrant settlement. The Technical Conference of Experts held in Geneva, February 28 - March 7, 1938, under the auspices of the International Labor Office of the League of Nations, reveal the following salient features of migration for settlement:[1]   1. Countries of immigration which are sparsely populated and which have vast undeveloped territories, are interested primarily in agricultural settlers. Referring especially to the Latin American States, the Report of the Experts points out that, in these countries, the institutions and funds established by the respective governments are limited in capacity. "It is perfectly comprehensible that in view of the limited resources placed at their disposal, the national settlement services should give preference to farmers who, being born and trained in the country, have more chance of settling successfully than persons coming from abroad."[2] In so far as these countries permit the introduction of alien settlers, it is limited to farmers "who are

---

1. *Technical and Financial International Co-operation With Regard to Migration for Settlement.* International Labor Office. Technical Conference of Experts. Geneva, 1938. Published in the United Kingdom for the International Labor Office, by P. S. King & Son, Ltd.

2. Ibid., p. 15.

skilled in special branches of agriculture in which the natives lack training or experience." All these countries seek "selected immigrants."

2. Any movement of migration for settlement must be supported both by the governments of the countries of immigration and those of emigration. The age of spontaneous and uncontrolled immigration is past. Land settlement can be promoted only after important development works have been carried out. This can be undertaken only by the State. Besides, the cost of establishing settlers has risen considerably. The immigrant would therefore require government subsidies in the form of free land, loans, food and medical attention for a certain period of time, and very often also transportation costs from his place of origin to the new settlement.

3. Private settlement organizations created for a social purpose, whether they are purely philanthropic, or such that bear dividends to shareholders, are unable, without government aid, to promote a new movement of migration for settlement. Of the purely philanthropic type, the largest and best known is the Jewish Colonization Association (JCA). This organization was established in 1889 by the late Baron de Hirsch of Paris who placed at its disposal practically his entire legacy. The JCA thus operated in the era of free immigration, and succeeded in establishing thousands of Jewish farmers in Argentina, and smaller numbers in other countries. In the last two decades, it has turned its attention primarily to Palestine, where it has aided Jewish colonization in cooperation with the Jewish Agency for Palestine.

Of the semi-commercial type, the two outstanding organizations which succeeded in the past, were the Hanseatische Kolonialgesellschaft, and the Koiga Kogyo Kaisha. These organizations received substantial aid from their respective governments. The first was created in 1897 under the auspices of the German Government and received a grant of half a million acres from the Brazilian State. The second was founded in 1917 at the initiative of the Japanese Government, from which it received since 1923 annual grants of 100,000 to 200,000 yen and subsidies equal to the costs of the immigrants' transport. Two other similar Japanese companies were formed in 1927 and 1928, namely, the Brazilian Development Company and the South American Development Company, for placement on the land of the Japanese immigrants already there. These organizations grew out of the Japanese Emigration Guilds, the latter being state subsidized.

4. The official representatives who spoke at the Conference of Experts in behalf of their respective governments, offered on the whole very attractive advantages to prospective alien agricultural settlers. At the same time, each of the speakers emphasized the desirability of "selected immigrants." They further stressed the need of international technical and financial cooperation for the promotion of migration with a view to settlement. It thus appears that present-day immigrant colonization is limited to selective agricultural settlement. Such an undertaking involves large sums of capital and can succeed only if supported by government subsidies and aided by international technical and financial agencies. In the light of these general considerations, we may now analyze the prospects of the various Jewish colonization projects.

All these projects for Jewish colonization have been suggested with a view to mass settlement on land. The Jewish settlers would form separate colonies, except in the case of Alaska, Ecuador, and the Dominican Republic where mixed or non-sectarian colonization was proposed. The settlers would be bound to remain on the farm and would not be allowed to engage in enterprises that might be in competition with the native population. The territories offered for Jewish settlement may be analyzed under the following headings:

A. *Territories that were considered unsuitable for European Settlers*

1. The territory in *British Guiana* that was offered in 1938 by Prime Minister Neville Chamberlain for Jewish settlement consisted mainly of forest and savanna, unexplored, wild and malaria-infested. Expert opinion with regard to this territory was divided. A commission that was sent in 1933 by the League of Nations to explore the possibility of settling Assyrians there, reported unfavorably. In 1939 an Anglo-American Commission visited British Guiana and it, too, stated that the territory was "not an ideal place for refugees from Middle European countries . . . |and was| not . . . suitable for immediate large scale settlement." However, this commission felt that a trial settlement project could be undertaken.[3] On the other hand, the London *Times* published

3. "Projects for Jewish Mass Colonization" *Jewish Affairs*, I:4, November, 1941. Published by the Institute of Jewish Affairs, American and World Jewish Congress, New York, p. 8.

what it considered an authoritative statement by A. O. Schwelin, declaring: the proposed territory "lends itself to development only by immigration of tropical labor, backed by a large amount of capital."[4]

2. The Government of *Ecuador* was ready in 1935 to place 1,200,000 acres of land for settlement of immigrants without regard as to race or nationality. Responsible Jewish organizations (*Hias, Hicem, Hilfsverein der Deutschen Juden*) indicated that the territory offered by the Government of Ecuador was not suitable for large scale settlement, and that it would require enormous expenditures to construct the necessary communications even for a small colonization enterprise. The higher altitude zone of that territory has a rarified atmosphere that would make life unbearable. The lowlands are torrid and malaria-infested.

3. The colony of *Tanganyika* that was suggested by the British government in 1938 for refugee settlement, proved to be handicapped by similar obstacles. J. H. Wellington, writing on the "Possibilities of Settlement in Africa," stated with reference to Tanganyika: "The government is evidently determined to allow European and Asiatic settlement only in so far as it will not clash with native interests."[5] The tsetse fly which covers most of that territory has a serious retarding effect on the latter's economic development. Some progress, however, was made by local health authorities in reclaiming many areas.[6] Prime Minister Chamberlain, in his statement before the House of Commons with regard to this project pointed out that "a scheme of small-scale settlement up to a total of 200 settlers is being considered," Lord Marley, on the other hand, stated that Tanganyika was not fit for mass colonization, and that it would be unwise to settle Jewish immigrants in a former German colony.

B. *Territories that were considered suitable for settlement, but not approved by the respective governments.*

4. In December 1938, the United States Secretary of the Interior, Mr. Harold I. Ickes, proposed a plan for settling refugees in *Alaska.* A bill for such a project was later introduced (March

---

4. Ibid., p. 9.

5. *Limits of Land Settlement: A report of Present-day Possibilities.* Prepared under the direction of Isaiah Bowman, President of The John Hopkins University. Council of Foreign Relations, New York, 1937, p. 262.

6. Ibid., p. 241.

1940) in Congress by Senator William H. King and Representative Frank R. Havenner. Opposition to the bill was expressed by Senators Reynolds and Bone, and also by the Alaska Delegate to Congress, Mr. Anthony Diamond. The King-Havenner Bill was referred to a sub-committee and was never brought before Congress.

5. The *Kimberley* district in north-western Australia was proposed for Jewish settlement by the Jewish Freeland League (organized in London, 1935). At present that territory is used for pastoral industry. Mr. J. Steinberg, secretay of the *League* and promoter of the plan stated that he would introduce a planned economy starting with a small number of selected and trained young men and women, and backed by a special Jewish financial institution. The settlement would be based on a balanced combination of pastoral, agricultural and secondary industry on cooperative lines[7] The plan met with a favorable response on the part of leading citizens of Australia. However, some experts consider the territory unsuitable for agricultural settlement. Griffith Taylor, reporting on "Possibilities of Settlement in Australia," indicated that Kimberley has the hottest climate of the continent, reaching an average of 85°F. In his opinion, "the future millions of Australia are going to find their dwelling places and occupations in the lands already known by 1865," i.e., in the southern and eastern areas.[8] A similar view was expressed in a pamphlet issued in 1936 by the Bank of New South Wales. In the Northern Territory and tropical Western Australia, the pamphlet stated: "Every attempt to establish agriculture, by capable men who have experimented for over a century, has been a failure."[9]

The Western Australian Government, though approving the plan in principle, made the following reservation: . . . "the first method of approach for successful settlement is by an extensive and effective pastoral occupation. . . . We would be reluctant to agree to altering any existing laws dealing with land settlement or pastoral occupation."[10] The Commonwealth Government of Australia has not yet given its approval of the project. Its

7. "A Jewish Settlement in the Kimberleys," by J. Steinberg. *The Australian Quarterly,* Vol. XII, No. 1, March 1940, p. 26.

8. *Limits of Land Settlement,* New York, 1937, p. 225.

9. *Empire Opportunities. A Survey of Possibilities of Overseas Settlement.* Contributed by the Dominions and other experts. London, 1938.

10. Quoted from *Jewish Affairs,* Vol. 1, No. 4, November, 1941, p. 11.

traditional attitude, according to the *Melbourne Sun*, is in opposition to group settlement in Australia.

C. *Territories that might be suitable for settlement but in which there was opposition on the part of the "natives."*

6. Portuguese *Angola* was considered by the Jewish Territorial Association in 1907 as a possibility for Jewish settlement. In 1912, the Portuguese Government approved of the plan. The following year, a commission of experts reported that it was possible to settle 250,000 Jews in that colony, provided the government would grant 7,500 square miles, exempt the settlers from taxes for a long term, and also if the project were subsidized by an organization possessing large capital. After the first world war, in 1931, the project was revived by a group of German Jews. But the opposition of the native and white population in Angola, forced the Portuguese government to abandon any scheme of Jewish mass colonization in that territory.

7. Lord Winterton, the British representative at the Evian Conference of 1938, stated at the closing session of that Conference that *Kenya* offered "the possibility of a small-scale settlement of Jewish refugees," and that "a scheme has been evolved for the acquisition of private land in the country." He added, however, that "there can be no question of mass immigration or of distributing land allotted for native occupation."[11] Very soon thereafter, protests against this plan were issued by the East African Indian National Congress, and by the big landowners and companies holding concessions in that territory. The scheme was quickly abandoned.

8. The French Colonial Minister, Marius Moutet, suggested in 1937 that *Madagascar* had good prospects for the settlement of Jews on land. The plan, he said, had been carefully studied by his ministry and the Colonial Governor. The Minister anticipated favorable results provided the following conditions were met: adequate financial backing; proper exploration of the territory; careful selection of the prospective settlers. In a subsequent statement to J. Jefroikin, President of the *Federation des Societes Juives*, the Colonial Minister maintained that "the importance of the French suggestion has been very much exaggerated. The

11. Ibid., p. 11.

question is only about the settling of individual families and, in exceptional cases of workers."

Leon Alter, who was a member of a Commission sent by the Polish government in May 1937 to investigate the territory, reported as follows: Even before the Commission had arrived in Madagascar, articles appeared in the local press protesting against the idea of Jewish colonization. The Governor General, Leon Cayla, told the Commission that as far as the center of the Island was concerned (since that was the most suitable area for settlement), it was occupied by the Hava tribes and would not be available for further settlement. "The Governor assumed that large-scale colonization by whites would probably encounter even stronger opposition from this indigenous element than do the Zionist settlements in Palestine on the part of the local Arabs. As far as he was concerned, he added, he was not prepared to tolerate such a situation.[12] At the Governer's suggestion, the Commission proceeded to investigate the northern part of the central area, called Ankaizina. In order to reach their destination, the members of the Commission travelled three days by road and were carried for another two days on shoulder by the natives. The local governor, then, informed them that there was no state land available for immigrant settlement, but some privately owned territory might be acquired. In Alter's opinion, that territory offered a possibility for a maximum settlement of 2,000 to 2,500 persons. The territory had no roads, and was infested with malaria.[13]

9. *Northern Rhodesia* was another British colony offered for Jewish settlement. In 1938, Prime Minister Chamberlain stated in Parliament that the Governor of the colony had reported favorably on the posibility of small-scale settlement. Captain R. D. Campbell, an expert attached to a commission that was sent to investigate the territory, submitted a plan for the creation of a Jewish state in the northwestern extremity of Northern Rhodesia. It was further reported that the British Government had proposed to settle 500 Jewish families in the colony. On the other hand, opposition to any immigration of Jewish refugees was voiced by the Legislative Council of the Colony, as well as by the Prime

12. *Madagascar,* by Eugene Hevesi. Issued by the Research Institute on Peace and Post-War Problems, American Jewish Committee, New York, May 1941, p. 29.
    13. Ibid.

Minister of neighboring Southern Rhodesia. Subsequently the British Government issued a statement that the reported proposal "to allow the immigration of 500 Jewish refugees was absolutely without foundation." The Governor of Northern Rhodesia announced to the Legislative Council that the proposal of the Colonial Secretary involved only 25 selected Jewish refugees trained in agriculture, and that provision would be made for the expatriation, within five years, of unsuitable refugees.[14]

D. *Territories that might offer various opportunities for settlement, but were merely suggested as possibilities without further negotiation or investigation.*

10-12. The French Colonial Minister, Marius Moutet, suggested in 1937 that there were prospects of land settlement for Jews in *New Caledonia, New Hebrides* and *French Guiana*, adding, however, that large capital was required and that only small-scale colonization was envisaged.

13-17. In 1934 the government of *Peru* made a formal offer of allowing Jewish refugee settlement in the province of Huanoco. In 1936, Congressman William I. Sirowitch announced that he had conferred with President Miguel Gomez of *Cuba* with regard to establishing on that island an industrial colony of German Jews. Another statement issued by the Congressman in May 1939, indicated that the new President of Cuba, Frederico Laredo Bru, would be in favor of forming a colony of 25,000 Jews. *Costa Rica* appeared in American newspapers in 1937 as another possibility for Jewish refugee colonization. *The Phillipine Islands* came into consideration in 1939 when President Quezon announced that his government would favor the settlement of 10,000 Jewish refugees on the Island of Mindanao. *Uruguay's* President, Dr. Gabriel Terra, offered in 1933 to permit 500 Jewish immigrant families to settle on land in his country.

18. Abyssinia, when it was still under Italian occupation, was another one of the territories officially suggested for Jewish mass settlement. The *Gran Consiglio de Fascismo* adopted a resolution on October 6, 1936, stating: "The Great Fascist Council does not exclude the possibility of controlled immigration of Jews into some zone of Abyssinia, also in order to draw off Jewish immigration

14. *Jewish Affairs,* November, 1941, p. 13.

from Palestine."[15] Newspaper reports in January 1939 indicated that the Abyssinia project had been suggested by the Council only as a possibility and that the Italian Government had subsequently regarded it impracticable.

E. *Territories in which colonization was started*

19. Of all the recent projects of Jewish immigration colonization, the Sosua settlement in the Dominican Republic is the only one that has thus far succeeded in getting started. At the Evian Conference of 1938, the Dominican Republic offered room for settling 100,000 refugees. The Refugee Economic Corporation of New York in cooperation with the President's Advisory Committee on Political Refugees, investigated the possibilities of the offer, and reported in its favor. Subsequently, the Dominican Repbulic Settlement Association (known as Dorsa) was organized in New York with an initial capital of $200,000 subscribed by the Agro-Joint (a subsidiary of the American Jewish Joint Distribution Committee). The President of the Dominican Republic, Generalissimo Rafael Trujillo, donated his Sosna estate of 26,000 acres. On January 30, 1940, an agreement was signed between the Dominican Government and Dorsa, and in March of that year the first six settlers arrived in the colony. The settlement, which is non-sectarian, now consists of 472 persons, of whom 104 are married couples, 158 single men, 38 single women and 68 children under the age of 15 years.

In 1942 the Brookings Institution made a survey of the Sosua colony and of the general possibilities of refugee settlement in the Dominican Republic. According to this survey, the native population, which is increasing at the rate of 50,000 a year, will need most of the arable land available. The surveyors therefore conclude that only a maximum of 5,000 refugees may be accommodated on land in the Dominican Republic.[16]

Common Features of all the Jewish Colonization Projects

The projects for Jewish mass colonization that were promoted in the past decade, as outlined above, have the following general features in common:

15. Ibid., p. 7.
16. *Refugee Settlement in the Dominican Republic.* Washington, D. C.: The Brookings Institution, 1942.

(a) After investigation of the possibilities for settlement in all the
proposed territories, it was revealed that at best only small-
scale enterprises could be undertaken.

(b) In each case, large sums of money was required.

(c) No government undertook to subsidize any of the colonization
schemes. On the contrary, several of the governments offered
their territories for Jewish settlement on condition that the
organizations sponsoring the projects would provide large
capital. All the offers made restricted the Jewish immigrants
to agricultural occupations.

(d) At the same time, the colonization of Jews on land requires
extensive as well as intensive preliminary training of the
prospective settlers.

(e) In the case of colonial territories, there was strong opposition
to Jewish refugee settlement on the part of the natives as well
as the established white population.

Conclusions

The multiplicity of projects for Jewish colonization is no doubt
symptomatic of the absolute need of finding a haven of refuge for the
masses of Jews who have been uprooted from their native countries
in Europe. Even if all the proposed territories were suitable for
colonization, the Jewish people could not possibly undertake the
promotion of so many schemes. Private philanthropy could not
muster the tremendous capital that would be required for such
undertakings. The result would be a dissipation of Jewish energy
and means without solving, or even alleviating, the problem of
Jewish mass migration.

As far as government subsidies are concerned, it appears that
the colonization policies prevailing in the countries of immigration
tend to favor the experienced farmer. The vast majority of Jewish
immigrants have to be trained and prepared for agricultural work
prior to their settlement on land. Jews have proven to be good
farmers wherever they have settled on land. However, it can hardly
be expected that every Jewish immigrant become a farmer in order
to be admitted to a given country. Yet this is the condition
underlying all the proposed plans of Jewish colonization. In this
era of controlled immigration, there may be room in some of the
suggested territories for only a very small number of Jewish
agricultural settlers.

On the other hand, there is not a single territory, outside of Palestine, where Jews could concentrate their energies and build a large-scale settlement commensurate with the needs of Jewish migration. Such a territory has not been discovered as yet, despite the diligent search made on four continents by governments and special commissions.

Even if a new territory for Jewish mass colonization were discovered in one of the colonial domains (the colonies are probably the only territories that might be available for that purpose), the Jewish people would not be psychologically or financially prepared to undertake a second enterprise of such magnitude, in addition to Palestine. Colonization of this type would be tantamount to establishing another Jewish homeland. It is hardly conceivable that a people could build two homelands at the same time.

1943

Communist Propaganda for Jews
The New Line

Since the outbreak of the present war, the Communist Party has carried on a special campaign to win adherents among Jews. Its success is rather questionable in view of its hitherto ineffective efforts, and particularly in view of the fact that it is incongruous for a movement advocating a dictatorship that persecutes Judaism and Zionism and is, in addition, tainted with a Hitler partnership, to gain support among Jews. As a matter of fact, many Party members and fellow travelers left after the Soviet-German pact was signed on August 23, 1939. Earl Browder, the general secretary of the Party, admitted as much when he said in April 1940, (*Freiheit*, New York Communist daily, May 2, 1940): "We have suffered losses in the latest period in our leadership in the Jewish field," and he stressed the fact that "the necessity of a big push forward in the Jewish field [is] of such immediate importance that we make it a general Party problem today."

The Communist drive is in line with its general policy of

developing "a new approach to the strengthening of our work in each of the particular national groups that comprise such a large part of the American people" (*Freiheit*, April 29, 1940). However, Browder has a special reason for giving "first attention to the work in the Jewish field." Declaring that "all of the issues of the day in the world and national political life present themselves in a sharp and aggravated form among the Jewish population," he emphasizes: "Do we realize the particular advantages that our position gives us in relation to the Jewish masses?" (*Ibid.*) Thus, the Communists are trying to utilize the Jewish position in the world today, just as they are with other groups, for the promotion of their own interests. This is part of the general line pursued by the Communist Party with the sole aim of defending the Soviet Union, a line followed in its activities among all sections of the American population.

Anti-Nazi Period

It has often been stated that the Communist Party in American receives its instructions from Moscow. Whether this is true or not is immaterial. But there can be no doubt that its policy runs parallel with the foreign policy of the Soviet Union, and that its tactics are applied in varying degree in the same direction. The unsteady course of Soviet policy cannot be easily foretold. In the words of the *New Masses* (Sept. 12, 1939, p. 13): "It would be foolhardy to attempt to predict the exact course of Soviet policy, which is always determined by the interests of the Soviet people. . . ." However, since the advent of Hitler, the pivotal issue in the international position of the Soviet Union has been the relationship of the latter to Nazi Germany. In 1934, that relationship had not yet been crystalized, but the basis upon which it was developing was symptomatic of subsequent results. Thus, Stalin declared at the Seventeenth All-Soviet Union Congress of the Communist Party, held that year, that "the main problem [of our relations with Germany] is not a question of fascism . . . the main question is the struggle that is taking place in the Third Reich between those who advocate cooperation with the Soviet Union," on the one hand, and those who oppose such a policy, on the other hand.

A year later, the line took a sharp turn, and militant anti-fascism became the chief slogan of the Comintern. The clarion call for a united front against fascism and nazism was issued by the General

Secretary of the Communist International, Georgi Dimitroff, at the Seventh World Congress held in Moscow in July and August, 1935. M. Ercoli, another spokesman at this Congress drew applause when he declared emphatically: "German fascism is the instigator of the most raging capitalist reaction, of bloody oppression of the workers, the toiling peasants, the national minorities and the entire German people. . . . To concentrate our battle fire against German fascism, as the principal instigator of war and the mortal enemy of the Soviet Union and the proletarian revolution, is the duty of every revolutionary" (*The Fight for Peace*, Workers Library Publishers, New York, 1935, p. 25).

The Communist Party in America promptly revamped its entire tactical apparatus in line with this new united front policy, which was maintained with varying intensity until the signing of the pact with Germany. As applied to the American scene, this united front policy urged the United States to "assume its rightful position of leadership in world affairs," denounced the isolationists, and supported President Roosevelt's foreign policies, the keynote of which was to quarantine the aggressor. Nazi Germany was the main target of Communist attack, and the boycott of German goods was advocated by the Communist Party. Hitherto, it had frowned upon such a method as a boycott, claiming that it would injure the German proletariat.

Since its very inception, the Communist Party has made strenuous efforts to win members among Jews. Jewish hatred of nazism furnished the Communists with additional appeals. Accordingly, The New York State Committee of the Communist Party, at a session held in March 1938, adopted a resolution which read in part: "As a result of the international offensive against the Jews, the Jewish people today are the natural enemies of fascism and can be readily mobilized into the antifascist front" (*Jewish Life,* April 1938, p. 5). The united front strategy was not merely to win Jewish membership for the Communist Party, but to penetrate and gain control of every Jewish organization. The Communists attempted to form cells in branches of the Workmen's Circle, some Y.M.H.A. and Y.W.H.A. groups, Jewish Centers, and Youth Division of the American Jewish Congress, a few local young people's leagues, and fraternal and benevolent associations. In a number of cases, they met with success. While they did not openly preach communism, they maneuvered some of these groups into joining such front organizations as the League for Peace and

Democracy, the American Youth Congress, and the Jewish People's Committee.

The Communist Party, its press and publications, did not miss an opportunity to describe the horrible deeds perpetrated by the Nazis against the German Jews. After the tragic pogroms in Germany on November 11, 1938, the Moscow *Pravda* of November 18, wrote: "The civilized world regards with repulsion and indignation the bestial wreaking of vengeance of the German fasicst on the helpless Jewish population. The fascists have revealed themselves as the vilest enemies of elementary human cultural values." *Nailebn* (N. Y.) devoted an entire article in an effort to prove that prominent persons in the Soviet Union had made protests against Nazi pogroms (Jan. 1939, pp. 14-16).

The New York State Communist Party felt its work among Jews important enough to establish a special Jewish Bureau and to issue an official monthly magazine entitled *Jewish Life*, which began publication in August 1937. The anti-Nazi line was kept in the forefront. John Arnold, one of its editors, reviewing the position of Jews in Germany in the March 1938 issue, wrote: "The five years of Hitler rule have been a hellish nightmare for the Jews of Germany . . . and is destroying the few limited rights that the Jews of Germany still possess." The all-embracing remedy put forward for these ills was collective security and a united front among all nationalities and groups including the Jews. Hence, Israel Amter tried to persuade his readers (*Jewish Life*, Oct. 1937, p. 17) that "the Communist program for the People's Front, for the unity of all anti-fascists in the struggle against reaction and fascism, meets the needs of the whole Jewish people."

The refugee problem was a particularly troublesome one for Communist apologists. Every democratic country in the world admitted German Jewish refugees in large or small numbers. The Soviet Union alone, which the Communists hailed as the liberator of the Jewish people, did not see fit to open its gates to persecuted Jews. The Communist Party did nothing to influence or petition the Soviet Government to aid Jewish refugees. When Communists were pressed for action by sympathizers, Earl Browder issued a statement that the Soviet Union had admitted more refugees than any other country. But that statement, being challenged by the editor of the *Day*, New York Jewish daily, was never substantiated by the Communists or corroborated by any other source. Two years later, in a speech delivered on April 21, 1940, Earl Browder still felt satisfied that the Soviet Union had done more than anybody else for the Jewish refugees. In a reminiscent mood, he stated: "I can remember a few years ago, everywhere I went . . . Communist sympathizers came to me and said: 'Tell me confidentially, why can't we get just a thousand Jewish refugees openly and demonstratively admitted into the Soviet Union? . . . *What a tremendous agitational and educational instrument that would be in our hands*' " (authors italics). The demonstrative and agitational value of such a move was apparently too great a temptation for Mr. Browder and he "had to answer, 'Comrades, don't be impatient. Don't be impatient. The time is coming and even today, don't forget that the Soviet Union, without any dramatics, very quietly already has more refugees than any other country in the world' " (*Freiheit*, April 30, 1940). As stated, this contention of Mr. Browder has never been proved by himself or anyone else.

The united front appeal among Jews met with very little success. Organizations which were engaged in activities vital to Jewish needs rejected the overtures of the Communists and their affiliates for so-called joint action. The American Jewish Congress, for example, refused to admit delegates for the Jewish People's Committee (a Communist "front") to its sessions in America or to the World Jewish Congress. The Young Poale Zion promptly withdrew from the American Youth Congress, after it learned that the latter was dominated by a Communist leadership. A few rabbis and some Jewish communal leaders who had joined the League for Peace and Democracy in the hope that they would be able to effect some good, eventually resigned from that organization when it became clear to them that the League was completely under the thumb of Communist organizers. Neither could the Communist Party itself boast a large Jewish membership. According to Earl Browder's testimony before the Dies Committee, on September 6, 1939, the Jews constituted only 2½% of the total membership of the Communist Party at the time (*The New York Times,* Sept. 7, 1939).

The New Front

The Nazi-Soviet pact cracked the Communist united front wide open. It caught the Communist Party unawares and bewildered its leadership as well as the rank and file. After the text of the pact was published and the party's spokesmen had given it their interpretations, it became clear that an entirely new policy in Soviet-German relationships had been formulated, one that extended far beyond the range of mere diplomacy. The keynote of the new front was sounded by Premier V. Molotoff in a speech which, as published by the *Daily Worker* of September 2, 1939, contained the following pertinent words: "Only enemies of Germany and the U.S.S.R. can strive to create and foment enmity between the peoples of these countries. *We have always stood for amity between the peoples of the Soveit Union and the German people*" (author's italics). The policy was henceforth to justify Hitlerism and place the blame for the war on Great Britain and France. The Moscow *Izvestia* was quite outspoken in an editorial on October 9, 1939, when it declared: "One may respect or hate Hitlerism just as any other system of political views. *This is a matter of taste.* But to undertake a war for 'annihilation of Hitlerism' means to commit criminal folly in politics" (Quoted in *The New York Times*, Oct. 10, 1939; author's italics). Molotoff again emphasized this policy when he declared: "We always held that a strong Germany was an indispensable condition for a durable peace in Europe. . . . Germany is striving to bring about an end to the war as quickly as possible, whereas England and France . . . want to continue the war and are against peace" (*The New York Times*, Nov. 1, 1939).

The Communist Party was a little tardy in catching up with the new line, but eventually it geared its propaganda machinery to act accordingly. The new front now has had the double task of upholding the foreign policy of the Soviet Union and whitewashing German agression. The Communists have, therefore, directed their attack against the Allies. They have apparently forgotten that only recently they had condemned Hitler as the "mortal enemy of the Soviet Union," and as an "imperialist aggressor . . . threatening . . . the position and national interest of England, France and the United States" (*Daily Worker*, Aug. 25, 1939). Their battle cries have now become, "Stop the War," "Support the Peace Policy of the Soviet Union," etc. They have been vociferous against conscription or any other measure for American preparedness, and they oppose any form of aid that might be given to Great Britain. Such steps toward defense or aid to Britain have been decried by them as "Hitlerization" of America.

A barrage of Communist propaganda was directed toward the American people, appealing to each particular group on the basis of what might seem its special interest. Irish youth were told that they had "nothing to gain by dying for British imperialist bandits," and that their "brothers in Ireland are already feeling the War-Lord's knife in their backs. . . . The Irish patriots . . . who are leading the struggle against war are being hung and imprisoned by the British bankers" (Young Communist League leaflet, New York, May 1940). In another leaflet issued by the Club Lincoln Square of the Y.C.L., the appeal was directed toward both the Irish and the Negroes with such headlines as "Britain hangs two IRA men," or "Negro farmers live in peonage."

The "young workers, farmers and students of America," were admonished to "beware of the agents of Wall Street in the ranks of labor. . . . They are the blood brothers of the European Social Democrats, the British Laborites and French Socialists, who sit in the war cabinets of Europe directing the murder of millions of youth" (C.Y.L. leaflet). Germany was not mentioned in this leaflet. The Finns, Poles, and Baltic groups in America were assured that the Soviet-Finnish war was a struggle of the Soviet Union against capitalist aggression, and that Stalin's occupation and subsequent annexation of a part of Poland and the Baltic states was a great act of liberation of oppressed peoples and of the working masses.

In approaching Jews with the new line, the Communist Party has found itself somewhat at a loss to justify its pro-Nazi sentiments. However, the Communist dialecticians have produced a remarkable formula, which is summarized by one of their spokesmen as follows: "It is true that the Jews hate Hitler and everything that Hitlerism stands for, but the Jews realize fully well that the war is being used by Hitler to rally the German people around himself. The sooner the German people will learn that the rest of the world is ready to help them get rid of Hitler, the sooner will they sweep out the Nazi vermin and rebuild Germany anew on the foundation of liberty and progress." Ergo, the formula continues: "Every additional country that joins the war against Germany gives Hitler an additional chance to argue that the German people must defend themselves against the whole world and that they must therefore support him in that effort." That is why, the argument concludes, the Jews don't want war against Hitler (S. Almazov in *Nailebn*, May 1940, pp. 3-4).

The new peace front, as applied to the Jewish field, has worked along the following lines: (1) It minimizes the danger of nazism and makes little or no reference to Germany; (2) it keeps hammering away at British imperialism, particularly in Palestine; (3) it champions the fight against anti-Semitism; and (4) it extols the benefits bestowed on the Jewish people by the Soviet Union. In their discussions of war and peace, of anti-Semitism or any other problem of Jewish interest, the Communist publications since the pact have minimized the atrocities committed by nazism against the Jews. It is also significant that the word nazism had been practically omitted from their vocabulary for a while. Only recently did their daily press begin to use the term "Nazi" more frequently.

Communist opposition to the building of the Jewish National Home in Palestine has always been relentless and unqualified. It denounced the Zionist movement as an outright capitalist enterprise and Jewish immigration into Palestine as a scheme to exploit the Arab masses, and it bewailed the lot of the so-called "landless" Arabs who were allegedly deprived of their possessions by the Jewish "intruders." The Communists in Palestine issued pamphlets in Arabic inciting the Arab population against the Jews. Zionism, of course, has been proscribed in the U.S.S.R. and its followers persecuted. Toward the end of the united front period, the Communists half-heartedly conceded the right of Jews to immigrate into Palestine only with the consent of the Arabs (B. Sherman, *The Communists in Palestine. The Mufti's Moscow Allies,* New York, 1939).

Now, the new Communist line on Palestine is no longer anti-Jewish but anti-British. The Jewish settlers are not at fault, they say, but it is British imperialism which has betrayed them. The *Freiheit* (April 23, 1940) prints heartrending reports that British soldiers "are . . . mowing down Jewish demonstrators," and that "the Jewish population is seething with rage." To emphasize this news, the *Freiheit* often spread such headlines as "British Storm troopers in Palestine," and the like (May 5, 1940). The Communist press also carried atrocity stories of the alleged "brutality" displayed by the British police against the inoffensive Jewish populace in Jerusalem and Tel Aviv, and in the colonies (*Freiheit*, Sept. 6, 1940). The Communists have forgotten the landless Arabs and are now denouncing Great Britain for limiting Jewish migration into Palestine. "One might think that Jewish land purchases," says I. Rennap in the *Freiheit* of April 19, 1940, "have been wholly responsible for the acute agrarian problem which is the root of the trouble in Palestine. This is not the case." And in order to leave no doubt in the reader's mind that he is a friend of the Jews in Palestine, Rennap emphasizes: "It should be noted that the new land regulations do nothing to prevent the grabbing of Arab peasant lands by Arab landlords. . . . Drastic restrictions of Jewish land purchases . . . will do very little to ameliorate the bad conditions of the Arabs as well as the Jews."

The Communists have thus seemingly taken up the cudgels for the Jewish settlement in Palestine. But instead of Zionism and Palestine, they now attack Zionist leadership. Thus, John Arnold, writing in the *Freiheit* on July 5, 1940, is convinced that "rank and file Zionists cannot help but feel disappointed at the bankruptcy of their leaders." This follows Arnold's claim on April 23 that "instead of arising to defend even Zionist interests, Zionist leadership has chosen to act as an apologist for British imperialism among the Jews even today." It seems that the Communists were not quite sure that their sudden concern about the welfare of the Jews in Palestine would gain much credence among the Jews in America, and they have, therefore, resorted to another scheme of trying to discredit the British and French Governments in the eyes of the Jewish people. They issued a cry that "British and French imperialism are persecuting refugees in England and France," and "85 per cent of the thousands of refugees interned in British concentration camps are Jews" (*Freiheit*, May 24 and Aug. 8, 1940). "The plight of the German refugees," they said, "victims of Nazi persecution, in England is a horrible one. . . . They are getting a severe dose of British Hitlerism in the name of war against Hitlerism." (*Ibid.*, July 19, 1940). Apparently they had nothing to say about the Jewish victims in the Nazi concentration camps in Germany, for they have been silent on that subject for quite a while. They discovered "British Hitlers," "French Hitlers," and "American Hitler's," but the original German Hitler seemed to have escaped their vigilance.

As the professed champions of the oppressed and persecuted, the Communists have paid particular attention to the problem of anti-Semitism. In the united front period, the Party had a very simple and direct anti-Nazi program of action for American Jews. It declared that "the main task confronting the Jewish people was the struggle against reaction and fascism . . . since the fate of the Jewish people is bound up with the victory of democracy and progress" (J. Soltin, *The Struggle against Anti-Semitism,* New York, 1938, pp. 8-9). And further: "This fight [against anti-Semitism] is and must be an integral part of the larger struggle against fascism. Every attempt to separate the two aspects of the struggle plays into the hands of the anti-Semites" (p. 20). That the Communists were more interested in the united front movement than in aiding Jews is evidenced by the fact that they carried on an untiring campaign against the departure of Jews from Nazi Germany, explaining that the proper solution was to fight nazism on the spot.

Since the advent of the Communist new policy, the question of anti-Semitism has been promptly tied up with the cry, "Stop the War!" Fascism and nazism are no longer the issue. United action is no longer necessary to combat nazism. According to Moses Miller, president of the Jewish People's Committee, "it is not the rulers of Britain and France who will destroy nazism. That is the task of the German people. They and they alone can solve the problem." But, Rabbi Miller declares, "the people of the world, particularly the Jewish people, must unite in order to see that the war is brought to an immediate halt," for "to support either side in this war . . . is to defend further anti-Semitism and further pogroms" (*A Jew Looks at War*, Jewish People's Committee, June 1940, p. 26.) How the war can be "brought to an immediate halt," without "supporting either side" is a secret that the Communists refuse to divulge. Furthermore, even if peace could be obtained immediately, it should be clear that, unless Hitler is defeated, the peace terms will be dictated by Nazi Germany. What, then, will be its effect upon the Jews of Europe? "It will be bad," the Communists say. But, "if the Allies defeat Hitler, it will be equally bad if not worse" (P. Novick, *Freiheit*, April, 5, 1940). In other words, they would rather have Hitler win the war.

"It is Good for Jews"

Since the "new front" came into vogue, and especially since Soviet Russia occupied part of Poland and the Baltic states, the Communists have emphasized the boon that the Soviet Union offers the Jewish people. Immediately after the pact was signed and while Hitler was timing his march into Poland, the Communists in New York hailed the treaty as the harbinger of peace and therefore a benefit to the Jews. "What is the prime interest of the Jews in Europe?" M. Katz asked in the *Freiheit* of August 26, 1939. "They are interested, above all, in peace. . . . One has to be a madman or a warmonger to dare say that the non-agression pact means war." After Hitler's conquest of Poland and Stalin's occupation of the eastern part of that country, the Communists greeted the Soviet Union as the liberator of persecuted Jews. They expressed no concern over the fate of the Jews who remained in Nazi Poland, doomed to certain annihilation. They also ignored the fact that the Soviet-German pact, which they had acclaimed as a bulwark of peace, was actually the spark that set off the European conflagration and was thus the direct cause of the extermination of hundreds of Jewish communities throughout Europe.

Following the partition of Poland as well as the acquisition of Baltic and Rumanian territories, there was no limit to Communist rejoicing. Their propaganda "shock troops" began to work feverishly. A flood of letters from individuals and press correspondents from the "liberated" territories, appeared daily in the New York Communist press. Their spokesmen addressed meetings and gatherings on the significance of this "Jewish liberation" (*Freiheit*, July 5, 25, 1940). The appeal was especially directed to the *landsmanshaften* of those territories in this country. A "people's conference" was convened under the auspices of Icor in New York on April 28, 1940, to which all *landsmanshaften* were invited. Subsequently, Icor issued another call to the *landsleit* of the Jews of the "liberated countries," urging them "to join the Icor and become a part of our family," and thus "help spread the truth about the Soviet Union" (*Freiheit*, July 25, 1940).

The greatest boast of the Communists for many years has been Biro-Bidjan, a far eastern province of the Soviet Union which was proclaimed a Jewish autonomous region by the Soviet Government in 1934. According to the late M. J. Olgin, the main reconstruction work for Jews in the territories recently occupied by Soviet Russia will also be effected in Biro-Bidjan. "Under these conditions," he wrote, "the Jewish autonomous region, Biro-Bidjan, with its vast potentialities, acquires greater significance. It is there where hundreds of thousands of new Jews can go in the very near future to start a new life in their own country" (from the *Freiheit* pamphlet, *M. J. Olgin,* Dec. 1939).

Biro-Bidjan has thus far served neither to alleviate the plight of the Jewish people in oppressed European countries, nor even to play any significant role in the improvement of conditions of the Jews in the Soviet Union. From the scanty information available from Soviet sources, it is learned that after twelve years of intensive colonization efforts there are now barely 25,000 Jews in that region, who comprise less than one-fourth of its population. The Jews of Soviet Russia did not care or had no real urge to go there. Furthermore, in spite of promises made by the Soviet Government in 1936 to transfer 1,000 Polish Jewish families to Biro-Bidjan, no Jews from abroad have been permitted to settle there. While the Communists claim that the undertaking has cost the Jewish people "nothing," "not a cent," Icor carries on a continuous campaign among American Jews, having collected tens of thousands of dollars for Biro-Bidjan. The Communists in America, however, have known how to utilize their "gigantic project," as an educational and practical propaganda method.

Front Organizations

The Communists do not always march under their own banner but often assume various guises in the form of organizations with innocent names. The most important planet in the Communist "solar system" was the American League Against War and Fascism, later changed to the American League for Peace and Democracy. The American Youth Congress is another "front" organization that the Communists have managed to control and use for their own interests as the occasion demanded. In the Jewish field, too, the Communists built up several "fronts," tinged in varying shades of red, pink or a neutral color to suit the tastes of the liberal, progressive "innocents."

One of the less disguised "fronts" is the Association for Jewish Colonization in the Soviet Union, better known as Icor. One need not quarrel with Icor's contention that it is not a Communist organization. One may take it at its word when it declares that "Icor has always been the only Jewish organization to defend the Soviet Union by word of mouth and in writing against all its enemies" (*Nailebn*, Jan. 1940). Its work has been carried on through a campaign apparatus which raises funds in America to settle Jews in Biro-Bidjan. Its Communist orientation is fully revealed in the pages of *Nailebn*, its official monthly publication, where one may find the same arguments for a united front, when that policy was in vogue, or, later for the justification of the Nazi-Soviet pact, that appeared in all the other Communist publications. To what extent Icor is interested in rendering aid to needy European Jews may be gauged by the nature of its latest project. In these days, when Jewish suffering in Europe and parts of the world has reached an unprecedented height, Icor has launched a campaign for a fund to erect a monument in Biro-Bidjan, something like a "Statue of Liberty," to celebrate the anticipated proclamation of the territory as a Jewish Soviet State (*Nailebn*, Aug. - Sept. 1940). This project, *Nailebn* comments, "is a great historical enterprise."

The same line and tactics have marked the activities of another front organization, the Jewish People's Committee. In the heyday of the People's Front and the anti-Nazi program, the Jewish People's Committee solemnly declared: "We protest against the Nazi government's cold, official pogrom with its sly, tongue-in-the-cheek legality which deprives most Jews of their means of livelihood and self-respect and is driving thousands to pauperism and suicide" (*America Challenges Anti-Semitism and Race Hatred*, Jewish People's Committee, Jan. 1939, p. 6). More recently, Moses Miller, president of the Jewish People's Committee, has, in effect, defended Hitler by placing the blame for the war on the Allies. "War was declared," he writes, "to force Hitler to keep his promise to march against the Soviet Union" (*A Jew Looks at War*, p. 21). There is not a word in protest or condemnation of Hitler's barbarous acts against the Jews in the Nazi-occupied countries or against the Nazi plans for Jews. Instead, Miller advises Jews not to support either side in this war, for "a victory for either side would be equally disastrous" (*Ibid.*, p. 27). Turning to the American scene, the Jewish People's Committee has been very busy fighting the conscription bill (Statement sent to Senators and Congressmen on July 30, 1940).

The Jewish People's Committee is supposed to be composed of a number of organizations and societies. However, its mainstay is the Jewish section of the International Workers Order. The I.W.O., which grew out of the dissident left-wing elements of the

Workmen's Circle, was organized in 1930. R. Salzman, the general secretary of the Jewish section, has described the I.W.O. as "an organization which is active in the class struggle and which often supports the activities of the Communist Party" (*On the History of the Fraternal Movement,* New York, I.W.O., 1936, p. 76). Thus, the I.W.O. was an ardent supporter of the united front policy, and its class struggle line has been adjusted to the new policy of the Communists. It is no longer directed against German fascism, but against "British imperialism." At its last convention, resolutions were passed for the support of the *Freiheit* "which is always at our service," for Icor, Yikuf, and the Jewish People's Committee. Jews were warned against being trapped into war, "which increases anti-Semitism." The secretary took pride in the fact that all the Trotzkyites had left the organization (*Freiheit,* June 12-17, 1940). But there was no word of condemnation against German aggression or against Nazi persecution of Jews. The tone and the highlights of the convention were furnished by Earl Browder, P. Novick and M. Katz, all functionaries of the Communist Party. Mr. William Wiener, former treasurer of the Communist Party, was re-elected president of the I.W.O.

Nor did the Communists neglect the cultural front. In addition to the Yiddish elementary schools of the I.W.O., which are under their direct influence, they have formed an apparently innocent body called Yikuf, the Yiddish Cultural Alliance, which functions on a world-wide basis. Some members of the Yikuf have protested that it is not a Communist organization, but the offical organ of the Jewish Buro of the Communist Party claims that "the Jewish Communists . . . were the first to see the necessity and possibilities of a united Yiddish cultural front," and they quote Dr. Zhitlowsky's statement that "the Communists have played a considerable role in the general preparations for the Yiddish Cultural Congress in Paris. Here in this country they undoubtedly stand in the front ranks of the active workers" (*Jewish Life,* Sept. 1937, p. 20). It is also interesting to note that Dr. Max Schatz-Anin, spiritual father of the world Yikuf, was the main Communist factotum during the transfer of Latvia to the U.S.S.R. Yikuf publishes a monthly magazine called *Yiddishe Kultur,* issued in New York.

Another literary venture of the "front" of the innocents is the monthly publication, *Equality,* which claims to be, "An Independent, Non-Sectarian Monthly Journal to Defend Democratic

Rights and Combat Racial and Religious Intolerance." In the days of collective security, *Equality* wrote in its first issue (May 1939, p. 15): "Out of sheer self-interest, if not for higher motives, the time has come to discard our isolationism, to acknowledge the mistake of a neutrality policy which has not made for neutrality, but for subsidization to the war makers." And in the September 1939 issue, it exclaimed: "If only the democratic powers collectively asserted their will." This yearning for collective security changed after the German-Soviet pact into a plea for isolation, for "peace mobilization," and, in June 1940, "to be on guard against the 'steps short of war' that lead inevitably to war's brink." Jews are now warned, practically in the same words used by all Communist publications, that "war will breed anti-Semitism," and that they must, therefore, "be in the forefront of the fight for peace" (Feb. 1940, p. 31).

After the demise of the League for Peace and Deocracy, which was conveniently and unceremoniously shelved at a secret session of its executive board on February 1, 1940, the Communist Party started a new "innocent" movement, the Emergency Peace Mobilization, which declared itself a permanent body at its congress held in Chicago during the Labor Day week-end, 1940. This congress sought to revive the old slogans of peace and democracy and to blend them with the latest mottoes, such as "Security at Home," "Jobs not Guns," and general anti-preparedness. The congress turned out to be an anti-conscription rally, staged with all the dramatic paraphernalia. It did not miss the opportunity to emphasize the Jewish angle and devoted a special panel to the question of Jews and the war "to discuss how best to organize the Jewish people in the fight for peace." It denounced the " American Hitlers," but not a word of condemnation was heard about the German Hitler. The Rev. John B. Thompson, who was elected national chairman of the American Peace Mobilization, the name of the permanent body, called upon Jews "to protect all minorities—including themselves," and counted "on a solid Jewish support to keep America out of war" (*Freiheit*, Sept. 5, 1940, p. 6). "Thus," wrote John Arnold in the same issue of the *Freiheit*, "the Emergency Peace Mobilization publicly scotched the lie of the anti-Semites who rant that Jews are warmongers." Apparently, to silence completely the anti-Semites, three Jews were included in the national council of the organization.

In spite of strenuous Communist efforts to gain adherents among Jews, they have exerted only a negligible influence upon Jewish community life. They did meet with relatively greater success during their anit-Nazi period, but, since the signing of the German-Soviet pact, their influence has rapidly declined. Jewish party leaders and rank-and-filers left the Party and its subsidiary organizations en bloc. Even such a veteran of the Communist Party as M. Epstein, editor of th *Freiheit,* resigned. Ephraim Schwartzman resigned as national secretary of the Jewish People's Committee. Yikuf also lost its most prominent members, including such writers as I. Opotashu, P. Hershbein, Dr. A. Mukdony, B. Z. Goldberg and H. Leivik. Such leading Jewish organizations as Junior Hadassah and Young Judea severed their affiliation with the American Youth Congress. The names of important Jewish organizations are absent from the Emergency Peace Mobilization, and only a few new "innocents," a testimony to their naiveté and to strenuous Communist efforts, have appeared at its sessions. Symptomatic of a sharp decline in the circulation of the Communist *Freiheit* is the fact that it has recently been compelled to raise its price from three to four cents and at the same time, carry on a vigorous campaign for contributions and new subscribers. In the issue of June 17, 1940, there was an urgent appeal to the "*Freiheit* Stakhanovists" to go out with "Olgin Boxes" in an emergency relief campaign for their paper. *Jewish Life* did not survive its first year, and *Der Hammer*, Yiddish Communist monthly, also expired with the October 1939 issue. Despite the vociferousness of Communist propaganda, designed to give the impression of numerical strength and effectiveness, their means of disseminating propaganda among Jews are weak, and their reading public is small. There are no pro-Communist publications in the Jewish field outside the Party organs and its affiliated or "innocent" groups.

This is not the place to summarize Jewish objections to Communism, but the very activities of all Jewish organizations are anti-Communist in their nature. A most relentless fight against Communists is being waged with telling effect in labor, religious and Zionist circles. Most American Jews, like most Americans, regard them as a nuisance rather than a menace. Only in New York do they constitute a problem. On the other hand, one should not overlook the fact that the small group of Communist diehards who carry on tenaciously in spite of their setbacks in the Jewish field are bound to get publicity, if not results.

1940

The Jewish Question in the Soviet Union

The volume under review consists of a collection of essays which were written by Solomon Goldelman on various occasions between 1930 and 1936.* The thoughts developed in these articles are not merely observations or comments on occasional events, but represent a critical analysis of the social and economic forces that have played a determining role in the life of the Jewish people in Soviet Russia. The essays are classified under three main headings: "Assimilation and Zionism," "The Jewish Question in Soviet Russia," and "Soviet-Zionism," each telling a dramatic tale of the pangs of a people caught in the maelstrom of the birth of a new social order. Goldelman, who is professor Economics at the new Ukrainian University at Mukacevo, Czechoslovakia, is a keen student of international affairs and an outstanding authority on contemporary Jewish history. While he does not subscribe to Soviet policies and methods, he is a friend of the Soviet people and has never attacked the Soviet government in speech or writing. It should also be noted that the author culled his information on Russian Jewry primarily from sources of Soviet publications and from Communist writers abroad. His studies are thus based on authorities whose sympathies for the Soviet regime no one will doubt. Communists have found it convenient to point to the fact that the Soviet government is by its very nature not anti-Semitic (a fact which nobody contests), and hence the Jewish problem is being automatically solved in Soviet Russia. But Goldelman shows that the non-anti-Semitism of the Soviet government has nothing to do with the Jewish Question. On the other hand, he

*Solomon Goldelman, *Löst der Kommunismus die Judenfrage?* (Does Communism Solve the Jewish Question?) Vienna: Verlag Heinrich Glanz, 1937.

272

demonstrates that neither the government nor the official leaders of Russian Jewry have made a direct attempt to meet the specific needs of the Jewish people in Soviet Russia. For the ruin of the Jews are not only the anti-Semites but also the assimilationists who divert the attention of the people from their inner economic, social and political problems and try to lead them into a land of false promises.

The Communist revolution, like previous cardinal changes in established society, created just another *Konjunktur* (a conjunction of events) which gave impetus to a new wave of assimilation, since the new system was in need of certain forces which the Jewish people possessed. The Jewish intellectuals, and some of the skilled artisans and workers who were useful for the new order of society, were allowed to enjoy the fruits of the Revolution. But those who were considered useless (and as late as 1930 there were 1,000,000 of them) were branded declassée and left to their own demise. That is the law of the Galut: Whenever we are needed for the development of a given state or society, we are invited, tolerated and even accorded special privileges. The moment we have fulfilled our function and are considered no longer useful, we are declared to be superfluous, are persecuted and exiled. This law, Goldelman maintains, operates with equal force in proletarian-industrial Russia as in capitalistic-industrial Western Europe. The Jewish problem, he concludes, is, therefore, a national issue, one of competition among nations and of exploitation of a minority people by the ruling majority.

So much for the theoretical side of the problem. What has actually been the lot of the Jewish people in Russia since the Revolution? Professor Goldelman reviews the role of the Jews in the industrialization of Soviet Russia and in the various colonization projects sponsored by the government, and he shows that in neither case was a serious effort made to strike at the root of the problem which lies in the peculiar position of the Jewish people in the diaspora. It is true that the Jews in Russia are not being persecuted or discriminated against, but at the same time, large masses of them are being used as objects in a state of affairs for which they are not fit, and yet they are not given a real opportunity to make an adequate adjustment. For over twelve years, a million Jews (i.e., two-fifths of the Jewish population), or as a Communist writer (Otto Heller) put it at the time, "almost a whole people," were employed, without civic rights, and on the verge of annihilation. And it was only when the first five year plan was already advanced (in 1930), that the authorities sought to recruit these helpless Jews as artisans and factory hands. The reason for this leniency was clearly stated by a Communist official, L. Singer: "The increase of the industrial proletariat has actually become a matter affecting the very life of Soviet economy. . . . Through our activity (to enlist Jewish youth in industry), we fulfill a very important State function." The declassed Jews were, thus, permitted to fill the vacant jobs in the rising industries, not for their own sake, but for the benefit of the State, and that only when the State was badly in need of them.

The Communists are wont to defend the position of the State, by pointing out that the Soviet government pursues a policy which is neither pro-Jewish nor anti-Jewish, but is proletarian and is applicable to all citizens alike. But that is the tragic irony of the situation: The Jewish question in Soviet Russia is thus being solved without regard to the particular problems of the Jews, as to how and when they need a solution. The experiments in agricultural colonization of the Soviet government, for which the Jews were the laboratory subjects, turned out to be even more tragic, because they were more promising. Professor Goldelman correctly terms these experiments "Soviet Zionism," for the promise made by the government to the Jews was nothing less than an *autonomous republic*, which was equivalent to a national homeland.

In this brief review, one cannot enter upon a detailed discussion of the necessity or value of these colonizational attempts. Goldelman has fully and adeqately analyzed the various grounds and motives underlying the government proclamations that purported to establish Jewish autonomous territories in Soviet Russia. In the first place it was a contest for Jewish foreign capital and for the support of the Jewish masses, especially the youth, abroad. This was to serve as an antidote to Zionism — a sort of counterplay in the game of Soviet anti-British policy. In the second place, and this was particularly true in the case of Birobidjan, the government was vitally interested in settling the wilds of the Taiga (Birobidjan) in anticipation of strategic complications around the Russo-Japanese border. By way of parenthesis, it will be of interest to quote the concluding lines of an article on "Three Years in the Jewish Autonomous Region," which appeared in *Forpost*, official Quarterly of Birobidjan, 1937, No. 2 (4), p. 115: "If the enemy shall dare touch even one foot of our Soviet holy land, he will have to record in his military chronicles the losses which he will have sustained in the battle with the patriots of Birobidjan. . . . The development and fortification of the Jewish Soviet State are put in the trustworthy hands of the flaming patriots of the Jewish autonomous region." Whether or not Goldelman's view is acceptable (though the reviewer is inclined to agree with his view), the liquidation of both colonizational projects, of the Crimea and only recently of Birobidjan, leaves one in bewilderment as to what was actually the intention of the government in uprooting thousands of Jewish families and transporting them to forsaken regions.

The Crimea project started out in high hopes, with a plan to settle 400,000 Jews, which in itself could be realized, if not for the sudden change in policy. The official explanation was that "Ukraine and the Crimea are the historical territories of other peoples and we (Communists) must not encroach upon their rights." Thus, the government declared the Jewish autonomous region in the Crimea as harmful to the indigenous peoples, and immediately upon the liquidation of this enterprise, it ventured on a new scheme of establishing a Jewish region in Birobidjan. A five year plan was devised to settle 100,000 Jews, but after eight years, the following results were obtained: 30,000 Jews were brought to Birobidjan and only 14,000 Jews remained, constituting less than 25% of the total population. (Compare these figures with the 200,000 Jews that entered and *remained* in Palestine during the same period of time, 1928-1936.) Now that Birobidjan, too, has come to a standstill, one wonders what new scheme is being fabricated at the expense of the Jewish masses in Soviet Russia. It should be pointed out that Professor Goldelman makes no indictment against the Soviet government. He repeatedly emphasizes the fact that the government is not anti-Jewish. But he clearly demonstrates that in the general interplay of forces, the Jewish people in Soviet Russia are being driven from pillar to post, their hopes aroused and frustrated, while their leadership is engaged in anti-religious campaigns and in playing assimilationist overtures.

1938

The Spirit That Always Negates

When Mephistopheles introduces himself to Faust, he says of himself, among other non-flattering remarks, "*Ich bin der Geist der stets verneint*" (I am the spirit that always negates). Ilya Ehrenburg's new introduction to the American reader by way of his obscure novel *Lasik Roischwantz*, only brings to light once more the negative aspect of his writings during that period.* In the early days of the Russian Revolution, Ehrenburg was roaming the capitals of Western Europe, pouring his invectives "right" and "left." He had no attachments and no sympathies. He was just against. And since he was also against the Bolsheviks, they expelled him from Russia twice after his brief trips home. When he was finally accepted, in the early thirties, as the foreign correspondent for Russian newspapers, and later repatriated to the Soviet Union, the Communist authorities knew exactly where he had stood. He had been in no-man's land waiting for the tide of battle to turn. But they also knew of his caustic, cynical pen which could become a useful weapon in their propaganda arsenal. Since then, Ehrenburg has never disillusioned his masters in the Kremlin. He has served them well, especially on the anti-Zionist and anti-American fronts.

The Hero, Lasik

The novel under review was written in Paris in 1927, after the Russian Revolution had already passed the periods of Civil War, Military Communism, and the *Nep* (New Economic Policy), introduced by Lenin as a stop-gap in the transition from bourgeois to proletarian society. Toward the end of 1925 the *Nep* was in retreat and on its way to liquidation. The decade of 1917-1927 had only a few bright spots of hope for the 2½ million Jews who remained within the boundaries of the Soviet Union. But even those few spots dimmed very fast, and the Jewish population was cast into the darkest period of their long sojourn in that country, overshadowing even the gloomiest of days under the Czars. During the rapid changes in the economic order, most Jews were tossed into the whirlpool of "delassed" citizens, where to be alive was considered a State crime. Poverty, degradation, starvation were

*Ilya Ehrenburg, *The Stormy Life of Lasik Roitschwanz.* Trans. from the Russian by Leonid Borochowicz and Gertrude Flor. New York: The Polyglot Library, 1960.

their lot. It was during those agonizing years that Ilya Ehrenburg, sitting in Paris, chose to write about "The Stormy Life" of a Russian Jew, named "Lasik Roitschwants." One need not dwell on the significance of the novel's title-name, or its folkloristic or pornographic implications. One may also dispose, at the very outset, of the literary qualities of this work without too much comment. There is in it not a single living character of flesh and blood; even a composite personality which may have been the author's intention to create, does not emerge. If the hero of the novel, Laski, were asked what he thought of himself as a literary creation, he would shrug his shoulders and say: "Who, me, a literary creation? I am a nothing or, as my defense counsel Landau would describe me, I am spun out of a pathological imagination — out of a spirit that always negates."

Dumb but Shrewd

There is nothing in the book that even intimates the struggle of the Jewish masses during those years — their aspiration for at least cultural autonomy, their hope to become an integral part of the builders of a new society, their excitement at the prospect of freedom that dawned on their horizon in the early days of the revolution. Lasik is just an individual coming from nowhere and going nowhere, unrelated to and unconcerned with the upheavals that welled up around him and his people. His greatest aspiration is securing a piece of sausage, preferably non-kosher, to satisfy his voracious appetite. If some good soul provided him with that for the rest of his life he would be completely contented. But since he has to take odd jobs to earn his daily sustenance, he runs into all kinds of difficulty.

For about a third of the book Lasik resides in the Soviet Union, always in trouble with "Natchalstvo" (Officialdom). He really has no ideological arguments with them, for he has nothing constructive to offer. "In the name of all that's being ridiculed," as he puts it, he pokes fun at the new order and at the officials for their ineptitude, inefficiency and stupidity. They catch on to him quickly, As one judge says: "He is dumb, but shrewd. He makes fun of us." (p. 19) Or, in the words of Petrow, the director of an institute, who shouts at him in exasperation: "You have made fun of everybody! To jail! To court!" (p. 92) Lasik therefore finds himself much too often eating his daily bread in the prisons of his home town Homel, or in

Tula, Kiev and Moscow. After he flees Russia together with his Jewish speculator-employer, who later leaves him in the lurch, Lasik wanders through several cities in Western Europe, and through their prisons — as a puppet advertiser, a fake rabbi, an imposter writer and artist, a lackey to a debauched millionaire, a Christian missionary — until he reaches Palestine, where his life ends in misery as he has lived it. The targets of his sarcasm and public exhibitionism are Prussian Junkerism, Jewish Orthodoxy, White Russian emigres, the British Empire and the Zionist enterprise, also modern art and the theater.

A Caricature of Jewish Characters

Lasik may appear sometimes as a sort of vagabond philosopher who is seeking absolute justice and true freedom. One gets the impression that the author tried to recreate in his hero the characters of Sholom Aleichem's "Tevyeh der Milchiger," with his delectable misquotations from the Bible and Talmud; Mendele's "Fishke der Krumer" and his tragic mishaps in life; Senderl in "The Travels of Benjamin the Third," who also ran afoul of the Russian gendarmerie; or Peretz's "Bontche Schweig," whose ideal was a hot bun with milk. But what a caricature Ehrenburg makes of his Lasik in the light of those great characters from the classics of Yiddish literature! His versions of Hassidic stories, whether of Levi Yitzhok of Berditchev, the Besht, or the Kotzker, lack the grace of folklore and the piety of the simple believer. An assimilationist from childhood, Ehrenburg has no use for those "superstitions" and the "obscurantist" customs of his people. His misquotations and elaborations are often crude blasphemies — a mixture of anti-religious propaganda, peppered with some moralizing which usually goes unnoticed by the listener. Under his pen, Jewish religious life in Frankfurt turns into a burlesque. In Palestine he sees only the profiteer, the American lady with diamonds, the corrupt official, or those who come to beg and die at the Wailing Wall. The heroic efforts of the pioneers he does not even notice. His humor is mainly a slapstick comedy of the type of "Three Stooges" in which children take an animal delight.

With such a name, it is hardly conceivable that *Lasik Roitschwantz* might in any way resemble his author. And yet, he does in many respects. Perhaps Ehrenburg did not anticipate the resemblance, which came into greater relief after he lapsed into the Bolshevik arms. For he himself might have been Lasik who was slapped around by the Communists for his desire to be "really free." Lasik, like Ehrenburg, does not fight for any great cause; he does not express any thoughts about human worth or the destiny of human society. He is just preoccupied with himself and his piece of sausage. How truly the author characterizes himself when he lets Lasik write in the foreword to a novel by a French author that a Russian publisher wants to pass along as Party propaganda: "To be sure, Alfonse Curose vacillates between two opposite camps, and does not succeed in putting his feet on safe ground." And then Lasik pats himself on the back for the clever introduction he has concocted: "I can cut up anything from the standpoint of Marxism, even a chicken stomach" (p. 108-9).

The People are Searching for Something

At the end of his life's journey, when he reaches Palestine, Lasik hopes to return home — to Homel. He tries to convince his *landsleit* that he "will collect a hundred signatures and send them by registered letter to all the Chief Commissars in Moscow, and they will send a real boat to pick us up. . . . To be sure," he tells them, "everything is bad and difficult there . . . However, the people are searching for something." (p. 300) Nevertheless, Ehrenburg, still standing on unsure ground, lets his hero pass away in Palestine, at Mother Rachel's Tomb, mourned only by a stubborn watchman, who at last perceives the innocent childish smile on Lasik's motionless face. Perhaps the author, deep in his heart, could not suppress a spark that yearned to unite with the eternal flame of Eretz Yisrael. Of course, that could have been only a fleeting thought. For, not long after he completed the book, Ehrenburg joined the victors of the proletarian revolution.

I admit I have ploughed through this whole tedious novel trying to find some justification for its existence. In the long string of episodes about Lasik's vagaries I found a Hassidic story, in the name of Levi Yitzhok, that might redeem the book from oblivion. Levi Yitzhok of Berditchev, so the story is told, was willing to forego the immediate coming of the Messiah in order to save the life of a simple poor Jew on earth. Alas, the author did not remember the moral of this tale when he joined the Bolshevik forces to bring the Communist Messiah. As for the poor Jew on earth, Ehrenburg has lent his pen for his complete obliteration.

1962

The Jewish Question in the Third Reich

Over three decades have now passed since the Nazis rose to power in Germany and, in the course of twelve years, extended their supremacy over Continental Europe with dire consequences for the free world. Theirs was a drive for world conquest, and in that drive their main target was the Jewish people, whom they sought to wipe off the face of the earth. Only the final victory of the Allied Nations put a stop to that mad scheme. Yet to this day we are still in search of an explanation for the Nazi intent, to begin with. Why, in their overall scheme, did they concentrate so much of their national resources and war potential on an all-out attack against the Jewish people? This question demands an answer, for the Nazi menace was not eliminated with the end of the war, either in Germany or in other parts of the world. One only has to listen to the 'army regulation' songs about future wars now chanted in the West German Panzer Division, to realize the magnitude of the menace. The West German soldiers reminisce with nostalgia about the "hot days and cold nights" they spent on the battle fields, far from their *Vaterland*, "in Poland, in Flanders, in burning deserts," beating back the enemy, and how they now yearn again for this combat unto death, "toward victory until the last fortress shall fall."[1] Warnings of this menace have come from responsible sources even in West Germany, including one of its leading philosophers, Karl Jaspers.[2]

1. Excerpts from a military 'song' recorded in *Der Spiegel,* May 2, 1966 (West German weekly), quoted by Z. Kamai in a Yiddish translation in the New York weekly, *Yiddisher Kemfer,* May 13, 1966, p. 5. (My English translation).

2. Cf. Karl Jaspers, *Wohin treibt die Bundesrepublik:* R. Piper & Co. Verlag, Munchen, 1966, pp. 108-109: Representative Arndt declared in the West German *Parlament,* ". . . 'wir können schon aus dem Grunde leider Gottes nicht sagen, das alles wiederhole sich nicht, weil hier bei uns in Deutschland Zeitungsblättchen erscheinen wie z.B. die

In it not within the province of this study to examine all the factors that may have entered into this phenomenon of contemporary history, especially the Nazi obsession, its tenacious fanaticism with regard to the Jews. This cannot be accounted for by the usual behavior of Jew-baiting on economic, political or religious grounds. For the Nazi phenomenon is not a problem of anti-Semitism in the historical sense of anti-Jewish action or sentiment. This is only one phase of it. Its roots lie deeper, in the development of German nationalism, its mysteries and ideologies, in the state of European society as a whole, and in the international community, even in certain concepts of science and religion. In this article an attempt will be made to analyse one major factor, namely, the Nazi concept of the 'Jewish Question' and its bearing on the war of the Third Reich against the Jews.

The fate of the Jewish people in the Third Reich was determined by many aspects of German nationalism, but primarily by the meaning the Nazis attached to the 'Jewish Question' and their preoccupation with it to the last rifle-sound of the war. And yet, their 'special treatment' (*Sonderbehandlung*) of the Jews in Germany and occupied Europe could have taken different forms besides extermination, as were indeed considered by the Party authorities during various stages of the war. Originally, the 'solution' to the 'Jewish question' was not to be sought during the years of armed conflict with the world. The problem was to be given only "basic scientific treatment in order to prepare the final all-European solution of the question by the Führer after the war."[3] What prompted the change is the role which the concept of the 'question' played in the destiny of the Nazi Party and State.

'Nationalzeitung,' bei der aus jeder Zeile der giftigste Antisemitismus schwitzt. . . . Was in der 'Nationalzeitung' steht, das ist die Sprache der potentiellen Morder von Morgen.'" (We cannot unfortunately say that nothing repeats itself. For here, among us in Germany, appear newspaper sheetlets as for example the 'Nationalzeitung,' in which the most poisonous anti-Semitism oozes out of every line. . . . What is written in the 'Nationalzeitung' is the language of the potential murderers of tomorrow).

3. Statement by Wilhelm Coblitz at a Conference of the *Institut für deutsche Ostarbeit*, held in Cracow, March, 1941. See, *Hitler's Professors,* by Max Weinreich. Yiddish Scientific Intitute (YIVO), New York, 1946, p. 96. This outstanding work on "Germany's Crimes Against the Jewish People" contains a wealth of documentary material, to which I will refer frequently in this essay, under the letters H. P. Note also a statement by Gerhard Kittel, one of the first German scholars to espouse the Nazi cause (*ibid.,* p. 244): "Violent extermination of Jewry is not a question that can be given serious consideration. If it did not succeed in the system of the Spanish Inquisition or the Russian pogroms, it certainly is not possible in the twentieth century. Furthermore, the idea lacks intrinsic meaning. An historical state of affairs (*Tatbestand*), as is the case with this people, may be resolved through the people's extermination at most in demagogic slogans, but never in history itself.

This was the *fatum* of the mythology of the Third Reich.[4] Later, "Himmler and also Goebbels *explained* that the 'final solution' was a task that could not have been postponed because *in world history* there was only one Adolf Hitler and because the war had presented a unique opportunity for 'solving the problem.' Later generations would have neither the strength nor the opportunity to finish with the Jews."[5] Indeed, they were ready to sacrifice much needed war material and even stake the outcome of the war itself in order to 'finish the job,' because the 'job' to them was a fatalistic necessity. And this is the phenomenon that we are trying to investigate. What we are trying to understand is: Why did the Third Reich with its super-powerful *Wehrmacht* consider the small, unarmed, stateless and scattered Jewish people as a threat to its existence? What was the "Jewish grip" that the Nazis wished "to save the German people from?"[6]

The Goal-World Conquest

One must bear in mind that the 'Jewish Question,' as conceived by the Nazis, had nothing to do with problems confronting the Jews living as minority groups in dispersion, their adjustment to a non-Jewish environment, their participation in the economic, political and social-cultural structures of the majority populations in the states of which they are a part. The Nazis were not interested in these matters, that is, they were not concerned with the Jews but only with the 'Jewish Question,' which for them was a problem of racial ideology embedded in a mythical *Weltanschauung.* Neither their own economic self-interests, as such, nor their people's emotional reaction, and certainly not religious considerations, played a decisive role, but only their ultimate goal—the glory of the Third Reich on its path to world conquest.[7]

The meaning of an historical situation is always in the sense that it presents us with a task which we are to master. To kill all the Jews, however, does not mean to master the task" (my translation).

4. Cf. Ernst Cassiver, "Judaism and the Modern Political Myths," *Contemporary Jewish REcord,* New York, April, 1944, Vol. VII:2, pp. 115-126. (Publ. by the American Jewish Committee).

5. Raul Hilberg, *The Destruction of European Jewry.* Quadrangle Books, Chicago, 1961, p. 266 (my italics).

6. Cf. HP., p. 25.

7. Cf. HP., p. 55. Professor Pete-Heinz Seraphim, Nazi ideologist and expert on East-European Jewry, wrote in 1938: "Anti-Semitism in Eastern Europe is preponderantly a result of conflicting economic interests, mixed up with emotional and sometimes religio-moral rejection. But goals and sentiments based on nationalism and enmity toward

Before this goal of the Nazis the 'Jewish Question' posed tremendous obstacles. It constituted a negation of their ideology, and yet they wanted to use it as an active force, a sort of secret weapon, for the attainment of their goal. In matters of State and in the conduct of the war, this 'question' could not therefore be made just a separate province of some special department. It was the crucial problem of the central Party and the State. The entire Nazi hierarchy, from the Führer down to the lowliest Dienstleiter and all the tremendous intellectual, scientific and cultural forces which they were able to muster among the people, concentrated on finding a solution to this paramount problem of Nazidom—the 'Jewish Question.' One of their leading historians of anti-Semitism, Dr. Clemens A. Hoberg, summed up this supreme effort in his report of a conference held in 1938: "National-Socialist scholarship," he said, "has to organize itself from all disciplines into a new totality in accord with the policy of the Jewish question. . . . This unity is therefore possible only . . . as the embracing universality of the German spirit in which anti-Semitism, instead of pure negation, is a constructive, necessary element of the whole."[8] To deal with this problem *systematically* and *thoroughly,* they set up many institutes, agencies, libraries, publications and periodic conferences, which were placed under direct control of the highest ruling authorities. Those agencies attracted or pressed into service a larges number of leading scientists, sociologists, historians, psychologists, and even theologians, and they became the German nation's laboratories of racial theory and practice.

Nazi Institutes for the Study of the Jewish Question

A brief review of some of the institutes, agencies, libraries and publications which the Nazis established for the study of the 'Jewish Question' will reveal how deeply and how fatally they were involved in it. No less a renowned philosopher than Martin Heidegger declared in 1933: "The National Socialist revolution was not merely the taking over of an already existing power in the state by another party sufficiently large to do so, but this revolution means the complete revolution of our German existence."[9] It was

minorities are no *Weltanschauung* and never can have its momentum." HP., p. 78, quoted from Seraphim's *Das Judentum im Osteuropäischen Raum,* p. 673.

8. HP., p. 55.
9. HP., p. 14.

therefore necessary to reshape the entire outlook of the German people in line with National Socialism through new research and through a new interpretation of history. In the early stages, the Nazis were not ready to take over the existing institutions of higher learning.[10] In October, 1935, they set up an agency of their own, the "Reich-Institute for the History of the New Germany," with a "Research Department on the Jewish Question," which became the focus of all the Institute's activities. The *Reichsinstitut,* declared Walter Frank, its director, "considers itself as the center of anti-Semitism in German science."[11] The kind of history that was written by the scholars of the department was, as Julius Streicher was "happy to ascertain", in the spirit of Adolf Hitler, who "said in the beginning of the movement: 'A fighter does not lecture, he speaks from the heart.'"[12] In the next eight years, until 1944, the fighter-scholars produced nine heavy volumes of research on the *Judenfrage* with contributions from thirty-five scientists, some of them world-famous in their respective fields.

About the same time, or a year later, Goebbels sponsored the "Institute for the Study of the Jewish Question," which gradually became, under cover, an agency for the Ministry of Public Enlightenment and Propaganda. And, not to be outdone by either Goebbels or Frank, Alfred Rosenberg, dissatisfied with the latter's *Forschungen zur Judenfrage,* especially its ideological aspects, founded in June, 1939, his own "Institute of the National Socialist Democratic Workers Party for Research into the Jewish Question." The advent of this agency and its ties with the Führer's overall plan are important to note. Hitler had dreamed of founding near Berchtesgaden a *Hohe Schule* (School for Higher Learning) as "the central place for National Socialist research, teaching and training."[13] While this had not materialized, Rosenberg was able to persuade the Führer to set up, in anticipation of the School, its basic department, and that was Rosenberg's Institute. Its inauguration took place at a Conference in March, 1941, in Frankfort am-Main, in the presence of representatives of the

<hr>

10. Cf. Karl Jaspers, *Rechenschaft und Ausblick.* R. Piper & Co. Verlag, Munchen, 1958: "Die Wissenschaft im Hitlerstaat," p. 218-224. The Party was basically hostile toward science, but it wanted to utilize it for its own purposes. It established Reich institutes, etc.

11. HP., pp. 54, 245, also see p. 46.

12 Ibid., p. 54.

13. Ibid., p. 98.

highest Party and State officials. Before that assemblage of dignitaries Rosenberg expounded on the universal implications of the Jewish question in the "great war," which was "also a cleansing biological world revolution," and was therefore "the cause of the entire European continent, the cause of the entire world."[14]

In the same year two other weapons were polished up and sharpened for use by the new establishment. Rosenberg's cheap smear-paper "Der Weltkampf" (est. 1924) was now turned over to the Party Central Publishing House for service to the Institute. It was converted under a slightly changed name, *Weltkampf*, into a 'respectable' scientific journal, "to be the mouthpiece of German and European scholarship," which looked upon this anti-Jewish "work as upon a 'world struggle' (*Weltkampf*), as upon a war."[15] The other weapon was the library and archives of Judaica and Hebraica attached to the Institute, comprising the sequestered famous Jewish and municipal libraries in Germany and abroad. This became the largest library of its kind in the world. But in the minds of the Nazis it was meant not for information on the life and creativity of the Jews, but for source material on the 'Jewish Question,' as was another smaller library that was attached to Frank's Institute, "in accordance with the principles of the National Socialist movement."[16] We need not follow here the formation and careers of all the other institutes, publications and agencies that served the same end, namely, the Nazi war against the Jews. There were similar institutions established under German domination in France, Denmark, Hungary, Italy, Croatia, and Lithuania, and a major "Institute for German Work in the East," located in Cracow, Poland, Gradually the old established institutions of higher learning were also brought into conformity and attuned to the 'problem.' As early as 1939 the political philosopher Bruno Amann indicated the general directive: "In the future," he wrote, "there should be no German university which would not have at least one chair on the Jewish question."[17]

Before we consider the specific Nazi aspects of the 'Jewish

14. Ibid., p. 101.
15. Ibid., p. 104.
16. Ibid., pp. 79, 104-105.
17. Ibid., p. 83.

Question,' however, we ought to look into one more institute which emphasized the *ecumenical* scope of the problem. It was mentioned earlier in this essay that one of the first scholars to embrace the Nazi cause was the theologian Gerhard Kittel, who expressed himself on the religious phase of the issue. Another pioneer in this field was professor Ernest Bergmann of the University of Leipzig, who, writing in 1933, placed "the Jewish question *sub specie aeternitatis* or, rather, by facing the cross."[18] But the one who undertook an organized campaign on the religious front was Walter Grundmann, research director of the "Institute for the Study of Jewish Influence in the Life of the German Church," formed in April, 1939, by a group of Land Churches.[19] His program was "the de-Judaization of Religious Life as the Task of German Theology and Church." This went to the extent of 'proving' that Jesus was not a Jew and of extirpating every Jewish element in the New Testament, as it was rewritten under the title of "God's Message."

What interests us most about that Institute is that it was kept under suspicious surveillance by the Nazi authorities, who would not even grant it permission to issue a magazine of its own. The Propaganda Ministry regarded "the endeavors of this organization . . . well meant. But," it explained, "there is no interest either in assimilating Christian teaching in National Socialism or in proving that a transformed (*umgestaltetes*) Christianity is not fundamentally Jewish." The Nazi relationship to Christianity was more correctly expressed by Bruno Amann, mentioned above, namely, that "the Jewish question . . . from the point of view of Weltanschauung would also be directed against the Protestant and Catholic denominations, in order to achieve uniform attitudes toward the great religious problem of the German folk in the spirit of the National Socialist revolution."[21] It is from this point of view and scope—*sub specie aeternitatis*, and in the mystic "spirit of the National Socialist revolution"—that we must approach the Nazi concept of the 'Jewish Question.'

18. HP., p. 63. Gerhard was the notorious son of the noted Biblical scholar R. Kittel. (See above, note 3).
19. Ibid.
20. Ibid., p. 67.
21. Ibid., p. 83.

One must not expect theoretical consistency from the Nazi professors. While they operated with mystic ideas of race, blood, folk and space, which they tried to fuse into a *mythos* of superstate, they proceeded in a pragmatic, utilitarian way to test the cogency of their theories by their results in application. The Nazi scholars were nimble dialecticians, who could produce a plausible theory for any contingent operation of state policy. Their concepts of race and folk, which seemed constant at first, underwent procrustean changes as suited their purpose. Even the term 'Jew' did not always mean the same thing in their 'scientific' jargon. What remained constant in their theoretical structure were two main ideas: 1) the supremacy of the German folk, and 2) its will to power. The 'Furor Teutonicus' rose again in the twentieth century as it did in the centuries of the Crusades and the Black Death, and once more the Germans set out to creat their 'Imperium Mundi' but with more dreadful fury than heretofore.[22] "The Teutons," declared Ernst Krieck in his *Folk unter dem Schicksal* (Folk Under Fate), "are the nobility folk of world history. If we want to prove this history again, we must remove from our existence Asiatism in any shape that has permeated our being... This is the racial renaissance."[23]

Furthermore, it should be noted that the Nazi rejection of intellectual honesty and moral principles was a basic ingredient of their *Weltanschauung,* camouflaged by a shady science of human evolution based on survival of the fittest and destruction of the foe. They designated it the National Socialist science, according to which the German or Teutonic folk was regarded as the most fitting 'species' of all human races, the only one destined to rule the world, even for the world's own sake. When they rose to power they proclaimed a National Socialist Revolution, that is, they transformed their racial *science of evolution* into an *instrument of revolution.* They undertook the premeditated, revolutionary advancement of their own supremacy through a direct extermination of all other races and groups whom they considered as inferior and hence unfit for survival. They viewed it as their destiny and the fate of the world, and therein lay the tragedy of the Nazi concept of the

---

22. Cf. Selma Stern, *The Spirit Returneth.* Jewish Publication Society of America, Philadelphia, 1946, p. 121ff.
23. HP., p. 74.

'Jewish Question' for the Germans themselves, for the Jewish people, and for mankind as a whole.

Those of us who have been brought up in the Anglo-Saxon mode of thinking will no doubt wonder what all this theoretical claptrap has to do with what the German did to the Jews or to other peoples in occupied Europe. But this is no wonder to the German mind. The scientific researches, conferences and institutes were no cover-up or dress-up affair. If one surveys judiciously this unique phenomenon—the stupendous amount of energy, ingenuity and material possessions spent by German scholarship on the 'Jewish Question', one will realize what a highgeared motive power those theories, philosophies and ideologies had generated for the destructive machinery of the Third Reich. Those theories (to be sure, not entirely sprung from Nazi brains) promulgated new ideas and concepts of human value, diametrically opposed to the Jewish and Christian religious precepts, which the Nazis strung together within their concept of the 'Jewish Question'. In the following paragraphs I shall briefly sketch some salient features of those new values.

The New Era

The Nazis proclaimed a New Universal Era for mandkind in which the rise and dominion of the Third Reich would advance man toward his goal of becoming a 'higher being', patterned after the image of the Nordic race. This was their 'Annunciation' of the salvation of man, in complete negation of the Jewish and Christian ideas of salvation. Jewish tradition had established a different kind of Universal Era, starting with Creation, when the kingdom of God made itself manifest, and leading toward the Messianic age (in the 'end of the days'), when that kingdom will be fulfilled through the salvation of man. Christianity, accepting creation as a starting point, set an historic date for man's salvation, namely, the advent of Jesus. As long as these Jewish and Christian ideals permeated the consciousness of man, the Nazis felt their goal was impossible of attainment. The 'Jewish Question' appeared to them as the anti-Reich, much as the anti-Christ is to the Christian. Speaking in such mystic terms, Bruno Amann wrote: "The Reich of the Teutonic racial soul rises against the anti-Reich of the Semitic-Bolshevik chaos."[24] Thus, the Nazis envisioned a new world order to be

---

24. HP., p. 83. The hyphenated adjective 'Bolshevik' is just to emphasize the Nazi view of the 'Jewish' source of the 'Chaos.'

created out of a presumed chaos by the 'saving' super-power of the Third Reich.

The Image of Man

The Nazi view of man rested on the proposition that there are by nature higher and lower races, whose destinies differ according to their respective biological evolution. There really are, they maintained, different 'species' (*Arten*) of people. This was the "deep mystery" of which Alfred Rosenberg spoke as he hailed the "new scientific *discovery*, which we call racial science." These were also "the eternal laws of selection," which Hitler discovered "in contradiction to the philosophy of pacifist-international democracy."[25] There was no doubt in their minds that the Teutonic race did not only belong to a higher species, but was the highest of all; and the dominion they sought over Europe, and eventually over the world, was not just for the survival of their species, but for the establishment and perpetuation of its supremacy. That was the Nazi self-image. But when they contemplated the 'Jewish Question', an entirely different image of man stared them in the face, one that expressed the dignity and equality of all men whose prototype was "created in the image of God." In their attempt to obliterate that image they chose to murder the people who first proclaimed it to the world, and that is how they anticipated the "final solution to the Jewish Question."

Greater Space

Paul Tillich characterized the Nazi mentality as being dominated by the concept of space, in contradistinction to the Jewish world-view which is in terms of historical time. This was probably meant in a limited sense of space, namely, as a principle of materiality versus spirituality. However, in Nazi ideology 'space' is a correlative term of 'race' and assumes the same fatalistic connotation as the latter, and that is: As the superior Teutonic *race* can grow and perpetuate itself only in an absolute condition of purity, so it can function only in an hermetically closed-in *space*, to the total exclusion of any other race-mixture.

25. Ibid., p. 26-27. Rosenberg's quotation is taken from his book, *Der Kampf um die Weltanschauung,* Munchen, 1938, Cf. also his *Mythus des 20. Jahrhunderts.* Hitler's words are taken from his speech at the Nuremberg Party Convention in 1933.

The Nazi race-science, therefore, called for a concomitant space-science, which was based on the idea of 'Greater Space'. In its first stages, the goal was "to overcome the mental and physical principles of the last two millenia, to revolutionize the European continent as a German-Teutonic continent and to strengthen and complete it as a bulwark of the new idea of national socialism."[26] This was written in 1940 by a Nazi scholar Freidrich Schmidt, in his book *Das Reich als Aufgabe*, that is, as the basic function of the Third Reich. The continent was not only to be made *Judenrein* but also purged of all "detrimental influence of such population elements alien to the [German] folk that constitute a danger to the Reich and the German folk community."[27] That included Poles, Czechs, Ukrainians and other indigenous populations.[28] Europe, especially the eastern region, was to become the 'Greater Space' of the German folk, expunged of all 'alien' admixtures.[29]

Negative Morality—Lying

To achieve its aims it was not enough for the Third Reich to have a *Wehrmacht*, mighty as it may have been in the *blitzkrieg* occupation of Europe. It was rather necessary to have a moral and legal justification in the eyes of the German folk itself and in the eyes of the soldier at the front who was to perform the 'job.' It needed a new set of values and a new basis in legislation that were in essence a negation of Jewish and Christian principles of morality. This aspect of the 'Jewish Question' loomed larger in the

26. HP., p. 126.
27. Ibid., p. 121.
28. Cf. Gerhard Jacobi. *Racial State.* Institute of Jewish Affairs of the American Jewish Congress and World Jewish Congress, New York, 1944, p. 31 ff. The German theories and policies with regard to alien races (that is, other than Jew, since the Nazis did not consider them as a race but a race-mixture, a 'racial type,' a 'sham people,' and the like) changed with the exigencies of the war, from enslavement to extinction, to refolking, Germanization, etc. Cf. HP., pp. 111, 112, 179, 184. Note Hitler's order to his people on the eve of the War: "have no pity. Have a brutal attitude... Kill without pity all men, women and children of the Polish race or language," (Quoted from the *New York Times,* Nov. 24, 1945, in HP., p. 183). Cf. further, Moshe Kaganowitch, *The Participation of the Jews in the Partisan Movement of Soviet Russia* (Yiddish), Rome, 1948, p. 10, 16, 21 ff. ". . . after the extermination of Jews there began a mass-extermination of the White-Russian and Polish population." And: "The Poles, White-Russians and Ukrainians would repeat with a shudder, 'As soon as the Germans are finished with the Jews they will get after us.'"
29. This is reflected also in the old slogan of 'Drang nach Osten' (vital drive toward the East). In a training course for *Ordnungspolizei,* entitled, *The Security of Europe,* the Führer presented its new meaning: "It is our task not to Germanize the East in the old sense, i.e., to impart to people dwelling there Geman language and German laws, but to see to it that in the East dwell solely people of real German, Teutonic blood" (HP., p. 130).

minds of the Nazi ideologists than any other phase of it. As will be indicated later, they were unable to solve it even after, or more so because, they eliminated the Jews by violence from their midst. Not that they had any moral compunctions or pangs of guilt about it, but because they could not translate a negative morality into a positive social force.

One of the elements of their negative morality was the 'untruth.' It is erroneous to assume that Hitler used 'the lie' just as a means of propaganda. In Nazi philosophy lying was a biological factor in the survival of the fittest and hence a 'morally' justifiable means of life.[30] Hitler did not invent this principle. But he and his professors refined it into a sharp instrument and used it not only against the Jews, but also in their dealings with the Czechs, the Poles, the Russians, with their own Axis partners, and with the rest of the world. It was at the basis of their scientific and philosophical research, and it played a part in their relations with their own German folk. Finally they lied to each other, until they started lying each to himself.

Negative Morality—Killing

The Biblical commandment, "Thou shalt not kill" was the greatest obstacle on the road to Nazi conquest of the world, not in terms of conflict in war, but killing as a way of life. This was to them the essence of the 'Jewish Question.' The prohibition to kill was viewed as a fundamental contradiction of Nazi racial theory. In the parlance of *Rassenkunde* "races originate as a result of natural or artificial breeding selections. For this purpose the breeder makes use of the same rigid selection, of isolation, and inconsiderate extinction (*Ausmerze*) of all descendants who do not fit into the breeding goal . . ."[31] This purposive 'breeding selection' which the Germans perfected through 'experimental genetics' on human beings, became the 'political biology' of the National Socialist movement and the Reich. In its practical application it was effected by means of two formidable instruments, fashioned by the Nazis, one, called *Euthanasia*, for the elimination of

---

30. Cf. Karl Jaspers, *op. cit.,* "Die Wissenschaft in Hitlerstaat," p. 218: ". . . Wahrheit und Nationalsozialismus schliessen einander aus. . . . Denn er musste in der Wissenschaft wie in der Kirche seinen Todfeind fühlen." (Truth and National Socialism exclude each other. . . . For in science as in the church it must have sensed its mortal enemy).
31. HP., p. 173, Cf. ibid., p. 27ff.

'undesirables,' killing the weak and unfit in order to strengthen their own race, and the other, called *Genocide* — exterminating other races to assure the 'Greater Space' for the Nordics alone. Thus the biological struggle for existence was turned by the Nazis into premediated murder, and killing was elevated into a law of the natural way of life, to be advanced by the science of political biology.[32] What this meant to the evolution of the German folk is that it had to be transformed into a nation of killers. From their goal of developing the superman the Nazis now proceeded to a new, 'higher goal,' the "superhumanly inhuman," as the fighters in the East were exhorted to become. Thereby they placed themselves outside the community of the human race, as conceived by the moral code of The Ten Commandments.

The Reich as Law-Giver

The Nuremberg Laws[33] and similar racial legislation enacted by the Third Reich before and during the war were not just a matter of internal affairs, as the Western world was prone to view them. They were meant as legislation for the human race as a whole, from beginning to end. The Reich which, in the mind of the Nazis, only the German folk could create, was conceived as the bearer of the new world order. Therefore, within the 'Greater Space' it was the sole lawmaker, and it would brook no "interference from powers that are alien to the space and do not belong to the folk."[34] The

32. This theory was developed by Carl Schmitt, "a renown professor of political science," whom Martin Buber took to task in his essay "Die Frage an den Einzelnen," published in 1936, when the discussion was still on a respectable academic level. Buber criticized Schmitt's political scientific thesis that the "friend-foe" relation among people is a fundamental criterion of the State. The concept 'foe', according to Schmitt, entails a real struggle within the state with "the possibility of physical killing," and that, he says, lends "to man's life its specifically *political* tension." (Cf. Martin Buber, *Das dialogische Prinzip*, Heidelberg, 1962, pp. 252-53). Among Schmitt's other contributions to political science was his study, "German Science of Law in the Struggle Against the Jewish Spirit." (Cf. HP., p. 40. not 78).

33. The two Nuremberg Laws adopted by the *Reichstag* at a special session of the Nazi Party Convention on September 15, 1935, in Nuremberg, were: "German Citizenship Law," and "The Law for the Protection of German Blood and Honor." Specifically, these laws made a distinction between 'Arians' and Jews or part-Jews, and declared all Jews as aliens, having thus deprived them of German citizenship and prohibited their intermarriage or even association with 'Arians.'

34. HP., p. 74. Quoted from a lecture read by Carl Schmitt at the University of Kiel, April 1, 1939. The scientific jargon of the title of the lecture is enlightening: "Völkerrechtliche Grossraumordnung mit Interventionsverbot für raumfremde Mächte." (The people's right for the arragement of Greater Space, with Prohibition of Intervention by Powers Alien to the Space). "Interventionsverbot (Prohibition of Intervention) was for him a scientific term establishing a truth, not just a wish.

aging Nazi philosopher, Karl Haushofer, President of the *Deutsche Akademie*, greeted this new theory of international law as "a planetary outlook . . . a high goal of mankind and *the* highest of German geo-politics."[35] And so, the Third Reich, as the new world law-maker, braced itself against the anti-Reich, that is, the 'Jewish Question.' As such, it arrogated unto itself the right of decree over the fate of other peoples—who shall live and who shall die, who shall dwell in his place and who shall be uprooted. This was the 'legal' ground from which sprang 'Euthanasia' and 'Genocide.' two Gorgon-heads on the Sheild of the Nazi State.[36]

The Jewish Question Rises from the Ashes

When the smoke of the gas chambers cleared away and the Nazis could look at their 'Greater Space' as it was shrinking in the last throes of the war, they suddenly realized that they had broken their secret weapon of prosecuting the war—the Jews of Europe. Without the Jews, the 'Jewish Question' grew paler and paler. It could not be sustained on the Jewish corpses, nor could it be re-assembled out of their ashes. Surveying the grim picture shortly before D-Day in March, 1944, the Nazis found that, the Jews having been eliminated, "the public at large considered the Jewish question settled . . . Young officers of twenty declare . . . that they had never yet seen a Jew. Consequently they find no interest, or only slight interest, in the problem, as it has been presented to them

35. Ibid., p. 34.

36. The mystic-historical basis for this law-making power was given a philosophical undercoat by Martin Heidegger. History for him was the hour when the New Era was decided by the Führer. That was fated. "The National Socialist revolution," he declared in November, 1933, "brings a complete revolution in our German existence. Doctrine and 'ideas' shall no longer govern your existence. The Führer himself, and only he, is the current and future reality of Germany, and his word is your law." (Martin Heidegger, *German Existentialism*, tr. by Dagobert D. Runes. Philosophical Library, New York, 1965, pp. 27-28). Commenting on Heidegger's historical perspective, Martin Buber wrote: "Here history no longer stands, as in all believing times, under divine judgment, but it itself . . . that sinister leading personality . . . assigns to the Coming One his way." (Cf. Buber, *Eclipse of God:* "Religion and Modern Thinking," tr. by Maurice S. Friedman. Harper Torchbooks, 1957, p. 77). Cf. also Hans Jonas, "Heidegger and Theology," *The Review of Metaphysics,* XVIII:2, December, 1964, pp. 207-233. Pointing to Heidegger's "fate-laden character of thinking as the self-unveiling history of being itself," Jonas assumes that the Christian "theologian should resist the attempt to treat his message as a matter of historic fate . . . as he must resist the idea of fate itself' (p. 215). Perhaps it was more than symbolic (to follow Buber's allusion to divine judgment) that when the German forces came close to Mount Sinai, in the battle of North Africa, they suffered a decisive defeat near the foot of the mountain where the ancient law-giver pronounced the divine law of true morality, which should govern men and nations.

up to now . . . Therefore the danger arises that the speeches of the Führer, who always begins his political messages with a detailed summary of the Jewish problem, lose so much of their penetrative power for the younger generation, and in their view, assume the character of a historical lecture."[37] But the old guard of Nazi leadership continued in the same groove. Facing the threat of final defeat, they now clung to a ghost of their secret weapon.

To recapture the momentum and to bolster the morale of their armed forces, the Nazis tried to conjure up the old spectre of world Jewish domination, ritual murder, Jewish Bolshevism and Capitalism, and all the cabal of classical anti-Semitism. They even tried to forge what they called "spiritual weapons . . . alongside with the sword. . ."[38] to convince the Allied Nations of their folly in fighting their German benefactors. Toward that end they had prepared for the convening of an international anti-Jewish Congress in July, 1944, even as the Allied forces were pounding away at the 'Fortress Europe.' That Congress was to adopt a "resolution . . . of unequivocal vow of allegiance to Germany's Jew-policies and demand a Europe free from Jews."[39] It was indeed the Nazi's last desperate attempt to use their secret weapon—the 'Jewish Question' . . . even in its disembodied garb.

That Congress never met. Europe was liberated. As the Teutonic fury was being tamed and crushed, and as the embattled areas came into view before the Allied armies, there lay buried in the soil of Europe six million Jews. But the 'spirit returneth.' Unbroken it came to life again in the surviving remnants—*Sheerit hapleta*—as they moved to reunite with their brethren in the Land of Israel and the rest of the free world.

Prospect in Retrospect

From the beginning of the Nazi rise to power in Germany, many leaders of the Jewish communities in the Western democratic countries tried to warn the free world of the impending calamity for mankind as a whole. But little did the free world then recognize the

37. HP., 237: Memorandum submitted to the Ministry of Propaganda by Wolf Meyer-Christian.

38. Ibid., pp. 207-208, 210ff. (Note the book *WHat Are We Fighting For?* published by the *Personalamt* of the German army, in January, 1944).

39. Ibid., p. 223.

true character of Hitler's pre-occupation with the 'Jewish Question.' The inevitable clash of forces came and brought dire results for European Jewry. It also took a great toll in human lives and suffering among other peoples, before the enemy was subdued. The Allied Nations lost at the hands of the Nazis untold millions not only in military combat, but also through enslavement, starvation and group annihilation. Did the defeat of the German armies at the end of the war also bring an end to the Nazi pre-occupation with the 'Jewish Question'? The answer may be found in the last words of Paul Tillich on the subject: "Remember what I said before: it happened to all, and it is still taking place."[40]

1966

40. Cf. Albert Hoschander Friedlander, "A Final Conversation with Paul Tillich," *Reconstructionist,* November 12, 1965, Vol. XXXI:14, p. 23.

Comments on Hannah Arendt's
View of the Jewish Condition

Professor Henry L. Feingold   July 3, 1980
c/o *Judaism*
15 East 84th Street
New York, N. Y. 10028

Dear Professor Feingold:

I have read your very insightful article "Arendt Revisited" (*Judaism*, Winter 1980), and I just want to comment on two small passages. You write: (1) "The problem is to account for the carping, jaundiced quality of her narrative in the early days of Zionism" (p. 126). (2) "Yet, if Arendt's posture was quixotic and her writing about Jews, especially their political culture, inaccurate and often unkind, she could also be remarkably prescient about what was in store for them. ... Her predictions ... all made with extraordinary precision at a very early date [1944], should alert us to the fact that we were dealing with no ordinary political thinker ... of brilliant insights and intuition" (p. 127). I don't mean to dwell on the question how Arendt's "inaccurate writing" about the "political culture" of the Jews squares with her "prescient" predictions about them, or how her "quixotic" posture shows "no ordinary political thinker." What baffles me is that you, like several others who have tried to rehabilitate her, have not come to grips with her morbid intellectual posture as such. For her real problem was lodged in her intellect, which was distorted by her vitriolic emotional outbursts. As Wilhelm Windelband has noted, "Philosophische Systeme wachsen nicht mit logischer, sondern mit psychologischer Notwendigkeit; aber sie erheben den Anspruch auf logische Geltung." In Arendt's case, her entire political philosophy is nothing but an attempt to give logical validity to her "pariah" relationship to society. To make a pariah mentality a logically consistent world outlook is a perversion of human reason, not to speak of human dignity. She created for herself a status of a "social outcast" and tried to "drum it" (the literal meaning of pariah) into everybody's mind that not only is it the most desirable and most noble position for the Jews to adopt, but that it is the only way they can sustain themselves among the nations — without a national existence of their own. This is the source of the "jaundiced quality" of her political philosophy for the Jews.

Arendt was infected with the jaundice of an extreme European individualism to which she tried to give a logical ground in order to justify her rejection of European society as well as her own people. It was a logic of *Selbstdenken* — an anomalous concept which Aristotle had reserved for the Prime Mover alone, and rightfully so; for a mortal who ventures in this kind of enterprise can only end in intellectual *Selbsmord.* This is what is so terribly repellent about her vituperations. It has no living spark of intellectual honesty; it oozes out of a "spirit that always negates," as Mephistopheles describes himself in Goethe's *Faust.*

As to her prescient predictions about the Jewish State, they were rather bad hindsight from which she drew wrong conclusions, for the events she "predicted" had been in formation and had been discussed at Zionist Congresses and written about in Zionist periodicals since the inception of that movement and especially since the beginning of the modern Yishuv in Palestine. Ezekiel Kaufmann wrote about the relationships of the Yishuv and the diaspora with deep insight and sound advice. And was it Arendt's discovery that Israel was dependent on America and American Jewry? Besides, what is wrong with it? It is but a matter of extent and balances. She might have discovered, if she had real insight into Israel's position in the Middle East, how much the United States is dependent on Israel, a situation which is being gradually recognized in American political circles. Her foretelling of the so-called "Masada Complex" was simply shooting in the dark, because she had no inkling what Masada meant in Jewish life. (Permit me to send you enclosed an article of mine on this subject).

To say that Martin Buber "shared much of her views [even] . . . regarding the Arab question" is, I believe, doing an injustice to Buber's memory. If there is any comparison between the two, it may be found in their younger days when each in his and her own way was swept along the stream of European Kultur. She spoke of her roots in German philosophy; but he described his own state more poignantly, which suited her condition even more strongly. "I lived," he said "in a world of confusion, a mythical habitation of roving souls with the fullness of spiritual agility but without Judaism, and thus without humanity. My first impulse toward my liberation came from Zionism." Poor Hannah. She never came out of that morass, though she retained her Hebrew name. Martin, on the other hand, "returned" to the Jewish fold through Zionism, and he remained faithful to it for the rest of his life. On the tenth anniversary of the State of Israel he worte: "I have accepted the form of the new Jewish communal being which has come out of the war, the State of Israel, as my own. . . . The commandment to serve the spirit is now to be fulfilled by us in this State and through it."

A final word. What intrigues me is that you yourself recognize that Arendt's malaise was her alienation not only "from European society but from the Jewish world as well." But you ascribe it to her "devotion to mind for mind's sake" and you want "to reclaim it." That is not a redeeming feature of her thoughts on Judaism and the Jewish people. Rather, it was the source of her malady: an individualistic mind for its own sake, detached from the realities of her people.

I am sincerely yours,
Alexander S. Kohanski

An Open Letter to Charles S. Isaacs

In the heat of the teachers' strike in New York City, with its racial tensions and anti-Semitic overtones, *The New York Times Magazine* (Nov. 24, 1968) published an article, "A J.H.S. 271 Teacher Tells It Like He Sees It," by Charles S. Isaacs. The Magazine noted that "the author, a teacher who opposed the New York teachers' strike, leads an eighth-grade algebra class at J.H.S. 271, a key school in the dispute." In his article, Mr. Isaacs mentions his background: "Grammar school in Brooklyn, *bar mitzvah*, suburban high school, Long Island University, marriage, law school at the University of Chicago. My father owns a parking lot, my mother is a working housewife. . . . In another day," he adds, "my 23rd birthday would not have found me teaching in the ghetto. This generation, though, has grown up at a unique time in history. I am not alone in being a contradiction to my upbringing." The following 'Open Letter' deals mainly with Jewish issues in the Black-White confrontation, also reminding Mr. Isaacs that he is a product of his upbringing rather than a contradiction to it.

I have read your article on J.H.S. 271 in today's *New York Times Magazine* with great interest. Allow me first to make a few preliminary remarks, before I go into what I consider to be the basic issue with reference to the role of the Jew in the entire complex of "community control." I recognize your idealism, integrity, and genuine desire to help the Black community to gain control of its own destiny. I furthermore recognize the right of the Black people to mold their own lives and to organize their community for effective action in order to bring about a real change for the better in their existing conditions. There is no doubt that they, on their part, recognize your willingness to help them, and that they know how to use your help. Second, I am not here passing judgment on the veracity of your story as far as factual information is concerned or on the light in which you painted it, whether or not there is enough illumination for an 'outsider' like myself to see it in proper perspective. I do not doubt your desire to be objective, in the sense of presenting an object-lesson to be learned about the struggle of a local Black Community to raise itself out of the slums.

The Underlying Forces in Black Power Movement

My comments are directed only to the question of Jewish-Black relations, which you have touched upon in your article. I say "touched upon" because you have only related what you have seen and not also, as the woman present at your meeting in Forest Hills pointed out, "what you haven't seen." By that I do not mean the anti-Semitic sheets that were distributed in Jewish teachers' schoolboxes before the 'event' or the slurs and threats during and after the 'event.' I take it, that you have not only not seen them, but that you honestly know nothing about them. What I do mean is that you have not seen the underlying forces operating in the Black Power movement in relation to the Jews who are helping to foster that power. Let me begin with a citation from your article. "We," that is Black and White teachers, you say, "form a mixture, not a solution—a *smorgasbord*, not a melting pot. The moment of truth came . . . when we decided to organize the faculty and elect a steering committee." When the question of parity representation between Black and White was raised, "Steve Mayer, a White teacher, pointed out that, in a vote on the question, the White majority would be deciding whether or not the Blacks were to have self-determination. Most of us recognized this as the colonial situation we all were determined to avoid, and the vote no longer was necessary. The two caucuses met separately, elected their representatives, and the steering committee was formed."

The iron logic of this argument is so self-evident that most likely everyone present must have felt ashamed for not having seen it himself, to begin with. But have you, who have analyzed the situation for us, seen also the logical consequence of the argument? When the Blacks become the majority on your faculty (and the day is not far off, judging from the tempo of the movement) will they accord the White minority the same consideration? Not by the logic of your argument for anti-colonialism and Black self-determination. For, if the present White majority on the staff is there only for the purpose of establishing *Black self-determination* (which in the final analysis, can be attained only through a Black majority), then after the goal has been achieved, the Whites will no longer be needed at all, not even as a minority, except for those few who may still serve the best interests of the Blacks as they, the Blacks, see fit. The rest will have to go, because they will have outlived their usefulness.

The Issue of Black Anti-Semitism

Moreover, they will be in the way of the new Black teachers and administrators who will have learned, in the transition period, how to fill *all* the positions by themselves. And of those who will be thus replaced, the Jewish teachers and administrators will be the first to go, as is already the case. This, my friend, is Black anti-Semitism. You couldn't possibly see it, because by your "own background" your knowledge of Jewish life and history is about the size of a *bar-*

mitzvah capsule; and one does not learn the real meaning of anti-Semitism just from the chanting of a *bar-mitzvah haftarah,* most likely not even comprehending its message. So, don't be amazed if you couldn't convince the Jewish parents in Forest Hills that you didn't see anti-Semitism in your Black school or in its local community. You really didn't; but the Jews of Forest Hills found it incredible that you couldn't. But you will protest, as you do in your article, that you never heard any anti-Semitic remarks against you and "have never experienced any racial or religious slur against me there, nor has anyone with whom I have spoken, nor have I seen any 'hate' literature besides that which is distributed by the U.F.T." Let me assure you once more that I do not sit in judgment over your testimony. You say you did not experience anti-Semitism in that school and community, and I take it that you didn't. But that is not really the issue. The officials of the local governing board, for example, say that they didn't know that almost all of the 19 dismissed teachers and administrators were Jews. It is not germane to the argument to muster evidence in refutation of such innocence. The fact is, the 19 or 18 and almost all of the other teachers "not wanted" by the Black community and your school *are* Jews. That is what counts, and that is most relevant to the issue of Black anit-Semitism there.

How Recognize Action Harmful to Jews

In order to explain the actual meaning of anti-Semitism, it will be more understandable if I don't use this term at all. As an object of 'experience,' it is evidently as diversified as are the individuals who do or do not claim to have experienced it. And to define anti-Semitism will also lead us nowhere, because each person's definition will be derived from his own experience or from that of a number of individuals, and we will just be moving in circles. So let us, instead, talk about what kind of action on the part of non-Jews—Blacks, in this case — may be identified as being against the vital interests of the Jewish people. And this we can learn best from Jewish history, not merely from the so-called "dark ages" or the Nazi Holocaust, which some are apt to regard as a non-repeatable horror, but from the more recent past and our own age as well, under all kinds of political and social conditions. Now, how do we recognize action which has been or may become injurious to the life and well-being of the Jewish people? Such action is not always manifested in "racial and religious slurs" or even threats to Jewish lives. Indeed, it is often pronounced and documented in seemingly good intentions to 'benefit' the Jews. But what such good intentions turn out to be are invitations to Jews to *serve* a king, an emperor, a state, the down-trodden masses, and the underprivileged classes—until such time as their services are no longer needed and they become "unwanted" (as the current phrase goes), and can be dispensed with. This has happened again and again where Jews, as a group, did not have solid ground to stand on, and were tossed around by the 'governing bodies' who had the 'power' to determine their lot. And that is how it came about that we have had masses of displaced Jews, declassed Jews, homeless Jews, jobless Jews, superfluous Jews—all driven from pillar to post.

"Not Wanted" — An Echo of the Past

Just think back for a moment on that organizing session of your faculty. What would have happened if, out of genuine conviction, you and Mr. Mayer had strongly supported the view in general open elections and had won the day? The two of you and quite a few others of the same view would have been declared saboteurs of the experimental project, and ushered out of the school unceremoniously. What you fail to recognize is that the caucus plan does not change your precarious position a bit, for the White caucus is not really on a par with the Black caucus. The Blacks have the administrator, the governing board and other forces in the community to back them up; they are part of them. But the Whites, and especially the Jewish teachers among them, are part of nothing, least of all the school and the community they are serving. They have no social, economic or any other communal ground to stand on, except a footstool from which they may promote Black self-determination. Do you really expect some thirty thousand Jewish teachers, comprising well over a hundred thousand souls, to place themselves on that same footstool? This, as you can well see, is not just a matter affecting a few Jewish teachers returning to a Black community school where they are "not wanted." It concerns masses of our people in all professions, businesses and all other walks of life.

What concerns us most is the "not wanted," which echoes horrid experiences of our people in the past, and which has now come to plague us in this land of opportunity, where we have every right and reason to feel free and wanted. Yes, you can say: "Here am I and 'forty percent' other Jewish teachers in a Black community school and *we* are wanted."* No, my friend, you are not wanted in that school either; but you are useful. Read over your article again very carefully, as if you had never read it before, and you will realize how useful you are to the 'new establishment' or the one you are helping to establish! Now, don't misunderstand me: Jewish life in America does not depend on whether or not we are wanted by the Blacks. I am just pointing out how this phrase characterizes their relationship with the Jews. You'll say then: "This is not alone a problem for Jews, but rather a general problem of the White-Black confrontation." But one must be able to recognize the specific in a general situation, if one is to "tell it like it is." And it is the vulnerable position of the Jews in this conflict and the role they play in it as a community and as individuals that concern us specifically.

An "Apartheid" Doctrine

Without further elaboration, let me refer to two instances which reflect on the Jewish position in this regard, one seemingly minor, but the other of considerable proportions. In a recent symposium on Black-White relations at Yale University, Sidney Hook (Jewish) professor at New York University, who is "chairman of an ad hoc faculty committee to frame a Negro studies program there," commented on "what he regarded as extraneous political and ideological considerations" by certain Black leaders. In response, Maulana Ron Karenga declared that the Black community is "a colony ruled by a mother country," and that it is now saying, "you can't make decisions for us." Professor Hook retorted that Mr. Karenga was advocating an "apartheid doctrine which made it impossible for people like me to help Black people get shoes, get food, get power." Mr. Karenga smiled: "You don't even understand what I was saying. *Your helping us is beside the point. You should be helping your own society.*" (Cf. *The New York Times*, May 13, 1968, p. 47. Italics mine).

---

*Those of us who read Jewish history know full well the significance of 'percentage Jews' in schools, universities, professions, etc. I cannot dwell here on the statistical fallacies of the so-called surveys of Black anti-Semitism and their percentages of Blacks and Jews involved or not involved. I will only state: we Jews are not statistical data, and the surveys tell nothing about the inner drive in the Black community and its potential.

You may just be wondering what all this has to do with Jews. Mr. Karenga said "your own society," not Jewish society! It has very much to do with Jews. Karenga was quite clear: he wants power to fill the university positions and to determine courses of study without the help of White ad hoc committees or any other help from Whites, except as the Blacks may see fit to use it. Otherwise he feels that White help will be a hindrance to him, much as your help will be to the Black caucus in your school if you ever go counter to its desires. This is Black self-determination and anti-colonialism, exactly in the sense in which you and Mr. Mayer spoke of at your faculty meeting. And when Black power begins to move into positions in the universities, as Black self-determination demands, the first to be forced out of those positions will be the Jewish professors and instructors, in the same manner in which the Jewish teachers were dismissed by your region—just by registered letter delivered at the noon hour: "You are not wanted!"

"Sell Out at Low Prices, or Else"

The second case-in-point of Black determination is that of Leonard Stein's furniture store in Washington, D. C. Since you are vitally interested in the Black power movement, you must have read about it in the *New York Times* of July 8, 1968: "Jews Troubled Over Negro Ties," by Irving Spiegel. You will recall that in the riots that followed the assassination of the Rev. Dr. King, more than 1200 Jewish merchants were burned out of their hard-earned life possessions. This was followed up by "Negro-sponsored threats that White (spell Jewish) merchants leave the area and sell out at ridiculously low rates or face further attack." I have seen an editorial (from which the above is quoted) describing the whole 'happening' as "clearly hooliganism," and identifying "the problems of the Negro with the problems of the Jew." This is tantamount to saying the interests of the victims of a pogrom are identical with those of the pogromists. The burning and looting of 1200 Jewish stores is apologetically called "hooliganism," to take the brunt off responsible Negro leadership. By comparison, sixty-five years ago, in the Kishinev pogrom in czarist Russia, a similar number (1500) of Jewish shops and homes was destroyed, and the whole civilized world raised its voice in horror of the outrage. Some people contend there is no comparison between Kishinev and Washington. Perhaps not, in a good many respects. But in both events, the Jews were assailed by elemental forces, and these are the same the world over in their destructiveness. And another similarity is that, in Washington as in Kishinev, there was no force outside the Jewish community, especially within the Black power movement, to counteract that elemental fury. On the contrary, the inner Black powers are learning fast how to utitize and channel it for self-determination. (You must have watched the David Susskind interview with Black youth, who had been or still are leaders of street gangs in the ghetto).

Why Hurt an Ally?

Now, what about Leonard Stein's furniture store I started with as a case in point? That store was not touched *during* the riots. It was burned and looted *two weeks after* the riots, by careful planning. Why this delayed action? Mr. Stein was *helping* the Black people toward self-determination. He employed Negro help only. As head of the B'nai Brith Council in the Washington area, he was an ardent fighter for civil rights. He "had no personal fears about working in the ghetto." He was sure it couldn't happen to him. And when it did happen, he was "perplexed and disheartened," but little did he know why. Like you and your Jewish co-workers in the Black community, Mr. Stein, too, could not see the real meaning of Black anti-Semitism. He didn't notice it even after he had been warned by the Blacks; there were "broad hints that it was coming." But he couldn't read the signs written in bold: "You, Mr. Stein, have seen the riots, the burning and the looting. Turn your business over to your Black employees 'at ridiculously low rates'; or you'll suffer the same fate!" Mr. Stein couldn't believe it. Was he not an 'ally' of the leaders of the Black movement? Why should they want to hurt an ally who is fighting for their self-determination? Perhaps he saw them in the same light as you did looking as Les Campbell. "When I first met Campbell," you relate in your article, "I hardly knew what to expect. . . . Two months of conversation and observation" dispelled your suspicion and you were gratified to learn: "Campbell wants to see the institutions that determine the lives of Black people controlled by those people, and not by White colonial masters, but he recognizes the role that can be played by White allies in the struggle." Clear enough! Only, you have missed the significance of the word "allies"; and, ironically, you still "hardly know what to expect." Perhaps Karenga's illuminating retort to Professor Hook will give you some insight. Remember his smile: "You don't even understand what I was saying. Your help is beside the point. You should be helping your own society."

Neither Morality Nor Justice

This is the real issue and this is what we, Jews, have at stake in the Black-White confrontation: can we help our own? We are not going to do it by charitable deeds, by throwing our money and best talents into a *smorgasbord* to be dished out by Black power. You will not be able to help yourself even to a piece of marinated herring out of it, when the 'restaurant' is manned fully by Black administrators and supervisors. When Mr. Stein and other Jewish leaders urge us not to withdraw from the civil rights fight because we Jews must uphold our tradition of moralilty and justice, they are speaking of 'charity' and not of true morality and real justice. For Mr. Stein, and many others with him, have failed to demand of their Negro 'allies' the assurance that Jews would not be burned out of their businesses or forced to turn them over to Blacks at ridiculously low rates. Instead, they just went ahead 'helping' Black self-determination, hoping for the best. That is neither morality nor justice.

In Jewish tradition, both these concepts and practices are based on reciprocity, on give and take, on mutual responsibility. The Hebrew idiom expresses it in essence: establish peace and justice "between man and his neighbor." *Between*, not on one side alone. And for us Jews to help build up Black Power and Black self-determination without the assurance of reciprocity for Jewish interests and Jewish self-determination, is utterly immoral and unjust—to both sides. There is a Jewish-Black confrontation of serious dimensions. Anyone who does not see it is just hiding his head in the sand. Insofar as they confront each other in their vital interests, they can work them out together with considerable advantage to both sides. But both sides must accept the 'togetherness' and each must assume responsibility for the interests of the other.

1969

Ecumenism: Dialogue or Dialectic

What I am writing here is a dialogue between a Jew and a Christian, or rather an attempt to clarify for myself what such a dialogue can possibly mean for either one or both of us. I ought to state, therefore, at the outset, that I do not speak for any organized group and do not represent an official trend of thought. Also, I do not speak from a point of view of Judaism to a point of view of Christianity. There is no dialogue between "isms" or "points of view." Dialogue can take place only between persons, even groups of persons, but as living, acting persons. Thus, when I enter in dialgoue with my Christian neighbor I do it as a living, practicing Jew with a living, practicing Christian. At the same time, one must not overlook the fact that I, as one of the Jewish faith, am a part of an entity which regards itself as a world people, and that my neighbor of the Christian faith is part of another entity which regards itself as a universal religion.

One more preliminary remark. Since my present dialogue is in the form of the written word, I have to presuppose a previous dialogue between my Christian neighbor and myself that might have taken place through the spoken word, in which each of us would have expressed, without formalisms, some element of relation to one another, as an " other." That is, I presume that such a relation already exists in some measure, at least, and that the present dialogue is between "one" who is a Jew and an "other" who is a Christian, neither of us questioning the actual, full existence of the other, as such. I will have more to say on this point later, but for the present I trust I have made myself understood that I do not regard the question of why one is a Jew and another a Christian as the subject of the dialogue.

In that preliminary dialogue, too, I for my part would have found a way of expressing my immediate relation to my "partner-in-speaking" to the effect, that I regard his Christian religion as the most important thing in his life, which I do not intend to diminish, as I do not want to impair any other of his life giving powers. And he would have found a way of expressing a similar relation to me. We would say it not on theological grounds, but as a basic element of the dialogical reality that occurred between us.

Since the conclusion of the Second Vatican Council there has been in the Western world a buoyant feeling that a new era has set in, called the "Era of Ecumenism." This is a good feeling, as it grows out of the modern conditions of man in an ever-shrinking world in which communication has become the dominant problem, both extensively and intensively. Ecumenism, therefore, insofar as it signifies a universalism which is to influence modern man for generations to come, must find ways of adjusting itself to the present era in new modes of thought, idioms of expression and inter-religious relations. For ecumenism itself is not new. The Christian religion from its very inception has always been a universal religion, even though it has undergone deep-seated divisions. What may be new about the present ecumenism is the Churches approach to the non-Christian faiths. However, ecumenism today means primarily the restoration of universal unity within divided Christendom itself, and only secondarily in relation to other religions. A Jew who is by his very faith outside this restoration process will say to himself: "I am not and cannot consider myself a part of this ecumenical movement, and yet it affects me because it affects my Christian neighbor. I therefore wonder what will be our neighborly relations when his Christian ecumenism will have been accomplished and how will it differ from our present relations?"

Internal Affairs

I put this question in the future form, because it is not the same question that was asked at the Vatican Council; nor is the answer given by the council directed toward it. And for that matter, one could not expect the council to have answered it, because such a question is not resolved by pronouncements. What the Vatican Council could and did pronounce in its relation to the Jews is with respect to a past occurrence at the origins of Christianity affecting a doctrinal point in the Christian religion, and within reason it tried to clarify that point so as to remove certain misunderstandings as far as the Jews of today are concerned. But this is still basically an internal Christian affair — the correction of a certain historical viewpoint (not shared by the Jews to begin with), but not a projection into the future. It does not address itself to the personal question I posed above. And yet, I maintain that the Vatican Council's statement on its relationship to the Jews of today is of utmost importance, not so much for the correction it has made, as for the avenue it has opened up for me and my Christian neighbor to meet in a new relation. But that relation can be neither just Christian nor Judaeo-Christian; it must be *between* Jew and Christian.

I as a Jew have always looked at Christianity as being

ecumenical, that is universal, and I need no new declarations concerning my Jewish past in order to find a proper relationship with my Christian neighbor. If I look for something new in the Vatican Council's ecumenism it is not what it says about the Jews but what it says about itself as a universal religion. For, as I pointed out in my preliminary remarks, I am a member of a world people which has its own religious faith, and my Christian neighbor is a member of a universal religion of his own. The decisive factor in our relations is what is meant by "world" and "universal." One has to view these terms in the light of the present era. What is the demand of the 20th Century with respect to universalism? Or to put it in ecumenical language, what does the present age expect of the new ecumenism that will enable it to build a better "universum" (oikoumene means the world-household) for all men to live in? It expects not universal inclusion but universal relation. Not all in one, but each standing on his own ground and yet being able to meet the other in human communication. Accordingly, a world people with a religious faith of its own is not an imperialistic nation that aims to embrace every other people within its orbit, but one which recognizes other peoples and religions in the world besides itself and is as vitally interested in their separate existence as it is in its own. By the same token, a universal religion is today not one which includes all human beings within its fold, but one which relates itself universally to other religions which are also universal and will remain so in their own right.

Man's Expectation

In such a relationship between universalia each religion is concerned with the unimpaired identity of the other as it is with its own identity. This is what I understand to be modern man's expectation from the new ecumenism, inside as well as outside the Christian church. We have long passed the age of "tolerance"; we are now in the age of "equality." Tolerance means that the one who is being tolerated is in need of the other who tolerates him, but the relationship is not reversible; whereas in equality both parties in the relation need each other and recognize that that need exists. When a great church such as Catholic Christianity finds it necessary to place among the schemata of its Ecumenical Council the consideration of its relations with the Jews, that church must surely feel a driving inner need for it. And if the Jews have responded to this show of concern with equal concern, they too must have an inner need for it. I think the need on both sides is real and can be met in time. But the meeting will not be in an all-inclusive ecumenism where one may eventually absorb the other, but rather in dialogue where both retain their mutual independence.

Ecumenism is not synonymous with dialogue. The first is the goal of the Christian Church, and in its striving toward that goal the church has cut out some channels in which the second may also flow between Christian and Jew. As far as the Jew is concerned, Christian ecumenism, as such, is not his goal. The relationship in dialogue, which is to be established, will emerge as the dialogue itself occurs in reality. But its pre-condition, the new Christian ecumenism, is not yet clear enough to indicate what direction that relationship will take. As the dialogue takes hold in moments of actual meeting of one with an "other," it will bring out the need for relationship on the part of both, the Christian and Jewish communities, which thus far has only been adumbrated or rather beclouded.

In Christian missionary literature addressed to Jews we often find the expression, with reference to Isaiah 1.18: "Come now, and let us reason together." If one is trying to convert someone, reasoning is the proper approach. But the prophet's intent is not that of reasoning but rather of telling his people to show their ways to God so that they may learn of His ways accordingly. The Hebrew word "v'nivakheha" in that verse means "let us show each other," as it is also used, for example, in Job 13.15: "I will show (okhiah) Him my ways." The difference between "reasoning" and "showing one's ways" is a difference between dialectic and dialogue. The same is true in relations between man and man, in our case, between Christian and Jew. If we are to carry on a dialogue, our talk should be about our respective ways to God and to man and not about the reason why we must go our separate ways. Let me illustrate it by an actual encounter.

Some time ago, a group of Christian Sunday school students and their two teachers of a neighboring Protestant church came to visit our synagogue, and I acted as their guide. We met in our chapel where I showed them the Torah scroll, spoke of some of its contents, described the main features of our worship, and so forth. There was some interlocution but only to clarify some minor points. When I finished and asked for questions or statements, there were none forthcoming. I thought I had done a fairly good job in conducting a "dialogue" with my Christian young neighbors and that I had conveyed my message. But it seemed that what I talked about was not really what concerned them.

No Longer Dialogue

For after a while, one student hesitatingly raised his hand. "Can you tell us," he queried, "why the Jews do not accept Christ?" Whatever answer I gave and whether or not it satisfied the questioner, my listeners and I were no longer in relation of dialogue. That particular kind of question as well as my reply was in the sphere of dialectic. If this give-and-take would continue on an adult level, for every reason I would give for my not accepting Christ my interlocutor would produce a counter-reason why I should accept him. This type of "reasoning with each other" could go on in a perfectly normal course of polite though pointed exchange, until one or the contrary position were overcome or, barring that, both sides would give up the argument stubbornly refusing to yield to each other. They would then part more estranged than when they first met, for each would be trying to weaken the other's position and they would regard each other as opponents in real life, not just disputants in a rational argument. Such is the nature of dialectic: Its aim is to resolve the contraries either by abolishing one of them or absorbing one into the other, or perhaps combining them both into a new unity. In dialogue, on the other hand, contraries are accepted as they are without one being overcome or absorbed by the other, but rather both bringing out their differences and fortifying each other's positions. Therefore, when I engage in dialgoue with my Christian neighbor, I should seek not only to learn of his way, but as he shows it to me I should also find him strengthened in his own belief. And the same should hold true in the case when he seeks to learn about my way.

Dialectic always looks for some common ground to stand on, some common principle on which both parties can agree as a basis for their discussion. But dialogue does not need a common starting point; it ensues when a person speaks with another person without preconceived principles or formulations. One starts with something that is of vital concern to him. The other listens and when he finds that he, too, has the same concern, he responds. The other may not even say anything but respond by listening so attentively that nothing else but the speaker exists for him at the moment. Then the dialogue emerges as a relation of mutuality and may extend into wider relations of communality. An actual encounter of this kind will illustrate my point. Recently I acted once again as guide to a group of students and their teachers from a nearby Episcopalian church who came to our synagogue to learn something about the ways of the Jewish religion. As I showed them the scroll of the Torah and the ceremonial objects of our services, and pointed out the Biblical motifs on the stained glass windows, I talked of things, ideas and ways which concern me, as a Jew, in worshipping God. But at the same time I also talked about and listened to things and ideas which concerned them, as Episcopalians, in their way of divine worship. There thus developed a brief dialogue between us about the interest each took in the concerns of the other. When we parted, each felt more faith, and the students and their teachers expressed that feeling to me. That was a true meeting in dialogue.

Between Communities

What is true of individuals or small groups of Christians and Jews entering in dialogue with each other also holds when their respective communities speak with one another on a matter of vital concern to each of them, even when they are not on the same ground. Regrettably, such communal encounters, which usually take place in public, have assumed the character of dialectic rather than dialogue. One such event of major proportions, which occurred some two years ago, caused great consternation in the ecumenical movement. The Jews and Christians had their separate grounds of concern in that event, but it was treated on a dialectic level, and the collision between the Jewish community and the Christian church was traumatic for the one and dumbfounding for the other. I am referring to the situation of the Jews in Israel in May of 1967, when they found themselves imperilled by genocide before they joined battle with the Arabs. The Christian churches of many denominations, with few exceptions of individual churchmen, stood by and looked on in silence. This so outraged the Jews who had been active in ecumenism that some left and many more were about to leave the movement.

I hope that my Jewish people and my Christian neighbors will bear with me if I consider that event in a calm, judicious manner, though it is surely not a matter of pure reasoning, nor is it merely a thing of the past. The issue involved has serious long-range implications, not so much for the ecumenical movement as for the success or failure of the dialogue between Jews and Christians, which that movement has hopefully opened up. And because I believe that dialogue is needed on the part of both communities, I do not think that we, Jews, should withdraw from this relationship. It is incorrect to assume that the spirit of ecumenism has descended upon us, and all one has to do is embrace or reject it as the case may be.

Ecumenism is yet to show itself in meaning, spirit and fact. Similarly, dialogue has not yet found its proper form to show its effect on the neighborhood level: and on the communal level it has not even reached a stage of primary relation. As for the event in Israel which caused the rift, I shall not speak of the church's failure to help, not because I condone its position but because the kind of help it might have offered at the moment of Israel's greatest peril would have been of no avail. Whatever help the church may render must be of a long range nature. Therefore, what I want to say to my Christian neighbor, and say it on a level of dialogue, not dialectic, has to do not with Israel but with the Christian church itself. That is, I want to learn from him the way a Christian acts according to his Christian precepts when a matter of vital import affects his fellowman who is not of the same religion, and what is the ground on which a Christian stands in that kind of situation. When the Christians, standing on their ground, were confronted by the Jews on what the latter considered as a breach in the spirit of ecumenism with regard to Israel, one official spokesman of the National Council of Churches explained: The Jewish community was "quite right in denouncing Christian churches for silence during the threats of genocide." But, he reasoned, "I think we were justified in not urging the Government to do more than it did in defense of Israel. We and they had to seek a proper balance in the area." (New York Times, Nov. 8, 1967). Whether this kind of reasoning is valid or not is a matter of dialectic, and that is not the kind of relationship we Jews, historically speaking, have good cause to pray for. The self-contradiction; of the explanation lies there in the open on its dialectic surface: If the Jewish community is "right in denouncing Christian churches" for their position, how can the same churches be "justified" in having taken that position?

Now two years have passed since the Six-Day-War and the

situation in the Middle East has been growing more critical for Israel's security every day with the continued onslaught by the Arab states and their commandos. Still the Christian churches, after prolonged dialogue with the Jewish community, have nothing to offer but "keeping things in balance." Once again we hear "the president of the two million-member Protestant denomination warn . . . that the Arab-Israel conflict in the Middle-East must not be permitted to injure relations between Jews and Christians in the United States, 'no matter to which side our sympathies may be directed.'" (The Jewish News, Feb. 9, 1969).

A note of consolation might have been detected in the words of a prominent Catholic leader of ecumenism, who crticized the American Christian community for "a generalized indifference to the welfare of Israel that shades off into hostility toward Israel." However, in commenting on the "fragility of Jewish-Christian relations," he noted an "over-expectation" in the Jewish community of what to expect from dialogue held thus far, and complained that some Jewish spokesmen "tend to overcharge the Christian community in this crisis." But what this Catholic spokesman complains about is the very burden of Christian ecumenism: Has it been really engaged in dialogue or only in dialectic? What should one, on either side, expect from dialogue? Just a balancing of the scales?

When a Christian stands in dialogical relation with a Jew who is in mortal danger, it is not the Christian's function to keep the balance between the Jew and the one who threatens him. For if he is in actual dialogue with the Jew, he, the Christian, is in the same scale with him and he must tip it for life against death. And if he fails him in that and the Jew dies, his Christian partner (and that's what he is in a dialogical relation) dies with him, because, not having acted, the partner has forfeited his confirmation as a Christian. I know that before the new ecumenism many Christian individuals did just that — confirmed themselves in dialogue with Jews in time of danger to the latter. But I am now speaking to the Christian church as a body in Christ. A church whose religion has deep concern for human beings cannot stand by as an outside observer and just seek a balance. For what does seeking a balance mean? It means calculating whether the Jew in the one scale is worth saving as compared with his adversary in the other scale who is there to destroy him. If the spokesman of a great national Christian organization recognizes that this is a case of "threats of genocide," how does one keep a balance on genocide? And how does this new ecumenism differ from the old, when the spiritual forces of the church proposed to save the soul of the Jew while the secular arm burned him alive? These questions the Christian church has to answer for itself, if it wants to address itself not only to the Jew but also to modern man in general.

Act of Relating

I, for my part, ask these questions without any ill-will. I genuinely want to speak with my Christian neighbor on this matter, not to argue or reason and certainly not to match wits with him. I just want to learn of his Christian way in relating himself to this kind of concern. And what is more important, I want to know how he carries such a concern into deed — for dialogue is man's deepest act of relating to fellowman. If it is not that, it is either dialectic or simply sentimental talk. I have no excessive expectations about dialogue between Christian and Jew, in the sense that it can take place constantly on all occasions and under all circumstances. But the test of true dialogue is in a moment of crisis. And one who has failed to respond and act in that moment has never experienced the relation in dialogue at all. If my Christian neighbor should ask me now: Is it possible for us to engage in dialogue again? I would say yes, but it will not come from the top in conference or convention. Perhaps we ought to make a new start — between "one" and an "other."

1969

To Ann Roiphe: A Communication

Passaic, N. J.
January 4, 1979

Dear Ms. Roiphe:

I read your article "Christmas Comes to a Jewish Home" (in the New York Times) with much interest and, if you will allow, with deep understanding. "Being a Jew who celebrates Christmas," you say, "... needs some explanation." But more important is the fact that your "grandfather deserves an explanation" and that when you "look at the tree lights [you] remember the light of the memorial candle. Somehow magical and sacred. [Your] mother's candle in memory of her beginnings and her past, and her family." These words reflect reverence for your ancestral past, a spirituality crying out for embodiment in some tangible present. You have chosen to transform it into the imagery of a Christmas tree. And yet, the image cannot contain your spirit, because your "tree" is not real, only "bright bulbs, an *artificial* snowbase, and *wax* Santa Claus candles." So you bring to mind the imagery of your grandfather's experiences in Russia and your mother's memorial candle — all very dear to you but without a spark left in them to rekindle your spirit. And again you seek comfort in "the bright bulbs and the artificial snowbase," which numb rather than warm your heart.

One Christmas eve, you recall, your cat played havoc with your tree. "A cat misunderstood the occasion. The destruction was terrible." You retrieved the animal's error and repaired the damage, alright. But when a human being misunderstands the occasion, the destruction may be catastrophic. You look for new symbols but again fall back on your grandfather's imagery. "The symbol of Jesus," you write, "is just a symbol, an excuse for human bravado against the void. I see humanity where my grandfather saw only the march of Cossacks." Does this explain why you celebrate Christmas, which is a symbol of Jesus? For Christmas celebrates the birth of Christ not of Scrooge in whom you wish to lodge your idea of humanity. Isn't it rather that your grandfather saw real marching, marauding Cossacks, whereas you see nothing but the *void* which you try to fill with symbolic bulbs and artificial snow? Ask a real believing Christian what he thinks of your "symbol of Jesus." How can one who celebrates Christmas not just for its "commercial glitter," as you say, be so insensitive to the foundation of Christianity?

To be sure, as you point out, it is a matter of education, "out of the ghetto, away from Heder into college, into philosophy and history and art ... into history of revolutions and ... isms." But Zionism, for example, also has an *ism* and is one of the greatest revolutionary movements in the annals of mankind. And so has Judaism an *ism* and a philosophy, a history and art. I teach philosophy in a college. My courses include Greek philosophy, nineteenth century German philosophy and — also Jewish philosophy. Yes, I went to Heder and on to college (at Southwestern in Memphis, Tenn., formerly Southwestern Presbyterian University). In a class on Religious Poetry, my Christian professor always called on me when the subject of biblical poetry was discussed. As the only Jew in the class (there were only eight of us in the College at that time), I was expected to know my Hebrew Bible. And the same is expected of me now by my professional colleagues.

In a course which I gave on Judaism, some Christian students (most students in this class were Christians) asked me about "the God of vengeance." I read to them about Christians who preached and prayed for vengeance in the New Testament (Luke 18, 1-8, Romans 3:5-6, Revelations 6:10 and 18-20). Then they asked me why Jews don't follow the NT precept of "turning the other cheek." I told them that in the first place it is not an original NT notion but is found in the Old Testament (Lamentations 3:30-31). Moreover, we Jews have already turned both cheeks "to those who smite us," and we have none left to turn any more. And they also protested, as you do, against the "cruel" God who smote the Egyptian firstborn children. I replied: The Jews did not invent child killing. It was the Egyptians who drowned the Jewish male infants in the Nile (see Exodus 1:15-16 and 22).

When you left the Seder table because you could no longer bear to hear the story of the "Egyptian soldiers being swallowed by the sea," you might in your solitude have contemplated the fate of the Jewish men, women, and children who would have been thrown into that same sea had the Egyptian soliders succeeded in overtaking them before they crossed it. Our Bible teaches that God is merciful and forgiving yet does not hold the guilty unanswerable for their crimes (Exodus 34:6-7). The historical lesson of the Exodus (and we learn the same lesson today) is that the enemies of the Jewish People must realize the hard way (they know no other way) that their perpetrations against Jewish life will not go unrequited. Your confession that you would wear the "yellow badge" is a noble sentiment, but it should also be known to you that the wearers of this badge in the ghettos and in the concentration camps of the holocaust fought their enemy with unsurpassed heroism. This is reality: the badge is only its symbol.

I trust that you will bear with me for writing you at this length. I don't as a rule, write "letters to the editor," but do respond occasionally to writers in a personal way of interhuman relationship. Permit me also to send you herewith a few items I have written on the subjects touched upon in this communication. They may be of interest to you.

Sincerely,
Alexander S. Kohanski

A Perspective on the Holocaust
And You Shall Teach It To Your Children

Can one speak of the Holocaust in perspective? That would require setting it at a distance, reducing its magnitude to normal dimensions, so that we may be able to comprehend it within the limited powers of human understanding. But no matter how far it recedes, the enormity and intensity of the devastation remains overwhelming. We search in vain for norms of the human psyche, for standards of social behavior, for ethical values or guides of religious belief to fathom the agony of a people marked for total annihilation. We ask repeatedly: What is the sense of it all? What is its recompense, and can it be rectified in the eyes of man or God? Yet if we succumb to its overwhelming force we cannot speak or write about it, and we certainly cannot teach it to our children; we can only stand before it in awe and be silent.

How to Gauge the Problem

Many of us have kept this pent-up silence for almost a generation. Attempts have been made to bring the Holocaust into proper perspective — whether religious, national or generally human — so that we might impart its meaning to the next generation. But we have been baffled by the many questions that keep welling up from the depths of the catastrophe each time we as much as touch its rim; and we can hardly say we have brought forth a plausible answer. Perhaps, then, a major difficulty lies in the way we look at the problem. In order to gain a perspective of the Jewish catastrophe in Europe we must seek not so much the answers to the many questions that have been raised as the meaning of the

317

questions themselves. For we cannot devise a measuring rod for answering a question unless we have first set a standard for asking it. Furthermore, when we propose to teach the meaning of the Holocaust to succeeding generations, we are not duty-bound to bring them the answers. Each generation must take upon itself to give its own answer through its very act of Jewish living. What we of the generation of the Holocaust can and ought to teach is our understanding of the question, for our own answer, too, can be found only in the living acts of our generation. All we can hope to convey to our youth, then, is our standard of gauging the nature of the problems.

Historical View

Another requisite for gaining a perspective in teaching about the Holocaust is to place it in a wider frame in relation to Jewish realities, that is "remember the days of old, consider the years of every generation," as we are taught in the Book of Deuteronomy (32.7). We are so distraught by the incomprehensible answers we have tried to put forth that we forget the recent Holocaust in Europe is not the only one that afflicted our people on that continent. We also over look the fact that we have been teaching our children about the Holocausts of past centuries, only we have presented them as history, that is receding so far in the past that we have lost sight of their true magnitude and have failed to understand their meaning in our life today. In the past 1,000 years the Jews of Europe suffered four Holocausts. The first three annihilated many communities in several lands, and the fourth embraced the whole continent. There may be no particular significance to the periodic recurrence of these catastrophies, but they did occur at intervals of about 300 years, the first in the 11th Century during the Crusades, the second in the 14th Century Black Death, the third in the 17th Century Ukrainian uprising against Poland and the fourth in the 20th Century during the Nazi domination over Europe. Each of these Holocausts cut deeply into the life energies of our people, and each was enormous in magnitude and inordinately cruel, when gauged by the size of the population and the advancement in means of destruction at the time. In each there was devastation as well as heroism, "Shoa Ug'vura," as the State of Israel has designated the Holocaust. There was heroism shown during the destruction and strength that came forth thereafter. In each there was an assertion of the Jewish "will to live" against the brute forces of "will to power." After each catastrophe the Jewish community of Europe renewed itself with greater vigor, rebuilt its ruins, struck new and deeper roots, and continued to weave its religious-cultural life across the path of history.

But why, we may ask, did we have to pay such a high price for our survival as a people, for the preservation of our way of life, for our particular mode of serving God? I do not know why this is so. I cannot even say that this is the way of Providence, for surely God has given us a way of life and not death, I would say, rather, it is the way of man. When it comes to matters of life and death, the human species, especially in its advanced stage of homo sapiens, seems to be unable to set for himself a proper standard of valuation. He gropes to reach even greater heights through willful destruction. This is the way of mankind as a whole. Other peoples, too have suffered evil and untold devastation at the hands of their fellow-men, only the Jewish people has been singled out time and again for "special treatment." This is the historical view of the Jewish catastrophe. The problem is whether we can gain some perspective in viewing the one which has occured in our own time.

An Incomprehensible Question

When we contemplate the events of the Holocaust in our time, whatever acquaintance we may have of them, they pass before us in images of pain, horror, death and destruction, and we ask: Why did this happen? Why did six million have to die? What sense can there be in their annihilation? We then look for the answer in an attempt at finding some meaning in death and destruction. But there is no answer in death. It is incomprehensible in terms of human knowledge, hope or aspiration as well as in terms of divine will in this life on earth. Yet this kind of no-answer does not assuage our troubled hearts, and we push our querying further. If there is justice in the world, why did it not manifest itself in the most trying hour of our time? Why was the destruction not prevented or at least stopped? If our question is directed to the powers of the free Western nations, who were in a position to do it, we know the answer. But this only makes our hearts the more troubled, and we ask the ulitmate question: If there is a God of Justice in the universe, why did He not prevent or stop the

Holocaust? And since He didn't then. . . .

I suspect that one who says that after Auschwitz he does not believe in God, did not believe in Him before Auschwitz either. For faith itself is the most trying of man's experiences, touching at the roots of his existence. A man of faith, then, will not deny God, but he may look at the Holocaust as a unique phenomenon of destructiveness which is outside the bounds of history and thus inexplicable to the rational mind. However, it did happen in the course of history, and it is bound up with all its fibres in the entire complex of events which led up to it as their culmination. Perhaps we are asking an incomprehensible question, that is we are again asking about the meaning of death, for which history can have no answer. Those who see the catastrophe as standing outside of human history are further troubled by another question: How is Jewish life possible after Auschwitz? What meaning can it possibly have now? This does not differ basically from the previous question, for as long as we see in Auschwitz only death and destruction we can derive no meaning of Jewish life from it either during or after the Holocaust. Addressing himself to the Jewish people in 1951, Martin Buber viewed the problem of the devastation as one of "dialogue between heaven and earth." Instead of the above question as to the meaning of Jewish life, he posed the following one: "In a time when there is an Auschwitz, how is it possible to have life with God? One might still believe in a God who permitted what has happened, but can one still speak to Him? Can one still call on Him?" As a man of undaunted faith, Buber did not seek to explain or to justify the catastrophe, only to find his way back to God who had concealed Himself from the world in a time of great calamity. He referred to the reply God had given to Job, who also demanded to know why his "rights were denied him." God replied, Buber said, but did not justify anything. Nothing was explained, nothing straightened out. The injustice did not become just, and the cruelty did not become kindness. Nothing happened except that man apprehended God's call again. And Buber concluded: "We still plead our case before God even now . . . His future appearance may be unlike any preceding one, yet we will again recognize our cruel and benevolent God."

Once more we have received an answer which does not satisfy because the question has not been put in proper perspective, and that is as a problem of Jewish life. If the life-giving forces of the Jewish people did not manifest themselves during the Holocaust, there can be no meaning of Jewish life issuing from it afterwards. To be sure, Buber veered away from the theme of death and destruction and phrased his question in terms of "life with God." This may serve those who seek the universal meaning of life in the face of human relations with the divine; but it does not tell the stricken Jewish people how its particular way of life can still be meaningful after what has happened to it in Auschwitz. More important, Buber does not remove the implication that God permitted this to happen to the Jewish people, in particular.

A Question of Jewish Life

Did God really conceal Himself and break off His dialogue with the Jewish people while the Holocaust was burning, thus permitting it to happen? I have heard this question in many forms but have not been able to understand exactly what is meant by it. If God were to prevent or stop the calamity, He would still have to do it through the instrumentality of human hands. The only ones who were in power to carry out His mission were the governments of the free Western nations. These governments were called upon by the leaders of American and world Jewry to intervene, but the heads of state did not heed the call. Translated into the language of "dialogue between heaven and earth," the voice of those who pleaded for rescue was the call of dialogue from heaven, and those who disregarded the plea were the ones who shut the dialogue off on earth. Not having responded to the call, the governments failed in their responsibility. But the dialogue between heaven and earth never ceased in the ghettos and concentration camps all over Europe. The Jewish people who suffered the calamity never stopped speaking with God even in their darkest hours. And this is the meaning of their dialogue: that in the face of death they asserted their will to live. If we want to understand the problem of the Jewish catastrophe and its meaning for future generations, our question ought to be, Can we find life through the suffering of the millions in the ghettos and the camps? When the reign of death spread over Europe during the Second World War, it appeared as if the apocalyptic end was near. But when it reached the Jewish ghettos and camps it received its refutation through an affirmation of life. Once more the Jewish "will to live" asserted itself at its highest against the destructive "will to power."

Under prevailing conditions of unsurpassed brute force it is incorrect to gauge what happened merely by the number who died or the manner in which they died. A more correct criterion is how they lived, how resolutely they affirmed Jewish life personally and collectively; how they celebrated their festivals, sang, prayed and studied; how they played, taught their children, and created works of art and letters. This was their dialogue with God. For when death is the order of the day, to strive to live even for an hour is a sublime act of being in the Divine Presence. Not death but life is the power that prevailed in the Jewish catastrophe in Europe. This upsurge of living forces in the Jewish people was manifest throughout their existence in the camps and the ghettos, as they resisted the forces of destruction actively or passively, as may have been the demand of the hour. Their heroic resistance was overshadowed, if not ignored, by many of the early chroniclers of the years of devastation and have been brought to full light only recently by those who look at the catastrophe in the perspective of Jewish living. The resistance came not so much out of the depth of despair as from the will to live. Who can fathom the living spirit of a people whose children sing in the following vein?

Song of a Child in the Warsaw Ghetto

I will be sad beginning tomorrow.
Today I will be joyous.
What's the use of sadness, tell me, what?
Cruel winds start to howl.
Why should I today mourn for tomorrow?
The tomorrow may be very beautiful and sunny;
Tomorrow the sun may shine for us again;
We shall then be sad no more.
I will be sad beginning tomorrow.
Tomorrow, not today. No, today I will be joyous.
And every day, no matter how bitter it may be,
I shall say:
I will be sad beginning tomorrow,
Not today. (My translation).

The late Nobel Prize poet Nelly Sachs poured out her laments over the "smoke" and the "dust" and the "sand" of the millions who died, and only in her last poems did she show some rays of light shining through the thick dust. Her visions of night and desolation then underwent a transformation into the mystery of life. Yet as early as 1944 a "distant" participant in Tel Aviv, who knew what was happening in the ghettos of Eastern Europe, wrote: "For many years we did not understand the meaning of this passive resistance on the part of our fellow Jews and our movement in Poland. We did not appreciate it as it deserved. We did not regard it as the miracle it was." In this perspective, the events of the Holocaust — the tragic, the heroic, the gloom and the light, above all the human frailties and the almost superhuman resistance — become a living legacy to be transmitted unto all generations to come.

1971

The Silent Witness of the Holocaust

November 23, 1976

Mrs. S. Kanner
260 Harrison
Passaic, N. J.

Dear Mrs. Kanner:

I have received the book *Meczenstwo Walka, Zaglada Zydow w Polsce, 1939-1945* (issued by the Polish Ministry of National Defense), which you left in my mailbox, and I wish to thank you for it. I will cherish it in my library as a monument to our martyred brethren in Poland.

I looked through the volume, every page of it, noticed your English translation of some of the captions, and was also able to decipher myself some of the Polish titles. But the pictures speak without words and grip one with their pent-up silence.

I have tried to absorb the faces of our men, women, and children, especially of the Partisan Fighters. Their countenances shine out of the pages, full of life, dignity, determination, pride, and defiance — for example, the elderly Jew with his beard well-groomed looking straight into the eyes of his murderer who points his gun at

323

him at close range. By contrast, the faces of the enemy are empty, congealed, even their grins or smiles — indistinguishable — look waxen; no human semblance left in them.

Much has been written and spoken about the Holocaust, but the heroism of our martyrs has not been fully revealed or perhaps not quite comprehended. May their names be a blessing unto all generations.

Cordially,
Alexander S. Kohanski

אהיה עצוב החל מחר,
לא היום.
(תרגום עברי מאת המחבר)

המשוררת נלי זק"ש, שזכתה בפרס נובל, שפכה כוסות תמרורים על "העשן," "העפר", ו"החול" של המליונים שמתו, אך לא הרגישה בשגב החיים שהקדישו. רק באחדים משיריה האחרונים, כאשר נצצו עליה קרני אור דרך עבי העשן, נהפכו מראותיה של חשך ושממה למסתורין של חיים. ברם, בארץ אבות יהודי פולני אחד, מ. נוישטאט, שהתבונן מרחוק ממקום מגוריו בתל אביב במעשי אחיו בגטאות של ארץ מולדתו, כתב עוד בשנת 1944: "במשך שנים רבות לא הבנו את הגבורה הפסיבית של אחינו בני ישראל ושל התנועה שלנו בפולין. לא הערכנו אותה כפי ערכה. לא ראינו את המופת שבה."

אם נביט גם אנחנו מתוך השקפה זו, כל קורות השואה — השממון וגם האור, הסבילות וההתקוממות, וכנגד כולם, בני עמנו בחולשתם ובהתגברותם — כל אלה הם מורשת חיים שעלינו להוריש לדורות שיבואו.

1973

והעממיים. ככה מללו הם את דו־שיחם עם האלקים. ומי ימלל את גבורתם ? מתוך
חייהם בתנאים כאלה גם נמצא את קנה המידה האמתי של עצם השואה : כשהמשטר
גוזר למוות מדי יום ביומו אז כל מאמץ יהודי להשאר בחיים אפילו שעה קלה הוא
מעשה גבורה של נפש רוממה. לא רק קצב המוות אלא גם ערך כביר של חיים שרר
בגטאות של אחינו היהודים. גם התקוממתם, אף כי אחרה לבוא מפני סיבות ששלטו,
באה לא מתוך יאוש אלא מתוך רצון החיים. מי יתעמק בלב עם סובל יסורים אשר
אחד מבניו כותב שיר כדהלן.

שיר של נער בגטו של וורשה

פון מארגן אן וועל איך זיין אומעטיק,

פון מארגן אַן !

היינט וועל איך פריילעך זיין !

וואס איז די פעולה פון אומעט — זאג מיר : וואס ?

די בייזע ווינטן הייבן אַן צו בלאָזן ?

צו וואס זאל איך היינט טרויערן וועגן מארגן ?

דער מארגן קען זיין אזוי שיין, אזוי זוניק.

מארגן קען די זון ווידער שיינען פאר אונדז;

מיר וועלן מער ניט דארפן אומעטיק זיין.

פון מארגן אַן וועל איך זיין אומעטיק.

פון מארגן, ניט היינט, ניין ! היינט וועל איך פריילעך זיין.

און יעדן טאג, ווי ביטער ער זאל ניט זיין,

וועל איך זאגן :

פון מארגן אַן וועל איך זיין אומעטיק,

ניט היינט.

אהיה עצוב החל מחר,

החל מחר !

היום אתעלז.

מה תכלית בעצב, אמר לי : מה ?

האם רוחות עז התחילו לפרץ ?

למה לי לבכות ליום מחר ?

אפשר למחר יהיה שמש ויופי,

מחר שוב תזרח השמש עלינו,

ולא נהיה עוד עצובים.

אהיה עצוב החל מחר,

ממחרת, לא היום לא ולא ! היום אתעלז.

ובכל יום, אף כי יהיה מר מאד,

אני אמר :

בשרש ישותו. איש האמונה אינו כופר בעיקר אף אם איננו יכול להבחין את מובן המקרה. ובכל זאת נודה שגם איש האמונה לא ירגע עד שיבין, ויהיה רק מקצת ממקרה הנורא הזה. פה אנו פוגעים בנקודה המרכזית של בעיתנו: על איזה מקרה מדובר כאן, על מקרה נורא של אבדון או על מקרה מופת של חיוב החיים? יש שואלים אפילו מנוקדת החיים, האם יש אפשרות לחיי עם יהודי אחרי אושביץ, ומה טעם יש לחיים כאלה אחרי שהעם סבל כליון של ששת מליונים? באמת אין הבדל בין השאלה הזאת ואלו ששאלנו למפרע. כל זמן שלא נכיר את תוקף החיים שפעם בלב היהודים בגטאות ובמחנות ההשמדה לא נגלה שום משמעות חיובית בעצם השואה או בתוצאותיה.

הדו־שיח עם האלקים

באחד מנאומיו בשנת 1951, מרטין בובר הסב את השאלה מחיי העם לשאלה של יהודי המתהלך עם אלקיו: "בזמן שיש אושביץ, איך אפשר לחיות בקרבת אלקים? אפילו אם אפשר עוד להאמין בא־ל שהרשה את המקרה, האם אפשר עוד לדבר אתו או לקרא בשמו?" כבעל אמונה שלמה, בובר לא השתדל לחרץ משפט דתי על השואה אלא לשוב אל האלקים שהסתתר מן התבל בעת השבר הגדול, והוא מסיים: "אנחנו נתפלל על זכותנו בפני השם גם עכשו... ואף־על־פי שהתגלותו בעתיד תהיה שונה מאלו שבעבר, נכיר עוד את אלקינו   והמיטיב." ככה בובר לא מצא תשובה לסבל העם, אלא הרחיק את השאלה מחיי העם בקרב בני אדם לנקודת־ראות אוניברסלית של זיקה בין אדם והשגחה האלקית שהסתתרה מבני האדם. אבל, האם באמת הסתתר הא־ל מן התבל והפסיק את דו־שיחו עם העם היהודי בעת שבערה הבערה? אם הא־ל רוצה לעכב בעלילה הוא עושה זאת על ידי אנשים עושי רצונו. אנשים כאלה בימי השואה היו ראשי המדינות החופשיות. מנהיגי קהלות היהודים פנו אליהם והפצירו בהם לעזור; אבל הם לא שמעו בקולם. אם נעתיק זה ללשון "דו־שיח בין שמים וארץ", כדברי בובר, קול השמים נשמע מפי היהודים שבקשו הצלה, אך ראשי המדינות הפסיקו את הדו־שיח עם אלקים וסרבו למלא את חובתם.

בגטאות ההשמדה, להפך, לא נפסק הדו־שיח בין הנאסרים והשמים. ולכן הבעיה הנכונה של השואה היא, איך למצוא ערך חיים בתוך הענויים של מליוני אחינו שעברו דרך הגטאות ומחנות הכליה. כאשר הסתערה שליטת העריץ בארצות אירופה נדמה כי העמים הגיעו לקץ אפוקליפטי. אך כאשר נקף השליט בשערי הגטאות של היהודים נתקלה בסתירה: "רצון החיים" של העם היהודי הכזיב את "רצון הכח" המחריב. כי כל מה שקרה שם אין לדון רק על־פי מספר הנהרגים או במידה שבה נהרגו, מפני שהאויב התנפל עליהם בכח אדיר ובכפתע פתאם עד שלא יכלו להתכונן למערכת הגנה, אפילו אם היו להם האמצעים הנחוצים. יותר נכון להעריך את אורח חייהם הפנימיים שערכו בתנאים תת־אנושיים שעומסו עליהם: איך שמרו על דתם ותרבותם, למדו את בניהם, חגגו חגיהם, שרו ושחקו, ויצרו דברי משא והגיון ומעשה אמן, ומעל כל אלה, איך התאמצו להגשים כל דק ורגע של חייהם הפרטיים

327

אחת מהשואות עשתה כלה בחלק גדול מקהלותינו וקצצה הרבה בנטיעות חיוניות של כל העם. בכולן הוכחו אכזריות נמרצת ומעשי חבלה שאין לשער, אם נעלה בחשבון את ממדי האוכלוסיה וכלי המשחית הפשוטים של הימים ההם. אך חשוב גם לציין שבכולן היתה גם גבורה של יהודים יחידים וגם של קבוצות שהתקוממו נגד המחבלים בזמן הפלילה ואחריה. ויותר מזה, רצון־החיים של העם היהודי התגבר אז כהכחשה ברצון הכח הגס. כעבור הזעם, הקהלות היהודיות באירופה חדשו את חייהן ביתר עוז, הקימו את חורבותיהם, הכו שרשים רעננים, והמשיכו לרקם את רקמתם הדתית־תרבותית לדור ודור.

גורלנו עלי אדמות

והנה נוצצת שאלה שמחרדת את הלב ונוקבת את המוח: מדוע נפל בגורלנו לשלם מחיר גבוה כזה בעד קיומנו כעם מיוחד ובעד דרכנו המיוחדת בעבודת הבורא? אין לי תשובה על שאלה זו, כי בכלל אין אדם יודע טיבה של שאלה גורלית. הפיטן ליום א׳ דסכות הגיד לנו: "שלמתי בזה רגל עלי אום שבעים." אפשר שגם זה גורלנו. בכל אופן אי־אפשר לאמר שזהו דרך ההשגחה, כי הלא היא צותה לנו לבחור בחיים ולא במות. יותר נכון לאמר שזהו דרך מין־האדם שלא למד להעריך את החיים שצווה לבחור בו, ויודע רק להשתלט ברחבי התבל על־ידי הרג וחרמה. הלא אנחנו היהודים לא היו היחידים שסבלו תחת ידי העריץ, היו אלפים ורבבות מגויי הארץ שאובדו על ידו; רק לרבות שעם ישראל נבדל ל"טיפול יוצא מן הכלל."

עד כאן המבט הגורלי־ההיסטורי, גורל חיי נצח של עם מלומד שואות וחרמות, המחדש תמיד את ימיו כקדם. אבל עוד לא ירדנו לעצם הבעיה של השואה שנתרחשה בימינו אנו, והיא: איך ליישר את מבטנו עליה ומה נגיד לבנינו. בזה לא נטפל בהסטוריה או בגורליות, אלא במה שאירע בחיי העם תחת סבל יסוריו: איך התקרב לאלקיו ונתרחק מיתר העמים. ובזה יש מבט שמעל־להיסטוריה.

תלונה נגד השמים

כששואלים: מדוע קרה המקרה? מדוע ולמה ירדו ששת מליוני בני עמנו לאבדון, ומה טעם יש בכליונם? אנו שואלים שאלות שאין להם מושג; כי לאמתו של־דבר אין טעם בכליון. אין מושג לשאלה מוחלטת של אבדון במונחים של הבנה אנושית, של תקוות וצפויים, אף לא במושגי השגחת האל בחיינו. וכששואלים: אם יש צדק בעולם, מדוע לא הופיע בעת אסוננו הכי גדול? ומדוע נתנו לפורצים להשתולל בנו ובעמים אחרים ולא מחו בידם בעוד מועד? אז, אם שאלות אלה כוונו נגד המעצמות הגדולות במערב, שהיה בכוחן לפעל, אנחנו יודעים את התשובה השלישית שקבלנו מהם. אבל זה רק מכווץ את לבנו ואנחנו מרימים את תלונותינו נגד השמים: אם יש אל בערפל, מדוע הרשה את המקרה, או לכל הפחות, מדוע לא עצר בעדו. ואם הרשה, ואם לא עצר, אז...

אני חושד, שאלה שאומרים "אחרי אושביץ אין אלקים בעולם" לא האמינו באלקים גם לפני אושביץ, כי הלא האמונה היא המבחן היותר חריף בחיי אדם שנוגע

סקירה על השואה והגבורה *

באתי לדבר אתכם על השואה מתוך שני מבטים, מבט של הסטוריה וגורל, ומבט שמעל להסטוריה. כלל גדול הוא בתולדות עמנו: כל מקום שאתה מוצא שואה, אתה מוצא גבורה. אבל כשמדברים על שואה בלי מצרים שבאה עלינו בימי הנאצים, האם אפשר לדבר עליה מתוך סיכוי כל־שהוא? לזה צריך להתרחק ממנה מרחק רב כדי לראות את הקוים המתלכדים בנקודת מראה אחת, להוריד אותה לממדים נורמליים ולהביא אותה תחת שלטון השכל המוגבל של בני אדם. ובכל זאת, כל מה שנתרחק מן השואה, פלצות הולכת ומתגברת עלינו. לשוא אנו מחפשים איזה חזון בדמיון אנושי, איזה חוק בתהליך חברתי, איזה ערך נימוסי או מורה־דרך דתי כדי לרדת לעמקו של סבל העם שנחתם לכליון. אנו שואלים פעמים אין מספר, היש טעם בזה? האם יש בו תמורה, או איך יצדק בעיני אלקים ואדם? ולמרות זה, אם נרשה לעצמנו להכנע תחת מעמסה זו, לא נוכל לדבר או לכתוב על השואה כלל, ואף לא נוכל לספר אדותיה לבנינו. נוכל רק לעמוד בפניה ביראה ובדום.

רבים מאתנו שמרו על דממה זו כמעט דור שלם. התאמצנו לפעמים לחוות השקפה על השואה בממדים דתיים, לאומיים, או כלל־אנושיים כדי לברר אותה לדור הצעיר. ובכל פעם פרצו קושיות שאין להן שחר; ומבלי מצוא פתרון, נרתענו אחור ודמנו. ובכל זאת, אם נעמיק להבין את המאמצים שלנו, אולי נבוא לדעת שאין אנו מתקשים בפתרון אלא בעצם הקושיא. אי־אפשר לפתור בעיה אי־מובנת. עלינו לרדת לתוך־תוכה של הבעיה ולהעלות ממנה משפט הנובע מנבכי מאורעותיה.

ועוד דבר: כשאנו מנסים לבאר את משמעות השואה לדורות שיבואו, אין בידינו לפענח להם את הסתור. תפקיד כזה מוטל על כל דור ודור לענות בעצמו בתוקף חייו היהודיים. מה שמוטל עלינו, הדור שראה בהרס עמנו, הוא להביע את גישתנו למשמעות הבעיה; מה שנוגע לפתרון שלנו, גם הוא יבוא רק למעשה בנפשנו ובחיינו.

בעית השואה

כדי לקבע את בעית השואה על תקונה, צריך שתראה באספקלריה של חיי עמנו למעשה בדורות שעברו. היינו כל כך נבוכים מן הפתרונים שאין להם שחר עד ששכחנו שהשואה בימינו לא היתה היחידה בתולדות עמנו ביבשת אירופה. ואף מה שהיינו מספרים לבנינו על שואות שעברו לא שמנו לב להן כהוגן, מפני שהעתקנו אותן לשיעורים בהיסטוריה ולא חשנו בשיעורן ולא הבנו את פשרן בחיינו אנו. במשך אלף השנים האחרונות היהודים באירופה נוגפו בארבע שואות. כל אחת משלש הראשונות החריבה קהלות עצומות בארצות מיוחדות, אך הרביעית כמעט הציתה את כל היבשת. נציין את העובדה, אפילו אם אין בה שום הוראה, שארבע השואות באו במחזורים של שלש מאות שנה: הראשונה במאה האחת־עשרה בזמן מסעי־הצלב, השניה במאה הארבע־עשרה בימי ״המות השחור״, השלישית במאה השבע־עשרה על ידי מורדי חמלניצקי, והאחרונה במאה העשרים על ידי הנאצים. כל

329

PART III

Zionism and the State of Israel

> Zionism and the renewal of the
> State of Israel in our time are
> manifestations of the everlasting
> verities of the Jewish people.

When Jewish Youth Responded to the Call

The Second Aliya in Erets Yisrael, 1904-1914

Toward the end of the nineteenth century, Jewish youth in Russia forgot the pogroms of the 80's and the antisemitic excesses of the Russian hooligans that were not only sanctioned by the czarist government, but also looked upon with equanimity by many leading lights among the Russian intelligentsia. Again the young souls became animated with the spirit of revolution and with the establishment of a better society in which all men would be equal, and hatred and oppression would be banished forever. The Russian revolutionary movement, which at that time began to assume sizable proportions, exerted a magnetic influence on the Jewish intellectuals and student youth and absorbed many of them into its maelstrom of action. The Jewish national movement had been dormant. The Hovevei Zion had struggled along with their program of small colonization efforts in Palestine, and the tiny Yishuv itself had not yet produced the vigorous voice that could summon Jewish youth of the Diaspora for greater deeds. The Bilu of 1882, that group of a handful of idealistic students who had given up their careers and went to Palestine to redeem their people, left no trace in the minds of the succeeding young generation. The latter stood ready to sacrifice itself on the altar of "universal brotherhood" for the liberation of the Russian masses.

The meteoric appearance of Herzl on the Jewish scene, to be sure, made a great dent among the Jews of Eastern Europe and aroused their hopes beyond expectation. But the youth was yearning for action, and it was perhaps due to the dominating personality of Herzl and to his policy of suspension of all practical activity in Palestine until the "Charter" was obtained, that left the young generation without an immediate goal for active self-expression. Instead of serving their own people, then, the Jewish intelligentsia, in large numbers, grouped themselves under the banner of the Russian revolution. It was the beginning of what is now called "Red assimilation." Marxism, which had been the Bible of the Russian revolutionists since the beginning, taught that the vanguard of the revolution was the industrial proletariat. Following this principle with blind faithfulness, and in spite of the fact that there was an insignificant number of Jewish industrial workers at the time (counting only some 40,000 in old Russia, in 1897), the Jewish revolutionaries began to organize their toiling brethren for the general class struggle. The leading force of that movement was the Bund (founded in Vilna in 1897) that strove to identify itself completely with the Russian masses and fought bitterly against every attempt to inject a Jewish national motive into its program, even though, as a matter of expediency, it carried on its work in the Yiddish language.

Nachman Syrkin

Now there were exceptions to the rule, and one of those intransigent spirits who would not succumb to mass ecstasy was Nachman Syrkin, the "lone fighter" on the Jewish national front, as Berl Katzenelson called him. What Syrkin grasped of the Zionist movement, as no one before him had apprehended, was its basic revolutionary character. The Jewish people had to be reorganized, its anomalous existence revitalized, its economic, cultural, and political life given a new foundation and renewed vigor. The Jewish worker and the Jewish farmer were not yet in existence, at least not in sufficient numbers, and therefore had to be created before they could be organized for the struggle. In brief, the Jewish people had to undergo an inner revolution in order to liberate itself from the shackles of the Galut, and that revolution was Zionism, or the upbuilding of the Jewish national homeland in Erets Yisrael. But Syrkin went further in his revolutionary interpretation of the Jewish national movement. Zionism as such, that is as viewed in its purely nationalistic aspect without the social implications, was insufficient to bring about a radical change in the life of the people. The new society that was to emerge in Palestine had to rest on an entirely different foundation — on a basis of social and economic justice and equality. Thus Syrkin posited two principles for Jewish national redemption — Zionism and

Socialism — and he sought to bring them together into one synthesis. Syrkin may not have solved this problem theoretically, but his comrades and followers succeeded in resolving it materially on the soil of Erets Yisrael.

Ber Borochov

At the beginning of the twentieth century, small groups of Jewish revolutionaries began to rethink their universal concepts and to turn their attention to the problems of their own peopple. The resurgent wave of pogroms in 1903 and the setback of the Russian revolution in 1905 shook them out of their hypnotic state of cosmopolitan assimiliation and brought them closer to the everyday realities of Jewish suffering. Those whose nerves were not shattered by the shock returned to their fold and placed themselves in the midst of Jewish self-defense, fighting for their people's life and honor which they now embraced as their own. Not many came back, but those who did were of a rare calibre — hardened under the sledge of the czarist Okhranka (secret police) and filled with revolutionary zeal and now also with a deep love of their people. The most outstanding of them was the erstwhile revolutionary Ber Borochov. At that time, the first Poalei Zion groups sprang up in the towns of the Jewish Pale, and Borochov soon emerged as their theoretical exponenet and practical leader. Thoroughly versed in Marxian dialectics which he had absorbed in the days of his general revolutionary activities, he tried to supply the tenets of Marx and Engels to the question of Jewish nationalism. By inference from the Marxian principle that the class struggle is determined by the relations of the *means* of production, Borochov reasoned that the national struggle is shaped by the relations of the *conditions* of production, such as geographical boundaries, control of natural resources, and the like. Both principles work together, and since the proletariat is the vanguard of every nation, the Jewish proletariat will liberate its people by means of the class struggle in its national homeland, whether the Jews were driven by an elemental, or as Borochov termed it in Russian-Yiddish, a *stychic* force.

These were youthful intellectual speculations that Borochov later modified in accordance with Jewish reality, after having delved deeper into the sources of his people's past and current intolerable conditions. Whether or not his theories were convincing, his fervor for the Jewish cause was contagious. Still the movement remained on a theoretical plane until, almost spontaneously, groups of Poalei Zion and others from Homel, Minsk, and other towns in Poland, Lithuania, and the Ukraine, banded together and set out for Palestine. That was the Second Aliya which started in 1904 and continued until the first World War, when their total reached 2,250. (The general Jewish immigration into Palestine for that period was some 18,000).

Joseph Vitkin

What prompted those young people to leave their homes, some of which were quite comfortable, and go to the bare hills and desolate plains of the ancient land, was an inner urge of pioneering — a determination to change the entire scheme of things that went into the make up of the "Jewish question." As if by divination of that urge which was coming to life among the youth in the diaspora, the earlier pioneers in Palestine issued a call signed by Joseph Vitkin, summoning the youth to come to their ancestral land and rebuild it. The efforts of the Bilu and their immediate successors had failed to lay the foundation for the national rebirth of the people and the country. Their colonies which were struggling for survival did not prepare the ground for the absorption of newcomers. In many instances the new arrivals were resented and rejected by the older settlers. Vitkin and his comrades realized that the national homeland would not be rebuilt unless new young blood was injected into the whole enterprise. Their message to the youth in the diaspora (in 1905) read in part as follows:

We must work and struggle to redeem the land and fight with the courage of a people for whom there is no retreat. . . . Awake, O youth of Israel! . . . . Your people lies in agony. Rush to its aid. . . . Arm yourselves with love of the land and of the people, with love of freedom, with great patience and come! . . . Know, brothers, your people is sick and unhappy. . . . Do not come to it with complaints or demands. Come, rather, to help and to awaken, and your greatest and loftiest reward will be the very realization of your goal. . . . Be ready to struggle. . . . Be prepared for the worst, but also for victory. And your victory will the victory of the people.

The pioneers of the Second Aliya who responded to Vitkin's call as well as to their inner urge came to Palestine to lay the foundation of a new national structure. They undertook to carry out by themselves all the menial tasks, hard labor, tilling the soil, drying the swamps and protecting their possessions against the attacks of marauders. Their motto was self-labor, and their ideal, the revival of the Hebrew language and culture in a new society based on principles of freedom and equality for all. They started the collective and cooperative settlements which have become a basis for the ever increasing absorptive capacity of the land. The blooming collectives and cooperatives, such as Degania and Kineret in the lower Galille, Nachlat Yehuda, Bir Yaacov, and En Ganim in Judea, and all the numerous colonies that have been modeled after them are living monuments to the unswerving faith of those pioneers in the truth of their undertaking. Each of those settlements was started by a handful of people. Toward the end of the period, in 1914, they became an important factor in the new Yishuv. While they cultivated their own settlements they also tilled the soil, worked and kept guard in the Jewish private colonies. In March 1915 one could count in Judea alone 2,381 of them as wage earners (including 941 Yemenites), 1,268 artisans, and 1,115 in other occupations, together 4,764 out of a total Jewish agricultural population of 7,400. (The entire Jewish Yishuv in Palestine in 1914 numbered some 105,000, of whom 12,000 lived in 45 colonies).

Aaron David Gordon

The man who, more than any other individual among the pioneers of the Second Aliya, embodied the aspirations of that movement and realized it in his personal life was Aaron David Gordon. He was the oldest in years among them, having come to the land at the advanced age of 48; but he was the youngest in spirit expressing the inner revolution that gripped an age-old people in its heroic effort to break the impass of its life in Galut. Gordon started life anew as a worker in the fields of Degania, regaining his strength and youth as he dedicated himself to the rebirth of his nation in its ancient homeland. He was a teacher and guide of his pioneering generation. His principle that each individual must regard himself as part of his people, and that both must realize themselves through work with nature, was rejuvenating to the entire movement.

337

The heritage of the Second Aliya has been woven into the fabric of the Yishuv, and it is still operative in it today. Many of its first pioneers of the Aliya are today still active, some of them occupying leading positions in the community. The Yishuv has since grown in numbers and strength through the Third and succeeding Aliyot, and now represents a united force with a common purpose to build and defend their land. That purpose is animated by the legacy of the pioneers of the Second Aliya.

1940

Borochov, Marxian Zionist

In the short span of his dynamic life, Ber Borochov (1881-1917) made many contributions to the thought and action of the Jewish labor movement of his own period and he has remained to this day, one of the leading exponents of Labor Zionist ideology. Borochov's most singular contribution is his economic interpretation of the Jewish problem. It is true, he was not the first to study contemporary Jewish life from the economic angle, but he went further than his predecessors, in applying the methods of dialectic materialism to the problems of the Jewish people.*

While Borochov was unquestionably a Marxian (at least in his earlier writings), and fully subscribed to the theory of dialectic materialism, he was realist enough, to allow certain elements of this theory to fall by the wayside as he went along searching for the significant and determining factors in Jewish history. For Borochov issued from the point of view of Jewish life which he had observed and studied at first hand, and applied the Marxian principles only as a *method* of investigation (as Engels himself correctly named it), and not as a dogma of absolute truth. Furthermore, Borochov was never at peace with the materialistic interpretation of history, least of all, in its application to Jewish reality. This was not due to Borochov's shortcomings as a thinker, but to the inner contradictions of materialism of whatever brand it

---

Nationalism and the Class Struggle, a Marxian Approach to the Jewish Problem. Selected writings by Ber Borochov translated from the Yiddish. Introduction by Abraham G. Duker. Poale Zion-Seire Zion and Young Poale Zion Alliance, New York, 1937.

may be. This is not the place to enter upon a discourse on the issue involved. Suffice it to point out, that Lenin, after writing lengthy dissertations on the materialist interpretation of history, arrived at the following conclusion: "To be a materialist means to recognize objective truth which is revealed to us through our organs of sensation," which is nothing but "sensationalism" pure and simple, leading into the quagmire of skepticism.

Borochov did not delve into this problem, but he touched upon another phase of materialism which is really the crux of the entire controversy. In the well-known Marxian sense, "materialism" excludes human will as a factor in the development of society, or for that matter, human history as a whole. It recognizes only the external, material objects, which are independent of man, as the determining forces of the social structure of mankind. In his earlier writings, Borochov tried to adhere to this principle having made an attempt to build the entire structure of Jewish national and class struggle on the foundation of the external interaction of the conditions of production, the relation of production and the forces of production, leaving out of account the element of human will in the entire process. In this respect, Borochov only extended the Marxian analysis of class relationship and applied it to relationships among nations. Class struggle, according to Marx, arises out of the conflict that prevails between the forces of production and the relations of production. The national struggle, Borochov reasons, emerges when there is a conflict between conditions of production, such as geographical boundaries, raw materials and other sources of production (which are the basis of national existence) on the one hand, and the forces of production on the other.

This cold, impersonal interpretation of nationalism never satisfied Borochov himself, or his followers. It somehow did not fit the history of the Jewish people. To fill the gap in the objective interpretation. Borochov introduced another principle, the "stychic process" whereby he sought to get to the core of the driving force in Jewish life. But the gap was only widened, for the "sytchic process," as Borochov conceived it, was also a blind, impersonal, though more elemental objective force, underlying the will to live and to be free. What was still lacking, was the unifying principle which kept the Jewish people together and which motivated, if not determined, their entire course of national existence. Borochov had recognized this deficiency in his theory from the very start, and he tried to introduce additional concepts such as group character, a

339

feeling of kinship, associated with a historical common past, a language, and political institutions, which help to cement and preserve the entity of a given people. But, he considered these merely as *instruments* of preservation which are the superstructures of the material base, namely of the conditions of production. Thus far, Borochov tried to maintain a consistent materialism, at the expense of inconsistent nationalism. Further observation of Jewish reality and especially of the labor colonization work in Palestine, however, led him to a different interpretation of the national urge. The purely materialistic concept of the "stychic process" gave way to a many-sided view which included the economic, political, and emotional elements as well. He ultimately accepted "the Zionist assertion that the *will* of our people" is, if not the sole determining factor, at least one of the most important factors in our national existence and our regeneration in Palestine.

The more significant contribution of Borochov's theory is evidenced by his application of the dialectic principle to the contemporary economic struggle of the Jewish people in the Diaspora. This principle, too, Borochov took over from Marxism, but he used it with great skill, and, what is more important, with deep insight into the Jewish problem. Borochov was the first who consistently applied the dialectic principle to the problem of the Jewish people, as an inner process. His analysis of the "Economic development of the Jews" is still a classic, notwithstanding the serious changes which this economy has undergone since that essay was written. Zionist thinkers before Borochov, notably Pinsker and Smolenskin indicated the anomalous economic position of the Jewish people in the diaspora, but it was Borochov, who pointed out the abnormal inner structure of Jewish economy and showed its effects upon the course of our Galut history.

In brief, Borochov's analysis reveals the fact that everywhere the Jews predominantly occupy the final levels of production, such as the needle trade, baking, printing, and similar trades which serve the consumer directly. The Jews are not rooted in the primary or basic stages of production, such as agriculture, mining, forestry and the like, which are close to nature and which constitute the economic foundations of organized society. Expressed in different terms, on the basis of the share of labor and land in human production, Borochov shows that Jewish occupations are predominant in the sphere of labor. Upon further classification of labor into mental and physical, it appears that the Jews are preponderant in the field of mental labor. The Jews, thus, occupy the higher rungs of the economic ladder (though not the highest) while the base and the lower stages are in the possession of the indigenous, non-Jewish population. National competition aggravates the situation to the detriment of the Jews. As soon as the indigenous occupants of the lower rungs begin to climb the ladder, the upper levels must be evacuated, and the Jews fall to the ground.

We see here both the inner contradictory process of Jewish economy, and its relation to the surrounding environment. Drawing this analysis to its logical conclusion, Borochov arrives at his theory of Jewish migration, which is the crux of the Jewish problem. The Jewish masses who are expelled, directly or indirectly, from a given country, and find a haven of refuge in another one, go through the same economic process in their newly adopted home, as in the country from which they were expelled. In order to survive in the new country, the immigrants must concentrate in large masses, as that facilitates their adaption to the new environment. On the other hand, mass concentration hinders the Jews from penetrating into the lower levels of production, and they only perpetuate the habits and occupations of their previous environment. In due time, national competition (between the Jewish masses and the other peoples of a given state) is bound to ensue, and the Jewish problem arises. Instead of decentralizing (in the occupations) in a given country, the Jews spread all over the world, creating for themselves in each country the same conditions which involve the same problem. In the dialectic process of national competition lurks another, equally potent factor of class struggle. This struggle goes on within the national unit of the Jewish people, as well as without, among the surrounding nations. The Jewish masses are passing from the middle and lower-classes into the working class. But, in order to survive, the Jewish workers must strike roots in the primary and basic levels of human production, and this they can achieve only in a land of their own. The result of the entire process is inevitable: *Concentrated settlement of the Jewish people in a central place.* By the same dialectic process which operates in human society as a whole, the redemption of the Jewish people devolves upon the masses of its own laboring class. It is Jewish labor that must regenerate itself in a homeland of its own where it will create the necessary conditions of production upon which a free people and a free society will be established.

Borochov's teachings exerted great influence on Labor Zionist thought. His writings, however, were in Russian and Yiddish, and were hitherto inaccessible to the English reader. The Young Poale Zion Alliance has now presented to the American public a small volume of his selected essays in an English translation. This selection, which is primarily intended for youth, reflects the main tenets of Borochov's theory, including his analysis of and observations on the cosmopolitan anti-national tendencies among intellectual radicals. The excellent introduction by Abraham G. Duker gives a full view of Borochov's background and of the social and economic trends of his period.

One should have liked to see more of Borochov's writings included in this volume, at least to make the text commensurate in size with the "Introduction." But, most likely, technical limitations did not allow for that. On the whole, it is a job well done. The reader who has not known Borochov will be gratified to come in contact through his selected essays, with a brilliant intellect, and a great Jewish personality who had devoted his life to the liberation of his own people.

1938

A. D. Gordon's Philosophy of Man and Nature

In this age of brutal, physical force and cynical negation of moral and ethical values, the message of A. D. Gordon may sound like a cry in the wilderness.* Who would heed a man who dedicated himself to a life of work in the arid fields of Palestine, and admonished his fellow men to do likewise, for he firmly believed that the regeneration of the human race may be achieved only by work and by "living nature." He abhorred war, oppression, or any form of domination of man over man. He sought freedom of the

*A. D. Gordon, *Selected Essays*. Trans. Frances Burnce from the Hebrew edition of N. Tradyon and A. Shohat. New York: League for Labor Palestine, 1938.

individual, of the group and of humanity as a whole. Above all, he yearned and labored for the rebirth of his own people in its ancient land. Gordon, perhaps more than any other individual of his period, symbolized the regeneration of the Jewish people on the soil of its homeland. He came to Palestine in 1904, after he had lived in his native Ukrainian village for 54 years, of which 23 years he spent as a minor official on the estate of his distant relative, the Baron Ginsburg. At this advanced age he broke with his past and started life anew as a common laborer in the agricultural settlements of Palestine. Later he joined the Kvutza (collective) Dagania, where he remained till the end of his life (1922). It will be inadequate to classify Gordon as a philosopher, a writer or a teacher. He disclaimed all these or any other appellations. As he says of himself: "I am not a publicist, nor a man of science; neither am I a poet. I am just a simple Jew with a simple Jewish heart and I want to write to you, my brothers and my friends, as a simple Jew writes a letter to his family on family affairs." Yet he developed a systematic and well integrated philosophy of nature, man and nation, which can be presented here only in bare outline.

Regeneration is the keynote of the life and works of A. D. Gordon. Primarily he dealt with the problems of regeneration of the Jewish people. But the principles which he promulgated are applicable to any other people, as well as to the human race as a whole. Man, he says, has become removed from the fountain of all living forces, which is nature, and that is the cause of our modern social ills. Man has become an automaton, thwarted in his self-expression, trying to comprehend nature through intellectual abstraction. Instead, man should *live* nature, expand his inner forces and thus realize himself fully in complete freedom.

How can man achieve this state of freedom? What medium shall he employ? And can each one attain it individually? Man can be redeemed and regenerated only through work. And by work Gordon meant a creative force that produces not only the means of sustenance, but new life and new values. Yet labor is regenerative only if it is self-labor without exploitation of others. Although he regarded mental and manual work as of equal importance, he emphasized physical labor on land as the most significant factor in the regeneration of the Jewish people. The individual, Gordon maintained, cannot redeem himself alone, apart from the group. This is a basic principle of his theory of nationalism. There is really no sharp line of demarcation between the individual and the group;

the two are organically interrelated and they cannot function or be conceived apart from each other. The "collective man" is a natural phenomenon of social evolution, as human society goes through the stages of the family unit, into the national unit and higher up into the unity of the human race, which is based on a harmonious relationship among the nations. This harmony will prevail if each nation will be allowed to develop its inner natural forces without at the same time encroaching upon the rights of other nations. True internationalism means justice to all nations. Gordon rejected the undue "self-criticism" of certain writers who advised the Jews to imitate what might be considered the "higher" culture of their neighbors, or to change their habits and become a "different nation." Neither of these prescriptions will place them on an equal basis with other nations. Only the self-realization of the Jewish people to the fullest extent of its inner capacities will rejuvenate and regenerate it as a nation. This can be achieved in its own homeland. The nation and the land must redeem each other.

Gordon exerted great influence on his own generation as well as on the succeeding generations of pioneers in Palestine. The volume under review contains only a part of the spiritual heritage which he bequeathed to posterity. The very difficult task of rendering Gordon's Essays into English was most ably performed by Dr. Frances Burnce with the assistance of Dr. E. Silberschlag. This volume will serve as a guide to those who seek deeper understanding and fuller appreciation of the work of the Jewish pioneers in Palestine. For in essence Gordon was the greatest pioneer of the national rebirth of his homeland and his people.

1939

Twenty Years Histadrut

Landmarks in the life of the Histadruth are significant stages in the growth and development not only of the Jewish labor movement in Palestine, but of the Yishuv as a whole. Born twenty years ago, on the threshold of the Third Aliyah, when pioneering youth began to surge into Palestine in large numbers, the Histadrut, has ever since maintained its role as the vanguard of

Jewish colonization and creative effort in the national homeland. At its foundation, on December 5th (Chanukah), 1920, it counted only 4,433 members. Three years later, at the close of the Halutz Aliyah (a year of economic crisis), its membership grew to 8,400. In 1926, when another crisis ensued at the end of the Fourth Aliyah, the Histadrut embraced 22,500 members and in 1930, after the riots of the preceeding year, its membership increased to 27,400. During the period of mass immigration (1930-1936), the Histadruth grew by leaps and bounds, counting in March, 1937, over 104,000 members who, together with their families, constituted 48% of the total Jewish population in Palestine. And now, at the turn of another decade, when the Yishuv is faced with the gravest crisis in its existence, the Histadruth is still on the increase, its membership reaching well over 120,000. This brief account in figures reveals a basic truth about the Histadrut, namely, that it had its inception in the actual needs of the time, and that its phenomenal growth and consolidation have had their source in the realities of the Yishuv.

Quest of Unity

Political parties are by nature always jealous of their identity and independence and are often a serious hindrance toward the unification of divergent elements. On the other hand, the parties in Zionism have been the driving forces of immigration, colonization and the general constructive work in the Yishuv. An attempt to unite the labor parties and groups extant at the time (Poale-Zion, Hapoel-Hatzair, Left-Poale-Zion and non-partisan groups) was made in the spring of 1919 at the conference in Petach Tikvah; but the effort was unsuccessful because the individual parties thought that such coordination infringed upon their sovereignty. Their differences and conflicts were so pronounced that for a time it seemed hopeless ever to attempt to unite them. Yet the common tasks that confronted them brought them together once more and unity was effected. The key for united action was presented by Joseph Trumpeldor in a call which he issued to all the labor groups. Without encroaching upon the independence of the existing parties, he summoned them to form an organization in which they would all be represented in proportion to their numerical strength, and which would engage in the economic, social and cultural activities that concerned all alike. Thus, the Histadrut Haovdim

Haklalit b'Eretz Israel (General Federation of Jewish Labor in Palestine) came into existence.

The process of unification on the basis of vital economic and social needs of the working population has continued ever since with remarkable success. Political parties, too, have united *Mapai,* including the Poale-Zion, Achdut-Avoda and Hapoel-Hatzair) while others have come to the fore (Hashomer Hatzair, Hapoel Hamizrachi, leftist groups and religious groups), and they are all represented in and united by the general Histadruth. At present, the membership of the Histadrut embraces left-wing and right-wing labor groups, General Zionists, religious Zionists, Yemenites and a variety of other non-partistan groups. Each of these parties and groups elects its representatives to the General Conference and has its share in the conduct of Histadrut affairs.

Colonizing Agency

The unique role on the Histadruth in the upbuilding of Palestine will be appreciated if one bears in mind the two-fold nature of its function. It is a trade-union as well as a colonizing agency. As a labor organization it is constituted of three national trade unions, the Agricultural Workers' Union (31,000 members), the Railway, Postal and Telegraph Workers' Union (600 members) and the Office Workers' Union (6,000 members) as well as of numerous local trade unions in every occupation, including the professions. As an agency promoting colonization work, it is organized, as of March 12, 1924, in a cooperative Workers' Association Ltd. (Hevrat Ovdim) with branches in all the agricultural, industrial and financial enterprises. The members of the Histadrut as individuals or colonies (particularly the Kvotzot) are the shareholders (of membership stock with voting power) in these enterprises. Preferred stock, bearing dividends but no voting power, is sold to the general public. "Hevrat Ovdim" as a body possesses the controlling number of shares (founders' stock, 41-50%) in each undertaking.

These undertakings cover every field of endeavor. Colonization of workers' settlements is promoted by "Nir," building of workers' houses and suburbs is carried on by "Shikun," public works by "Solel Boneh," Plantation of orange groves by "Yakhin." Various co-operative shops are fostered by "Merkaz Hakooperatsia," work at the ports of Tel-Aviv and Haifa is undertaken by "Nachshon," marketing of agricultural products by "Tnuva," promotion of consumers' co-operative by "Hamashbir," and transportation and communication lines are handled by "Eged Hameuhad." Other enterprises are included among the economic functions of the Histadrut, but they are too many to be enumerated here.

Financial Institution

The magnitude of these enterprises may be gauged from the fact that 12 major establishments have a combined capital of about $5,000,000 with a total turnover for one year (1937) of more than $36,000,000. The chief financial instrument which is operative in all the economic functions of the Histadrut is its Workers' bank (Bank Hapoalim) with a registered capital of close to one million dollars, deposits of about two and a half million dollars and a capital turnover, for one year, of $62,000,000. What is the national significance of these institutions? Much has been written and said about the absorptive capacity of Palestine. Experts on colonization have been baffled by the rate of increase in population through immigration and the rapid establishment of the newcomers on a sound economic basis. In six years, from 1930 to 1936, a Jewish population of 200,000 has absorbed in its midst another 200,000 who came to Palestine from many lands.

The Yishuv has its own peculiar laws of expansion which are best explained by what is known as the "dynamic principle" of colonization: the more people arrive in the country, the more ground they prepare for others to come. This dynamism in the rebuilding of Palestine has gained its greatest tempo through the co-operative and collective enterprises of the Histadrut. A clause in the constitution of the Kibbutz Hameuhad, a large unit of collective settlements, states as one of its aims "the constant expansion of the Kibbutz and the steady absorption of the workers' Alliyah." This is an imperative of all the economic undertakings of the Histadrut. There is never a lack of space for a newcomer in a Kvutza or Kibbutz. When there are not enough beds, two sleep in one bed, and when there is not enough food, they share their meals, until, after a period of transition, the new arrivals are settled permanently and become productive forces in new avenues of employment. Therein lies a great secret of the absorptive capacity of Palestine. In a pioneering country, such as Palestine has been for the past two decades and still is, one might not expect to find social and educational institutions developed according to modern progressive standards. Yet, the Histadrut has been the vanguard in this field as well. Social medicine, unemployment insurance, emergency unemployment relief and work, immigrant aid, elementary and secondary schools, vocational training, adult education and the promotion of art, music, and the theater, have been fostered by the Histadrut since its inception.

The Kupat Holim (Sick Fund) which was started by the agricultural workers eight years prior to the formation of the Histadrut and was subsequently incorporated into the latter, is now the most efficient and progressive health institution in Palestine. Toward the end of 1938, Kupat Holim reached a membership of 81,000. During that year it gave medical service to 140,000 patients, Jews and Arabs, in 186 settlements at an expenditure of over $1,000,000. Perhaps the most progressive feature of this institution is the fact that its medical and clerical staff are members of the Histadrut and, as such, also full-fledged members of Kupat Holim, enjoying all its privileges and sharing in its obligations. There have been many critical periods in the Yishuv in the past twenty years, which resulted in unemployment. In the course of the riots in 1936-1939, and since the beginning of the present war, the unemployment situation reached alarming proportions at various stages of the general economic index. One may say without exaggeration that the Histadrut has staved off many a calamity by establishing the Pidyon Avoda (emergency unemployment fund,) in addition to its regular unemployment fund. Pidyon Avoda is a voluntary tax levied from all members of the Histadrut in proportion to their earning capacity. In six years (1933-1939) this special fund, together with the other unemployment funds of the Histadrut raised a total of $1,398,000, and attracted large sums of national and private capital for investment in public works which created millions of work days for the unemployed.

It is beyond the scope of this article to describe in detail the accomplishments of the various educational and cultural institutions, the daily press, periodicals and other publications of the Histadrut. Suffice it to point out that they have played an important role in the training and prepartation of the pioneers, the newcomers as well as the young native generation, for their arduous task of settling and building a homeland in Palestine. Youth has been given particular attention in the organization of Hanoar Haoved (Working Youth) which maintains vocational work shops, general courses of study and seminars, agricultural training groups, camps and a health resort, and facilitates the settlement of young workers on land. Among other colonies, Na'an, Migdal, Sheikh-Avreikh and the new Tel-Hai have been established by members of Hanoar Haoved.

Women's Role

One of the basic principles of the labor movement in Palestine is hagshama atzmit (self-realization) which the Halutzim have to attain in their lives, individually as well as collectively. For the Halutza, the woman pioneer, this principle has been doubly difficult to realize. The place of the woman in the Kvutza or Moshav, or for that matter in all the undertakings of labor colonization, was undetermined at first. Her old role in the kitchen was unbearable to her, for she wanted to have an equal share in every phase of creating the new forms of life in the pioneering Yishuv. After many years of struggle against the hard reality of colonizing experiments and the prejudices that had prevailed among her male comrades, the woman attained her position of equality in the workers' society. The Moatzat Hapoalot, or Women's Council, is now an autonomous body within the framework of the Histadrut, representing the female membership which is about 30 per cent of the total. Among the functions of the Women's Council are: training of immigrant girls in agricultural and industrial occupations and helping them obtain suitable employment; establishing cooperative institutions to relieve the working woman from household duties; raising the standard of living and promoting the cultural needs of its membership. The position of the pioneer woman in the Yishuv is now coming closer to the ideal visualized by one of labor Palestine's immortal leaders, A. D. Gordon, namely that the woman's role in modern society should be in accordacne with her specific natural capacities, physical as well as psychological. This is equality of opportunity for self-realization in the true sense of the word.

National Responsibility

In the two decades of its existence, the Histadrut has proven to be a potent, if not the most potent, factor in the building of the

Yishuv, bearing responsibility for the national enterprise as a whole. Leaders of the labor movement have held responsible positions in the Vaad Leumi (I. Ben Zvi as president), in the Zionist Executive and the Jewish Agency (David Ben Gurion as chairman of the Executive, and the late Haim Arlosoroff and now Moshe Shertok as successive heads of the Political Department). Being a member of the International Cooperative League and of the Trade Union International, the Histadrut has been able to make effective representations of the Jewish cause in Palestine before the world labor movement and particularly in Bitish labor circles. The members of the Histadrut have always been among the first to contribute to the Keren Hayesod, Keren Kayemeth and other national funds. The same feeling of responsibility motivated the attempts made by the Histadrut to come to an understanding with the Arab people. True, the key to a solution of this intricate problem has not been discovered as yet, but the Histadrut has made a distinct contribution toward a rapprochement with the Arabs, in so far as it organized Arab workers' clubs, conducted education activities among them and helped in protecting their interests and raising their standard of living.

Finally, the members of the Histadrut and the organization as a whole, have been in the forefront of Jewish self-defense in Palestine, having protected heriocally their own colonies as well as private possessions, and even Arab and Christian settlements, against rioting Arab bands. And now, as the world conflagration approaches the shores of Palestine, the Histadrut together with the Yishuv has mobilized its forces and stands ready to defend the national homeland to the last man.

1941

Two Anchors on Our
Line of Defense

Cleveland Jewry is being called upon once more to give of its substance, and give generously to the Jewish Welfare Fund which has now started its annual drive. It will be well in this connection to review the proceedings of the United Palestine Appeal Conference held in this city a few weeks ago, since the U. P. A. is a constitutent part of the United Jewish Appeal which, in turn, is one of the main beneficiaries of the local Jewish Welfare Fund. It is not the purpose here to repeat the utterings of all those who spoke at the Conference, though some of those utterings were truly great and made a lasting impression. What is intended here is to bring home the basic problem dealt with at the Conference, which was in the main, the problem of our general line of defense.

A Measure of Consolation

Before proceeding with this discussion, mention should be made of a few unique phenomena of this Conference, which grew out of the existing world conflict. We have been used to receiving messages at our Conventions from official and semi-official spokesmen of various governments, and this Conference was no exception to the rule. But there was a difference in the situation. The messages and greetings we received now, came from governments who are engaged in a struggle for the life or death of their peoples. Many of those governments are now in exile, while their countries are overrun by the Nazi hordes who are bent on exterminating their populations. They are now suffering or threatened with a fate similar to that of the Jewish people. The encouragement and sympathy for our cause which they expressed in their greetings are thus more genuine, since they have become fellow sufferers. Let us not be misunderstood; we do not rejoice in the calamity of the conquered nations, although there is a good old Hebrew saying: "Tzarat rabim hatzee n'hama." (A universal misfortune is a measure of consolation). But our consolation is in the fact that the suffering nations have become more attuned to appreciating our misfortunes—that they are now in a better position to understand us.

Another encouraging sign that became manifest at this Conference was the type of addresses delivered before the delegates by the non-Jewish speakers. We always invited among the speakers at our national conventions a few of the select Gentiles, those whom we call in the very expressive Hebrew phrase, Hasseedei umot ho-olam (the pious among the Gentiles) to say a few words to us. Most of those speakers, in all their sincerity, though with much naivite, would come and tell us what a great and noble race we were, that we had given to the world the Bible and the

Prophets, and that Jewish persecution was a crime against the Commandments of God and against the tenets of Christianity. The more sensitive among us would listen to their praises with mixed feelings. They sang paeans to our past glory, which no one disputed and about which the non-Jewish world cared very little. But what about our present, which is full of controversy and which has been the butt of many national and international conflicts? Very few would touch upon it.

At this last conference, however, more than on previous occasions, our Gentile friends spoke of us in our presence, in terms of our vital, everyday needs. When Professor Albright of John Hopkins University, who spoke on the "Role of Palestine in the Rehabilitation of the Near East." confessed before the audience that he had recently become a convinced political Zionist, he motivated his conversion by a penetrating analysis of our position among the nations of the world today, from which he drew the inevitable conclusion. And when Senator Barkley stated in his unequivocal manner that the Palestinian Jews might fight under the flag of any democratic nation but that it would be more desirable and more honorable for them to fight under their own blue and white flag, his words rang with sincerity and conviction. And our own Mayor Lausche, who spoke with simplicity and deep sympathy, drew an apt comparison between the Jewish aspirations in Palestine and the struggle for liberation of the small European peoples, of one of which he is a descendant.

Global Front

The U. P. A. Conference was convened for the purpose of rallying the American Jewish forces in support of our national homeland in Palestine. Many people might ask   (and some did ask), should we not concentrate all our efforts on national defense in this country, rather than divert our energies to a distant territory where only a comparatively small number of Jews lives? In a crisis such as the American people faces today, such reasoning may appear sound, since it calls attention to the danger at home—and there is nothing closer to a person than his own home. But there is a fallacy in this type of arugment. What many Americans (and many Jews among them) had failed to realize prior to our entry into this war, was the very thing that President Roosevelt had emphasized repeatedly, namely, that the war is being fought on a world front and that there is no separate American line of defense. Rabbi Silver stated it very clearly and emphatically, when he declared that should Palestine fall into enemy hands, it would be as serious a blow to the American and British war efforts as the fall of Singapore might be. As to our own Jewish position in this world, the defeat of Palestine would spell the greatest calamity in our life everywhere, including the United States. Our front is far flung, encompassing the entire Globe, but we have only two bases of operation, two anchors on our line of defense—Palestine and America.

Wherein lies the strength of the Yishuv in Palestine? Our population there is only a little over half a million souls. But what it lacks in numbers, it makes up in courage, discipline and organization. A few years ago, when the Refugees of German persecution started coming into Palestine in larger numbers, there appeared a declaration in the Hebrew press in Tel Aviv, which bore the very trenchant caption: "Pleeteem lo nihyeh od" (We shall not be refugees again). Palestine is their last stand;—they will not move from there, but will defend it to the last man. On that, the entire Yishuv is united. But even more remarkable than this is the fact that our defense forces in Palestine are recruited on a volunteer basis, not only in political, economic and social defense work, but also in the military service. The contributions made by the Yishuv toward national funds (Keren Hayesod, Keren Kayemeth, etc.) are ten times larger per capita than those made by American Jewry. We have in the Palestine Jewish community the highest concentration and the greatest expression of our will to live and our will to be free as a people.

We often ask ourselves, what does Palestine mean to the American Jew? What can it offer to us here in our everyday life? Speakers at the Conference pleaded that Palestine should become a matter of personal concern to every one of us here, not only as a haven of refuge for our European brethren, but as as stronghold for our own self-defense. It is not difficult to conceive from the trend of events, how a free, self-reliant, Jewish commonwealth in Palestine may help our battle against prejudice, defamation and even persecution in this country. Every Jew should bear that in mind when he is called upon to make his contribution to the United Palestine Appeal (or the Welfare Fund). He will be buying an insurance policy for his own security in this country as well.

Yet there is another aspect of our reconstruction work in Palestine which should not be overlooked in the least. It was Spinoza who pointed out in contrast with the Rambam, that the genius of ancient Israel was not prophecy (and we may add, in contrast with Karl Marx—not profits), but the capacity to build a higher level of social life. From the point of view of world history, it is perhaps our destiny, or if you will, our mission, to return to Palestine and establish there the new form of society which will serve as a model for the other nations to emulate. Thus, the tiny hilly country on the eastern shores of the Mediterranian basin may yet be destined once more to give the world a renewed creed in the dignity and freedom of man, such as was promulgated in our Scriptures some 3,000 years ago. For, the reconstruction of our national life in Palestine, in so far as it is sound and lasting, is based on the concepts of a just social order, of cooperative living, of creative self-labor, of freedom for all peoples on earth. The world which is now engulfed in this struggle against oppression and slavery, will not be able to rise from its ruins if it tries to re-establish itself on the foundations of the old order. The thinking minds of the democratic nations have already begun to realize it, and they are in search of new forms for the society that is to emerge out of the present chaos. Perhaps—and this is not far-fetched—Palestine will show the way.

Can Palestine do it alone? The answer is, "No." We have in Jewish lore, and for that matter in our history, the concept of a triune—that of the People, the Land and the Torah. Neither one ever functions properly without the other two. The land, Palestine, is there to be reclaimed and redeemed, but only a small segment of our people is now in that land to do it on the spot. The rest of our people is scattered in all corners of the earth. Most of our communities in the other parts of the world have been destroyed, or are on the verge of annihilation. The one corner where we can do most is the United States of America. Here lies our second anchor and base of operation. We need not apologize for our national aspirations in Palestine, as we need not protest our American patriotism. We have lived in this country nearly three hundred years and have had our share, together with the pioneers of other groups, in building and developing the economic, cultural as well as political resources of the land. We have taken an active part in the wars of America, and we have served the interests of this country with valor and distinction. The time has passed when Zionists, or any one working for the rebuilding of Palestine, might be accused of dual nationalism. The Gentiles understand this even better than a good many of our own brethern. We are fortunate enough in having the material possessions necessary for the erection of strongholds both here and in Eretz Israel. What we still lack is sufficient moral and spiritual fortitude in applying ourselves to this task with unrelenting determination. In this respect we stand in unfavorable contrast with the Jewish community of Palestine. American Jewry, to say the least, is not nearly so well united, and what is more ominous, not so disciplined as is the Palestine Yishuv.

Given the people and the land, we must complete the triune of Jewish survival by reviving the Torah, in its broadest sense, comprising our entire religious, social and cultural heritage which has kept us alive as individuals as well as a people. We are told that British Jewry has risen to greater heights during this war in strengthening its inner communal life, enhancing its cultural and spiritual activity and also in increasing its efforts on behalf of Palestine. The Jews of America may well take that as an example. We need not and must not sacrifice our communal well being, our organizations and institutions in this country, in order to fortify our position in Palestine. For these institutions are the bastions of our strength, the forces that weld us together so that we may carry on our fight on all fronts.

1942

Creation of the Third
Jewish Commonwealth

"The Jewish State is essential to the world; it will therefore be created." These prophetic words Herzl worte in 1895 in the preface to his *Judenstaat.* On November 29, 1947, the United Nations General Assembly, by a vote of 33 to 13, approved the establishment of the Jewish State in a partitioned Palestine. The Third Jewish Commonwealth has thus arisen in the midst of a world still torn asunder by the aftermath of war. That the two great contending forces in the world today—the United States and Soviet Russia—were able to compose their differences on the formation of the Jewish State, is a good omen for humanity's yearning for peace. The Palestine parition plan, said Dr. Oswaldo Aranha, retiring president of the U. N. General Assembly, is a "bold and historic experiment which will be one of the greatest factors in avoiding unrest in international relations." Once again, out of Zion may yet come the word and the deed for true and lasting peace.

Spontaneous Jubilation

The Yishuv in Palestine burst forth in spontaneous celebration as the news reached the country. Even British soldiers were carried along by the jubilant spirit and joined the celebrants in the streets. They permitted the merrymakers to ride on their armored cars. At the same time the Haganah and the entire Yishuv is bracing up to meet the wave of Arab riots which started sporadically in several sections of Palestine and which may spread at the instigation of the ex-Mufti. *For the Displaced Persons* (who may now be called "Delayed Pioneers") in European lands, the day the United Nations approved the Palestine plan is the beginning of their real liberation. In *Belzen*, British zone, seven thousand Jews sang and danced amidst great rejoicing. In *Rome*, at the Arch of Titus — symbol of destruction of ancient Judea—five thousand Jews gathered in a mass meeting, which ended in a parade under the Arch. In *Munich*, three thousand DP's jammed the Opera House for a mass celebration. The Jews in *Vienna* went on a mass pilgrimage to the grave of Theordor Herzl, ending a week-long celebration. In the *American Zone*, the Central Committee of Liberated Jews declared a two-day holiday. *In London*, tangible expression of support to the reborn Jewish State was given at a conference of the Jewish National Fund at which $30,000 was raised. The 33 nations voting for partition were inscribed in the JNF Golden Book, as were also the Jewish State, and Great Britain for her past services to the Jewish people The Jewish Agency raised the Zion flag over its building. *In Budapest*, the Jewish flag was raised over the Jewish Community Council building and festivities continued for a week. Demonstrators paraded through the streets of *Bucharest*, shouting "Long Live the

Jewish State." Mass-meetings and special thanksgiving services were held in communities throughout the United States and Canada, in Latin America, South Africa and Australia.

Unity in Variety

Jewish organizations of different outlook hailed the U. N. decision on the establishment of the Jewish State. The American Zionist Emergency Council called it "a milestone in the history of the world." Judge Joseph Proskauer, president of the American Jewish Committee, greeted with satisfaction the contribution of the U. S. delegation toward the Palestine solution. He emphasized, however, the Committee's position that "there can be no political identification of Jews outside of Palestine with whatever government may there be constituted." Mrs. Joseph Welt, president of the National Council of Jewish Women termed the U. N. decision "a necessary part of any program that will enable Jews of the world to rebuild their lives in freedom and security." Justice Meir Steinbrick, national chairman of the Anti-Defamation League, said the new state will help eliminate antagonism between Jews and non-Jews in many parts of the world and deprive anti-semites in this country of fuel to feed the fires of anti-semitism. Masada, the Zionist Youth Organization, resolved, at its recent convention, to back the Haganah and declared that an attack on Jews in the Middle East would constitute an attack on American Jewish youth.

Arab Reaction

The threat of bloodshed and massacre of Jews, issued by some spokesmen of Arab countries, does not seem to reflect the unaminous reaction of the Arabs in the Middle East, although serious trouble is brewing and will no doubt issue from the Arab Higher Committee of Palestine and Arab League headquarters. Fighting, arson and looting is going on in Jerusalem, Haifa and other parts of the country. However, Arab leaders disclaim responsibility, blaming "lawless elements" for the trouble. In Nathania a delegation of Arab notables called on Mayor Ben-Ami, congratulating him on the establishment of the Jewish State and expressing hope for cooperation between Jews and Arabs. The Iraqi government issued a communique in which it instructed the people "to preserve order and tranquility." The government in

Egypt assured the Jewish population of protection of life and property. In Syria and Lebanon demonstrations went off without anti-Jewish violence.

Role of Britain

The British Government informed the United States of its intention to terminate the mandate in May of 1948, at which time it expects the United Nations to assume responsibility for the administration of Palestine. In the meantime, the Colonial Secretary declared, British troops will be responsible for law and order in the country, and if necessary, the armed forces will be augmented. It is expected that the five-man commission appointed by the U. N. General Assembly to carry out the partition plan in Palestine will be on its way there within a couple of weeks. The Governments represented on the Commission are: Bolivia, Czechoslovakia, Denmark, Panama, and the Philippines.

1947

Israel and American Jewry

Presented here is the first response to questions posed in a letter to the Jewish Community Bulletin by Rabbi Morris Goldstein and published in last week's issue. His inquiry called for views as to how Jewish life in America may be enriched through the inspiration of spiritual benefits from creation of Israel. The Bulletin will welcome constructive letters on the subject. The following is the reaction of a recognized San Francisco leader in Jewish education (Ed.).

Rabbi Morris Goldstein, in his letter to the editor last week, has posed some very pertinent questions before American Jewry, all of which may be summed up in one major proposition: That Israel may become a source for spiritual enrichment of Jewish life in Amrica. And, indeed, Israel can become such a source if our ties with it will be woven out of the proper fabric, enabling the spirit to flow to and fro freely. What Israel has already demonstrated in the process of gaining its independence is a spiritual force that manifests itself rarely in the history of mankind. The American people experienced the same kind of spirituality in its war of independence more than a century and a half ago. But in this country we are now too far removed from that spirit in time and too often also in thought. The demonstration Israel has given to us and to the rest of the world is that Jews have an equal right to live in freedom as a nation and that they are willing to grant the same right to others, regardless of race, creed, or color. This should help bring back to every one of us in America the original tenets of our own democracy.

Give and Take Basis

Another principle demonstrated by Israel in its struggle for freedom is that one must find spiritual strength in oneself. If American Jewry is to revitalize its life it must seek spiritual forces within its own community. One cannot live on borrowed spirituality and be free. I would consider the relationship between the Jews of America and the Jews of Israel as one of "give and take." A similar relationship existed between the Jewish community of Babylonia and that of Palestine during the Second Commonwealth, to the enrichment of both sides. There are several areas in the creative life of Israel that may bring forth great values for us in America as well. In this short comment only two such values may be mentioned, namely, the Bible and the Hebrew language.

A Human Laboratory

In the life and labor of the halutzim in Israel one may see the realization of the social and ethical teachings of the Torah and the Prophets. There the Bible is becoming a way of life in actuality. Perhaps once more in the history of man that small country is destined to become the human laboratory for great religious and ethical experiences. Our own reading and teaching of the Bible will assume far greater significance in our everyday life if we can show at least in one corner on earth how teachings are translated into practice. The other area, the Hebrew language, is of equal importance for the spritiual revival of the Jewish community. Its religion, culture, and tradition, which are the sustenance of American Jewry, originated in that language. The renaissance of Hebrew in Israel may thus serve us here as an inspiration to intensify the cultivation of our national tongue in our schools and institutes of higher learning for the study of the hebraic sources of our heritage.   1949

Reflections on Jewish-Arab Relations

Rabbi Jack J. Cohen* has tried to take Jewish-Arab relations from the impossible prongs of a 'dilemma' into the open arena of 'problems.' Prior to the Six Days, he maintains. Israel was in a dilemma in relation to its neighboring Arab states, and especially to the Arab refugees. If she retaliated against the Arab raids on her territory with a show of force, she would earn the condemnation of the United Nations for lack of restraint. If she did not retaliate she would jeopardize her security. If she allowed the refugees to return she would again endanger her security; if she did not allow this she would be charged with "being inhumane, insensitive to human suffering..." After the Six Days, Rabbi Cohen holds. "All this has now been rendered a matter for historical reflection." Instead of having a dilemma, he says, Israel is "now confronted by a set of genuine problems," which, he postulates, are derived from the Jewish majority's treatment of the Arab minority in their common state. And that, he argues, is a matter of morality, not of security, and thus the 'dilemma' has disappeared.

Entangled in one Horn of the Dilemma

Rabbi Cohen's main difficulty, to begin with, lies in his dissociation of security from morality, and in putting them on two separate horns of a dilemma. But even if this were so, everyone knows that a dilemma can be solved only by taking hold of both horns at the same time. Instead, Rabbi Cohen circumvents the horn of security and becomes entangled in the horn of morality, further complicating it by a new dilemma for majority-minority relationships. For the latter is not as clear-cut a problem as he would like it to be, that is, of a Jewish majority having in its 'power' (he emphasized that word many times) and therefore "a grave responsibility" to do right by its Arab minority. In fact, the question of security always comes back to demand its resolution vis-a-vis the Arabs even *in* Israel. Since Rabbi Cohen formulates and develops the issue of morality without regard to security, he has not really escaped either horn of his dilemma. Out of his love

*See, "Arabs and Jews: From Dilemma to Problems," by Jack J. Cohen, *Reconstructionist,* Oct. 6, 1967.

for Israel, his passionate sense of righteousness, and out of his deep desire to defend the good name of the Jews before the world, Rabbi Cohen sees the goodness of his people, and he earnestly seeks a way of rendering it more effective in relation to their Arab neighbors, and at the same time convince the latter of it. Unfortunately, the overall impression obtained from his article is that the Jews in Israel, officially and unofficially, do not behave toward their Arab minority on a proper level of humaness and morality. And he advises that, if the Jews did rise to the proper level, their Arab neighbors would drop their resentments, cease their opposition to the State and start loving it together with the Jewish majority as their common homeland. Not only that; he feels "Israel's position internationally, and possibly even in the eyes of the other Arab states, could be strengthened." Yet the latter, he says, is "immaterial to the point" he is trying to make. "For the treatment of Israel's own Arabs by the State and the Jewish majority is a moral question in its own right."

Rabbi Cohen's line of reasoning proceeds for the most part of his essay on theoretical grounds. When he does "descend from theory to actuality," his balance of evidence hardly supports his conclusions. If we added up and evaluated all his "buts" of favorable "Jewish treatment of the Arabs in the State of Israel," we would find them far outweighing his instances of unfavorable treatment. However, that is not the main burden of his argument in the light of the issue he has raised, namely (as he quotes the prophet), that "a righteous man shall live by his faith." The essence is in the ground of his argument , and his analysis of both theory and actuality rests on a ground of some very serious historical misconceptions and factual non-existents. These are of decisive, vital importance to the Jewish position in Israel and in the Middle East as a whole. I can only touch upon them here very briefly.

State of Israel No Charitable Enterprise

Rabbi Cohen looks at the historical events that led up to the final establishment of the State of Israel from a charitable viewpoint, and he even does "not want to be uncharitable to Israel's stand toward its Arab population . . ." Since, according to his view, the State of Israel was created by the UN as a charitable, humane enterprise for the Jewish homeless, why should the Jews, who are now the majority and possess the 'power,' not show the same charitable spirit toward their Arab minority and give them all the privileges they feel are coming to them, even "UJA funds?" But charity, we must remember, is not the foundation of morality; it is the other way around. And indeed, the Jews did not return to their ancient homeland to establish it as a charitable institution, but rather to rebuild it as a state on very high moral grounds. If the Bible is to be quoted to remind us of our moral obligations, then let us go to the source of it.

The Jews are an historical people and they have the moral, legal, and every other right to their land, Eretz Yisrael, with or without the Balfour Declaration, the Mandate or UN resolutions. All these were only instrumentalities for helping to fulfill that right, which had to take its natural course in the events of our time anyhow. The League of Nations Mandate did not establish that right, it only confirmed it. And Weizmann poignantly made it clear to the British statesmen even before they took over. "The Jews," he said, "will go to Palestine anyhow, whether you want it or not. There is no power on earth that can stop [them] . . . You gentlemen can make it easy for them; you can make it difficult." The Gherer Rebbe expressed it in one phrase. When told by the governor of Jerusalem (no friend of the Jews) how much His Majesty's Government supported the Jewish homeland, the Rebbe said," *mehekke teise.*" When asked what he meant, he clarified: "We have a mandate over Eretz Yisrael from the *Ribono-shelolom*; if Great Britain wants to add its signature to advance that mandate's validity, *mehekhe teise* no harm."

Israel Established by Jews Not by UN

It is, therefore, historically erroneous to say, as Rabbi Cohen puts it, that "Israel was established by the UN to solve the problem of Jewish homelessness, to enable the Jewish people to house all those Jews unwanted elsewhere . . ." For the State of Israel was in fact not established by the United Nations or even with its aid, which was not forthcoming anyway when needed most. The partition plan voted by the UN in November, 1947, was an adjudication between two contending parties for the same territory (all of it, not just "large portions of Palestine," as Rabbi Cohen thinks). The UN decided on partition and drew up an agreement, which the Jews accepted, but which the Arabs did not accept. And here is the basic moral issue.

Wrong Assumption and Incorrect Moral Implication

Rabbi Cohen's second major historical error is that he assumes "that the Jews have come home into an area which was occupied in their absence by another people who have earned the right to live there *as a people*" (his italics). This, he says, also entails a moral issue, and the burden falls on the Jews. But he makes a wrong assumption and implicates the moral issue incorrectly. The area was *not occupied* by another people when the Jews came there. If that were so they could not have founded a single colony in that territory, 'homeland' or no homeland. There were Arab's living in the area. This is not the same as being occupied by another people. The Jews saw their homeland lying waste, the largest portions of its territory uninhabited, desolate, neglected, and they returned to rebuild it for themselves. And the true moral implication of their coming is this: in their relation to the Arabs and Jews agreed, and have lived up to this agreement, not to deprive the inhabitants of their possessions and not to exploit them for the rebuilding of the Jewish homeland.

One may ask, with whom did the Jews make that agreement? The answer is, with those who at the time recognized their right to the land and offered to help them exercise it. But the Arabs did not agree, one may retort. That is begging the question. You cannot enter into an agreement with someone who does not recognize your right to negotiate the terms of agreement. The right itself is not negotiable. But who, one will ask, bestowed that right on the Jews? That is the burden of the issue and the crux of Rabbi Cohen's fallacy. If we stand on his ground, that it was the UN or Great Britain or some other world Power which gave the Jews the right to settle in Palestine, because they "were not wanted elsewhere," then the Arabs can say, "We don't want them either." Is this a moral ground to stand on? What kind of moral relationship is this among peoples when everyone has a right to keep the Jews out if unwanted, and the Jews should have no right to their own ancestral land? No human power or combination of powers could give them the right. They have it, the same as any other people has a right to a land, and they have had that right for millennia, regardless how many of them had lived there at the given time, or who else may have lived there at the same time. And the only ones who can exercise that right for the Jews are they themselves.

As for the 'earned' right of the Arabs to live there *as a people*,

Rabbi Cohen well knows that the Jews have repeatedly called upon them to join forces in the rebuilding of the land, and in rebuilding themselves in the land and in the entire Middle Eastern region (a very essential factor in the question of rights) for their mutual benefits as 'peoples.' And Rabbi Cohen also knows that the Arabs in and out of Palestine have spurned this offer and refused to enter upon a covenant. These reminders are not just "a matter for historical reflection," as Rabbi Cohen suggests. The history of the State of Israel is still in the making. It did not start with UN resolutions and will not end with them. For what was the Six Day War if not but another battle (as Aba Eban prefers to call it) in the prolonged struggle of the Jewish people to enter into a covenant with their Arab neighbors?

Which Arab Case?

We now come to Rabbi Cohen's argument on behalf of the Arabs residing in Israel. He construes an Arab case which is non-existent and calls upon the Jews of Israel to act 'humanely' and 'morally' toward it, as if it did exist. But morality deals with real people and their actual claims, not hypothetical ones. In presenting the case of the Arabs, he postulates that the Jews are the conquerors and the Arabs the conquered, and that the Jewish majority is powerful and the Arab minority powerless. Neither is a correct assumption in fact or in the complexity of the situation. (He reiterates his fallacious argument when he tries to advise Israel on the "common mistake of conquering peoples.") And then he produces an hypothetically downtrodden Israeli Arab who says to the Jews as follows: "'If, however, you wish to make a new beginning for our two peoples—and for mankind as a whole—then at least acknowledge that power confers no right and that Palestine belongs equally to Jews and Arabs who live here and who may yet be privileged to come.'" Is this an actual case? Do the Arabs in Israel recognize "that Palestine belongs equally to Jews" and to them? And, which Palestine are they talking about, the partitioned one, the truncated one, the whole of it or the entire area of ancient Eretz Yisrael? (The last name, Rabbi Cohen admits, would never pass the lips of an Israeli Arab.) Rabbi Cohen knows this is not the case. In the next section immediately following the above quotation; he says: "Arabs, unfortunately, do not argue in this vein. They are unprepared to acknowledge any Jewish claim to

Eretz Yisrael." Then what is his argument for the Arab case all about? Are they ready to acknowledge Jewish claims to Israel, if not to *Eretz Yisrael*? Their actual case exludes all Jewish claims, because they have not recognized the Jewish *right*, and without that there can be no mutuality and no covenant. The irony of it is that the superscription of that section, which starts with the last quote, reads: "Jews Cannot Afford To Be Insensitive" (meaning, to the moral issue). No. indeed!

Equal Rights Derive from Common Destiny

The actual present Arab case is this: the Jews cannot deal with the Arabs in Israel alone without anticipating the outcome of their relation with the Arabs in the other states. Rabbi Cohen asks a rhetorical question. "How can we speak of the equality of [Israel's] citizens if one group is more equal than any other?" But the rights of the Arabs cannot come from sheer equality of citizenship with the Jews in a common country. They must share a *common destiny*, and thereby acquire not just 'equal' but *common rights*. At present, the Jews *are* in fact 'more equal' (to use this phrase), because their lives are at stake, and not the lives of the Arabs. It is as basic as that. When the State of Israel (common to both Jews and Arabs) is threatened by the Arabs of the other states, it is the Jewish citizens, not the Arabs, who are threatened with annihilation. The majority-minority basis on which Rabbi Cohen rests his entire case for the Arabs is seen by him just as a matter of humaneness, abstracted from the issue of security. Sitting in Jerusalem he ought to know that without security firmly established, the Israel Arab minority may, in one fateful turn of battle, join the invading Arab armies and bring the direst consequences upon the Jewish citizens with whom they now seek equality.

Meaning of Jewish State

Rabbi Cohen does not grasp the full import of the majority-minority relationship, because he is still under the spell of United Nations resolutions. He views the birth of the State of Israel as a "peculiar genesis," fathered by the UN, instead of as a natural outgrowth of the life and toil and sacrifice of the Jewish people themselves. And that is why he does not gauge the character of the adjustment required in the majority-minority status. He thinks the Six Days have established a new Jewish-Arab relationship. They have not. They have only brought about new conditions on which that permanent relationship (which the Jews have always wanted and have always maintained) can now be assured. This is the essence of Israel's demand for direct negotiations with the Arabs, which can take place only upon the latter's recognition of *Jewish* rights. Rabbi Cohen says, "The problem of the 'Jewish State' [in quotation marks] is a ticklish one," and he seeks a new meaning for it. The Jewish State, I submit, is not in quotation marks, and it is not a problem. It may only be considered as a problem by one who questions its right to exist. Its meaning, furthermore, is simple, and has been made crystal clear from the days of Pinsker, Herzl, Weizmann and the pioneers in the land, to our own day. It means *the rights of the Jewish people.* The Arabs are not concerned with Israel as a state; they are concerned with the fact that the *Jews* claim their right to it, and they (the Arabs) refuse to recognize that right. If Rabbi Cohen could cast off the spell of UN resolutions, he would see this stark actuality; not only did the United Nations not give birth to the State of Israel, but its very partition design has miscarried. And now the Jews know, as they have known all along, but as the Arabs have yet to realize, that neither of them can depend on instrumentalities of the UN or other Powers for an adjudication of their respective claims. Both parties concerned have to sit together and do it themselves, by drawing up a lasting covenant between them and live up to it.

Morality and Security Inseparable

This, in substance, is the moral issue of the situation in Israel and in the Middle East as a whole. That issue cannot be separated from the issue of security, for the two can be solved only together and at the same time. As for the Arabs in Israel, they will have a case in *morality* if they begin to work for the state's *security*. They can do it now, through their existing civic, professional and religious organizations, by making it known to their Arab brothers throughout the Middle East that they would join with their Jewish co-citizens in a common destiny, and that they, like the Jewish citizens, are seeking a negotiated peace between Israel and the other states for the security and well-being of all nations, Israel among them, in the entire Middle East Region. Toward that end the Arabs in Israel have to start working in earnest, without preconditions and on their own initiative. That is sharing in a common destiny, and that will make their equality real and enduring.

1968

The Masada Complex, In Whose Mind?

In *Newsweek* of March 19, 1973, the political analyst Stewart Alsop reported about an encounter he had had with Prime Minister Golda Meir as she was speaking at a luncheon for the Washington Press. "Toward the end of the lunch," he wrote, "after utterly demolishing a journalist who had asked a critical question, she suddenly turned to me and fixed me with a basilisk eye, 'And you, Mr. Aslop,' she said. 'You say that we have a Masada complex.'" Mrs. Meir was referring to a piece Aslop had written for the same magazine, July 12, 1971, under the title "The Masada Complex."

"'It is true,' she said. We do have a Masada complex. We have a pogrom complex. We have a Hitler complex,'" and she finished with some remarks about Israel's indominitable will not to "surrender to the dark terror of the Jewish past."

Apparently, Mr. Aslop was impressed by Mrs. Meir's "moving oration," as he called it, but he did not seem to grasp the reality of her words. For in the rest of his article he goes on with his analysis as if she had not spoken at all, following the same old track of blaming Israeli "intransigence" and lauding Arab "sweet reasonableness" that is characteristic of all Arab apologists here and abroad. He writes, for example, it "took courage, coming from an Arab leader," for King Hussein, though he "did not exactly say so, but hinted broadly," to intimate that he "would be willing to concede to the Israelis the right to maintain 'security settlements' on the west bank . . . In return (for) a sliver of sovereign territory through East Jerusalem." How Mr. Alsop derived such concrete concessions from broad hints is hard to tell, if we remember what the King did say exactly all along about putting an end to Israel's sovereignty or, as he called it, to "de-Zionize Israel," which escaped Mr. Aslop's attention.

367

Similarly, Mr. Alsop reports, with deep concern for President Anwar Sadat's political future, the latter's readiness "for an interim agreement" if he could only get "a prior commitment that Israel would at some point *agree to negotiate* the evacuation of all Egyptian territory seized in the 1967 war" (my emphasis). Again, Mr. Alsop failed to mention that Israel is ready to negotiate with Sadat anything he might want, any time, any place, but without prior commitments. For what Sadat really wants, and actually said so, is not "a prior commitment to negotiate the evacuation," but rather a prior committment to evacuate without negotiation, and not just at "some point" but at definite points according to his own time table. Yes, he would negotiate how it's to be done, if one could call that negotiation.

Ignores Basics

What is most incomprehensible about Mr. Alsop's analysis is that he sees the entire Arab-Israeli conflict as merely a dispute over "a sliver of sovereignty" in a piece of territory, ignoring the deeper large-scale and long-range implications that precipitated this dispute and many others. At the same time, he invokes a newly contrived rule of "no holding of territory gained through conquest," which is an ad hoc rule applied to Israel but to no other country in the Middle East or in the rest of the modern world. For, if this rule is a valid basis for demanding Israel's evacuation of all occupied territory, why is Hussein entitled to sovereignty in East Jerusalem and, for that matter, on the West Bank, which never belonged to him, but which he conquered in the war of 1948 and held by force of arms until it was liberated by the Israelis in 1967? But I am not going to dwell on the numerous discrepancies and inconsistencies of this argument. I have cited these remarkable instances of so-called "objective" political reporting and analyzing not in order to enter into a debate with Mr. Aslop about his long-range view of the Middle-East situation, but to point out his misconception of the meaning of Masada in the life of the Jewish people and in Israel's conflict with her Arab neighbors.

Its Own Masada

He ends his report on the same note, as he writes: "The stock Israeli answer is that 'We can see only to the horizon.' To the horizon," he muses, "it is easy to see that Israel can hold what she has. But beyond the horizon, it may be that Israel is creating its own Masada." What Mr. Alsop fails to realize is that Masada does not lie beyond Israel's horizon but, literally and figuratively, on its horizon, and that what Israel wants is to be able to determine that her Masada does not flare up again as a "complex" in the minds of the Arab leaders. For, while Masada, as a symbol of Jewish self-emancipation and self-determination, is in the land of Israel, the "Masada Complex," as a fixation to destroy Israel, is in the minds of her Arab neighbors. Now, since Masada is an actual historic event, we shall examine briefly what meaning a so-called complex may have in connection with this event in its historical perspective.

Last to Fall

Masada, which now is in ruins, is an ancient Jewish fortress on a high mountain top on the western shore of the Dead Sea. It was the last stronghold to fall in the seven-year war against Rome. After the destruction of Jerusalem in that war, many Judean warriors and their families joined their compatriots in Masada, where they made their last stand. The Romans laid siege to the fortress, and when the Judeans saw that they could hold out no longer, they decided to take their own lives rather than be taken captive. When the Romans finally penetrated the walls, they found all men, women, and children inside dead. This was in the year 73 C.E. The fall of Masada thus marked the end of Jewish national independence, in ancient times, a condition which lasted for almost 1,900 years until the rebirth of the State of Israel in 1948. What has been of paramount value about Masada in the memory of the Jewish people is that it represents the spirit of national freedom for which Jews—young and old, men, women, and children—are willing to give their lives, no matter what the odds are against them. In this spirit the defense forces of the State of Israel adopted as their motto "Masada shall not fall again!"

Freedom, Dignity

There is nothing morbid about this memory. It was not a nation committing suicide, as Mr. Aslop seems to imply by associating it with a psychotic "complex." Rather, it was a conscious, well-disciplined act of a group of Jewish warriors, fighting for the freedom and dignity of their people, who chose to die at their own hands rather than fall into the hands of the Romans. For they knew well what the latter had in store for them—brutal murder, a life of shame for their women and children in slavery, or being devoured by wild beasts in the arenas of Rome.

In the subsequent history of Jewish martyrdom there were many instances of similar acts on the part of groups of Jews, even entire congregations, who wanted to avoid defilement by their tormentors. During the holocuat in Nazi Europe there were comparatively very few Jewish suicides. But one night in a Jewish orphanage, several hundred maidens took their own lives in order to escape deportation to an army camp for a life of dishonor.

A Masada Act

We may call this a Masada act, in that the girls chose death when they were faced with a life of shame. In Jewish tradition this is considered Kiddush Hashem, the consecration of the Divine Name. Now if there is a certain "complex" to be associated with the name of Masada, it is the kind that Mrs. Meir spoke of at that luncheon in Washington, when she grouped it together with the "pogrom complex," the "Hitler complex," and the like. These are not psychotic states of the Jewish people, but rather of certain Gentile potentates, at whose hands the Jews have suffered greivously. Those rulers have a consuming passion to wipe the Jews off the face of the earth. We need not dig here into their reasons or motives. To them Masada may represent the old Roman slogan Hierosolyma est perdita (Jerusalem is laid waste), which reverberated in 19th Century Europe under the intitials HEP! HEP!

Around this slogan they may spin a cluster of delusions until it grows into a complex, and when such a complex becomes attached to a social or national ideology, it may assume extremely destructive dimensions. Such was Hitler's delusion of nazism as well as Nasser's delusion of Pan-Arabism, which is now being emulated by Muammar Kaddafi. Those obsessed with this kind of complex see what they call the "Jewish Question" as a spectre standing astride their road to conquest. It is remarkable how they all yearn to stage a "Masada" as their "final solution" to this question, and how remarkably alike their methods are. They instigate a reckless war of annihilation, and when they lose the war, they conjure up a ghost of a so-called Jewish menace to world peace. In 1944, when Hitler was facing total defeat in his war against the Allies, he was still preoccupied with his "final solution" to the Jewish question. Having realized that he could not finish this job if he lost the war, he contrived to convene an international anti-Jewish congress for the purpose of enlisting the aid of the other nations and their "unequivocal vow of allegiance to Germany's Jew-policies and demand a Europe free from Jews." That congress did not take place only because Europe was liberated in good time.

In 1967 Nasser was set to wage a war of extinction against Israel, and when he suffered total defeat, he started a campaign to enlist world sympathy and to gain support for his scheme under various pretexts, through diplomatic channels, notably in the United Nations and from the Great Powers. This goal is still being pursued by his successors in Egypt, in Syria and in Lybia.

There is yet another, even more significant parallel among the goals and methods of these would-be conquerors. Their aim is to make their respective domains free from all other ethnic elements, and their first step is to make their own lands Judenrein. When Hitler sent forth his troops to conquer the eastern regions of Europe he ordered them "to see to it that in the East shall dwell people only of real German, Teutonic blood."

In Arab Lands

The same policy has been pursued to this day by the Arab leaders in the Middle East. They have made their lands practically devoid of Jewish inhabitants, after having expropriated, incarcerated and expelled them from their midst. It is noteworthy that states like Jordan and Saudi Arabia have never permitted a Jew to set foot on their soil. And now that the hundreds of thousands of those uprooted Jews have found a new home—a real home—in their ancestral homeland in Israel, the same Arab leaders are bent on staging a "Masada" as their final act of extirpating all non-Arab elements from their region.

This is the open, declared policy of the Husseins, the Sadats, the Kaddafis, not-withstanding the dubious concessions and reconcilations which some well-meaning Western political analysts may try to find in their "broad hints." Israel's reply to all such hints is, If you really mean to be conciliatory, then let us get together and reconcile our differences. This is a simple, normal demand of a people that has no delusions and is not obsessed by complexes about its position in the Middle East. For Israel is resolved that its homeland is and will continue to be in that region, as it has been for millenia in the past. But Israel also wants to make sure that the Arab leaders in the neighboring lands do not try once more to break out with their "Masada Complex," and that is why it lets it be known to them that "Masada shall not fall again!"

1973

Note

There is a parallel of the Masada mass suicide in the history of Spain. About 145 years after Masada, the Romans invaded Spain (218 common era); but it took them 200 years to subdue the indomitable Celtiberian tribes who lived in what is now called Castile. The struggle of those tribes against the Romans is symbolized by the City of Numancia, which the Romans had besieged for a year and a half. When the Numancians could hold out no longer, rather than surrender they (all 6000) committed suicide, and as the Romans entered the city they did not find a single person alive to tell the story of that collective act. In Spanish folk-consciousness Numancia has become synonymous with "extreme heroism."

Jews, Arabs, and Zionists in the Middle East

This month in Jerusalem the Ministry of Posts issued a commemorative stamp for the 20th anniversary of the "Exodus of Iraqi Jews to Israel." The exodus was called "Operation Ezra and Nehemia" in reminiscence of the return of the exiles from Babylon in the sixth and fifth centuries before the Common Era. More than two decades ago, another operation, called "Magic Carpet," rescued the Jews from Yemen and transported them by plane to Israel. These and other undertakings to liberate the Jews from Arab countries have been going on at an increasing pace ever since the establishment of the State. By the end of 1967, the Jewish community in Israel included over half a million immigrants who were born in Arab lands in Asia and Africa. Today there are very few Jews left in the Mid-Eastern Arab states. I will describe their condition in the paragraphs below. But first let us take account of the climate of opinion with regard to the Jews in the Middle East that is being generated by the Arabs and their leftist supporters in the United States and abroad.

372

In a recent TV appearance an Arab commando spokesman and his American "advocate" protested that the Palestinian Arabs are not fighting the Jews but the Zionists. All they want, they said, is to establish Palestine as a non-racial, inter-religious state in which Jews, Christians and Moslems would live together in freedom and justice. The new slogan now is not a "Jewish State" and not a "Moslem State" but a "Palestinian Entity." This motto was picked up by the New Left of various denominations, including some Jewish young extremists who have joined the chorus of protesters against "Zionism" and "American Imperialism." Thus, the World Youth Assembly held in July at the United Nations, which was dominated by the Soviet Arab-leftist bloc, forced through a resolution demanding the creation of "a unitary democratic state in Palestine," rejecting even such an innocent amendment as "a just and lasting peace in the Middle East in acordance with the Security Council resolution of November, 1967."

Nothing Changed

Nothing has changed in the leftist opposition, new or old, to the Zionist movement and the State of Israel or, for that matter, to all values in Jewish life. We hear the same slogans, denunciations and vituperations and we see the same maneuvering that have come from communist and other leftist quarters for decades in the past. The more significant aspect of the latest slogan, however, is the ideological and historical ground on which the Arabs base their reasoning. Their argument is that, if not for anti-Semitism in the western countries, there would be no need for a Jewish State. And since the West is responsible for Jewish persecutions, it should be the western states' responsibility to solve this problem in their own territories and not impose it on the Arab Middle East. The Arab states, they claim, have always treated their Jewish inhabitants well and protected their interests. If the Zionists had not come to disturb the Arab world, the Jews would continue to live there happily as ever before. This claim, too, is an old one, but in recent years it has been converted into a subtle tool of political strategy to destroy the State of Israel.

Shortly after the 1967 War, the World Islamic Conference, meeting on Sept. 22 in Amman, chided "the Jewish communities living in Islamic countries that [they] do not appreciate the

Moslems' good treatment and protection over the centuries." About two months later, King Hussein broadcast this lesson in history in a speech at Georgetown University, during his official visit to the United States (New York Times, Nov. 7, 1967). He purported to express the sentiments, though contrary to the resolutions, of the Arab heads of state who attended the Khartoum Conference in September. In his appeal to history he tried to evoke nostalgic memories of a romantic ideal of peace and serenity in Jewish-Arab relations in the Moslem countries which, he said, the Zionists have so rudely disturbed. His pathos reached a climax in his challenge to Israel: "Who is responsible for disturbing the peace in that part of the world? . . . as for us," he proclaimed, "there has always been and will always be a place for the Jews in the Arab world. [N. B. No Jews are permitted to set foot in Hussin's Kingdom . . .] We have always recognized the legitimate right of the Jews as a people." He was so carried away by his noble sentiment that he forgot to square it with his earlier statement in the same speech that, if not for the State of Israel "the process of [Jewish] assimilation would have gone on peacefully, as it had in the Arab world for centuries . . ."

False Statements

Needless to say that neither statement is historically correct, unless he meant the forced conversion of Jewish orphans to Islam, as imposed by the government in Yemen. But to continue with the Arabs' sweet reasonableness. "The Jews of Israel have a choice." Hussein went on: "the choice of living with us peacefully and eternally as they have in the past, or of remaining an isolated outpost in the Arab world." And he closed with the following solemn peroration: "A permanent peace will come when Arab and Jew can live together, as they have in the past, in peace, friendship, and religious liberty." All the Jews have to do, then, is to "de-Zionize Isreal" (Hussein's phrase), which is tantamount to the liquidation of the Jewish State.

It would be futile to try to correct the Arab leaders on the true meaning and function of Zionism in Jewish life, but they certainly can stand corrected on the historical facts of Jewish life in the Arab world. The general attitude of Islam toward the Jews is more correctly reflected in an editorial in the Moroccan daily Al-Ma'asah of June 22, 1967: "Let us not delude ourselves. There are no Zionists, only Jews. The holy *Koran* itself even alluded to this when it said: 'In thy search for sworn haters of the believers in Allah, thou wilt find more are Jews'. . . . We demand the heads of those Jews who are traitors to the Moslems." (See "Persecution of Jews in Arab Lands." Ministry of Foreign Affairs. Information Division, Jerusalem, January 1969). This enmity resulting in mistreatment and persecution goes back to the earliest contacts between Jews and Arabs in Morocco, Tunisia and Algeria, formerly known as the Maghreb. As recorded by Andre N. Chouraqui, a native of that area, in his book *The History of the Jews of North Africa,* "Under Islam [in the dark ages of the 7-9th centuries] the stubborn Jews who clung to their ancestral faith were subjected to such repression, restriction and humiliation as to exceed anything in Europe" (p. 39). And further: "Virtual outcasts of inferior status, the Jews became the victims of every crisis," and were "at the mercy of the mob" (p. 50). In recent years, since these countries gained independence, the fate of the Jewish inhabitants was determined by the mood and political expediency of the rulers and by the fury of the mobs. In three years' time (1960-1963) Algeria was almost emptied of its 130,000 Jews. Morocco lost half of its Jewish population which counted 250,000 in 1947, and Tunisia had only 16,000 Jews in 1965 out of 120,000 in 1942.

600,000 in Israel

After the pogroms of 1945 and 1948, Libya's 30,000 Jews left en masse for Israel, except for 3,000 who remained in that country. Today Israel counts among its population over 600,000 Jews who originated in North Africa. Nasser's persecution of Egyptian Jewry (report of the American Jewish Congress) has continued throughout his regime through economic restrictions, denationalization, expropriation, incarceration and expulsion—all in accord with the pan-Arab goal laid down in his book *The Philosophy of the Revolution.* Egypt is now practically "Judenrein." Iraq, which had an old Jewish settlement since Babylonian times and numbered 120,000 souls in 1948, has hardly 2,000 left now. They are kept as hostages by the government, subject to mistreatment, arrest and execution as may be expedient to official policy. The 3,000 Jews remaining in Syria, out of 30,000 in 1943, are not in much better condition than those in Iraq. Lebanon is the only country where the Jewish population of some 6,000 has remained constant, but their lives are restricted politically and economically.

There have never been any Jews in the Kingdom of Jordan and their entry there is prohibited, notwithstanding Hussein's pretension that "Arab and Jew can live together in peace . . . friendship, and religious liberty." Saudi Arabia, without any pretension, simply forbids any Jew to touch its soil, even for transit in diplomatic service of a foreign government. Prior to 1948, 70,000 Jews lived in Yemen under the most abject conditions, deprived even of such elementary rights as walking on a sidewalk or riding on a horse. As mentioned before, the majority of them were transferred to Israel in "Operation Magic Carpet," leaving a few hundred behind who chose to convert to Islam in order to be able to remain in their native land. There may be a hundred Jews remaining in Yemen scattered in several villages.

Hard Facts

Such is the idyl of "eternal peace," "good treatment and protection," which the Arab states have accorded to their Jewish inhabitants. Indeed, if not for Zionism, these Jews, driven by their Moslem "benefactors" from pillar to post, degraded, dispossessed, and exiled, would still be wandering about, knocking at the closed gates of every country in the world, as their European brethren did before and after the Second World War. Now the remarkable thing is that the Zionist movement did not strike deep roots among the Jews of North Africa and Asia. What meaning, then, could Zionism have for Jews in the Arab world? It is important that we clarify this matter to ourselves, as Jews, even though we shall never convince others of its true import. For the common notion is that Zionism is a European vintage grafted unto the Arab vineyard but foreign to its climate.

The term "Zionism" has been bandied around by friend and foe so that all too frequently it has been taken as a mere slogan or ideological weapon in the battle of words. That, however, should not detain us here, for our concern is not with mere words, but with the realities of Jewish life in the world, and specifically in the Middle East. It is noteworthy that the two classic pamphlets which gave the greatest impetus to the formation of the Zionist organization, namely, Pinsker's "Auto-Emancipation" and Herzl's

"The Jewish State," do not deal with Zionism or even exclusively with Palestine. Pinsker did not mention Zionism at all, and Herzl spoke in his Preface only passingly of "the attempts of the Zionists," but regarded them as inadequate for the solution of the Jewish problem. Nor did either of them contemplate a Zionist organization as the driving force to realize his ideas. Pinsker recommended a Congress of Jewish Notables, and Herzl proposed The Society of Jews, The World Zionist Organization that was founded under Herzl's Initative later in 1897, in Basel, was the expression of the will of the Jewish masses and their representatives at that gathering. The word Zionism then assumed the same meaning as that of self-liberation enunciated in those two pamphlets, and that is: The Jews must assert themselves as a people and establish for themselves a land of their own where they could determine their destiny free from domination by others.

But historically speaking, the word Zionism has another, more specific connotation. It is derived from the name of Mount Zion in Jerusalem on which King David built his citadel and established the capital of his kingdom. Zion has come to be identified with Jerusalem, and the city of Jerusalem with the Jewish State, the same as, for example, the White House signifies Washington, and Washington, the United States. It is therefore natural that when the Jewish people started on their road to self-liberation in a land of their own that the land of their choice was their ancient Homeland in Zion, and that the movement organized for its realization was named Zionism. It is the movement of self-liberation.

There is yet another meaning to the word Zionsim which is perhaps the most fundamental of all, and that is the right of the Jewish people to their ancient homeland Eretz Israel. When we speak of rights we usually tend to think in terms of codes of law, national or international, and that is why the argument with reference to the Jewish State often degenerates into a controversy over legal interpretations of the British Mandate over Palestine, resolutions of the League of Nations or the United Nations, and similar international documents. I will come to the value of such resolutions and documents shortly, but first I want to establish the principle of Jewish rights to Eretz Israel. That principle is inherent in Zionism or Jewish self-liberation, as it declares: A right which cannot be put in question for any other people, must not be put in question also for the Jewish people.

Every other people has a right to a particular territory which it has chosen for itself in the course of history through peaceful or martial means (and there is no people on earth that has not used both means), and identified itself with it as its homeland. The Jewish people has the same right to what it has chosen for itself as its historical homeland. No human power can bestow this right on others or take it away from them, for it is a human right in itself, unquestionable and inalienable. As far as the Jewish people is concerned, this right, too, exists within this people, asserts itself through this people, and is maintained and defended by this people. This is true of Jews in all parts of the world—all those who want to assert this right and go up to Israel and participate in the furtherance of its development and security. It is especially true of the Jews who have come or may yet come to Israel from Arab lands in the Middle East, because their homeland is situated in that region. It is not a matter of just requiting the Jews of Europe for their sufferings at the hand of anti-Semites. And if that were so, history and recent events have shown that the Arab states have excelled in anti-Jewish excesses no less than their European counterparts. But we are speaking here of primary rights, not of compensations.

Inalienable Right

Taking the Middle East as the oldest known inhabited region on earth, the Jewish people, who had its origin in this region and who has lived there in large or small numbers ever since for thousands of years, certainly longer than any of the modern Arab nations, has the same inalienable right to a land of its own in this very same region as the Arab states have. To put in question the right of the State of Israel to exist at a time when Arab states have been only recently firmly established and new ones are still coming into existence, is a spurious issue. If self-liberation cannot be questioned for the Arab peoples in the Middle East, it also must not be questioned for the Jewish people in that area. Nevertheless, we find that this issue persists in the minds of persons who are concerned with the Middle East conflict on governmental and inter-governmental levels. That, I submit, is due primarily to its entanglement with the role of the United Nations in the whole complex of events, and with the concomitant problem of the Arab refugees. If we are to understand the true import of Zionism as Jewish self-liberation, we must clarify this matter on both counts.

The first pertains to the question, "Who created the State of Israel?" and the second to the question, "Who created the Arab refugee problem?"

It is historically erroneous to say that Israel was established by the United Nations as a haven of refuge for persecuted European Jews. On this ground the Arabs argue: "If the UN wants to be magnanimous toward the suffering European Jews, that is a European problem; let the UN find a haven of refuge for them in Europe, not in our Middle East. Our Jews are treated well and they don't need a state of their own." I have already dealt with this fraudulent distortion of Jewish life in the Arab states in the past and in recent times. But the main contention of the Arabs in this argument is that the Jewish people have no right to their homeland in the Middle East unless the UN gave them that right, and further, that since the UN established the Jewish State it can also abolish it. Neither contention is correct.

Created by Jews

Israel was created by the Jewish people and not by the UN or even with its aid, which was not forthcoming anyway when needed most. Furthermore, the Jewish people have had this right to establish their state with or without the UN, the same as any other people enjoys this kind of right. What took place at the United Nations General Assembly on Nov. 29, 1947, was the adjudication of a territorial dispute and not the bestowal of a right which already existed prior to the dispute. It should be borne in mind that in the dispute between the Jews and the Arabs, each party to the dispute claimed the whole territory of Palestine for itself. When they appeared before the United Nations in 1947, the latter adjudicated their claims through a partition plan, so that "the Mandate for Palestine shall terminate . . . Independent Arab and Jewish states . . . shall come into existence in Palestine . . ." The Jews accepted the plan, proclaimed their independence and named their State Israel. The Arabs rejected it and to this day they insist on their claim to the whole of Palestine.

What is important to remember in this entire drama is that neither the League of Nations after the first World War nor the United Nations after the second World War ever undertook to establish ab initio the rights of the Jewish people to its national homeland, Eretz Israel. As said, this right always existed as inalienable with the people. The international tribunals only confirmed it so that the world might know that this right exists. Witness the Preamble of the Mandate for Palestine issued in 1922 by the League of Nations: "Whereas recognition has thereby been given to the historical connection of the Jewish people with Palestine and to the grounds for reconstituting their national home in that country." And in articles 2 and 4 of the Mandate the right is further recognized with reference to the Administration of the territory and of a Jewish "public body" that would act on behalf of all the Jews in the rebuilding of their homeland. There is no mention of persecuted Jews or "haven of refuge." The homeland was meant and has always meant to be for all Jews throughout the world who want to exercise their right to Eretz Israel and rebuild it as their State.

Yishuv a State

The second important thing to bear in mind is that the Jewish Community in Palestine, then known as the Yishuv, had been building itself up as a functioning state in fact, though not in name, through decades of colonizing enterprise and internal organization, long before the partition resolution of the UN. That resolution, as said, only tried to settle the dispute over territorial boundaries between Jews and Arabs. But since the Arabs did not accept the partition plan and the UN failed to enforce it, the plan as such, miscarried, and the acutal territorial divisions were decided on the field of battle.

If there is any doubt in any one's mind as to who created the Jewish State, one need only read the record of events that followed the partition resolution. Not only did the UN fail to carry out its own resolution, but it tried every way to prevent the Jews from proclaiming their State. There was maneuvering going on among the Big Powers to replace partition with a new "trusteeship plan," a "temporary truce," or just delay, while the Arab armies were attacking Palestine from within and from without. But the Jewish leaders at Lake Success and the Yishuv in Eretz Israel did not yield. They knew that they alone would have to fight their battles and defend their right. As Chaim Weizmann described those fateful days in his autobiography "Trial and Error" (p. 476): "It was plain to me that retreat would be fatal. Our only chance now, as in the past, was to create facts, to confront the world with these facts, and to build on their foundation. Independence is never given to a people; it has to be earned; and having been earned, it has to be defended." This is Zionism.

Refugee Issue

And now we come to the problem of the Arab refugees, which came about in the course of the Jewish War of Liberation. Everybody knows it, but few want to believe it: Israel did not drive any Arabs out of the land; they left at the instigation and insistence of their own leadership, the Arab Higher Committee, directed from Damascus and Cairo. This is a fact which can be ascertained by anyone who cares to read Arab documents instead of Arab propaganda. (See the comprehensive article "The Arab Refugees," by Herbert Parzen, "Jewish Social Studies," Oct. 1969). Furthermore, as David Ben Gurion attested in his letter of Dec. 6, 1967, to President de Gaulle: "After the establishment of the Jewish State on May 14, 1948, not a single Arab was expelled from the country. . . . All those who are referred to today as 'refugees' left their homes during the period of the British Mandate. Large numbers of Arabs began to leave within two days of the General Assembly resolution . . . calling for partition. . . . When guerrilla warfare in the cities grew worse . . . the Arab residents were requested by their Jewish neighbors, and by the Haganah as well, to remain. On instruction from the Mufti in Egypt, however, nearly all of them fled" (idib., 322).

One need say nothing further about the Arab refugee problem except that it can be adjusted only through negotiation between Israel and the Arab states concerned, taking into consideration the fact that those states, as described above, have expropriated their Jewish inhabitants and forced them out of their native lands, and that Israel gathered them in by the hundreds of thousands. The adjustment must be governed by the principle of mutuality that exists between free, independent nations. This, too, is Zionism.

Homeland Claim

A final word about the Arab claim that Palestine is their homeland and they have a prior right to it. The Jews, and we may now say, especially the Zionists, never denied the rights of the Arabs to live in their settlements in Palestine and enjoy the bounties of the land as they and their neighbors may develop it.

They do, however, deny that Palestine was an Arab state. And yet, the Zionist Organization always recognized that there was a conflict of interest between Jew and Arab in Palestine as to which of them would eventually constitute the majority population and hence exercise governmental control of the land. That is, both peoples had national aspirations in Palestine, each seeking self-determination and sovereignty.

But this was not a matter of abstract theoretical nationalism. The conflict took place in a given territory between given populations, and even though the comparative number of Jews and Arabs changed in the course of time, the size of the territory remained the same. That territory, it must be remembered, was then not just the cut-out kangaroo-shaped piece of land that was designated in the UN partition plan as the Jewish State. It extended over the entire area on both sides of the Jordan River, bounded by Syria, Lebanon, Iraq, Saudi Arabia, and Egypt, quite a sizable land, which was known since Biblical times as Eretz Israel. This was the land which was entrusted to the British Government with the mandate "to secure the establishment [therein] of the Jewish national home." From the very start of the Balfour Declaration and the Mandate, the Jews called upon the Arabs in Palestine to make common cause in the rebuilding of the land, which had been lying desolate and waste for centuries. The Jewish colonizing agencies sought to enter upon a covenant with their Arab neighbors for the benefit of both peoples. The Arabs spurned the offer and continually refused to even negotiate the proposition. When the Jews finally realized that there was an impasse to the conflict, they agreed to a partitioning of the territory, so that each people could constitute its own independent state in it.

The idea of partition, it should be pointed out, did not just come at the end of the Mandate period. It was first put into effect by Great Britain (in 1920) even before Britain was accorded the Mandate, when it severed the larger eastern portion across the Jordan and excluded Jewish colonization from it.

Other partition plans came up in subsequent years but never materialized, until the one of 1947 was adopted by the United Nations. Partition was thus accepted by the Jews as a policy of adjudicating between their rightful claim and the rightful claim of the Arabs to the same territory — the whole territory — Eretz Israel, including Transjordan. There was enough room there — and there still is — for both peoples to have their respective independent states. But again, the Arabs wanted and still want all of it, and they vowed to drive the Jews out of there at the point of the sword. The outcome of three attempts that they have made in the past two decades to achieve their goal is well known. And during those years, Israel has grown ever stronger and more resolute to thwart their design. In this the Jewish State has the support of World Jewry. For, the right of Israel to exist is not determined by outside powers, big or small. No one can give this right to the Jews or take it away from them. It is theirs and it is for them to bring it to fruition and protect it.

1970

And These Words Which We Hear Today

One of the sins for which we ask forgiveness in these Days of Awe is for words "uttered with our lips" (bevituy sefatayim). This is a rather strange confession, since all speech comes through the lips. No doubt, the author of the "long confession" had in mind two biblical references, one in Leviticus (5.4), "If one swears through an utterance of his lips to do good or evil . . . and it escapes his attention"; and the other in Proverbs (14.23), "And the words of the lips are only a lack." The first is when a person confuses the intent of his words, and the second when his words are just meaningless. So grave is this kind of fault in human conduct that the same prayer stresses it many times in different ways, such as words spoken "with unclean lips," "with the chatter of our lips," in making "a false promise" or "with clear knowledge and deceit"—at least 14 transgressions that may be committed with our tongue, all leading up to "the sin that we have sinned with confusion of the mind." It is remarkable that, despite our modern developments of sharpened analytical thought, deepened psychological insight and refined language arts, we are still unable to overcome the transgressions of the lips in our national and world affairs, not to speak of our private dealings. Indeed, with those means at our disposal we have sunk ever more deeply into a morass

383

of a complexity of legislation that lends itself to conflicting interpretation, a profusion of guidelines that change frequently and a proliferation of questionnaires, forms and reports that stagger the imagination and overwhelm our physical and mental endurance. We have buried directness and simplicity under a heap of equivocal talk and, to that extent, have lost our bearings in reality. In the following presentation I will limit myself to the talk that is going on concerning the conflict in the Middle East and the impressions created in the public mind through the use of certain stock words and phrases in trying to resolve this conflict. The root of so many "misconceptions and misunderstandings" (to use the words of a recent confession by an American statesman) between all the parties concerned stems from a "confusion of the mind" engendered by a misapplication of old words to new conditions— words that have outlived their original significance or have been given connotations contrary to accepted usage in western civilization.

Client-Advocate Relation in a Global Conflict

Although everyone knows that the basic conflict in the Middle East is of a global character, in that each of the big powers tries to maintain a dominant role in that region, it nevertheless has been portrayed to the public merely as a struggle between Jews and Arabs over a piece of territory or, more recently, over so-called "conquered territory." This skewed perspective has given rise to two false notions—namely, that the local contending parties are clients of the big powers, and that the latter are only acting as mediators, trying to resolve their clients' wrangling. If this metaphor of advocate-client relationship may be used at all, it is more correct to see it in reverse order. To begin with, the big powers are not mediators but interested parties to the conflict, and in this respect they are the clients of Israel and the Arab states, respectively, the first as advocate of the interests of the United States, and the second those of the Soviet Union. The real issue of reassessment now before the American government, therefore, should be whether it is to its advantage to change "attorneys"— that is, to put its entire trust in the Arab states to uphold its global concerns in that region. Seen in this light, the actual differences between Israel and the American government are a matter of joint approach or, better, a joint long-range policy in relation to the

Arabs. In the past number of years such a policy worked to the benefit of both partners, though not contracted officially by written agreement. But the new American "reassessment" tends to disregard this working relationship in the mistaken hope that the United States will gain more from the Arab side. This is where the "misconceptions and misunderstandings" really lie.

Negotiations, Opportunities

Two of the most troublesome words bandied about in recent dealings with the Middle East situation are "negotiation" and "opportunity." The word "negotiate," as understood in the Western mode of thought means to resolve a difficulty (*negotium*) between two or more parties through compromise, give and take and mutual concession on the ground that the parties involved recognize each other's worth and treat each other's vital interest with due regard. Another meaning of this word, mostly used in common speech, is "to get around" an obstacle, such as, for example, a driver of a car in congested traffic may try to negotiate a particularly irksome corner in order to avoid running into it. A third meaning, though not often used, is simply "to be busy" (*negotsus*—full of business, a busy-body), trying to gain advantage of the other side by complicating or beclouding the issue. In the entire course of Jewish-Arab confrontation, which has lasted almost a hundred years, and especially during the period of the British Mandate and thereafter to this day (more than half a century), the Arab leaders have never entered into negotiations with Israel, as this term is understood in the international community — namely, direct discussion with a view toward reaching a mutual accommodation. Rather, they used this word in the second and third meaning, always aiming to get around the Israelis or to confound and confuse the purpose at hand. Since 1967, after they had failed in open battle, the Arab states created a task force of so-called "moderates," first under King Hussein (at the Khartum Conference) and more recently under Yasir Arafat (at the Rabat Conference) to prepare for the destruction of Israel through a mist of words of "sweet reasonableness." Thus Hussein has been speaking with nostaligia about Jewish-Arab "peaceful co-existence" in Arab lands in the past (which hardly ever existed), and Arafat has been propagandizing an ideal "Democratic State in Palestine" including Jews (as many as he may allow to remain there) after the dissolution of the Jewish State. Such is the actual role which the Arab leaders want to assign to the Palestine Liberation Organization in their "negotiations" with Israel.

Lost Opportunity

Each time an attempt at negotiation failed, the mediators broadcast the notion that Israel had lost a rare opportunity for peace. And thus we become ever more entangled with an illusive word in our assessment of the situation, the word "opportunity." It is being dangled before us, both in retrospect and prospect, as if the mediators had created the necessary conditions for real peace, or even a way to peace. Notwithstanding this illusion, Israel is being chided for its so-called "inflexibility," and warned of "tragic consequences" if again it should fail to heed the signs of the time. But what possible significance can this word have in the context of real negotiations? It can only mean that Israel should have grasped, or should now grasp, even the slightest offer by the Arab states for mutual recognition and accommodation of their respective claims. Yet, if we examine the whole range of Jewish-Arab relations since the early days of the Yishuv in **Palestine**, we shall look in vain for such an approach on the part of the Arabs. They simply never allowed an opportunity for a settlement to arise, except on their own terms. No matter what avenue of compromise Israel has tried, the response has always been Arab total demands, Arab threats and Arab cries of "aggression;" when their threats were thwarted.

A Just and Lasting Peace

Perhaps the most pernicious phrase that has gained currency in the diplomatic language of the leading statesmen is "a just and lasting peace" for the Middle East. It sounds so comforting and reassuring of their "good offices" that no one in good conscience may question it. But, even taking it at face value, how is it possible to arrange a just and lasting peace in one region while the rest of the world is embroiled in all kinds of large or small turmoil? The two main factors that militate against a peace settlement in that area — namely, the conflicting interests of the big powers and the avowed enmity of the Arab states toward Isreal — will continue for an unpredictable length of time. (President Sadat has vowed repeatedly that there will be no peace with Israel in this generation, or the next. . .). The best Israel may expect in this juncture of world events is an accommodation with its Arab neighbors on fixed boundaries within which it may continue to develop its inner life and look with extreme watchfulness to a better climate in international relations. For, in the final analysis, the eruption of large-scale fighting in the Middle East does not depend on Israel or the Arabs themselves, but rather on the big powers facing each other in the global arena. It is no longer a secret that the Arab military actions against Israel in 1967 and 1973 were planned and instigated overtly or covertly by the Soviet Union. Whether new fighting will break out even after the Arabs and Israel reach some agreement will depend not on the agreement, as such, but on the American stance vis-a-vis Russia's maneuvering on the Asian-African front. It is a specious argument to suggest that another Arab-Israeli war will be the cause of a world conflagration. It is the other way around. If and when the big powers reach an impasse with regard to their vital interests and find themselves on the brink of an armed clash, the first bombshells will fall in the Aisan-African enclave known as the Middle East.

Threat of a Third World War

In the international arena, the term war is used almost exclusively in the sense of an armed struggle between nations. The fear of the use of atomic weapons in such a struggle looms so large in our consciousness that we hardly stop to think of other kinds of international warfare that may threaten our existence. In fact, we already are in the midst of the Third World War — a real war, though of a different character, with a different logistic and strategy than in the past. If a big country like the United States, which considers itself the greatest power on earth, is in constant danger of being paralyzed by an Arab oil embargo, then we are in a state of global war. It would be foolhardy to put the blame for such an embargo on Israel. The danger to America lies in the very fact that the embargo threat hangs over it, regardless of Israel's role in the Middle East. Any other juncture of world events, not even originating in that area but unfavorable to the Arabs, may prompt the latter to carry out their threat. As compared with the first two world wars, the term war now assumes a new meaning. A brief glance at some of their basic differences will give us an insight into Israel's position in the new constellation of forces. The first two wars produced certain conditions which were favorable to the rebirth and growth of the Jewish State in its ancient homeland. World War I was fought for a redistribution of dependent territories among the contending big powers. In this process the Jewish people succeeded in reclaiming its right in Palestine and to accelerate its settlement there, which culminated in the proclamation of the independent state of Israel. The Second World War was a struggle for the supremacy of scientific-technological control of the globe. In the first war, the weight of *man-power* was decisive, whereas in the second the deciding factor was a highly sophisticated *fire-power*, first on the part of Germany and later of the Allied nations. When Israel was established after the second war, it was able to maintain its position and defeat its enemy's overwhelming man-power, because it quickly developed a superior technologically trained defense force. The Third World War, in which all nations are now engaged, is for the supremacy of *economic power*, fought directly with economic-financial weapons on a global scale. Not a rifle-shot need be fired or a missile explode in order to bring a country or a group of countries to total subjugation.

Another important characteristic of this war is that, unlike the other two wars, it is a triangular confrontation of two superpowers forming the two lateral sides, still relying on fire-power, and the Third World, notably the Arabs, forming the base, but using purely economic force. Insofar as the Arabs may gain the upper hand over the other two sides (experts on oil reserves in the Soviet Union estimate that by 1980 that country, too, will become dependent in large measure on Middle East oil), they will not have to resort to a military attack against Israel at all. The latter may succumb under economic pressure, which is now the basic strategy of the Arab boycott. In order for Israel to be able to counter these measures, it must renew its pioneering spirit of former days in all walks of life, restrain its run-away economy of private enterprise and shape its life once more in forms of the kibbutz and kvutza — of the cooperative movement that was the driving force of its early development and still constitutes the backbone of its survival.

A Right to Exist

When the powers in the United Nations line up against Israel's interests in relation to the Arabs, some of them who want to show their sympathy for Israel, even though they fail to support it, declare that they recognize its "right to exist." This non-descript slogan, intended to assuage Jewish fears, does more harm to Israel's cause than do direct attacks coming from its bitterest enemies. For to say that Israel has a right to exist implies that such a right may be put into question and that there is some super-authority or one of the big nations that may grant or deny it at will. This whole notion emanates from a gross historical misconception of how the Jewish State came into being, at whose pleasure it exists and who guarantees its survival: Without going into a detailed account of past events, suffice it here to say that the Jewish State was established by the Jewish people on the basis of its historic right to the land of Israel, both human and divine (if one wants to invoke superior powers). This right to a homeland is not bestowed by some judicial tribunal, but exists in and of itself through historical developments of nations, peoples or ethnic groups, and is inherent in every communal entity. When applied to the Jewish people, it means that this people has the same natural and divine right to its own land as does any other people on earth. It is ironical that no one every found it necessary to declare that Jordan or Syria or Kuwait, or any other of the 20 Arab nations that came into being about the same time as Israel, has a "right to exist. . . " It should be known that neither the United Nations nor its predecessor, the League of Nations, first established the right of the Jewish people to its own land, but rather recognized its existence as of old. This is amply borne out by the preamble to the Mandate in 1922 and by the partition resolution of the United Nations in 1947. The latter only adjudicated a territorial dispute between the Jews and the Arabs, but never questioned their rights to exist within national states of their own. Furthermore, the defense of this right for the Jews was never undertaken by the U.N., but was left to the Yishuv in Israel with the help of their brethren in other lands, from the inception of the State to this day and in days to come. The only right that Israel expects to receive from others is mutual cooperation and due regard for its vital interests, as part of the community of nations.

Our Goals and Our Words

The goals that we seek through a settlement of the Arab-Israeli conflict in the Middle East are essentially the same as those sought by all contending nations in other parts of the globe. The responsibility rests on the big powers even more than on the local nations in the area. These goals may be attained if the big powers will try to come to a mutual understanding not only between themselves but also with the small nations. The words they may use in projecting their policies will play a vital role in determining the outcome. This is not a time for equivocation. Their words must be grounded in the realities and reflect the interests of all peoples concerned.

1975

The First Zionist Congress
On Its Eightieth Anniversary

The First Zionist Congress was convened by Theodor Herzl on Aug. 29-31, 1897, in Basel, Switzerland, with 197 delegates coming from Jewish habitations in many parts of the world. The Zionist movement, or even the term "Zionism," was not born at this Congress. Rather, it was a confluence of divergent streams of an earlier Jewish national awakening which sprang from the sources of East-European Jewry and which also spilled over in small rivulets in the West. The delegates had all been confirmed Zionists, most of them of long standing, and some, including the founder of the Congress, who became recent adherents. As we look at it now through the eyes of its participants and observers at the time, there unfolds before us the drama of Jewish life in Eastern and Western Europe at the end of the 19th Century, which gave the immediate impulse toward convening this assembly. There were internal as well as external factors that brought it into being. However, the latter were the leadership's primary concen and thus dominated the sessions almost to the end. The purpose of the Congress was outlined by Theodor Herzl in his opening address, which received thunderous applause. Yet the mood was set by Max Nordau, second in command, who painted a moving, masterful, but very grim picture of Jewish material and moral suffering in many lands, caused by external forces of economic restrictions and governmental oppression in the East, and by social and political disabilities in the West — a dichotomy which set the two branches of Jewry apart even in their first attempts toward unification.

390

The inner life of the Jewish masses in Eastern Europe, their cultural, religious and national aspirations were at the time strange to the Western Jews, as the latter's manner and approach to Zionism were little appreciated by the Easterners. As Chaim Weizmann summed up the difference, the Eastern representatives "were the spokesmen of the Russian Jewish masses who sought in Zionism self-expression and not merely rescue . . . [To the Westerners] all this was rather alien at first . . . The fact that the heart of Jewry was fixed, by every bond of affection and tradition, on Palestine, seemed beyond the understanding of the Westerners. The enormous practical significance of this fixation, its unique and irreplaceable power to awaken the energies of the Jewish people, escaped them." The contrast was also markedly noted by Nordau, although on a different level. In the East he found the *Judennot* (Jewish suffering) in the dire poverty of its masses, people starving and fighting to eke out a bare existence, which was true enough. In the West he saw the *Judennot* in the moral degradation of the emancipated Jew. "The men of 1792," he said in reference to the decree of September, 1791, which granted full civic rights to French Jewry, "emancipated us on the basis of cavalier principles." Now this so-called emanicipated Jew "is crippled inside and a sham outside, which makes him ridiculous and repulsive to the high-minded esthetic person. . . . This is the moral suffering of the Jews, which is more painful than the physical because it affects . . . proud and sensitive people." Nordau's speech struck home among the delegates of both camps, who met it with enthusiastic applause. Ahad Haam, who was a very critical observer at this Congress, wrote shortly after it to Nordau: "In your address at Basel, which will remain unforgettable, . . . you have confirmed some of the views which I had expressed in my book [*Al Parashat Derachim*, which he sent with his letter], but which were then considered paradoxical. You can imagine how pleased I was . . . that these same views, presented by you in such beautiful form, were received by everybody with enthusiasm." And Weizmann, who otherwise did not think very highly of Nordau's brand of Zionism, wrote of his speech (in *Trial and Error*): "For the first time the Jewish problem was presented forcefully before a European forum . . . It was a bugle call sounded all over the world, and the world took note."

In order to grasp the full impact of Nordau's address on the assembly and its reverberations in the press, we must understand the connection between Jewish emancipation and Zionism in Western Europe and the specific character of the "Jewish Problem" there at the time. Emancipation meant the removal of all restrictions against the participation of Jews in civic life and granting them the rights and duties that are enjoyed by all the other citizens in a given country. In Western Eueope, this process began in earnest in 1791 in France and was fulfilled thereafter in various measures in other countries in Western and Central Europe. But in Eastern Europe, and especially in Russia, this did not materialize until after the Russian Revolution and the end of World War I.

Now a remarkable thing occurred in the West. When the Jews were still deprived of their civic and political rights, no one questioned their existence as a nation or people. Indeed, the term "Jewish nation" was commonly used by statesmen and political writers in designating their identity. But with the promotion of emancipation the Jews were expected to pay for it with the price of their nationhood. The slogan was: Nothing for the Jews as a people, everything for the Jew as an individual. This opened the gates of the Ghetto, but at the same time it also broke down the walls of the Jewish communities. Assimilation now beckoned to those who wanted to shed also their social disabilities and to throw themselves into the general stream of social, cultural and political life. But it did not take them very long to discover that they were not acceptable in the positions to which they aspired, and that social and political freedom were not within their reach. Very soon, the anti-Jewish forces, ever active throughout this period, organized themselves not only to minimize what had been granted officially but also to reverse the entire process, and make things even worse than before.

'Anti-Semitism' Coined

The the Jews realized that the price of nationhood which they had to pay had robbed them of their internal forces to maintain their identity and fight their common battles, and that they were thus exposed to external exigencies which were beyond their control. The name given to this onslaught on the Western Jews was "anti-Semitism," which was coined in 1879 by Wilhelm Marr, a popular Jew-baiter in Germany. In the same period, during the wars of Napoleon and after his defeat there ensued a national awakening among the indigent peoples in central and southern Europe which brought in its wake the independence and consolidation of several countries, such as the Germanic states. Italy and Greece. The spirit of nationalism also began to make itself felt among some of the estranged intelligentsia in the Jewish population. This is how the Zionist idea took root among the Jews in the West. It is of interest to note that the term "Zionism" is a Germanic form of the word Zion which was first introduced in 1890 by a native Viennese Jew, Nathan Birnbaum, who propagated Jewish nationalism in his weekly magazine, "Selbstemanzipation." Anti-Semitism, then, was identified with the "Jewish Problem" as a manifestation of Gentile reaction to the emancipation of the Jews in Western Europe, and Zionism was the answer of some of those Jews to this problem. By contrast, in Eastern Europe, where emancipation was not even in sight, the problem was not that of anti-Semitism but simply of a relentless, continuous drive by governmental authorities to eliminate the Jewish population from their midst. To the Eastern Jews, therefore, Zionism meant the strengthening of national-cultural life from within in order to gather strength for rebuilding themselves in their ancient homeland in Palestine. In later years, when Weizmann was working toward obtaining the Balfour Declaration, he wrote a letter to Lady Crewe, once more delineating the character of East-European Zionism in the following words: "We who come from Russia, where a most modern and perfect machine is set up to crush the Jewish body and soul, are least afraid of so-called anti-Semitism. We have seen too much of it. . . . We have the right to be treated as normal human beings, capable of entering into the family of nations as an equal, and to be masters of our own destiny. We hate equally anti-Semitism and philo-Semitism. Both are degrading."

These were the two sides of the Jewish Problem. And thus, returning now to the mood at the Zionist Congress, the Westerners responded to Nordau, who was one of their own, as he aroused them to the moral suffering of their notables, which was caused by anti-Semitism. The Easterners, on the other hand, reacted to his portrayal of the dire needs of their oppressed masses. Chayim Nachman Bialik expressed the feelings of those masses in his poem

"Mikraei Zion," which he wrote "in remembrance of the Congress in Basel":

Your people's woes brought you together
From the dispersion in the Exile.
Their bitter sigh aroused you and, behold,
The great moment came:
The sweet, the bright, the warm tear
Welled up from the depths;
The tear we had hoped for so long.

Concept Crystallized

In the midst of this outpouring of enthusiasm gratitude and tumultuous applause, Theodor Herzl stood in complete command, surveying both camps with a keen eye, a warm heart and unsurpassing intuition, and fully aware of the inner tensions that were bound to put roadblocks on his way to the goal. He saw all the facets of the Jewish Problem, externally in its Eastern and Western settings, and also internally as a problem of rejuvenating the national cultural spirit of Judaism. Herzl came to accept the full import of the Zionist idea within a short span of less than two years, between the time he wrote his Judenstaat in 1895 and convened the Congress in 1897. In that pamphlet he spoke only of the inevitable need of a Jewish State to solve the problem. Zionism was not his means, and Palestine was only one of the possible goals. As late as July, 1896, speaking before the Maccabeean Club in London, his emphasis was still on "the acquisition of a territory under the law of nations (voelkerrechtlich), be it Palestine or some other place." But, as he continued speaking, writing, and corresponding with proponents and opponents in preparation for the Congress, his concept of a Jewish State crystallized into the Zionist idea as it was understood by the veteran Zionists.

The final formulation of this idea, known as the Basel Program, reads: "The aim of Zionsim is to create for the Jewish people a home in Palestine secured by public law" (oeffentlichrechtlich gesichert). This text was ironed out by a special committee and adopted by the plenum, but its key phrase — "secured by public law" — expressed the essence of Herzl's approach to the Jewish problem and of his concept of the World Zionist Organization which was founded at this Congress as the instrument of its realization. We must bear in mind that Herzl, like most other Western Jews, was awakened to the Jewish national idea through personal experiences with anti-Semitism yet in his young days, and most dramatically when he witnessed the outrageous behavior of the judges and the mob at the Dreyfus trial in Paris. Therefore, to him Zionism was the antidote to anti-Semitism, which was the common enemy of the Jews. Thus he defined the Jewish nation as "a historically identifiable group of people who belong together and who are held together by a common enemy." Moreover, his very idea of a Jewish State came to him from his observations of the anomalies of emancipation and its accompanying anti-Semitism.

Historical Meaning

"This is the historical meaning of Jewish emancipation — that through it we have become state-minded again," he commented in one of his early speeches. He also portrayed this anomaly in his play "Das neue Ghetto," which, by the way, was at first rejected by every producer (1894), but was later staged (1898) in Vienna with acclaim — a change in public opinion that reflected Herzl's influence after he had espoused the Zionist idea. Despite this limited background and deep-seated traumatic experiences, Herzl was able to rise above them and scan the entire range and scope of his people's problem within and without. He certainly was aware of it throughout the sessions of the Congress, when he came into contact with the Russian delegation, which was the largest at that assembly.

Of these people he later wrote: "Seventy of our delegates came from Russia, and it was patent to all of us that they represented the views and sentiments of the five million Jews in that country. And what a humiliation for us, who had taken our superiority for granted! . . . They possess that inner unity which has disappeared from among the Westerners. They are steeped in Jewish national sentiment, though without national narrowness and intolerance. They are not tortured by the idea of assimilation, but their essential being is simple and unshattered . . . They manage to remain erect and genuine." He saw Zionism personified. The deepening of his nationalism was evident in his opening address. "Zionism," he stated, "is the homecoming to Judaism before the return to the Jewish land." And further: "The Congress will also concern itself with the spiritual means of reviving and cultivating the national consciousness . . . We have no intention of giving up even one iota of our inherited culture, but are thinking of continuing to deepen it." He then spoke with gratitude of the agricultural settlements up to that time in Palestine and Argentina as outposts of the national movement.

Stressed Self-Help

However, these were maintained through the benevolence of individual philanthropists (Baron Edmund de Rothschild and Baron de Hirsch, respectively), and he warned: "A people can be helped only by itself, and if it cannot do that, then it cannot be helped. We, Zionists, want to arouse the people toward self-help. In this we must not raise premature, unhealthy hopes. For this reason, it is of highest value that our transactions be public, as this Congress purports them to be." In this last statement Herzl asserted what he considered to be the main, if not the sole, purpose of the Congress, and that is the formation of a national representative body that would bring the Jewish problem before public opinion, but would guide the people toward helping itself. All other items on the agenda at the time had to give way to this singular task. This single-mindedness of purpose had its ground in Herzl's conception of the role of the World Zionist Organization, to be formed at this Congress, on the road ahead of him. The Congress, for him, was not just an open forum for making the Jewish case known to the world, but, more important, for demanding from the world powers its rectification. Colonization of outlying territories in Asia and Africa was then getting into high gear as part of the national policies of the great powers. Any attempts by Jews to colonize in Palestine thus became a matter of political realism and could not be left in the hands of philanthropists. Herzl saw in the colonial competition among the big powers a juncture of events that could serve the Jewish cause if properly exploited. But in order to get the attention of the world statesmen, the Jews needed a representative body that would gain recognition in the eyes of those statesmen. Such a body, therefore, had to be organized according to European parliamentary standards, not discounting the formalities of protocol, with a definite program and steady course of action. This new body was the World Zionist Organization which emerged from the first Congress. It became a political factor in relations with the world powers, not just in dealings with the government in control of Palestine at the time. For the Jewish problem, as Herzl wanted everyone to know, was a problem not only for the Jews but for the world as well.

Opened the Doors

In the political arena, whether in local, national, or international relations, one who wants to come to an agreement with another party must have negotiable goods to offer to that party. Herzl understood this thoroughly. From the very start, even in his "Judenstaat," he spoke tirelessly of the benefits that an independent Jewish territory would bring not only to the Jews but, perhaps, even more so to the countries from which they would emigrate. It did not matter whether the particular benefits he offered at the time were appreciated by the nations of the world. What mattered was that they took him seriously, and he was able, for the first time in the history of the Diaspora, to "open the doors" (the front, not the back doors) of European chancelleries and royal courts to the cause of the Jewish people, as a people. And after he opened those doors, they remained open also for his successors when new political junctures became auspicious for the Jewish people. This was the essence of Herzl's political Zionism, which he substituted for the philanthropic Zionism of his time. And this holds true for all time as it did in his day, in the days of the Balfour Declaration or now in times of American involvement in the Middle East. The State of Israel has offered and can continue to offer many advantages to the United States Government on the basis of mutual interests. And now as before, this has to be brought forcefully to the attention of the democratic world, particularly, to the American people.

When the first Zionist Congress adjourned, Herzl wrote in his diary: "Today I have founded the Jewish State. Today many would laugh at these words, but in five years — certainly in 50 years — everyone will understand this." These prophetic words were fulfilled 50 years later, in November, 1947, when the powers of the world, assembled in the United Nations, gave recognition to the formation of a Jewish State, now the State of Israel.

1977

Historical Background of Israel-Arab Negotiations

It is not my intention to trace the development of relations between Jews and their neighbors in Palestine or the middle East back to antiquity, but a few references to biblical times will shed some light on the nature of that relationship throughout history, even from the days of Abraham to our own time. The first encounter between Abraham and the Philistine King Abimelech concerned the possession of certain water wells dug by Abraham and demolished by Abimelech's servants. However, when Abimelech saw that Abraham had prospered in all his undertakings and had dug a new well, he proposed a peace treaty with him, and with their "children and grandchildren." While Abraham accepted the proposition he also reminded Abimelech about the water wells that his "servants had robbed" him of. The Philistine king played innocent, claiming that he "did not know who had done that thing." Abraham did not pursue the matter further, but gave Abimelech "seven lambs in witness that he [Abraham] had dug this well. . . . and they both swore to it" (Genesis 21:22-30). This solomen treaty did not last very long, for we read shortly thereafter that Abimelech made trouble for Abraham's son, Issac, when the latter, who lived in Gerar (a Philistine province), also prospered like his father. "The Philistines then became envious of him and they demolished all the wells that his father had dug and they filled them with dirt. And Abimelech said to Isaac, 'Get out of our midst because you are exceedingly more prosperous than we are'" (ibid., 26:12-16). Isaac then moved to the valley of Gerar, but the Philistines were not satisfied and continued to quarrel with him over Abraham's wells which he opened up again, until he removed himself entirely from the region and returned to his father's settlement in Beer Sheva (ibid., vv. 17-22).

Abraham's encounter with his neighboring countries was in a battle against the four kings from Mesopotamia who had ruled over the five kings in the valley of the Dead Sea. When the latter revolted, the four kings attacked them, took away their possessions and led their people together with Abraham's nephew Lot into captivity. Abraham organized his household army, overtook the four kings near Damascus, recaptured the possessions and rescued Lot and the rest of the captives. Yet when Abraham returned home from his victorious engagement, he was still fearful for his security. Nachmanides comments, Abraham was afraid that the four kings might gather a larger army and come back to fight him and he would not be able to overcome them. Then God assured him, "Do not fear, Abram, I will be your shield" (ibid., 14:1-16, 15:1).

Another war, characteristic of international relations in the Middle East, took place between Ahab, king of Israel (the ancient northern Jewish kingdom), and his neighbor to the north, Ben-Hadad, king of Aram (today's Syria). Ben-Hadad besieged Samaria and demanded of Ahab a heavy personal ransom, which the king of Israel was ready to grant. However, when Ben-Hadad saw how easily Ahab had submitted, he tightened up the conditions, and told him that the houses of Israel would be searched for hidden treasures. Ahab rejected this demand and Aram's army attacked Samaria. When the Aramaeans were defeated, an unknown prophet said to Ahab: "Go and fortify yourself and be sure that you know what you ought to do, for when a year rolls around, the king of Aram will come up against you again" (1 Kings 20:20-22). And indeed, the following year Aram returned with a larger army and fought Israel at Afekah, and when it was again defeated and Ben-Hadad fled to a hiding place in the city, his advisors fell upon a scheme of playing on the Jewish moral precept of mercy. "We have heard," they said to Ben-Hadad, "that the kings of the house of Israel are merciful kings. Let us dress in sackcloth and put ropes on our heads and go out to the king of Israel; perhaps he will save your life" (v. 31). And the scheme worked. Ahab greeted Ben-Hadad as his brother and brought him in a chariot to Samaria. Ben-Hadad proposed to make a covenant with Ahab: "'I will return the cities that my father took from your father, and you may set up market places in Damascus, as my father had done in Samaria' .... And he [Ahab] made a covenant with him and sent him away" (vv. 33-34). But there was a prophet in Israel who rebuked Ahab for his lack of good judgment. "Thus said the Lord," the prophet warned, "because you let go out of your hand the man I had marked for destruction, you will lose your life for his life and the lives of your people for his people. And the King of Israel went home sullen and became depressed" (vv. 42-43). Three years later Israel and Aram fought over a piece of territory in Ramot Gilead and Ahab fell in battle (ibid., 22:3, 34-37).

These few references to antiquity display a pattern of internal and external relations between the Jewish people and their neighbors in the Middle East that has repeated itself through the ages to this day. To dig a well one must possess land, and its ownership must have the ability to enforce it against the possible betrayal by the other party. When we now consider the position of the State of Israel in the same region in modern times, we must take into account the aims and aspirations of the two parties in dispute, namely, the Jews and the Arabs, and how they have encountered each other in peace and in war since the inception of the Jewish resettlement in that region about a century ago.

A Conflict of National Aspirations

Toward the end of the nineteenth century Jews started to migrate into Palestine not just to find a haven of refuge for a number of homeless individuals, but rather to rebuild their ancient homeland. This is the essence of Zionism which came as a response to Jewish emancipation in certain European countries at that time. The governments that embraced the principle of emancipation for Jews were willing to grant them political and economic equality on an individual level but not for the Jewish people as a national entity. The price that the Jews were expected to pay for their individual equality was to become absorbed as members of the dominant ethnic group in each country, which would lead them to complete assimilation. The paradox of this condition was that even those Jews who were ready to pay that price were hindered by a factor that could not be legislated in their favor, namely, their being accepted by the dominant population as truly equal on a social level. Thus official emancipation of the Jews in Western Europe, under the best of circumstances, intensified the anti-Jewish social forces that undermined also the slight gains that the Jews had made politically and economically. In Eastern Europe even this modicum of freedom was never instituted until after the first World War, and there too it was vitiated by a combination of social, economic, and religious factors that the local governments fostered to the detriment of the Jewish population. Internally, Jewish communal adherence weakened, as large segments that were blinded by the lustre of Western enlightenment and its promises of individual freedom, became estranged from their own people and broke their ties with it culturally, nationally, and even religiously and ethnically. The national urge of those who remained within the

Jewish fold, having been thwarted from without, lay dormant until in due time it burst forth into a drive for a return to Zion, out of which emerged the Zionist Movement.

As we proceed with an analysis of Israel-Arab relations in modern times, we may bear in mind two major tenets of Zionism: (1) The Jews constitute a national entity with all rights, privileges, and obligations like any other nation in existence. (2) In order to function as such an entity in its internal affairs as well as in its international relations, it must have a territory with definite boundaries that it may call its own and within which it may determine its national life and exercise its constituent authority internally and externally independently of outside forces. The classic formulations of these two tenets have come down to us in Leon Pinsker's *Auto-Emancipation,* in Theodor Herzl's *The Jewish State*, and in Ahad Haam's (Asher Ginzburg's) series of essays on "The Way of the Spirit" ("דרך הרוח," in his published works על פרשת דרכים., Berlin, 1930, vols. 1 & 2). The World Zionist Organization, founded by Herzl at the end of the last century, served as the instrumentality to bring those ideas into fruition in the ancient homeland of the Jewish people, in Erets Israel.

The Palestinian Arabs were opposed to Jewish resettlement in their midst from its very inception in 1882, but the conflict was then between neighbors and not between governmental or national forces, for there was no national movement among the Arabs at the time to counteract Jewish national aspirations. To be sure, there were Arab attacks against Jewish colonies, but the Jews learned to organize their self-defense and to work out their differences with the Arabs on a local scale. The national conflict between the two sides began to develop during the first World War, after the issuance (November 2, 1917) of the Balfour Declaration for the establishment of a Jewish National Home in Palestine. As the British armed forces were liberating the territory from Turkish rule, the Arabs in the region started to organize themselves for a presentation of their national claims before the forthcoming Peace Conference. In anticipation of these events, Haim Weizmann, representing the World Zionist Organization, took the initiative in trying to reach an understanding with the Arabs for their mutual national interests in the Middle East. Thus came into existence the first official agreement between Jews and Arabs on a national level. The man who emerged as the recognized Arab leader at the time was Emir Feisal, son of King Hussein of Hedjaz, who represented and acted on behalf of his father's kingdom. After a series of negotiations, in which British authorities took part, Weizmann and Feisal signed a "Treaty of Friendship" (January 3, 1919), in which, among other things, they pledged mutual support and close collaboration for the development of the Arab State [that is to be formed in the region] and Palestine, . . . [where they will] carry out the Balfour Declaration. . . . The Zionist Organization is. . . [to] assist the Arab State in producing the means for developing the natural resources and economic possibilities thereof. The parties thereto agree to act in complete accord and harmony on all matters embraced herein before the Peace Conference.[1]

But less than three months later, when Feisal submitted the Arab claims for an independent national existence before the Supreme Council of the Peace Conference in Paris, he forgot his "Treaty of Friendship" with the Jews and had this to say with regard to Palestine:

On account of its universal character, I shall set Palestine aside for the mutual consideration of all parties. With this exception, I ask for the independence of the Arab areas [in the Middle East] enumerated in our memorandum.[2]

The Zionist deputation presented the Jewish claims before the Peace Conference on February 23. The Allied Powers looked upon those claims with favor and they received "quite a good Press in France." Then an interview with Emir Feisal appeared in the Paris *Matin* that "was frankly hostile." A meeting was arranged between Feisal and Felix Frankfurter (who was a member of the American Zionist deputation), followed up with a letter from Feisal (March 3, 1919) in which he tried apolegetically to assure Frankfurter that the Arabs "will wish the Jews a most hearty welcome home" and he praised Weizmann who "has been a great helper of our cause," further expressing the "hope that the Arabs may soon be in a position to make the Jews some return for their kindness."[3] Whatever the internal maneuvers may have been in

<hr>

1. *Jews and Arabs in Palestine.* Ed. Enzo Sereni and A. E. Asheri. New York, Hechalutz Press, 1936, pp. 44a-46a.
2. Ibid., p. 46a.
3. Haim Weizmann, *Trial and Error.* New York: Harper and Brothers, 1949, pp. 245-46.

the Arab camp that made Feisal break his promises of the "Treaty of Friendship" with Weizmann, it is quite obvious that from the start his intention was only to utilize the Zionists' good standing with the Allied Powers for the promotion of his own cause, and if and when that was achieved he would try to "make the Jews some return for their kindness." It should further be noted that Feisal had added a condition to his Treaty with Weizmann that "If the Arabs are estasblished as I have asked in my manifesto of January 4. . . . I will carry out what is written in this agreement. If changes are made, I cannot be answerable for failure to carry out this agreement."[4] Well, he violated the spirit and letter of the agreement even before he knew what direction his Arab cause might take at the Peace Conference in Paris. A year later (in May 1920) the Arab Congress in Damascus proclaimed him King of Syria (including Palestine), and he ascended the throne without a thought of keeping his promise to help the Jews carry out the Balfour Declaration. He took charge of both Syria and parts of Palestine and became rather intransigent about his newly acquired prerogatives, which, fortunately for the Jewish cause, were soon abrogated by the French Mandate over Syria (in July 1920).[5]

From this first major process of negotiation between Jewish and Arab representative in which an agreement was signed and promptly broken by the Arab side, we may draw a few significant conclusions as to the possibility of reaching a meaningful signed treaty with any of the Arab leaders in the near future.

(1) *Palestine.* Feisal acted on behalf of his father's kingdom alone, without the consent of the Palestinian Arab spokesmen, who never accepted his propositions with regard to the Balfour Declaration, whatever his own intentions may have been on this matter at the time. Their position was completely antagonistic to the Jewish aspirations, as their Council had formulated it at the end of the first World War, to wit: (a) Palestine had been promised by the Allies to the Arabs, and the proposal of creating a Jewish National Home there was in violation of this promise. (b) The Christians as well as the Mohammedans could not agree to let the Holy Land fall into Jewish hands. (c) The Jews are an alien element in the country and thus tend to create such conditions that

4. Weizmann, *op. cit.*, p. 247.
5. Cf. Adolf Bohm, *Die Zionistische Bewegung.* Jerusalem: Hozaah Ivrith, 1937, vol. II, pp. 138-39. Typically, Feisal blamed Arab opposition to the Zionists as the cause of his downfall in Damascus.

would make it impossible for the Arabs to develop their own autonomous national life.[6]

(2) *The Middle East as a Whole.* With the best of his intentions, Feisal promised to help the Jews attain their goal in Palestine only if and when he would realize his aim to establish a united Arab country in the Middle East with himself as its head. But his grand plan failed, and the Allied Powers gave him only the kingdom of Iraq (in 1921). Then as the region was carved up into smaller Arab states, it became clear that the Jewish position in Palestine assumed the proportions of a regional and international problem in the entire Middle East. Jewish interests were thus not determined exclusively in relation to the Arab population in Palestine, but also and especially in relations with the other Arab states, each of which aimed at extending its dominion or influence over the region as a whole. This was further complicated by the rivalries of the Big Powers in that area and their leanings toward Arab demands regarding the abandonment of the Balfour Declaration. Whatever promises, hints, or intimations various Arab spokesmen may make toward a negotiated settlement with the Jews they are all aimed at a utilization of Jewish influence and creative skills for their own purposes in their drive to extend their rule over the entire region. The Arabs consider the Jews a foreign element in the Middle East, and they all want to eliminate them from their midst.

(3) *Terror as a National Policy.* It was during Feisal's brief reign in Syria that the Arab Councils started a campaign of terror against the Jewish settlements in Palestine in order to exert pressure on the Allied Powers to annul the Balfour Declaration. The first Jewish leader to fall in this campaign was Captain Joseph Trumpeldor, who guarded with his small Jewish garrison the village of Tel Hai, in Upper Galilee, that was then unoccupied by either British or French troops. He was shot by a bedouin terrorist, reportedly upon orders from Damascus. It should be noted that orders of terror issuing from Damascus were also applied against the Christian population in Lebanon, in order to undermine the French bid for a mandate over that country. This policy has since been pursued by Palestinian and outside Arab task forces with ever increasing severity under various commands but with the unanimous encouragement, training, and material support

6. *Jews and Arabs in Palestine*, p. 54, and, with reference to the "McMahon Declaration of October 24, 1915," pp. 35a and the "Sykes-Picot Agreement" of May 16, 1916, pp. 38a.

of several Arab states. The major outbreaks in Palestine in 1921, 1929, 1936, and 1939, and since the establishment of the State of Israel inside and outside that territory, have all had the same end in view — the elimination of the Jewish national entity from the Middle East. A corollary of this policy has been that the other Arab states have imposed oppressive measures against their respective Jewish populations that had lived in their midst for centuries and millenia, by abrogating their civil rights, expropriating their possessions, incarcerating them without due course of law, and expelling them from their countries, so that out of tens and hundreds of thousands of Jews who had lived there before the Jewish State was established there are now only a few hundred or a few thousand left in each of those countries.[7]

(4) *Arab double play.* The double play that the Arabs showed in their negotiations came to light not only in their attitude toward the Jews, but also in their relations with the Big Powers who supported their cause. This was revealed, rather ironically, in connection with the British White Paper of 1939, which gave the Arabs practically everything they had asked for, namely, the scrapping of the Balfour Declaration and a plan for the establishment of an Arab State in Palestine within five years. It will be recalled that that White Paper was issued as a result of a Tripartite Conference of British, Arab, and Jewish representatives, held at the St. James Palace in London, in February 1939. The British yielded to the Arab demands in the hope that in the event of a world war (which was already looming on the horizon), the Arab states that had been newly formed under British protectorates or mandates, would support the British cause. Yet when the war broke out in September of that year, the Arab countries promptly deserted the Allied Powers and went over to the German side or remained neutral with an "ill-concealed hostility" toward Great Britain. On the other hand, the twenty-first World Zionist Congress, meeting in Geneva in August 1939, pledged support to England in her war efforts, despite her White Paper which the Congress rejected outright.

To cap the series of ironic events that followed the ill-boding White Paper, some members of the Arab delegations, after having emerged triumphantly from the Tripartite Conference, sought to placate the Jews with new promises. At the Conference the Arabs refused to sit with the Jews in the same room or even to enter and

7. For a fuller description of this state of affairs, see my essay "Jews, Arabs, and Zionists in the Middle East," in this volume.

leave the St. James Palace through the same door. But as soon as
the Conference was over, they did not hesitate to meet the Jewish
delegates face to face, when their interests prompted them to do so.
One Arab leader after another became solicitous of Jewish help for
their respective ambitions, promising in return to mitigate the
effects of the White Paper (shades of Feisal who hoped " to make
the Jews some return for their kindness"). The most significant
aspect of the Tripartite Conference was the revelation not just of
the utter futility of negotiating with the Arabs, but more so of the
anger involved in such an enterprise, especially when a Big Power
is a partner in the deal. As it became evident during those
negotiations, the British and Arab representatives had already
agreed in advance on their plan to dismantle the Jewish Homeland
and to establish an Arab State. Why then did they call the
Conference? Its purpose was revealed when one day between
sessions, the Foreign Secretary, Lord Halifax, called in Dr.
Weizmann and advised him to accept "the inevitable" and
"renounce [publicly] your rights under the Mandate and under the
various instruments deriving from it."[8] Obviously the purpose of
the Conference was to break down the resistance of the Jews in a
peaceful way, this time, through a voluntary disclaimer of their
rights. Of course, Weizamnn stoutly refused to act in such a
"disgraceful manner." The situation was saved through the
rejection of the White Paper by the Mandates Commission of the
League of Nations. But what actually prevented its immediate
coming into force was the outbreak of the second World War.
Nevertheless, its implications were strongly felt after the war,
when there was no longer the League of Nations to stem the tide of
anti-Jewish action, and a new international authority had not yet
come into existence to step into the breach. Then another prospect
opened up for the Zionist cause, and that was the presentation of a
Palestine partition plan before the newly formed United Nations
Special Committee on Palestine, at Lake Success, in October-
November, 1947.

The Palestine Partition Plan

Before I proceed with the events at Lake Success, it will be
instructive to review some of the basic factors of Jewish-Arab

8. Weizmann, *Trial and Error*, pp. 403-404.

relations that played a part in the development of the Jewish Yishuv in Palestine up to 1947. As said, the Palestinian Arabs were antagonistic to the rebuilding of the Jewish National Home right from the start (1882) and they did not relent but rather intensified their opposition as the Yishuv grew and prospered. Between the two wars, as the Arab countries gained political influence in the region, they used every possible stratagem in trying to force the Big Powers to abandon the Jewish cause. Whether they used terror or negotiation, their goal was the same — to abrogate all promises for a Jewish Homeland and to reduce the Jewish population in the entire area to a small insignificant community, just enough to serve their own interests. Yet, notwithstanding all their schemes, and despite the fact that the Mandatory Power favored their side, the Jewish Yishuv in Palestine was able to vastly increase its population, build new towns and villages, establish industrial, agricultural, and business enterprises, create religious, social and cultural institutions, all of which constituted a self-governing Jewish national entity, or a Jewish State in the making. Now what is important about this entire undertaking is that it was accomplished not by political negotiations with the Arabs, but by a process of accommodation to the ever changing circumstances in the region and in the world situation in general. The Jews mustered enough strength to defend themselves against Arab attacks, and found ways of circumventing the Arab political schemes by practical means of building and fortifying their positions, and by working with some Arab elements who were willing to cooperate (notably in the field of labor), and thus increased in due time also their political status in the land. Just to cite a few statistical examples: From 1920 to 1947, that is during the most turbulent years of Arab riots and periodic attempts by the Mandatory Government to curtail the Yishuv's growth, the Jewish population in Palestine rose from 55,000 or 9.7% of the total to 550,000 or 33% of the total. Agricultural Jewish settlements increased from 43 (in 1914) to 276, and industrial enterprises and small shops grew from 2,475 (in 1929) to 6,300. During the same period the Arab population in Palestine also increased considerably and its industrial and agricultural enterprises advanced greatly.[9] What all this signifies is that on a local level, without political

9. Cf. *A Survey of Facts and Opinions on Problems of Post-War Jewry in Europe and Palestine.* Ed. Alexander S. Kohanski. New York: American Jewish Conference, 1943, pp. 85 and 90.

negotiations, commissions of inquiry, and all the other Big Power intergovernmental paraphernalia, the Jews and the Arabs in Palestine learned how to accommodate each other so that both sides benefited from the Jewish return to their homeland. We may thus question the wisdom of continued efforts on the part of the State of Israel to seek a negotiated settlement of all their differences with the neighboring Arab states. This became evident especially when the Partition Plan was negotiated before the United Nations at Lake Success in 1947.

To start with, it should be pointed out that a proposal for partitioning Palestine between the two contending parties was first broached to Weizmann by the Peel Commission (formed by England to investigate the 1936 Arab riots) "at a session held *in camera* on January 8, 1937."[10] Based on the Peel Report then, the British Government issued a White Paper in July 1937, in which partition was mentioned officially. But before the Zionist Executive had a chance to discuss with the British the precise terms of the plan, it was scuttled, and instead the Tripartite Conference, mentioned earlier, was convened and Great Britain issued a new White Paper (in 1939) designed to put an end to Jewish aspirations for their National Home altogether. With these preludes in the background, when the Arab representatives came to Lake Success in 1947, they were convinced that they could repeat the same performance as they did in 1939, and they refused to accept the United Nations Resolution of November 29, 1947 for the establishment of two separate states in Palestine, one Jewish and one Arab. The Zionist representation accepted the plan, even though the territorial distribution was not advantageous to them.

This is how the Jewish State was conceived officially. But it is erroneous to view its birth simply as due to the efforts of the United Nations, although full recognition and praise should be given to those of its member nations, notably the United States under the personal leadership of President Harry S. Truman, who tipped the scale in its favor. After the vote on November 29th, the Arabs launched an armed attack on the Yishuv and the hostile forces in the UN banded together in an attempt to reverse the partition decision. Even the American Delegation reversed itself and proposed suspension of partition and the formation of a trusteeship

10. Weizmann, *op. cit.*, p. 385.

over Palestine when the Mandate ended on May 15, 1948. When that failed to pass, another stratagem was tried, to declare a "Temporary Truce," without political decisions, provided the Jews refrained from proclaiming their State in the meantime. But the Yishuv had already repulsed the Arab armies on many fronts and set up their own governmental authority in areas that the Mandate had evacuated. The Zionist delegation at the UN stood fast and, following Weizmann's advice "to create facts and confront the world with these facts," started preparing for the proclamation of the Jewish State on May 15, 1948. At the same time Weizmann addressed a letter to President Truman making "a bid for the [American] recognition of the Jewish State as soon as it was proclaimed." And once more, President Truman took matters into hand and on the same day the U. S. Government recognized "the Provisional Government as the *de facto* authority of the new State of Israel."[11] Thus the Jewish State was created by the heroic sacrifices of the Yishuv on the battlefields and by the resolute decision of its leaders to pursue their goal of national independence without being distracted from its course by further dubious negotiations.

Peace with Egypt

What has happened since the Jewish War of Independence is now history and need not be recited here. The State of Israel has flourished, but its Arab neighboring states have never relented their drive, through terror and wars, to wipe it off the map. Not being able to defeat it in open warfare, one of its major antagonists, Egypt, was persuaded to try peaceful negotiation. Its prospects may be guaged by a careful study of the documents that have accumulated around the "Peace Treaty" that was signed on March 26, 1979, in Washington, by President Anwar Sadat of Egypt, Prime Minister Menachem Begin of Israel, and witnessed by President Jimmy Carter of the United States.[12] From the very first step, when Sadat appeared before the Knesset in Jerusalem on November 20, 1977, it became clear that nothing had changed in Arab opposition to the Jewish national revival in their ancient Homeland. Sadat let the Jewish Parliament know unequivocally

11. Ibid., pp. 476-78.
12. For the texts of those documents see *Myths and Facts of 1982: A concise Record of the Arab-Israeli Conflict.* Ed. Leonard J. Davis and Moshe Decter. Washington, D. C.: Near East Report, 1982, pp. 218-40.

that he regarded the Jews as strangers in the Middle East, and that they set up their state in a land that did not belong to them. He admitted that he and the other Arab leaders had rejected the State of Israel, and even refused to talk with its representatives or sit with them at the same negotiating table. But now, in a spirit of "tolerance and respect for rights," like that of the Califs of old whom he brought up as an example, he said that he was ready to accept the world's recognition that "Israel has become a *fait accompli*," and that he would abide by "all the international guarantees" received by Israel from the Superpowers. He wanted to live in peace with Israel. The word "peace" he repeated seventy-four times in his speech without giving it any substantive meaning for the Jewish State, except emphasizing that "Israel obtains all kinds of guarantees . . . [to] live in the region in security and safety." And then he stated his price: Israel's "complete withdrawal [not just the removal of its troops] from the Arab territories occupied after 1967, . . . including Arab Jerusalem." The Palestinian people to exercise their right of return and their right to establish "their own state." "Jerusalem . . . should be a free and open city for all believers." He called these demands "facts" that are not negotiable.[13]

Sadat's "sacred message" (as he called it) to Israel then was that it should "give up once and for all the dream of conquest," "withdraw from all occupied territories," and "respect the rights" of the Palestinian Arabs to form their independent state there; and that in return the Arab nations will show "tolerance" toward the Jews living in that "part of the world." Not a word was said about the rights and needs of the Israelis. These things were transmuted into an empty word "peace" which he drummed into their ears seventy-four times in order to arouse in them false hopes for real friendship. When he spoke of the Arabs who fled from Palestine during the Jewish War of Independence (nobody chased them out) that they have the right to return, he did not think of the hundreds of thousands of Jews who were driven out of Egypt and the other Arab countries, whether they too had the right of return. And while he lectured Israel not to "dream of conquest" and to do "justice" to the Palestinians, he failed to mention the injustices done them by Jordan, that had ruled the West Bank by conquest and held their refugees in tents of squalor for twenty years until Israel delivered

13. See ibid., p. 18.

them in 1967. Nor did he allude to the oppressive rule of Egypt over the Gaza strip, which did not belong to it. During that period it never occurred to Jordan and Egypt to grant the Palestinians national independence in the West Bank and Gaza, which Sadat now claimed as their indisputable right. In sum, Sadat demanded justice and rights for the Arabs without negotiation, but for the Jews he could only promise to negotiate international guarantees for peace and security.

In response to Sadat's passionate, self-righteous oration, Prime Minister Menachem Beign said with dignity: "It is my obligation to tell our guest . . . of our ties between our Nation and this land. . . . We did not take strange land, we returned to our homeland." And he also reminded his guest how little trust the Jews may be expected to place in international guarantees. When "our people . . . were being destroyed," he said, "no one came to our saving—not from the East and not from the West. . . . We shall never again place our nation in such danger." And as to Sadat's demand for Israel's withdrawal from the occupied territories "without negotiation," Begin replied: "I propose that everything is open to negotiation; . . . everything is given to negotiation between the Jewish nation and the Arab nation." Most important, "Let us conduct the negotiations as equals. . . . All nations in the region are equal; and each one will have to relate to one another with honor, and in the spirit of openness, of readiness to listen one to another to facts and to points and to expectations."

In the Peace Treaty between Israel and Egypt that was finally signed on March 26, 1979, Egypt was accorded the return of the entire Sinai peninsula with its highways, airfield, and oil wells that Israel had built and cultivated, including the Jewish settlements on the Mediteranean shore, which Israel agreed to evacuate. The problem of a new Arab state that Sadat had demanded was left open, but enough was stipulated in the Treaty to tie Israel with certain obligations for future consideration by a tripartite representation of Egypt, Jordan, and Israel, with the participation of Palestinian spokesmen. These points are many and definite, but their language is often vague and equivocal, lending itself to contrary interpretations. The danger of such a Treaty is that Israel will be expected to abide by it regardless of how it is interpreted, whereas the Arabs states who, besides Egypt, are not parties to this Treaty (and even condemned it), may reject it outright. And Sadat already indicated that in the future, whether in war or in peace, he would support the other Arab states. Apart from that, the tangible issues of territorial return, military deployment, and population removal, were decided in Egypt's favor and have been carried out by Israel to the letter of the document; whereas the less tangible clauses, such as economic, cultural, and other social exchanges that might accrue to Israel's benefit have not yet been put into effect. As far as Israel is concerned, the "Peace Treaty" of 1979 has turned out to be nothing but a "peace of paper."

Concluding Observations

The basic conflict between Israel and its Arab neighbors is not so much a matter of adjustments between the Jews and the Palestinians, as it is between the State of Israel and the Arab states in the Middle East as a whole. A new Arab state on the West Bank and Gaza has no prospect of maintaining itself in that small area, economically or politically, especially in the face of the surrounding Arab countries each of which has an eye on its absorption or dismemberment. If the Arabs themselves felt such a state could survive they would have created it when they controlled the area before 1967.

From the Peace Treaty of 1979 as well as from all previous negotiations with the Arabs, directly or indirectly (and there have been some direct conversations between Israeli and Arab leaders in the past), we may learn that they have all tended to impose on Israel commitments in favor of Arab demands, by which Israel would have to abide, but at best could exact from the Arab states only vague promises to Israel, which they never intended to fulfill.

The negotiation apparatus as a means of resolving the conflict between Israel and the Arabs has proved to be a broken reed, on which Israel dare not lean. Instead Israel should try to make accommodations with its Arab neighbors, whenever and wherever possible, inside and outside of Palestine, on a one-to-one basis, on concrete, tangible issues in a give-and-take manner on the spot, without entanglements in unwarranted commitments for the future. This process has worked within the State of Israel on a small scale, and it may be applied also in relation with the Arab states on a larger scale.

1982, revised 1986

PART IV
Jewish Education

413

The Jewish education of our youth is toward the future. And the future lies in the community to which our youth belongs.

Jewish Education and the Community

Our Sages in the Talmud remember with great fondness the man, Yehoshua ben Gamala, who founded the elementary Hebrew School in ancient Palestine. "For, if not for him," they say, "Torah would have been forgotten in Israel." The founders of the Bangor Hebrew School will be remembered by the present generation and by generations to come with equal affection. One may visualize the small Jewish community of Bangor some four or five decades ago as a pioneering settlement, struggling on the up-hill in search of economic security. While the head of the family was preoccupied in his daily toil he could hardly pay attention to the Jewish upbringing of his children. Perhaps he spent some spare moments in the evening or on a week-end to instruct his son in the rudiments of "saying ivri." If he was a little affluent he may have engaged a "house rebbe" to prepare his boy for Bar Mitzvah. As in the days of yore, before the time of Yehoshua ben Gamala, the Jewish upbringing of the young generation was in parental hands. With the establishment of the Hebrew School, this function became a community responsibility.

Communal responsibility for Jewish education means primarily that the Jewish upbringing of the young generation must be rooted in the religious, cultural and social life and needs of our people. These are the major factors of Jewish survival; they form the practical basis of Jewish education. The question is often raised as to the practical value of studying Hebrew, Jewish history, literature or other elements of the Hebrew School curriculum. The answer lies in the *aim* of Jewish education, and that is, to relate the child to the Jewish group in its historical and contemporary development, as well as in its hopes and aspirations for the future. As an individual, unrelated to Jewish group life, one may find no practical value in Jewish studies, except perhaps as an extension of one's liberal education. Thus, one who is interested in languages may also study Hebrew as another language; one who likes history may also become interested in Jewish history, and similarly in Jewish literature. But then one sees no practical use for these subjects in everyday life. On the other hand, Jewish studies assume practical meaning only in the light of group experience, that is, in so far as the individual identifies himself with his group and shares in its communal life. The community's responsibility is, therefore, to bring to the fore the group demand for Jewish education and to create the general atmosphere in which its importance and practical value may be recognized. But here the responsibility does not end.

In our own State of Maine, the Maine Jewish Council has launched a program of education with the same end in view, namely, to develop standards and to advance the principles and needs of Jewish education in all the communities in this state, in line with national endeavors. This program, like that of the Bureaus in large cities, is a cooperative enterprise. All our communities may participate in it with a sense of common responsibility for the Jewish upbringing of our children in the small towns as well as in the larger cities in our state. If we accept the tenet, which has been brought to our attention by the exigencies of our time, that Jewish education is essentially a process of relating the individual to his largest group life, then each of our communities must not isolate its Hebrew Schools and other educational institutions within its own limited confines. In this respect, the responsibility of each community for Jewish education also involves the obligation on its part to join forces with other communities for the achievement of the common goal.

1947

The Teacher in the Jewish School*

The theme of our Conference today is "The Role of the Teacher in Jewish Education." One might well say, the teacher's position is quite obvious — it is at the foundation of the school. But in reality

*Address at the Jewish Teachers Conference in San Francisco, September 7, 1952.

this cannot always be taken for granted; nor is the teacher's role self-evident from the tasks he may be called upon to perform in a given school. At this gathering we propose to take stock of the structure and functions of this foundation upon which stands the edifice of Jewish education.

How important is the teacher in the life of our people? A Talmudic story illustrates his role. "Rab," the story tells, "came to a certain place where he ordained a fast because there was a drought. The precentor of the congregation conducted the service, and when he uttered the words 'He causes the wind to blow,' the wind at once blew; and when he uttered the words 'He causes the rain to fall,' at once the rain fell. Rab said to him, What is your exceptional merit? He answered, I am an elementary teacher, and I instruct the children of the poor exactly the same as I teach the children of the rich.'' This legend signifies the power the teacher possesses by virtue of his vocation. He can influence the course of natural events. Some modern theories to the contrary notwithstanding, the teacher determines the course of the child's nature, directly or indirectly. And this is not to be taken metaphysically but in a very real phychological and sociological sense. It is particularly true in the Jewish community where the religious school is the major, if not the sole, factor in the Jewish upbringing of the young generation. The teacher's influence upon his pupils in the school may penetrate to the very roots of their beings as Jews. This may be brought home more forcefully if we realize that the vast majority of American Jews today knows or does not know, practices or does not practice, Judaism to the extent that the teachers had transmitted, or failed to transmit, Jewish values to the children in the religious schools of a generation ago. For very little was transmitted to them through the home. Today, even more so than in the past, the character of Jewish life and thus its future strength and vitality are being wrought by the teachers in the Jewish schools.

What are the teacher's responsibilities in the school? Because of the great importance attached to the teacher's role, Jewish tradition from Talmudic days to the present has made supreme demands of the teaching profession. However, it is significant that those demands were put forth by the sages and teachers themselves; that is, the high standards of character, devotion, purity of heart and purpose, were self-imposed. In similar manner, we of the teaching profession, whether by vocation or avocation, are gathered here to set for ourselves some guiding principles in meeting our responsibilities toward Jewish youth of today. I would offer as the first of such principles the teacher's own belief in what he proposes to teach. Again, because the school is the strongest citadel wherein the spirit of our people may dwell with a sense of completeness and self-realization, it must be permeated with an atmosphere of our people's faith and of faith in our people. This atmosphere has to be created by the teachers. Hence, what they try to impart to their pupils must have meaning in their own personal lives — identification with the Jewish people, love of learning, religious practice, and participation in Jewish communal affairs. The primary function of the Jewish teacher in relation to his pupils is to influence them or, if you will, to indoctrinate them. I know this word "indoctrination" is anathema to educators of a certain modern school of thought. Even the word "influence" is banned from their vocabulary. But when we instruct in matters of faith, normative precepts of right conduct, and in the history and destiny of a people, we are indoctrinating, or else our teaching is meaningless. In the Sabbath morning prayers, when the Sefer-Torah is returned to the ark we recite, perhaps unwittingly, "I have given you a good doctrine; ye shall not forsake my Torah." The Hebrew original for the word "doctrine" is "lekah," meaning that which is taken to be true, or an accepted truth. It is only right that a Jewish teacher should ask himself how many truths of Judaism he himself has accepted before he ventures to instruct the young in the Jewish faith.

Another aspect of the relationship between teacher and pupil may be evaluated in terms of aims, and that from the pupil's viewpoint. We are all familiar with the principle that education; should be in consonance with the child's interests or needs. While no one may dispute this principle in essence, there are differences of opinion on two major implications. First, since the Jewish school can hope to meet only a few of the child's needs, the question is what shall be the choice of interests and of subject matter. Second, who shall make the choice — the child, the teacher, the parents, the congregation, the community, or perhaps all of them together? Time does not permit us now to discuss these two fundamental issues. For our immediate purpose we might consider what the child expects from the Jewish school. We are in the habit of deploring the children's reluctance to attend religious school. If this general notion were broken down into particular instances, we would find that certain children do not like certain things in certain Jewish schools. Upon further investigation we may even discover that all children do not like some things in all schools. This would be no great problem if their dislikes were just treated for what they are in their individual cases in the course of routine or special administrative procedure. That is, when children are dissatisfied with certain apsects of the school we try to adjust them as well as the school to our educational goals. Our difficulties, however, arise when we posit the children's dissatisfactions as universal premises for our school program. Then we are apt to lose sight of the purposes of Jewish education and to convert our schools into something which may be neither Jewish nor educational in character. We become unduly concerned with attracting the children or as we say, 'making them like school,' at any price, and we allow ourselves to be sidetracked from our primary goals. In our zeal for gaining numbers we promise all sorts of diversionary activity, and the role of the teacher then becomes that of an entertainer. If he tries to teach under such circumstances his relationship with the pupils becomes untenable.

I believe that we ought to free ourselves from the notion that children do not like to come to our religious schools. Even though there is an element of truth in it, we cannot possibly build anything of value on such an assumption. Rather, we ought to take as our premise the thing that the child wants when he does come to religious school. In my estimation, the child who attends our school basically wants to learn. By this I mean, he wants to gain new experiences, to explore new vistas, to master new situations. True, he may not always accept the subject-matter we give him or he may resist the manner of its presentation. This will require improvement in our curriculum planning and teaching methods, but always with a veiw to meeting the child's real interest, and that is, learning. The natural relationship between teacher and pupil is just what these two terms signify in their co-relative meaning, namely, a learning situation. The question a teacher should ask himself after each class session is, "have the children learned anything" or "have I taught them anything" at this session? From this relationship will issue true friendship, enjoyment, proper attitudes and, what we generally aim for, happiness. How should the teacher relate himself to parents? No doubt the school and the home are intimately connected in the child's Jewish upbringing. Jewish knowledge and observance or their absence at home, shape in large measure the child's attitude toward the school. We are fully aware of the wide gaps or total voids of Judasim that prevail in many, if not most, of our pupil's homes, which have affected the Jewish school. While the number of pupils in our schools has grown in proportion to the Jewish population in the past two or three decades, the quality as well as the quantity of instruction has greatly diminshed. For several generations we have been winding our way along the lines of a cone-shaped spiral, constricting the periphery of Jewish learning at the turn of each generation. If this trend continues, we shall reach before long the apex at zero. The process must be reversed. We must start to intensify, deepen and at the same time broaden the content of the Jewish school. The question, of course, is with whom shall we start.

Some maintain that we must first educate the parents. This may mean that we propagandize the parents on the value of Jewish education, or that we actually teach them the precepts and practices of Judaism. The former is comparatively simple, whatever it may be worth. The latter, however, if it is meant as a springboard for the reversing of the trend in Jewish education, is an unrealistic approach to the problem. Even if it were feasible, by the time the parents become properly educated their children will have grown up and have children of their own and we shall thus be moving in a vicious circle. As for propagandizing the parents, while necessary, it will not by itself give them the intrinsic meaning of Jewish education or of Judaism. The truth of the matter is that, except for those who consider themselves outside the Jewish fold, parents desire to give their children a Jewish upbringing of some kind. One may go even further and say that on the whole they want them to receive a good Jewish education. To that extent they need not be propagandized. What parents may not know is the content and meaning of a good Jewish education or the type of schooling required for its achievement. They entrust their children to the teachers and educators for guidance and instruction. Where, then, shall be begin? We must begin with ourselves as teachers. We must first train ourselves before we can train our pupils. I have enough confidence in human beings to believe that a person who undertakes to teach wants to do his best for his pupils. When he fails, it is due in most cases to lack of self-preparation and, what is more important, to his unwillingness to put himself to the test. When a candidate applies to me for a teaching position, I usually ask him what he has done or is willing to do for himself in Jewish learning. This is not so much to examine him for actual knowledge as to ascertain his attitude toward the acquiring of knowledge. His answer as a rule reveals to what extent he possesses the traits of a teacher.

One of the main qualities of a teacher is love of children. In general human relations, this is an application of the dictum in our Torah — "Love thy neighbor as thyself." It will be instructive, however, to apply here Hillel's formulation of this precept. With deep insight into human psychology, Hillel stated: "That which is hateful to you do not do unto others." The love of a teacher, as teacher, for a child expresses itself through teaching him. Therefore, one who hates to be taught should not undertake to teach others. Such a person could not show very much love for his pupils. Another important trait of a teacher is love of learning — in our case, love of Jewish learning. I do not share the view, which has become standard among educators, that all we should try to inculcate in our children is proper attitudes. The tendency among those educators is to deprecate knowledge and learning as "bookish," "cramming," "obsolete," and "authoritarian." I think this veiw is a major obstacle to progress in our schools. If we do not impart basic Jewish knowledge from the very sources of Judaism to our children, they cannot possibly develop proper attitudes toward Jewish values. For attitudes, as such, cannot be taught; they are a by-product of learning real things. If the teacher loves the subject of his instruction, loves Jewish learning, he will be able in the teaching process to convey to his students the right attitudes towared Jewish realities. A third major characteristic of a teacher is youthfulness. This trait is not to be associated with physical age or even with mental age. It is the quality of constant inquiry, of searching for knowledge, of wonderment about the mysteries of the world yet to be unraveled. Such a teacher studies together with his pupils. He is their true companion. There are teachers in our schools who possess these traits and other qualities in varying degrees; some, indeed, to a high degree. What they lack is sufficient Jewish knowledge, especially from its sources. There are many teachers who have attained a high level in the general American culture but who do not possess or pursue Jewish culture. The influence of such teachers is bound to be adverse to Judaism, despite their good intentions to direct their pupils toward Jewish learning; for they exemplify a Jewishness that is pale and insignificant by comparison with the dominant culture. If, then, the teacher is to assume the responsibility that is his in the Jewish school, he must devote as much time as possible to self-advancement in the field of Jewish learning and to the acquiring of proper teaching methods and techniques specifically applied to that field.

In my discussion of the teacher's role in the school, I have referred to the Jewish Religious School in general, embracing all types of Sunday Schools and Hebrew Schools. However, since almost all representatives at this Conference come from the Sunday School, a word should be said about the place of this type of school in Jewish education. The proper designation of the Sunday School should be the "one-day-a-week religious school," as differentiated from the three days or five days a week. I do not negate the value of the Sunday School. The children come to us that morning rested over the week-end from public school and are receptive to new learning. The Sunday session can therefore be utilized for effective instruction. However, one session a week is wholly insufficient for an adequate education of any kind. It is now common knowledge that the sum-total of Sunday School experiences leaves the child only with some vague notions about Judaism. We tell him that it is his heritage. But does he own it? It may be well for us to heed Goethe's admonition: "What you have inherited from your fathers you must acquire anew in order to possess it." We cannot possibly transmit the Jewish spiritual heritage to our children if we do not allow them sufficient time to acquire it personally. Jewish educators throughout the country cherish the hope that the one-day-a-week school, which is today the predominant educational institution for the majority of our children, will pass from the scene of American Jewish life, and will be replaced by more intensive as well as extensive schools. This, too, can be accomplished by the Jewish teacher if he realizes the full import of his calling. In this respect, the Sunday School teacher can perform two important functions: utilize the limited Sunday morning session for maximum teaching, and imbue the children with a desire for greater, more extensive learning.

There is a Talmudic saying, "It is possible that a person may acquire his reward of the world to come in a single hour" (Yosh koneh olamo beshaa ahat). That is, one may perform in one hour a deed so great that it will assure his entire future. The teacher in the Sunday School may attempt just that. In the hour or two he has the children with him, he may find moments when he can convey to them the full impact of his Jewish teaching. But then, the teacher must be well prepared for that hour; and he must guard every moment of it that it shall not be wasted with extraneous "activities" or other irrelevancies. Another Talmudic saying is appropriate to the second function assigned to the Sunday School teacher. Says Rabbi Tarfon: "it is not incumbent upon you to complete the work; but neither are you at liberty to shun it" (Lo alecha hamlacha ligmor . . .). We have to have faith that, if we do our share of the task and do it well, our children, coming out of our schools, will continue to advance in Jewish learning for the enrichment of their lives. I know that you have all come to this conference to seek through common deliberation the best ways of serving the children entrusted to you in your schools. I hope that when you leave this gathering you will have gained renewed faith in the future of your work.

1952

Torah on One Foot? Yes, But. . .

This story is well known. When someone asked Hillel to teach him the whole Torah while standing on one foot, the sage instructed him patiently: "What is hateful to you, don't do to your neighbor. . . . The rest go and study." We usually admire Hillel's brilliant instruction for its brevity and succinctness. However, many of us overlook the admonition in the second part of his reply, namely, "go and study." What Hillel really tried to convey to his impatient interrogator is that there are no shortcuts to the knowledge of Judaism. If our generation is perplexed about the values of Jewish religion, culture, tradition or any other aspect of Jewish life, it is an indication that there is yearning for Jewish knowledge. The difficulty lies in the way many persons go about trying to satisfy their thirst for such knowledge. They want to have a quick answer to every troubling question, without taking the trouble to acquire even a rudimentary acquaintance with the underlying bases of their questions. Such an approach does not lead to an understanding and appreciation of Jewish life. On the contrary, it only adds to their perplexity and increases their impatience. What our generation needs, then, is basic knowledge of Judaism. This need is for all—young and old, rich and poor. In the city of San Francisco, this need is being met by two major institutions—The Jewish Education Society and the College of Jewish Studies.

The Jewish Education Society is a central community agency rendering service in the field of Jewish education. Its main object is the advancement of Jewish education on a high level of pedagogic standards, regardless of the type of school or its sponsorship. Each of its affiliated schools determines its own religious character. The Society helps in the developing of curricula; it supplies teachers for Hebrew schools; it gives professional guidance and supervision; and it coordinates the programs of its affiliated schools—Hebrew schools as well as Sunday Schools. The Jewish Education Society's viewpoint is that of the community as a whole. The Jewish community has a vital stake in the Jewish upbringing of its yuoung generation. How to make such upbringing adequate to the needs of the child, is one of the Society's major concerns. The Society therefore urges parents to send their children to a Jewish school at least three days a week, and if possible, five days a week. It further urges that the children start at a young age, simultaneously with their entrance to public school. Is this asking too much of the children or their parents? It depends upon the value one places on Jewish education: It is essential to the child's wellbeing, to his sense of freedom and security as an American Jew? Those who think that it is will realize that Judaism cannot be transmitted in a capsule while the child is "standing on one foot" in the school, extending the other foot outside. The child must learn to experience his Jewishness and thus learn to appreciate its values in his everyday life as an individual and as a member of the community. This is a slow process of growth, which can be advanced best if the implanting begins at a tender age, and the cultivation continues in adequate time for many years.

The second institution of Jewish learning, the College of Jewish Studies, aims among other things to meet the needs of adult Jewish education in this community. The College was founded in the fall of 1949 by the Jewish Education Society and the Board of Rabbis of Northern California, in cooperation with congregations Beth Israel, Beth Sholom, Emanu-El, and Sherith Israel, and the Jewish Community Center. For a proper understanding and appreciation of Jewish life and values one must go to the sources of Judaism—to the spiritual creations of the Jewish people throughout the ages. If one wants to know how Jewish values may become meaningful in our everyday life, one must first learn to know what those values are, and what are their mainsprings that have sustained Jewish life. This requires study—patient, systematic and continuous learning. This is not an undertaking just for scholars. It is a matter of basic knowledge that anyone who seeks may acquire.

The College offers systematic courses on Jewish life and lore, in history, Bible, religion, literature, art, music, Hebrew language, which are accessible to everyone. Sessions are held on Monday and Wednesday evenings, at 639-14th Avenue. Each term course is given once a week for ten successive weeks. The winter term will Start January 7th. Registration will take place Monday to Thursday, December 17-20. Here is an invitation to Jewish learning, extended to all adult persons in our community. The College has another primary aim, and that is to train Sunday School teachers. There are, no doubt, many young men and women of ability who feel that they can make a contribution toward the enhancement of Jewish life by instructing the young. To those the College offers a systematic training course in Judaica and in the principles and methods of education. In modern times, the quest for knowledge may begin with a telephone call. A cordial invitation is therefore extended to all who are interested, to call Skyline 1-6987, or to inquire in person at 639-14th Avenue, at the offices of the Jewish Education Society and the College of Jewish Studies.

1951

Concerning the "Experiment with the One-Bond Method"

Since Abraham N. Franzblau published his article on the One-Bond Method of teaching Hebrew in the 1950-51 Winter-Spring issue of this magazine, most of us who had serious misgivings about the validity of his method have been looking forward to a report on its application in an actual class situation. Such a report has now been presented *Jewish Education*, Spring, 1953) by Rebecca Lister. According to the report, the children of Mrs.

Lister's class have learned what they were supposed to learn, namely, reading in English at sight from a given Hebrew textbook. They do not, and are not supposed to, know the sound of a Hebrew sentence, word or letter. More specifically, the children have learned to look at certain Hebrew word-signs and read them in English for comprehension. Since this was an experiment in teaching Hebrew language, one would like to know how much of this language the children have learned by the One-Bond Method. How well are they able to utilize vocabulary, recognize grammatical forms and, generally, what have they retained, the English content of the stories or the Hebrew language? Mrs. Lister is silent on too many points in the experiment for the reader to be able to draw proper conclusions from her description. She does not indicate, for example, how large a vocabulary the students have mastered in the course of two years. It is possible that they have memorized certain sentences or whole stories, without knowing the meaning of most of the words or their structural variations. I once observed a class that was learning Humash by the translation-at-sight method (in old Heder-fashion). Some of the students recited a given portion in English with remarkable accuracy; but they knew only a few Hebrew words of the whole portion.

Similarly, Mrs. Lister mentions that "the ability to establish a relationship between a word and its root . . . became apparent . . ." But she does not tell how many grammatical forms and of what complexity the children have learned to identify and utilize without Hebrew articulation. Sometimes she writes in the potential mode, and the reader is not sure whether a particular technique was actually applied. Thus, she states: "Without a formal attempt at grammar, the teacher may indicate that the kometz hay ending usually indicates feminine gender." Did she teach that to her pupils, and if so, with what results? Mrs. Lister spends about one column to describe specifically "How the Method Works." The rest of her report is very much "traditional." The techniques she mentions in connection with the acquisition of grammar, review, or testing, are not new or peculiar to the One-Bond Method. They have been used with varying degrees of success by many other methods. Most revealing, however, is her section on "Incidental Learning of Writing." "One day," she relates, "the children asked if they could write the Hebrew words. . . . The writing continued for a while and one of the children said 'I can write most of these words without looking at the blackboard.' Another child remarked 'So what! That's what I've been doing right along.'" This *enfant terrible,* who has been doing it right along, has spoiled the Method. For "writing is not inherent in the One-Bond Method." Yet, "children continued to write on their own initiative." (Earlier, on Page 50, Mrs. Lister stated: "Cursive writing is not employed. The children need not learn this bond.") One wonders whether the writing, which is not a product of the Method but which was practiced nevertheless, was not responsible for a considerable part of the learning and retentiveness. More important, however, would be to know what prompted the children to ask for writing experience, and why the teacher did not utilize this natural interest for teaching purposes. Another question that comes to one's mind is whether the children were ever curious to find out what the Hebrew words sound like. It is not likely that 10-11 year olds would go through a Hebrew course for two years and be satisfied to remain in the dark about such an intriguing matter. And, if they did raise the question, what did the teacher do about it? Besides Hebrew "for comprehension," Mrs. Lister reports, the children also learned prayers and *brochos* by transliteration. "Occasionally," she says, "while reading from the prayerbook, a child would say, 'Doesn't this word mean . . .'?" But how could the child tell the meaning of a Hebrew word in transliteration? When he saw the word-sign 'ato,' for example, in the Hebrew textbook, he always pronounced it "you." How could he identify the English word-sign "atoh" with "the word you?" And how could a child, "While reading Gilenu . . . sound a word in Hebrew," when he never learned to pronounce words in Hebrew characters? Apparently, there must have been some instruction in the reading of Hebrew text in the original, which, again, is not in accordance with the One-Bond Method.

The most serious omission from the report is an account of what transpired in "the control classes which were taught by the traditional method." It would have been instructive if the teacher of one of those classes were allowed to describe her actual method and procedure. From the scanty reference to the control classes by the principal of the school, one gets the impression that those classes were not conducted with too much enthusiasm or even proper attention to their needs. They were probably just tolerated alongside the One-Bond classes. For lack of a comparative report of the Lynbrook School, I may point out that in the Hebrew School system of San Francisco, there are students who have studied under somewhat similar conditions, namely, in two 50-minute sessions of Hebrew instruction per week (plus a 30-minute period on Sunday morning for prayers), for two years. The students, who were 8-9 years of age when they started in September 1951, began with Chomsky's Sippuri Aleph Part I as their very first primer. The instruction was by the so-called "traditional method." Without entering into great detail, their record as of the end of May, 1953, shows the following achievements: They have completed Sippuri Aleph, Parts I and II and about one-third of Sippuri Sheni (revised mimeographed edition). They can read the Hebrew text with accuracy and fair fluency and they understand what they read without translation. They can single out the roots of verbs and they know the grammatical forms of the present, past and some of the future tense, and several of the noun possessives. They can answer questions in Hebrew and, toward the end of the second year, they started to compose a simple Hebrew story.

What, then, is the comparative merit of the One-Bond approach? As a method, its validity has not been proved, if one were to judge by the report of the Lynbrook experiment. But assuming that the method is sound (or shall we say, "good to look at?"), the question still remains: What is its purpose? Is the goal aimed at by this method a desirable one? As developed in his major article some two years ago, Dr. Franzblau's ultimate goal is to make available to the young generation of American Jewry the vast field of Hebrew culture. His more immediate aim is to enable the student to translate a Hebrew text into English at sight, without articulating the Hebrew language itself. In my opinion, the former aim is superfluous while the latter is undesirable. Surely Dr. Franzblau is aware of the fact that many Hebrew works have already been translated into English and are therefore available to the American Jew in his native tongue. The casual reader of a Hebrew text, trained by the "One-Bond Method," even if this method should prove most successful, will hardly improve in his English translation upon those of the masters. It is more likely that such a reader will not even obtain the correct meaning of the original Hebrew, especially of its idiom which abounds in literature. What purpose, then, is there in learning to read Hebrew word-signs in English at sight?

One may agree with Dr. Franzblau that "ours is not, and will probably never be, a Hebrew speaking milieu in America," and that "the clue to the whole problem [of teaching Hebrew] is *reading.*" But his aim and method do not follow this clue. He uses the term "reading" in a restricted sense, namely, *looking* at symbols and deriving their *meaning*. "If the child," he asks rhetorically, "grasps the complete meaning of each sentence, paragraph or story which he reads silently in Hebrew, even though he cannot pronounce it, and can translate it perfectly into English. . . can anyone say that this child is not reading Hebrew?" The answer is, No, this child does not read Hebrew; he reads English in square-shaped signs. For "the essence of language" is not just "meaning," as Dr. Franzblaum maintains. All forms of expression — painting, music, architecture, etc. — essentially have meaning. What differentiates language from the other media, is that its meaning is conveyed through word-sound, not to speak of syntax, idiom and aesthetic form. Language is word-articulation, whether it is spoken or read. Even in silent reading there is kinaesthetic enunciation. One who is looking at Hebrew word-signs, but is not articulating in Hebrew, is not reading this language. From the point of view of Jewish culture, translation-at-sight has no intrinsic value. Hebrew is the creation of the Jewish people and is thus one of its treasures to be transmitted to the young generation. A treasure, like a precious stone, can be genuine only in the original. If it is presented in imitation, it ceases to be a treasure and becomes undesirable. Whether in method or purpose, the One-Bond approach does not promise salvation from the ills we have been suffering in trying to teach Hebrew to our children.

1953

Jewish Educational Content and the Jewish Child

The theme of our Teachers' Conference this year—"What Do We Teach and How?"—assumes special significance in view of the fact that our schools now enjoy an abundance of pupil enrollment, exceeding by far the enrollment of previous years. However, when we want to gauge the success or effectiveness of our educational institutions, the sheer weight of numbers is no valid criterion. On the contrary, this quantitative growth may cause much concern to those of us who find our schools unable to meet the increased need. For our schools are too often inadequate not only in physical accommodations and frequency of instruction, but also, and especially so, in matters of content and skills of teaching. These deficiencies are not to be charged against any particular type of school—be it the Sunday School, afternoon or all-day Hebrew School—or to any specific educational movement, as such. All our schools face them to a greater or lesser degree. What is important, therefore, is that we all face them together, that we recognize our collective responsibility to search for a solution to our common problem.

Problem of Motivation

In asking, "What shall we teach?" one must also ask, "What for?" I shall, therefore, consider some aspects of purpose as well as of content. The goal of all education, it is generally maintained, is the child. Our concern, that is, is the child's development of character, integration of personality, growth, happiness. The child's interests and needs at every age level are the springboard and culmination of his schooling. These aims and purposes have given rise to what is known as the "child-centered" school as opposed to the so-called "content" school. What is meant by these contrasting views was well expressed by a leading educator in the following statement: "When we say, 'The teacher teaches the boy geography,' the direct object in this sentence, grammar notwithstanding, should be *the boy* and not *geography*." Hence, in the child-centered school, geography will be omitted if it is not to the boy's interests and need; whereas, in the content school, it will be taught regardless of his need. The implication of either alternative for Jewish education is quite obvious. The one may discard much if not all of Jewish content, while the other may do violence to the child's personal interests. This conflict cannot be resolved as long as the child is taken to be the sole aim of education. Indeed, this conflict has been of much concern to Jewish educators in the past two decades, especially since the beginning of the decline of intensive education, such as was exemplified by the communal Hebrew School or Talmud Torah. The main reason for the decline, so the argument goes, is that the Jewish school has not been meeting the needs of the American Jewish child. Much evidence can be marshaled to substantiate this contention, if one views the evidence from the vantage-point of the pupil's reaction to the actual teachings in many of our schools.

What need, for example, does the child have for the study of Jewish history? Some teachers have been hard put in trying to show that the past may convey important lessons for the present. But this is just begging the question. For the child, if he is the only measure of all things that are taught him, may not see the need either for the lesson or for its appliction. All of us who have taught European Jewish history in the upper grades are well familiar with the strong resistance offered by children to this course of study. They do not want this phase of Jewish life brought home to them and they resent and reject all possible comparison with their own life in America. There are many factors that may account for our failure to persuade the student otherwise. The most important one, I believe, is that we try to appeal only to their own interests. I should say, parenthetically, that I am not discussing here a methodological question of making Jewish history interesting to the pupil, that is, entertaining, palatable, or even exciting. Our concern is to make it meaningful and valuable to him, so that he will really accept it as his own.

Another knotty question, more difficult to answer than the previous one, is "Why learn Hebrew?" Some try to motivate this subject-matter by pointing to the State of Israel in which Hebrew is the native tongue and which the students might someday visit. This is a remote, long-range goal realizable only by a minute fraction of our students. While it may excite their imagination for a moment, it can hardly serve as the bedrock upon which such a difficult subject as Hebrew may be grounded. A more immediate motivating factor, the Prayer Book, has all but ceased to be of practical import in learning Hebrew, even for mechanical reading. In most synagogues, the cantor is the only one who recites the prayers in Hebrew. The Rabbi, with an eye to meeting the needs of youth, leads congregational responsive reading only in English. How then can the synagogue service influence these same youths toward a desire for Hebrew study? Not unless they all want to become cantors, which is very unlikely. Again, the appeal to the child's personal interest falls short of its mark.

Or let us take another important subject in our curriculum, the Bible. What reason can we give the child that it is to his interest to know the Holy Scriptures? Some teachers would bring the words of Torah and Prophets down to the level of the pupil's everyday experience. That is a very good approach. But, from the point of view of the child's personal development, why does he have to go to this ancient and difficult source, when he can find many contemporary writings on similar subject-matter which may be more suitable to him in style and mode of thought? In fact, our schools have been supplied with many a book purporting to give a modern version of the Bible as literature, story, or legend. The actual text, even in translation, is rarely taught to our pupils. This omission is our tacit concession to them on the question of Bible study, when we try to gear content to their interests.

Desire for Happiness Not Adequate as Motivation

As a corollary of the "child-centered" idea there developed a theory of "happiness" as the aim of education. This theory gives people such a comfortable feeling that one who ventures to dispel some illusions about it may well be risking his professional reputation, if not his very career. But since I have risked both in recent years in order to bring Jewish education up to its proper level, I will not be in any greater jeopardy by saying a few words also about this notion of happiness. We all want our children to be happy, well-adjusted human beings. All of us, parents and teachers alike, are ready to do everything within our means to help them secure the maximum of joy in life. But as a theory, a *Weltanschauung*, a primary purpose of Jewish education, this goal has played havoc with many of our youth as well as our schools.

No one can guarantee happiness to another person, and no educational system can claim such power of assurance. At best, the school, and for that matter the home, can help the child to develop capacities for meeting life situations with fortitude and a sense of gratification. But when it comes down to the actual satisfaction of the child's personal needs which will make him happy, the Jewish school has been quite at a loss in trying to make its content meet those needs. The "happiness theory" asserts that the child will accept Jewish life if it is presented to him as a pleasurable experience. In actual application, any subject-matter that does not fit into this pattern is relegated to the background or omitted entirely, and the child's whole stay in the school becomes one continuous holiday celebration. Of course, we want, and we do have, joyous moments in Jewish life; and I do not mean to minimize the value of holidays as a source of joy. But Jewish life is not always a holiday. What happens in a time of adversity? Is the child, especially when he grows up and faces the world by himself, able to meet it? His impulse would be first to shrink from and then to reject his Jewishness altogether. It is not, he discovers, the ever joyous festival that was pictured to him by the school.

The Child and the Community

Here I come to my point of departure from the above mentioned theories. The Jewish school has a task to perform which exceeds the mere gratification of the child's personal interests. Its foundation is in the Jewish community, of which the child is an integral, active factor. That is, the child is to satisfy not only his personal needs but also the needs of the community. The two may sometimes be in conflict. Such conflict, however, can be resolved only if the interests and needs of the group are considered equal in importance with those of the child. Our school must therefore be bi-focal, that is, child-centered and community-centered at the same time. And both foci must be located in the historical continuity of our people. These are the living realities of Jewish education. The inseparable relationship between child and people was never questioned in past generations. Therefore, the problem of making Jewish life acceptable to the child through pleasurable experience or otherwise, never arose in the Jewish school. The child is the bearer of the future of his people. His people's life is his own life, in joy or in sorrow. Our sages of the Talmud expressed this relationship with Messianic vision. "Said Rav Yehuda in the name of Rav: What is the meaning of the verse, 'Touch not Mine anointed ones, and do My prophets no harm'? My anointed ones are the school children, and My prophets are the scholars" (*Sabbath*, 119:2). The school children, according to our sages, are the Messiahs or redeemers of their people.

Unless we ourselves, as teachers and leaders in Jewish education, accept this basic principle of child-people relationship, we really have nothing of Jewish content to teach our children. For content, or subject-matter of instruction, is only a phrase used to express the life and experiences of our people as they have come down to us in the written word and oral traditions.

When we say we want to transmit this content to our children, we mean that we want to continue the integral, inseparable relationship between them and their people. Content is not to be regarded just as an instrument for the child's character development, or general happiness. That is where the conflict arises. If it were just an instrument, there may be better, more attractive, and more highly tempered instruments, whereby those purposes might be achieved even with greater facility than through Jewish content. Jewish experience (and all experience is of the past) which we call the content of our teaching, has character of its own—having objective existence outside the schoolroom and its pupils. This is the object or subject-matter of instruction. But so is the child and his interests the object of our teaching. In our school, the child is to meet Jewish content as a living reality and grow and develop with it, that is, learn to recognize his relationship with his people. That is why our subject-matter should be taught, as far as possible, from its sources and not in paraphrase. A few illustrations will clarify the meaning of content as a living reality.

In the Hebrew Junior High School in San Francisco, children were studying Hebrew literature. They came across Hillel's famous statement: "If I am not for myself, who is for me?; and if I am for myself alone, what am I?; and if not now, when?" The teacher explained: This statement is not to be taken just as a wise maxim of an ancient sage. It has a life history which is reflected in the character of the man who pronounced it, in the turbulent times of the first century before the Common Era when Hillel lived, taught and guided his people, and in the yearning and accomplishments of the modern Halutzim in Israel who adopted it as one of their own mottoes. The class continued with a story about Hillel's patience, taken from the Talmud. After some discussion about the Talmud in general, its origin, character and composition, the children wanted to know whether the story in their book was identical with the Talmudic text. The teacher read to them from the *Masekhet Shabbat* (31:b) where the story is related, while they compared it word for word with their book. When they discovered the identity of the texts, they stopped for a moment in complete silence. They came up to the teacher's desk to look at the *Masekhet*, touched it, leafed it in great wonderment. Then one said, "We have studied the Talmud." Through an identity of "words," the children experienced an identification with their people of past generations. This is content.

Earlier I spoke of difficulties we encountered in motivating the study of Hebrew. We could overcome many an obstacle if we ourselves realized that the Hebrew language expresses the life and character of the Jewish people, and that, without a knowledge of this language, our youth cannot adequately understand and appreciate the character of our people. I do not mean only the ideas and values which are treasured in Hebrew writings. I mean the very nature of the language, its word formation, syntax, idiom, which conveys the essence of the Jewish character. Here, too, we teach content through the "word." I realize that I am speaking to a group of teachers, the vast majority of whom do not know Hebrew. That is not their fault, for they cannot be held responsible for what they had not been taught in their childhood. But as teachers and leaders in Jewish education today, they have an obligation to see to it that the present young generation shall receive proper instruction in the Heberew language and in the original Hebrew sources of Jewish content.

The entire subject-matter or content of instruction in our school may be expressed in one word, which we all know, but which we use in our classrooms much too seldom. That word is *Torah.* What we teach is Torah, in its widest all-inclusive sense; and our children should be made aware of it. They should know that they come to our schools to learn not just reading, translation, coloring and the like, but Torah—the life and length of our days as a people.

1954

A Community Endeavor
in Jewish Education

In a paper presented at the 1947 annual meeting of the American Association for Jewish Education, in Baltimore, Md., Jacob Lown, then Chairman of the Maine Jewish Council's Education Committee, charted the road which the Council had envisioned for its educational program in the State of Maine. Originally, he pointed out, the Council was formed for the purpose of coordinating fund-raising endeavors for overseas needs. Seven years later, it found it necessary also to embark upon a state-wide program of Jewish education. "Thus," he said, "the Council

435

started with *gemilut hasadim* and expanded into the field of Torah." This juxtaposition of two traditional fundamentals of Jewish existence, namely, learning and kind deeds, characterized the educational pursuits of the Maine Jewish Council when Philip W. Lown was its president, from 1945 to 1949.

One Community

The Jewish Community of Maine was then, and still is, a composite of three large centers in Portland, Bangor, and Lewiston-Auburn and some twenty-five small towns and hamlets, comprising a total of about 9,000 Jews in a general population of 900,000, spread over an expanse of 33,215 square miles, from Aroostok County in the north to Biddeford-Saco and the Atlantic Ocean in the south, a stretch of 250 miles. One may appropriately speak of the Jews of Maine as one community, whether inchoate or closely organized, for they are largely homogeneous, of traditional stock, and with a sense of kinship and mutual belonging. This may not be evident from the manner or degree of their formal communal organizations and institutions on a state-wide basis. On the contrary, the latter, insofar as they were brought into existence and functioned periodically, were the overt expressions of that sense of belonging that the Jews of Maine feel toward each other. At other times, when no state-wide organization was in operation, that feeling lay dormant, but it was no less potent. Thus, whether the Jews of Maine yielded to the demand of the hour and constituted themselves into a modern organized body, or preferred, on other occasions, to function more loosely and informally through personal association, both modes of operation were equally the manifestations of a communal entity, such as Maine Jewry has always been. The following account of the Jewish educational activities in the State of Maine will cover a brief span of three-and-a-half years, 1945-1949, when the entire Jewish community was formally organized in a representative body, the Maine Jewish Council. For, it was during that period that state-wide educational functions were undertaken and carried to a degree of fruition.

The New Program

What united the Jews of Maine for the first time formally, as pointed out above, was the ago-old tradition of *gemilut hasadim*— doing a kind deed for their needy brothers. They had been doing this for a long time, separately in each locality and individually, on a level of personal charity. But in 1938, the impact of the nazi onslaught against the Jews of Germany drew them closer together for a concerted effort, and they formed the Maine Jewish Committee (later named the Maine Jewish Council). While greater unity was thus achieved, the purpose in the succeeding seven years remained the same, namely, *gemilut hasadim* for overseas need. Then a new transformation took place. In 1945, the Maine Jewish Council extended its functions beyond those of fund-raising into the field of education and communal relations. It will be difficult to ascertain the reason for this change from objective data, first, because such data is very scant and second (and this is more important) because the motives for a change could not have arisen from objective data alone. The subjective element is, therefore, the more valid criterion for gauging the forces that brought about the expanded program.

In announcing this program, as President of the Council, Philip W. Lown, expressed that subjective feeling, perhaps for the entire community, when he said: "We recognized that Jewish education was still a step-child in the American Jewish communities. We realized that Jewish education means learning to live intelligently as Jewish Americans. We felt that Jewish knowledge is a source of personal dignity and security and that Jewish education can counteract the demoralizing effects of anti-Semitism. We became convinced that a sincere pride in our great heritage, a pride that comes through knowledge and proper attitudes, would furnish to our people the shock absorbers against the impact of these turbulent times." One must bear in mind that when this program was launched there had been Hebrew schools functioning in the three large cities in the State and there was a modicum of sporadic Jewish teaching in some of the small towns. What was the innovation that the Maine Jewish Council tried to bring about? There were some differences in outlook on the matter and, without elaborating on shades of opinion, two major trends may be noted here. One was that the Maine Jewish Council could serve only the small towns and villages which did not have any educational facilities, and the other was that it could and should serve all areas in the State, the large towns as well as the small ones. The second view reflected the principle that Jewish education is not only a communal responsibility but also a communal need, that is, all segments and localities of the community need it alike and that such need can be met only by a combined effort of a communal character, in the case of Maine, on a state-wide level. Under Philip Lown's leadership, the latter view seemed to prevail and for the time being became the basis of the Council's educational endeavors.

Another important factor that came into play at the very inception of the program was that, in assuming the new burden, the Maine Jewish Council was placed in a dual role: on the one hand, as the fund-raising arm of the United Jewish Appeal, and on the other hand, as the educational agency of Maine Jewry. In the eyes of many, neither role could justify the other. And even though the new program was greeted with enthusiasm by the Jews of Maine as a whole, the fund-raising role of the Council, paradoxically, counteracted its educational efforts. The paradox was that, while the fund-raising arm supplied the means for the educational enterprise, it stamped that enterprise as a *gemilat hesed*—as a charitable deed for the needy—and hence, as a diversion of means from the greater need, namely, Jewish reconstruction overseas. As will be indicated later, this dualism was never resolved. The program was, nevertheless, inaugurated in the hope that in due time and as a result of marked gains, Maine Jewry would accept it as its own, in and for itself.

Stages of Development

In the first stages, the emphasis, naturally, had to be placed on establishing educational facilities in the small towns and outlying districts where none had existed. Because of the small size of each locality and the distances involved the one-day-a-week session, commonly known as the Sunday School, was considered as the only type of school feasible in those areas. Within the first year, by the end of 1945, a network of Sunday Schools was established in eight centrally located towns, in Waterville, Augusta, Presque-Isle, Bidderford-Saco (which later expanded into a week-day Hebrew School), Bath, Rockland, Calais-St. Stephen, and Gardiner. A curriculum was designed by the Council's Executive Director especially to suit the needs and levels of the student body and geared to instruction by laymen, who staffed all those schools. The executive director also visited the schools periodically and provided pedagogic and administrative guidance and materials to the teaching personnel and the school committees.

The eight schools soon reached a total enrollment of 111 students (46 boys and 65 girls), or 90% of all the children of school-age, between 5½ and 17 years. They were divided into four groups: Alef, 5½-7 years; Bet, 8-10 years; Gimmel, 11-13 years; and Dallet, 14 years and up, forming a total of 19 classes that met every Sunday, 10 to 12 in the morning. For those who lived too far away from the school centers, a course of home study was provided, following the same curriculum and guided by the Council office. At the time, 10 boys and girls, ages 6-14 engaged in the home studies. All expeditures for school facilities, equipment and supplies were defrayed by the local school committees. The students paid for their textbooks and materials. With the exception of one shcool, there was no charge for registration or tuition. Parallel with the schools, a series of public lectures was sponsored by the Maine Jewish Council in several centrally located towns, and adult cultural groups were organized in Biddeford-Saco, Calais, Bath, Lewiston-Auburn. Gardiner, Pittsfield, and Rumford. These groups comprised a total of some 70 men and women, who met regularly weekly, bi-weekly or monthly and engaged in a program of self-study of Jewish life and lore, prepared, guided and directed by the Council's Executive Director. Another educational medium was provided through the Council's newly founded monthly publication, *The Gazette*, which contained articles on literature, the Bible and Talmud, Jewish life in the past and present, book reviews and current events. The office of the Council also served as the agency for spreading Jewish books for young and old.

The Hebrew Schools

The second step in advancing Jewish education on a communal, state-wide level was to involve the existing Hebrew Schools of the large towns in the program as a whole. Each of these schools had its own principal and teaching staff and a local education committee to guide its affairs. In November 1946, the professionals and some lay representatives of the Hebrew Schools of Portland, Bangor, Lewiston-Auburn, and Bidderford-Saco met in Augusta, under the auspices of the Council's Education Committee, to consider their mutual interests and their relationship to the state-wide program. The factual situation in those schools at the time, more than any other factor, pointed to their need for a central agency, not only to coordinate their efforts, but also to render consultation and guidance to each of them locally. For in that year, all the four Hebrew Schools had acquired new professional staffs—principals and teachers. The turn-over of teachers was almost a perennial occurrence, and at the end of every two or three years the principle, too, was changed. The joint meeting in Augusta had a salutary effect on all of them, first, in the mere fact that they met as colleagues and co-workers in the same field and, second, in that they realized that their respective interests somehow rested on the foundations of Jewish education in the State as a whole. A similar meeting of the lay Sunday School teachers at the end of the first year, held in Waterville, revealed their interdependence and need for sharing their educational experiences as well as their call for central planning, guidance and coordination.

In the subsequent years of the Council's operation in this field, service was rendered to the Hebrew schools in the form of observation and consultation, as called upon, while the Sunday Schools and the adult cultural functions continued under the Council's direct guidance and supervision. In turn, the principals of the Hebrew schools, the local rabbis and some lay leaders helped the Council in its adult educational program as speakers and lecturers at cultural meetings and as contributors of literary articles in its monthly publication.

The Portland Survey

Toward the end of 1948, the executive director was requested to make a survey of Jewish education in the city of Portland, under the auspices of the local Jewish Federation. The immediate demand for such a survey was prompted by the formation of a new congregation with a religious Conservative orientation. Maine Jewry, as indicated above, was very largely of a traditional Orthodox outlook, and its educational and communal institutions bore the imprint of that outlook. The Hebrew schools as well as the Sunday schools were thus conducted in the spirit of Orthodox observance of custom and ritual. In Portland, where there were four synagogues serving a population of some 4,000 souls, the Hebrew School could function as the central educational institution for all the congregations, because they were all Orthodox in character. In 1948, a Conservative movement came into being and established a congregation of its own. Thereupon, the central Hebrew school, with its Orthodox orientation and five-day a week session, came under close scrutiny as to its ability to serve all segments of the Jewish population. Parenthetically, it should be mentioned that a feeling of separation from the Hebrew school had prevailed in the community for some time, for since 1942 there existed a local Sunday school for 5-8 year olds, sponsored by the Jewish Community Center, with no connection to the Hebrew school and with no direct transition from one to the other.

The Federation's Survey Committee, under the chairmanship of Joseph Larkin, who was also a leading member of the Maine Jewish Council, did not purport to analyze the religious leanings of the Jews of Portland, but only their educational needs and the manner in which those needs could best be satisfied. We shall not record here the details of the Survey, its findings or recommendations. However, two salient facts revealed the necessity for a statewide educational agency. While Portland is the largest city in the State and has also the largest Jewish population, it is still not sizable enough to have a central bureau of its own to coordinate the divergent trends in Jewish education, which already in 1948 had made themselves strongly felt. The second and even more revealing fact was the high aspiration that the Jews of Portland (and this was most likely typical of the state as a whole) had for the Jewish education of their children. That, too, could not be cultivated, adequately interpreted and met by Portland Jewry alone and on its own.

The parents' high educational goal was indicated by the response to a questionnaire presented in a house-to-house canvass to 331 families with school-age children, 5-18 years, which constituted perhaps 80% of the Jewish school-child population in the city. When asked what subjects parents considered of primary importance in the Jewish education of their children, two-thirds of the responses included "all items of ritual and ceremony, all items of history and contemporary Jewish life, a reading knowledge of elementary Hebrew, a knowledge of Yiddish, and Jewish literature in English." Equally high was the percentage of those who desired a Jewish education beyond the proverbial Bar-Mitzvah age, even beyond high school, in courses of study in higher Jewish schools, adult education or college. The surveyor came to the conclusion that there was "a receptivity among the parents for an intensive, as well as extensive, Jewish educational program" in Portland.

However, he further observed, "many of them may not realize the implication of this in terms of years of study for their children, number of hours per day, or days per week. These matters have to be interpreted to the parents, taking their own conception of Jewish education as a starting point."

Reporting on the outcome of the Survey early in 1949, Israel Bernstein, President of the Jewish Federation of Portland and a past President and Honarary President of the Maine Jewish Council, indicated that the main tenet of the surveyor's recommendations had been adopted by the Federation's Board of Directors, to wit: "'A program of Jewish education, no matter by whom sponsored, must be related to the Jewish Community as a body, of which the individual is an integral part. It is therefore the responsibility of the community as an organized entity to provide for Jewish education and also give it general direction and guidance. The Jewish Federation of Portland should establish an Education Committee with the following functions: a) To promote general interest and social demand for Jewish education; b) to coordinate the plans of all agencies and organizations that are engaged in Jewish education work; c) to advise the Federation Board of Directors on the financial needs of the educational agencies; and d) to work in conjunction with the education department of the Maine Jewish Council.' On this sound foundation," Mr. Bernstein concluded, "can well and securely rest a new communal system of Jewish Education in Portland." But the pivotal point of this recommendation—item d)—faded out even before the entire survey could be acted on. That year, the Maine Jewish Council and its education department ceased to exist.

The dissolution of the Council was primarily due to the fact that the raising of funds for overseas needs had remained its dominant purpose. It has not transformed itself into a communal agency of mutual concern among all segments and localities in the State. Its educational services in the small towns and even in the large centers were still regarded by one section or another as an act of *gemilut hasadim*, and not as a common need. Thus, the inner contradiction between charity and learning had not been overcome, and when the pressure of the former had somewhat relaxed, the latter was suspended altogether. The fund-raising function became decentralized again and the educational program, having depended on that function, lost its financial basis of operation.

Camp Lown

In the same year (1945) that the Maine Jewish Council started its state-wide educational activities, another institution of educational import was established under its auspices and general direction, and that was a children's summer camp, located on the shores of one of the Belgrade Lakes, near Oakland, Maine. The camp was conceived as an integral part of the Council's educational program. It was named *Camp Lown*, in honor of the family of Philip W. Lown, who had rendered outstanding service in all phases of Jewish life in the State. Its objective was to create the kind of environment that would be most conducive to the Jewish upbringing of the young generation. As stated in its first formulation of purpose, issued in October, 1945: "In Camp Lown [the Maine Jewish Council] hopes to create an environment of Jewish living—a life pulsating with Jewish tradition, with the observance of customs and ceremonies of the Sabbath and holidays, vibrating with song and dance, and permeated with the ideals of the Jewish heritage. What is equally important, such an environment is to become an integral part of the general American environment; the child will associate his Jewish living with his Americanism, without conflict or incongruity. The children who will have experienced this type of living in camp, will bring back to their homes and Jewish schools a new message of dynamic Jewish life."

The camp was originally intended only for the children of the State of Maine, and its first year of operation, in 1946, was conducted on that basis. It has an enrollment of 105 boys and girls, ages 7-13 years, who came from 21 towns and rural sections in all parts of the State. The campers differed widely in their Jewish background, 36 of them having attended Hebrew School, 30 having had one year in the newly founded Sunday schools, and the rest, no Jewish education at all. Those coming from small towns and rural sections had had little or no opportunity to meet other Jewish children of their respective ages, except in the one-day a week classes of the Sunday schools, where such had existed at the time. It was the aim of the camp to weld them into a Jewish children community, at least for the camping season.

The program of activities was diversified, covering the usual camp functions, such as sports, crafts, dramatics, and the like, but permeated with the unifying spirit of Jewish living. It included, for example, a course of study in Hebrew on a voluntary basis, which was nevertheless attended by over 90% of the campers. Characterizing the program as a whole, the camp director pointed out in his report at the end of the season: "What we tried to avoid, and I believe succeeded in, is drawing a line of demarcation between Jewish and general elements in the program. We did not have so-called 'Jewish content' and general 'American content'. It was an integral program of American Jewish living that found expression in a variety of forms; and the campers accepted it as such." This was, of course, made possible by a dedicated counselor staff, most of whom had a sound knowledge of Judaica and were personally committed to the ideals of Jewish life. It was further enhanced by the whole-hearted support rendered by Philip W. Lown, President; Saul G. Chason, Chairman, and the other officers and members of the Camp Committee. A goodly number of the campers who attended that first year and following seasons, later joined as members of the camp staff and thereby helped to develop a Camp Lown tradition that has lasted now for almost an entire generation. In the course of time, the camp extended its enrollment to several states on the eastern seaboard, virtually from Maine to Florida. It has modified its program in line with the demands of the hour. Its basic character, however, has remained the same—that of a Jewish cultural camp, steeped in the spirit and practices of American Jewish traditions.

Camp Lown has been in continuous operation since its inception. Apparently, it was not affected by the dissolution of its parent body, the Maine Jewish Council, and that could be ascribed to the fact that it had established itself on the fundamental principle of Torah, independently of *gemilut hasadim*. Not that the element of kind deeds was lacking in the camp administration. Quite the contrary, it offered scholarships where needed and the campers themselves participated in functions at camp, which contributed to the needs of others in this country and abroad. But its underlying principle of Torah—Jewish learning—was accepted as an end in itself, as a personal need shared and met by all, together, and not as a charitable deed offered by one to the other. This is the way of Torah alongside *gemilut hasadim* and, combined with *avodah*, worship, it is one of the "three things on which the world rests."

As one looks back twenty years ago on the eduational efforts of the Maine Jewish Council—the tremendous amount of energy expended by its lay and professional workers—one wishes to find some tangible, lasting values resulting from that entire undertaking. Those values, again, cannot be measured by the criteria of organizational continuity or statistical data. In 1945, when the Maine Jewish Council projected new or additional goals on its horizon, there was something vital stirring the Jews of Maine as they reached out for those goals. They then turned their attention to the inner side of Jewish needs, trying also to help themselves while they continued helping others. In this process, the best forces in the community came to the fore and their effort revealed their genuine concern with the pulsating realities affecting every phase of their communal interests. And this is of lasting value, for the genuinely real begets the real. The young generation that came under its influence will, no doubt, find their own proper ways and means of coping with the realities of Jewish life in their native State.

1966

Origin and Function of Modern Tenets in Jewish Education

In the past few decades of Jewish education in the United States, there has accumulated a body of principles which has been accepted without questioning in most of our educational institutions. We may call those principles the dogmas of modern Jewish education. A dogma is a principle of knowledge that is posited at the basis of a system of thought without accounting for the origin of that principle, its presuppositions and implications. In religion, a dogma may be an article of faith; in philosophy it may be a concept of reason; in education it often is a concept and method of instruction. All dogmas are teleological, that is, they anticipate a desirable end, or purpose, be it the confirmation of belief, the ascertainment of necessity in reason, or the development of character. Assuming that these ends are worthy of our pursuit, our concern is whether the underlying principles, when put to the test, will not fail us on the way to our goal. For what makes a dogma questionable is that it often contains hidden elements which militate against the very purpose for which it has been posited. Our task is to analyze those elements with a view to discovering their origin and function in theory and practice.

The Object of Instruction

A major dogmatic principle adopted in Jewish education from the general field is that we teach "the child" and not "subject matter." This is the well known doctrine of the "child centered" school as distinguished from the "content school." As one leading educator phrased it: "When we say, 'the teacher teaches the boy geography,' the direct object of this sentence, grammar notwithstanding, should be *the boy* and not *geography*." In teaching the boy, then, we are concerned with his "character" development, his "personality," needs, and adjustments. It would follow that if geography or any other subject did not contribute to those needs, it should be eliminated from the curriculum. More important, whatever the content of the curriculum may be, it should be geared to the boy's needs, interests and adjustment in life. A corollary of this principle is that we teach the "whole child." For if the child is the direct object of instruction, there would be no character or personality unless the child as a whole constituted that object. This educational principle sounds so plausible, so self evident, that its dogmatic nature is hardly suspected by modern educators, even by those who feel a need for remodeling their entire educational structure now in existence. Thus we hear again of "substantial changes" recently contemplated by Jewish educators, who declare: "We must educate the total child—there can be no compartmentalization—the Jewish self is his total self so that character education becomes a primary concern of the educational process."* This principle is interrelated with two others, so that any one of the three forms a presupposition of the other two, and together they constitute a sort of tripod foundation of modern Jewish educational theory.

---

*This quotation and others in the same context are taken from *The Record*, Winter 1965, issued by the Northern N. J. Region of the United Synagogue of America. They represent the basic views of many modern educators.

Adjustment and Change

The second dogmatic principle is that "we teach the child how to live in the present." The educational process, thus, has two factors, the child and his surrounding present, and teaching consists of adjusting the former to the latter. Consequently, we should teach the child only such elements of the past as will serve his present needs. As envisioned by the planners of the "new" Jewish education, "subject matter in our schools can be evaluated only by the relevancy of the subject matter to life situations and practical application." The third dogmatic principle is that of constant change in the child's present environment. The two factors in the educational process—the child and his present environment—can therefore be adjusted only by means of an experimental curriculum, that is, the adjustment of the child to his environemnt is always in the nature of experimentation. One can never tell what the constantly changing present may demand of the child in the next moment. Symptomatic of this approach is the fact that for the past two decades, at least, a recurrent theme at the annual conference of the National Council for Jewish Education, has been "Jewish Education in a changing Community," without coming to rest on a single abiding element. From this approach also stems the indeterminateness of content in the Jewish schools, for the teacher has to change constantly his choice of past elements to suit the child's ever changing present needs. The three dogmas stated above—that the direct object of teaching is the total child for his adjustment to an ever changing present by means of an experimental curriculum—are grounded in erroneous conceptions of all three factors in the educational process; the object of teaching, the present, and the meaning of change.

Teacher-Pupil Correlation

Truthfully, we do not and cannot teach the child in part or in toto. The child is not and cannot be the object of our teaching. Teaching is only one term in the correlation of teaching-learning, and the teacher, as such, does not exist independently of the child-learner, as such. Furthermore, both teacher and child do exist independently of each other as persons, and their teacher-learner correlation comes into being only when the former teaches *something* to the latter. Without that something the correlation is not there, and the one is not a teacher nor the other a learner. That something has an objective reality of its own. It does not originate with the teacher and certainly not with the learner. The former acquired it and transmits it to the latter. This is what is meant by tradition, which is the subject matter of all learning, whether of the sciences, the humanities, or religious-ethical precepts. In the process, that is, when the two meet in a teacher-learner correlation, they both may put their personal stamp on the subject matter. They may introduce new insights and may even create new subject matter. But in order for the new to have objective validity, it must rest on tradition.

Pure Subjectivism

What we can and should teach, then, is content, not the child. Many modern educators have deprecated this primary factor in the educative process, with deplorable results. This is not just a matter of shift in emphasis. There is a basic difference that shows up at every phase of the child's career in our shcools. The educator, referred to above, who changed the meaning of the sentence, "the teacher teaches the boy geography," to indicate that the boy is the direct object of our teaching, did not only create a grammatical oddity; he also introduced an objective anomaly. For, he disregarded "geography" or the content, and still thought that he could just "teach the boy." The educational process was thus converted into pure subjectivism—opinion, attitude, character development, personality growth. This is bound to happen in every educational system where the child is posited as the direct object of teaching. Strange as it may seem, the child, in such a system, becomes depersonalized. Instead of teaching things to the child, the teacher makes him the *thing* to be taught. This is the hidden fallacy of the dogma: while speaking in terms of personality growth, it overlooks the child as a *person*. The fallacy is more striking when the teacher claims he can and should teach the total child.

The Child as a Person

To speak of the total child can have meaning only if the child is regarded as a person, that is, a socially oriented individual in his home and community environment. A person is one who assumes responsibility within and toward his group—in our case, one who assumes the mitzvot (commandments) of Jewish life. Of course, the child cannot be expected to be fully aware of his social orientation and responsibility; but he has to have some awareness of them at every stage of his development, varying with the degree of his maturity. This awareness can be fostered only by the home and community, the latter insofar as the child participates in it and comes under its influence. It is what the home and community expect of the child that makes a difference in his education in school. This leads us to the fundamental issue in Jewish education, namely, who is responsible for it? The answer given throughout our history has been unmistakable: it is the responsibility of the parents, and that is, not just to send the child to school and bear the costs, but also to see to it that child learns, in other words, make him aware of his responsibility for the mitzvot of life. This idea is expressed in the meaning of bar-mitzvah.

In Jewish tradition, learning has always been regarded as a *mitzvah* in the simple sense of the word. In the teacher-learner correlation, which involves two persons, there are two distinct mitzvot, teaching on the part of the teacher and learning on the part of the child. As long as the child is not yet a bar-mitzvah (regardless of chronological age), that is, unable to fulfill his obligations altogether by himself, the responsibility devolves on the parents to see to it that he carries out that mitzvah. Jewish learning is thus *not toward* bar-mitzvah; it is the mitzvah itself. When the child is of tender age and therefore not ready to assume the full burden, his parents carry that burden with him. When he becomes of age, that is, bar-mitzvah, he assumes the mitzvah of learning on his own responsibility. But when the school steps in and takes over that responsibility, presumably to make the child into a "person," it undertakes an impossible task.

Function of the School

The "child oriented" school claims it can perform that task— teach character development, personality growth, in a word, make the child into a person. And this is, in effect, what the educators who contemplate "new changes" in Jewish education purport to do. "We recognize," they say, "that in vital areas, what the Jewish school is doing is not supplementing or supplanting the family or the secular school, or society at large, but, rather, that the school is

449

actually the *sole* agency in the area of imparting morals, ethics, patterns of conduct, and, in other words, Judaism." Even more far-reaching is their contention that Jewish education; will thus "become more related to the thought processes, to the feelings and life situations of the child, it will become more enjoyable and by becoming more enjoyable will have succeeded in reducing, or eliminating absolutely, resistance to Jewish education by furnishing the ultimate satisfaction in showing relevancy."

If the Jewish school is the *sole* agency for doing all this, it does supplant the family and society, which are the natural agents in molding the child as a person. What relevancy can the child find in those teachings if they are not demanded or expected by home and society and do not emanate from them? How will those teachings be made relevant, to whom and to what? If the school is the sole agency, there remains only one higher instance of appeal for relevancy, and that is the child himself, his pleasure and self-interest. Even if the school succeeded in founding a children's society of its own that would presumably exercise the desired influence on the individual, it would still be only a limited, artificial scheme and would hardly have relevancy to actual everyday living. It would not, in any event, represent "the life situations of the child" that the new approach envisions. For a school, ultimately, can only reflect the ideas and ideals of the society in which it operates. It cannot become a substitute for the natural agencies of home and community. In a voluntary, democratic society, such as the Jewish community, this is certainly the case. The school, therefore, cannot claim to teach the total child or even a major portion of him. Apart from the fact that the child is involved in the school only for short intervals of time, even when increased to a maximum, the child as a whole—as a person—does not grow out of the school. On the contrary, he comes as a person *to* the school, and throughout his career there he continues to interact with it as person to person. The child as a whole, as a person, orients himself at every level of his growth toward his home and community, and not toward his school, no matter how promising its teachings may be for his "pleasure" and "happiness." The school simply cannot fulfill such promise. If there is to be a rethinking of the goals and practices in contemporary Jewish education (and that is most necessary) it should be in the spirit of "shuva Yisrael"—a return to some of the fundamental tenets that have always been valid in Jewish life. One such tenet is that the parents, the home, are primarily and ultimately responsible for the Jewish upbringing of their children. The school, supported by home and community, will impart to the child the necessary subject matter that will help the parents and society to shape his Jewish personality. If we look around, we shall find that parents are waiting to be awakened toward that responsibility.

The End Result of Teaching

The second dogma of modern Jewish education—that we teach the child for adjustment to his present—has also been beset with difficulties in theory as well as in practice. Its underlying assumption is that all genuine learning comes through experience and is for experience. Since experience is factually in the present, the child learns through the present for the present, that is, he finds himself in a series of successive moments of interaction with his environment and at each step he learns to adjust to a given situation. What prompts him to "learn" is the urge to satisfy his impulses and desires. The function of the teacher is, then, to set up the conditions of learning—the factors of environment—so that through interaction with them the child will "learn" how to satisfy his desires. This is the biological interpretation of learning, which has been adopted in modern education in general, and applied to Jewish education in particular. It is significant that the examples illustrating this process are usually drawn from the behavior of animals and human infants. In experiments with cats, for instance, it was shown that the animal learns through trial and error to go through the correct channels of a maze in order to reach for food placed at the other end. Experiments with small children show similar results, namely, adaptation to the environment in order to satisfy a natural desire. On the negative side, if a child experiences an unpleasant encounter with environment, he will avoid it. The child who burns his finger by playing with the flame of a candle, will learn not to do it again. The learning process, according to this theory, has two phases: the pleasure of the interaction and the satisfaction of the desire. The learner will accept the process and its results if they are pleasant and gratifying and he will reject them if they are unpleasant and ungratifying. Applied to the Jewish school, it would follow that the child will accept his Jewishness if the learning process is pleasant and he finds it satisfying, and he will reject his Jewishness if the process is unpleasant and unsatisfying.

451

Educative Norms and Standards

There is no question that on the biological level, rejection of a process will occur if it does not satisfy a desire, although it is not true that the process itself must always be pleasant in order to be accepted in pursuit of a desired end. The more decisive factors are the extent to which the end result is worthwhile and the child's capacity to attain it. A child may get into a fight to obtain a toy and come out of it scratched up, yet satisfied with holding the toy in his hand. To him the end result was worthwhile even though the process was unpleasant. And, having learned it, he will repeat the process in pursuit of other desires he considers worthwhile. But the real educational question, which modern educators have failed to answer satisfactorily, is whether the child is capable of determining the actual worth-whileness of all his desires even on a biological level (such as, food and hygiene habits), not to speak of the social-ethical level. What if the child gets into a fight to obtain a gun? Obviously, by our social standards and common sense, both the desire and the means of satisfying it are considered improper. What is the educative process and what is the educator's function in that kind of situation, or, for that matter, in any situation where standards of conduct and proper goals are to be taught? If we are to direct the child on the proper path, how do we teach him and toward what end?

In reality, we cannot teach the child proper ends by experience alone or by training him to adjust to the present. (There may be nothing wrong in the child obtaining the gun at present. It is his future use of it that may be disastrous). When it comes to education of proper ends, the problem is not whether the child accepts or rejects a given educative process, but whether he accepts a *norm* for that process, not set by himself. Similarly, it is no longer then a question of satisfying a desire, but of setting a goal *to be desired*. On this level of education we deal with norms, standards and goals, which do not grow out of the mere biological desires of the child. They may be, and often are, even in conflict with his desires.

Teaching Is for the Future

This places the child in a social setting, and what we teach him are the norms established by society in the past and the goals to be pursued by him as a member of that society, for the future. This is especially the case in the field of Jewish education, where our teachings have meaning only in relation to the Jewish people or community, as a whole. What we teach is historical past, and our goal is its continuity into the future. The present can never be a goal, for in order even to grasp it we would first have to delimit it. Is the present the few hours the child spends in school, the day he passes at home and at play? Is it to be measured in intervals of weeks and months filled with a variety of activities, or by years and decades comprising a complex of events? Unless we think in terms of past and future, we do not know where the present begins or ends. And yet, there is a present factor in the educative process, and that is the child himself. The child *is* the present to whom the past is being taught with an outlook toward the future. He is the present, means that he is the bearer of the past into the future. And that future is not just the child's; it is his and his people's together, inseparably. Such an outlook makes a fundamental difference in the teacher-learner correlation in the Jewish school, on the one hand, and between the school and the home and community, on the other hand.

Condition of Acceptance of Jewishness

The present is the child. If, then, the teacher teaches for an adjustment to the present, the teaching process is reduced to an adjustment of the child to himself. He becomes the criterion of what is and what is not desirable and acceptable, on the basis of his pleasure and happiness. What is problematic in this approach is not that parents and teachers seek the child's happiness in association with Jewish living, but that pleasure is made a criterion and happiness a condition of the child's acceptance of his Jewishness. The goal of education is thus not the objective reality of his Jewishness but his subjective feeling of fleeting moments of pleasure and happiness. The real goal, which is a striving for the future, is over-shadowed, because pleasure and happiness, being changeable, subjective emotions, are in themselves aimless. For, even if the Jewish school should succeed in making all instruction momentarily most pleasant and in showing the child that it is all relevant to his happiness, there would always be a wider field open to him where he might seek greater pleasure and more promise of happiness than he could find in his Jewishness. This is the paradox, or paralogism, of the dogma that the child is taught Judasim for his adjustment to the present. His acceptance of the teaching is predicated on his happiness, and his happiness is predicated on his acceptance of the teaching. The truth of the matter is that neither the acceptance nor the happiness is determined by the school. The child and the adult members constitute the Jewish community for good or for bad, for happiness or adversity. The child's acceptance of his Jewishness, in different degrees and on different levels of his development, comes from the home and community. The school can only deepen its meaning by relating the past to him and lead him, pointing toward the future. The Jewish present, as far as the school is concerned, is the child himself, as a person, molded by his Jewish home and society.

Change and Experiment

The third dogma of Jewish education, namely, experimentation, grows out of the fallacies of the other two dogmas. The child, as a present reality, is a changing being. If he is the object of our teaching for his adjustment to the present, the teaching is by its very nature and application a constantly changing process, a perpetual experiment. Symptomatic of this approach is the preoccupation with methodology in the Jewish schools. Poor results are attributed to wrong methods rather than to the fact that the school is trying to teach the wrong thing. Hence there is continual experimentation with new methods. But there is yet a deeper fallacy in this outlook and that is the very concept of change. The modern Jewish school sees the child placed in a changing community and, since it has to adjust the child to the present, it feels it must continually change the teaching along with the changing community. In such a teaching process nothing abides. The community changes, the child changes, and the adjustment which is the presumed purpose of instruction, also changes. What it is that stays on, that the teacher hands over to the child for him to carry along out of school, neither the educator nor the learner is quite sure. Because, out of a welter of incessant changes no abiding element can be procured, except perhaps a statistical probability.

This statistical concept of change is erroneous because change cannot be conceived without a constant that changes. Even the most general statement, "it changes," posits an "it" that undergoes change. More specifically, in human affairs change does not just happen by "it-self." It is man "him-self" who brings about change, whether by producing new technological conditions or by direct transformation of social relations, or both. It then devolves on man to decide which of the changes he has produced are to be continued and cultivated into new constants, and which are to be discarded or further modified. The proper guage is the past, because it is the only thing that abides, even in its various metamorphoses. The true criterion for new constants is the desirable aim set toward the future. When we look to the past for that which abides, we must be able to discern in it the eternal verities, unchangeable in themselvs. These are the things we can teach to our children. For we cannot teach that which is in ceaseless formation. We can only teach that of the past which has been formed and abides.

Practical Application

There are two major areas in the Jewish school curriculum, which are directly affected by the theoretical outlook discussed above, namely, the Hebrew language and Bible. In the following sections an attempt will be made to analyze the educational content and methods of instruction of each of these areas.

The Hebrew Language

The question of purpose and function of the Hebrew language in the Jewish school in America has vexed educators for many decades and especially since the rebirth of the State of Israel in 1948. Whatever purpose Hebrew had had in the past, with the establishment of the State it assumed new dimensions and thus created an effervescent condition that to this day has not yet found its equilibrium. Heretofore, Hebrew was regarded, for the most part, as a holy tongue of prayer and ritual or as a language of books, but not for everyday use. The impact of the reborn State of Israel on the American Jewish community has brought, among many other values, a new awareness of the Hebrew language as a vernacular. While the study of Hebrew as a spoken language has not assumed mass proportions in the United States, it has become a widespread goal and a new motivation in the Hebrew school curriculum. In extreme cases, Hebrew has not only beocme the basis for the study of Judaism but has also been posited as the *sine-qua-non* for the very existence of the Jewish people. Without Hebrew, it is argued, the Jewish community cannot survive. While there is an element of truth in this assertion, the historical facts have been blurred, and the real function of Hebrew in Diaspora education has been misconstrued.

The Alexandrian Argument

The proponents of Hebrew as an absolute goal and medium in Jewish education argue from the history of the Jewish community in Alexandria, Egypt, which flourished in the first centuries before and after the common era and disappeared without exerting an influence on Jewish life in subsequent generations. This, it is said, was due to the fact that Alexandrian Jewry did not cultivate the Hebrew language, and that even its leading scholar and Biblical exegete, Philo, hardly knew the Bible in the original. While the historical facts have been corroborated in the main, the advocates of Hebrew have slanted the causal relationships out of their true perspective. Alexandrian Jewry left no trace in Jewish life not because it did not speak or know Hebrew, but because it was estranged from the mainstream of Jewish thought, which was rabbinic Judaism. It did not cultivate the Hebrew language because it had no need for it. Its mode of thinging was throughly Hellenized and the Greek language was for it the more appropriate medium of expression. The neglect of Hebrew in Alexandria was not the cause, but the result, of its severance from the vital forces of Judaism. Philo's philosophical writings were not preserved by the Jews not because they were not written in Hebrew, but because they had no Hebrew thought and spirit. The major works of Saadia and Maimonides were also not written in the Hebrew language, yet they became the spiritual possession of Jewry throughout the ages. Philo's writings, on the other hand, were attuned to the current Greek philosophies, which, having come into contact with Jewish religious precepts, laid the foundation of Christiantiy. This is why it was the Patristic Church that preserved Philo's writings for posterity.

Hebrew, as such, will not assure the survival of the Jewish people, but, on the contrary, the people will retain the Hebrew language as one of its treasures as long as it will serve its spiritual needs, which have their source in Jewish tradition. Neither will Hebrew be cultivated as a vernacular merely to serve as a bridge between American Jewry and Israel. That may be done by a limited number of persons, scholars, tourists, and the like. But as a spoken language it can never become the goal and medium of Jewish education in America. In general, Jewish life here cannot flourish as a dependent on borrowed spirituality from Israel or anywhere else. It must find vitality within itself and draw sustenance from the sources of its heritage. This task devolves equally on the Jewish community in Israel and in the Diaspora. The bond between the two will then be woven out of a spiritual substance that will never break. But that is not a matter of linguistics.

Hebrew in the Jewish School

The proposed role of Hebrew as an absolute goal and a medium of instruction lies at the root of the difference between the "child centered" and the "content centered" Jewish schools. The former, which considers the child as the object of teaching, claims it can teach every child in Hebrew. For its goal is to develop attitudes, pleasurable experiences, and (Hebrew being in vogue) an adjustment to the present. The amount of Hebrew learned does not really matter here. The so-called "conversational Hebrew," which many schools have introduced under various guises, may well serve this purpose. It is pleasant, popular, meets an immediate desire, and makes no great demands on the student. Simple observation of the products of those schools will reveal the fallacy of making Hebrew the goal and medium of learning. Too many students have come out of those schools losing both ends: they did not learn the Hebrew language and they forfeited the Jewish heritage.

On the other hand, the school that undertakes to teach Hebrew to the child for the purpose of learning Hebraic source material, realizes that not every child can or will learn the language sufficiently to enable him to reach those sources in the original. Such a school must therefore establish a unified curriculum with parallel classes for those who will learn Hebrew as part of that curriculum, and those who will not take, or take to, the Hebrew language. The latter will receive their instruction entirely in their native language, which in our case is English. But even those who will take Hebrew on the elementary and high school level will master it only for the reading of original source material or text. Discussion and interpretation have to be conducted in the native tongue, if the source material is to have basic validity for the

457

learner. This has been the Hebraic tradition of Jewish education in the Diaspora through the ages, beginning with the Second Commonwealth. As will be shown later in the section on teaching the Bible, *targum*— translation became a fundamental principle of instruction yet in the days of Ezra. Hebrew, thus, has an important place in the curriculum of the American Jewish school insofar as it enables the learner to reach the sources of Judaism in the original, but not as a vernacular or medium of teaching when it comes to giving interpretation, significance and meaning to the text.

Historical Motive of the Tarbut Schools

There was a short period in modern Jewish history when Hebrew was introduced in our schools as a spoken language and sole medium of instruction. That was during the first three or four decades of the present century in Eastern Europe, in the *Heder Metukan* and the *Tarbut Gymnasia.* But there, the time and conditions of Jewish life demanded it. Those schools were in reality *hachsharot,* preparatory stations, for settlement in Eretz Israel, where the Hebrew language had already taken root as a vernacular. In the Tarbut schools Hebrew was taught as a "natural" language for "over there." Even those who had dreamed of autonomous Jewish communities in Poland, Lithuania, Czechoslovakia, where Hebrew would become "native" to the young generation, soon discovered that their hopes could be realized only "over there," in Eretz. The Hebrew poet A. Broides, writing in honor of the twentieth anniversary of the Tarbut Gymnasia in Poland, admonished the graduates as follows:

> For the morrow will find you in throngs on the road
> Arm in arm; your 'wakening song will resound.
> Remember that Eretz will harness for backbreaking work
> To bring life to the swamps, to the rocks in the ground" (my transl.).

That was the true aspiration of those schools, and rightfully so. But right or wrong, that has never been applicable to the Jewish school in the United States. We and they have the same roots, and together we look to a wider tomorrow, for us here and for them over there.

Teaching the Bible

The teaching of Bible in the Jewish school has often been posited primarily as a problem in language preparation. While that is partially true when the Bible is taught in the orginial, it is not the real issue when related to the curriculum as a whole. If the function of Hebrew in our school is properly evaluated, as analyzed above, the question of language preparation is resolved by teaching the Bible in the original only to those students who can or will be prepared for it linguistically; provided again, that the preparation is only for reading of the Hebrew text and not also for discussion and interpretation in Hebrew. Those who cannot or will not be prepared for the original, should be taught Bible in a standard English translation. The real question, then, in Bible teaching is not a matter of linguistics but of content and purpose. And here, as in the case of the Hebrew language, the basic dogmas of modern Jewish education are reflected in what happens in the classroom.

Bible as Aggada

Those who take the child as the object of instruction teach him Bible as story, *aggada*, covering the narrative portions, mostly in paraphrase or abbreviation. They maintain that the story is best suited to the child's interests. It is simple, pleasant, entertaining, and gives him the feeling or "attitude" of learning Torah. Actually, he is learning only Bible stories of the same type he was taught in nursery or kindergarten. And when the teacher tries to derive some moral lesson from those stories, on the level of the child's modern thinking, he runs into difficulty with archeology or the historicity of events, especially those that occurred miraculously. This difficulty arises from the empirical approach to the Bible, that is, trying to derive universal precepts from the experience of individuals or the people as a whole, as related in the story. When challenged on historical or naturalistic grounds, the teacher feels constrained either to accept the event literally as a miracle or to reject it entirely as legend. His is especially toubled when he equates the miraculous with the supernatural. The two most debated events, in this respect, are the Exodus from Egypt and Revelation at Sinai. Indeed, one may view these happenings as miracles, but there is nothing in Scripture to indicate that they occurred supernaturally. But even when viewed as miracles, they would cause no difficulty if the Bible were not presented as story. For miracles, as such, neither prove nor disprove God's existence, His presence or His commands. The Rambam sensed this problem of Biblical exegesis and he noted in the *Mishneh Torah* (I:8). "The wonders that Moses performed in the wilderness were done to meet certain needs and not to prove the truth of his prophecy." Hegel held a similar view: since miracles are sensate, that is, non-spiritual, experiences, they cannot confirm the spiritual, as such.

A miracle may be considered as an unusual event in the life of an individual or a people that occurred at a time and place most needed, yet least expected. The miracle of Exodus, for example, was that when the Jewish people found themselves between the sea and the pursuing Egyptian army, something unusual and least expected happened at that moment, which saved their lives. The unusual thing was that the waters split or receded just in time for them to escape their pursuers. The believer will say with Scripture that it was Divine intervention. But there is nothing in the Biblical text to suggest that the sea was split by supernatural means. It was a "strong eastern wind" blowing "all night" that pushed the waters aside. And yet, the teacher who relates the event as mere story finds himself in a dilemma of either accepting Exodus as a supernatural miracle or relegating it to the realm of fable. A more controversial discussion is often heard about the verse in Exodus 31: 18, where it says: The Lord "gave Moses the two tablets of the Pact, stone tablets inscribed by the finger of God." It is as if the whole drama of Revelation hinged on the question whether God, *kiveyachol,* wrote with His finger or not. That is very disturbing to the "story teller," indeed; and since such a thing is inconceivable to a naturalist, the whole story is viewed by him as a fable and thus Revelation itself is put in jeopardy.

Bible as Halacha

A totally different view of the matter is taken by the teacher in the "content centered" school, for he teaches the Bible to the child, and he teaches it not as *aggada* but as *halacha*. This teacher is not perturbed by that passage in Exodus. One who accepts the Rabbinic interpretation of the Divine in the Bible as non-corporeal and non-anthropomorphic, finds no difficulty with "the finger of God" any more than with "the word of God," or with His blowing "the breath of life" into Adam's nostrils. In characteristic fashion, the ancient Mechilta on Exodus and, later, Rashi do not comment on the passage at all. Ibn Ezra explains it as speaking in terms of "human custom," and the Rambam classifies it among the expressions which the Sages designated as "comparing the creature to its Creator," and, he adds, "they [the Sages] were sure that no doubt or confusion would arise from it." (*Guide*, I:47).

In the school, then where the content of the Bible, and not the child, is made the object of instruction, the teacher will not seek so much the narrative portions of *aggada*, as he will emphasize the eternal verities enunciated in what is generally identified as *halacha*—the way of life—and he will expound those verities as the moral, ethical, and religious precepts that are true for all time and not merely for the child's adjustment to the fleeting moment. These verities are stated in the Bible directly as laws, statutes, teachings and commandments, and are not derived from the empirical data of individuals or the nation. One would be hard put, for example, to learn the commandment "thou shalt not covet" from the life and behavior of King David. That does not mean that the Bible should not be taught as history. On the contrary, the laws and commandments should be presented in their historical context. Otherwise, they might appear as mere abstractions, perhaps inapplicable in human affairs. The teachings of the Biblical verities are exemplified in the history of the people, positively and negatively. But they are neither proved nor disproved by the historical events, and while archeological findings may throw some valuable light on the historicity of certain occurrences, they do not affect the basic teachings of the Bible, as such. To try to base the teaching of the Bible, especially in our elementary and intermediate schools, on archeological evidence or the lack of it, is a diversion from the true aim of Jewish education.

Bilingual Method

The Bible, particularly the Torah, is the pedagogic book, par exellence, for the moral upbringing of man. It was composed as such: its language, style and very structure bear the earmarks of a book designed for instruction. The arch of the Pentateuch, if one may visualize it that way architecturally, with the book of Leviticus as its keystone, is built as an everlasting span to carry an historic people across the ages. The ancient Rabbis found the proper pedagogic approach to the study of the Bible by devising the method of *Pardes*. As is well known, this word is an acronym of the letters *Peh* in *Peshat* (simple meaning of text), *Resh* in *Remez* (allusion), *Dallet* in *Drush* (interpretation), and *Samech* in *Sod* (hidden meaning). The first pertains to the reading of the given text and the other three are what is called exegesis, hermeneutics or interpretation.

Pardes, taken as a whole, means that each generation not only reads "out of the Torah", but also reads "into it." The languages of instruction were determined by these two goals. Reading out of the Torah is *mikra* or the original content. Reading into the Torah is *targum* or translation in the broad sense of the word. Each generation translates the original text into its own idiom, in the light of its cumulative knowledge even seeking "hidden meanings" through speculative reason. But the interpretation must not go contrary to the text—the targum must be derived from the mikra. While the mikra was preserved in its traditional purity, in the *Masorah*, neither adding to nor subtracting from the text, the targum or interpretation was given free reign in thought and imagination. Thus was established the fundamental pedagogic principle of studying the Torah in two languages: reading twice in the original Hebrew text and once in translation (שנים מקרא ואחד תרגום).

The bilingual problem of teaching the Torah is not peculiar to modern Jewish education. It goes back to the days of the prophets. Jeremiah (10: 11) already found it necessary to address his people in Aramaic. A generation or two later, in the days of Daniel and Ezra, Aramaic became a dominant language and *targum* (translation) was adopted as the prevailing method of interpretation. Commenting on *Nehemiah* 8:8, Rav Ika bar Abin said in the name of Rav Hananniel, in the name of Rav: "It is written, 'and they read in the book of Divine Law with interpretation.' 'They read' means reading the text of the Torah, and 'with interpretation' means translation." (Megilla, 3 a). Rashi comments on the same verse in Nehemiah, which further states, "'they made it intelligible and explained the text to the people,' meaning, they translated the words of the Torah to the people." This bilingual method of studying the Torah has continued in various languages through the years of Dispersion, to this day. To try now to reverse this course and interpret the Bible to our children in the American Jewish schools in Hebrew is to do violence both to the original text and its exegesis. Even with proper language preparation, the student who is taught by the Ivrit-beIvrit method (perhaps with some exceptions in the all-day schools), may at best read a verse in Hebrew and render it in "other Hebrew words." He cannot possibly discuss the verse adequately or understand the teacher's interpretation (assuming the teacher himself can do it) in Hebrew. And, just to read a verse of the Bible in Hebrew and paraphrase it in simpler Hebrew, can hardly be construed as Bible study. The proper way to teach the Bible to those who are adequately prepared linguistically is to read the text in the original with understanding of *peshat* (basic meaning) and then discuss and interpret it in the student's native language. Those who do not or cannot receive the necessary Hebraic grounding, should study the Bible in a standard English translation.

1966

PART V
Philatelic Briefs

Otte Wallish
Menorah

The Art of the
Stamps of Israel

In a recent reveiw of an art exhibit, John Canaday, of the New York Times, pointed out the difference in public interest between paintings and stamps. From the collector's point of view, he wrote, "paintings are meant to be looked at and enjoyed for the enrichment of our lives; stamps are meant to be recognized and may be collected for their rarity." Basically a stamp need only indicate the fact that a certain fee was paid for postal services in a given country. Any other information presented on a postal issue and how such information is arranged and designed graphically or pictorially, are not of the essence of stamps as such. And yet, all countries started very early in their postal history to use stamps for purposes other than purely postal service. One may find on stamps of every period many aspects of life of a nation, its history, geography, industry, agriculture, as well as social, cultural and religious ideas. More recently, attention has also been given to the artistic side of stamp making. Indeed, there is an increasing awareness among philatelists and the public at large of the esthetic quality of stamps. Famous works of arts reproduced on postage have become leading collectors' items among topicalists. In this field, France and the Vatican are particularly outstanding. Many of the African stamps are illuminated with brilliant colors of exotic flowers, birds and animals. Last year, these beautiful values were featured in a special issue of Life lmagazine. (The stamps of Israel, by the way, were not included in that issue.)

Like every other country, Israel has utilized its postage to convey messages of national and world import. It has portrayed its historic struggle for independence, its great moments in Biblical and other days, its industrial, agricultural and scientific advancement, and its cultural and ideal strivings. At the same time, from its very inception Israel has laid stress on the artistic production of its postal values. The art expressed on Israeli stamps is not a reproduction of famous works; nor is it just a copying of objects in their natural surroundings; but each design is an artistic creation in its own right. One might say, in the stamps of Israel one can discern the beginnings of an Israeli art, indigenous to the land and the people, even though most of the designers originate from other countries and and studied in the art schools of Europe. As a result, there is a marked influence of modern and "modernistic" (to use a common term) painting on the artists in Israel. Some critics maintain that they are all of European vintage and that there is no Israeli or Jewish art identifiable as such. Be this as it may, out of the welter of Expressionism, Pointilism, Cubism, Constructivism and all the Abstractionist offshoots (and they have all left their mark), there emerges in Israel an art bearing the unmistakable impress of Hebraic tradition.

The Hebraic tradition rests on two elements — conciseness and immediacy. These are primary elements, embedded in the spirit of the Hebrew language and the Bible, and expressed in Jewish art through the ages. For, while the Torah prohibits graven images, decorative arts have been cultivated on sacred objects from the days of the Tabernacle in the wilderness to the modern synagogue. In art, then, as in other cultural-spiritual values, Israel has turned, or returned, to original sources, even though it utilizes technical media garnered from other climes. The element of "conciseness" expresses the essential — "the little that contains a lot." The Kabbalists named it "the Secret of Condensed Reality" סוד הצמצום . The element of "immediacy" expresses the capacity to perceive reality in its essence and momentarily. It is perhaps no accident that the city of Safed, the cradle of Kabbala, has become a favorite abode of Israeli artists. For Kabbala, with all its mystic speculation, is striving to reach the essence of reality in its Divine manifestations. Neither of the two elements — conciseness or immediacy — is to be confused with modern abstraction in art. "Abstractionsim" started out as a movement of liberation — freedom from natural form, color, line, or space. It ended, however, as a trend in escape from reality. There are some artists in Israel who follow the same trend. Nevertheless, one gains the feeling that the artistic colony there is sobering up from the abstractionist hallucinations. The Talmudic Sages noted long ago: "The very air of the Land of Israel engenders wisdom"

אוירא דארץ ישראל מחכים. Those artists, like the designers of Israel's postage, who have become intoxicated with that air — breathing from the countryside, the lake and the seashore, even from the industrial and cultural intensity, have come very close to expressing a high degree of the essence of reality.

Many artists have been called upon by the Israeli Ministry of Posts to design its stamps in the course of the past thirteen years since the inception of the State. Those artists vary in their creative expression, background and training. Most of them came from European schools and studios; but some, the younger ones, have had their apprenticeship in Isreal's art school, Bezalel, or in the ateliers of older masters. In the following notes, the discussion will center on the artistic qualities of a few of the designers who have been most active in the production of Israel's postal values. (Numbers in the text refer to Scott catalog).

Otte Wallish is a prolific, diversified artist. He designed the first stamps of the State of Israel, the Doar Ivri, whose appearance, as he said, marked the greatest event in his personal life. Between that series and his latest set of the 1960 Provisionals and the 25th Zionist Congress issue, Wallish created a veritable art gallery of postal values — the Definitive Coins, the third, fourth, sixth, ninth, and tenth Independence sets, Petach Tiqvah (22), UPU (31-2), Festivals 1952, Menorah With Tribes (55), Tabim (88-9), Postage Due, Defense (124-6), Refugees (178-9), others. On the whole, Wallish is more interested in design than in color, his intent being on delineation of events and ideas. By profession an advertizing, commercial artist, he tends toward story telling and display. But he tells his story direct to the point, in realistic, often literal, style. One can see, for example, the tale of heroic fighting, ruin and supreme sacrifice in some of his Independence issues, in which he depicts battle-scarred scenery at Yad Mordecai, Safed and Degannia (62-4), or at Gesher and Yehiam (84-5). His directness is sometimes in the manner of poster advertizing, as in his illustration of verses from *Song of Songs* — Festivals (66-9). He sacrifices pictorial completeness to stress the literal meaning of "fig" and "nut" in the verse, by drawing the fruits in full color, but sketching their leaves only in bare outline, thus creating a direct poster-like effect.

When Wallish does not tell a story, he uses symbols to point up an idea of Israel's striving or accomplishment. His Defense stamps (124-6) have a sword and olive branch, pointing to security and peace. His Tenth Independence (142) shows a stylized Menorah with the central branch blossoming forth into ten green leaves, symbolic of Israel's miraculous development in ten short years. While most of his stamps are in monochrome, he also has some fine color combinations in flat juxtaposition, as for example, in Tabim (88-9). Wallish's greatest achievement, however, is the Menorah With Tribes (55), which is, in this writer's opinion, the most beautiful of all Israeli issues to date. majestic in conception, design and color shading, this stamp reflects in quiet repose Israel's past glory, and is a worthy symbol of the new State as the unifying force among the various tribes.

G. Hamori is a sensitive colorist in a wide range of subject-matter. He has produced such items as Bilu (72), the Pictorial Airs (C9-15), Festivals 1953 (75-7), Teachers (91), Seventh Independence (93), Red Magen-David (104), The Twelve Tribes (105-16), Technion (118), Einstein (117), and others. His landscapes are a faithful reproduction of the Israeli countryside, as in the Airmail set. But his other designs are highly imaginative in the use of line as well as color. Hamori shows a keen eye for nuances in shading. In the Magen-David Adom, flat greens and gray-whites pass through interchangeably a wide gamut of fine gradations. And even finer shading of greens, syncopated with flaming reds of the burning Menorah, is displayed in the Seventh Independence stamp (93). His most effective color scheme is in the Twelve Tribes set. When grouped together, the variations on each value blend into harmony with those of the rest, from the faintest tinge to the deepest hue.

Other leading colorists among Israel's stamp designers are the *Shamir* brothers, *Maxim* and *Gabriel*, who work together as a team on all their assignments. They designed Approach to Jerusalem (26), Festivals 19-49 (28-30). Tel-Aviv (44), Parachute (92), Eighth Independence (119), Citrus (120), Bezalel (127), Tenth Industry Exhibition (144), Bialik, Shalom Aleichem, Tel-Aviv (160) Jubilee of Three Colonies (165-7), and Herzl (183). In almost all of their issues, the Shamir brothers succeed in creating a bright pictorial effect that attracts attention. One cannot help but notice the stamp. This they achieve by developing the design around a central bright-colored spot. In its simplest form, the bright spot, as for instance in the Citrus issue, is of two juicy red oranges; in the Eighth Independence it is a blue-and-white ribbon fluttering through the air and forming the figure 8. More subtle designing and of greater pictorial value are the Bezalel and Tel-Aviv (160) issues. In the former, the golden yellow central part of the architectural design is reinforced by a bright yellow Bezalel beaker in the lower right. The Tel-Aviv stamp, which delineates several public institutions, has very fine structural detail brought into relief against flat green on blue with shadings of brown and gray, half framed in a wide brown border — all grouped on several levels around a central white illumination. Even in their portrait stamps — Shalom Aleichem, Bialik — there is a spot illumination on the face, reflected in bright shading of green or brown in the central background and deepening in tone toward the edge. The same illumination is carried out on the tabs of these items. In some designs — Tenth Anniversary of Industry, Bezalel — they make effective use of the Dufy (French Modernist) two-dimensional style of pen-and-ink or brush line on flat colors. The impression is highly suggestive of reality and immediacy.

In the Three Colonies, the Shamir brothers bring their style of central lighting to a high degree of refinement and greatest achievement. Notwithstanding that these landscapes are done in monochrome, the color on each stamp is so varied in its gamut of shading that the total picture appears as a symphoney of hues. Each landscape stands out like an aquatint in blue — Degania, brown — Yesod Hamaalch, or green — Merhavia. The three are the finest example of Israeli landscape painting.

1961

Israel Reflected in Special Cancellations in 1960

Industrial Expansion

The Israel Government Yearbook of 1960-61 puts the year 1958 as "a turning point and signpost in the development of industry and crafts. Till then, efforts were spent mainly on producing consumer goods; that objective has been fully met, and production for export will be the primary interest now" (p. 104).

The special cancellation on the "Dedication of the Diamond Center" in Jerusalem, marked an important landmark in the continued growth of the diamond trade. After Belgium, Israel is now the second largest export of semi-precious stones, having risen from about nine million dollars in 1950 to $46,000,000 in 1959. The "Third Fruit Exhibition" cancellation of November 3 in Haifa revealed the great variety of new and old fruits now being cultivated in Israel for local consumption as well as for shipment abroad. Fruit growing is spread over 400,000 dunams of land, with new plantations opening as the need grows. Bananas topped the export list in 1959-60, with 4,500 tons going to Cyprus, Greece, and Malta. Flowers are also becoming more abundant in Israel's export. Estimates for 1960 were over 15,000,000 bulbs and cut flowers. A quarter million gladioli went to Great Britain, Germany, Switzerland, and of all places, Holland. The *Hag Haperach* (Flower Festival) cancellation of April 13 in Haifa highlighted this activity.

Israel's industrial expansion is reflected in very large measure in its paper production, especially paper packaging, which is the bulk of this enterprise. The "Packaging Exhibition in Israel" cancellation of June 2 in Tel Aviv tells of great strides made despite many handicaps in procuring raw materials and other difficulties. While the output grew from 15 Kilo per capita in 1954 to 29 Kilo in 1960, the supply is still short of satisfying local needs, not to speak of the increasing demand for packaging goods for exports. Water, as is well known, is becoming the greatest concern of the age not only in Israel but also all over the Globe. The expected increase of 20,000,000 cubic meter of water supply for the year in Israel did not materialize fully because of drought, low precipitation, and the falling off in the flow at Yarkon's springs. Some settlements are not yet self-sufficient in their water supply, and the fruit plantations, especially, require increasingly larger amounts. There has been a slowdown in the annual water increment from 15% to 5% in 1958-59 and to as low as 1.3% in 1959-60. One can thus appreciate the

Packaging   Air Force

472

alarming slogan on a cancellation of July 15 in Tel Aviv: "Spare the water, citizen, heed/This from heaven has been decreed."

A remarkable advance was made in Israel's air transport and its infant aviation industry. "The best for flying/Fly in the Air Force" reads a slogan cancellation of August 1 in Tel Aviv. Understandably, it is Israel's Air Force that has given stimulus to the aircraft industry, which now aims to become an independent producer in the field. Until now production was tied to foreign licenses, notably from France, for the making of parts and jet-propelled training planes, or for repair and overhauling jobs for Israel's air force and foreign clients. Civil aviation over national and international routes by Arkia and El-Al, repectively, has shown extended activity. With the general growth of industry and some prosperity, there has been a substantial increase in motor vehicles on the streets, roads, and highways of the country. And, alas, with such an increase, traffic accidents went up in alarming proportion. It is said that Israel now has the highest accident rate in the world. One may then surmise the significance of the slogan cancellation used in Jerusalem, Tel Aviv, Haifa, Beer Sheba, and Tiberias during the month of January 1960: "Join the drive against death on the roads." In 1959 there was a liberalization of policy on the production and import of passenger cars. Rationing was suspended and concessions were made on imports of new cars in preference to used ones. As a result, there was an increased import from 1,100 cars in 1957 to 2,300 in 1959. At the same time the auto industry took on new life. Local assembly plants produced 3,820 cars in 1959 compared with 2,500 in 1958 for internal use as well as for export (1,780 in 1959 against 670 in 1958). The abrupt cessation of the "Renault" agreement did not halt development. The American Ford, Kaiser-Frazer, and Studebaker stepped into the breach. Negotiation with a European company for the assemblage of heavy trucks was in progress. Israel's auto industry was on the way to becoming an independent enterprise. In 1960 proposals were also made for the manufacture of a popular car, the Sabra, which has since reached the American market. As to safety on the roads, not only have special cancellations been issued, but special steps have been taken by the government for the prevention of accidents. More stringent traffic laws have been enacted, and a program of road improvement and widening of highways has been set in motion.

Financial resources are naturally the main problem in Israel's expanding economy. Furthermore, the specter of a runaway inflation is ever present. Only recently, as reported in *Haaretz* of November 9, 1961, Levi Eshkol, Minister of Finance, was questioned in the Knesset concerning rumors about the devaluation of the Israeli Pound. The Minister, of course, denied the allegation. But all realize that a sound fiscal policy is essential for a healthy economic expansion. The government authorities are therefore intent on attracting among other resources local capital from the citizens themselves by stimulating savings accounts. Three slogan cancellations on this subject were in use in 1960. Most prominently featured was "Save today for tomorrow," sponsored by the Savings Authority (Reshut Hahisahon), December 16-30 in Jerusalem and other places. More specific slogans were: "Open a checking account in Bank Hadoar," and "Save in Bank Hadoar," both cancelled on August 1 in Haifa and Jerusalem, respectively. The Bank Hadoar (Post Office Bank) was established in 1953 for clearing services, savings accounts, postal money orders, payment of government salaries, and settlement of accounts for the National Insurance Institute. About a third of its 74,000 depositors in 1959-60 were minors, which gives the bank a family basis. Bank Hadoar also plays an important part in the program of planned industrialization, which is now the primary task of the Ministry of Commerce and Industry.

2. *Culture, Philately, Sports*

The filming of "Exodus" in Israel was regarded of financial importance and was given every possible cooperation by the government and the local authorities. Six Israeli actors and more than one thousand auxiliaries participated together with Hollywood stars. The public followed their movements with keen interest in the press, which carried reports, illustrations, interviews with director Otto Preminger and leading actors. The Post Office Department honored the event with a special cancellation "Exodus — On location in Israel" in Hebrew and English, May 20 to June 5 in Jerusalem. The year 1960 marked the 200th anniversary of the death of Israel Baal-Shem-Tov, founder of the Hassidic Movement. While the issuance of a commemorative stamp ws postponed till August 1961, the event was given prominence in Israel by an "Exhibition of Hassidism," and a special cancellation on September 5, 1960, opening day, in Tel

Aviv. Two stamp exhibits took place during the year, which received special cancellations: The "Ghana Philatelic Exhibition" opening on June 7 in Jerusalem, and "Taviv National Stamp Exhibition" October 9-19 in Tel Aviv. The assistance rendered by the State of Israel in Ghana's economic, scientific, and cultural development since the latter gained independence in 1957, has been quite substantial. The Ghana stamp exhibition in Jerusalem was thus another link in the chain of cooperation and the fostering of close ties with the newly born African states. It is also of interest to note that the Israeli artist Miriam Karoli, designer of postal issues (Ships, Youth Aliva, etc.) designed the 5/-value of Ghana's latest National Founders Day set, issued September 21, 1961. Besides the first-day covers of the Taviv stamp and Souvenir sheet, there were three other cancellations connected with that show: a slogan on October 2 in Tel Aviv, reading "Attend the National Stamp Exhibit Taviv," October 9-19, a special cancellation *Taviv* (Hebrew and English) on the opening day, October 9, Tel Aviv (besides the first day cover); and another special, Youth Day, National Stamp Exhibition Taviv," October 18. Covers used by the Philatelic Services for mailing Taviv orders carried a square block imprint in English, "Greeting from 'Taviv' National Stamp Exhibition, Tel Aviv, 1960" and the Hebrew word "Taviv" and the year 721. Postal services have increased in the course of the year in keeping with the general development of the economy, and, like in many other countries, the holiday season taxes the post offices to capacity. There was thus the timely slogan on August 28 (before the Jewish New Year) in Jerusalem and other cities, "Be early in sending your letters and greetings for the holidays," with a clock dial indicating 20 before the twelfth hour.

Peace of Jerusalem   Taviv Stamp Exhibit

"Gadna" (G'dud Noar Ivri) is a youth organization of pre-military age, engaged in command training, sports, marksmanship, and sea and air exercises. It received a special cancellation for a "Shooting contest, Gadna, Lag b'Omer," May 15, 1960, Rishon

Lezion, with insignia of bow and arrow and two rifles over a target. Another sport event, the annual hiking pilgrimage to Jerusalem, had two specials on April 4, with a humorous cartoon depicting a hiking couple with the inscription "Hulda — We are all going up to Jerusalem," and a similar wording on another cancellation for those who started from Eshtaol. The march lasted four days with 11,000 participants, young and old, even to the advanced age of 93.

3. *Health Services*

When Hadassah was preparing to move its medical center to Ain Karem, outside Jerusalem, the government appointed a committee to study the effect of that move on the medical facilities in the Capital. The committee recommended that the Sief Building be converted into a hospital to be maintained jointly by the Ministry of Health and the Municipality. To emphasize this extended service in the city, the "Dedication of the Medical Center in Jerusalem," August 3, 1960, was marked with a special cancellation in Hebrew and English. The same month witnessed the "Cornerstone laying for the School of Dentistry — Hadassah — Jerusalem," which was given a special cancellation on August 8, also in English and Hebrew. A cancellation was dedicated to the drive against infantile paralysis between April 15 and May 15 in Jerusalem, Tel Aviv, and Haifa, reading: "Fight against the silencing of children — Join the March of Prutot." It should be pointed out that in 1959-60 the rate of infantile paralysis and other contagious diseases diminished to a very low point. At the end of each year, the Red Magen David holds its annual lottery to raise funds for its manifold needs. This is usually promoted by a special cancellation, which was used this year December 1-27 in Tel Aviv, announcing "Red Magen David Lottery Month." Many attractive prizes, including a car are in store for the lucky winers. An advertisement for the lottery for 1961, which appeared recently in *Haaretz*, tells of a fortunate young couple who won the car last year just before their wedding. As practical young people, they sold the car and used the money for a new home — a most welcome wedding gift.

4. *National and World Jewish Organizations*

The State of Israel has sought to keep alive its relationships with Jewish organizations that have contributed toward its establishment and that still play an important part in the advancement of its welfare. On the national level. The United Jewish Appeal—Keren Hayesod received a slogan cancellation February 1, which was used through the month in Jerusalem, Tel Aviv, and Haifa, reading in English and Hebrew: "Your Contribution to the United Campaign Helps in Building the Land," with the letters "KH" and "Kof-Heh" in an oval. The accomplishments of "Women in Israel" were represented in an exhibit October 26 in Tel Aviv, sponsored by the "Moetzet Hapoalot—Pioneer Women," the women's division of the Histadrut. On this occasion due recognition was given to the Pioneer Women Organization of the United States for outstanding help to its sister group in Israel. The American body was organized in New York in 1925, and it thus celebrated its 35th anniversary in connection with the special exhibit. The cancellation was in Hebrew and English on the opening day of the exhibit.

A third national event honored with a postmark was the Ninth Conference of the Histadrut, opened February 3 in Tel Aviv, also celebrating its 40th anniversary. The Histadrut, or The General Federation of Labor in Israel, was founded in 1920 and it now counts in its membership almost two-thirds of the total Jewish population. The members represent all political parties and shades of opinion. During the Mandate period it was regarded as "The Labor Commonwealth in the Making." A special post office operated at the conference February 3-5. Three world bodies of the Zionist Movement held their conferences in Jerusalem during 1960. Special postmarks were thus accorded to "The World Conference of the Keren Hayesod — United Jewish Appeal," December 21; "The World Conference of the Jewish National fund," December 14 (in Hebrew and French, with KKL emblem); and "The 25th Zionist Congress," December 27 (in Hebrew and English with letters "Kaf-Heh" in a circle silhouetting Herzl's profile). The significance of those three gatherings in the life of the country was reflected in some of their resolutions. The Keren Hayesod called on World Jewry to recognize the "overriding historic necessity of raising one-thousand-million dollars in the coming decade to . . . assure the absorption of the third million of Israel's population." The Jewish national fund, with a representation from 28 countries, gained new impetus by a redefinition of its functions. Since all the unsettled land in Israel is now owned by the State, the original JNF task of buying land as "the perpetual possession of the Jewish people" has lost its practical meaning. The Conference therefore called to the attention of world Jewry that the land in Israel is still largely barren, and it invited Jews everywhere to "unite in making the stones and the sand into good soil." The JNF, with its great popular appeal, has thus opened new vistas for itself in Israel.

After the establishment of the State of Israel, the World Zionist Congress held its 5-year periodic sessions in Jerusalem (the 23rd Congress in 1951, the 24th in 1956, and the 25th in 1960-61). Many are the problems that have beset this body vis-a-vis the actual existence of the State. Foremost is the need to revaluate its own purposes and functions, now that it can no longer be regarded as the governing arm of a "State-on-the-way," as it was called heretofore. Thus some new trends of thought were noted at the 25th Congress, especially with regard to immigration and Jewish education. Another world body that met in Israel that year was The World Jewish Congress in connection with the "Celebration of South American Jewry in Israel." This was marked by a cancellation on March 3, with an emblem of a globe and Magen David. This manner of celebration was an innovation in the relationship of the State of Israel with Jewish communities in the diaspora. There has been concern in Israel that the young Israeli generation had shown a tendency to forget or ignore its origin from the Jewish communities in the diaspora and had evinced little desire to continue its contacts with them in the present. Steps were taken to check this trend as early as 1958, when the Ministry of Education launched a campaign to stimulate "Jewish awareness" among the youth of the land. Special guidelines for teachers were prepared to advance in the elementary schools "a knowledge of the Jewish heritage that grew through the two millennia of dispersion," and to spread "more detailed knowledge of Jewish communities in other parts of the world." The following year a similar program was launched on the High School level. The recognition given in 1960 to the South American Jewish communities by the World Jewish Congress and the State of Israel was part of the larger campaign. It helped to renew the old bonds with those communities and to cement new ties of mutual understanding and cooperation. Plans were also laid for honoring each year a different segment of world Jewry in a similar manner. Another gathering of world import marked with a special cancellation was the "Conference of Jewish Journalists" on December 26 in Jerusalem. This was also part of the effort to bring together responsible Jewish spokesmen from many lands for a better understanding between them and the State. The fifth world body that was honored in a similar manner was WIZO, "Women's International Zionist Organization," on the occasion of its fortieth anniversary December 9 in Tel Aviv. The cancellation was in Hebrew and English, with the figure 40 enclosing the Wizo emblem. This organization is the second largest in the Zionist movement and is engaged in social welfare, and in vocational and agricultural training in Israel. It was founded in 1920 in London by a group of women including Vera Weizmann and Rebecca Ziff, now world head of the organization.

Medical Center   Second International   Pioneer Women

5. *International Conferences*

The ancient world recognized the strategic position of Israel (or Canaan, Palestine) as it lay astride the military and commercial routes connecting three continents. That small country was the bone of contention between kings and emperors from the days of Abraham (when the four Chaldean Kings defeated the five kings in Canaan) through the times of the Persians, the Greeks, and the Romans, the Mohammedans and the Crusaders, to the days of the British Mandate. Now the land of Israel is coveted by its neighboring Arab states; but it is also the focal point on which all the three continents converge their cooperative efforts for economic, social, scientific, and cultural development. Six international gatherings took place in 1960 in Israel, which highlighted its role for peaceful pursuits. "The Council of the Socialist International" met in Haifa on April 25, and was postmarked with a special cancellation in Hebrew and English with an emblem of a semi-globe topped by a sailboat on the high seas placed in a triangle.

Significantly, it chose Israel for its first meeting ever held outside Europe because of Israel's proximity to the newly established states in Africa and Asia, whose economic and social democratic problems were in the main issued on the Council's agenda. Its host was the Mapai, Israel's leading labor party, which is a member of this body, known as The Second International. During the Mandate period and subsequently, the Mapai and the Histadrut received great moral and practical support from many members of the Council in Western lands.

An "International Seminar Conference on Housing" was held May 5 at Bitan Aharon (Kfar Vitkin) and was postmarked in Hebrew and English with an outline drawing of a brick house. A "World Seminar on Services to Universities" was held on July 17 in Jerusalem and received a postal cancellation in Hebrew and French, with an emblem of a globe and an oil lamp. "The Third International Congress of State Lotteries" met April 14 in Tel Aviv and was commemorated with a cancellation in Hebrew and French with the emblem "peh" (for the Hebrew word "Payis," meaning lottery). Though not a conference, the World Refugee Year was observed by a dual issue of a pair of stamps on a special first day-cover, marking the event in Hebrew and English with the world emblem as part of the international undertaking. Israel also contributed 25,000 refugee stamps to the sponsoring International Committee.

A far-reaching assembly was "The International Conference on Science in the Advancement of New States," convened August 15 in Rehobot, at the initiative of Abba Eban, President of the Weizmann Institute of Science and Minister of Education The cancellation was in Hebrew and English with an emblem of the Eastern Hemisphere and a torch rising out of Africa. Thirty Western countries sent some of their greatest scientists who met with the leaders of the new African and Asian states. At the closing session on August 25 it was decided to establish a permanent committee to channel requests for help from scientists in Western lands. "The Fifteenth Congress of the International Union of Local Authorities (UILA)" chose Israel for its first meeting held outside of Europe since its founding in 1913. This Congress, which met November 16 in Tel Aviv, was the largest not specifically Jewish gathering ever convened in Israel. Thirty-three countries, from Austria to Yugoslavia, were represented by 677 mayors of local municipalities, small, large, and of metropolitan size, including 75 from the United States. Its theme, "The task of local government in developmental areas," found Israel especially suitable for its purpose. The Assembly regarded that land as an ideal laboratory for the building of new towns and villages in areas previously considered unfit for settlement. As is customary with the UILA, its flag was deposited in the Congress city, Tel Aviv, for two years until the next session. The postal cancellation was in Hebrew and English, with the name "Israel" over the Menorah emblem in the center.

6. *Zionist Leaders*

"The 80th Birthday of Zeev Jabotinsky" was observed by a special postmark with a modified State emblem, on November 2, at the Metzudat Zeev Jabotinsky Museum in Tel Aviv. Vladimir Jabotinsky (1880-1940) was a great force in the Zionist Movement, particularly in World War I. He was instrumental in the formation of the Jewish Legion that fought alongside the British forces in the liberation of Palestine from the Turks. Later, in 1923, Jabotinsky and his followers broke away from the World Zionist Congress and founded a separate organization known as "Zionist Revisionist."

7. *Towns and Settlements*

The "25th Anniversary of Nahariya, The Pioneer Township of Western Galilee" was marked by a cancellation on April 15, with an emblem of sun rays and a tower by the sea. Situated on the Mediterranean north of Haifa, Nahariya has earned the reputation of being the family resort of the nation. It caters especially to the tourist trade. The following month, on May 15, "The Twelfth Anniversary of the Liberation of Western Galilee" (in the war of 1948) was celebrated with a special marking in Nahariya, with the city's sun rays emblem. Kiryat Zanz, a Hassidic colony, was given a new obliterator on April 19 with a scroll-like Hebrew inscription (from the Yom Kippur liturgy), "And you said, here I will dwell for a long time and sustain you through my blessing." A slogan cancellation was imprinted June 16 to July 15 in Jerusalem, reading in Hebrew and English, "Pray for the Peace of Jerusalem" (Psalm 12:6), with the city emblem and leaves between the two lines. As part of the Herzl Year, commemorating his birth centennial, which was observed in Israel in 1960, the village of

Herzlia was elevated to the status of a municipality. The cancellation "Herzliah Cilty" on May 5 expresses the industrial, agricultural, and sea-faring advancements of the town that are drawn in its emblem. This is the only town in the world named for Theodor Herzl, the founder of the World Zionist Organization and father of the Jewish State. Established in 1925 by "The American Zionist Commonwealth," it is now a thriving city with three suburbs of some well-to-do residents (though very few Americans) with luxurious homes. It is considered the nation's favorite playground, its beaches being frequented by 40,000 to 50,000 visitors on a summer week-end.

8. *Post Office Openings*

The opening of a new post office or the establishment of a mobile postal service is marked in Israel by a special cancellation. The twenty-one markings of this type that appeared in 1960 reveal certain population trends in the country, as new post offices are opened in a given area when the increase in settlement warrants a separate service. Thus the greatest expansion was shown in the *Coastal Plain* (Sharon Valley): Gelil Yam, March 1; Enat, March 28; Kfar Yasif, April 24; Rishpon, May 4; Tira, May 8; Savyon, June 5; Kefar Yavne, June 17; Neurim, September 1; Universita Bar Ilan, September 18; Bet Yehoshua, December 11; and Lev Hasharon (mobile post), December 15. In *Jezreel Valley* (The Emek): Mizpe Biryya, May 9; Hayogev, May 22; and Hevel Megiddo (mobile post), December 20. In *The Negev*: Udim, June 19; and Avedat, June 11. In *Jerusalem Region*: Yar Hakedoshim (near Mt. Herzl), June 19; Mount Zion, September 18 (both for tourists); and Shimshon (mobile post), December 21. Other openings: Yaar Simhoni, June 13; and Ashrat (Western Galilee), December 20. As of March 31, 1961, there were in Israel 65 Post Offices, 49 P.O. Branches, 218 Postal Agencies, and 29 Mobile Postal Routes, serving a total of 200,000 addresses in 550 Jewish and Arab settlements. It is the declared goal of the Ministry of Posts to have "regular distribution of mail in every inhabited place in the country."

References: Slogans taken from the original cancellation; also from the *Jerusalem Post, The Government Year Book, 1960-1961. The Holy Land Philatelist,* and *The Israel Philatelist, 1960.*

1961

Art on Israeli Stamps

Israel proclaimed its independence on May 15, 1948. The following day it issued its first set of postage stamps, to emphasize symbolically as well as actually the sovereignty of the new State. This set is known as "Doar Ivri" (Hebrew Post), because at the time of its printing, twelve days prior to its issue, the name of the State had not yet been known. Its motif, designed by Otte Wallish of Tel Aviv, was taken from several ancient Hebrew coins struck in the first and second centuries C.E. The new State thus sought to identify itself with the spirit of revolt against foreign rule that prevailed in ancient Judea, as it had in the modern Israel. There were two major outbreaks against Roman rule in Judea: The First Revolt (War of the Second Temple — 66-70 C.E.), and the Second Revolt (War of Bar Kochba — 132-135 C.E.). As a sign of their independence, even though short-lived, the leaders of those revolts struck coins, marking the years of redemption. Some of those coins, which show high quality of artistic design and workmanship, were reproduced on the Doar Ivri set (Scott, 1-9).

Each of the first six values has a different coin, depicting Jewish religious symbols, such as, a seven-branch palmtree, a vine leaf and its reverse, an amphora with lid, a bunch of grapes for first fruit on Pentecost, a chalice of the sacred vessels, and a palm branch with citron for the Feast of Tabernacles. The inscriptions point to the events of the struggle: "For Zion's Redemption," "Zion's Freedom," and "Year Three," on the first three values with coins of the First Revolt; "One Year After Israel's Redemption," on the next three values, all of the Second Revolt. The higher values (7-9) repeat the chalice of number five and its reverse, three pomegranates, with the inscription "Holy Jerusalem, Israel Shekel, Year Two," or Three, or Four, respectively, all of the First Revolt. The first five values were also used later in the year (1948) for the "provisional" postage-due set (J 1-5) with the overprint "D'mei Doar." The ancient coin motif was used again by the same designer, Otto Wallish, on the definitive stamps issued in Israel in four sets, in 1949 (17-22), 1950 (38-43), 1952 (56-61) and in 1954 (80-83), known as the Second, Third, Fourth and Fifth Coinage Series. The second series repeats four of the Doar Ivri designs and adds two new ones on the last two values, namely, "Second Year of Israel's Freedom," with an amphora, and "For Israel's Redemption" with a palm branch and citron. The 10 Pruta

Flying Scroll

value appeared also in an imperforate sheet, Tabul (16), commemorating the first anniversary of the stamps of Israel exhibition, held in Tel Aviv on May 1, 1949.

The third coin series is a revised edition of the second, with the same values and the same coin designs, but with a change in the inscriptions on the left side of the stamps (not on the coins) from "First Revolt" to "War of the Second Temple," and from "Second Revolt" to "War of Bar Kochba." These ancient wars of liberation are more commonly known under the latter two designations, which most likely accounts for the revision. The first four values of this set were later used for the "provisional" Official Stamps (01-4) issued in 1952, with the overprint "Bul Sherut." The fourth series has six additional values printed on the same designs as the previous series. The last of the definitive coinage stamps has four additional values, 80, 95, 100, and 125 Prutot. One has a coin design of the Wars of the Maccabees against Syrian-Greek rule, 168 B.C.E., and the other three are new coins of the other two revolts. The first has the inscription "The Hasmonean Era" and a coin with a flower design and the words "King Jehonathan," who was one of the Maccabean rulers in ancient Judea. It has been pointed out by numismatic scholars that the coins of this period bear symbols of foreign origin, such as, flowers, cornucopiae, anchors and the like, in contrast with the coins of later periods which have Jewish symbols. The next value has a coin with three ears of wheat and the inscription "Quarter Shekel" of the War of the Second Temple. The third stamp has the Temple facade with the Holy Ark and the inscription "Jerusalem," and the last value has a Jewish harp with the words "Second Year of Israel's Freedom," both from the War of Bar Kochba. The coin of the second value, the 95 Prutot, was used again by Otte Wallish as the basic design for the new "provisionals" issued January 6, 1960 (186-177), when Israel changed its monetary unit from Pruta (1000 to the IP) to Agora (100 to the IP).

Ancient Seals

An oval seal of a "Flying Scroll" forms the design of the first Festival set issued in 1948 (10-14). The seal was used by the kings in ancient Juda on pottery for wine and oil, and bears the inscription "For the King," indicating that those were receptacles for the collection of taxes in kind. Another reproduction of ancient seals appears on the Festival set of 1959 designed by Miriam Karoly (129-131). One stamp has the likeness of a very graceful horse with the inscription "For Temech Son of Meknamelech," the other has a lion with the words "For Shema Servant of Jeroboam," and the third has two deer in juxtaposition, reading "For Netanyahu Son of Avadyahu." It is surmised that the three seals are from the days of Jeroboam the Second, king of Israel in the 8th century B.C.E.

3. *Ancient Jewish Art*

In the Valley of Jezreel, known since biblical times as the granary of the Holy Land, there stand the remains of a synagogue built in the sixth century C.E. It is called the Bet-Alfa synagogue, because it is in the modern colony of that name. Synagogal art has adhered to the biblical stricture against "graven images" as stated in the Second Commandment. The art of the Bet-Alfa is thus of pure design, the Zodiac, animals, birds and fruit arranged in a floor mosaic. Except for a few breaks in the tiles, the design has been preserved almost intact. The first major reproduction of a section of that mosaic was that of the "Sun chariot surrounded by the

Zodiac," which appeared on the Tabul sheet (132) in 1952. The stamps, designed in four sectional triangles by E. Errel of Tel Aviv follows the original very closely, deviating only in conciseness of delineation and lettering.

Other synagogues and tombstones in Israel and neighboring areas have yielded objects of art which have been utilized by stamp designers. The first definitive airmails (C1-6), by Otte Wallish, have ancient drawings of birds from various sources. There is a pair of doves picking on grapes (C1) from a third century clay lamp, now in "Museum Haaretz," in Tel Aviv. The second value has an eagle carved on a tomb in second century Bet-Shearim, northern Israel. There is an ostrich-like bird of the Bet Alfa mosaic (C3); a dove found in many decorations on Holy Arks (C4); a painted eagle from a tomb in Moreisha, southern Israel, of the second century B.C.E. (C5); and a dove with branch, like Noah's dove, from the mosaic of a fourth century synagogue in Geresh, Jordan (C6). Three other synagogues of more recent times in Jerusalem, Petach-Tikva and Safad (of Ari the Kabbalist) furnished the elaborate decorations of their Holy Arks for designs on the Festival set of 1953 (75-77), by G. Hamori.

Architectural Relics

For almost nineteen centuries the Triumphal Arch of Titus has stood near the Coliseum in Rome, its bas-relief bearing witness to the fall of Jerusalem and the destruction of the Second Temple in 70 C.E. Among the objects sculptured on the south wall of the Arch is the only known replica of the seven-branched Menorah that was in use in the second temple in Jerusalem. The bas-relief depicts the Menorah and other sacred vessels being carried into captivity by the victorious Roman legions. From this bas-relief new-born Israel modeled the Menorah on its State emblem, as a symbol of the people's unconquerable spirit. This Menorah with full emblem was first incorporated in the upper left corner of three stamps, designed by M & G Shamir for the Festival set in 1949 (28-30), and again in the lower right corner of one stamp by M. Kara in the Independence set of 1950 (34). The Shamir brothers also used the Menorah with emblem in a circle over the figure of a ribboned 8 in their Eighth Independence design (119). Wind-Struski placed it on the right side of five tall anemons on the Fifth Independence issue (73), and G. Hamori used it for his main

486

theme, with the Menorah lit up, on the Seventh Independence stamp (93). In addition, the Menorah emblem appears on all but one of the tabs or the Independence stamps from 1951 to 1961. The Tenth Independence (142) has a highly stylized Menorah, which suggests the original very remotely. The most outstanding Menorah design, surrounded by symbols of the Twelve Tribes, is Otte Wallish's definitive 1000 prutot (55), issued in 1952. it is majestically conceived and expresses the ingathering of the people from the various communities unified within the State of Israel. Some remains of ancient structures in Israel, dating back to the Roman period, the Crusades and later centuries, have been sketched in stylized, suggestive outline on three of the latest airmail sets, designed by Friedel Stern (C 18-20, 21-23, 24-26). In the first set, there is a corner view of a lone Corinthian capital standing in the commercial center in Ascalon, on the Mediterranean shore; a tower of Tiberias' ancient wall; and an old winding street in Safad. In the second set, the city of Akko is represented by its famous "Inn of the Columns," built in the 18th century by the conqueror Achmed-Jazzar out of columns taken from Byzantine and Roman buildings all over the country. In the Capernaum stamp are delineated four Corinthian columns and broken capitals with parts of a remaining wall of the richly ornamented "Centurion's Synagogue" (mentioned in the New Testament, Luke, VII:5), which was built in the first century and probably destroyed by an earthquake in the sixth century.

The third set, issued in October, 1961, has a sketch of the "Tomb of Jethro" at Kfar Hitim, which is sacred to the Druse religion; an old mill outside Jerusalem, at Yemin-Moshe, built in 1857 by Sir Moses Montefiore to encourage settlement of Jews on country sites; and a view of the old city of Jaffa. A more realistic view of the city of Tiberias and its "Tomb of Rabbi Meir," a second century Talmudic sage, is portrayed by G. Hamori on an airmail stamp issued in 1956 (C 17). A unique art treasure reproduced on an Israel stamp is a Jewish postman riding on a horse, which is part of an engraving depicting a huge procession, led by the postman in Prague in honor of the birth of a prince in 1741. The stamp was issued on the occasion of the National Stamp Exhibition held October 9, 1960, in Tel Aviv (Taviv 187). It also appeared perforated on a souvenir sheet (187a) with about a third of the original engraving.

1962

References

1. *The Holy Land Philatelist*. various issues in 1960 and 1961.

2. *The Israel Philatelist*, XIII: 2. p. 539 f. "The Arch of Titus and the Menorah," by Irving Wittow.

3. *Catalogue* No. 6, 1960, Ministry of Posts, Philatelic Services, Israel.

4. Descriptive Folders of the Philatelic Services, Israel.

5. "Highlights of Jewish History on Israel Stamps," by Helene Lande Blumkin. Pamphlet from *Jeshurun Yearbook*, New York, 1957.

6. "Israel's Coinage — Ancient and New," by Leo Kadman, Tel Aviv. *The Holy Land Philatelist*. Oct-Nov, 1959, p. 1252; Dec Jan, 1959/60, p. 1268.

7. Archeology and the Bible, by George A. Barton, Philadelphia, 1925.

8. *Steinmatzky's Palestine Guide*, by Zev Vilnay, Jerusalem, 1935 (for a description of places of antiquity).

Memorial Shrine to the victims of the Holocaust, Jerusalem

Israel's Two Commemoratives of "Devastation and Heroic Resistance" Hashoa Vehagvura

In the twentieth year after the uprising of the Warsaw Ghetto, Israel released two postage stamps in memory of the heroic resistance of European Jewry against their German slaughterers. The date of issuance, the 26th of Nisan — April 30, 1962, was on the eve of the "Day of Heroes and Martyrs," proclaimed by the Knesset as a national Memorial Day.

Yad Vashem

Twenty years is a short span in the history of a people. The open wounds are still gaping in the minds of the survivors and of those who had indirect contact with the holocaust. And yet, there has been a strong current among Jews everywhere to forget and let life return to normal. The State of Israel, therefore, appropriately decreed a Day of Remembrance to be observed annually by its own inhabitants. It has also designated one of the hills in Jerusalem as "The Mountain of Martyrs" on which is erected a Memorial Tent containing the Grave of the Unknown Martyr in memory of the Six Million. Near the casket of ashes stands an Eternal Light which is kindled daily by either a representative of one of the liquidated communities, a prominent person or a student. Nearby is Memorial Square, where the closing ceremony of the Day of Remembrance is held in the presence of the President, statesmen and a large assemblage. A replica of the Eternal Light has been fashioned in two sizes — a small replica, by the artist M. Zabari, for every Jewish household; and a larger replica, by Miss Z. Schatz, for synagogues and public institutions in Israel and throughout the Diaspora — so that none may forget. All these monuments are in the care of "Yad Vashem" (a monument and a memorial, so named from a verse in Isaiah, 56:5), which was established by the Knesset in 1953, as the Authority for the Remembrance of the Devastation and Heroism.[1]

What Do We Remember?

It should be noted that the remembrance in Yad Vashem as well as on the commemorative stamps is not only of the holocaust (Shoah) but also of heroism (Gvurah). It is to the credit of Israel's Parliament that it gave due recognition to the heroic resistance of European Jewry under Nazi domination. There has been a tendency among some sociologists, psychologists and other writers of late to minimize the struggle or, at best, to ignore the memory of the Jewish fighters against the Nazis and their collaborators. In their cool appraisal of the events these writers reached a decision that the Jewish people did not resist — and they just wonder why! They can find no answer to their inquiry because of their incomprehensible approach to the most unique phenomenon in the annals of mankind, unprecedented even in the history of Jewish martyrdom. This is not the place to discuss or refute all those writings, but one such work must be touched upon, even though briefly, as it purports to be an objective, scientific study of the holocaust.

Did the Jews Resist?

Raul Hilberg, in his book, *The Destruction of the European Jews*, contends that the Jewish population offered no resistance to the Nazi perpetrators, and when such resistance was taken it was "only in a few cases, locally, and at the last moment." And, not only did the Jews not resist, but, according to Hilberg's peculiar theory of "interaction" between perpetrators and victims, they (the victims) cooperated with the murderers and thus hastened their own destruction. This whole process, he maintains, was due to the Jewish ghetto mentality which throughout history sought compliance with the evil decrees or their alleviation, but not resistance. Physical resistance especially, he claims, has been "completely absent in two thousand years of Jewish ghetto history." If this so-called scientific interpretation of the events of 1941-1943, the blackest years in Jewish existence, were correct, the "Day of Remembrance" would be a gruesome, horrid experience, and the sooner forgotten the better. We certainly would not be justified in, nor could we find the proper way of, relating these events to our children, to whom we want to entrust the "Day of Remembrance" as a spiritual inheritance. Hilberg's thesis is fallacious, his historical evidence incorrectly adduced and some facts wrongly stated. It is not true, to begin with, that physical resistance has been "completely absent in two thousand years of Jewish ghetto history." The annals of the Jewish communities in the Diaspora are replete with accounts of organized Jewish fighting against their tormentors in major and minor encounters, in pogroms and frontal attacks. In 1944 a two volume anthology, *Sefer Hagvura* (The Book of Heroism), was issued in Tel Aviv, replete with Jewish heroic deeds against their enemies from the days of Masada in ancient Judea to the end of the 19th century in czarist Russia. How can a serious historian or sociologist overlook those deeds in an appraisal of Jewish life in the Dispersion?

The Ghettos

What is even more spurious is Hilberg's contention that European Jewry responded to the Nazi action with a ghetto mentality. The Jews of post World War I in Eastern Europe, and certainly in Western Europe, were not ghetto-minded, as was amply attested by their valiant fight for political, cultural and economic rights in their native lands. Furthermore, the Jews under German occupation did not dwell in ghettos, as we understand these historically. The word "ghetto" employed by the Nazis was a diabolic euphemism for the "Concentration Centers" they erected for the Jews as transfer depots to the death camps. It had no resemblance to the medieval or modern ghetto, where Jews lived voluntarily or under compulsion for their own protection and internal organization. Nor did the Nazis just make pogroms on the ghettos, in which case the Jews might have organized self-defense squads, as they had done against pogromists in many towns in Russia. The correct appraisal of the situation is that the German Wehrmacht waged a total war against the Jewish people which was in the nature of a military exercise preparatory to the full-scale war of annihilation Hitler had planned for all inhabitants of Poland,

White Russia and the Ukraine. His aim was to fulfill the German "Drang nach Osten" (penetration of the East), to create the Greater Space for Folksdeutsche, and "to see to it that in the East shall dwell people only of real German, Teutonic blood." The Jews, as happened before in world conflagrations, were just the first victims of this mad scheme. In this perspective one may understand more readily the behavior of the Jewish people under Nazi occupation.

A Fight for Life

In case of sudden attack a people does not respond by rushing into a suicidal offensive against the enemy. The first reaction is to strengthen itself from within to be able to absorb the initial blows. When the Germans blitzed the Soviet Union in June, 1941, with devastating effect on the military forces and civilian population, the Russians abandoned whole armies on their Western front and retreated to the interior before they were able to recover from the blow and take a stand. A whole people does not fight a war for death; it fights for life. The Jews of Europe did the same. They lost the fight, and it is easy to dub them ghetto-minded, cooperators, paralyzed with fear, incapable or unwilling to resist. Not at all! The Jews resisted from the very beginning of the Nazi onslaught; only their resistance assumed different forms at various stages of the war. Their toll at each stage was enormous, because the military odds against them were tremendous. One must remember that the Germans introduced a new type of warfare in their initial attack namely, lightening speed (blitz) and encirclement. They applied the same technique against the Jews. In a matter of days they encircled whole Jewish communities, transferred them to newly established concentration centers (ghettos), killed off many of their leaders and intellectuals, isolated the centers from each other, and started a systematic program of starving them to death. The normal response of the Jewish people, like of any other people, was to regroup their forces within the ghettos and establish underground contacts for immediate survival — to obtain food, medical care, clothing, to provide education for their children and cultural functions for adults, even entertainment to dispel their gloom. This was resistance of the first order. A people that loses its will to live cannot fight. The Nazis tried but could not break that will. It is remarkable that very few Jews in the ghettos and camps committed suicide. When death is the order of the day and the hour, to live is an act of heroism. "For many years," wrote Neustadt from Tel Aviv in 1944, "we did not understand the meaning of this passive heroism on the part of our fellow Jews and of our movement in Poland. We did not appreciate it as it deserved. We did not regard it as the miracle is was."

Physical Resistance

Now some sociologists, psychologists and other writers persistently query why the Jews did not take up active resistance, why they did not fight back. Amidst all their theoretical, objective, scientific "pilpul" these writers fail to see the stark reality of the situation. The Jews did not fight in the early stages because they had no guns! And when they did obtain whatever guns and ammunition they could, in mortal risk at every step, and when they were able to establish some bases of operation, they fought with a courage and valor that astounded even the antagonistic indigenous underground. This was not only true of the fighters in the Warsaw Ghetto in April, 1943. Jewish resistance started long before, as early as December, 1941, and reached well organized proportions through 1943, in occupied Poland, White Russia and the Ukraine.[3]

For who can fathom the soul of a people whose children sing in the following vein?

I will be sad beginning tomorrow,
Today I will be joyous.
What's the use of sadness, tell me,
what?
Cruel winds start to howl.
Why should I today mourn for
tommorrow?
The morrow may be very beautiful
and sunny.
Tommorrow the sun may shine for
us again;
We shall then be sad no more.
I will be sad beginning tommorrow,
Tommorrow, not today. No, Today
I will be joyous.

493

> And every day, no matter how bitter
>   it may be,
> I shall say:
> I will be sad beginning tommorrow,
> Not today.
> (Translated from the Yiddish by the
> writer).[9]

The catastrophe of European Jewry under Nazi rule was the severest in the history of our people, having struck more deeply and more devastatingly than the War with Rome at the end of the Second Temple (66-70 C.E.) or the Hadrianic persecutions in the days of Rabbi Akiba and Bar Kochba sixty years later. The heroism shown by our people, men, women and children, during the Nazi catastrophe outranks the exploits of the fighters in those earlier wars, great as the latter were in their own right. Describing only one of the many organized groups of fighters in Nazi Europe, M. Neustadt, mentioned above, wrote: "Just a few weeks ago we received detailed information about a partisan organization of Jewish youths operating in Western Galicia and calling themselves 'The Fighting Pioneers'. This report tells about persons well known to us and about their deeds of heroism in freeing prisoners, in blowing up bridges and Nazi enterprises, in acts of retaliation, etc. We have descriptions of deeds which sound like veritable legends." Descriptions of this kind abound in the chronicles gathered and published during and after the holocaust. These are the things about the destruction and heroism we ought and want to remember. The two commemorative stamps issued in Israel will help those of us who treasure them in our collections to keep this memory alive.

Designing the Commemoratives

The stamps, of two denominations, were designed, one by Cyla Menussy and Chava Ornan (0.12 ag), and the other by Jacob Zim (0.55 ag). Mrs. Menussy was born in Israel and Mrs. Ornan in Czechoslovakia. Mr. Zim is a native of Poland. Ornan and Zim are the only survivors of their families who had been in Nazi concentration camps. All three are graphic artists now residing in Tel Aviv. The designing of postage stamps on this theme no doubt posed some artistic and personal difficulties, especially for the two who had themselves experienced the Nazi horrors. For how could one arrest a torrent of painful memories, and how could one bind the searing wounds of a martyred people, to give them adequate expression in a few strokes on the size of a "commemorative," even adding the tab? This problem was also faced by many poets and writers who tried to give literary form to national calamity now and in the past. This type of creativity lies in the field of the sublime, and few have been able to rise to that height. Perhaps a word about the nature of sublime art will help us guage the magnitude of the problem.

Sublime Art

When the artist contemplates an overwhelming elemental force that threatens man's very existence without being able physically to avert it, he may experience the surge of a moral or spiritual power that surpasses the destructive physcial elements. The artist must then find the proper medium and shape it in graphic, plastic or lingual form, showing the interplay of both forces, but giving sway to the moral over the physical. This requires a certain distance from the destructive force in space and time. The closer one is to the pending or actual calamity, the greater must be one's moral force to surpass the physical in sublime art. The highest expression of this kind ever attained in the field of poetry is found in Ch. N. Bialik's Hebrew poems of "Pain and Wrath" which he wrote following the pogroms in Russia in 1903. While not all that he had to say then applies to the Jewish catastrophe under Nazi dominion, certain passages, quoted below in this writer's English translation, well up from the depths of Jewish martyrdom through the ages. They are therefore appropriate in our contemplation of the Devastation and Heroism that these stamps commemorate.

In "The City of Slaughter," describing one of the scenes of martyrdom, Bialik wrote:

> In the twilight of the eve, when
> Toward west the sun declines behind the wall.
> Enwrapped in clouds of flaming red like blood,
> Open quietly the gate and walk into the stall.
> A horrid darkness will engulf you there,
> An abysmal, hidden fright;

Around you terror hovers clinging to the walls
And cramped up in the stillness of the night.

* * *

And the last hushed cry, a shrill tortured gasp
O'er your head is there congealed still sobbing,
As if grief eternal groaning from the ground
Were seething there and throbbing.
It must be that a spirit laden
With heavy sorrows and searing pain
Imprisoned itself with its affliction
And will not move from there again.

* * *

It wants to weep but cannot weep;
Its pent-up groan it cannot utter.
And strangled by its quiet grief,
it wanes and withers in its flutter.
it spreads its wing o'er the sainted martyrs
Who lie as shadows on the ground
it hides its head beneath a wing
And laments without a sound.

In his poem "O, Heavens Seek for Me Compassion," Bialik
cried out:

Cursed be he who says revenge is bliss!
Such revenge, for blood of infants gored,
Has not designed yet even Satan or his horde.
Let the blood sink to the abyss;
Let it penetrate down from the girth,
Fill the dark bowels, and sap
The tottering foundations of the earth!

The Shema and Yizkor

In the pictorial arts the task is more difficult to accomplish. The
designers of the two commemorative stamps used elements of
Jewish traditional value — The "Shema" and the "Yizkor"

496

(Memorial) candle. These have been great moral factors in the life of the people in observing solemn occasions. The Jewish outcry "Shema Yisrael!" in time of personal or national adveristy is the expression of an abiding faith in the Divine Presence that will never depart or forsake. Menussy and Oran, then, conceived of fire shaped out of the Hebrew letters " Shema Yisrael." Against a pitch black background rises a glowing red and yellow flame — a beacon of hope in the darkness of night. Like the Burning Bush in the Wilderness of old, the flame of the "Shema" burns but does not consume. On the bottom of the stamp the irregular letters of the words "Hashoa Vehagevoura" lead from the deep shadow of "Shoa" into the bright light of "Gevoura." The slender shape of the entire design conveys the feeling of elevation — approximating the sublime.

Of a more sublimate conception is the design of six candles for the Six Million by Jacob Zim. It grips and tears at one's innermost and cleanses one's spirit until the elements of physical destruction fade into nothingness. The motif is the "Yizkor" candle, hallowed in Jewish tradition as the symbol of the immortality of the soul. Like the Jewish spirit which did not bend before the Nazi perpetators, the six pale-white candles stand erect, though their bodies are consumed in part, sending their quiet flames upward againt a blue-black deep. Blood drips over the yellow badge of the Magen David at the foot of the candles, but the Hebrew letters of "Israel" reborn, firm and clear, wash the blood away. The tab bears the inscription "These I remember..." While the source of this phrase is Psalm 42:5, where the Psalmist yearns for the glory of Jerusalem that lay desolate, the text also refers to the Yom Kippur service in memory of the Ten Holy Martyrs in the days of Rabbi Akiba: "These I remember and my soul pours forth, that the insolent devoured us like a cake unturned." On the First Day Cover of the two commemoratives there is an imprint of the Ner Tamid (eternal light) replica, taken from the Memorial Tent in Jerusalem. On its base is inscribed the Hebrew verse from Isaiah, 56:5 —"And I shall establish for them a monument and a memorial . . . that shall not be cut down."

1963

References

1. "Yad Vashem," in *Sefer Hashana Shel Haitonaim.* (Journalists Year-book) 5721, Tel Aviv, 1960, Page 128.

497

2. *The Last Stand,* Published by the Poalei Zion Organization of American, April, 1944, Page 9, 14.

3. *The Ghettos in Uprising* (Yiddish), by L. Shpizman, published by the Central Committee of Poalei Zion-Zeirei Zion, New York, 1944, Page 25.

4. *Hitler's Professors,* by Max Weinreich, Yiddish Scientific Institute-Yivo, New York, 1946, Page 130.

5. *Hitler's Ten Year War on the Jews,* by Institute of Jewish Affairs of the American Jewish Congress — World Jewish Congress. New York, 1943.

6. *Blessed is the Match*, The Story of Jewish Resistance, by Marie Syrkin. Jewish Publication Society of America, Philadelphia, 1947.

7. *The Participation of Jews in the Partisan Movement of Soviet Russia* (Yiddish), by Moshe Kaganowich. Published by the Central Historical Committee at the Union of Partisans "Pachach" in Italy, Rome, 1948.

8. *Sefer Hagvurah* (Hebrew), an historical anthology of Jewish heroism, arranged by Israel Heilprin, Tel Aviv, vol. I, 1941; Vol. II, 1944.

9. *Froien in di Ghettos* (Women in the Ghettos), edited by L. Spizman, Pioneer Women's Organization. New York, 1946, page 70.

The Israel Festival Stamps, 1948-1965

Festival 1950, by Arthur Szyk

Moadim Lesimha — Joyous Festivals

The Festival Series, called in Hebrew, "*Moadim Lesimha*" (festivals for rejoicing) started the first year after the establishment of the State of Israel, in 1948. In keeping with the custom of extending greetings on New Year's Eve, the stamps bear the inscription "*Moadim Lesimha*" and the Jewish calendar year, which are also repeated on the tabs and the First Day covers. The greeting is derived from the Kiddush — the blessing over wine recited on Holidays: *"And thou, O Lord our God, hast given us in love festivals for rejoicing . . ."* However, the more traditional Jewish New Year greeting is *"Leshana Tova Tikatevu"* (May you be inscribed for a good year), or in short, *"Leshana Tova"* (for a good year), which is also given on some First Day covers. On other holidays, such as Tabernacles, etc., the traditional usage is the Yiddish greeting *"Gut Yom-Tov"* (Good Holiday) or the Hebrew *"Hag Sameah"* (Happy Festival).

Jewish Calendar

In the Jewish calendar the Universal Era is traditionally counted from Creation, which was completed on the first Rosh Hashana (New Year). Computing Biblical chronology and with some Messianic speculation, the Sages of the Talmud arrived at a fixed calendar (cf. *Avoda Zara*, 9-10; and *Sanhedrin*, 97). Thus the year one of the Common Era corresponded to the year 3761 of the Universal Era, and the common year 1948, when the State of Israel was founded and the first Festival stamps were issued, was 5708 of the Jewish calendar. The year is written on the stamps and tabs in Hebrew letters, giving its numerical value, but omitting the thousands, which are assumed to be generally known; as for example, 5708 is written 708. To calculate the common year from the Hebrew number, add 1240. Thus the Hebrew year 725 plus 1240 equals 1965 or, starting in the fall, 1964-1965.

Agricultural Year of Biblical Origin

The Jewish New Year is in the Fall, usually in September, as its calendar is based on the agricultural year. The first month is called Tishrei, and Rosh Hashana (New Year) has been observed on the first two days in Israel and by most of the other Jewish communities from ancient times to the present. The main Biblical sources for the High Holidays and the three Pilgrimage Festivals are in *Leviticus*, 23 and *Deuteronomy*, 16. But there are many other verses and passages in the Torah, the Prophets and Writings, referring to the holidays and their national-religious significance, and especially to the joyous character of their observance. Some of those verses are quoted on the tabs and First Day covers of the Festival stamps, thus tying present-day celebrations with their Biblical origins. The stamps are issued each year prior to New

Year's day, and the cancellation is dated from a few days to over a month in advance.

Four Motifs

The Festival stamps issued from 1948 to 1965 or in the Hebrew years, 5709 to 5726, may be classified according to four major motifs, each reflecting a certain spiritual or economic aspect of the young State. These motifs are: 1) Historical Continuity in the Land of Israel; 2) The Land and Its Produce; 3) Spiritual Values of Traditional Observance; and 4) Universal Ideas. It should be pointed out that in Jewish tradition the holdiays have a twofold significance, one religious-national and the other economic-agricultural, blending together in a unique experience of joy and thanksgiving. The natural and spiritual are inseparable in the life of the people. The three Pilgrimage Festival — Passover, Pentecost, and Tabernacles — had their origin in the perennial pursuits of the Jewish farmer in the ancient land. But each festival was also associated with some major historic event that impressed itself upon the memory of the people and was recalled each year at the celebration of these festivals.

Passover, the spring holiday of rejuvenated nature, reminded the Israelites of their exodus from Egypt and liberation from enslavement through the redeeming power of divine Providence. Shavuot (Pentecost) came at the time of the ripening of the fruit, seven weeks after Passover, and it also signified the time when the people stood at Mount Sinai to receive the Torah—the constitution that welded them into a nation. Succot, (Tabernacles) was *The Festival* of the agricultural year, the time of ingathering of all the produce of the good land that the Lord had given them as an inheritance. In this season the farmer's booths in the fields also reminded the people of the booths (succot) in which they dwelt as they wandered in the wilderness under the guidance of the Lord through Moses His servant. While the Torah details the national and economic laws governing the festivals and prescribes their ritual observances, the Biblical emphasis is on their joyous, life-giving and life-sustaining powers. *"And thou shalt rejoice in thy festivals"* is a constant Biblical refrain when speaking of the holidays.

The second thing to bear in mind about the Jewish holidays is that they have also been set aside as "appointed times" (literal meaning of *"moadim"*) for meditation, for a searching after one's deeds through the year, and for "*a return*" to the good ways that the Lord has taught man in relation to his fellow-man and to his Creator. In the course of generations, these ideas have become dominant, especially in the observance of Rosh Hashana (New Year) and Yom Kippur (Day of Atonement), even though these holidays had been closely related to the season of "*ingathering of the fruit*" and, in point of time, are still celebrated that season. Both moments, the spiritual-reflective and the natural-earthly, find their expression in the four motifs of Israel's Fesitval stamps.

1. *Historical Continuity 1948, 1949, 1957, 1960, 1961, 1964*

The first two festival issues, designed by Otte Wallish and M. G. Shamir respectively indicate two ways in which the new State identifies itself with the past. One is by presenting relics of Jewish life in the land through the generations; the other is by portraying its national heroes, defenders and fighters for freedom. The six stamps of New Year 1948 show a "*flying scroll*" with the word "*L'melech*" (for the King), which was a royal seal used by the kings of Judah on wine and oil vessels for the collection of taxes in kind. The stamp has the inscription "*Joyous Festivals*" and the year. On the First Day cover is a simple arabesque and the cancellation specifies "*first day of festival stamp.*" In the following year, 1949, the theme of three festival stamps is national defense, each bearing the State emblem and respectively the insignia of the Defence Army, the Navy, and the Air Force, which are also shown on the First Day cover. The cancellation again specifies "*first day of festival stamp.*" The stamp further points out that the year 5710 is "*the second year of the State,*" probably an allusion to a similar inscription on an ancient coin of Bar Kochba, namely, "*Second year of Israel's liberation.*" That coin was later depicted on the definitive set of stamps of 1950. These two themes of past relics and independence recur on subsequent festival issues with greater elaboration.

In 1957 three stamps show ancient seals, probably used by kings and others. The emblem on each is enlarged by the artist, Miriam Karoly, in stylized form above the seal, and the ancient inscription of ownership is transliterated on the tab in modern Hebrew characters: "*To temech son of Miknemelech*" 50 prutot, "*To Shema servant of Jeroboam*" 160 prutot, and "*To Netanyahu son of Obadyahu*" 300 prutot. On the 1964 issue, Chava Ornan and

501

Cyla Menusy designed three polychome glass vessels of the 1-3 centuries in Israel, recalling a highly developed glass industry of the time. The tabs bear the emblem of Museum Haaretz in Tel Aviv, and the cover shows the Glass Pavilion of the Museum in which a large collection of ancient glass work is on permanent exhibit.

Two other issues of the same motif present kings and heroes of Israel. Three stamps of 1960, designed by A. Calderon, give a symbolic presentation of the characters of the first three kings of Israel. It was they who laid the foundation and consolidated the ancient Jewish kingdom: Saul the warrior, David the Psalmist, Solomon the wise judge and Temple builder. In 1961 the same artist presented three heroes of old: the legendary Samson, who subdued the Philistines with torch and foxes, Judah Maccabee who freed his people from Syrian-Helenistic rule with sword and shield and the pitcher of oil he found in the Holy Temple after liberation, Bar Kochba, with bow and arrow, who fought against the Romans and re-established an independent Israel in 132-135 of the Common Era. These stamps with flying scrolls, ancient seals, glasswork and the like, as well as kings and heroes of old, point to a flourishing, vibrant and viable Jewish community in Israel in days of national independence or under foreign rule. And now, as the reborn State of Israel takes account before every New Year of its own phenomenal development, it can see in those relics and records the high level of advancement that former generations had attained in the land. Thus present-day Israelis can truly regard themselves as the generation of *"The Return"* to the land of their forefathers — in historical continuity.

2. *The Land and Its Produce: 1952, 1954, 1958, 1959*

"A land that flows with milk and honey," was the report given of Canaan by Joshua and Caleb, two of the twelve Princes whom Moses had sent to scout the country (Numbers, 14:8). The Torah further relates that as a sample of the land's fertility the scouts brought with them a huge cluster of grapes *"carried by two on a rod."* This is portrayed by G. Hamori on the festival stamp of 1954, quoting the words of Joshua and Caleb on the tab. The cover has a quotation from Deuteronomy, 16:14, *"And thou shalt rejoice in thy festival."* In another passage in the Torah, Moses praises the land for the *"Seven Species"* that became known as

most characteristic of its natural bounty: *"A land of wheat and barley, and vines and fig-trees and pomegranates; a land of olive-trees and honey . . ."* (Deut., 8:8). These are depicted by Zvi Narkis on two sets, the first four species on the stamps of 1958 and the last three in 1959. On the tabs is the verse quoted above, with the word for each species given in the color of the respective stamp. Biblical poetry is, on the whole, rich in metaphors of nature. This is particularly so in the book *"Songs of Songs,"* which is resplendent with pastoral beauty. On the four festival stamps of 1952 Otte Wallish sketches some vegetation of the land, giving the appropriate verse from *"Song of Songs"* that describes each item. The numerical values of the big Hebrew letters in the four verses, the Tav (in the word for fig), Shin (lily of the valley), Yod (dove), and Gimmel (nuts), compose the Hebrew year 713. The tabs give chapter and verse of the respective quotations, the inscription *"Joyous Festivals"* and the year.

3. *Traditional Observance: 1950, 1951, 1953, 1956*

The fruit of the land is closely related to the ceremonial and ritual at home and synagogue. These observances have remained basically the same since ancient time, in accordance with Biblical instructions. On Tabernacles, for example, *"four kinds"* are assembled in the Llav (palm branch, willow, myrtle) and Etrog (citrus), They are displayed during the recitation of *"Songs of Praise"* (Hallel) at morning services to remind worshippers that the blessings of nature are given by diving Providence. (Cf, Leviticus, 23:40). These *"four kinds"* are the central theme of two festival stamps in 1950, designed by the great miniaturist, Arthur Szyk. The tabs bear an inscription from the prophet Nahum, (2:1), *" Celebrate your festivals, O Judah!"* The cover design is composed of the names and emblems of the Twelve Tribes with the Hebrew year in the center. This is perhaps symbolic of the ingathering of the exiles, as Tabernacles is the ingathering of the crops, as the same prophet further proclaims: *"For the Lord has returned the splendor of Jacob as well as the splendor of Israel."* (2:3) The serenity and quiet beauty of the stamps reflect the everlasting values of the holiday.

In ancient times wind, string and concussion instruments were used in connection with holiday observances and other festive occasions. Since the destruction of the Temple musical instruments have been prohibited at services in traditional synagogues. An exception has been made for the Shofar (ram's horn), which has retained its special function of announcing the advent of the New Moon and the New Year, and also as a reminder of its use at Mount Sinai, at the giving of the Torah. Two sets of festival stamps, designed by Miriam Karoly, portray men and women playing seven different instruments as recorded in various passages of the Bible. Some of those instruments were used by Miriam after the crossing of the Red Sea, by King David and the Israelites in celebration of the return of the Ark of the Lord, or by the Levites in the Temple in Jerusalem. (Exodus, 15:20; II Samuel, Psalm 150, etc.) The four stamps of 1955 display timbrels and cymbals, the horn, trumpet, and harp. Those of 1956 show the lyre, sistra, and the pipe. On the tabs are the verses in which the respective instruments are mentioned. The prophet Nahum's joyous proclamation *"Celebrate your festivals, O Judah!"* is again inscribed on the covers of both sets. Other traditional themes of the holdiay season are used on the stamps of 1951, designed by Wind-Strusky (5 & 40 prutot), and M. Kara (15 prutot). Rosh Hashana is symbolized by doves carrying New Year greetings. Yom Kippur is represented by the Torah Scroll, expressing the idea of return to God's teachings, Succot is depicted by the fruit of the land. Torah and Avodah (worship) are the themes of the three stamps of 1953, by G. Hamori. He symbolized the holiday season by delineating three Holy Arks of the famous synagogues in Jerusalem, Safed and Petah Tiqua. The tabs and cover bear the words *"for you and gladness and cheerful seasons,"* quoted from the prophet Zachariah (8:19), who further prophesied that divine glory will return unto Zion and that the fast days will be turned into days of gladness.

4. *Universal Ideas 1962, 1963, 1965*

The ideal of peace and end of evil, prophesied by Isaiah, has long since become the universal goal of mankind. Three verses of this prophecy in chapter eleven, 6-8, are illustrated by Chava Ornan and Cyla Menusy on the festival issue of 1962. Inscribed on the stamps and the tabs the verses read: *"And the wolf shall dwell with the lamb," "and the leopard shall lie down with the kid," "and the sucking child shall play over the hole of the asp."* The cover displays a green olive branch and the words *"joyous festivals."* Repentance and divine forgiveness are expressed by the artist,

Jean David, on three stamps of 1963, through illustrations of three verses from the Book of Jonah. This Book, which deals with that basic idea, is read as the Haftara at afternoon services on Yom Kippur. This set is the only one in the Festival series to-date that does not have the phrase *"joyous festivals"* or the year on the stamps, but only on the tabs. The tabs further have the appropriate verse for each picture; tempest on the sea; Jonah inside the fish with the city of Nineveh in the background; and the sun beating down on the recalcitrant prophet who felt sorry for himself but not for the great metropolis. The most universal concept, creation of the world, is expressed pictorially by A. Calderon on the latest festival issue of six stamps in 1965. Following the Biblical text of Genesis 1, the artist delineates in a few stylized strokes each element of creation: Light, Firmament, Vegetation, the Constellations, Sea-life and Fowl, and Animal-life and Man. The Hebrew word for each element, the greeting *"Joyous Festivals"* and the year appear on the respective stamps. The tabs have the general inscription *"Creation of the World"* in Hebrew and French and the corresponding number for each of the six days. These stamps symbolize how the first New Year, at the completion of creation, started the Universal Era which, according to tradition, is to pass into the era of Universal Peace.

Designers of the Festival Series

1948 Otte Wallish, Flying Scroll
1949 M & G. Shamir, Defense
1950 Arthur Szyk, Lulav and Etrog
1951 Wind-Strusky, Doves and Torah M. Kara, Fruit
1952 Otte Wallish, Dates
1953 G. Hamori, Holy Arks
1954 G. Hamori, Grapes
1955-56 Miriam Karoly, Instruments
1967 Miriam Karoli, Seals
1958 Zvi Narkis, Four Species
1959 Zvi Narkis, Three Species
1960 A. Calderon, Kings
1961 A. Calderon, Heroes
1962 Chava Ornan & Clya Menusy, Isaiah
1963 Jean David, Jonah
1964 Chava Ornan & Cyla Menusy, Glass Vessels
1965 A. Calderon, Creation   1966

Source of the JFK Stamp Design

On May 4, 1964 David Lidman, writing in the New York Times, revealed for the first time how the source of the John F. Kennedy Memorial stamp was discovered by one of the designers, William Seno, of the Raymond Loewy—William Smith firm in New York. "The designers," Lidman wrote, "studied hundreds of photographs of Kennedy, seeking a portrait that would capture his character and personality. The full-face photograph chosen was found by accident by Mr. Seno in an advertisement in the Bergen (N. J.) Evening Record." Being a New Jersey resident, this bit of information to me struck home, and I immediately started to track down the place and date of the publication. With the courteous help of the New Jersey Telephone Information Service, I learned that the name of the daily was "The Record," published by The Bergen Evening Record Corp. with headquarters in Hackensack, N. J. A call to The Record confirmed the appearance of the advertisement, but the date was very difficult to ascertain. It was several months ago, and the copy was just an ad, which was not kept on file. If I wanted, I was assured, I could visit the office and make a search through the volumes of recent issues, that is, five or six months of daily newspapers. I then betook myself to the main office of the paper at 150 River St., Hackensack, N. J. Fortunatley, a young man of the office staff pressed his remarkable memory and suggested that the ad—he had a vivid recollection of it—had appeared earlier in the year, in February. It was an announcement of a Kennedy movie offered for sale by a Hollywood producer. With that he pulled out the filmed February issues of the newspaper and started rolling the pages from first to last. The ad did not show up. Back and forth we rolled the film, peering at every page for a square spot of about 5 by 4 inches. Suddenly it came into full view on page 63, next to the last page of Tuesday, February 18. There, in the left corner, was the youthful Kennedy portrait, identical with that of the memorial stamp. Underneath the picture the ad read: "Not a Sad, Solemn Eulogy, but a 200 ft. 8 mm movie filled with Action. Life! and Vigor!!"

When I left the office of The Record I had under my arm all the 20 bulky copies of the February 18th issue that were still available for sale. In the following days I pasted the advertisements and other pertinent data on maximum cards for first day cancellations. A few of the small copies I sent to Boston, the city of the first day of issue. The large items and some additional small ones I kept for first day cancellation in Hackensack. May 29 was for me, as it was for many fellow collectors, John F. Kennedy philatelic day. I made the rounds to several post offices in my town and neighboring communities, to the United Nations Building and the Kennedy Interantional Airport in New York. I had a variety of covers and maximum cards for cancellation, but my prize copy was the Kennedy picture of the " ad" in The Record, which I sought to have postmarked in Hackensack. N. J.

Several disappointments in post offices earlier in the day made me apprehensive of the success of my mission to Hackensack. However, my trip to the post office there went smoothly; I even found a parking place two doors away! The building was one of the newer structures and it made a cheerful impression on me. But, would the clerk be as cheerfully accommodating? I walked inside and took a quick glance at the faces of the men standing behind the service windows. At the Parcel Post window a middle-aged postal clerk was performing his duties with affable dexterity. He was patient, kind and solicitous of the wishes of his customers—a true servant of the people. From this gentle person I received most perfect double-circle cancellations—"Hackensack, N. J. May 29, 1964, USPO"—tying copy with plate blocks and singles on all the items I presented to him. I cherish these items in my Kennedy collection as well as the memory of the gentleman who canceled them for me.

1964

"Old Glory"

U. S. Stamps Tell Her Story

American stamp collectors recall somewhat ruefully that not until 1957 was there a commemorative stamp issued by the P.O. Department honoring our National Flag. And not until January 1963, was there such a stamp released as a regular issue. There were also comments in the philatelic press to the effect that it took some prodding before the PMG yielded to the rising demand for a Flag stamp. It was then that I became interested in finding out to what extent the U.S.postal issues prior to 1957 had the national emblem as part of their designs. My research led me to a new topical in my collection—the American flag on U.S. postage stamps.

My personal interest in collecting Flag stamps is in the story behind them, and in what they reveal about the growth of the country, its history, aspirations, local color, personalities, and other forces that have gone into the making of the American nation. That story, as reflected in the Flag stamps issued from 1869 to date, is a fascinating one. I have found no fewer than 54 items in this series, not counting variations, imperforates, souvenir sheets, and the like. In many of these the Flag is a prominent feature of the design; in some it is hardly noticeable, although it is definitely there. When in doubt as to its identity, I inquired from the source, such as the custodian of a National or State building, and received very helpful information.

For purposes of this collection I arranged the entire series in seven groups, as follows: 1) Stamps showing the origin and development of the Flag from Revolutionary days to the present. 2) Special stamps honoring the Flag as such. 3) Presidents and national heroes whose portraits are draped by the Flag. 4) National, State and territorial buildings flying the Flag. 5) American vessels flying the Flag. 6) Military posts and battles displaying the Flag. 7) Commemorative events in which the Flag is displayed. 8) An interesting sub-topic is the U. S. Flag on foreign stamps, of which there is a large selection, but which is not included in this description.

My collection consists of single mint copies, variations, souvenirs, and in the special Flag issues also of FDC and matched plate blocks. I have designed my own albums and lay-outs, and have supplied typewritten descriptions pasted in color frames as part of the design on each page. In the historical section I have also added pictures of the Flag in its different stages of development.

Origin and Development of the American Flag

a) Flags of the Revolution were adapted from local and colonial emblems and used by military units on posts and in battles. Three of those flags have been incorporated in stamp designs. Bunker Hill (Massachusetts); an anchor with the word "Hope" (Rhode Island); and the "Liberty or Death" banner in the Battle of White Plains (N. Y.). The direct forerunner of the Stars and Stripes was the Grand Union Flag, or Cambridge Flag, hoisted by General Washington in January 1776 at Cambridge, Mass. as the Standard of the Continental Army. It had 13 red and white stripes and the red and white crosses of the "mother country" in a blue canton. There is no U. S. stamp bearing a facsimile of that Flag.

b) The National Flag came into being through an Act of the Continental Congress on June 14, 1777. This Act prescribed 13 alternate red and white stripes and 13 white stars in a blue field, but it did not indicate their sizes or specific arrangement on the banner. Traditionally, Betsy Ross, a flag maker in Philadelphia, is credited with the design of the first Flag—13 stars in a circle on a blue union with 13 alternate red and white stripes (as shown on the Betsy Ross stamp, No. 1004). This credit is based on a claim made by her grandson, William C. Candy, and attested by her daughters and other persons. Another claimant of this historic distinction was Francis Hopkinson, a member of the Continental Congress from Philadelphia. There is, however, no historical evidence for either claim. Following the centennial celebration of the first Flag Act, in 1877, June 14 was observed as Flag Day in various regions. In 1916 President Wilson proclaimed it as National Flag Day to be observed annually.

c) The Second Flag Act was passed by Congress on January 13, 1794, establishing the emblem of 15 stars and stripes, corresponding to the number of States in the Union at the time. This Flag, with the stars arranged in five staggered rows of three each, appears on the stamp honoring Francis Scott Key, No. 962.

d) When, in 1818, the number of States reached 20, it was realized that adding more stripes for each new State would make the size of the flag unwieldy. At the suggestion of Capt. Samuel C. Reid, USN, Congress passed The Third Flag Act, April 4, restoring the original 13 stripes and ruling that a star be added for each new State on the Fourth of July following its admission. This Act is still in force.

e) Additional stars, and hence the re-arrangement of the canton, appeared with each new State, until the 48-star emblem (six rows of eight stars each) came into existence in 1912 with the admission of Arizona and New Mexico. This flag is presented on many

509

stamps and particularly on the first special Flag issue of 1957. In 1912 President William Howard Taft issued an order establishing the proportional dimensions of the national Flag, but withdrew it a few months later. President Woodrow Wilson re-issued the order in 1916, thus setting the dimension of the horizontal length at 1.9 of the vertical width. The blue canton, or union, was fixed in width at seven of the 13 stripes, and in length, at 0.76 of its width. The 49th star was added in 1959 and the 50th in 1960, after the admission of Alaska and Hawaii.

f) Some of the popular names of the Flag have interesting origins. It is known as "Stars and Stripes" for its design; "Star Spangled Banner," so named in 1814 by Francis Scott Key, author of the National Anthem; and "Old Glory," the name first given to a Flag on a ship by a young sea captain, William C. Driver of Salem, Mass. The originals of the last two are now in the Smithsonian Institution.

2. *Special Stamps Honoring the Flag*

The first postage stamp featuring the national emblem was issued in 1869. It shows the Eagle resting on the Shield and Flags grouped on the sides. On top are 13 stars arranged in a semicircle. However, the first stamp to honor the Flag in a design by itself appeared 88 years later, on July 4, 1957. It displays the 48-star Flag—six rows of eight stars each—flying from a pole. Underneath is the inscription "Long May It Wave." The stamp was also the first to be printed in natural colors on the Giori press. The flag of July 4, 1959 was issued to commemorate Alaska's admission as the 49th State in 1958. The 49-star union is arranged in seven staggering rows of seven stars each. Similarly a special commemorative Flag stamp was issued July 4, 1960, upon the admission of Alaska as the 50th State in 1959. The 50 stars are arranged in five rows of six each and four inter-spacing rows of five each. The Flag of the regular issue appeared on January 9, 1963, when the new 5c first-class postal rate went into effect. The central design is an unfurled 50-star emblem over a picture of the White House, which also flies its own Flag from the top. This is the first American stamp without the words "U.S." and "Postage," it being assumed that the Flag in natural colors and the White House are in themselves sufficient to symbolize the nation.

3. *Presidents and National Heroes*

The George Washington 2c regular issue of January 17, 1903 has his portrait (by Stuart) draped by two flags. Abraham Lincoln of the same issue, January 20, 1903, has his picture (by Brady) decorated by Flags in the upper corners. *Gen. Casimir Pulaski,* Polish patriot and hero of the American Revolution, was commemorated on the 150th anniversary of his death (1779) by an issue of January 16, 1931. The Polish and U.S. banners are in the upper corners over an oval portrait of the General. *LaFayette's* 175th anniversary of arrival in America (1777) was honored on June 13, 1952. The American and French flags are displayed on the sides of the Marquis' portrait. *Betsy Ross,* already mentioned in this article, was commemorated on the 200th anniversary of her birth, January 2, 1952, with a stamp showing her purported design of the first American Flag as she spread it out before the Flag Committee consisting of George Washington, Robert Morris and George Ross. *Francis Scott Key,* also mentioned above, appears on a stamp issued August 9, 1948, with two Flags draping his picture—one, flowing over Ft. McHenry, is the 15-star-and-stripe of his day when he wrote the National Anthem (September 14, 1814). The other, the 48-star and 13 stripes is of the time of issue. By Presidential Proclamation, the national Flag is now flown over the Fort in Maryland, and by tradition over Key's grave, day and night.

4. *Buildings Flying the Flag*

The fourth section of our discussion of U. S. stamp depicts the National Emblem. Three of the National Capital Sesquicentennial issues commemorating the establishing of Washington as the nation's Captial in 1800, display the Flag: on the White House, issued June 12, 1950; at the Supreme Court, August 2; and over the Capitol, November 22. By Presidential Proclamation, the Flag is flown over the Capitol day and night. The stamp "Women in Our Armed Services," September 11, 1952, shows the Flag over the Capitol in the background. Two of the *Franklin D. Roosevelt* series of 1945 have the Flag—one on the White House (3c, June 27) and the other on the Hyde Park residence (1c, July 26). The 10c airmail issued August 30, 1947, primarily for mail to Latin America, has the Flag on the left top corner of the Pan American Building in Washington, D. C. States and territories honored on stamps have the national emblem flown over buildings of old Capitols or historical edifices. These are: *Vermont*, issued March 4, 1941 150th anniversary of admission to Statehood; and *Iowa Territory Centennial*, August 24, 1938, which has a flag over the Old Capitol Building in Iowa City, which is now the principal administrative unit of the University of Iowa. *La Fortaleza*, Palace of the Governors in Puerto Rico, issued in tribute to U. S. territories November 25, 1937, showing the U. S. Flag on top of the castle. Since 1952, when the Commonwealth of Puerto Rico was established, both the U. S. and Puerto-Rican emblems have been flown from the Fortaleza. The U. S. Flag flies on top of the *Palace of Governors*, Santa Fe, N. M. (regular 1¼c issue, June 17, 1960), which since 1909 has been the main seat of the Museum of New Mexico. The design is by the late Santa Fe photographer Tyler Dingee, from one of his own photos taken before 1959.

5. *The Flag on Ships*

In the *Navy* issue of 1936-37, the Flag is flown from a top mast on a sailboat of the Revolutionary War, between pictures of Captains John Paul Jones and John Barry (1c, December 5). The 3c has a Flag on the left of a sail vessel of Civil War days, between portraits of Commodores David G. Faragut and David D. Foster (February 18). The *Constitution* or " Old Ironsides," issued October 21, 1947, on the 150th anniversary of its launching in 1797, flies the Flag at midlevel on the left; 16 stars of the number of States at the time are arched over the boat. The 100th anniversary of Commodore *Matthew C. Perry's* negotiations with Japan for trade in 1953, issued on July 14, 1953, shows one of his vessels anchored in Tokyo Bay flying the American Flag against the background of a full moon. *The Hudson-Fulton* of September 25, 1909, on the tercentenary of the discovery of the Hudson River and the centenary of steam navigation, has an American Flag on the "S.S. Clermont" on the right. The sailboat on the left is Henry Hudson's "Half Moon," probably flying the British emblem. *The Golden Gate* 20c regular issue of May 1, 1923 has a Flag unfurled on the left promontory as ships pass through the Gate. *Savannah*, on the 125th anniversary of the first steamship crossing the Atlantic Ocean in 1819, issued May 22, 1944, flies the national emblem on the front mast and the ship's ensign in the center. *Soo Locks* of June 28, 1955, on the centennial of transportation on the Great Lakes, shows a Flag on the left side of the large steamer. *Louisana State* sesquicentennial of April 30, 1962 has a boat with a Flag on the left front. On Novermber 22, 1935, a 25c airmail was issued especially for use by *Transpacific* airmail service to Hawaii, Guam, and the Philippines, which was inaugurated November 25. The same design without date was issued February 15, 1937 in 20c and 50c denominations for airmail to China. These *China Clipper* stamps have a boat on the right, covered partly by the numeral, flying a Flag on the front mast. The 10c *Parcel Post* of December 12, 1912 has a Flag on a mail tender beside a large steamship. This is one of a set of twelve such stamps put on sale January 1, 1913, and is the only U. S. Parcel Post series ever issued. By order of June 26, 1913 further printing of distinctive Parcel Post stamps was discontinued.

6. *Military Posts and Battles*

The *Continental Flag* of 13 stars and stripes and the "Liberty or Death" ensign are displayed on the 150th anniversary issue of the Battle of White Plains, October 18, 1926, mentioned previously among the Flags of the Revolution. This has also been issued in a souvenir sheet of 25 to commemorate the International Philatelic Exhibition in New York, October 16-23, 1926. *Washington's Headquarters* in Newburgh, N. Y., issued April 19, 1933, on the 150th anniversary of the Proclamation of Peace which ended the War of Independence in 1783, displays the Flag from a pole at Hasbrouk House that was used as Headquarters. The same stamp had a special printing on March 15, 1935, ungummed, under authority of PMG James A. Farley, "for a limited time in full sheets as printed blocks thereof, to meet the requirements of collectors and others who may be interested." (From "Postal Bulletin" No. 70782). Catalogues note that this special issue is identifiable only in pairs or blocks of four, showing wide gutters between the stamps. However, one can detect on the Farley issue a lighter shade of purple than on the regular one. Arkansas Post with the American Flag is shown on the *Arkansas State Centennial* of June 15, 1936. The Stephen Watts *Kearny Expedition*, issued October 16, 1946, on the centenary of Kearny's entry into Santa Fe, N. M. In 1846, has the Flag raised in front of the Palace of Governors. The design is from a painting "Capture of Santa Fe" by Kenneth M. Chapman. *Fort Kearny's* centenary of founding in

Nebraska, September 22, 1948, flies the Flag from a pole in the center of the Fort. The Flag is also in the center of *Fort Bliss*, in Texas, issued on its centenary, November 5, 1948. The dramatic raising of the American Emblem on Mount Suribachi, *Iwo Jima*, is pictured on the stamp issued July 11, 1945, in honor of the U. S. Marines who recaptured the island February 23 of that year.

7. *Commemorative Events*

The earliest of historical events to be commemorated on a stamp was "Fremont on the Rocky Mountains" issued June 17, 1898 at the Trans-Mississippi Exposition in Omaha, Neb. *John Charles Fremont*, explorer, first U. S. Senator from California in 1850, first Presidential candidate of the Republican Party in 1856, and Union General in the Civil War in 1861, is pictured on the stamp standing on the Rockies as he raises the American Flag in his right hand. Two of his companions stand on a lower level apparently each waving a small Flag. The design is from an old engraving. The *First Transcontinental Railroad*, issued May 10, 1944, on the 75th anniversary of its completion, depicts the celebration at Promontory, Utah on May 10, 1869, after driving in the last spike. The Flag is flying from a pole on the right. The scene is from the painting "Golden Spike Ceremony" by John McQuarrie. The first of the *Sesquicentennial Lincoln* commemorative series, Lincoln-Douglas Debates, August 7, 1958, has the Flag unfurled on the left of the speaker's platform. Two Flags are flown from cords on the sides of *Jupiter* 7c airmail, August 15, 1959, commemorating the 100th anniversary of carrying mail by the Balloon Jupiter from LaFayette to Crawfordsville, Ind. The *Victory* issue of March 3, 1919, on the successful completion of the First World War, presents a standing figure of Liberty Victorious with the Flags of five Allied Nations. In the back center is the American Flag; on the left, the British and Belgian; and on the right, the French and Italian Flags. *Michigan State Centennial* of November 1, 1935 (also in souvenir sheet with three other items, on the 'Third International Philatelic Exhibition of 1936) has the State Seal in the center and the national and State Flags on the sides. *Texas State Centennial*, December 29, 1945, features the American and Texan Flags as the principal design. A ray from the 28th star of the national Emblem pierces into the canton of the other Flag forming the "Lone Star" of Texas. Though not a full banner, a portion of the red and white stripes of the Flag appears as the background on the *Girl Scouts* 50th anniversary issue of July 24, 1962.

I wish to acknowledge the cordial response to my inquiries I received from several sources: Wallace L. Whitcomb, Sergeant at Arms, from his office at the Capitol of the State of Vermont; Bruce T. Ellis, Associate Director for History, Museum of New Mexico, Santa Fe; Ken Donnelson, from his Univeristy Relations Office at the "Old Capitol" Building, State University of Iowa, Iowa City; and Charles F. Zimmerman, Special Assistant to the Governor, La Fortaleza, San Juan, Puerto Rico. Their helpful information and the careful attention they gave to my communications have extended the horizon of my philatelic interests. This is the saga of "Old Glory" on American postal issues to date. As one peers at the stamps through the collector's magnifying glass, one envisions the colorful panorama of the American landscape, the struggle for liberation, and the array of events since then, though long past, that still give ferment to our national life today. It is interesting to note that many of the Flag issues were designed from paintings, engravings and photographs by early American artists. These add not only to the aesthetic enjoyment of the spectator but also to the delight of the lover of Americana.

1963

Bibliography

The Writings of Alexander S. Kohanski, 1917-1986

Books

1. An Outline of Contemporary Palestine. New York: New York Metropolitan Avukah, 1933. Mimeographed.

2. *Lossky's Theory of Knowledge.* A Dissertation for the degree of Doctor of Philosophy. Complete manuscript of 202 pages deposited in the library of Vanderbilt University, 1936. Printed in part by Menonite Press, Scottdale, Pa., 1936.

3. *A Survey of Facts and Opinions on Problems of Post-War Jewry and Palestine* (writer and editor). New York: The American Jewish Conference. 1943.

4. *The Jewish Social Service Quarterly* (editor). New York: The National Conference of Jewish Social Welfare, Dec. 1943 to Sept. 1945, vol. 20:2 to 22:1.

5. *The American Jewish Conference: Its Organization and Proceedings of the First Session, 1943* (writer and editor). New York: American Jewish Conference, 1944.

6. *The American Jewish Conference: Proceedings of the Second Session. 1944* (editor). New York: American Jewish Conference, 1945.

7. *The Gazette* (writer and editor). Monthly, Lewiston, Me.: The Maine Jewish Council, Oct. 1945 to Dec. 1947, vols. I:1 to III:3.

8. *Curriculum for Jewish Religious Schools.* San Francisco: Asko Press, 1949. Fourth Printing 1953. Mimeographed.

9. *Hammakor.* Hebrew Reader, Alef. Illustrated by Dorothy D. Kohanski. San Francisco: Asko Press, 1950. Second Edition 1955.

10. *From Kishinev to Babi Yar.* Cedar Grove, N.J.: Asko Press, 1968.

11. *An Analytical Interpretation of Martin Buber's I and Thou.* Woodbury, N. Y.: Barron's Educational Series, 1975.

12. *Philosophy and Technology: Toward a New Orientation*

in Modern Thinking. New York: Philosophical Library, 1977.

13. *Tsava'ah: The Ethical Will of Rabbi Joseph Moses Abraham Levinski, the Tsaddik of Lazday.* Third Hebrew Edition. Edited and with an Introduction, Translation, and Commentary by Alexander S. Kohanski. Preface and Family Charts by Dorothy D. Kohanski. Passaic, N. J., Asko Press, 1982.

14. *Martin Buber's Philosophy of Interhuman Relation.* Teaneck, N. J.: Fairleigh Dickinson University Press. London and Toronto: Associated University Presses, 1982.

15. *The Greek Mode of Thought in Western Philosophy.* Teaneck, N. J.: Fairleigh Dickinson University Press. London and Toronto: Associated University Presses, 1984.

Essays, Lectures, Addresses, Poems

Items that have no publisher have not been printed heretofore.

1917-1926

16. Hamilhama, 1917.
17. On a Nomen Is Main Leed, 1923.
18. Du Laidst, 1924.
19. Shpritsn Funken, 1924.
20. Oign Tsvei, 1924.
21. Main Leed. From Solomon Ibn Gabirol, "Melitsati Beda' agati," 1924.
22. Es Zogt tsu Mir die Erd. From Solomon Ibn Gabirol, "Netosh Lu," 1924.
23. Dos Leed fun Ritters Toit, 1925.
24. Through My Window, 1925.
25. Honimun, 1926.
26. Shikzal, 1926.

27. "The Song in the Jewish School Today," *The Hebrew Watchman*, Memphis, Tenn., 14 October 1927.
28. Tsu F.Sh., 1927.
29. Freeling in Memphis, 1927.
30. Tsu. . . , 1927.
31. Aheen. . . , 1927.
32. Tsurik in Memphis, 1927.
33. Einzam, 1927.
34. Lebensfreid, 1927.
35. Lebn, 1928.
36. Tsu S. B., 1928.
37. "Einfuhlung and Painting." Master's Thesis, Vanderbilt University, 1928. Mimeographed.
38. *Torchbearer Annual* (associate editor), New York Metropolitan Avukah, June 1932.
39. "Problems of Organization," *Torchbearer Annual*, June 1932.
40. The Yiddish Theater in New York, 1932-33 (unfinished), 1933.
41. The Jewish Social Worker and Labor Zionism. A Statement prepared for the Jewish Social Workers Chapter of the League for Labor Palestine, New York, 1935.
42. "Summary: The Problem and Its Solution," in *Jews and Arabs in Palestine*, edited by Enzo Sereni and R. E. Asheri. New York: Hechalutz Press, 1936.
43. "Nicolai Onufreievich Lossky's Theory of Knowledge," abstract of doctoral thesis, Bulletin of Vanderbilt University, 15 August 1936.

44. "Role of the League," *Jewish Frontier*, June 1937.
45. "Borochov: Marxian Zionist," *Jewish Frontier*, February 1938.
46. "Solomon Goldelman, *Löst der Kommunismus die Judenfrage?*" (review), *Jewish Social Service Quarterly*, June 1938.

47. "A. D. Gordon, *Selected Essays*" (review), *Jewish Social Service Quarterly*, March 1939, pp. 336-37.

48. "The Jewish Community in America," *Aufbau*, October 1940.

49. A Silver Wedding Anniversary, 1940.

50. When Jewish Youth Responded to the Call, 1940.

51. "Communist Propaganda for Jews," *Contemporary Jewish Record*, Sept.-Oct. 1940, pp. 470-83.

52. "Federation," *The Universal Jewish Encyclopedia*, 5(1940):265.

53. "Fraternal Orders," *The Universal Jewish Encyclopedia*, 5(1940): 419-23.

54. "Hashomer Hatzair," *The Universal Jewish Encyclopedia*, 5(1940):236.

55. "Hechler," *The Universal Jewish Encyclopedia*, 5(1940):287.

56. "Looking Into the Future," trans. from the Yiddish of B. Weinryb's review of *Jewish Fate and Future* by Arthur Ruppin, *Jewish Frontier*, January 1941.

57. Youth Aliyah. Dramatic Children's Story with Song and Dance, July 1940.

58. "The Yishuv in Palestine Braces Up to Meet the War Emergency: A Survey of Economic Conditions," *The Hebrew Watchman*, Memphis, Tenn., January 1940.

59. "Twenty Years Histadrut," *The New Palestine*, 10 January 1941, pp. 9-10.

60. "Rumania in Revolt;" (editorial), *Jewish Frontier*, February 1941.

61. "Another Alaska Bill" (editorial), *Jewish Frontier*, February 1941.

62. "Israel Goldstein's *Toward a Solution*" (review), *Jewish Frontier*, June 1941.

63. In the Rifle Academy, 1941.

64. "Spirit of the Maccabees" (1941), *The Gazette*. Published by the Maine Jewish Council, December 1946.

65. "Two Anchors on Our Line of Defense," *The Cleveland Jewish Center Bulletin*, 6 March 1942.

66. "Effects of the War on the Jewish Community: A Survey," *Jewish Social Service Quarterly*, December 1943, pp. 67-80.

67. "Migration and Colonization," *A Survey of Facts and Opinions* (see item 3).

68. "Jewish Representation in Peace Negotiations," *A Survey of Facts and Opinions* (see item 3).

69. "Palestine," *A Survey of Facts and Opinions*, (see item 3).

70. "Aide-Memoire on Jewish Refugees, 1933-1943," prepared for The American Jewish Conference, included by the Hon. Immanuel Celler of New York as part of his speech in the House of Representatives, Monday, January 24, 1944. Printed in *The Congressional Record*: Proceedings and Debates of the 78th Congress, Second Session.

71. "Commission on Post-War," in *Report of the Interim Committee* of The American Jewish Conference, 1 November 1944, pp. 89-121.

72. "The Essence of Weizmann's Zionism," by I. Elazari-Volcani. Trans. from the Hebrew, in *Chaim Weizmann: Statesman, Scientist and Builder of the Jewish Commonwealth*, edited by Meier Weisgall. New York: Dial Press, 1944, pp. 238-53.

73. "The Jewish Case at San Francisco" (United Nations Conference), *Jewish Frontier*, May 1945, pp. 11-14.

74. "Jewish Representation at the United Nations Conference in San Francisco," Radio address over WINS. New York, 2 June 1945 (Disk).

75. "Central and Western Europe," Review of the Year 5705 (1945-1946), *American Jewish Yearbook*, 47(1945-46): 375-90.

76. *Queen Esther*. Lewiston, Me: Asko Press, 1946. Revised 1986.

1947-1956

77. "Ode to Zion." From Yehudah Halevi, "Ziyon Halo Tishali," *The Gazette*, Feb.-Mar. 1947.

78. "A New Song: Passover Hymn." From Yehudah Halevi, "Shira Hadasha," *The Gazette*, April 1947.

79. Fair at Sight. From Yehudah Halevi, "Yefat Mareh," 1947.

80. On His Bad Luck. From Abraham Ibn Ezra, "Al Ro'a Mazalo," 1947.

81. "In the City of Murder." From Chayyim Nachman Bialik,

"B'ir haharega" (excerpt), *The Gazette*, May 1947. First half in *From Kishinev to Babi Yar*, Asko Press, 1968.

82. "Jewish Education and the Community," *The Gazette*, October 1947. Also in *Bangor Hebrew School Fortieth Anniversary, 1907-1947*1, Bangor, Me., 2 October 1947.

83. "Creation of the Third Jewish Commonwealth," *The Gazette*, Nov.-Dec. 1947.

84. *A Survey of Jewish Education in Portland, Maine.* The Jewish Federation of Portland, Me., 1948. Mimeographed.

85. "Spiritual Influence from Israel," (Israel and American Jewry), *Jewish Community Bulletin*, San Francisco, 17 January 1949.

86. "Thoughts on Jewish Education." *Jewish Community Bulletin*, San Francisco, 7 October 1959.

87. Educational Responsibility of the Emergent Jewish Community, 1949. Address at Conference of the Western Region of the American Association for Jewish Education, San Francisco 3 March 1949.

88. "First National Education Conclave," *Jewish Community Bulletin*, San Francisco, 19 January 1951.

89. "Center Show Poses Question of Jewish Art" (Purim Megillah), *Jewish Community Bulletin*, San Francisco, 6 April 1951.

90. "A Biblical Film in the Spirit of the Book," *Jewish Community Bulletin*, San Francisco, 29 June 1951.

91. "Torah on One Foot? Yes . . . But," *B'nai B'rith Bulletin*, San Francisco, December 1951.

92. "On the Slaughter." From Chayyim Nachman Bialik, "Al Hashekhita," 1951. In *From Kishinev to Babi Yar*, 1968.

93. "An Existential Approach," article review of Will Herberg's *Judaism and Modern Man, Jewish Frontier*, February 1952, pp. 25-28.

94. "Jewish Education in San Francisco," *Jewish Education*, Summer 1952, pp. 54-57.

95. "Content of the Jewish School: Report of a Panel," *Jewish Education*, Winter 1952, pp. 60-62.

96. The Teacher in the Jewish School. Address at the Jewish

Teachers Conference in San Francisco, 7 September 1952.

97. "Concerning the "Experiment with the One-Bond Method,'" *Jewish Education*, Fall 1953, pp. 58-60.

98. "Jewish Educational Content and the Jewish Child," *Reconstructionist*, 29 January 1954, pp. 25-28.

1957-1966

99. "The Art of the Stamps of Israel," *The Israel Philatelist*, March and June 1961.

100. Humash or Bible, What's the Difference? Conversation at a Game of Dreidel, 1961.

101. "Babi Yar." From the Russian of Yevgeny Yevtushenko, *Jewish News* (N. J.), 24 September 1961. *Reconstructionist*, 6 April 1962, pp. 15-19. In *From Kishinev to Babi Yar*, 1968, pp. 25-28.

102. "Israel Reflected in Special Cancellations in 1960," *Israel Philatelist*, December 1961, March 1962, March 1963.

103. "Art on Israeli Stamps," *Israel Philatelist*, February, 1962. *Fine Art Philatelist*, Muskagee, Okla., Nov.-Dec., 1981.

104. "The Spirit that always Negates," article review of Ilya Ehrenburg's *The Stormy Life of Lasik Roitschwantz*, *Reconstructionist*, 2 February 1962, pp. 19-22.

105. "Old Glory — U. S. Stamps Tell Her Story," *Linn's Weekly Stamp News*, 30 September and 7 October 1963.

106. "Israel's Two Commemoratives of Devastation and Heroic Resistance," *Israel Philatelist*, Nov.-Dec. 1963.

107. "Source of JFK Stamp Design," *Linn's Weekly Stamp News*, 28 September 1964.

108. "Two Views on 'Babi Yar,'" comments, *Jewish News* (N. J.), 13 September 1963.

109. "A Critique of Religious Humanism," article review of Eugene Kohn's *Religious Humanism: A Jewish Interpretation, Reconstructionist*, 11 and 25 June 1965.

110. "Martin Buber: An Appreciation," *Jewish News* (N. J.), 2 July 1965.

111. To Mordecai M. Kaplan on His Eighty-fifth Birthday, 1966.

112. "The Israel Festival Stamps, 1948-1965," *Israel Philatelist*, Sept.-Oct. and Nov.-Dec. 1966.

113. "Origin and Function of Modern Tenets in Jewish Education," *Jewish Education*, Spring-Summer 1966, pp. 143-54.

114. "Concept of the Jewish Question in the Third Reich," *Jewish News* (N. J.), 9 September 1966. In *The Jewish Catastrophe in Europe* (abbreviated), ed. Judah Pilch, 1968. ch. 2 pp. 39-46.

1967-1976

115. "A Community Endeavor in Jewish Education, in *Philip W. Lown Jubilee Volume*, ed. Judah Pilch, 1967, pp. 15-25.

116. "Hermann Cohen and Mordecai M. Kaplan," *Jewish Social Studies*, 29:3 (July 1967): 155-70.

117. "From Kishinev to Babi Yar," *Jewish News (N. J.), 29 September 1967 (see item 10).*

118. *"Jewish Life in Europe between the Two World Wars, 1919-1939," in The Jewish Catastrophe in Europe*, 1968, chap. 1, pp. 9-38.

119. "Reflections on Jewish-Arab Relations," *Reconstructionist*, 23 February 1968, pp. 7-12.

120. "A Song of a child in the Warsaw Ghetto," trans. from the Yiddish in *Froien in the Ghettos*, ed. I. Shpizman. New York: Pioneer Women's Organization of America, 1940.

121. Shir shel Na'ar Bagheto she Varsho. Trans. from the Yiddish, 1973, (see above 120).

122. "With Sunrise." From Chayyim Nachman Bialik, "Im Shamesh," in *From Kishinev to Babi Yar* (see item 10).

123. "Conversation." From Yevgeny Yevtushenko, "Razgovor," in *From Kishinev to Babi Yar* (see item 10).

124. "Ecumenism: Dialogue or Dialectic," *Jewish News* (N. J.), 12 September 1969.

125. "An Open Letter to Charles S. Isaacs," *Reconstructionist*, 28 September 1969, pp. 13-19.

126. "Jews, Arabs, and Zionists in the Middle East," *Jewish News* (N. J.), 25 September 1970.

127. "A Perspective on the Holocaust," *Jewish News* (N. J.), 17 September 1971.

128. "Martin Buber's Restructuring of Society Into a State of Anocracy," *Jewish Social Studies*, 24:1 (January 1972): 42-57.

129. "Martin Buber Speaks to Jewish Youth of the Meaning of Return (Teshuvah)," *Jewish News* (N. J.), 7 September 1972.

130. Is Buber a Personalist? Reflections on Harold M. Schulweis's "Buber's Broken Dialogue" (*Reconstructionist*, December 1972), 1973.

131. Sekira al Hashoa, 1973. Lecture at the Summer Seminar (Hashavua Haivri) of the Histadrut Ivrit, 1973.

132. "The Masada Complex, In Whose Mind?" *Jewish News* (N. J.), 20 September 1973.

133. "Einstein's Metamathematics," *Philosophia Mathematica*, ed. J. Fang, Winter 1973, pp. 165-81.

134. Is Nietzsche a Metaphysician?" Paper read at the Spring Conference of the N. J. Regional Philosophical Association, at Rider College, Trenton, N. J., 28 April, 1973.

135. Postscript on Nietzsche's Metaphysics, 30 April 1973.

136. Some Observations on a Discussion between Norbert Samuelson and Shubert Spero Concerning Maimonides' Concept of Relations as Divine Attributes (see *Judaism*, Winter 1973), 1973.

137. Lididee Shalom Shtern, 1974

138. "A Sanctuary in the Forest: The Pond." From Chayyim Nachman Bialik, "Habereikha," *Jewish News* (N. J.), 12 September 1974.

139. "Di Keniglekhe Kroin." From Solomon Ibn Gabirol, "Keter Malkhut," *Yiddisher Kemfer*, 27 September 1974.

140. My Song. From Solomon Ibn Gabirol, "Melitsati," 1974.

141. I am the Master. From Solomon Ibn Gabirol, "Anee Hasar," 1974.

142. Nocturne. From Solomon Ibn Gabirol, "Anee Ha'ish," 1974.

143. On the high Seas. From Yehudah Halevi, "Belev Yam So'er," 1974.

144. Max Scheler's Metaphysical Anthropology, 1974.

145. "And These Words Which We Hear Today," *Jewish News* (N. J.), 4 September 1975.

146. "Martin Buber's Philosophy of Judaism," *Judaism,* Winter 1975, pp. 69-81.

147. "Martin Buber's Approach to Jesus," *Princeton Seminar Bulletin*, Winter 1975, pp. 103-115.

148. Kant's Moral Problem of Freedom. Paper read at the Conference of the New Jersey Regional Philosophical Association, at Kean College of New Jersey, 1 May 1976.

149. Un az der Malakh vet Fregn. From Chayyim Nachman Bialik, "V'im Yishal Hamalakh," 1976.

150. "Mordecai M. Kaplan's Vision of a Modern Judaism," *Jewish News* (N. J.), 23 September 1976.

151. Correspondence with Kaplan on His "Vision of a Modern Judaism," 13 October 1976.

152. Silent Witnesses of the Holocaust, 23 September 1976.

1977-1986

153. The American Revolution and the Age of Enlightenment. Lecture at the Townsend Lecture Series, Kean College of New Jersey, 13 April 1977.

154. Reflections on a Philosophy of Technology. Paper read at the Second University of Delaware Philosophy and Technology Conference, June 17-18, 1977.

155. "First Zionist Congress on Its Eightieth Anniversary," *Jewish News* (N. J.), 18 September 1977. Lecture at the Adult Education Institute of Adas Israel, Passaic, N. J., 1977. Also included in Lecture on "Theodor Herzl, Eighty Years Later," at the Lecture Series of Temple Judea, Laguna Hills, California, 13 November 1984.

156. "Martin Buber's Way in Judaism," *Jewish News* (N. J.), 28 September 1978.

157. Martin Buber and the Quest of Scientific Knowledge. Paper read at the Conference of the New Jersey Regional Philosophical Association, at Livingston College, N. J., 2 December 1978, in observance of Buber's Centennial of Birth.

158. Mishnato shel Martin Buber al Hayahadut. Lecture at "Hashavuah Ha'ivri" of the Histadrut Ivrit of America, at

Gibber's Summer Hotel, Kiamesha Lake, N. Y., 10 July 1978.

159. "Albert Einstein's Humanism: A tribute on his Centennial of Birth," Lecture at the Adult Education Institute of Adas Israel, Passaic, N. J., Winter 1979.

160. *Animated Had Gadya* (Hebrew and English), illustrated. Passaic, N. J.: Asko Press, 1979.

161. The Problem of Modernity: To Establish the Bounds of Human Freedom, 1979.

162. "Perform the Miracle." From the Yiddish of Alexander Spiegelblatt's *Volkenbremen*. Tel Aviv: Di Goldene Keyt, 1979, p. 13.

163. "Captive." From Alexander Spiegelblatt (see 162), p. 16.

164. "Icicles." From Alexander Spiegelblatt (se 162), p. 32.

165. A Note on Buber's Approach to Jesus, 1980.

166. Comments on Hannah Arendt's View of the Jewish Condition, 3 July 1980. A communication.

167. "From the Jewish Heritage in Spain: Pilgrimage to the Statue of Solomon Ibn Gabirol," *Jewish News* (N. J.), 4 September 1980.

168. *The Art of Philosophizing* (manuscript 256 pages), 1981.

169. "Remembering the Abiding Faith of Our Forebears: An Account of an Ethical Will," *Jewish News* (N. J.), 24 September 1981. Lecture at Adult Education Institute of Adas Israel, Passaic, N. J. Winter 1981.

170. The Legacy of Rabbi Yehudah Hakohen of Budvich. Address at the Kahanski Family Reunion at the Sheraton Heights, Hasbrouck Heights, N. J., July 4 1982.

171. My Religious Belief, 30 July 1984.

172. Observations on Hans Reichenbach's Ethical Imperative, 20 September 1984.

173. Come, My Friend. From Hebrew Liturgy, "Lekha Dodi," 1985.

174. Tsu der Huppa, 1985.

175. Historical Background of Arab-Israel Negotiations. Lecture at Adult Education Institute of Adas Israel, Passaic, N. J., 15 December 1982. Revised 1986.